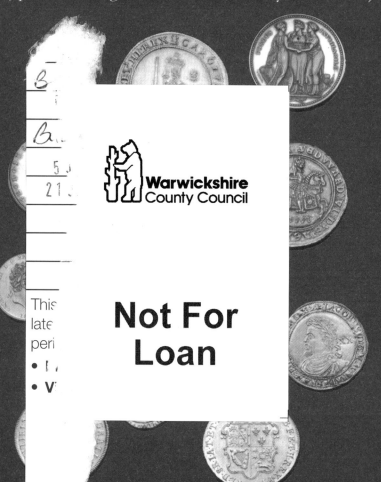

B
B
5
21

This
late
peri

• I
• V

D1395307

The British Numismatic Society
www.britnumsoc.org

*Sharing and expanding knowledge of British Coinage
from the Iron Age to the 21st Century*

**To enquire about membership
email: membershipsecretary@britnumsoc.org**

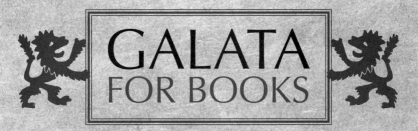

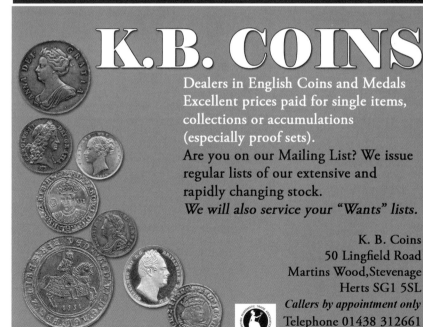

SELLING YOUR COINS & BANKNOTES?

Warwick and Warwick have an expanding requirement for coin and banknote collections, British and worldwide and for coins and notes of individual value. Our customer base is increasing dramatically and we need an ever larger supply of quality material to keep pace with demand. The market has never been stronger and if you are considering the sale of your collection, now is the time to act.

FREE VALUATIONS

We will provide a free, professional and without obligation valuation of your collection. Either we will make you a fair, binding private treaty offer, or we will recommend inclusion of your property in our next specialist public auction.

FREE TRANSPORTATION

We can arrange insured transportation of your collection to our Warwick offices completely free of charge. If you decline our offer, we ask you to cover the return carriage costs only.

FREE VISITS

Visits by our valuers are possible anywhere in the country or abroad, usually within 48 hours, in order to value larger collections. Please telephone for details.

VALUATION DAYS

We are staging a series of valuation days and will be visiting all areas of England, Scotland, Wales and Ireland during the coming months. Please visit our website or telephone for further details.

EXCELLENT PRICES

Because of the strength of our customer base we are in a position to offer prices that we feel sure will exceed your expectations.

ACT NOW

Telephone or email Richard Beale today with details of your property.

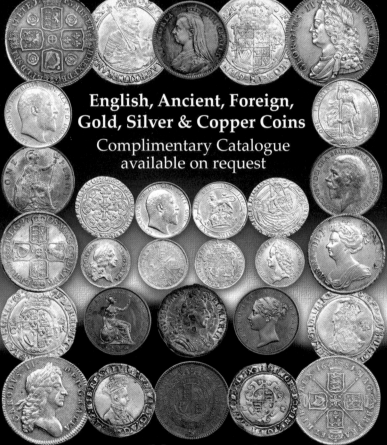

Standard Catalogue of British Coins

COINS OF
ENGLAND
AND
THE UNITED KINGDOM

48th Edition

SPINK

LONDON

A Catalogue of the Coins of Great Britain
and Ireland
first published 1929

Standard Catalogue of British Coins
Coins of England and the United Kingdom
48th edition, 2013

© Spink & Son Ltd, 2012
69 Southampton Row, Bloomsbury
London WC1B 4ET

Typeset by Design to Print UK Ltd,
9 & 10 Riverview Business Park, Forest Row, East Sussex RH18 5DW
www.designtoprintuk.com
Printed and bound in Malta
by Gutenberg Press Ltd

ISBN 978-1-907427-24-4

2013 Auction Calendar

Coins / Antiquities: Printed Catalogue
eAuction: Antiquities, Collectables & Coins

Sale Dates:	Last Date For Entries:
12th January 2013 - eAuction	28th December 2012
9th February 2013 - eAuction	25th January 2013
2nd March 2013 - eAuction	15th February 2013
14th March 2013 - Coins	7th February 2013
15th March 2013 - Antiquities	7th February 2013
6th April 2013 - eAuction	22nd March 2013
4th May 2013 - eAuction	19th April 2013
8th June 2013 - eAuction	24th May 2013
20th June 2013 - Coins	16th May 2013
21st June 2013 - Antiquities	16th May 2013
6th July 2013 - eAuction	21st June 2013
3rd August 2013 - eAuction	19th July 2013
14th September 2013 - eAuction	30th August 2013
5th October 2013 - eAuction	20th September 2013
31st October 2013 - Coins	27th September 2013
1st November 2013 - Antiquities	27th September 2013
9th November 2013 - eAuction	25th October 2013
7th December 2013 - eAuction	22nd November 2013

Please contact us for further information regarding consignment.

Enquiries:
+44 (0) 1708 222824
+44 (0) 1708 225689 fax
info@timelineauctions.com

TimeLine Auctions Limited
Berry Lodge
St Mary's Lane
Upminster, RM14 3PH, UK

*Sales may be filled before their last date for entries; you are advised to submit material as early as possible. The management of TimeLine Auctions Limited reserve the right to alter the dates of sale.

CONTENTS

ACKNOWLEDGEMENTS

We wish to acknowledge the valuable contributions of the following who have submitted information and provided photographs which have greatly enhanced this edition.

Richard Abdy *(The British Museum)*
Tony Abramson
Dr Martin Allen *(Fitzwilliam Museum)*
Dr Mark Blackburn *(Fitzwilliam Museum)*
Joe Bispham
Nigel Clark
Chris Comber
Barrie Cook *(The British Museum)*
Geoff Cope
Simon Cope
Jonathan Cope
Dave Craddock
Joe Cribb *(The British Museum)*
Mike Cuddeford
Paul Davies
Paul Dawson
Tim Everson
Stephen Fass
David Fletcher
Michael Freeman
Glen Gittoes
Megan Gooch
Eric Green
Dave Greenhalgh
David Guest

Peter Hendra
Steve Hill
Dr John Hulett
Peter Jackson
Richard Kelleher *(The British Museum)*
Geoff Kitchen
Ian Leins *(The British Museum)*
Joe Linzalone
Neil Paisley *(Colin Cooke Coins)*
Rob Pearce
Nigel Prevost
Mark Rasmussen
The Schneider Family
Dr Irving Schneider
May Sinclair
Peter D Spencer
Andrew Wayne
Tim Webb-Ware
Walter Wilkinson
Barry Williams
Gareth Williams *(The British Museum)*
Antony Wilson
Paul & Bente R. Withers
Peter Woodhead

Museums/Institutions
The Trustees of the British Museum, London
The Fitzwilliam Museum, Cambridge

Photography
Richard Hodges
Paul & Bente R. Withers
Wioletta Madaj

ABBREVIATIONS

Archb.	Archbishop	laur.	laureate
Æ	bronze	mm.	mintmark
Æ	silver	mon.	monogram
Ν	gold	O., obv.	obverse
Bp.	Bishop	p.	new penny, pence
BV	bullion value	pl	plume
cuir.	cuirassed	quat.	quatrefoil
d.	penny, pence	qtr.	quarter
diad.	diademed	rad.	radiate
dr.	draped	R., rev.	reverse
ex.	exergue	r.	right
grs.	grains	s.	shillings
hd.	headstg.	stg.	standing
i.c.	inner circle	trun.	truncation
illus.	illustration	var.	variety
l.	left	wt.	weight

Another eventful year passes by, noteworthy for the Olympic and Paralympic Games in London in the summer. The release of numerous new coins to mark the games has sparked new interest in collecting coins, especially the range of new 50 pence designs. I set about trying to form a complete set of these coins from change and am still missing one. There appears to have been enormous interest in this series and they are actually quite hard to find in change so I have resorted to asking shopkeepers to look out for them on my behalf!

The summer seems a distant memory now as we drift into the winter months, we continue to experience major financial problems around the globe and there remains a great deal of uncertainty; this is reflected in the continued high price of gold sitting currently at £1092 per ounce, around the same price as one year ago. The market for British coins remains very strong in general but the trends which have been developing gradually over the last few years have become more pronounced and sharply focused.

There has been a gradual change in collecting habits over a long period of time where more emphasis is being placed on condition than outright scarcity. One of the underlying reasons is simply that there are many more collectors of British coins now than ever before. Linked to this is the fact that there is a finite supply of coins on the market, especially those surviving in the higher grades, and competition for these pieces is fierce. The large collections formed in past by collectors such as Lockett, Murdoch and Montagu etc are simply not possible these days without enormous wealth, even with substantial sums of money the coins themselves are simply not around in sufficient quantity to satisfy the existing demand. The trend now is to form smaller collections of individually selected high grade coins which are considered the finest known of their type and not necessarily to form a collection of anything specific such as crowns or shillings. This has resulted in a general downturn of interest in lower grade coins. It is quite probable that the general economic downturn has had a direct impact and that collectors with less disposable income are simply not spending as much as they used to on the middle grade coins, whereas wealthy individuals are diverting a percentage of their cash into high grade coins as an alternative to low-yield deposit accounts and traditional forms of investment.

The obvious effect on prices is that coins in the higher grades of EF and UNC continue to climb at much higher rates than in the lower grades of F and VF, many of which have not moved at all.

In general, in this new edition, prices for hammered coins are up around 7.5% overall, mostly in VF grade. In particular, Saxon coins remain strong and Tudor coins have experienced a surge. Milled coins are up around 6.5% overall but the price increases are nearly all in the EF and UNC grades which is what the current market clearly wants.

Demand for sovereigns is at an unprecedented level, the recent sale of the Bentley collection highlighted the demand not only for quality but also for scarcity in this area with collectors competing for the elusive rarities which only come onto the market once in a lifetime.

Forgeries have become a hot topic recently; we have seen a number of extremely good copies of classic British rarities finding their way into the market place. The old warning 'Caveat Emptor' or 'Let the buyer beware' springs to mind. We can not recommend strongly enough that you should always buy coins from reputable dealers who will guarantee the coin as genuine and who are happy to refund you should you have any doubts. The British Numismatic Trade Association (BNTA) represents the interests of more than eighty numismatic firms throughout the UK and whose members are bound by a code of ethics, look out for the BNTA logo.

The cover coin chosen this year is a celtic gold stater of Tasciovanus, king of the Catuvellauni, a tribe of ancient Britain which occupied the modern day counties of Hertfordshire, Bedfordshire and Cambridgeshire, centred around Verlamion (St. Albans).

This particular coin was found by a metal detector in Cambridgeshire in 2011 and sold at the Spink auction in December 2011 for £6500 + premium.

The background of the cover is a drawing by Mark Gridley, an artist who produced a series of superb reconstructed drawings of Iron-Age settlements for Oxford Archaeology Unit.

The workmanship of the coin engravers of the Iron-age period is outstanding; the Celts were clearly talented artists and experts in working with metal. The abstract designs we encounter on Celtic coins would no doubt have had a clearer meaning to the people of the day, the designs can be quite complex and full of hidden images with faces, eyes, wheels, stars, comets, animals etc. Often when the coins are rotated the designs remain balanced and often reveal more hidden imagery. Celtic coins offer fantastic variety, fascinating history and great value for money. Because they frequently turn up in hoards they can be very affordable and a modest type collection can be built up relatively easily.

As for other changes in the this edition, we have taken the decision to remove prices for uncirculated copper coins of George IV and Victoria. Truly uncirculated coins with no wear and full lustre for this period are virtually impossible to find. It is therefore misleading to try to suggest accurate prices for coins which hardly ever trade on the market.

The tendency to include minute varieties in recent editions has had to be reigned in with a view to publishing specialised handbooks for collectors of varieties. The catalogue is overcrowded in places and is becoming difficult to use in order to distinguish one basic type from another. We must not lose our way in our aim to provide a succinct catalogue which is easy to use, with this in mind we are in the process of compiling information for a new edition of English Silver Coinage since 1649 so we would welcome information of new varieties which can be included in this new edition. We will, therefore, gradually be removing a lot of the minor varieties from this book. We also aim to publish, in due course, a specialised handbook for English gold coins.

Last year we announced that we would be separating the Decimal issues into a separate volume for this edition, for a number of reasons we have not done this but it will happen next year.

We hope that you continue to find collecting English coins interesting, rewarding and profitable. The market conditions over the last five years have made for very interesting movements in the prices of coins, not just in the UK but worldwide and we look forward to what the next year has to bring.

Philip Skingley

Editor, Coins of England

INTRODUCTION

Arrangement

The arrangement of this catalogue is not completely uniform, but generally it is divided into metals (gold, silver, copper, etc) under each reign, then into coinages, denominations and varieties. In the Celtic section the uninscribed coins are listed before the dynastic coins; under Charles II all the hammered coins precede the milled coinage; the reign of George III is divided into coins issued up to 1816 and the new coinage from 1816 to the end of the reign; and under Elizabeth II the decimal issues are separated from the pre-decimal *(£.s.d.)* coinages.

Every major coin type is listed though not every variety. We have endeavoured to give rather more coverage to the varieties of relatively common coins, such as the pennies of Edward I, II and III, than to the very much rarer coins of, for instance, King Offa of Mercia.

Values

The values given represent the range of retail prices at which coins are being offered for sale at the time of going to press and **not** the price which a dealer will pay for those coins. These prices are based on our knowledge of the numismatic market, the current demand for particular coins, recent auction sale prices and, in those cases where certain coins have not appeared for sale for some years, our estimation of what they would be likely to sell at today, bearing in mind their rarity and appeal in relation to somewhat similar coins where a current value is known. Values are given for two grades of preservation from the Celtic period onwards and three to four grades of preservation for coins of the 17th to the 20th century.

Collectors normally require coins in the best condition they can afford and, except in the case of a really rare coin, a piece that is considerably worn is not wanted and has little value. The values given in the catalogue are for the exact state of preservation stated at the head of each column and bearing in mind that a score of identical coins in varying states of wear could be lined up in descending order from mint condition (FDC, *fleur de coin*), through very fine (VF) to *poor* state. It will be realized that only in certain instances will the values given apply to particular coins. A 'fine' (F) coin may be worth anything between one quarter and a half of the price quoted for a 'very fine' (VF); on the other hand, a piece in really mint condition will be valued substantially higher than the price quoted for 'extremely fine' (EF). The designation BV has been adopted for coins whose value on the market has yet to exceed its bullion value. Purchasing sovereigns, catalogued as BV, will attract a dealers' premium.

We emphasize again that the purpose of this catalogue is to give a general value for a particular class of coin in a specified state of preservation, and also to give the collector an idea of the range and value of coins in the English series. The value of any particular piece depends on three things:

Its exact design, legend, mintmark or date.

Its exact state of preservation; this is of prime importance.

The demand for it in the market at any given time.

Some minor varieties are much scarcer than others and, as the number of coins issued varies considerably from year to year, coins of certain dates and mintmarks are rarer and of more value than other pieces of similar type. The prices given for any type are for the commonest variety, mintmark or date of that type.

The Scope

Coin collecting, numismatics, is a fascinating hobby. It requires very little physical exertion and only as much mental effort as one wishes or is able to put into it at any time. There is vast scope and boundless ramifications and byways encompassing not only things historical and geographical, but also touching on economics, metallurgy, heraldry, literature, the fine arts, politics, military history and many other disciplines. This catalogue is solely concerned with British coinage from its earliest times right up to date. From the start the beginner should appreciate that the coinage of our own nation may be seen as a small but very important part of the whole story of world currency.

The first coins, made of electrum, a natural alloy of gold and silver, were issued in western Asia Minor (Lydia) in the later seventh century B.C. Over the next century or so coinage of gold and silver spread across the Aegean to mainland Greece, southwards to the eastern Mediterranean lands and eventually westward to the Greek colonies in southern Italy, Sicily (Magna Graecia) and beyond. The coins of the Greeks are noted for their beautiful, sometimes exquisite craftsmanship, with many of the coin types depicting the patron deities of their cities. Coins of Philip II of Macedon (359-336 B.C.), father of Alexander the Great, circulated amongst the Celtic peoples of the Danubian Basin and were widely copied through central Europe and by the Gauls in France. Gold Gaulish staters were reaching Britain around the beginning of the first century B.C. and the earliest gold to be struck in the island must have been produced shortly afterwards. Although their types and designs copy the Apollo head and racing charioteer of Philip II's gold coins, they are stylistically much removed from the original representation and very individually Celtic in concept.

The coins of the Romans cover some seven centuries and include an enormous number of different types that were current throughout a major part of the civilized world from Spain to Syria and from the Rhine in the north to the Sudan in the south. The Roman province of Britain was part of this vast empire for four hundred years from AD 43 until the early fifth century. Innumerable Roman coins have been recovered from sites in this country, most being made of brass or bronze. Many of these are quite inexpensive and very collectable. In recent years many hoards of gold and silver coins have been found, usually by use of metal detectors.

Following the revival of commerce after the Dark Ages, coinage in Western Europe was virtually restricted to silver until the thirteenth century, though gold was still being minted in Byzantium and in the Islamic world. In the Middle Ages many European cities had their own distinctive coinage and money was issued not only by the kings but also by nobles, bishops and abbots. From the time of the later Crusades gold returned to the West, and the artistic developments of the Renaissance in the fifteenth century brought improved portraiture and new minting techniques.

Large silver crown-size thalers were first minted at Joachimsthal in Bohemia early in the sixteenth century. The substantial shipments of silver coming to Europe from the mines of Spanish America over the next couple of centuries led to a fine series of larger coins being issued by the European states and cities. The larger size allowed greater artistic freedom in the designs and the portraits on the coins.

Both Germany and Italy became unified nation states during the later nineteenth century, thereby substantially reducing the number of mints and coin types. Balancing the reduction in European minting authorities were the new coins that were issued by the independent states of South and Central America. Since the 1950s many new nations have established their independence and their coinage provides a large field for the collector of modern coins.

It can be seen that the scope for the collector is truly vast, but besides the general run of official coinage there is also the large series of token coins—small change unofficially produced to supplement the inadequate supply of authorized currency. These tokens were issued by merchants, innkeepers and manufacturers in many towns and villages in the seventeenth, eighteenth and nineteenth centuries and many collectors specialize in their local issues.

Some coins have designs of a commemorative nature; an example being the Royal Wedding crown of 1981, but there are also large numbers of commemorative medals which, though never intended for use as coinage, are sometimes confused with coins because they are metal objects of a similar shape and sometimes a similar size to coins. This is another interesting field for collectors as these medals often have excellent portraits of famous men or women, or they may commemorate important events or scientific discoveries. Other metallic objects of coin-like appearance that can be confusing for the beginner are reckoning counters, advertising tickets, various other tickets and passes, and items such as brass coin weights.

Minting processes

From the time of the earliest Greek coins in the late seventh century BC to about the middle of the sixteenth century AD, coins were made by hand. The method of manufacture was simple. The obverse and reverse designs were engraved or punched into the prepared ends of two bars of bronze or iron, shaped or tapered to the diameter of the required coin. The obverse die, known as the *pile*, was usually spiked so that it could be anchored firmly into a block of wood or metal. The reverse die, the *trussel*, was held by hand or grasped by tongs.

The coin was struck by placing a metal blank between the two dies and striking the trussel with a hammer. Thus, all coinage struck by this method is known as 'hammered'. Some dies are known to have been hinged so there would be an exact register between the upper and lower die. Usually a 'pair of dies' consisted of one obverse die (normally the more difficult to make because it had the finer detail, such as the ruler's portrait) and two reverse dies. This was because the shaft of iron bearing the reverse design eventually split under the constant hammering; two reverse dies were usually needed to last out the life of the obverse die.

Some time toward the middle of the sixteenth century, experiments, first in Germany and later in France, resulted in the manufacture of coins by machinery.

The term 'milled', which is applied to all machine-made coins, comes from the type of machinery used – the mill and screw press. With this machinery the obverse die was fixed as the lower die and the reverse die brought down into contact with the blank by heavy vertical pressure applied by a screw or worm-drive connected to a cross bar with heavy weights at each end. These weights usually had long leather thongs attached which allowed a more powerful force to be applied by the operators who revolved the arms of the press. New blanks were placed on the lower die and the struck coins were removed by hand. The screw press brought more pressure to bear on the blanks and this pressure was evenly applied, producing a far better and sharper coin.

Various attempts were made during the reigns of Elizabeth I and Charles I to introduce this type of machinery with its vastly superior products. Unfortunately problems associated with the manufacture of blanks to a uniform weight greatly reduced the rate of striking and the hand manufacture of coins continued until the Restoration in 1660, when Charles II brought to London from Holland the Roettiers brothers and their improved screw press.

The first English coins made for circulation by this new method were the silver crowns of 1662, which bore an inscription on the edge, DECVS ET TVTAMEN, 'an ornament and a safeguard', a reference to the fact that the new coins could not be clipped, a crime made easy by the thin and often badly struck hammered coins.

The mill and screw press was used until new steam-powered machinery made by Boulton and Watt was installed in the new mint on Tower Hill in London. This machinery had been used most successfully by Boulton to strike the large 'cartwheel' two- and one- penny pieces of 1797 and other coins, including 'overstriking' Spanish *eight-reale* pieces into Bank of England 'dollars' since the old Mint presses were not able to exert sufficient power to do this. This new machinery was first used at the Mint to strike the 'new coinage' halfcrowns of 1816, and it operated at a far greater speed than the old type of mill and screw presses and achieved a greater sharpness of design.

The very latest coining presses now operating at the Royal Mint at Llantrisant in South Wales, are capable of striking at a rate of up to 800 coins a minute.

Condition

One of the more difficult problems for the beginner is to assess accurately the condition of a coin. A common fault among collectors is to overgrade and, consequently, to overvalue their coins.

Most dealers will gladly spare a few minutes to help new collectors. Many dealers issue price lists with illustrations, enabling collectors to see exactly what the coins look like and how they have been graded.

Coins cannot always be graded according to precise rules. Hammered coins often look weak or worn on the high parts of the portrait and the tops of the letters; this can be due to weak striking or worn dies and is not always attributable to wear through long use in circulation. Milled coins usually leave the Mint sharply struck so that genuine wear is easier to detect. However a x5 or x10 magnifying glass is essential, especially when grading coins of Edward VII and George V where the relief is very low on the portraits and some skill is required to distinguish between an uncirculated coin and one in EF condition.

The condition or grade of preservation of a coin is usually of greater importance than its rarity. By this we mean that a common coin in superb condition is often more desirable and more highly priced than a rarity in poor condition. Coins that have been pierced or mounted as a piece of jewellery generally have little interest to collectors.

One must also be on the lookout for coins that have been 'plugged', i.e. that have been pierced at some time and have had the hole filled in, sometimes with the missing design or letters re-engraved.

Badly cleaned coins will often display a complexity of fine interlaced lines and such coins have a greatly reduced value. It is also known for coins to be tooled or re-engraved on the high parts of the hair, in order to 'increase' the grade of coin and its value. In general it is better to have a slightly more worn coin than a better example with such damage.

Cleaning coins

Speaking generally, *do not* clean coins. More coins are ruined by injudicious cleaning than through any other cause, and a badly cleaned coin loses much of its value. A nicely toned piece is usually considered desirable. Really dirty gold and silver can, however, be carefully washed in soap and water. Copper coins should never be cleaned or washed, they may be lightly brushed with a brush that is not too harsh.

Buying and selling coins

Exchanging coins with other collectors, searching around the antique shops, telling your relatives and friends that you are interested in coins, or even trying to find your own with a metal detector, are all ways of adding to your collection. However, the time will come when the serious collector needs to acquire specific coins or requires advice on the authenticity or value of a coin.

At this point an expert is needed, and the services of a reputable coin dealer are necessary. There are now a large number of coin dealers in the UK, many of whom belong to the B.N.T.A. (The British Numismatic Trade Association) or the I.A.P.N. (The International Association of Professional Numismatists) and a glance through the 'yellow pages' under 'coin dealer' or 'numismatist' will often provide local information. Many dealers publish their own lists of coins. Studying these lists is a good way for a collector to learn about coins and to classify and catalogue their own collections.

The Standard Catalogue of Coins of England and the UK has been published since 1929. It serves as a price guide for all coin collectors. Spink also publish books on many aspects of English, Greek, Roman and Byzantine coins and on British tokens which serve as a valuable source of information for coin collectors. Our books are available directly from Spink or through reputable booksellers. Many branches of W. H. Smith, and other High Street booksellers, stock copies of *The Standard Catalogue*.

Numismatic Clubs and Societies

There are well over one hundred numismatic societies and clubs in the British Isles. For details of how to contact them see page 562. Joining one is the best way to meet fellow enthusiasts, learn about your coins and other series and acquire coins in a friendly and informative way.

Useful suggestions

Security and insurance. The careful collector should not keep valuable coins at home unless they are insured and have adequate protection. Local police and insurance companies will give advice on what precautions may be necessary.

Most insurance companies will accept a valuation based on *The Standard Catalogue*. It is usually possible to have the amount added to a householder's contents policy but particularly valuable individual coins may have to be separately listed. A 'Fire, Burglary and Theft' policy will cover loss only from the insured's address, but an 'All Risks' policy will usually cover accidental damage and loss anywhere within the U.K.

For coins deposited with a bank or placed in a safe-deposit box a lower insurance premium is usually payable.

Keeping a record. All collectors are advised to have an up-to-date record of their collection and, if possible, photographs of the more important and more easily identifiable coins. This should be kept in a separate place from the collection so that a list and photographs can be given to the police should loss occur. Note the price paid, from whom purchased, the date of acquisition and the condition of the coin.

Storage and handling. New collectors should get into the habit of handling coins by the edge. This is especially important as far as highly polished proof coins are concerned.

Collectors may initially keep their coins in paper or plastic envelopes housed in boxes, albums or special containers. Many collectors will eventually wish to own a hardwood coin cabinet in which the collection can be properly arranged and displayed. If a home-made cabinet is being constructed avoid using oak and cedar wood; mahogany, walnut and rosewood are ideal. It is important that coins are not kept in a humid atmosphere; especial care must be taken with copper and bronze coins which are very susceptible to damp or condensation which may result in a green verdigris forming on them.

From beginner to numismatist

The new collector can best advance to becoming an experienced numismatist by examining as many coins as possible, noting their distinctive features and by learning to use the many books of reference that are available. It will be an advantage to join a local numismatic society, as this will provide an opportunity for meeting other enthusiasts and obtaining advice from more experienced collectors. Most societies have a varied programme of lectures, exhibitions and occasional auctions of members' duplicates.

Those who become members of one or both of the national societies, the Royal Numismatic Society and the British Numismatic Society, receive an annual journal containing authoritative papers and have access to the societies' library and programme of lectures.

Many museums have coin collections available for study, although they may not always be displayed, and a number of museum curators are qualified numismatists.

SOME NUMISMATIC TERMS EXPLAINED

Obverse	That side of the coin which normally shows the monarch's head or name.
Reverse	The side opposite to the obverse, the 'Tails'.
Blank	The coin as a blank piece of metal, i.e. before it is struck.
Flan	The whole piece of metal after striking.
Type	The main, central design.
Legend	The inscription. Coins lacking a legend are called 'mute' or anepigraphic.
Field	That flat part of the coin between the main design and the inscription or edge.
Exergue	That part of the coin below the main design, usually separated by a horizontal line, and normally occupied by the date.
Die	The block of metal, with design cut into it, which actually impresses the coin blank with the design.
Die variety	Coin showing slight variation of design.
Mule	A coin with the current type on one side and the previous (and usually obsolete) type on the other side, or a piece struck from two dies that are not normally used together.
Graining or reeding	The crenellations around the edge of the coin, commonly known as 'milling'.
Proof	Carefully struck coin from special dies with a mirror-like or matt surface. (In this country 'Proof' is not a term used to describe the state of preservation, but the method of striking.)
Hammered	Refers to the old craft method of striking a coin between dies hammered by hand.
Milled	Coins struck by dies worked in a coining press. The presses were hand powered from 1560-1800, powered by steam from 1790 and by electricity from 1895.

CELTIC COINAGE

The Celtic or Ancient British issues are amongst the most interesting and varied of all British coins. They are our earliest coins and are the product of a society that left no historical sources of its own. It is therefore often difficult to be specific about for whom, when or where they were produced. Despite only being used for approximately a hundred and fifty years they do provide a rich variety of designs and types in gold, silver and bronze. Collectors looking for a theme to concentrate on may find the coins of one tribe, an individual ruler or a particular phase in the coinage interesting.

Grading Celtic Coins

The majority of Celtic coins were struck by hand, sometimes resulting in a loss of definition through weak striking. In addition, the design on the dies was often bigger than the blank flan employed, resulting in the loss of some of the design. Coins with full legends are generally more valuable than examples with incomplete legends. Bronze coins in good condition (VF or better) and especially toned examples attract a premium. Factors that detract from a coin's value are chips, scratches and verdigris on bronze coins. It is important to take into account these factors as well as the amount of wear on a coin when assessing its grade.

	Cunobelin Bronze Unit	Epaticcus Silver Unit	Cunobelin Gold Stater
Fine			
Very Fine			

Plated Coins

Plated gold staters, quarter staters and silver units are recorded for many known types. They vary considerably in the quality of their production and are usually priced at around a quarter of the substantive types value. Their exact purpose or relation to the type they copy is not fully understood.

References and Select Bibliography.

M   Mack, R.P. (1975) 3rd edition, The Coinage of Ancient Britain.
V   Van Arsdell, R.D. (1989), Celtic Coinage of Britain.
BMC   Hobbs, R. (1996), British Iron Age Coins in the British Museum.

de Jersey, P. (1996), Celtic Coinage in Britain. *A good general introduction to the series.*
Nash, D. (1987), Coinage in the Celtic World. *Sets the coinage in its social context.*

The layout of the following list is derived from the standard works by Mack, Van Arsdell and the British Museum Catalogue by Richard Hobbs. References are made to these works where possible, in the case of the last work it should be noted that the British Museum collection is not exhaustive, and therefore should not be used to assess the rarity of a coin. More detailed information than that given here can be gained from these works.

IMPORTED COINAGE

The earliest coins to circulate in Britain were made in northern Gaul (Belgica) and imported into the south-east of England from around 150 B.C. onwards. They were principally the product of two tribal groups in this region, the Ambiani and Suessiones. In Britain these types are known as Gallo-Belgic A to F. The first type Gallo-Belgic A is ultimately derived from the Macedonian gold staters (M) of Philip II (359-336 B.C.)

The reasons why they were imported are not fully understood. However, the context for their importation is one of close social, political and economic ties between Britain and Gaul. Within this cross-channel relationship they undoubtedly had various functions, such as payment for military service or mercenaries, in exchanges between the elite of each society: in cementing alliances for example, or as gifts in a system of exchange.

Numbers in brackets following each entry refer to numbers employed in previous editions of this catalogue.

GALLO-BELGIC ISSUES

2	4	5	7

		F £	VF £
From *c*.150 B.C. – *c*.50 B.C.			
1	**Gold Stater.** Gallo-Belgic A. (Ambiani). Good copy of Macedonian stater, large flan. Laureate head of Apollo r. R. Horse l. *M. 1; V. 10. (1)*	1500	6500
2	Similar, but head and horse l. *M. 3; V. 12. (1)*	1250	5000
3	B. (Ambiani). Somewhat similar to 1, but small flan and 'defaced' *obv.* die. R. Horse r. *M. 5; V. 30. (3)*	575	1850
4	— Similar, but with lyre between horse's legs. *M. 7; V. 33. (3)*	650	2250
5	C. (Ambiani), *Stater.* Disintegrated Apollo head. R. horse. *M. 26; V. 44. (5)*	275	900
6	**Gold Quarter Stater.** Gallo-Belgic A. Similar to 1. *M. 2; V .15. (2)*	325	1050
7	— Similar to 2. *M. 4; V. 20. (2)*	300	850
8	B. Similar to 3. *M. 6; V. 35. (4)*	275	800
9	— Similar. R. Two horses l. with lyre between legs. *M. 8; V. 37. (4)*	150	400
10	D. Portions of Apollo head R. A mixture of stars, crescents, pellets, zig-zag lines; often referred to as 'Geometric' types,(See also British 'O', S. 46.). *M. 37, 39, 41, 41a, 42; V. 65/7/9/146. (6)*	85	210

From c.50 B.C.

11

		F £	VF £
11	**Gold Stater.** Gallo-Belgic E. (Ambiani). Blank obv. R. Disjointed curved horse r., pellet below, zig-zag in exergue. *M. 27; V. 52, 54. (7)*	175	375
12	F. (Suessiones). Devolved Apollo head r. R. Disjointed horse r. With triple-tail. *M. 34a; V. 85. (8)*	525	1650
13	Xc. Blank except for VE monogram at edge of coin, R. S below horse r. *M. 82; V. 87-1. (9)*.............	350	1050

Armorican (Channel Islands and N.W. Gaul, c.75-50 B.C.)

14	**Billon Stater.** Class I. Head r. R. Horse, boar below, remains of driver with Victory above, lash ends in or two loops, or 'gate'. *(12)*.........................	35	160
15	— Class II. Head r. R. Horse, boar below, remains of Victory only, lash ends in small cross of four pellets. *(13)*	30	150
16	— Class III. Head r., anchor-shaped nose. R. Somewhat similar to Class I. *(14)*...............	30	150
17	— Class IV. Head r. R. Horse with reins, lyre shape below, driver holds vertical pole, lash ends in three prongs. *(15)*	35	160
18	— Class V. Head r. R. Similar to last, lash ends in long cross with four pellets. *(16)*................	45	200
19	— Class VI. Head r. R. Horse, boar below, lash ends in 'ladder' *(17)*	50	225
20	**Billon Quarter Stater.** Similar types to above. *(18)*..............	45	185

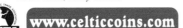

CELTIC COINS STRUCK IN BRITAIN

Coin production in Britain began at the very end of the second century B.C. with the cast potin coinage of Kent (Nos 62-64). Inspired by Gaulish issues and ultimately derived from the potin coins of Massalia (Marseilles) in southern Gaul, the precise function and period of use of this coinage is not fully understood. The domestic production of gold coins started around 70 B.C., these issues are traditionally known as British A-P and are derived from imported Gallo-Belgic issues. Broadly contemporary with these issues are quarter staters, silver units, and bronze units. Recent work by John Sills has further enhanced our understanding of this crucial early period with the identification of two new British staters (Insular Belgic C or Kentish A and the Ingoldisthorpe type) and their related quarters and a Westerham quarter stater. The Insular Belgic C or Kentish A type derived from Gallo-Belgic C now becomes the first British stater.

EARLY UNINSCRIBED COINAGE

20A   20B

		F £	VF £
20A	**Gold Stater.** Insuler Belgic C/Kentish A type. Devolved Apollo head r. R. Disjointed horse r, a rosette behind or in front, or both. *M. —; V. —; BMC —*	550	1850
20B	Ingoldisthorpe type. Similar to last, as illustration. *M.—; V.—; BMC— ..*	450	1500

21   22   23   24

21	British A. Westerham type. Devolved Apollo head r. R. Disjointed horse l. large pellet below. *M. 28, 29; V. 200, 202; BMC 1-32 (19)*	225	575
22	B. Chute type. Similar to 9 but crab-like object below horse. *M. 32; V. 1205; BMC 35-76. (20)*	150	375
23	C. Yarmouth type. Similar to 9 but star-like object in front of horse. *M. 31; V. 1220; BMC 78-85. (21)*	750	2500
24	D. Cheriton type. Similar to Chute type but with large crescent face. *M. 33; V. 1215; BMC 86-128. (22)*	250	675
25	E. Waldingfield type. Annulet and pellet below horse. *M. 48; V. 1462; BMC — —. (23)*	825	2650

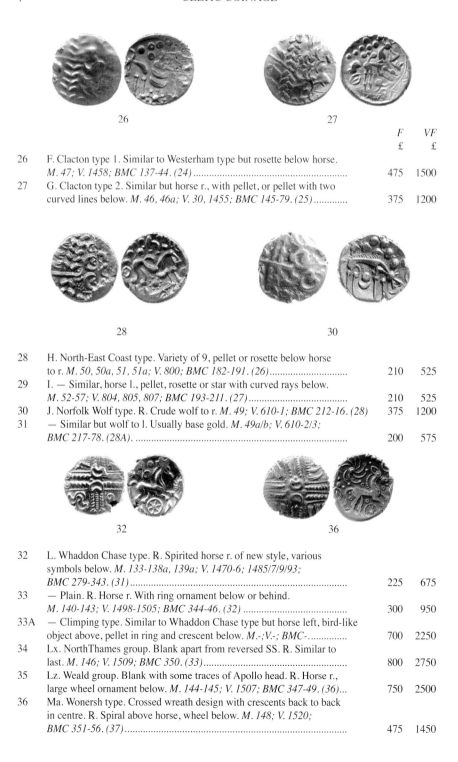

26   27

		F £	VF £
26	F. Clacton type 1. Similar to Westerham type but rosette below horse. *M. 47; V. 1458; BMC 137-44. (24)*	475	1500
27	G. Clacton type 2. Similar but horse r., with pellet, or pellet with two curved lines below. *M. 46, 46a; V. 30, 1455; BMC 145-79. (25)*	375	1200

28   30

		F	VF
28	H. North-East Coast type. Variety of 9, pellet or rosette below horse to r. *M. 50, 50a, 51, 51a; V. 800; BMC 182-191. (26)*	210	525
29	I. — Similar, horse l., pellet, rosette or star with curved rays below. *M. 52-57; V. 804, 805, 807; BMC 193-211. (27)*	210	525
30	J. Norfolk Wolf type. R. Crude wolf to r. *M. 49; V. 610-1; BMC 212-16. (28)*	375	1200
31	— Similar but wolf to l. Usually base gold. *M. 49a/b; V. 610-2/3; BMC 217-78. (28A).*	200	575

32   36

		F	VF
32	L. Whaddon Chase type. R. Spirited horse r. of new style, various symbols below. *M. 133-138a, 139a; V. 1470-6; 1485/7/9/93; BMC 279-343. (31)*	225	675
33	— Plain. R. Horse r. With ring ornament below or behind. *M. 140-143; V. 1498-1505; BMC 344-46. (32)*	300	950
33A	— Climping type. Similar to Whaddon Chase type but horse left, bird-like object above, pellet in ring and crescent below. *M.-;V.-; BMC-.*	700	2250
34	Lx. NorthThames group. Blank apart from reversed SS. R. Similar to last. *M. 146; V. 1509; BMC 350. (33)*	800	2750
35	Lz. Weald group. Blank with some traces of Apollo head. R. Horse r., large wheel ornament below. *M. 144-145; V. 1507; BMC 347-49. (36)*	750	2500
36	Ma. Wonersh type. Crossed wreath design with crescents back to back in centre. R. Spiral above horse, wheel below. *M. 148; V. 1520; BMC 351-56. (37)*	475	1450

37 38

		F £	VF £

37 Mb. Savernake Forest type. Similar but *obv.* plain or almost blank.
 M. 62; V. 1526; BMC 361-64 .... 185 550

38 Qa. British 'Remic' type. Crude laureate head. R. Triple-tailed horse,
 wheel below. *M. 58, 60, 61; V. 210-214; BMC 445-58. (41)* 250 750

39 Qb. — Similar, but *obv.* blank. *M. 59; V. 216; BMC 461-76. (42)* 200 575

39A **Gold Quarter Stater.** Insuler Belgic C/Kentish A type. Similar to Gallo-Belgic D,
 but with rosette in field on obverse. *M. —; V.—; BMC —* 300 950

39B Ingoldisthorpe type. Similar to last but with sperm-like objects in field.
 M.—; V.—; BMC— 325 975

39C British A. Westerham type. Similar to last but of cruder style, or with
 L-shapes in field on rev. *M.—; V.—; BMC—* 275 850

40 British D. Cheriton type. Similar to Stater, large crescent
 face. R. Cross motif with pellets. *M. —; V. 143 var; BMC 129-136* 250 800

41 F/G. Clacton type. Plain, traces of pattern. R. Ornamental cross with
 pellets. *M. 35; V. 1460; BMC 180-1. (43A)* 175 475

42 H. Crescent design and pellets. R. Horse r. *M. —; V. —; BMC 192* 180 525

43 44 45

43 Lx. N.Thames group. Floral pattern on wreath. R. Horse l. or r. *M. 76;*
 V. 234; BMC 365-370. (44) 180 525

44 Ly. N.Kent group. Blank. R. Horse l. or r. *M. 78; V. 158; BMC 371-3. (45)* 165 425

45 Lz. Weald group. Spiral design on wreath. R. Horse l. or r. *M. 77; V. 250;*
 BMC 548-50. (46) 165 425

46 47 48

46 O. Geometric type. Unintelligible patterns (some blank on obv.).
 M. 40, 43-45; V. 143, 1225/27/29; BMC 410-32. (49) 75 175

47 P. Trophy type. Blank. R. Trophy design. *M. 36, 38; V. 145-7;*
 BMC 435-44. (50) 125 300

48 Qc. British 'Remic' type. Head or wreath pattern. R. Triple-tailed horse,
 l. or r. *M. 63-67; 69-75; V. 220-32, 36, 42-6, 56; BMC 478-546. (51)* 135 375

49 Xd. Head l. of good style, horned serpent behind ear. R. Horse l. *M. 79;*
 V. 78; BMC 571-575. (11) 325 950

51   53

		F £	*VF* £
50	**Silver Unit** Lx. Head l.or r. R. Horse l. or r. *M. 280, 435, 436, 438, 441; V. 80, 1546, 1549, 1555; BMC 376-382. (53)*	90	350
51	— Head l. R. Stag r. with long horns. *M. 437; V. 1552; BMC 383-7. (54)*	90	350
52	— **Silver Half Unit.** Two horses or two beasts. *M. 272, 442, 443, 445; V. 474, 1626, 1643, 1948; BMC 389-400. (55)*	85	325
53	Lz. Danebury group. Head r. with hair of long curves. R. Horse l., flower above. *M. 88; V. 262; BMC 580-82*	125	450

54   54A

54	— Helmeted head r. R. Horse r. wheel below. *M. 89; V. 264; BMC 583 -592. (58)*	90	350
54A	Cruciform pattern with ornaments in angles. R. Horse l., ear of corn between legs, crescents and pellets above, *M.—; V.—; BMC—*	135	525
55	— **Silver Quarter Unit.** As last. *M. 90; V. 268; BMC 642-43. (59)*	50	175

56   61

56	— Head r. R. Horse r. star above, wheel below. *M. —; V. 280; BMC 595-601*	75	225
57	— Head l., pellet in ring in front. R. Horse l. or r. *M. —; V. 284; BMC 610-630*	50	175
58	— Serpent looking back. R. Horse l. *M. —; V. 286; BMC 631-33*	85	275
59	— **Silver Quarter Unit.** Cross pattern. R. Two-tailed horse. *M. 119; V. 482; BMC 654-56. (56C). (Formerly attributed to Verica)*	40	150
60	**Bronze Unit.** Lx. Winged horse l. R. Winged horse l. *M. 446; V. 1629; BMC 401 (78)*	65	275
61	Chichester Cock type. Head r. R. Head r. surmounted by cock. *M. —; V. — BMC 657-59*	75	300

POTIN
(Cast Copper/Tin alloy)

62

		F £	VF £
62	**Unit.** Thurrock type.Head l. R. Bull butting l. or r. *M. —; V. 1402-42; BMC 660-666. (84A)*	20	70

63   64

63	Class I type. Crude head. R. Lines representing bull *(Allen types A-L.)* M. 9-22a; V. 104, 106, 108, 112, 114, 115, 117, 119, 120, 122, 123, 125, 127, 129, 131, 133; BMC 667-714. (83)..	25	75
64	Class II type. Smaller flan, large central pellet. *(Allen types M-P.)* M. 23-25; V. 135-39; BMC 715-23. (84)	20	60

CELTIC DYNASTIC AND LATER UNINSCRIBED COINAGE

From Julius Caesar's expeditions to Britain in 55/54 B.C. and his conquest of Gaul in 52 B.C. to the Claudian invasion in 43 A.D., southern Britain was increasingly drawn into the orbit of the Roman world. This process is reflected not only in the coins but also in what we know about their issuers and the tribes they ruled. Latin legends begin to appear for the first time and increasingly accompany objects and designs drawn from the classical world. A lot of what we know about the Celtic tribes and their rulers, beyond just their names on coins, is drawn from contemporary and slightly later Roman historical sources. A great deal however is still uncertain and almost all attributions to either tribes or historically attested individuals have to be seen as tentative.

The coin producing tribes of Britain can be divided into two groups, those of the core and those of the periphery. The tribes of the core, the Atrebates/Regni, Trinovantes/Catuvellauni and Cantii, by virtue of their geographical location controlled contact with the Roman world. Unlike the tribes of the periphery they widely employed Latin legends, classical designs and used bronze coinage in addition to gold and silver.

Following the Roman invasion of 43 A.D. it is likely that some coinage continued to be produced for a short time. However in 61 A.D. with the death of King Prasutagus and the suppression of the Boudiccan revolt that followed, it is likely that Celtic coinage came to an end.

TRIBAL/MINT MAP

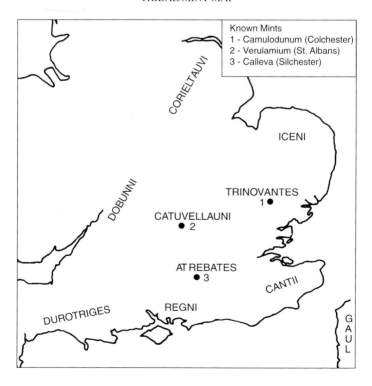

Known Mints
1 - Camulodunum (Colchester)
2 - Verulamium (St. Albans)
3 - Calleva (Silchester)

ATREBATES AND REGNI

The joint tribal area of these two groups corresponds roughly with Berkshire and Sussex and parts of northern and eastern Hampshire. The Atrebatic portion being in the north of this region with its main centre at Calleva (Silchester). The Regni occupying the southern part of the region centred around Chichester.

COMMIUS
(Mid to Late 1st Century B.C.)

The first inscribed staters to appear in Britain, closely resemble British Q staters (no.38) and are inscribed 'COMMIOS'. Staters and silver units with an inscribed 'E' are also thought to be related. Traditionally this Commius was thought to be the Gaulish chieftain who Caesar refers to in De Bello Gallico, as firstly serving him in his expeditions to Britain and finally fleeing to Britain c.50 B.C. This attribution does however present chronological problems, and the appearance of a few early staters reading 'COM COMMIOS' suggests that the Commius who issued coins is more likely to have been the son of Caesar's Commius.

65

		F £	*VF* £
65	**Gold Stater.** Devolved Apollo head r. R. COMMIOS around triple tailed horse r., wheel below. *M. 92; V. 350; BMC 724-29. (85)*	350	1050

66
67

66	Similar, but 'E' symbol above horse instead of legend. *M. —;V. 352. BMC 730*	375	1100
67	**Gold Quarter Stater.** Blank except for digamma. R. Horse l. *M. 83; V. 353-5; BMC —. (10)*	135	350

69

69	**Silver Unit.** Head l. R. Horse l. Mostly with 'E' symbol above. *M. —;V. 355; BMC 731-58. (57)*	35	135

70

70	**Silver Minim.** Similar to Unit. *M. —; V. 358-5; BMC 759-60*	35	130

TINCOMARUS or TINCOMMIUS
(Late 1st Century B.C. – Early 1st Century A.D.)

Successor to Commius and on his coins styled as 'COM.F' (son of Commius). Early coins of the reign like his predecessors are very obivously Celtic in their style. However later coins exhibit an increasing tendancy towards Roman designs. Indeed Tincommius is recorded as a supliant king of the Roman emperor Augustus (Res Gestae, xxxii), finally fleeing to Rome in the early 1st century A.D. The discovery of the Alton Hoard in 1996 brought to light gold staters with the new legend TINCOMARVS.

72   73

		F £	*VF* £
71	**Gold Stater.** *Celtic style*. Devolved Apollo head r. R. TINC COMM. F. around horse. *M. 93; V. 362; BMC —. (86)*	750	2250
72	Similar but legend reads TINCOMARVS. *M. 94; V. 363; BMC 761-765. (86)*	525	1750
73	**Gold Quarter Stater.** Spiral with pellet centre. R. Horse r. T above. *M. 81; V. 366; BMC 781-797. (46)*	125	325

74   75

74	TINCOM, zig-zag ornament below. R. Horse l. *M. 95; V. 365; BMC 798-810. (87)*	150	425
75	**Gold Stater.** *Classical style.* TINC(O) on a sunk tablet. R. Horseman with javelin r. often with CF in field. *M. 96-98; V. 375-76; BMC 765-769. (88)*	450	1250

76   77

76	COM.(F). on a sunk tablet. R. Horseman with javelin r. TIN in field *M. 100; V. 385; BMC 770-774. (88)*	300	900
77	**Gold Quarter Stater.** TINC on a tablet, C above, A or B below. R. Winged head (Medusa?) facing. *M. 97; V. 378; BMC 811-826. (89)*	210	625
78	TIN on tablet. R. Boar l. *M. 99; V. 379; BMC 827-837. (90)*	120	325

79   83

		F £	VF £
79	COMF on tablet. R. Horse r. TIN around. *M. 101; V. 387; BMC 838-841. (90)*	125	350
80	— R. Horse l. TIC around. *M. 102; V. 388; BMC 842-851. (90)*	125	350
81	COM on tablet. R. Horse l. T above. *M. 103; V. 389; BMC 852-3. (90)*..	135	375
82	COMF on tablet. R. Horse r. TINC around. *M. 104; V. 390; BMC 854-879. (90)*	120	325
83	**Silver Unit.** Laureate head r. TINCOM in front, V behind. R. Eagle stg. on snake. *M. 105; V. 397; BMC 880-905. (91)*...	40	180
84	Laureate head l. R. Bull l. TINC around. *M. 106; V. 396; BMC 906-910. (91A)*	45	190
85	Laureate head r. R. Bull r. TIN(C) around. *M. —; V. 381; BMC 911-925. (92B)*..	40	175
86	Facing head. R. Bull l. TINC around. *M. —; V. 370; BMC 926-29 (92)*..	45	190

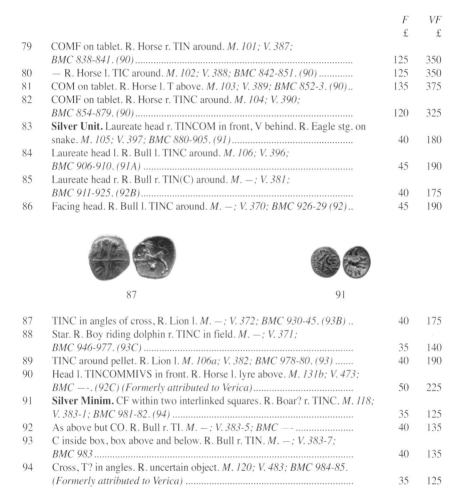

87   91

87	TINC in angles of cross, R. Lion l. *M. —; V. 372; BMC 930-45. (93B)* ..	40	175
88	Star. R. Boy riding dolphin r. TINC in field. *M. —; V. 371; BMC 946-977. (93C)*	35	140
89	TINC around pellet. R. Lion l. *M. 106a; V. 382; BMC 978-80. (93)*	40	190
90	Head l. TINCOMMIVS in front. R. Horse l. lyre above. *M. 131b; V. 473; BMC —. (92C) (Formerly attributed to Verica)*.....................................	50	225
91	**Silver Minim.** CF within two interlinked squares. R. Boar? r. TINC. *M. 118; V. 383-1; BMC 981-82. (94)*	35	125
92	As above but CO. R. Bull r. TI. *M. —; V. 383-5; BMC —-*	40	135
93	C inside box, box above and below. R. Bull r. TIN. *M. —; V. 383-7; BMC 983*	40	135
94	Cross, T? in angles. R. uncertain object. *M. 120; V. 483; BMC 984-85. (Formerly attributed to Verica)*	35	125

EPPILLUS

(Later 1st Century B.C. – Early 1st Century A.D.)

His reign is likely to have coincided with that of Tincommius's, who also claimed to be a son of Commius. Two coinages appear in his name, one for Kent and one minted at Calleva (Silchester, Hants.) in the northern part of the territory of the Atrebates and Regni. The coins of Calleva conform to the southern denominational structure of gold and silver with fractions of each, whilst the Kentish series is distinctly tri-metallic, replacing the silver minim with bronze. A joint coinage was issued by Eppillus and Verica. It is not understood if Eppillus held both territories simultaneously.

COINAGE STRUCK AT CALLEVA

		F £	VF £

95   96

No.	Description	F £	VF £
95	**Gold Stater.** Devolved Apollo head r. R. EPPI COMMI F around horse. *M. —; V. 405; BMC —*	1850	6500
96	**Gold Quarter Stater.** CALLEV, star above and below. R. Hound r. EPPI. *M. 107; V. 407-08; BMC 986-1005. (95)*	125	350

97   98

No.	Description	F £	VF £
97	COMM F EPPILV, around crescent. R. Horse r. *M. —; V. 409; BMC 1006-1009. (95A)*	135	375
98	EPPI COMF in two lines. R. Winged horse r. *M. 302; V. 435; BMC 1010-15. (129)*	135	375

99   100

No.	Description	F £	VF £
99	**Silver Unit.** Crescent REX CALLE above and below. R. Eagle r. EPP. *M. 108; V .415. BMC 1016-1060. (96)*	40	175
100	Bearded hd. r. in wreath. R. Boar r. EPPI(L) F CO(M). *M. —; V. 416; BMC 1061-87. (96A)*	40	175
101	Bearded hd. in pellet border. R. Lion r. EPP COMF. *M. 305; V. 417; BMC 1088-1115. (131)*	40	175
102	**Silver Minim.** Floral cross. R. Eagle r. EPPI. *M. —; V. 420; BMC 1116-17*	45	165
103	Spiral and pellets. R. Ram r. EPP. *M. —; V. 421; BMC 1118-20. (96C)* ...	45	165
104	Bulls head facing. R. Ram r. EPP. *M. —; V. 422; BMC 1121-24. (96D)* ..	50	175
105	Wreath pattern. R. Boar r. EPP. *M. —; V. 423; BMC —-*	55	185
106	Crescent cross. R. Hand holding trident. *M. —; V. 487; BMC —. (111C)*	50	175

KENTISH TYPES

107

		F £	VF £
107	**Gold Stater.** COMF within wreath. R. Horseman l. EPPILLVS above. M. 300; V. 430; BMC 1125-26. (127)	1850	6500
108	Victory holding wreath l., within wreath. R. Horseman r. holding carnyx, F EPPI COM below. M. 301; V. 431; BMC 1127-28. (128)	2500	8500
109	**Gold Quarter Stater.** Crossed wreaths, EPPI in angles. R. Horse l. M. 303; V. 436; BMC 1129. (130)	425	1350
110	COMF in pellet border. R. Horse r. EPPI. M. 304; V. 437; BMC 1130-31. (130)	350	1050
111	**Silver Unit.** Head l. EPPIL in field. R. Horseman holding carnyx, EPPILL. M. 306; V. 441; BMC 1132. (131)	275	900
112	**Bronze Unit.** Bow cross, EPPI COMF around. R. Eagle facing. M. 309; V. 450; BMC 1137-38. (134)	45	250
113	Bull r., EPPI COF around. R. eagle facing. M. 310; V. 451; BMC 1139-41. (134)	45	250
114	Head l., EPPI in front. R. Victory l. holding wreath and standard. M. 311; V. 452; BMC 1142. (133)	50	275
115	Bearded hd. r., EPPI CF. R. Biga r. CF. M. 312; V. 453; BMC —	60	325

JOINT TYPES OF EPPILUS AND VERICA

116	**Silver Unit.** Head l. CO VIR in front. R. Victory, EP. M. 307; V. 442; BMC 1133-34. (132)	425	1350

117

117	Head r. VIR CO in front. R. Capricorn l. EPPI COMF. M. 308/a; V. 443; BMC 1135-36. (132)	250	825

VERICA

(c.10.-c.40 A.D.)

The exact details of Verica's succession and relationship to Eppillus and Tincommius are not fully understood. However by c.10 A.D. it seems likely that Verica was the sole ruler of the southern region. His close contact with Rome, both political and economic, seen in the increasing use of classical designs on his coins, culminated in his flight to Rome in c.42 A.D. to seek assistance from Claudius.

		F	*VF*
		£	£
118	**Gold Stater.** COM:F on tablet. Ŗ. Horseman r. holding spear, VIR below. *M. 109; V. 460; BMC 1143-44. (97)*	325	950
119	COM.F. on tablet, pellet in ring ornament above and below. Ŗ. Similar to last. *M.121; 461; BMC 1146-53. (97)*	325	950

120

121

120	COM.F on tablet. Ŗ. Horseman r. holding spear, VIR above, REX below. *M. 121 var; V. 500; BMC 1155-58. (98)*	275	750
121	Vine-leaf dividing VI RI. Ŗ. Horseman r. with shield and spear. COF in field. *M. 125; V. 520-1; BMC 1159-73. (99)*	350	1000
122	Similar, reads VE RI. *M. 125; V. 520-5/7; BMC 1174-76. (99)*	350	1050
123	**Gold Quarter Stater.** COMF on tablet. Ŗ. Horse l. VIR. *M. 111; V. 465; BMC 1177-78. (100)*	150	400

124

124	COMF on tablet, pellet in ring ornament above and below Ŗ. Horse r. VI. *M. 112; V. 466; BMC 1179-1206. (100)*	130	300
125	COMF on tablet, pellet border. Ŗ. Horse r. VI above. *M. 113; V. 467; BMC 1207-16. (100)*	135	325

126

128

126	COM FILI. in two lines, scroll in between. Ŗ. Horse r. VIR(I) above. *M. 114; V. 468; BMC 1217-22. (100)*	140	375
127	VERI COMF, crescent above, star below. Ŗ. Horse r. REX below. *M. 122; V. 501; BMC 1223-36. (101)*	140	375
128	VERI beneath vine-leaf. Ŗ. Horseman r. with sword and shield, FRX in field. *M. 124; V. 525; BMC 1237-38. (102)*	250	900
129	COM, horseman r. Ŗ. Seated figure, VERICA around. *M. 126; V. 526; BMC 1239. (103)*	525	1750
130	Similar to last. Ŗ. Laureate bust r., VIRI in front. *M. 127; V. 527; BMC 1240. (103)*	475	1500

	F	*VF*
	£	£

131 **Silver Unit.** COMF, crescent and or pellet in ring above and below. R. Boar r.
VI(RI) below. *M. 115; V. 470/72; BMC 1241-1331. (104)* 40   160

132   133

132 VERICA COMMI F around pellet in ring. R. Lion r. REX below.
M. 123; V. 505; BMC 1332-1359. (105) 45   185
133 COMMI F, horseman with shield r. R. VERI CA, mounted warrior with
spear r. *M. 128; V. 530; BMC 1360-92. (106)* 45   185

134   137

134 Two cornucopiae, COMMI F. R. Figure seated r. VERICA. *M. 129;
V. 531; BMC 1393-1419. (107)*.. 40   160
135 Bust r. VIRI. R. Figure seated l. *M. 130; V. 532; BMC 1420. (108)* 100   425
136 Naked figure l. R. Laureate bust r., COMMI F. *M. 131; V. 533;
BMC 1421-49. (108)* 40   160
137 VERICA REX, bull r. R. Figure stg. l., COMMI F. *M. —; V. 506;
BMC 1450-84. (108B)* 40   150
138 COMF, in tablet and scroll. R. Eagle facing, VI RI. *M. —; V. 471;
BMC 1485-1505. (104A)* 40   150
139 VIRIC across field, ornaments above and below. R. Pegasus r., star
design below. *M. —; V. —; BMC —. (104B)* 75   325
140 Head r. Verica. R. COMMI F., eagle l. *M. 131A; V. 534; BMC —. (108A)* 90   375
141 **Silver Minim.** COF in tablet, R. Facing head (Medusa?), VE below. *M. —;
V. 384; BMC 1506. (94A). (Formerly attributed to Tincommius)*.............. 40   160
142 Head r. R. Horse r., VIRICO. *M. 116; V. 480; BMC —. (109)* 40   160
143 Pellet and ring pattern. R. Lion r. VIR. *M. 120a/c; V. 484;
BMC 1514-17. (109)*.. 35   135
144 VIRIC reversed. R. Boar r. *M. —; V. 485; BMC 1518* 35   135
145 Cross. R. Trident. *M. —; V. 486-1; BMC —-*.. 45   175
146 Uncertain. R. Boar r. *M. 120b; V. 510-1; BMC —. (109)* 30   120
147 Crescent cross. R. Boar r. *M. —; V. 510-5; BMC 1521-23. (109)* 35   140
148 VIR VAR in tablets. R. Winged horse r. CO. *M. 120d; V. 511;
BMC 1507-12. (109)* 35   140

149   150

149 Vine-leaf, CFO. R. Horse r. VERI CA. *M. —; V. 550; BMC 1524-25* 35   140
150 CF in torc. R. Head r. VERIC. *M. 132; V. 551; BMC 1526-33. (111A)*.... 30   135

		F £	VF £
151	Altar, CF, R. Bulls head facing, VERICA. *M. 120e; V. 552; BMC 1534-37. (109)*	55	225
152	Temple, CF. R. Bull r, VER REX. *M. —; V. 553; BMC 1538-41*	30	135

153 154

153	Cornucopia, VER COM. R. Lion r. *M. —; V. 554; BMC 1542*	35	150
154	Two cornucopiae. R. Eagle l. *M. —; V. 555; BMC 1543-58*	30	100
155	Floral pattern, CF. R. Lion r. *M.—; V. 556; BMC 1559-63. (111E)*	35	140
156	Sphinx r., CF, R. dog curled up, VERI. *M. —; V. 557; BMC 1564-68. (109B)*	30	135
157	VERI. R. Urn, COMMI F. *M. —; V. 559; BMC —-*	40	160
158	A in star. R. Bird r. *M. 316; V. 561; BMC 1569-71*	50	200
159	Urn, Rex. R. Eagle r., VERRICA COMMI F. *M. —; V. 563; BMC 1572-78. (109C)*	30	110
160	VIR inside tablet. R. Boars head r. *M. 117; V. 564; BMC 1579-81. (109A)*	30	130
161	Cross. R. bull l. *M. —; V. —; BMC 1582*	35	150
162	Boars head r., CF, R. Eagle, VE. *M. —; V. —; BMC 1583-86*	30	120
163	Head r, COMM IF., R. Sphinx, R VE. *M. —; V. —; BMC 1587-89*	35	150
164	A in tablet. R. Boar r. VI CO. *M. —; V. —; BMC 1590*	50	200
	The two following coins are possibly issues of Epatticus.		
165	Bull r. R. Eagle with snake l. *M. —; V. 512; BMC 2366-70*	35	150
166	Bust r. R. dog r. *M. —; V. 558; BMC 2371-74*	40	160

CANTII

The Cantii, who gave their name to Kent, occupied a similar area to that of the modern county. Caesar considered this the most civilised part of Britain and the early production of potin units in Kent can be seen as indicative of this. A number of Kentish rulers for whom we have coins, appear to be dynasts from the two neighbouring kingdoms, who were involved in struggles to acquire territory. Eppillus (see Atrebates and Regni) produced coins specifically for circulation in Kent and like those of Cunobelin they circulated widely.

EARLY UNINSCRIBED

167	**Gold Stater.** Ly. Blank. R. Horse l. numerous ring ornaments in field. *M. 293; V. 142; BMC 2472. (34)*	575	2000
168	Blank. R. Horse r. numerous ornaments in field. *M. 294; V. 157; BMC— (34)*	575	2000

169 170

169	Lz. Blank. R. Horse l., box with cross hatching below. *M. 84, 292; V. 150, 144; BMC 2466-68. (35)*	625	2250
170	**Gold Quarter Stater.** Ly. Blank. R. Horse r., pentagram below. *M. 285; V. 163; BMC 2473-74. (45)*	130	325

171   173   176

		F £	VF £
171	Blank. R. Horse r., 'V' shape above. *M. 284; V. 170; BMC 2475-77. (45)*	125	300
172	Lz. Blank. R. Horse l., 'V' shape above. *M. 85; V. 151; BMC 2469-70. (47)*	125	300
173	**Silver Unit.** Curved star. R. Horse r. Pentagram below. *M. 272a; V. 164; BMC —. (56)*	130	425
174	Serpent torc. R. Horse r., box with cross hatching below. *cf Mossop 8; BMC 2478*	175	600
175	**Silver Half Unit.** Spiral of three arms. R. Horse l. *M. —; V. —; BMC 2479*	75	275
176	**Bronze Unit.** Various animal types, R. Various animal types. *M. 295-96, 316a-d; V. 154/167; BMC 2480-91. (80/141-44)*	40	165

DUBNOVELLAUNUS
(Late 1st Century B.C.)

Likely to be the same Dubnovellaunus recorded on coins in Essex (see Trinovantes / Catuvellauni). The two coinages share the same denominational structure and have some stylistic similarities. It has been suggested that Dubnovellaunus is the British king of that name mentioned along with Tincommius as a client king in the Res Gestae of the Roman emperor Augustus.

177   180

177	**Gold Stater.** Blank. R. Horse r., bucranium above, serpent like object below, DUBNOV[ELLAUNUS] or similar around. *M. 282; V. 169; BMC 2492-96. (118)*	275	850
178	— R. Horse r., but without bucranium and with wheel below. *M. 283; V. 176; BMC 2497-98. (118)*	425	1350
179	**Silver Unit.** Winged animal r. R. Horse l., DVBNO. *M. 286; V. 171; BMC 2499-2501. (119)*	120	375
180	Winged animal l. R. Seated fig. l., holding hammer, DVBNO. *M. 287; V. 178; BMC 2502-03. (119)*	125	400
181	**Bronze Unit.** Horse r. R. Lion l., DVBN. *M. 290; V. 166; BMC 2504-06. (122).*	65	250
182	Boar l., DVBNO. R. Horseman r. *M. 291; V. 181; BMC 2507-08. (121).*	65	250
183	Boar r., DVBNO. R. Eagle facing. *M. 289; V. 180; BMC 2509-10. (121)*	60	240

VOSENOS
(Late 1st Century B.C./ Early 1st Century A.D.)
Little is known of this ruler who issued coins in a characteristically Kentish style similar to those of Dubnovellaunus.

	F £	VF £

184   **Gold Stater.** Blank. R. Horse l., bucranium above, serpent like object below., [VOSE]NOS. *M. 297; V. 184; BMC 2511-12. (123)* 2000   6000

185

185   **Gold Quarter Stater.** Blank. R. Horse r., VOSI below. *M. 298; V. 185; BMC 2514-15. (124)*.. 450   1350

186   **Silver Unit.** Horse and griffin. R. Horse r., retrograde legend. *M. 299a; V. 186; BMC —. (125)* 175   650

"SA" or "SAM"
(Late 1st Century B.C./ Early 1st Century A.D.)
An historically unattested individual whose coins are stylistically associated with those of Dubnovellaunus and Vosenos. His coins have been predominantly found in north Kent

187   **Silver Unit.** Head l., R. Horse l., SA below. *M. —; V. —; BMC —*.......... 200   750

187A   **Bronze Unit.** Boar l., R. Horse l., SA below. *M. 299; V. 187; BMC 2516-19. (126)*   85   300

187B

187B   Horse l., SAM below. R. Horse l., SAM below. *M. —; V. —; BMC —* 90   375

AMMINUS
(Early 1st Century A.D.)
Issued a coinage stylistically distinct from other Kentish types and with strong affinities to those of Cunobelin. Indeed it has been suggested that he is the Adminius recorded by Suetonius, as a son of Cunobelin. The enigmatic legend DVN or DVNO may be an unknown mint site.

189

188   **Silver Unit.** Plant, AMMINUS around. R. Winged horse r., DVN. *M. 313; V. 192; BMC 2522-23. (136)*.. 100   400

189   (Last year 190). A in wreath. R. Capricorn r., S AM (I). *M. 314; V. 194; BMC 2520-21. (137)* 95   350

190   **Bronze Unit.** (Last year 189). AM in wreath. R. Horse r., DVNO. *M. —; V. 193; BMC ——* 90   325

191   Head r. R. Hippocamp r., AM. *M. 315; V. 195; BMC 2524. (139)*........... 90   325

TRINOVANTES AND CATUVELLAUNI

Occupying the broad area of Essex, southern Suffolk, Bedfordshire, Buckinghamshire, Hertfordshire, parts of Oxfordshire, Cambridgeshire and Northamptonshire, they are likely to have been two separate tribes for most of their history. The Trinovantes were originally located in the eastern half of this area, with their main centre at Camulodunum (Colchester). The original Catuvellauni heartland was further west, with their main centre at Verulamium (St.Albans). The whole area eventually came under the control of Cunobelin at the end of the period.

TRINOVANTES

ADDEDOMAROS
(Late 1st Century B.C.)

Unknown to history, he appears to have been a contemporary of Tasciovanus. The design of his staters is based on the Whaddon Chase type (No.32) which circulated widely in this region.

200

		F £	VF £
200	**Gold Stater.** Crossed wreath. R. Horse r., wheel below, AθθIIDOM above. *M. 266; V. 1605; BMC 2390-94. (148)*	300	950

201   202

201	Six armed spiral. R. Horse r., cornucopia below, AθθIIDOM above. *M. 267; V. 1620; BMC 2396-2404. (148)*	250	725
202	Two opposed crescents. R. Horse r., branch below, spiral or wheel above, AθθDIIDOM. *M. 268; V. 1635; BMC 2405-2415. (149)*	325	1050

203   204

203	**Gold Quarter Stater.** Circular flower pattern. R. Horse r. *M. 271; V. 1608; BMC 2416. (44)*	175	500
204	Cross shaped flower pattern. R. Horse r. *M. 270; V. 1623; BMC 2417-21. (44)*	150	375
205	Two opposed crescents. R. Horse r., AθθDIIDOM around. *M. 269; V. 1638; BMC 2422-24. (150)*	225	800
206	**Bronze Unit.** Head l. R. Horse l. *M. 274; V. 1615/46 BMC 2450-60. (77)*	35	125

DUBNOVELLAUNUS
(Late 1st Century B.C./ Early 1st Century A.D.)

Dubnovellaunus is likely to have been the successor to Addedomaros, with whom his coins are stylistically related. It is not clear if he was the same Dubnovellaunus who also issued coins in Kent (see Cantii) or if he is the same Dumnobeallaunos mentioned in the Res Gestae of the emperor Augustus c.AD14.

207   208

		F £	VF £
207	**Gold Stater.** Two crescents on wreath. R. Horse l., leaf below, pellet in ring, DVBNOVAIIAVNOS above. *M. 275; V. 1650; BMC 2425-40. (152)*	325	900
208	**Gold Quarter Stater.** Similar. *M. 276; V. 1660; BMC 2442. (153)*	150	425

210

209	**Silver Unit.** Head l., DVBNO. R. Winged horse r., lattice box below. *M. 288; V. 165; BMC 2443-44. (120)*..	130	400
210	Head l., legend ?, R. Horse l. DVB[NOV]. *M. 278; V. 1667; BMC 2445. (154)*..	125	375
211	**Bronze Unit.** Head l., R. Horse l., DVBNO above. *M. 281; V. 1669; BMC 2446-48. (154)*..	50	175
212	Head r., R. Horse l. *M. 277; V. 1665; BMC 2461-65. (154)*	50	175

DIRAS
(Late 1st Century B.C./ Early 1st Century A.D.)

An historically unattested ruler, responsible for a gold stater related stylistically to Dubnovellaunus's.

213

213	**Gold Stater.** Blank. R. Horse r., DIRAS? above, yoke like object above. *M. 279; V. 162; BMC 2449. (151)*	2250	6750

CATUVELLAUNI

TASCIOVANUS
(Late 1st Century B.C./ Early 1st Century A.D.)

The early gold coins of Tasciovanus, like those of his contemporary Addedomaros, are based on the Whaddon Chase stater. Verulamium (St.Albans) appears to have been his principal mint, appearing as VER or VERL on the coinage. Staters and quarter staters inscribed CAM (Camulodunum/ Colchester) are known and perhaps suggest brief or weak control of the territory to the east. The later coins of Tasciovanus use increasingly Romanised designs. The adoption of the title RICON, perhaps a Celtic equivalent to the Latin REX (King), can be seen as a parallel move to that of his contemporary Tincommius to the south.

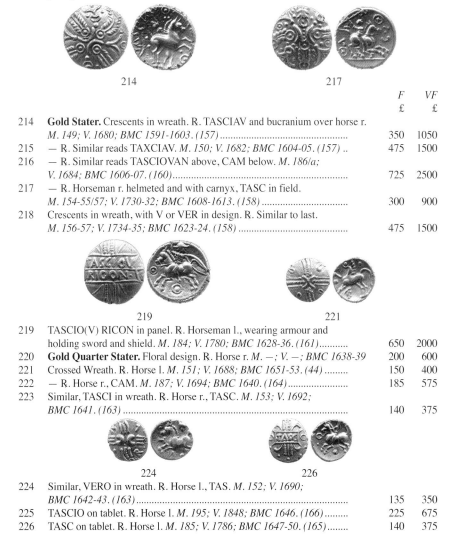

214   217

		F £	VF £
214	**Gold Stater.** Crescents in wreath. R. TASCIAV and bucranium over horse r. M. 149; V. 1680; BMC 1591-1603. (157)	350	1050
215	— R. Similar reads TAXCIAV. M. 150; V. 1682; BMC 1604-05. (157)	475	1500
216	— R. Similar reads TASCIOVAN above, CAM below. M. 186/a; V. 1684; BMC 1606-07. (160)	725	2500
217	— R. Horseman r. helmeted and with carnyx, TASC in field. M. 154-55/57; V. 1730-32; BMC 1608-1613. (158)	300	900
218	Crescents in wreath, with V or VER in design. R. Similar to last. M. 156-57; V. 1734-35; BMC 1623-24. (158)	475	1500

219   221

219	TASCIO(V) RICON in panel. R. Horseman l., wearing armour and holding sword and shield. M. 184; V. 1780; BMC 1628-36. (161)	650	2000
220	**Gold Quarter Stater.** Floral design. R. Horse r. M. —; V. —; BMC 1638-39	200	600
221	Crossed Wreath. R. Horse l. M. 151; V. 1688; BMC 1651-53. (44)	150	400
222	— R. Horse r., CAM. M. 187; V. 1694; BMC 1640. (164)	185	575
223	Similar, TASCI in wreath. R. Horse r., TASC. M. 153; V. 1692; BMC 1641. (163)	140	375

224   226

224	Similar, VERO in wreath. R. Horse l., TAS. M. 152; V. 1690; BMC 1642-43. (163)	135	350
225	TASCIO on tablet. R. Horse l. M. 195; V. 1848; BMC 1646. (166)	225	675
226	TASC on tablet. R. Horse l. M. 185; V. 1786; BMC 1647-50. (165)	140	375

		F	*VF*
		£	£
227	**Silver Unit.** Head l. R. Horse r. *M. —; V. 1698; BMC 1654*	65	200
228	Cross and box. R. Horse r., VER in front. *M. —; V. —; BMC 1655*	65	225
229	Cross and crescent. R. Horse l., TASCI. *M. —; V. —; BMC 1665-57*	65	200
230	Bearded head l. R. Horseman r., TASCIO. *M. 158; V. 1745;*		
	BMC 1667-68. (167)	75	300
231	Winged horse l., TAS. R. Griffin r., within circle of pellets. *M. 159;*		
	V. 1790; BMC 1660. (168)	70	250
232	Eagle stg. l., TASCIA. R. Griffin r. *M. 160; V. 1792; BMC 1658-59. (169)*	75	300
233	VER in beaded circle. R. Horse r., TASCIA. *M. 161; V. 1699;*		
	BMC 1670-73. (170)	70	275
234	— R. Naked horseman. *M. 162; V. 1747; BMC 1674-76. (171)*	70	275

235   238

		F	*VF*
235	Laureate hd. r., TASCIA. R. Bull l. *M. 163; V. 1794; BMC 1681-82. (172)*	70	275
236	Cross and box, VERL. R. Boar r. TAS. *M. 164; V. 1796;*		
	BMC 1661-62. (173)	70	275
237	TASC in panel. R. Winged horse l. *M. 165; V. 1798; BMC 1664-65. (174)*	70	250
238	— R. Horseman l., carrying long shield. *M. 166; V. 1800;*		
	BMC 1677-79. (174)	75	300
239	Two crescents. R. Winged griffin, VIR. *M. —; V. —; BMC 1666*	85	325
240	Head r., TAS?. R. Horseman r. *M. —; V. —; BMC 1669*	75	300

241

		F	*VF*
241	**Bronze Double Unit.** Head r., TASCIA, VA. R. Horseman r. *M. 178; V. 1818;*		
	BMC 1685-87. (190)	110	425

242

		F	*VF*
242	**Bronze Unit.** Two heads in profile, one bearded. R. Ram l., TASC. *M. 167;*		
	V. 1705; BMC 1711-13. (178)	35	140
243	Bearded head r. VER(L). R. Horse l., VIIR or VER. *M. 168; V. 1707;*		
	BMC 1714-21. (179)	30	130
244	Bearded head r. R. Horse l., TAS. *M. 169; V. 1709; BMC 1722-23. (179)*	35	140
245	Head r., TASC. R. Winged horse l., VER. *M. 170; V. 1711;*		
	BMC 1688-89. (180)	30	130
246	— R. Horseman r., holding carnyx, VIR. *M. 171; V. 1750;*		
	BMC 1724-27. (182)	30	130

247

		F £	VF £
247	VERLAMIO between rays of star. R. Bull l. *M. 172; V. 1808;* *BMC 1745-51. (183)*	30	125
248	Similar without legend. R. Bull r. *M. 174; V. 1810; BMC 1752-55. (185)*	35	140
249	Similar. R. Horse l., TASCI. *M. 175; V. 1812; BMC 1709-10. (186)*	35	140
250	Head r., TASCIO. R. Lion r., TA SCI. *M. 176; V. 1814; BMC 1736-38.* *(188)*	30	135
251	Head r. R. Figure std. l., VER below. *M. 177; V. 1816; BMC 1739-44.* *(189)*	35	140
252	Cross and Crescents. R. Boar r., VER. *M. 179; V. 1713;* *BMC 1702-05. (191)*	30	135
253	Laureate head r. R. Horse l., VIR. *M. 180; V. 1820; BMC 1706-08. (192)*	30	135
254	Raised band across centre, VER or VERL below. R. Horse grazing r. *M. 183a; V. 1717; BMC —. (193)*	40	150
255	**Bronze Fractional Unit.** Animal r. R. Sphinx l. *M. 181; V. 1824;* *BMC 1760-61. (198)*	40	160
256	Head l., VER. R. Goat r. *M. 182; V. 1715; BMC 1765-68. (199)*	30	140
257	Head r. R. Boar r, *M. 183; V. 1826; BMC 1762-64. (199)*	30	140
258	Head l. R. Animal with curved tail. *M. 183b, c; V. 1822; BMC 1759.* *(200)*	35	150

ASSOCIATES OF TASCIOVANUS
(Early 1st Century A.D.)

Towards the end of his reign, a number of joint issues bearing his name and the name of either Sego or Dias appear. In addition coins similar in style to those of Tasciovanus appear with either the name Andoco or Rues. It has been suggested that these issues belong to a period of struggle following the death of Tasciovanus and are all rival contestants for the throne. Another theory is that they are associates or sub-kings of Tasciovanus responsible for areas within the wider territory.

SEGO

259

259	**Gold Stater.** TASCIO in tablet, annulets above. R. Horseman with carnyx r., SEGO. *M. 194; V. 1845; BMC 1625-27. (162)*	1500	5000

260

		F £	VF £
260	**Silver Unit.** SEGO on panel. R. Horseman r. *M. 196; V. 1851;* *BMC 1684. (176)*	375	1350
261	**Bronze Unit.** Star shaped pattern. R. Winged sphinx l., SEGO. *M. 173; V. 1855;* *BMC 1690. (184)*	120	375

ANDOCO

262

262	**Gold Stater.** Crescents in wreath. R. Bucranium over horse r., AND below. *M. 197; V. 1860; BMC 2011-14. (202)*	725	2250
263	**Gold Quarter Stater.** Crossed wreaths, ANDO in angles. R. Horse l. *M. 198;* *V. 1863; BMC 2015-17. (203)*...	200	650

264

264	**Silver Unit.** Bearded head l. R. Winged horse l., ANDOC. *M. 199; V. 1868;* *BMC 2018. (204)*	110	375

265

265	**Bronze Unit.** Head r., ANDOCO. R. Horse r., ANDOCO. *M. 200; V. 1871;* *BMC 2019-20. (205)*...	45	175
266	Head r., TAS ANDO. R. Horse r. *M. 175a; V. 1873; BMC —. (187)*	60	250

DIAS

267   268

267	**Silver Unit.** Saltire over cross within square. R. Boar r., TASC DIAS. *M. —; V. —; BMC 1663. (173A)*..	95	275
268	DIAS CO, in star. R. Horse l., VIR. *M. 188; V. 1877; BMC 1683. (177).*	100	300

269

		F £	VF £
269	**Bronze Unit.** Bearded head r., DIAS TASC. R. Centaur r., playing pan pipes. M. 192; V. 1882; BMC 1728-35. (197)	50	250

RUES

270	**Bronze Unit.** Lion r., RVII. R. Eagle. M. 189; V. 1890; BMC 1691. (194)	45	225
271	— R. Similar reads RVE. M. 189; V. 1890-3; BMC 1692. (194)	40	200

272   273

272	Bearded head r., RVIIS. R. Horseman r., VIR. M. 190; V. 1892; BMC 1698-1701. (195)...	45	225
273	RVIIS on tablet. R. Winged sphinx l. M. 191; V. 1895; BMC 1693-97. (196)	45	225
274	**Bronze Fractional Unit.** Annulet within square with curved sides. R. Eagle l.,RVII. M. 193; V. 1903; BMC 1756-58. (201)............................	60	275

CUNOBELIN

(Early 1st Century A.D. to c.40 A.D.)

Styled as son of Tasciovanus on some of his coins, Cunobelin appears to have ruled over the unified territories of the Trinovantes and Catuvellauni, with additional territory in Kent. His aggressive policy of expansion that involved members of family eventually lead to Roman concern over the extent of his power. Following his death just prior to 43 AD, the emperor Claudius took the decision to invade Britain.

During his long reign an extensive issue of gold, silver and bronze coins used ever increasingly Romanised designs. It has been estimated from a study of known dies that around one million of his gold corn ear staters were produced. His main centre and mint was at Camulodunum (Colchester) appearing as the mint signature CAMV. The names SOLIDV and AGR appear on a few coins associated with Cunobelin and are likely to represent personal names.

280   281

280	**Gold Stater.** Biga type. CAMVL on panel. R. Two horses l., wheel below, CVNOBELIN. M. 201; V. 1910; BMC 1769-71. (207)............................	750	2250
281	Linear type. Corn ear dividing CA MV. R. Horse r., branch above, CVN. M. 210; V. 1925; BMC 1772-76. (208)..	300	800

		F	*VF*
		£	£

282   — Similar, privy mark 'x' above a letter in *obv.* legend. *M. 210a;*
       VA 1925-3/5; BMC 1777-81. (208)..   350   1050

283   285

283   Wild type. Corn ear dividing CA MV. R. Horse r., branch above.,
       CVN(O). *M. 211/2; V. 1931/33; BMC 1784-92/1804-08. (208)*..............   300   800
284   — Similar, heart shaped object between horses forelegs. *M. 211 var;*
       V. 1931-3; BMC 1793. (208)...   575   1750
285   — Similar, privy mark pellet or pellet triangle above a letter(s) in *obv.*
       legend. *M. —; V. 1931-5/7/9; BMC 1797-1803. (208)*   325   850

286   288

286   Plastic type. Corn ear dividing CA MV. R. Horse r., branch above.,
       CVNO. *M. 203/13; V. 2010-1/3/5; BMC 1809-11/15-23. (208)*..............   275   700
287   — Similar, 'B' in front of horse. *M. —; V. 2010-7; BMC 1813. (208)*.....   475   1500

289   290

288   Classic type. Corn ear dividing CA MV. R. Horse r., branch above.,
       CVNO. *M. 206-07; V. 2025/27; BMC 1827-31/33. (208)*   375   1100
289   — Similar, horse l., lis like object above. *M. 208; V. 2029;*
       BMC 1834-35. (209)   600   1850
290   Gold Quarter Stater. Biga type. Similar to 280. *M. 202; V. 1913;*
       BMC 1836/A. (210)...   225   675

292   296

292   Linear type. Similar to 281. *M. 209; V. 1927; BMC 1837-42. (211)*   135   300
293   Wild type. Similar to 283. *M. —; V. 1935; BMC 1843-44. (211)*   135   300
294   Plastic type. Similar to 286. *M. 204; V. 2015; BMC 1846-48. (211)*   130   300
295   — Similar but corn ear dividing CAM CVN. *M. 205; V. 2017;*
       BMC 1845. (212)   150   375
296   Classic type. Similar to 288. *M. —; V. 2038; BMC —. (211)*   150   475

299

		F £	VF £
299	**Silver Unit.** Two bull headed serpents, inter twined. R. Horse l., CVNO. M. 214; V. 1947; BMC 1856. (213)	80	350
300	Curled serpent inside wheel. R. Winged horse l., CVN. M. —; V. —; BMC 1857	80	375
301	CVN on panel R. Horse l., (C)M. M. 255; V. 1949; BMC 1858-59. (228)	65	225
302	CVNO BELI on two panels. R. CVN below horseman r. M. 216/7; V. 1951/53; BMC 1862. (215)	70	225
303	Head l., CAMVL. R. CVNO beneath Victory std. r. M. 215; V. 2045; BMV 1863-65. (214)	75	250

304   305

304	Two leaves dividing CVN. R. Horseman r., CAM. M. 218; V. 2047; BMC 1866-67. (216)	70	225
305	Flower dividing CAMV. R. CVNO below horse r. M. 219; V. 2049; BMC1867A. (217)	80	325
306	CVNO on panel. R. CAMV on panel below griffin. M. 234; V. 2051; BMC 1868-69. (218)	75	300
307	CAMVL on panel. R. CVNO below centaur l. carrying palm. M. 234a; V. 1918; BMC —. (219)	75	300
308	CAMVL on panel. R. Figure seated l. holding wine amphora, CVNOBE. M. —; V. —; BMC —. (219A)	70	225
309	Plant, CVNOBELINVS. R. Figure stg. r. holding club and thunderbolt dividing CA MV. M. —; V.—; BMC 1897. (219B)	80	350
310	Laur. hd. r., CVNOBELINVS. R. Winged horse springing l., CAMV below. M. —; V. —; BMC —. (219C)	80	350
311	CVNO on panel, wreath around. R. Winged horse r., TASC F. M. 235; V. 2053; BMC 1870. (220)	85	350

312   313

312	Head r., CVNOBELINI. R. Horse r., TASCIO. M. 236; V. 2055; BMC 1871-73. (221)	60	225
313	Winged bust r., CVNO. R. Sphinx std. l., TASCIO. M. 237; V. 2057; BMC 1874-78. (222)	45	150

314

316

		F £	VF £
314	Draped female fig. r., TASCIIOVAN. R. Figure std. r. playing lyre, tree behind. *M. 238; V. 2059; BMC 1879-82. (223)*	70	250
315	Figure stg. l., holding club and lionskin., CVNO. R. Female rider r., TASCIOVA. *M. 239; V. 2061; BMC 1884-85. (224)*	60	225
316	Female head r., CVNOBELINVS. R. Victory r., TASCIO(VAN). *M. —; V. —; BMC 1883. (224A)*	60	225
317	Fig. r. carrying dead animal, CVNOBELINVS. R. Fig. stg. holding bow, dog at side, TASCIIOVANI. *M. 240; V. 2063; BMC 1886-88. (225)*	70	240

318

318	CVNO on panel, horn above, dolphin below. R. Fig. stg. r. altar behind. *M. 241/41a; V. 2065; BMC 1889-90. (226)*	85	325
319	CVN on panel. R. Fig. holding club walking r., CVN. *M. 254; V. 2067; BMC 1891-92. (227)*	75	275
320	CVN in wreath. R. CAM, dog? trampling on serpent r. *M. 256; V. 2069; BMC 1893. (229)*	85	325
321	Winged horse l., CVN. R. Std. fig. r. *M. 258; V. 2071; BMC 1896. (230)*	80	325
322	CVNO in angles of cross. R. Capricorn r., CVNO. *M. —; V. —; BMC 1898*	80	325

BRONZE

323	Head l., CVNO. R. Boar l., branch above. *M. 220; V. 1969; BMC—. (232)*	35	140
324	CVNOB ELINI in two panels. R. Victory std. l., TASC. *M. 221; V. 1971; BMC 1921-27. (233)*	30	120
325	Winged horse l., CAM. R. Winged Victory stg l., CVN. *M. 222; V. 1973; BMC 1938-43. (234)*	30	125

326

326	Bearded head facing R. Boar l., CVN. *M.223; V.1963; BMC 1904-05. (235)*	35	135
327	Ram-headed animal coiled up in double ornamental circle. R. Animal l., CAM. *M. 224; V. 1965; BMC —. (236)*	35	140
328	Griffin r., CAMV. R. Horse r., CVN. *M. 225; V. 2081; BMC 1909-12. (237)*	30	125
329	Bearded head l., CAMV. R. CVN or CVNO below horse l. *M. 226, 229; V. 2085/2131; BMC 1900-01. (238)*	30	125
330	Laureate head r., CVNO. R. CVN below bull butting l. *M. 227; V. 2083; BMC 1902-03. (239)*	35	135
331	Crude head r., CVN. R. Figure stg. l., CVN. *M. 228; V. 2135; BMC —. (240)*	35	140

332

		F £	VF £
332	CAMVL / ODVNO in two panels. ℞. CVNO beneath sphinx crouching l. *M. 230; V. 1977; BMC 1928-30. (241)*	30	125
333	Winged horse l., CAMV. ℞. Victory stg. r. divides CV NO. *M. 231; V. 1979; BMC 1931-34. (242)*	30	125
334	Victory walking r. ℞. CVN below, horseman r. *M. 232; V. 1981; BMC 1935. (243)*	35	140
335	Head l., CAM. ℞. CVNO below eagle. *M. 233; V. 2087; BMC —. (244)*	35	140

336   337

336	Head l., CVNOBELINI. ℞. Centaur r., TASCIOVANI.F. *M. 242; V. 2089; BMC 1968-71. (245)*	25	110
337	Helmeted bust r. ℞. TASCIIOVANII above, sow stg. r., F below. *M. 243; V. 2091; BMC 1956-60. (246)*	30	120
338	Horseman galloping r. holding dart and shield, CVNOB. ℞. Warrior stg. l., TASCIIOVANTIS. *M. 244; V. 2093; BMC 1961-67. (247)*	25	110

339   340

339	Helmeted bust l., CVOBELINVS REX. ℞. TASC FIL below boar l., std. on haunches. *M. 245; V. 1983; BMC 1952-55. (248)*	30	130
340	Bare head r., CVNOBELINVS REX. ℞. TASC below bull butting r. *M. 246; V. 2095; BMC 1944-51. (249)*	30	120
341	Bare head l., CVNO. ℞. TASC below bull stg. r. *M. 247; V. 1985; BMC —. (250)*	35	135

342   343

342	Head l., CVNOBELIN. ℞. Metal worker std. r. holding hammer, working on a vase, TASCIO. *M. 248; V. 2097; BMC 1972-83. (251)*	30	125
343	Winged horse r., CVNO. ℞. Victory r. sacrificing bull, TASCI. *M. 249; V. 2099; BMC 1913-19. (252)*	25	110
344	CVNO on panel within wreath. ℞. CAMV below horse, prancing r. *M. 250; V. 2101; BMC 1987-90. (253)*	30	130

345   346

		F £	VF £
345	Bearded head of Jupiter Ammon l., CVNOBELIN. R. CAM below horseman galloping r. *M. 251; V. 2103; BMC 1984-86. (254)*	35	140
346	Janus head, CVNO below. R. CAMV on panel below, sow std. r. beneath a tree. *M. 252; V. 2105; BMC 1998-2003. (255)*	35	135

347

347	Bearded head of Jupiter Ammon r., CVNOB. R. CAM on panel below lion crouched r. *M. 253; V. 2107; BMC 1991-97. (256)*	30	125
348	Sphinx r., CVNO. R. Fig stg. l. divides CA M. *M. 260; V. 2109; BMC 2004-09. (257)*	35	135
349	Horse r. R. CVN below horseman r. *M. 261; V. 1987; BMC 1936-47. (258)*	40	150
350	Animal l. looking back. R. CVN below horse l. *M. 233a; V. 1967; BMC —. (259)*	35	140
350A	Ship, CVN below. R. Fig. r. dividing S E. *M. —; V. 1989; BMC 2010.*	135	575

"SOLIDV"

351

351	**Silver Unit.** SOLIDV in centre of looped circle. R, Stg. fig. l., CVNO. *M. 259; V. 2073; BMC 1894-95. (231)*	325	1000

"AGR"

352   353

352	**Gold Quarter Stater**. Corn ear dividing CAM CVN. R. Horse r., branch above., AGR below *M. —; V. —; BMC 1854*	350	1100
353	— R. Horse r., branch above., cross and A below. *M. —; V. —; BMC 1855*	375	1350

354

				F	VF
				£	£
354	**Silver Unit.** AGR inside wreath. R. Female dog r., AGR below. *M. —; V. —;*				
	BMC 1899			250	850

EPATICCUS
(1st Half 1st Century A.D.)

Epaticcus, styled as a son of Tasciovanus on his coins, was most probably a brother of Cunobelin. The corn ear employed on his staters is similar to that of his brother's produced at Colchester. His coins appear in northern Atrebatic territory and conform to the area's denominational structure. It seems likely that Epaticcus's coinage reflects an incursion into Atrebatic territory by the Trinovantian/Catuvellaunian dynasty.

355

355	**Gold Stater.** Corn ear dividing TAS CIF. R. Horseman r., with spear and shield. EPATI. *M. 262; V. 575; BMC 2021-23. (112)*	975	3500

356   357

356	**Silver Unit.** Head of Hercules r., EPAT(I). R. Eagle stg. on snake. *M. 263; V. 580; BMC 2024-2268/2270-76. (113)*....................................	30	95
357	Victory seated r. TASCIOV. R. Boar r., EPAT. *M. 263a; V. 581; BMC 2294-2328. (114)*	35	135

358

358	Bearded head l., TASCIO. R. EPATI below lion r. *M. —; V. 582; BMC 2329*..	110	375
359	EPATI inside panel. R. Lion r. *M. —; V. 583; BMC 2330. (114A)*............	95	350

360   361

360	**Silver Minim.** EPATI. R. Boars head r., TA. *M. 264; V. 585; BMC 2331-46. (115)*	35	125
361	TA inside star. R. Winged horse r., EPA below. *M. —; V. 560; BMC 2351-57. (116)*	35	135
362	Helmeted head r. R. Horse r., E below. *M. —; V. —; BMC 2358-63*	35	135
363	EPATI. R. Winged horse r., cross below. *M. —; V .—; BMC 2365*	40	150

CARATACUS
(1st Half 1st Century A.D.)

Coins inscribed CARA have been traditionally associated with the historically attested son of Cunobelin, Caratacus the leader of British resistance against Rome. His coins appear in the same area as those of Epaticcus and he may have been his successor.

364   364A

		F £	VF £
364	**Silver Unit.** Head of Hercules r., CARA. R. Eagle stg. on snake. *M. 265; V. 593; BMC 2376-84. (117)*	125	450
364A	**Silver Minim.** CARA around pellet in ring. R. Winged horse r. *M. —; V. 595; BMC 2385-89. (117A)*	85	275

DUROTRIGES
(Mid 1st Century B.C. to Mid 1st Century A.D.)

The Durotriges inhabited West Hampshire, Dorset and adjoining parts of Somerset and Wiltshire. Their coinage is one of the most distinctive in Britain due to its rapid debasement. The disappearance of precious metals from the coinage should perhaps be linked to the declining trade between the south-west and western Gaul, following the Roman conquest of the Gaul. Hengistbury Head is the probable mint site of the cast bronzes. Coins inscribed CRAB have been traditionally associated with the tribe.

UNINSCRIBED

365	**Silver Stater.** White Gold type. Derived from Westerham stater (no. 21). *M. 317; V. 1235, 52, 54, 55; BMC 2525-2731. (60)*	110	350

366   368

366	Silver type. Similar. *M. 317; V. 1235, 52, 54, 55; BMC 2525-2731. (60)*	35	125
367	Billon type. Similar. *M. 317; V. 1235, 52, 54, 55; BMC 2525-2731. (60)*	25	60
368	**Silver Quarter Stater.** Geometric type. Crescent design. R. Zig-zag pattern. *M. 319; V. 1242/29; BMC 2734-79. (61). Quality of metal varies, obv. almost blank on later issues*	25	75

369   371

		F £	VF £
369	Starfish type. Spiral. R. Zig-zag pattern. *M. 320; V. 1270; BMC 2780-81 (61A)*	45	180
370	Hampshire Thin Flan type. Crude head of lines and pellets. R. Stylised horse l. *M. 321; V. 1280; BMC 2782-87. (62)*	50	200
371	**Bronze Stater.** Struck Bronze type. Similar to No.365-67. *M. 318; V. 1290; BMC 2790-2859. (81)*	20	50

372

372	Cast Bronze type. Many varities, as illustration. *M. 322-70; V. 1322-70; BMC 2860-2936. (82)*	25	125

"CRAB"

373

373	**Silver Unit.** CRAB in angles of cross. R. Eagle. *M. 371; V. 1285; BMC 2788. (145)*	225	750
373A	**Silver Minim.** CRAB on tablet. R. Star shape. *M. 372; V. 1286; BMC 2789. (146)*	125	375

DOBUNNI
(Mid 1st Century B.C. to Mid 1st Century A.D.)

Dobunnic territory stretched over Gloucestershire, Hereford and Worcester and into parts of
Somerset, Wiltshire and Gwent. The earliest Dobunnic coins are developed from the British Q stater,
and have the distinctive tree-like motif of the tribe on the obverse. The inscribed coinage is difficult
to arrange chronologically and it may be that some of the rulers named held different parts of the
territory simultaneously.

UNINSCRIBED

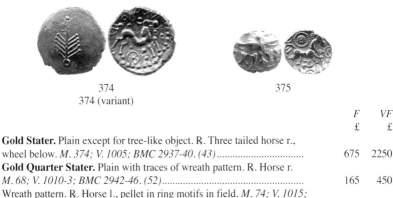

374
374 (variant)

375

		F £	*VF* £
374	**Gold Stater.** Plain except for tree-like object. R. Three tailed horse r., wheel below. *M. 374; V. 1005; BMC 2937-40. (43)*	675	2250
375	**Gold Quarter Stater.** Plain with traces of wreath pattern. R. Horse r. *M. 68; V. 1010-3; BMC 2942-46. (52)*	165	450
376	Wreath pattern. R. Horse l., pellet in ring motifs in field. *M. 74; V. 1015; BMC 2949. (51)*	165	450

377   378

377	**Silver Unit.** Allen types A-F/I-J. Regular series. Head r. R. Triple-tailed horse l. or r. *M. 374a, b/75/76, 378a-384; V. 1020/45/49/74/78/95/1135/1137; BMC 2950-3011. (63-64). Style becomes progressively more abstract, from-*	30	110
378	Allen types L-O. Irregular series. Similar to last. *M. 377-384d; V. 1170-85; BMC 3012-22. (63-64)*	40	150

INSCRIBED
The following types are not arranged chronologically.

ANTED

379

379	**Gold Stater.** Dobunnic emblem. R. ANTED or ANTEDRIG over triple tailed horse r., wheel below. *M. 385-86; V. 1062-69; BMC 3023-3031. (260)*	525	1500

	F £	VF £

380 **Silver Unit.** Crude head r. R̶. ANTED over horse. *M. 387; V. 1082; BMC 3032-38. (261)* 35 125

EISV

381 **Gold Stater.** Dobunnic emblem. R̶. EISV or EISVRIG over triple tailed horse r., wheel below. *M. 388; V. 1105; BMC 3039-42. (262)* 625 1850

382 **Silver Unit.** Crude head r. R̶. Horse l., EISV. *M. 389; V. 1110; BMC 3043-55. (263)* 30 110

INAM or INARA

383 **Gold Stater.** Dobunnic emblem. R̶. INAM or INARA over triple tailed horse r., wheel below. *M. 390; V. 1140; BMC 3056. (264)* 1100 3750

CATTI

384 **Gold Stater.** Dobunnic emblem. R̶. CATTI over triple tailed horse r., wheel below. *M. 391; V. 1130; BMC 3057-60. (265)* 525 1500

COMUX

385 **Gold Stater.** Dobunnic emblem. R̶. COMVX retrograde, over triple tailed horse r., wheel below. *M. 392; V. 1092; BMC 3061-63. (266)* 1100 3750

CORIO

386 **Gold Stater.** Dobunnic emblem. R̶. CORIO over triple tailed horse r., wheel below. *M. 393; V. 1035; BMC 3064-3133. (267)* 525 1500

387 **Gold Quarter Stater.** COR in centre. R̶. Horse r., without legend. *M. 394; V. 1039; BMC 3134. (268)* 425 1250

BODVOC

388   389

	F	VF
	£	£

388   **Gold Stater.** BODVOC across field. R. Horse r., without legend. *M. 395;*
       V. 1052; BMC 3135-42. (269)   800   2500

389   **Silver Unit.** Head l., BODVOC. R. Horse r., without legend. *M. 396; V. 1057;*
       BMC 3143-45. (270)   135   450

CORIELTAUVI

The Corieltauvi, formerly known as the Coritani, occupied Lincolnshire and adjoining parts of Yorkshire, Northamptonshire, Leicestershire and Nottinghamshire. The earliest staters, the South Ferriby type, are developed from Gallo-Belgic C staters, and are associated with the silver Boar/ Horse types. The distinctive dish shaped scyphate coinages have no parallels in Britain and stand apart from the main series. The later inscribed issues present a complex system of inscriptions. It has been suggested that some of the later inscriptions refer to pairs of names, possibly joint rulers or moneyers and rulers.

EARLY UNINSCRIBED
(Mid to Late 1st Century B.C.)

390   393

390   **Gold Stater.** South Ferriby type. Crude laureate head. R. Disjointed horse l.,
       rosette or star below, anchor shape and pellets above. *M. 449-50;*
       V. 809-815/19; BMC 3146-3179. (30)   200   425
391   Wheel type. Similar, but wheel below horse. *M. 449c; V. 817; BMC 3180*   425   1350
392   Kite type. Similar to 390, but diamond shape containing pellets above,
       spiral below horse. *M. 447; V. 825; BMC 3181-84. (29)*   225   700
393   Domino type. Similar to last, but with rectangle containing pellets.
       M. 448; V. 829; BMC 3185-86. (29)   210   550

| | 394 | | 395 |

	F	VF
	£	£
394	Trefoil type. Trefoil with central rosette of seven pellets. R. Similar to 390. *M. 450a; V. 821; BMC — . (30A)*	1350	5250
395	North Lincolnshire Scyphate type. Stylised boar r. or l. R. Large S symbol with pellets and rings in field. *M. —; V. —; BMC 3187-93*	200	450

* chipped or cracked specimens are often encountered and are worth less

396

| 396 | **Silver Unit.** Boar/Horse type I.Boar r., large pellet and ring motif above, reversed S below. R. Horse l. or r., pellet in ring above. *M. 405-06, 451; V. 855-60, 864, 867; BMC 3194-3214. (66)* | 40 | 150 |
| 397 | Boar Horse type II. Vestiges of boar on obv. R. Horse l. or r. *M. 410, 452-53; V. 875-877; BMC 3214-27. (68)* | 30 | 90 |

398 399

398	Boar Horse type III. Blank. R. Horse l.or r. *M. 453-54; V. 884-77; BMC 3228-35. (69)*	20	65
399	**Silver Fractional Unit.** Similar to 396-97. *M. 406a, 451a; V. 862/66; BMC 3236-3250. (67)*	25	80
400	Similar to 398. *M. —; V. 877-81; BMC 3251-55. (70/71)*	25	70
401	Pattern/Horse. Flower pattern. R. Horse l. *M. —; V. —; BMC 3256-57*	70	300

INSCRIBED

(Early to Mid 1st Century A.D.)

The following types are not arranged chronologically.

AVN COST

402 403

		F £	VF £
402	**Gold Stater.** Crude wreath design. R. Disjointed horse l., AVN COST. *M. 457;V. 910; BMC 3258. (286)*	450	1500
403	**Silver Unit.** Remains of wreath or blank. R. AVN COST, horse l. *M. 458; V. 914; BMC 3261-66. (287)*..	25	85
403A	**Silver Unit.** Inscription between three lines. R. Horse l. AVN. *M. -; V-; BMC-.*	100	350
404	**Silver Fractional Unit.** Similar. *M. —; l V. 918; BMC 3267-68. (288)* ..	30	85

ESVP RASV

405

405	**Gold Stater.** Crude wreath design. R. Disjointed horse l., IISVP RASV. *M. 456b; V. 920; BMC 3269. (289)*	375	1200
406	**Silver Unit.** Similar. *M. 456c; V. 924; BMC 3272-73. (290)*	50	175

VEP

407

407	**Gold Stater.** Blank or with traces of wreath. R. Disjointed horse l., VEP. *M. —; V. 905; BMC 3274-75. (296)*	475	1600
408	**Silver Unit.** Blank or with traces of wreath. R. VEP, horse r. *M. —; V. 963; BMC 3277-82. (297)*...	30	100
409	**Silver Half Unit.** Similar. *M. 464b; V. 967; BMC 3283-3295. (298)*	25	80

VEP CORF

410   412

		F £	VF £
410	**Gold Stater.** Crude wreath design. R. Disjointed horse l., VEP CORF.		
	M. 459, 460; V. 930/40/60; BMC 3296-3304. (291)	300	900
411	**Silver Unit.** Similar. *M. 460b/464; V. 934/50; BMC 3305-14. (292)*	30	110
412	Similar but VEPOC (M)ES, pellet in ring below horse. *M. —; V. 955;*		
	BMC —. (294)	40	135
413	**Silver Half Unit.** Similar. *M. 464a; V. 938/58; BMC 3316-24. (293/95)*	30	80

DVMNO TIGIR SENO

414   415

414	**Gold Stater.** DVMN(OC) across wreath. R. Horse l., TIGIR SENO. *M. 461;*		
	V. 972; BMC 3325-27. (299)	650	2250
415	**Silver Unit.** DVMNOC in two lines. R. Horse r., TIGIR SENO. *M. 462;*		
	V. 974; BMC 3328-29. (300)	150	475

VOLISIOS DVMNOCOVEROS

416

416	**Gold Stater.** VOLISIOS between three lines in wreath. R. Horse r. or l.,		
	DVMNOCOVEROS. *M. 463/a; V. 978-80; BMC 3330-3336. (301)*	325	900
417	**Silver Unit.** Similar. R. Horse r., DVMNOCO. *M. 463a; V. 980;*		
	BMC 3339. (302)	175	575
418	**Silver Half Unit.** Similar. *M. 465; V. 984; BMC 3340-41. (303)*	75	250

VOLISIOS DVMNOVELLAUNOS

419

		F £	VF £
419	**Gold Stater.** VOLISIOS between three lines in wreath. R. Horse r. or l., DVMNOVELAVNOS. *M. 466; V .988; BMC 3342-43. (304)*	400	1350
420	**Silver Half Unit.** As last but DVMNOVE. *M. 467; V. 992; BMC 3344-46. (305)*	120	375

VOLISIOS CARTIVEL

420A	**Gold Stater.** VOLISIOS between three lines in wreath. R. Horse l. CARTILLAVNOS. *M-; VA 933; BMC -*	1350	4500
421	**Silver Half Unit.** VOLISIOS between three lines in wreath. R. Horse r., CARTILEV. *M. 468; V. 994; BMC 3347-48. (306)*	250	850

IAT ISO E

422	**Silver Unit.** IAT ISO (retrograde)on tablet, rosettes above and below. R. Horse r., E above. *M. 416; V. 998; BMC 3349-51. (284)*	135	450

CAT

422A	**Silver Unit.** Boar r., pellet ring above, CAT above. R. Horse r. *M. —; V. —; BMC 3352*	175	650

LAT ISON

423

423	**Gold Stater.** LAT ISO(N) in two lines retrograde. R. Horse r., ISO in box above, N below. *M. —; V. —; BMC —. Only recorded as an AE/AV plated core, as illustrated.*	*Extremely rare*

ICENI

The Iceni, centered on Norfolk but also occupying neighbouring parts of Suffolk and Cambridgeshire, are well attested in the post conquest period as the tribe who under Boudicca revolted against Roman rule. Their earliest coins are likely to have been the British J staters, Norfolk Wolf type (no.30/31), replaced around the mid first century B.C. by the Snettisham, Freckenham and Irstead type gold staters and quarter staters. Contemporary with these are silver Boar/Horse and Face/Horse units and fractions. The introduction of legends around the beginning of the millennia led to the adoption of a new obverse design of back to back crescents. The continuation of the coinage after the Roman invasion is attested by the coins of King Prasutagus. Some of the Face/Horse units (no.434) have been attributed to Queen Boudicca.

EARLY UNINSCRIBED
(Mid to Late 1st Century B.C.)

424

		F £	VF £
424	**Gold Stater.** Snettisham type. Blank or with traces of pellet cross. R. Horse r., serpent like pellet in ring motif above. *M. —; V .—; BMC 3353-59....*	575	1750
425	Similar. Blank or with 3 short curved lines. R. Horse r., symbol above more degraded. *M. —; V. —; BMC 3360-83*	375	1200

426   427

426	Freckenham type. Two opposed crescents with stars or pellets in field. R. Horse r., various symbols in field. *M. 397/99; V. 620; BMC 3384-89. (38)*	300	900
427	Similar. Blank or with traces of pellet cross. R. Horse r., wheel or arch containing pellets above. *M. 400; V. 624; BMC 3390-95. (40)*	350	1050

428

428	Similar. Trefoil on cross design. R. Similar. *M. 401-03; V. 626; BMC 3396-3419. (39)*	325	950

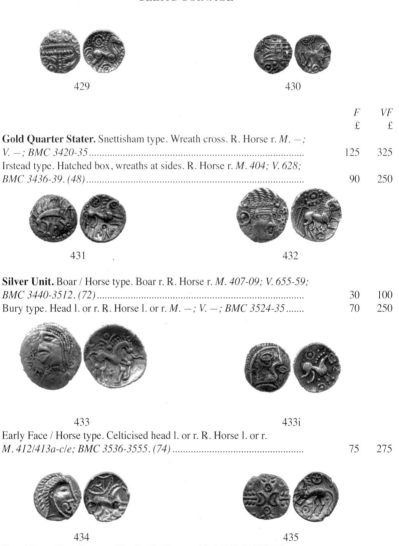

429   430

		F £	VF £
429	**Gold Quarter Stater.** Snettisham type. Wreath cross. R. Horse r. *M.* —; *V.* —; *BMC 3420-35*	125	325
430	Irstead type. Hatched box, wreaths at sides. R. Horse r. *M. 404; V. 628; BMC 3436-39. (48)*	90	250

431   432

431	**Silver Unit.** Boar / Horse type. Boar r. R. Horse r. *M. 407-09; V. 655-59; BMC 3440-3512. (72)*	30	100
432	Bury type. Head l. or r. R. Horse l. or r. *M.* —; *V.* —; *BMC 3524-35*	70	250

433   433i

433	Early Face / Horse type. Celticised head l. or r. R. Horse l. or r. *M. 412/413a-c/e; BMC 3536-3555. (74)*	75	275

434   435

434	Face / Horse Regular type. Head r. R. Horse r. *M. 413/d; V. 790-94; BMC 3556-3759. (74). Attributed to Queen Boudicca by R.D. van Arsdell*	45	165
435	Early Pattern / Horse type. Cross of two opposed crescents. R. Horse l. or r. *M. 414-15; V. 675-79; BMC 3763-74. (75)*	30	100

436

436	ECEN symbol type. Two opposed crescents. R. Horse r. *M. 429; V. 752; BMC 4297-4325*	25	75

	F £	VF £

437 **Silver Half Unit.** Boar / Horse type. Similar to 431. *M. 411; V. 661;*
BMC 3513-20. (73) 25 75
438 **Silver Fractional Unit.** Early Pattern / Horse type. Similar to 435. *M. 417/a;*
V. 681-83; BMC 3775-89. (76/A) 25 75

INSCRIBED
(Early to Mid 1st Century A.D.)
The following types are not arranged chronologically.

CAN DVRO

439

439 **Silver Unit.** Boar. R. Horse r., CAN(S) above, DVRO below. *M. 434; V. 663;*
BMC 3521-23. (271) 80 325

ANTED

440

440 **Gold Stater.** Triple crescent design. R. Horse r., ANTED monongram below.
M. 418; V. 705; BMC 3790. (272) 525 1500

441

441 **Silver Unit.** Two opposed crescents. R. Horse r., ANTED. *M. 419-21;*
V. 710-11/15; BMC 3791-4025. (273) 25 70
442 **Silver Fractional Unit.** Similar to last. *M. 422; V. 720; BMC 4028-31. (274)* 25 85

ECEN

443

		F	VF
		£	£
443	**Gold Stater.** Triple crescent design. R. Horse r., ECEN below. *M. —; V. 725; BMC 4032*	750	2250
443A	**Silver Unit.** Two opposed crescents. R, Horse r., ECEN. *M. 424; V. 730; BMC 4033-4215. (275)*	25	70
443B	**Silver Half Unit.** Similar to last. *M. 431; V. 736; BMC 4216-17. (276)* .	20	65

EDN

444	**Silver Unit.** Two opposed crescents. R, Horse r., ED, E, EI or EDN. *M. 423, 425b; V. 734/40; BMC 4219-81. (277)*	25	70

ECE

444A	**Gold Stater** Triple crescent design R. Horse r., ECE. *M. — ; V. — ;*	950	3000

445

445	**Silver Unit.** Two opposed crescents. R, Horse r., ECE. *M. 425-28; V. 761-66; BMC 4348-4538. (278-80)*	20	70

SAENU

446	**Silver Unit.** Two opposed crescents. R. Horse r., SAENV. *M. 433; V. 770; BMC 4540-57. (281)*	30	110

AESU

447

447	**Silver Unit.** Two opposed crescents. R. Horse r., AESV. *M. 432; V. 775; BMC 4558-72. (282)*	30	110

ALE SCA

448	**Silver Unit.** Boar r., ALE. R. Horse r., SCA. *M. 469; V. 996; BMC 4576*	150	575

AEDIC SIA

		F £	VF £
449	**Silver Unit.** AEDIC in two lines. ℞. Horse r., SIA? below. *M.—; V.—;* *BMC 4581*	200	750

PRASUTAGUS

450

| 450 | **Silver Unit.** Romanised head l., SUB RII PRASTO. ℞. Rearing horse r.,
ESICO FECIT. *M. 434a; V. 780; BMC 4577-80. (283)*............................ | 475 | 1750 |

This legend translates as "Under King Prasto, Esico made me", giving the name of both King and moneyer.

The systematic conquest of Britain by the Romans began in A.D. 43 when the Emperor Claudius (41-54), anxious to enhance his military reputation, authorized an invasion in which he personally participated, albeit in a purely symbolic role. The initial military contact between the two cultures had taken place almost a century before when Julius Caesar, during the course of his conquest of Celtic Gaul, led expeditions to the island in 55 and 54 B.C. Although no actual Roman occupation of Britain resulted from Caesar's reconnoitring campaigns, commercial intercourse was certainly accelerated, as evidenced by the 'Romanization' of the British Celtic coinage in the final decades of its production.

The Claudian conquest, commencing in A.D. 43, brought about a complete change in the nature of the currency circulating in Britain and ushered in a period lasting more than three and a half centuries during which Roman coinage was the only official medium of exchange. Local copies of the money brought with them by the four legions of the invasion army began to appear at a very early stage, the most popular type for imitation being the well-known Claudian copper as with reverse type fighting Minerva. Some of these copies are well-executed and of a style not much inferior to the prototype, suggesting that their local minting may have been officially sanctioned by the Roman government in order to make good a shortage of currency in the newly-conquered territory. Other examples are of much poorer style and execution and are frequently well below the normal weight of a Claudian as (usually between 10 and 11 grams). These copies must have been issued unofficially and provide evidence of the huge demand for this type of currency in a population which had never before experienced the benefits of having base metal coins available for small everyday transactions. In the decades that followed, the boundaries of the Roman province of Britannia were continually pushed further north and west until, under the celebrated Flavian governor Gnaeus Julius Agricola, the Roman army even penetrated to northern Scotland (A.D. 83/4). A few years later, under Trajan, the northern frontier was established along the Tyne-Solway line, a barrier made permanent by the construction of Hadrian's Wall following the emperor's visit to the province in 122. For a brief period in the mid-2nd century the frontier was temporarily advanced to the Forth-Clyde line with the building of the Antonine Wall, though this seems to have been abandoned early in the reign of Marcus Aurelius (ca. 163) when the Hadrianic barrier was re-commissioned and became the permanent frontier. The security thus provided to the now-peaceful province in the south facilitated urban expansion and the development of commerce. The new prosperity brought a flood of Roman coinage into the island-province and it was no longer necessary for shortages to be made good by large scale local imitation.

Until the mid-3rd century the production of Roman coinage remained the prerogative of the mint in the capital, with only occasional issues from provincial centres to serve short-term local needs. But with the deepening political and economic crisis in the third quarter of the century there was a dramatic decentralization of minting operations, with permanent establishments being set up in many important cities in the western as well as the eastern provinces. Britain, however, still remained without an official mint at this time and in the dark days of the 270s, when the separatist Gallic Empire to which Britain belonged was close to collapse, large scale production of imitative antoniniani (commonly called 'barbarous radiates') occurred in the province. The integrity and prestige of the Empire was, to some extent, restored by a rapid succession of Illyrian 'soldier emperors', until the situation was finally stabilized by Diocletian (A.D. 284-305) who established the tetrarchy system under which governmental responsibility was shared by four rulers. By the end of the 3rd century Britain had been reorganized into a civil diocese of four provinces: it had already been subdivided into Britannia Superior and Britannia Inferior almost a hundred years before, under Septimius Severus or Caracalla.

It was left to the colourful and enigmatic usurper Carausius (A.D. 287-293) to establish mints in Britain. It was, of course, vital for him to do so as his dominion was mostly confined to the island-province. Londinium (London) was his principal mint, with a secondary establishment at a place usually signing itself 'C' (probably Camulodunum, modern Colchester). After the downfall of Carausius' murderer and successor Allectus (293-296) Britain was restored to the central government, an event commemorated by the celebrated gold medallion of Constantius I showing the Caesar riding alongside the Thames approaching the gateway of the city of Londinium. At this point the mysterious 'C' mint disappears from the picture. Londinium, on the other hand, retained its status as an official mint under Diocletian's tetrarchy and its successors down to A.D. 325, when it was closed by Constantine the Great who regarded it as superfluous to his needs. In nearly four decades of existence as a Roman mint Londinium had produced a varied and extensive coinage in the names of almost all the emperors, empresses and Caesars of the period. It was destined never again to be active during Roman times, unless the extremely rare gold and silver issues of the late 4th century usurper Magnus Maximus, signed AVG, AVGOB and AVGPS, are correctly attributed to Londinium under its late Roman name of Augusta.

The termination of Roman rule in the British provinces is traditionally dated to A.D. 410 when the emperor Honorius, in response to an appeal for aid from his British subjects, told them to arrange for their own defence as best they might ('Rescript of Honorius'). In reality, the end probably came quite gradually. As the machinery of government ground to a halt and the soldiers stopped receiving their pay there would have been a steady drift of population away from the semi-ruinous cities and military installations to the countryside, where they could better provide for themselves through farming. Under these conditions the need for coinage would have been drastically reduced, as a primitive economy based on barter would largely have replaced the complex monetary economy of the late Roman period. In any case the supply of coinage from the Continent would now have dried up. The few monetary transactions which still took place were made with worn-out coins from earlier periods augmented by local imitations, production of which in Britain had resumed in the mid-4th century. Such was the pitiful end of the long tradition of Roman coinage in the remote island-province of Britannia. More than two centuries of 'Dark Ages' were to elapse before England's new rulers, the Anglo-Saxons, commenced the issue of gold thrymsas, the designs of many of which were based on late Roman types.

As Rome's Imperial coinage provided the currency needs of this country over a period of almost four centuries no representative collection of British coins is complete without some examples of these important issues. The following listing is divided into four categories: 1. Regular Roman issues, all of which would have been legal tender in Britain after A.D. 43; 2. Issues with types referring specifically to the province of Britannia, usually in commemoration of military campaigns in the north; 3. Official Roman coinage struck in Britain; 4. Imitations of Roman coins produced in Britain, all but possibly some of the earliest being of unofficial origin. The reference 'R.R.C.' is to the listing of the type in Michael Crawford's *Roman Republican Coinage* (Cambridge, 1974); and 'R.I.C.' to *The Roman Imperial Coinage* (London, 1923-1994, in ten volumes).

For more detailed collectors' information on Roman coinage, including a more comprehensive listing of types, the reader is referred to *Roman Coins and their Values Volumes 1, 2 and 3* by David R. Sear. A complete catalogue of silver issues may be found in the 5 volumes of *Roman Silver Coins* (H.A. Seaby and C.E. King) which provides a quick and convenient reference and is especially aimed at the collector. Gilbert Askew's *The Coinage of Roman Britain* (2nd edition) concentrates on those issues which are particularly associated with the Roman province of Britannia, but does not provide valuations. More recent works on this subject include R. Reece's *Coinage in Roman Britain* and *The Coinage of Roman Britain,* and also David R. Sear's *The History and Coinage of the Roman Imperators, 49—27 BC* which is devoted to the vital two decades of transition from Republic to Empire.

The standard works on the coinages of the Roman Republic and the Roman Empire have already been mentioned *(Roman Republican Coinage and Roman Imperial Coinage).* These monumental publications are essential to the advanced collector and student and their importance cannot be overstated. The British Museum Catalogues (3 volumes of Republican, 6 volumes of Imperial recently reprinted by SPINK) are also vital. They contain superb interpretive material in their introductions and are very fully illustrated. A similar work is Anne S. Robertson's *Roman Imperial Coins in the Hunter Coin Cabinet,* in 5 volumes (volume 4 is especially important for the later 3rd century coinage). For more general reading we may recommend J.P.C. Kent and M. & A. Hirmer's *Roman Coins,* undoubtedly the most lavishly illustrated book on the subject; C.H.V. Sutherland's *Roman Coins;* and R.A.G. Carson's *Coins of the Roman Empire.* Finally, for a most useful single-volume work on interpretation and background information, we would suggest A *Dictionary of Ancient Roman Coins* by John Melville Jones.

1. REGULAR ROMAN ISSUES

A token selection of the types of Roman coins which might be found on Romano-British archaeological sites. Many of the rarer emperors and empresses have been omitted and the types listed often represent only one of hundreds of variant forms which might be encountered.

		F	VF
		£	£
451	**THE REPUBLIC: P. Aelius Paetus** (moneyer), 138 B.C. Æ *denarius*. Helmeted hd. of Roma r. Rev. The Dioscuri galloping r. R.R.C. 233/1 ... *Although dating from long before the Roman conquest many Republican coins circulated well into the Imperial period and found their way to Britain where they are often represented in early hoards.*	20	60
452	**L. Thorius Balbus** (moneyer), 105 B.C. Æ denarius. Hd. of Juno Sospita r., clad in goat's skin. Rev. Bull charging r. *R.R.C. 316/1.*	25	70
453	**Q. Antonius Balbus** (moneyer), 83-82 B.C. Æ *denarius*. Laur. hd. of Jupiter r. Rev. Victory in quadriga r. *R.R.C. 364/1.*	25	70

454   456

454	**C. Calpurnius Piso** (moneyer), 67 B.C. Æ *denarius*. Laur. hd. of Apollo r. Rev. Horseman galloping r., holding palm-branch. *R.R.C. 408/1a.*	30	70
455	**Mn. Acilius Glabrio** (moneyer), 49 B.C. Æ *denarius*. Laur. hd. of Salus r. Rev. Valetudo stg. l., holding snake and resting on column. *R.R.C. 442/1.*	20	60
456	**Julius Caesar** (dictator), visited Britain 55 and 54 B.C., died 44 B.C. Æ *denarius*. CAESAR. Elephant r. Rev. Priestly emblems. *R.R.C. 443/1....*	75	175
456A	— Wreathed hd. of Caesar r. Rev. P. SEPVLLIVS MACER. Venus stg. l., holding Victory and sceptre. *R.R.C. 480/9.*	300	800
457	**Mark Antony** (triumvir), died 30 B.C. Æ *denarius*. Galley r. Rev. LEG. II. Legionary eagle between two standards. *R.R.C. 544/14.*	50	125

458   459

458	**Octavian** (triumvir), named Augustus 27 B.C. Æ *denarius*. Bare hd. of Octavian r. Rev. IMP. CAESAR. Trophy set on prow. *R.I.C. 265a.*	90	200
459	**THE EMPIRE: Augustus,** 27 B.C.-A.D. 14. Æ *denarius*. Rev. C. L. CAESARES AVGVSTI F COS DESIG PRINC IVVENT. The emperor's grandsons, Gaius and Lucius, stg. facing, with spears and shields. *R.I.C. 207.* *Almost all the coins in the Roman Imperial series have a head or bust of the emperor, empress or prince as their obverse type. Therefore, in most instances only the reverses will be described in the following listings.*	60	140

		F	VF
		£	£
460	Æ as. ROM. ET AVG. The altar of Lugdunum. *R.I.C. 230.*	50	125
460A	Æ quadrans. Obv. Anvil. Rev. Moneyers' inscription around large S. C. *R.I.C. 443.*........................	15	35
461	**Augustus and Agrippa,** general and designated heir of Augustus, died 12 B.C. Æ *dupondius.* Obv. Their hds. back to back. Rev. COL. NEM. Crocodile r., chained to palm-branch. *R.I.C. 159.* .... *See also no. 468.*	60	150
462	**Divus Augustus,** deified A.D. 14. Æ as. PROVIDENT S. C. Large altar. *R.I.C. 81.*........................	60	150
463	**Tiberius,** A.D. 14-37. *N aureus.* PONTIF MAXIM. Livia (?) seated r., holding sceptre and branch. *R.I.C. 29*....................	400	1100

464 467

464	*R denarius.* Similar. *R.I.C. 30.*................................	80	175
	This type is commonly referred to as the 'Tribute Penny' of the Bible (Matthew 22, 17-21).		
464A	Æ *as.* Inscription around large S. C. *R.I.C. 44*............	55	140
465	**Livia,** wife of Augustus, mother of Tiberius. Æ *dupondius.* Obv. Veiled bust of Livia as Pietas r. Rev. Inscription of Drusus Caesar around large S. C. *R.I.C. 43.*........................	150	375
466	**Drusus,** son of Tiberius. Æ *as.* Inscription around large S. C. *R.I.C. 45.*	65	175
467	**Caligula,** A.D. 37-41. Æ *as.* VESTA S. C. Vesta seated l. *R.I.C. 38.*	85	240

468

468	**Agrippa,** grandfather of Caligula, died 12 B.C. Æ *as.* S. C. Neptune stg. l., holding dolphin and trident. *R.I.C. 58.*.................................. *See also no. 461 and under Category 4.*	60	180
469	**Germanicus,** father of Caligula, brother of Claudius, died A.D. 19. Æ *as.* Inscription of Caligula around large S. C. *R.I.C. 35*................................	75	175
470	**Agrippina Senior,** mother of Caligula, died A.D. 33. Æ *sestertius.* S.P.Q.R. MEMORIAE AGRIPPINAE. Carpentum drawn l. by two mules. *R.I.C. 55.*	250	850

471   474

		F £	VF £
471	**Claudius,** A.D. 41-54, initiated the conquest of Britain by his invasion in		
	A.D. 43. Æ *as*. LIBERTAS AVGVSTA S. C. Libertas stg. r., holding pileus.		
	R.I.C. 113.	65	175
471A	Æ *quadrans*. Obv. Hand holding scales. Rev. Inscription around large		
	S. C. *R.I.C. 85.*	15	35

See also under Categories 2 and 4.

472   **Nero Claudius Drusus,** father of Claudius, died 9 B.C. Æ *sestertius*.
TI. CLAVDIVS CAESAR AVG. P. M. TR .P. IMP. P. P. S. C. Claudius seated
l. on curule chair amidst arms. *R.I.C. 109.* 130   450
See also under Category 4.

473   **Antonia,** mother of Claudius, died A.D. 37. Æ *dupondius*. TI. CLAVDIVS
CAESAR AVG P.M. TR. P. IMP. S. C. Claudius stg. l., holding simpulum.
R.I.C. 92. 100   275
See also under Category 4.

474   **Nero,** 54-68, emperor at the time of Queen Boudicca's rebellion in Britain.
Ν *aureus*. SALVS. Salus seated l. *R.I.C. 66.* 550   1300

475   Ν *denarius*. IVPPITER CVSTOS. Jupiter seated l. *R.I.C. 53.* 85   275

476   Æ *sestertius*. ROMA S. C. Roma seated l., holding Victory and parazonium.
R.I.C. 274. 150   475

476A   Æ *as*. S. C. Victory hovering l., holding shield inscribed S. P. Q. R. *R.I.C. 312.*   60   160

477   **Galba,** 68-69. Ν *denarius*. S.P.Q.R. / OB / C.S. within oak-wreath. *R.I.C. 167.*   100   275

478   **Otho,** 69. Ν *denarius*. SECVRITAS P. R. Securitas stg. l. *R.I.C. 10.*   200   550

479   **Vitellius,** 69. Ν denarius. CONCORDIA P. R. Concordia seated l. *R.I.C. 90.*   100   250

480   **Vespasian,** 69-79, commanded Legio II in the Claudian invasion of Britain
(43) and appointed Agricola to governorship of the province in 77/8. Ν *aureus*.
ANNONA AVG. Annona seated l. *R.I.C. 131a*   500   1200

481

481   Ν *denarius*. VICTORIA AVGVSTI. Victory advancing r., crowning standard.
R.I.C. 52. 30   80

481A   Æ *dupondius*. FELICITAS PVBLICA S. C. Felicitas stg. l. *R.I.C. 554...*   40   110

482   **Titus,** 79-81 (Caesar 69-79). Ν *denarius*. TR. P. IX. IMP. XV. COS. VIII.
P. P. Thunderbolt on throne. *R.I.C. 23a.*   50   140

483   485

		F	VF
		£	£

483 **Domitian,** 81-96 (Caesar 69-81), recalled Agricola in 83/4 and abandoned the conquest of northern Scotland (ca. 87). *Æ denarius.* IMP. XIX. COS. XIIII. CENS. P. P. P. Minerva stg. l., resting on spear. *R.I.C. 140*........... 25 75

484 *Æ dupondius.* VIRTVTI AVGVSTI S. C. Virtus stg. r. *R.I.C. 393*.......... 35 85

484A *Æ as.* MONETA AVGVSTI S. C. Moneta stg. l. *R.I.C. 354b.* 35 85

485 **Nerva,** 96-98. *Æ denarius.* AEQVITAS AVGVST. Aequitas stg. l. *R.I.C. 13.* 50 120

485A *Æ as.* LIBERTAS PVBLICA S. C. Libertas stg. l. *R.I.C. 86*................... 55 140

486 **Trajan,** 98-117, established the northern frontier in Britain along the Tyne-Solway line (ca. 100). *Æ aureus.* P. M. TR. P. COS. VI. P. P. S. P. Q. R. Genius stg. l., holding patera and corn-ears. *R.I.C. 347.* 450 1100

487   489

487 *Æ denarius.* COS. V. P. P. S. P. Q. R. OPTIMO PRINC. Military trophy. *R.I.C. 147.* 25 75

488 *Æ sestertius.* S. P. Q. R. OPTIMO PRINCIPI S. C. Spes walking l., holding flower. *R.I.C. 519.* 50 175

488A *Æ dupondius.* SENATVS POPVLVSQVE ROMANVS S. C. Emperor advancing between two trophies. *R.I.C. 676.* 50 100

489 **Hadrian,** 117-138, visited Britain in 122 and initiated the construction of a fortified frontier line (Hadrian's Wall). *Æ aureus.* HISPANIA. Hispania reclining l. *R.I.C. 305*............... 500 1200

490 *Æ denarius.* P. M. TR. P. COS. III. Roma stg. l., holding Victory and spear. *R.I.C. 76*............... 30 85

491 *Æ sestertius.* COS. III. S. C. Neptune stg. r., holding dolphin and trident, foot on prow. *R.I.C. 632.* 50 175

491A *Æ as.* FELICITATI AVG COS. III. P. P. S. C. Galley travelling l. over waves. *R.I.C. 719*............... 40 120
See also under Category 2.

492 **Sabina,** wife of Hadrian. *Æ denarius.* IVNONI REGINAE. Juno stg. l. *R.I.C. 395a*............... 40 120

493 **Aelius Caesar,** heir of Hadrian, 136-138. *Æ denarius.* CONCORD. TR. POT. COS. II. Concordia seated l. *R.I.C. 436.* 75 200

493A *Æ as.* TR. POT. COS. II. S. C. Spes walking l., holding flower. *R.I.C. 1067.* 50 130

	F	VF
	£	£

494   **Antoninus Pius,** 138-161, ordered the expansion of the Roman province
to include southern Scotland and constructed the Antonine Wall on the
Forth-Clyde line (beginning ca. 143). An uprising in northern Britain in the
150s results in a permanent withdrawal to the Hadrianic frontier early in
the next reign. *N aureus.* COS. IIII. Togate emperor stg. l., holding globe.
R.I.C. 233b.   400   900

495   *R denarius.* PIETATI AVG. COS. IIII. Pietas stg. l. between two children,
holding two more in her arms. *R.I.C. 313c*   25   70

496

496   *Æ sestertius.* SALVS AVG. S. C. Salus stg. l. at altar, feeding snake.
R.I.C. 635.   40   160

496A   *Æ dupondius.* TR. POT. XX. COS. IIII. S. C. Providentia stg. l., pointing
at globe at her feet and holding sceptre. *R.I.C. 2025*   25   60
See also under Categories 2 and 3.

497   **Antoninus Pius and Marcus Aurelius Caesar.** *R denarius.* Obv. Laur.
hd. of Antoninus Pius r. Rev. AVRELIVS CAESAR AVG PII F. COS. Bare
hd. of young Marcus Aurelius r. *R.I.C. 417a*   50   130

498   501

498   **Divus Antoninus Pius,** deified 161. *R denarius.* CONSECRATIO.
Four-storeyed crematorium of Antoninus Pius. *R.I.C. 436.*   25   75

499   **Diva Faustina Senior,** wife of Antoninus Pius, deified 141. *R denarius.*
AETERNITAS. Aeternitas stg. l., holding globe and billowing veil. *R.I.C. 351.*   25   75

499A   *Æ sestertius.* AVGVSTA S. C. Ceres stg. l., holding two torches. *R.I.C. 1120.*   30   110

500   **Marcus Aurelius,** 161-180 (Caesar 139-161), re-established Hadrian's Wall
as the permanent northern frontier of the province, ca. 163. *N aureus.*
PROV. DEOR. TR. P. XV. COS. III. Providentia stg. l., holding globe and
cornucopiae. *R.I.C. 19.*   450   950

501   *R denarius.* PIETAS AVG. Priestly emblems. *R.I.C. 424a.*   25   75

501A   — SALVTI AVG. COS. III. Salus stg. l. at altar, feeding snake. *R.I.C. 222.*   20   70

502   *Æ sestertius.* CONCORD. AVGVSTOR. TR. P. XVI. COS. III. S. C. Marcus
Aurelius and Lucius Verus stg. face to face, clasping hands. *R.I.C. 826..*   40   160

502A   *Æ as.* HONOS TR. POT. II. COS. II. S. C. Honos stg. r. *R.I.C. 1271a.* ..   30   75

	F £	VF £

503　**Divus Marcus Aurelius,** deified 180. Æ *denarius.* CONSECRATIO.
Eagle stg. r. on altar. *R.I.C. 272.* ....　25　70

504　　　　　　　　　506A

504　**Faustina Junior,** daughter of Antoninus Pius, wife of Marcus Aurelius.
Æ *denarius.* FECVNDITAS. Fecunditas stg. r., holding sceptre and child.
R.I.C. 677. ....　25　60

504A　Æ *sestertius.* HILARITAS S. C. Hilaritas stg. l. *R.I.C. 1642.* ....　35　120

505　**Diva Faustina Junior,** deified 175. Æ *as.* S. C. Crescent and seven stars.
R.I.C. 1714. ....　35　80

506　**Lucius Verus,** 161-169. Æ denarius. PAX TR. P. VI. IMP. IIII. COS. II.
Pax stg. l. *R.I.C. 561.* ....　30　80

506A　Æ *dupondius.* TR. P. IIII. IMP. II. COS. II. S. C. Mars stg. r., resting on
spear and shield. *R.I.C. 1387.* ....　35　95

507　**Lucilla,** daughter of Marcus Aurelius, wife of Lucius Verus. Æ *denarius.*
IVNONI LVCINAE. Juno stg. l., holding child in swaddling clothes.
R.I.C. 771. ....　30　75

507A　Æ *sestertius.* PIETAS S. C. Pietas stg. l., altar at feet. *R.I.C. 1756.* ....　35　120

508　**Commodus,** 177-192 (Caesar 175-177), major warfare on the British
frontier early in the reign; situation restored by Ulpius Marcellus in 184/5,
followed by unrest in the British legions. Æ *denarius.* LIB. AVG. IIII. TR.
P. VI. IMP. IIII. COS. III. P. P. Liberalitas stg. l. *R.I.C. 22* ....　30　80

509　　　　　　　　　511

509　Æ *sestertius.* IOVI VICTORI IMP. III. COS. II. P. P. S. C. Jupiter seated l.
R.I.C. 1612. ....　40　140

509A　Æ *as.* ANN. AVG. TR. P. VII. IMP. IIII. COS. III. P. P. S. C. Annona stg. l.,
modius at feet. *R.I.C. 339.* ....　25　70
See also under Category 2.

510　**Crispina,** wife of Commodus. Æ *denarius.* CONCORDIA. Clasped hands.
R.I.C. 279. ....　30　75

511　**Pertinax,** January-March 193, formerly governor of Britain, ca. 185-7. Æ
denarius. PROVID. DEOR. COS. II. Providentia stg l., reaching up to star.
R.I.C. 11a. ....　250　600

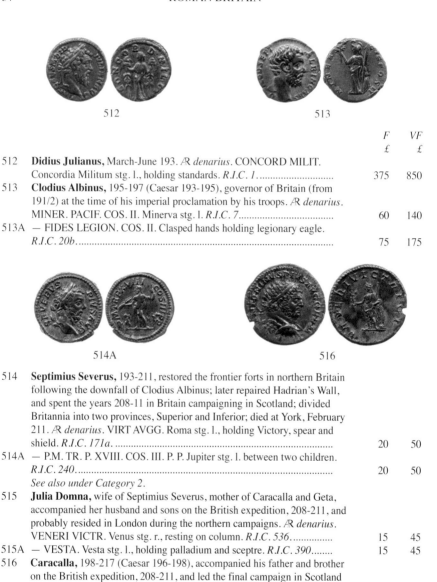

512   513

	F £	*VF* £
512 **Didius Julianus,** March-June 193. Æ *denarius*. CONCORD MILIT. Concordia Militum stg. l., holding standards. *R.I.C. 1.*	375	850
513 **Clodius Albinus,** 195-197 (Caesar 193-195), governor of Britain (from 191/2) at the time of his imperial proclamation by his troops. Æ *denarius*. MINER. PACIF. COS. II. Minerva stg. l. *R.I.C. 7*	60	140
513A — FIDES LEGION. COS. II. Clasped hands holding legionary eagle. *R.I.C. 20b.*	75	175

514A   516

514 **Septimius Severus,** 193-211, restored the frontier forts in northern Britain following the downfall of Clodius Albinus; later repaired Hadrian's Wall, and spent the years 208-11 in Britain campaigning in Scotland; divided Britannia into two provinces, Superior and Inferior; died at York, February 211. Æ *denarius*. VIRT AVGG. Roma stg. l., holding Victory, spear and shield. *R.I.C. 171a.*	20	50
514A — P.M. TR. P. XVIII. COS. III. P. P. Jupiter stg. l. between two children. *R.I.C. 240.*	20	50
See also under Category 2.		
515 **Julia Domna,** wife of Septimius Severus, mother of Caracalla and Geta, accompanied her husband and sons on the British expedition, 208-211, and probably resided in London during the northern campaigns. Æ *denarius*. VENERI VICTR. Venus stg. r., resting on column. *R.I.C. 536.*	15	45
515A — VESTA. Vesta stg. l., holding palladium and sceptre. *R.I.C. 390.*	15	45
516 **Caracalla,** 198-217 (Caesar 196-198), accompanied his father and brother on the British expedition, 208-211, and led the final campaign in Scotland in 210 during Severus' illness; made frontier dispositions before returning to Rome and finalized his father's arrangements for the division of Britain into two provinces. Æ *antoninianus* (*double denarius,* introduced in 215). VENVS VICTRIX. Venus stg. l., holding Victory and resting on shield. *R.I.C. 311c.*	30	75
517 Æ *denarius*. PART. MAX. PONT. TR. P. IIII. Trophy with two captives at base. *R.I.C. 54b.*	15	50
517A — P. M. TR. P. XV. COS. III. P. P. Hercules stg. l., holding olive-branch and club. *R.I.C. 192.*	15	50
See also under Category 2.		

		F £	VF £

518 **Plautilla,** wife of Caracalla. Æ *denarius*. PROPAGO IMPERI. Caracalla
and Plautilla clasping hands. *R.I.C. 362.* 25 75

519   522

519 **Geta,** 209-212 (Caesar 198-209), accompanied his father and brother on
the British expedition, 208-211, and took charge of the civil administration
in London during the northern campaigns. Æ *denarius*. PRINC. IVVENTVTIS.
Prince stg. l. beside trophy, holding branch and spear. *R.I.C. 18.* 20 50

519A — FORT RED TR. P. III. COS. II. Fortuna seated l. *R.I.C. 75.* 25 65
See also under Category 2.

520 **Macrinus,** 217-218. Æ *denarius*. PROVIDENTIA DEORVM. Providentia
stg. l., globe at feet. *R.I.C. 80.* 35 110

521 **Diadumenian,** 218 (Caesar 217-218). Æ *denarius*. PRINC. IVVENTVTIS.
Prince stg. l., two standards behind. *R.I.C. 109.* 70 175

522 **Elagabalus,** 218-222. Æ *antoninianus*. MARS VICTOR. Mars advancing r.
R.I.C. 122. .... 22 55

522A Æ *denarius*. P. M. TR. P. III. COS. III. P. P. Jupiter seated l., eagle at feet
R.I.C. 27. .... 20 40

523 **Julia Paula,** first wife of Elagabalus. Æ *denarius*. CONCORDIA.
Concordia seated l. *R.I.C. 211.* 40 100

524 **Aquilia Severa,** second wife of Elagabalus. Æ *denarius*. CONCORDIA.
Concordia stg. l., altar at feet. *R.I.C. 226.* 60 150

525 **Julia Soaemias,** mother of Elagabalus. Æ *denarius*. VENVS CAELESTIS.
Venus seated l., child at feet. *R.I.C. 243.* 30 75

526 **Julia Maesa,** grandmother of Elagabalus and Severus Alexander. Æ
denarius. SAECVLI FELICITAS. Felicitas stg. l., altar at feet. *R.I.C. 271.* 25 60

527 **Severus Alexander,** 222-235 (Caesar 221-222). Æ *denarius*.
PAX AETERNA AVG. Pax stg. l. *R.I.C. 165.* 15 40

527A — P. M. TR. P. XIII. COS. III. P. P. Sol advancing l., holding whip. *R.I.C. 123.* 15 40

528

528 Æ *sestertius*. MARS VLTOR S. C. Mars advancing r., with spear and shield.
R.I.C. 635. .... 30 85

	F	*VF*
	£	£

529   **Orbiana,** wife of Severus Alexander. Æ *denarius*. CONCORDIA AVGG.
Concordia seated l. *R.I.C. 319.* 70   175

530   **Julia Mamaea,** mother of Severus Alexander. Æ *denarius*. VESTA.
Vesta stg. l. *R.I.C. 362.* 20   50

530A Æ *sestertius*. FELICITAS PVBLICA S. C. Felicitas stg. facing, hd. l.,
resting on column. *R.I.C. 676.* 30   85

531A

531   **Maximinus I,** 235-238. Æ *denarius*. PAX AVGVSTI. Pax stg. l. *R.I.C. 12.*   20   50

531A Æ *sestertius*. SALVS AVGVSTI S. C. Salus seated l., feeding snake arising
from altar. *R.I.C. 85.* 30   85

532   **Maximus Caesar,** son of Maximinus I. Æ *denarius*. PRINC IVVENTVTIS.
Prince stg. l., two standards behind. *R.I.C. 3.* 50   175

533   **Gordian I Africanus,** March-April 238, governor of Britannia Inferior
late in the reign of Caracalla. Æ *denarius*. P. M. TR. P. COS. P. P. Togate
emperor stg. l. *R.I.C. 1.* 250   650

534   **Gordian II Africanus,** March-April 238. Æ *denarius*. VIRTVS AVGG.
Virtus stg. l., with shield and spear. *R.I.C. 3.* 250   650

535   **Balbinus,** April-July 238. Æ *antoninianus*. FIDES MVTVA AVGG.
Clasped hands. *R.I.C. 11.* 75   175

535A Æ *denarius*. PROVIDENTIA DEORVM. Providentia stg. l., globe at feet.
R.I.C. 7. 50   140

536   **Pupienus,** April-July 238. Æ *antoninianus*. AMOR MVTVVS AVGG.
Clasped hands. *R.I.C. 9a.* 75   175

536A Æ *denarius*. PAX PVBLICA. Pax seated l. *R.I.C. 4.* 50   140

537

537   **Gordian III,** 238-244 (Caesar 238). Æ *antoninianus*. LAETITIA AVG. N.
Laetitia stg. l. *R.I.C. 86.* 15   30

538   Æ *denarius*. DIANA LVCIFERA. Diana stg. r., holding torch. *R.I.C. 127.*   15   30

538A Æ *sestertius*. AETERNITATI AVG. S.C. Sol stg. l., holding globe. *R.I.C. 297a.*   22   65

539

		F	VF
		£	£

539 **Philip I,** 244-249. Æ *antoninianus*. ROMAE AETERNAE. Roma seated l.
  R.I.C. 65. .... 12 30

539A Æ *sestertius*. SECVRIT. ORBIS S. C. Securitas seated l. *R.I.C. 190.* 25 75

540 **Otacilia Severa,** wife of Philip I. Æ *antoninianus*. PIETAS AVGVSTAE.
  Pietas stg. l. *R.I.C. 125c.* 15 40

540A Æ *sestertius*. CONCORDIA AVGG. S. C. Concordia seated l. *R.I.C. 203a.* 25 75

541 **Philip II,** 247-249 (Caesar 244-247). Æ *antoninianus*. PRINCIPI IVVENT.
  Prince stg. l., holding globe and spear. *R.I.C. 218d.* 20 50

541A Æ *sestertius*. PAX AETERNA S. C. Pax stg. l. *R.I.C. 268c.* 25 80

542   543

542 **Trajan Decius,** 249-251. Æ *antoninianus*. DACIA. Dacia stg. l., holding
  staff with ass's hd. *R.I.C. 12b.* 15 35

542A Æ *sestertius*. PANNONIAE S. C. The two Pannoniae stg., each holding
  standard. *R.I.C. 124a.* 25 75

543 **Herennia Etruscilla,** wife of Trajan Decius. Æ *antoninianus*. PVDICITIA
  AVG. Pudicitia stg. l. *R.I.C. 58b.* 15 35

544 **Herennius Etruscus,** 251 (Caesar 250-251). Æ *antoninianus*. PIETAS
  AVGG. Mercury stg. l., holding purse and caduceus. *R.I.C. 142b.* 25 65

545 **Hostilian,** 251 (Caesar 251). Æ *antoninianus*. PRINCIPI IVVENTVTIS.
  Apollo seated l., holding branch. *R.I.C. 180.* 35 85

546 **Trebonianus Gallus,** 251-253. Æ *antoninianus*. FELICITAS PVBLICA.
  Felicitas stg. l., resting on column. *R.I.C. 34A.* 12 30

546A Æ *sestertius*. SALVS AVGG S. C. Salus stg. r., feeding snake held in her
  arms. *R.I.C. 121a.* 25 75

547 **Volusian,** 251-253 (Caesar 251). Æ *antoninianus*. VIRTVS AVGG.
  Virtus stg. l. *R.I.C. 186.* 12 30

548 **Aemilian,** 253. Æ *antoninianus*. PACI AVG. Pax stg. l., resting on column.
  R.I.C. 8. .... 50 120

549 **Valerian,** 253-260. Billon antoninianus. FIDES MILITVM. Fides stg. r.,
  holding two standards. *R.I.C. 241* 8 20

550 **Diva Mariniana,** wife of Valerian, deified 253. Billon *antoninianus*.
  CONSECRATIO. Empress seated on peacock flying r. *R.I.C. 6* 45 110

		F	*VF*
		£	£

551 **Gallienus,** 253-268, during whose reign Rome temporarily lost control
over Britain when Postumus rebelled and established the independent
Gallic Empire in 260. Billon *antoninianus*. VIRT GALLIENI AVG.
Emperor advancing r., captive at feet. *R.I.C. 54.* 10   25

552

552	— DIANAE CONS. AVG. Doe l. *R.I.C. 176.*	8	20

552A — SOLI INVICTO. Sol stg. l., holding globe. *R.I.C. 658.* 8   18
553 **Salonina,** wife of Gallienus. Billon *antoninianus*. VENVS FELIX. Venus
seated l., child at feet. *R.I.C. 7.* 8   20
553A — IVNONI CONS. AVG. Doe l. *R.I.C. 16.* 8   20
554 **Valerian Junior,** son of Gallienus, Caesar 256-258. Billon *antoninianus*.
IOVI CRESCENTI. Infant Jupiter seated on goat r. *R.I.C. 13.* 15   35
555 **Divus Valerian Junior,** deified 258. Billon *antoninianus*. CONSECRATIO.
Large altar. *R.I.C. 24.* 12   30
556 **Saloninus,** 260 (Caesar 258-260). Billon *antoninianus*. PIETAS AVG.
Priestly emblems. *R.I.C. 9.* 12   30
557 **Macrianus,** usurper in the East, 260-261. Billon *antoninianus*. SOL.
INVICTO. Sol stg. l., holding globe. *R.I.C. 12.* 35   85
558 **Quietus,** usurper in the East, 260-261. Billon *antoninianus*.
INDVLGENTIAE AVG. Indulgentia seated l. *R.I.C. 5.* 35   85

559

559 **Postumus,** usurper in the West, 260-268, founder of the 'Gallic Empire'
which temporarily detached Britain from the rule of the central government,
a state of affairs which continued until Aurelian's defeat of Tetricus in
273. Billon *antoninianus*. HERC. DEVSONIENSI. Hercules stg. r. *R.I.C. 64.* 12   30
560 — MONETA AVG. Moneta stg. l. *R.I.C. 75.* 10   25
560A *Æ sestertius*. FIDES MILITVM. Fides stg. l., holding two standards.
R.I.C. 128. 50   140
561 **Laelianus,** usurper in the West, 268. Billon *antoninianus*. VICTORIA AVG.
Victory advancing r. *R.I.C. 9.* 110   275
562 **Marius,** usurper in the West, 268. Billon *antoninianus*. CONCORDIA
MILITVM. Clasped hands. *R.I.C. 7.* 35   85
563 **Victorinus,** usurper in the West, 268-270. Billon *antoninianus*. INVICTVS.
Sol advancing l. *R.I.C. 114.* 8   20

		F £	VF £

564   **Tetricus,** usurper in the West, 270-273, defeated by Aurelian, thus ending
the 'Gallic Empire' and the isolation of Britain from the authority of Rome.
Billon *antoninianus*. LAETITIA AVGG. Laetitia stg. l. *R.I.C. 87.*   8   25
See also under Category 4.

565   **Tetricus Junior,** son of Tetricus, Caesar 270-273. Billon *antoninianus*.
SPES PVBLICA. Spes walking l., holding flower *R.I.C. 272.*   8   20
See also under Category 4.

566   **Claudius II Gothicus,** 268-270. Billon *antoninianus*. IOVI STATORI.
Jupiter stg. r. *R.I.C. 52.*   8   20

567   **Divus Claudius II,** deified 270. Billon *antoninianus*. CONSECRATIO.
Large altar. *R.I.C. 261.*   8   20
See also under Category 4.

568   **Quintillus,** 270. Billon *antoninianus*. DIANA LVCIF. Diana stg. r.,
holding torch. *R.I.C. 49.*   18   45

569   **Aurelian,** 270-275, restored Britain to the rule of the central government
through his defeat of Tetricus in 273; possibly began construction of the
chain of 'Saxon Shore' forts on the eastern and southern coastlines. Billon
antoninianus. ORIENS AVG. Sol stg. l. between two captives. *R.I.C. 63.*   10   25

569A   — RESTITVT. ORBIS. Female stg. r., presenting wreath to emperor stg. l.
R.I.C. 399.   10   25

570   **Aurelian and Vabalathus,** ruler of Palmyra 267-272 and usurper in the
East from 271. Billon *antoninianus*. Obv. Laur. bust of Vabalathus r. Rev.
Rad. bust of Aurelian r. *R.I.C. 381.*   25   70

571   574A

571   **Severina,** wife of Aurelian. Billon *antoninianus*. PROVIDEN. DEOR.
Concordia (or Fides) Militum stg. r., facing Sol stg. l. *R.I.C. 9.*   18   45

572   **Tacitus,** 275-276. Billon *antoninianus*. SECVRIT. PERP. Securitas stg. l.,
leaning on column. *R.I.C. 163.*   15   35

573   **Florian,** 276. Billon *antoninianus*. LAETITIA FVND. Laetitia stg. l.
R.I.C. 34.   30   75

574   **Probus,** 276-282, suppressed governor's revolt in Britain and lifted
restrictions on viticulture in Britain and Gaul. Billon *antoninianus*.
ADVENTVS PROBI AVG. Emperor on horseback l., captive seated
before. *R.I.C. 160.*   10   25

574A   — VICTORIA GERM. Trophy between two captives. *R.I.C. 222.*   15   40

575   **Carus,** 282-283. Billon *antoninianus*. PAX EXERCITI. Pax stg. l., holding
olive-branch and standard. *R.I.C. 75.*   15   40

576   **Divus Carus,** deified 283. Billon *antoninianus*. CONSECRATIO. Eagle
facing, hd. l. *R.I.C. 28.*   18   45

577   **Carinus,** 283-285 (Caesar 282-283). Billon *antoninianus*. SAECVLI
FELICITAS. Emperor stg. r. *R.I.C. 214.*   12   35

	F	*VF*
	£	£

578 **Magnia Urbica,** wife of Carinus. Billon *antoninianus*. VENVS VICTRIX.
Venus stg. l., holding helmet, shield at feet. *R.I.C. 343*............................ 60 150

579 **Numerian,** 283-284 (Caesar 282-283). Billon *antoninianus*. CLEMENTIA
TEMP. Emperor stg. r., receiving globe from Jupiter stg. l. *R.I.C. 463*.... 15 40

580 **Diocletian,** 284-305. Æ *argenteus*. VIRTVS MILITVM. The four tetrarchs
sacrificing before gateway of military camp. *R.I.C. 27a (Rome)*............. 100 200

581 Billon *antoninianus*. IOVI CONSERVAT AVGG. Jupiter stg. l. *R.I.C. 162*. 10 25

582 Æ *follis*. GENIO POPVLI ROMANI. Genius stg. l. R.I.C. 14a *(Alexandria)*. 10 30

582A — (post-abdication coinage, after 305). PROVIDENTIA DEORVM QVIES
AVGG. Quies and Providentia stg. facing each other. *R.I.C. 676a (Treveri)*. 22 65
See also under Category 3.

583 **Maximian,** 286-305 and 306-308, failed in his attempts to suppress the
usurpation of Carausius in Britain. Æ *argenteus*. VICTORIA SARMAT. The
four tetrarchs sacrificing before gateway of military camp. *R.I.C. 37b (Rome)*. 100 200

584

584 Billon *antoninianus*. SALVS AVGG. Salus stg. r., feeding snake held in
her arms. *R.I.C. 417*.. 8 20

585 Æ *follis*. SAC. MON. VRB. AVGG. ET CAESS. NN. Moneta stg. l.
R.I.C. 105b (Rome). 12 35

585A — (second reign). CONSERVATORES VRB SVAE. Roma seated in
hexastyle temple. *R.I.C. 84b (Ticinum)*. 12 35
See also under Category 3.
[For coins of the usurpers Carausius and Allectus see under Category 3]

586 **Constantius I,** 305-306 (Caesar 293-305), invaded Britain 296 and defeated
the usurper Allectus, thus restoring the island to the rule of the central
government; Britain now divided into four provinces and the northern
frontier defences reconstructed; died at York, July 306. Æ *argenteus*.
PROVIDENTIA AVGG. The four tetrarchs sacrificing before gateway
of military camp. *R.I.C. 11a (Rome)*... 110 220

587

587 Æ *follis*. GENIO POPVLI ROMANI. Genius stg. l. *R.I.C. 26a (Aquileia)*. 12 35

587A — SALVIS AVGG. ET CAESS. FEL. KART. Carthage stg. l., holding
fruits. *R.I.C. 30a (Carthage)*.. 15 40
See also under Category 3.

588

	F	VF
	£	£

588   **Galerius,** 305-311 (Caesar 293-305). Æ argenteus. VIRTVS MILITVM.
The four tetrarchs sacrificing before gateway of military camp.
R.I.C. 15b (Ticinum). .... | 100 | 200

588A   — XC / VI in wreath. *R.I.C. 16b (Carthage).* .... | 150 | 350

589   Æ *follis.* GENIO AVGG ET CAESARVM NN. Genius stg. l. *R.I.C. 11b
(Cyzicus).* .... | 12 | 35

589A   — GENIO IMPERATORIS. Genius stg. l. *R.I.C. 101a (Alexandria)*...... | 8 | 25
See also under Category 3.

590   **Galeria Valeria,** wife of Galerius. Æ *follis.* VENERI VICTRICI. Venus
stg. l. *R.I.C. 110 (Alexandria).*................................. | 35 | 85

591   **Severus II,** 306-307 (Caesar 305-306). Æ *follis.* FIDES MILITVM. Fides
seated l. *R.I.C. 73 (Ticinum).* .... | 35 | 85
See also under Category 3.

592   **Maximinus II,** 310-313 (Caesar 305-310). Æ *follis.* GENIO CAESARIS.
Genius stg. l. *R.I.C. 64 (Alexandria).* .... | 8 | 25

592A   — GENIO POP. ROM. Genius stg. l. *R.I.C. 845a (Treveri).* .... | 8 | 20
See also under Category 3.

593

593   **Maxentius,** 306-312 (Caesar 306). Æ *follis.* CONSERV. VRB. SVAE.
Roma seated in hexastyle temple. *R.I.C. 210 (Rome).* .... | 10 | 30

594   **Romulus,** son of Maxentius, deified 309. Æ *quarter follis.* AETERNAE
MEMORIAE. Temple with domed roof. *R.I.C. 58 (Ostia).* .... | 35 | 85

595   **Licinius,** 308-324. Æ *follis.* GENIO AVGVSTI. Genius stg. l. *R.I.C. 198b
(Siscia).* .... | 8 | 20

595A   Æ 3. IOVI CONSERVATORI AVGG. Jupiter stg. l. *R.I.C. 24 (Nicomedia).* | 8 | 20
See also under Category 3.

596   **Licinius Junior,** son of Licinius, Caesar 317-324. Æ 3. CAESARVM
NOSTRORVM around wreath containing VOT. / V. *R.I.C. 92 (Thessalonica).* | 8 | 22

597   **Constantine I, the Great,** 307-337 (Caesar 306-307), campaigned with
his father Constantius I against the Picts in northern Britain, summer 306,
and proclaimed emperor by the legions at York on Constantius' death
in July; closed the London mint early in 325 ending almost four decades
of operation. Æ *follis.* GENIO POP ROM. Genius stg. l. *R.I.C. 719b (Treveri).* | 12 | 35

598   — SOLI INVICTO COMITI. Sol stg. l. *R.I.C. 307 (Lugdunum).* .... | 6 | 18

598A   Æ 3. PROVIDENTIAE AVGG. Gateway of military camp. *R.I.C. 153
(Thessalonica)*................................. | 5 | 15

599   600

		F	VF
		£	£
599	— VIRTVS EXERCIT. Trophy between two captives. *R.I.C. 280 (Treveri)*.	12	30
599A	Æ 3/4. GLORIA EXERCITVS. Two soldiers stg. either side of two standards. *R.I.C. 518 (Treveri)*...	4	12
	See also under Category 3.		
600	**'Urbs Roma'**, after 330. Æ 3/4. Obv. Helmeted bust of Roma l. Rev. She-wolf l., suckling twins. *R.I.C. 195 (Nicomedia)*................................	5	15

601   604

601	**'Constantinopolis'**, after 330. Æ 3/4. Obv. Helmeted bust of Constantinopolis l. Rev. Victory stg. l., foot on prow. *R.I.C. 339 (Rome)*.	5	15
602	**Fausta,** wife of Constantine I. Æ 3. SALVS REIPVBLICAE. Empress stg. l., holding two children. *R.I.C. 459 (Treveri)*.....................................	18	45
	See also under Category 3.		
603	**Helena,** mother of Constantine I. Æ 3. SECVRITAS REIPVBLICE. Empress stg. l., holding branch. *R.I.C. 38 (Alexandria)*...........................	18	40
603A	Æ 4 (posthumous issue, 337-340). PAX PVBLICA. Pax stg. l. *R.I.C. 78 (Treveri)*.	10	25
	See also under Category 3.		
604	**Theodora,** second wife of Constantius I. Æ 4 (posthumous issue, 337-340). PIETAS ROMANA. Pietas stg. r., holding child. R.I.C. 43 *(Treveri)*......	12	30
605	**Crispus,** eldest son of Constantine I, Caesar 317-326. Æ 3. CAESARVM NOSTRORVM around wreath containing VOT. / V. *R.I.C. 68 (Aquileia)*.	8	20
	See also under Category 3.		
606	**Delmatius,** nephew of Constantine I, Caesar 335-337. Æ 3/4. GLORIA EXERCITVS. Two soldiers stg. either side of two standards. *R.I.C. 90 (Antioch)*.	18	45
607	**Hanniballianus,** nephew of Constantine I, Rex 335-337. Æ 4. SECVRITAS PVBLICA. River-god Euphrates reclining r. *R.I.C. 147 (Constantinople)*.	100	225
608	**Constantine II,** 337-340 (Caesar 317-337). Æ 3. BEATA TRANQVILLITAS. Altar inscribed VOT / IS / XX. *R.I.C. 312 (Treveri)*.	8	20
608A	Æ 3/4. GLORIA EXERCITVS. Two soldiers stg. either side of standard. *R.I.C. 392 (Rome)*.	4	10
	See also under Category 3.		
609	**Constans,** 337-350 (Caesar 333-337), visited Britain in 343, the last reigning emperor to do so. Æ 2. FEL. TEMP. REPARATIO. Soldier r., dragging barbarian from hut beneath tree. *R.I.C. 103 (Aquileia)*.............	10	30

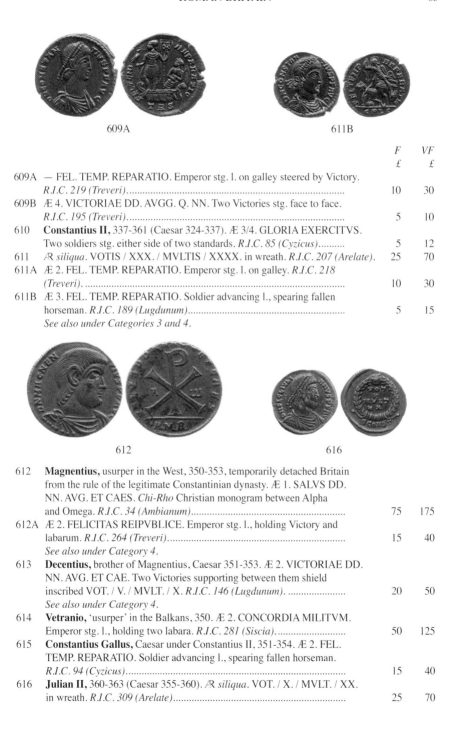

609A   611B

	F £	VF £

609A — FEL. TEMP. REPARATIO. Emperor stg. l. on galley steered by Victory. *R.I.C. 219 (Treveri)* 10 30

609B Æ 4. VICTORIAE DD. AVGG. Q. NN. Two Victories stg. face to face. *R.I.C. 195 (Treveri)* 5 10

610 **Constantius II,** 337-361 (Caesar 324-337). Æ 3/4. GLORIA EXERCITVS. Two soldiers stg. either side of two standards. *R.I.C. 85 (Cyzicus)* 5 12

611 Æ *siliqua.* VOTIS / XXX. / MVLTIS / XXXX. in wreath. *R.I.C. 207 (Arelate).* 25 70

611A Æ 2. FEL. TEMP. REPARATIO. Emperor stg. l. on galley. *R.I.C. 218 (Treveri).* 10 30

611B Æ 3. FEL. TEMP. REPARATIO. Soldier advancing l., spearing fallen horseman. *R.I.C. 189 (Lugdunum)* 5 15

See also under Categories 3 and 4.

612   616

612 **Magnentius,** usurper in the West, 350-353, temporarily detached Britain from the rule of the legitimate Constantinian dynasty. Æ 1. SALVS DD. NN. AVG. ET CAES. *Chi-Rho* Christian monogram between Alpha and Omega. *R.I.C. 34 (Ambianum)* 75 175

612A Æ 2. FELICITAS REIPVBLICE. Emperor stg. l., holding Victory and labarum. *R.I.C. 264 (Treveri)* 15 40

See also under Category 4.

613 **Decentius,** brother of Magnentius, Caesar 351-353. Æ 2. VICTORIAE DD. NN. AVG. ET CAE. Two Victories supporting between them shield inscribed VOT. / V. / MVLT. / X. *R.I.C. 146 (Lugdunum).* 20 50

See also under Category 4.

614 **Vetranio,** 'usurper' in the Balkans, 350. Æ 2. CONCORDIA MILITVM. Emperor stg. l., holding two labara. *R.I.C. 281 (Siscia)* 50 125

615 **Constantius Gallus,** Caesar under Constantius II, 351-354. Æ 2. FEL. TEMP. REPARATIO. Soldier advancing l., spearing fallen horseman. *R.I.C. 94 (Cyzicus)* 15 40

616 **Julian II,** 360-363 (Caesar 355-360). Æ *siliqua.* VOT. / X. / MVLT. / XX. in wreath. *R.I.C. 309 (Arelate)* 25 70

F	*VF*
£	£

617   Æ 1. SECVRITAS REIPVB. Bull stg. r. *R.I.C. 411 (Siscia).*   45   140
617A Æ 3. VOT. / X. / MVLT. / XX. in wreath. *R.I.C. 108 (Sirmium)*.............   8   25
618   **Jovian,** 363-364. Æ 3. VOT. / V. / MVLT. / X. in wreath. *R.I.C. 426 (Siscia).*   12   35

619

619   **Valentinian I,** 364-375 (in the West), during whose reign the Roman
      province of Britannia was devastated by the simultaneous attack of hordes
      of invaders on several fronts (the 'Barbarian Conspiracy'); order eventually
      restored by Count Theodosius, father of the future emperor . *N solidus.*
      RESTITVTOR REIPVBLICAE. Emperor stg. r., holding standard and
      Victory. *R.I.C. 2b (Antioch).*   120   275
619A Æ 3. GLORIA ROMANORVM. Emperor advancing r., dragging
      barbarian and holding labarum. *R.I.C. 14a (Siscia).*   5   15
619B — SECVRITAS REIPVBLICAE. Victory advancing l. *R.I.C. 32a (Treveri).*   5   15
620   **Valens,** 364-378 (in the East). *R siliqua.* VRBS ROMA. Roma seated l.
      R.I.C. 27e (Treveri).   25   70
620A Æ 3. SECVRITAS REIPVBLICAE. Victory advancing l. *R.I.C. 42b
      (Constantinople).*   5   15
621   **Procopius,** usurper in the East, 365-366. Æ 3. REPARATIO FEL. TEMP.
      Emperor stg. r., holding standard and shield. *R.I.C. 17a (Constantinople).*   50   125
622   **Gratian,** 367-383 (in the West), overthrown by Magnus Maximus who
      had been proclaimed emperor by the army in Britain. *R siliqua.* VRBS
      ROMA. Roma seated l. *R.I.C. 27f (Treveri).*   30   75
623   **Valentinian II,** 375-392 (in the West). Æ 2. REPARATIO REIPVB.
      Emperor stg. l., raising kneeling female figure. *R.I.C. 20c (Arelate).*   10   30
623A Æ 4. SALVS REIPVBLICAE. Victory advancing l., dragging barbarian.
      R.I.C. 20a (Alexandria).   5   12
624   **Theodosius I,** the Great, 379-395 (in the East), son of the Count Theodosius
      who had cleared Britain of barbarian invaders in the reign of Valentinian I;
      the Emperor Theodosiua twice restored Britain to the rule of the central
      government, by his defeat of the usurpers Magnus Maximus (in 388) and
      Eugenius (in 394). *R siliqua.* CONCORDIA AVGGG. Constantinopolis
      enthroned facing, foot on prow. *R.I.C. 55a (Treveri).*   30   75

624A

624A — VIRTVS ROMANORVM. Roma enthroned facing. *R.I.C. (Aquileia) 28d.*   30   75
624B Æ 2. VIRTVS EXERCIT. Emperor stg. r., foot on captive, holding
      labarum and globe. *R.I.C. 24b (Heraclea)*...............   12   35

	F	VF
	£	£

625 **Aelia Flaccilla,** wife of Theodosius I. Æ 2. SALVS REIPVBLICAE.
Victory seated r., inscribing Christian monogram on shield set on cippus.
R.I.C. 81 (Constantinople) 25 65

626   627

626 **Magnus Maximus,** usurper in the West, 383-388, proclaimed emperor
by the army in Britain, invaded Gaul, and overthrew the legitimate western
emperor Gratian; possibly reopened the London mint for a brief issue of
precious metal coinage (Rudyard Kipling presented a rather fanciful
version of his career in "Puck of Pook's Hill"). Æ *siliqua*. VIRTVS
ROMANORVM. Roma enthroned facing. *R.I.C. 84b (Treveri)*.............. 35 95
See also under Category 3.

627 **Flavius Victor,** son of Magnus Maximus, co-emperor 387-388. Æ 4.
SPES ROMANORVM. Gateway of military camp. *RIC 55b (Aquileia).* 40 100

628 **Eugenius,** usurper in the West, 392-394, recognized in Britain until his
defeat by Theodosius the Great. Æ *siliqua*. VIRTVS ROMANORVM.
Roma seated l. on cuirass. *R.I.C. 106d (Treveri).* 120 275

629   631

629 **Arcadius,** 395-408 (in the East, co-emperor with his father Theodosius I
from 383). Æ *solidus*. VICTORIA AVGGG. Emperor stg. r., foot on
captive, holding standard and Victory. *R.I.C. 1205 (Milan).* 100 250

629A Æ 2. GLORIA ROMANORVM. Emperor stg. l., holding standard and
shield, captive at feet. *R.I.C. 41 (Antioch)*... 15 40

630 **Honorius,** 395-423 (in the West, co-emperor with his father Theodosius I
and brother Arcadius from 393), this reign saw the end of Roman rule in
Britain following a succession of usurpations in the province, culminating
in that of Constantine III against whom the Britons rebelled in 409;
Honorius' celebrated 'Rescript' of the following year instructed the
provincials to look to their own defence as he was no longer able to assist
them. Æ *solidus*. VICTORIA AVGGG. Emperor stg. r., foot on captive,
holding standard and Victory. *R.I.C. 1287 (Ravenna).*............................. 100 250

630A Æ *siliqua*. VIRTVS ROMANORVM. Roma seated l. on cuirass.
R.I.C. 1228 (Milan)... 35 85

631 **Constantine III,** usurper in the West, 407-411, proclaimed emperor by the
army in Britain, but his authority rejected by the Romano-Britons two years
later, thus effectively ending 366 years of Roman rule in Britain. Æ *siliqua*.
VICTORIA AVGGG. Roma enthroned l. *R.I.C. 1532 (Treveri)*.............. 150 325

	F	VF
	£	£

632   **Valentinian III,** 425-455 (in the West), during whose reign the Saxon
conquest of the former Roman province commenced, following the final
unsuccessful appeal of the Romano-Britons for help addressed to the general
Aetius in 446. *N solidus.* VICTORIA AVGGG. Emperor stg. facing, foot
on human-headed serpent. *R.I.C. 2010 (Ravenna).*   125   300

632A Æ 4. VOT. PVB. Gateway of military camp. *R.I.C. 2123 (Rome).*   25   75

2. ISSUES WITH TYPES REFERRING SPECIFICALLY TO THE PROVINCE OF BRITANNIA

Struck in Rome, unless otherwise indicated. These usually commemorate military operations in the
northern frontier region of the province or beyond.

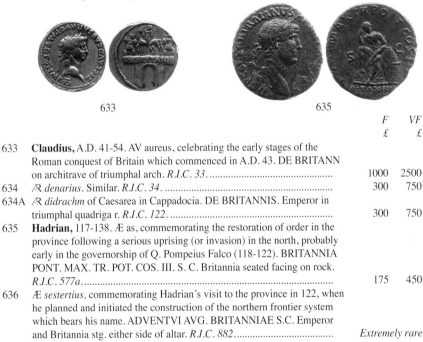

633   635

	F	VF
	£	£

633   **Claudius,** A.D. 41-54. AV aureus, celebrating the early stages of the
Roman conquest of Britain which commenced in A.D. 43. DE BRITANN
on architrave of triumphal arch. *R.I.C. 33.*   1000   2500

634   *R denarius.* Similar. *R.I.C. 34.*   300   750

634A *R didrachm* of Caesarea in Cappadocia. DE BRITANNIS. Emperor in
triumphal quadriga r. *R.I.C. 122.*   300   750

635   **Hadrian,** 117-138. Æ as, commemorating the restoration of order in the
province following a serious uprising (or invasion) in the north, probably
early in the governorship of Q. Pompeius Falco (118-122). BRITANNIA
PONT. MAX. TR. POT. COS. III. S. C. Britannia seated facing on rock.
R.I.C. 577a.   175   450

636   Æ *sestertius,* commemorating Hadrian's visit to the province in 122, when
he planned and initiated the construction of the northern frontier system
which bears his name. ADVENTVI AVG. BRITANNIAE S.C. Emperor
and Britannia stg. either side of altar. *R.I.C. 882* ....   *Extremely rare*

637

637   — BRITANNIA S. C. Britannia seated facing, foot resting on rock.
R.I.C. 845. ....   *Extremely rare*

		F	VF
		£	£

637A   Æ *dupondius* or as. *Similar. R.I.C. 846*..   *Extremely rare*

638   Æ *sestertius,* commemorating Hadrian's attention to the legionary garrison strength of the province, principally his transfer of *VI Victrix* from Germany in 122. EXERC. BRITANNICVS S. C. Emperor on horseback r., addressing gathering of troops. *R.I.C. 912.* ....   *Extremely rare*

638A   — EXERC. BRITANNICVS S.C. Emperor stg. r. on tribunal, addressing gathering of troops. *R.I.C. 913.* ....   *Extremely rare*

639   **Antoninus Pius,** 138-161. *Æ aureus,* commemorating the conquests in Scotland by the governor Q. Lollius Urbicus (138/9-142/3) at which time construction of the Antonine Wall was begun. BRITAN. IMPERATOR II. Victory stg. l. on globe. *R.I.C. 113*..   800   2000

640

640   Æ *sestertius.* BRITANNIA S. C. Britannia seated l. on rock, holding standard. *R.I.C. 742.*   550   1400

641   — BRITAN. IMPERATOR II. S. C. Helmeted Britannia seated l., foot on rock. *R.I.C. 743*..   550   1450

642   — BRITAN. IMPERATOR II. S. C. Britannia seated l. on globe above waves, holding standard. *R.I.C. 744.*   650   1700

643   — BRITAN. IMPERATOR II. S. C. Victory stg. l. on globe. *R.I.C. 719.*   200   500

643A   — BRITANNIA IMPERATOR II. S. C. Britannia seated l. on rock, holding standard. *R.I.C. 745.*   550   1400

644   Æ *as.* IMPERATOR II. S. C. Victory hovering l., holding shield inscribed BRI / TAN. *R.I.C. 732.*   90   225

645   Æ *dupondius,* commemorating the quelling of a serious uprising in the north, ca. 154/5, necessitating the evacuation of the recently constructed Antonine Wall in Scotland. BRITANNIA COS. IIII. S. C. Britannia seated l. on rock, shield and vexillum in background. *R.I.C. 930.*   80   200

		F	*VF*
		£	£

646 Æ *as.* Similar. *R.I.C. 934.* 75   185

Many specimens of this type are carelessly struck on inadequate flans.
Moreover, they have been found in significant quantities on Romano-British
sites, notably in Coventina's Well at Carrawburgh fort on Hadrian's Wall,
raising the interesting possibility that they may have been issued from a
temporary mint in Britain. The style of the engraving is quite regular,
indicating that even if locally produced these coins would have been struck
from normal Roman dies brought to Britain especially for this purpose.
See under Category 3.

647 **Commodus,** 177-192. Æ *sestertius,* commemorating the victories in
Scotland of the governor Ulpius Marcellus in 184/5. These were in
retribution for a major barbarian invasion several years earlier resulting
in serious damage to Hadrian's Wall, which had been temporarily overrun,
and the defeat and death of an unknown governor. BRITT. P. M. TR. P.
VIIII. IMP. VII. COS. IIII. P. P. S. C. Britannia stg. l., holding curved
sword and helmet. *R.I.C. 437.* ....   *Extremely rare*

648

648 — VICT. BRIT. P. M. TR. P. VIIII. (or X.) IMP. VII. COS. IIII. P. P. S. C.
Victory seated r., about to inscribe shield. *R.I.C. 440, 452* 120   300

649

649 **Septimius Severus,** 193-211. N *aureus,* commemorating the success of
the punitive Roman campaigns in Scotland during 209 and 210 culminating
in the illness and death of Severus at York in Feb. 211. VICTORIAE BRIT.
Victory advancing l. *R.I.C. 334.* 1200   3000

650 — VICTORIAE BRIT. Victory advancing r., leading child by hand.
R.I.C. 302. 1500   3500

651 Æ *denarius.* VICTORIAE BRIT. Victory advancing r. *R.I.C. 332.* 40   90

651A — VICTORIAE BRIT. Victory stg. facing beside palm-tree with shield
attached. *R.I.C. 336.* 40   90

651B — VICTORIAE BRIT. Victory stg. l. *R.I.C. 333.* 40   90

651C — VICTORIAE BRIT. Victory seated l., holding shield. *R.I.C. 335.* 40   85

652

		F £	VF £
652	Æ *sestertius*. VICTORIAE BRITTANNICAE S. C. Two Victories placing shield on palm-tree with captives at base. *R.I.C. 818*.............................	300	875
653	— P. M. TR. P. XVIII. COS. III. P. P. S. C. Similar. *R.I.C. 796*.	175	400
654	Æ *dupondius*. VICT. BRIT. P. M. TR. P. XIX. COS. III. P. P. S. C. Victory stg. r. between two captives, holding vexillum. *R.I.C. 809*.	100	275
655	Æ *as*. VICTORIAE BRITTANNICAE S. C. Similar. *R.I.C. 837a*...........	100	275
656	Billon *tetradrachm* of Alexandria in Egypt. NEIKH KATA BRET. Nike flying l. *Milne 2726*.	*Extremely rare*	
657	**Caracalla,** 198-217. *N aureus*, commemorating the victories achieved by the Romans in Scotland during the campaigns led jointly by Severus and Caracalla in 209, and by Caracalla alone the following year during his father's illness. VICTORIAE BRIT. Victory seated l., holding shield. *R.I.C. 174*..	1200	3000

658   659A

		F £	VF £
658	Æ *denarius*. VICTORIAE BRIT. Victory advancing l. *R.I.C. 231*.	40	85
658A	— VICTORIAE BRIT. Victory advancing r., holding trophy. *R.I.C. 231A*.	40	85
659	Æ *sestertius*. VICTORIAE BRITTANNICAE S. C. Victory stg. r., erecting trophy to r. of which Britannia stands facing, captive at feet. *R.I.C. 464*.	250	675
659A	— VICT. BRIT. TR. P. XIIII. COS. III. S.C. Similar. *Cf. R.I.C. 483c*.	225	600
660	Æ *dupondius*. VICTORIAE BRITTANNICAE S. C. Victory stg. r., inscribing shield set on palm-tree. *R.I.C. 467*............................	100	275
661	Æ *as*. VICT. BRIT. TR. P. XIIII. COS. III. S. C. Similar. *R.I.C. 490*.......	100	250
662	**Geta,** 209-212. Æ *denarius,* commemorating the victories achieved by his father and brother in Scotland in 209-10 while he and his mother were resident in London. VICTORIAE BRIT. Victory stg. l. *R.I.C. 92*............	40	85
662A	— VICTORIAE BRIT. Victory advancing r. *R.I.C. 91*.	40	85

663

		F	VF
		£	£
663	Æ *sestertius*. VICTORIAE BRITTANNICAE S. C. Victory seated r., inscribing shield set on knee. *R.I.C. 166.*	300	750
663A	— VICT. BRIT. TR. P. III. COS. II. S. C. Similar. *R.I.C. 172b.*	250	600
664	Æ *as*. VICTORIAE BRITTANNICAE S. C. Victory seated l., balancing shield on knee. *R.I.C. 191a*	100	275
665	Billon *tetradrachm* of Alexandria in Egypt. NEIKH KATA BRETAN. Nike advancing l. *B.M.C. (Alexandria) 1481.*	*Extremely rare*	

3. OFFICIAL ROMAN COINAGE STRUCK IN BRITAIN

The London mint, and the associated 'C' mint (possibly Colchester), were created by the usurper Carausius soon after his seizure of Britain in 287. Prior to this, in the mid-2nd century, there may have been minting of 'Britannia' asses of Antoninus Pius in the province using dies brought from Rome, though this has not been firmly established. After the downfall of the rebel British regime in 296 the minting establishment in London (though not the subsidiary mint) was retained by the tetrarchal government and the succeeding Constantinian administration. Early in 325, however, Constantine the Great closed the London mint after almost four decades of operation. A possible brief revival under the usurper Magnus Maximus has been postulated for gold and silver coins marked 'AVG', 'AVGOB' and 'AVGPS', though the attribution has not received universal acceptance.

666	**Antoninus Pius,** 138-161. Æ *as*, struck in northern Britain (?) in 155. BRITANNIA COS. IIII. S. C. Britannia seated l. on rock, shield and vexillum in background. *R.I.C. 930*	80	200
	Many poorly struck examples of this type have been found on Romano-British sites, notably at Brocolitia (Carrawburgh) fort on Hadrian's Wall in Northumberland, where no fewer than 327 specimens were discovered in the great votive deposit in the well which formed part of the shrine of the water-nymph Coventina. There appears to be a very real possibility that many of these 'Britannia' asses had been issued from a temporary mint in Britain, most likely situated in the north. The dies, however, are quite regular, and would thus have been brought from Rome to the island province for the express purpose of supplementing the money supply at a time of crisis.		
667	**Carausius,** usurper in Britain and northwestern Gaul, A.D. 287-293. N *aureus,* London. CONSERVAT. AVG. Jupiter stg. l., eagle at feet, ML in ex. *R.I.C. 1*	5000	12500
668	R *denarius,* London. EXPECTATE VENI. Britannia stg. r. and emperor l., clasping hands, RSR in ex. *R.I.C. 555*	450	1200

669   672A

	F	VF
	£	£

669 — RENOVAT. ROMANO. She-wolf r., suckling twins, RSR in ex.
R.I.C. 571.. 350 900

670 Billon *antoninianus*, London. COMES AVG. Victory stg. l., S—P in field,
ML in ex. *R.I.C. 14*. 45 110

670A — HILARITAS AVG. Hilaritas stg. l., B—E in field, MLXXI in ex. *R.I.C. 41.* 30 80

671 — LAETITIA AVG. Laetitia stg. l., F—O in field, ML in ex. *R.I.C. 50.*. 30 80

671A — LEG. II. AVG. Capricorn l., ML in ex. *R.I.C. 58*................................ 80 195
Legio II Augusta was stationed at Isca (Caerleon in South Wales).

672 — LEG. XX. V. V. Boar stg. r. *R.I.C. 82.* 80 195
*Legio XX Valeria Victrix was stationed at Deva (Chester in the northwest
Midlands).*

672A — PAX AVG. Pax stg. l., F—O in field, ML in ex. *R.I.C. 101.* 25 70

673 — Similar, but without mint mark. *R.I.C. 880.* 25 65

673A — PROVIDENT. AVG. Providentia stg. l., B—E in field, MLXXI in ex.
R.I.C. 149.. 30 80

674 — SALVS AVGGG. Salus stg. r., feeding snake held in her arms, S—P
in field, ML in ex. *R.I.C. 164*.. 30 80
*The reverse legends with triple-ending (AVGGG.) presumably are
subsequent to Carausius' recognition by Diocletian and Maximian in 289
following the failure of the latter's attempt to dislodge the usurper from
his island stronghold.*

674A — TEMPORVM FELICITAS. Felicitas stg. l., B—E in field, ML in ex.
R.I.C. 172.. 25 70

675 — VIRTVS AVGGG. Mars (or Virtus) stg. r., holding spear and shield,
S—P in field, MLXXI in ex. *R.I.C. 183.* 30 80

676 Billon *antoninianus*, Colchester (?). CONCORDIA MILIT. Emperor stg.
r. and Concordia l., clasping hands, C in ex. *R.I.C. 205.* 55 130

676A — EXPECTATE VENI. Britannia stg. r. and emperor l., clasping hands,
MSC in ex. *R.I.C. 216*.. 100 250

677 — FELICITAS AVG. Galley with mast and rowers, CXXI in ex. *R.I.C. 221.* 80 200

677A — FORTVNA RAEDVX. Fortuna seated l., SPC in ex. *R.I.C. 237.* 40 100

678 — LAETITIA AVG. Laetitia stg. l., globe at feet, S—P in field, C in ex.
R.I.C. 255.. 30 80

678A —-MONETA AVG. Moneta stg. l., CXXI in ex. *R.I.C. 287.* 30 80

679 — ORIENS AVG. Sol stg. l., C in ex. *R.I.C. 293*.................................... 35 85

679A — PAX AVGGG. Pax stg. l., S—P in field, MC in ex. *R.I.C. 335*........... 30 70

680

| | *F* | *VF* |
| | £ | £ |

680   — PROVID. AVG. Providentia stg. l., S—P in field, C in ex. *R.I.C. 353.*   30   80
680A — SALVS AVG. Salus stg. l. at altar, feeding snake, S—C in field,
C in ex. *R.I.C. 396.*   30   80
681   — SPES PVBLICA. Spes walking l., holding flower, S—P in field,
C in ex. *R.I.C. 413.*   30   80
681A — VICTORIA AVG. Victory advancing l., captive at feet, MC in ex.
R.I.C. 429.   35   85
682   **Carausius, Diocletian and Maximian,** after 289. Billon *antoninianus,*
Colchester (?). Obv. CARAVSIVS ET FRATRES SVI. Conjoined busts
of the three emperors l. Rev. PAX AVGGG. Pax stg. l., S—P in field,
C in ex. *R.I.C. 1.*   800   2000

682A   684A

682A — MONETA AVGGG. Moneta stg. l., S—P in field, C in ex. *R.I.C. —.* .   1000   2500
*See also nos. 693-4 and 698-700 as well as regular Carausian types with
the triple-ending 'AVGGG.' on reverse.*
683   **Allectus,** usurper in Britain, 293-296. *N aureus,* London. ORIENS AVG.
Sol stg. l. between two captives, ML in ex. *R.I.C. 4*   7000   17500
684   Æ *antoninianus,* London. LAETITIA AVG. Laetitia l., S—A in field,
MSL in ex. *R.I.C. 22.*   30   80
684A — PAX AVG. Pax stg. l., S—A in field, ML in ex. *R.I.C. 28.*   35   80
685   — PROVID. AVG. Providentia stg. l., holding globe and cornucopiae,
S—P in field, ML in ex. *R.I.C. 36.*   35   85
685A — SALVS AVG. Salus stg. r., feeding snake held in her arms, S—A in
field, MSL in ex. *R.I.C. 42*   30   80
686   — TEMPOR. FELICITAS. Felicitas stg. l., S—A in field, ML in ex. *R.I.C. 47.*   30   80
686A — VICTORIA AVG. Victory advancing l., S—P in field, ML in ex. *R.I.C. 48.*   30   80
687   Æ *antoninianus,* Colchester (?). AEQVITAS AVG. Aequitas stg. l., S—P
in field, C in ex. *R.I.C. 63.*   30   80
687A — FIDES MILITVM. Fides stg. l., holding two standards, S—P in field,
C in ex. *R.I.C. 69.*   30   80

688A

	F £	VF £
688 — LAETITIA AVG. Laetitia stg. l., S—P in field, CL in ex. *R.I.C. 79.*.. *This form of mint mark has given rise to the alternative identification of this mint as Clausentum (Bitterne, Hants.)*	40	100
688A — MONETA AVG. Moneta stg. l., S—P in field, C in ex. *R.I.C. 82.*......	40	95
689 — PAX AVG. Pax stg. l., S—P in field, C in ex. *R.I.C. 86.*	35	80
689A — PROVIDENTIA AVG. Providentia stg. l., globe at feet, S—P in field, C in ex. *R.I.C. 111.*................................	30	80
690 — TEMPORVM FELIC. Felicitas stg. l., S—P in field, CL in ex. *R.I.C. 117.*	40	100
690A — VIRTVS AVG. Mars stg. r., holding spear and shield, S—P in field, C in ex. *R.I.C. 121.*	30	80
691 Æ '*quinarius*', London. VIRTVS AVG. Galley l., QL in ex. *R.I.C. 55.*.... *An experimental denomination issued only during this reign, the types of the so-called 'quinarius' would seem to indicate that it was in some way associated with the operations of the fleet upon which the survival of the rebel regime in Britain was totally dependent.*	30	85

692   693

692 Æ '*quinarius*', Colchester (?). LAETITIA AVG. Galley r., QC in ex. *R.I.C. 124.*..............................	35	85
692A — VIRTVS AVG. Galley l., QC in ex. *R.I.C. 128.*.................................	35	85
693 **Diocletian,** 284-305. Billon *antoninianus* of London, struck by Carausius between 289 and 293. PAX AVGGG. Pax stg. l., S—P in field, MLXXI in ex. *R.I.C. 9.*................................	35	85
694 Billon *antoninianus* of Colchester (?), same date. PROVID AVGGG. Providentia stg. l., globe at feet, S—P in field, C in ex. *R.I.C. 22*............	35	85

695

		F £	VF £

695 Æ *follis*, London. GENIO POPVLI ROMANI. Genius stg. l., LON in ex.
R.I.C. *1a*.. 125 275
*By the time the central government had recovered control of Britain in 296
the antoninianus had been replaced by the larger follis under Diocletian's
sweeping currency reform. London was retained as an official imperial
mint, but the secondary British establishment (at Colchester?) was now
abandoned. Except for its initial issue in 297 (marked 'LON') the London
mint under the tetrarchic government produced only unsigned folles
throughout its first decade of operation. Perhaps Constantius did not
wish to draw attention to his employment of a mint which had been the
creation of a rebel regime.*

696 — Similar, but without mint mark. *R.I.C. 6a.* 15 35

697 — (post-abdication coinage, after 305). PROVIDENTIA DEORVM
QVIES AVGG. Quies and Providentia stg. facing each other (no mint mark).
R.I.C. 77a.... 30 65

697A

697A — QVIES AVGG. Quies stg. l., holding branch and sceptre, PLN in ex.
R.I.C. 98.... 20 50

698 **Maximian,** 286-305 and 306-308. Æ' *aureus* of London, struck by
Carausius between 289 and 293. SALVS AVGGG. Salus stg. r., feeding
snake held in her arms, ML in ex. *R.I.C. 32.* .... *Extremely rare*

699 Billon *antoninianus* of London, same date. PROVIDENTIA AVGGG.
Providentia stg. l., S—P in field, MLXXI in ex. *R.I.C. 37.*...................... 35 85

700 Billon *antoninianus* of Colchester (?), same date. PAX AVGGG. Pax stg.
l., S—P in field, C in ex. *R.I.C. 42.* 35 85

701 Æ *follis*, London. GENIO POPVLI ROMANI. Genius stg. l., LON in ex.
R.I.C. 2.... 100 250

702 — Similar, but without mint mark. *R.I.C. 23b.* 15 35

703 — (post-abdication coinage, after 305). PROVIDENTIA DEORVM
QVIES AVGG. Quies and Providentia stg. facing each other (no mint mark).
R.I.C. 77b.... 30 65

704

		F	*VF*
		£	£

704 — (second reign). GENIO POP. ROM. Genius stg. l., PLN in ex. *R.I.C. 90*. 20 40
704A — HERCVLI CONSERVATORI. Hercules stg. l., resting on club,
PLN in ex. *R.I.C. 91*. 30 75
705 **Constantius I,** 305-306 (Caesar 293-305). Æ *follis,* London (as Caesar).
GENIO POPVLI ROMANI. Genius stg. l., LON in ex. *R.I.C. 4a*.......... 110 275

706

706 — Similar, but without mint mark. *R.I.C. 30*. 15 35
707 — (as Augustus). Similar. *R.I.C. 52a*. 20 45
708 **Divus Constantius I,** deified 306. Æ *follis,* London. MEMORIA FELIX.
Altar flanked by eagles, PLN in ex. *R.I.C. 110*....................................... 20 50
709 **Galerius,** 305-311 (Caesar 293-305). Æ *follis,* London (as Caesar).
GENIO POPVLI ROMANI. Genius stg. l., LON in ex. *R.I.C. 4b*.......... 110 275
710 — Similar, but without mint mark. *R.I.C. 15*. 10 25
711 — (as Augustus). Similar. *R.I.C. 42*. 12 30
711A — GENIO POP. ROM. Genius stg. l., PLN in ex. *R.I.C. 86*................... 18 45
712 **Severus II,** 306-307 (Caesar 305-306). Æ *follis,* London (as Caesar).
GENIO POPVLI ROMANI. Genius stg. l. (no mint mark). *R.I.C. 58a* ... 35 85
713 — (as Augustus). Similar. *R.I.C. 52c*....................................... 35 85
714 **Maximinus II,** 310-313 (Caesar 305-310). Æ *follis,* London (as Caesar).
GENIO POPVLI ROMANI. Genius stg. l. (no mint mark). *R.I.C. 57*..... 15 40
715 —-GENIO POP. ROM. Genius stg. l., PLN in ex. *R.I.C. 89a*.............. 15 40
716 — (as Augustus). Similar, but with star in r. field. *R.I.C. 209b*............... 12 30
717 **Licinius,** 308-324. Æ *follis,* London. GENIO POP. ROM. Genius stg. l.,
star in r. field, PLN in ex. *R.I.C. 209c*. 12 30
717A — Similar, but with S—F in field. *R.I.C. 3*. 8 20
718 — SOLI INVICTO COMITI. Sol stg. l., holding globe, S—P in field,
MSL in ex. *R.I.C. 79*.. 10 25
719 **Constantine I, the Great,** 307-337 (Caesar 306-307). Æ *follis,* London
(as Caesar). GENIO POPVLI ROMANI. Genius stg. l. (no mint mark).
R.I.C. 72.. 25 65
719A — GENIO POP. ROM. Genius stg. l., PLN in ex. *R.I.C. 88b*.................. 15 35

		F	*VF*
		£	£

720 — PRINCIPI IVVENTVTIS. Prince stg. l., holding standards, PLN in ex. *R.I.C. 97*...................... 25 60

721 — (as Augustus). ADVENTVS AVG. Emperor on horseback l., captive on ground before, star in r. field, PLN in ex. *R.I.C. 133*...................... 22 55

722 — COMITI AVGG. NN. Sol stg. l., holding globe and whip, same mint mark. *R.I.C. 155*...................... 18 45

723 — CONCORD. MILIT. Concordia stg. l., holding standards, same mint mark. *R.I.C. 195*...................... 15 40

724 — MARTI CONSERVATORI. Mars. stg. r., holding spear and shield, star in l. field, PLN in ex. *R.I.C. 254.*...................... 15 35

724A — SOLI INVICTO COMITI. Sol stg. l., holding globe, S—F in field, MLL in ex. *R.I.C. 27*...................... 10 25

725 Æ 3, London. VICTORIAE LAETAE PRINC. PERP. Two Victories supporting shield, inscribed VOT. / P. R., over altar, PLN in ex. *R.I.C. 159.* 10 25

726

726 — VIRTVS EXERCIT. Vexillum, inscribed VOT. / XX., between two captives, PLN in ex. R.I.C. 191...................... 10 25

727 — BEAT. TRANQLITAS. Altar, inscribed VOT / IS / XX., surmounted by globe and three stars, PLON in ex. *R.I.C. 267*...................... 10 25

727A — SARMATIA DEVICTA. Victory advancing r., trampling captive, PLON and crescent in ex. *R.I.C. 289*...................... 20 45

728 — PROVIDENTIAE AVGG. Gateway of military camp, PLON in ex. *R.I.C. 293*...................... 10 25

729 **Fausta,** wife of Constantine I. Æ 3, London. SALVS REIPVBLICAE. Empress stg. l., holding two children, PLON in ex. *R.I.C. 300*...................... 60 150

730 **Helena,** mother of Constantine I. Æ 3, London. SECVRITAS REIPVBLICE. Empress stg. l., holding branch, PLON in ex. *R.I.C. 299.*...................... 60 150

731 **Crispus,** eldest son of Constantine I, Caesar 317-326. Æ 3, London. SOLI INVICTO COMITI. Sol stg. l., holding globe, crescent in l. field, PLN in ex. *R.I.C. 144.*...................... 12 30

731A — VIRTVS EXERCIT. Vexillum, inscribed VOT. / XX., between two captives, PLN in ex. *R.I.C. 194.*...................... 12 30

732 — BEATA TRANQVILLITAS. Altar, inscribed VOT / IS / XX., surmounted by globe and three stars, P—A in field, PLON in ex. *R.I.C. 211.* 12 30

733 — CAESARVM NOSTRORVM around wreath containing VOT. / X., PLON and crescent in ex. *R.I.C. 291*...................... 12 30

734   737A

		F £	VF £
734	— PROVIDENTIAE CAESS. Gateway of military camp, PLON in ex. *R.I.C. 295.*	10	25
735	**Constantine II,** 337-340 (Caesar 317-337). Æ 3, London (as Caesar). CLARITAS REIPVBLICAE. Sol stg. l., holding globe, crescent in l. field, PLN in ex. *R.I.C. 131.*	12	30
736	— VICTORIAE LAETAE PRINC. PERP. Two Victories supporting shield, inscribed VOT. / P. R., over altar ornamented with wreath, PLN in ex. *R.I.C. 182.*	12	30
737	— VIRTVS EXERCIT. Vexillum, inscribed VOT. / XX., between two captives, PLON in ex. *R.I.C. 190.*	12	30
737A	— BEATA TRANQVILLITAS. Altar, inscribed VOT / IS / XX., surmounted by globe and three stars, PLON in ex. *R.I.C. 236.*	10	25
738	— CAESARVM NOSTRORVM around wreath containing VOT. / X., PLON and crescent in ex. *R.I.C. 292.*	10	25
738A	— PROVIDENTIAE CAESS. Gateway of military camp, PLON in ex. *R.I.C. 296.*	10	25
739	**Constantius II,** 337-361 (Caesar 324-337). Æ 3, London (as Caesar). PROVIDENTIAE CAESS. Gateway of military camp, PLON in ex. *R.I.C. 298.*	25	60
740	**Magnus Maximus,** usurper in the West, 383-388. *N solidus,* London (?). RESTITVTOR REIPVBLICAE. Emperor stg. r., holding labarum and Victory, AVG in ex. *R.I.C. 1.*		*Unique*

The attribution to London of this rare series has not been firmly established, though Maximus was certainly proclaimed emperor in Britain and it is well attested that the principal city of the British provinces bore the name 'Augusta' in the late Roman period (Ammianus Marcellinus XXVII, 8, 7; XXVIII, 3, 7).

741

		F £	VF £
741	— VICTORIA AVGG. Two emperors enthroned facing, Victory hovering in background between them, AVGOB in ex. *R.I.C. 2b.*	5000	10000

Maximus appears to have struck a similar type in the name of the eastern emperor Theodosius I (cf. R.I.C. 2a), though it is presently known only from a silver-gilt specimen preserved in the British Museum.

		F £	VF £
742	Æ *siliqua,* London (?). VOT. / V. / MVLT. / X. within wreath, AVG below. *R.I.C. 4.*	850	2000
742A	— VICTORIA AVGG. Victory advancing l., AVGPS in ex. *R.I.C. 3.*	750	1750

4. IMITATIONS OF ROMAN COINS PRODUCED IN BRITAIN

At certain periods during the three and a half centuries of its occupation Roman Britain seems to have been the source of much local imitation of the official imported coinage. This began soon after the Claudian invasion in A.D. 43 when significant quantities of sestertii, dupondii and asses (especially the last) were produced in the newly conquered territory, as evidenced by the frequency of their occurrence in archaeological finds. The technical excellence of many of these 'copies', together with the surprising extent of their minting, would seem to indicate that some, at least, of these coins were produced with official sanction in order to make good an unexpected deficiency in the currency supply. Others are much poorer and well below weight, representing the 'unofficial' branch of this operation, some of it probably emanating from territory as yet unconquered. As conditions in the new province settled down rapid Romanization and urbanization of British society brought a general increase in wealth, and with it a much greater volume of currency flowing into the country. Local imitation now virtually ceased, except for the occasional activities of criminal counterfeiters, and this state of affairs lasted down to the great political crisis and financial collapse of the second half of the 3rd century. At this point large scale minting of imitations of the debased antoniniani of the late 260s and early 270s began in Britain and in the other northwestern provinces, all of which had been seriousy affected by the political dislocation of this turbulent era. This class of imitations is usually referred to as 'barbarous radiates', the emperor's spiky crown being a constant and conspicuous feature of the obverses. Most frequently copied were the antoniniani of the Gallic rulers Tetricus Senior and Tetricus Junior (ca. 270-273) and the posthumous issues of Claudius Gothicus (died 270). The quality of the 'barbarous radiates' is variable in the extreme, some exhibiting what appears to be a revival of Celtic art forms, others so tiny that it is virtually impossible to see anything of the design. Their production appears to have ended abruptly with Aurelian's reconquest of the western provinces in 273. A similar phenomenon, though on a lesser scale, occurred in the middle decades of the following century when normal life in Britain was again disrupted, not only by usurpation but additionally by foreign invasion. With supplies of currency from the Continent temporarily disrupted local imitation, particularly of the 'Æ 2' and 'Æ 3' issues of Constantius II and the usurper Magnentius, began in earnest. How long this continued is difficult to determine as life in the island province was now subject to increasingly frequent episodes of dislocation. By now urban life in Britain was in serious decline and when Roman rule ended early in the 5th century, bringing a total cessation of currency supplies, the catastrophic decline in monetary commerce in the former provinces rendered it no longer necessary for the deficiency to be made good.

		F	VF
		£	£
743	**Agrippa,** died 12 B.C. Æ as, of irregular British mintage, imitating the Roman issue made under Agrippa's grandson Caligula, A.D. 37-41. S. C. Neptune stg. l., holding dolphin and trident.	40	100
	The large official issue of Agrippa asses was made shortly before the Claudian invasion of Britain in A.D. 43 and would thus have comprised a significant proportion of the 'aes' in circulation at this time. In consequence, it would soon have become familiar to the new provincials providing an ideal prototype for imitation.		
744	**Claudius,** 41-54. Æ *sestertius,* of irregular British mintage. SPES AVGVSTA S. C. Spes walking l., holding flower.	75	250
745	Æ *dupondius,* of irregular British mintage. CERES AVGVSTA S. C. Ceres enthroned l., holding corn- ears and torch.	35	100

746

	F	VF
	£	£

746 Æ *as*, of irregular British mintage. S. C. Minerva advancing r., brandishing
spear and holding shield. 30 85
*This is by far the commonest of the Claudian imitations and the prototypes
must have represented the bulk of the aes coinage carried by the legions at
the time of the invasion. The martial type may well have been specially
selected as a suitable theme for the initial import of coinage into the newly
conquered territory.*

747 **Nero Claudius Drusus,** father of Claudius, died 9 B.C. Æ *sestertius,* of
irregular British mintage. TI. CLAVDIVS CAESAR AVG. P. M. TR .P.
IMP. S. C. Claudius seated l. on curule chair amidst arms 85 300
*This type was issued by Claudius half a century after his father's death and
would thus have been prominently represented in the initial wave of coinage
imported into the new province.*

748 **Antonia,** mother of Claudius, died A.D. 37. Æ *dupondius,* of irregular British
mintage. TI. CLAVDIVS AVG P.M. TR. P. IMP. P. P. S. C. Claudius
stg. l., holding simpulum. 60 175
*Another Claudian issue for a deceased parent, this represents one of only
two dupondius types struck during this reign and would have entered
Britain in significant quantities at the time of the invasion in A.D. 43.*

749A   749B

749C

749 **'Barbarous radiates',** ca. 270-273. British and Continental imitations of
billon *antoniniani,* principally of Divus Claudius II (A), Tetricus Senior
(B) and Tetricus Junior (C). The inscriptions are usually blundered and
the types sometimes unrecognizable. British mintage can only be
established by provenance. 5 10

750 **Barbarous 4th century,** mostly of the second half of the century, and principally
imitated from 'Æ 2' and 'Æ 3' issues of the later Constantinian period, notably those
of Constantius II ('soldier spearing fallen horseman' type), and the usurpers
Magnentius and Decentius ('two Victories' type). The copies, especially those of
Magnentius and Decentius, are often of excellent style and execution, though the
legends frequently contain small errors. Those of Constantius II are sometimes very
barbarous and poorly struck, occasionally over regular issues of the earlier
Constantinian period. Again, the likelihood of British mintage can only be established
by provenance. 5-8 10-15

Grading of Hammered Coins

As the name suggests, hammered coins were struck by hand with a hammer. This can lead to the coin being struck off centre, double struck, weak in the design, suffer cracks or flan defects. It is important to take these factors into account when assessing the grade of this series. Value is considerably reduced if the coin is holed, pierced, plugged or mounted.

Extremely Fine
Design and legends sharp and clear.

Very Fine
Design and legends still clear but with slight evidence of wear and/or minor damage.

Fine
Showing quite a lot of wear but still with design and legends distinguishable.

William I PAXS type penny

Henry VIII 1st coinage gold Angel

Edward VI silver shilling

EARLY & MIDDLE ANGLO-SAXON KINGDOMS & MINTS (C.650-973)

Approximate extent of Danelaw

Approximate extent of Hiberno-Norse Kingdom of York

NORTHUMBRIA

York

Lincoln

Chester

Derby • Newark (?)
• Nottingham

Stafford

Shrewsbury

Leicester • Stamford (?)

Tamworth

Norwich

EAST ANGLIA
• Thetford

MERCIA

Northampton • Huntingdon

Warwick

Newport • Bedford

Hereford

Buckingham • Hertford

Maldon

Gloucester • Oxford

Malmesbury • Wallingford • London

Bath

Rochester

Canterbury •

Wilton

Winchester

KENT

Lympne

Dover

Barnstaple

Langport

Shaftesbury

Southampton

Lewes

WESSEX

Exeter •

Bridport •

Wareham

Chichester

Totnes

EARLY ANGLO-SAXON PERIOD, *c*. 600-*c*. 775

The withdrawal of Roman forces from Britain early in the 5th century A.D. and the gradual decline of central administration resulted in a rapid deterioration of the money supply. The arrival of Teutonic raiders and settlers, even in relatively small numbers, disrupted life and it was probably not until late in the 6th century that renewed political, cultural and commercial links with the kingdom of the Merovingian Franks led to the appearance of small quantities of Merovingian gold *tremisses* (one-third solidus) in England. A purse containing 37 such pieces (plus 3 gold blanks and 2 ingots) was found in the Sutton Hoo ship-burial. Native Anglo-Saxon gold *thrymsas* were minted from about the 630s, initially in the style of their continental prototypes or copied from obsolete Roman coinage and later in pure Anglo-Saxon style. The mixed Crondall hoard of 101 gold coins (1 Byzantine, 24 Merovingian or Frankish, 69 Anglo-Saxon, 7 others) gives structure to the arrangement of thrymsas. By the middle of the 7th century the gold coinage was being increasingly debased with silver, and gold had been superseded entirely by about 675.

These silver coins, contemporary with the *deniers or denarii* of the Merovingian Franks, are the first English pennies, though they are commonly known today as *sceats* or *sceattas* (pronounced 'skeats' or 'shatters' a term more correctly translated as 'treasure' or 'wealth'; the singular is *sceat* not *sceatta*, which is the adjective). They provide important material for the student of Anglo-Saxon art. Indeed, it could be said that, until recently, the largely anonymous, anepigraphic, nature of the sceatta coinage detracted from its numismatic character, however, Anna Gannon's work on the subtle iconography of this period has elevated its status significantly.

Though the earliest ('primary') sceats are a transition from the gold thrymsa coinage, coins of new ('secondary') style were soon developed which were also copied, and issued in substantial numbers (probably tens of millions) as a trading currency, by the Frisians of the Low Countries ('Continental'), evidencing the significant volume of North Sea trade, and their central role in the economic resurgence. Early coins are of good silver content, though the quality deteriorates early in the 8th century, with weights then averaging around 1.00gms. The secondary sceats exist in numerous varied types, though the survival rate, generally is low and for some types, extremely low. Many can be regarded as propaganda during the Conversion Period, though the iconography is often, and probably intentionally, ambiguous, to broaden their appeal to differing cultural traditions in Anglo-Saxon England. As well as the official issues there are mules and other varieties, which may be contemporary imitations; there is no clear line of demarcation. The 'eclectic' types are those which do not sit comfortably in the current, alphabetic, Serial classification. Many of the sceats were issued at the time of Aethelbald King of Mercia, (A.D. 716-757) who was overlord of the southern English, but as few bear inscriptions it is only in recent years that research has permitted their correct dating and the attribution of certain types to specific areas. The Aston Rowant (Oxon.) hoard of 324 sceats, deposited *c*. 710, separates the primary and secondary phases.

Through recent detector finds and continued research, a definitive classification is evolving but remains fluid. The arrangement given below is informed by Michael Metcalf's work on the series, developing Rigold's alphabetical classification. In this listing, the primary sceats are followed by the Continental then the secondary and, finally, the eclectic. This is not chronologically precise as there is some overlap, but has been adopted for ease of reference and identification. This list is more extensive than previously published in *Coins of England* but is not exhaustive. The catalogue numbers previously in use have been retained for the thrymsas and primary sceats but the secondary and Continental have been renumbered (the 'old' S. number given in brackets) as the issues regarded as 'eclectic' have now been given a separate section. The reference 'B.M.C.' is to the type given in *British Museum Catalogue: Anglo-Saxon Coins*. The reference *M* is to an illustration, and *M. p.* to a page, in Metcalf (below).

Major works of reference include:

Metcalf, D. M. *Thrymsas and Sceattas in the Ashmolean Museum*, Vols I-III.
Gannon, A. *The Iconography of Early Anglo-Saxon Coinage* (2003)
Rigold, S. E. *'The two primary series of sceattas'*, B.N.J., XXX (1960).
Sutherland, C. H. V. *Anglo-Saxon Gold Coinage in the light of the Crondall Hoard* (1948).
Abramson, T. *Sceattas, An Illustrated Guide* (2006)
Op den Velde, W. & Klaassen, C. J. F. *Sceattas and Merovingian Deniers from Domburg and Westenschovwen*. (2004).

Previous years' catalogue number is shown in brackets where applicable.

ᚠ ᚪ ᚦ ᛖ ᚱ ᛣ · ᚷ ᛈ ᚾ ᚻ ᛁ ᚩ ᛋ ᚸ ᛄ ᛏ ᛒ ᛗ ᚪ ᚷ ᚷ ᚺ ᚷ ᚠ ᚠ ᚹ ᚪ

f u th o r k z w h n i j jh p x s t b e m l ng d oe a Æ ea y

Early Anglo-Saxon Runes (Futhark)

GOLD

752

		F	*VF*
		£	£

A.   Early pieces, of uncertain monetary status

751   Thrymsa. Name and portrait of Bishop Liudhard (chaplain to Queen Bertha
        of Kent). R. Cross. .... *Extremely rare*

752   Solidus. Imitating solidi of Roman rulers. Blundered legends, some
        with runes. .... *Extremely rare*

753   754   758

B.   Crondall types, *c*.620 – *c*.645

Twelve different types, which are almost certainly English, were found in the Crondall hoard
of 1828. All are thrysmas, containing 40-70% gold.

753   'Witmen' type. Bust r. with trident. R. Cross. Legend normally blundered.
        M. 1-21 1250   4000

754   London-derived type. Head r. with pseudo-legend. R. Cross. Pseudo-legend.
        M. 22-32 1350   5000

755   'Licius' type. Elegant imitation of Roman triens. Bust l. R. VOT XX.
        M. 33-41 2000   7500

756   'LEMC' type. Head l. R. Maltese cross with letters L, E, M, C in angles,
        or cross on steps. *M. 42-9* 1500   5750

757   'LONDINIV' type. Facing bust, crosslets l. and r. R. Tall cross,
        LONDVNIV and pseudo-legend around. *M. 51-7* 2000   7500

758   Eadbald of Kent (616-40) London. Bust r. AVDVARLD REGES. R. Cross on
        globule, LONDENVS. Usually garbled. *M. 50* 2500   9500

758A   — Canterbury. As 758 but DOROVERNVS M. *M-* 2750   10500

759   Other crude types, usually with head or bust, R. Cross. *M. 58-72* 900   3000

C.   Ultra-Crondall types, *c*.620 – 655?

Thrymsas not represented in the Crondall hoard, but probably of the same date range.

760   761   762

760   'Benutigo' type. Bust r., blundered legend. R. Cross on steps, runic
        legend (Benutigoii?) 2000   7250

761   'Wuneetton' type. Bust r., cross before. R. Cross. Blundered legend
        (WVNEETON or similar). *M. 77* 1350   4250

762   'York' type. Stylised face, crosslets to l. and r., squared pattern beneath. R.
        Cross. Blundered legend. *M. 76* 2000   7500

762A   — similar, but rev. with four 'faces' around central square. *M. p.51* 2250   8500

D.   **Post-Crondall types, *c*.655 – *c*.675**

Pale gold types, visibly debased and sometimes almost silvery, containing 10-35% gold. The description "standard" is a reference to the Roman legionary ensign bearing the legend e.g. VOTIS X MVLTIS XX also carried in Anglo-Saxon episcopal processions. The legend is reduced to TOTII on the coinage and may be described as the "votive standard".

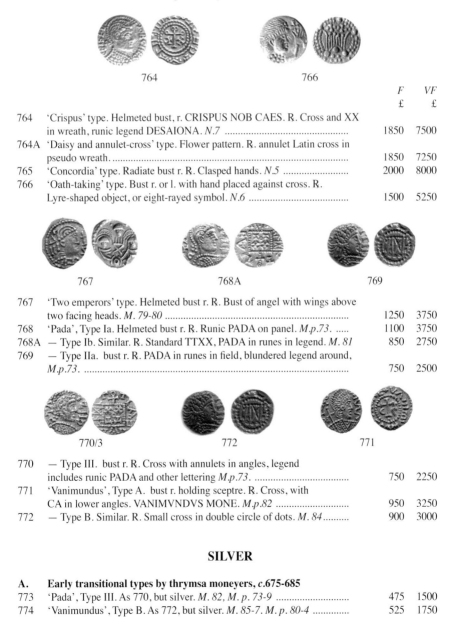

764   766

		F £	VF £
764	'Crispus' type. Helmeted bust, r. CRISPUS NOB CAES. Ŗ. Cross and XX in wreath, runic legend DESAIONA. *N.7*	1850	7500
764A	'Daisy and annulet-cross' type. Flower pattern. Ŗ. annulet Latin cross in pseudo wreath.	1850	7250
765	'Concordia' type. Radiate bust r. Ŗ. Clasped hands. *N.5*	2000	8000
766	'Oath-taking' type. Bust r. or l. with hand placed against cross. Ŗ. Lyre-shaped object, or eight-rayed symbol. *N.6*	1500	5250

767   768A   769

767	'Two emperors' type. Helmeted bust r. Ŗ. Bust of angel with wings above two facing heads. *M. 79-80*	1250	3750
768	'Pada', Type Ia. Helmeted bust r. Ŗ. Runic PADA on panel. *M.p.73.*	1100	3750
768A	— Type Ib. Similar. Ŗ. Standard TTXX, PADA in runes in legend. *M. 81*	850	2750
769	— Type IIa. bust r. Ŗ. PADA in runes in field, blundered legend around, *M.p.73.*	750	2500

770/3   772   771

770	— Type III. bust r. Ŗ. Cross with annulets in angles, legend includes runic PADA and other lettering *M.p.73.*	750	2250
771	'Vanimundus', Type A. bust r. holding sceptre. Ŗ. Cross, with CA in lower angles. VANIMVNDVS MONE. *M.p.82*	950	3250
772	— Type B. Similar. Ŗ. Small cross in double circle of dots. *M. 84*	900	3000

SILVER

A.   **Early transitional types by thrymsa moneyers, *c*.675-685**

773	'Pada', Type III. As 770, but silver. *M. 82, M. p. 73-9*	475	1500
774	'Vanimundus', Type B. As 772, but silver. *M. 85-7. M. p. 80-4*	525	1750

B.   Primary Sceattas, *c*.680 – *c*.710

Minted in various regions of south-eastern and eastern England.

775: varieties A1   A2   A3

	F £	VF £
775 Series A 2a. Radiate bust r., TIC. R. Standard, TOTII. The varieties are:		
A1, TIIC. R. Rounded 'horns' on reverse standard;	200	500
A2, TIC. R. Square horns;	85	225
A3, —, R. Row of pellets behind head. *B.M.C.2a, M. 89-94, M. p. 85-93*	85	225

776   777   777A

776 Series BX. Diademed bust r., VANTAVMA or similar. R. Bird r. above cross on steps, annulets and pellets in field vary. *B.M.C. 26. M. 97-9, M. p. 99*	110	275
777 — BI. Diademed head r. within serpent circle. R. Bird r. on cross. *B.M.C. 27a. M. 100-106.*	50	125
777A — BII. Similar but simplified legend VAVAVA. R. Crosslet or annulet beside bird. *M. 113-6.*	60	135

777B, two styles   778

777B — BIIIA, Type 27a. Diademed head r. with either protruding jaw or pointed nose, symbols before, serpent circle. R. Full bodied or linear bird on cross within serpent circle, annulets either side, pellets below. *M. p. 158-65*	65	150
778 — BZ. Abstract facing head. R. Simplified bird on cross in linear style, blundered legend. *BMC 29a, M. 138-9. M. p. 136-7*	90	240

779 C1   779 C2   779 CZ

779 Series C. Radiate bust r., similar to 775 but runic ᚠᛗᛣᚠ replaces TIC. R. Variety C1, standard, TOTII; variety C2, four crosses around standard. *B.M.C. 2b. M. 117-125, M. P. 106-12*	50	120
779A Series CZ. Radiate bust r., similar to 779 but R. large cross pattée abuts 'standard'. *M132-2, M. p. 113.*		

780

	F £	VF £

| 780 | King Aethelred of Mercia? (674-704). Degenerate head. R. Æthiliræd in runes in two lines. *M. 134-5, M. p. 120-4* .... | 175 | 575 |

781: various styles

781 Series F. Bust r., with pelleted helmet, blundered legend. R. Small cross on steps, arrangement of surrounding annulets and letters "T" and "I" varies *M. 136-7, M. p. 125-32* 70 200

782: various styles

782 Series Z. Broad facing portrait (Christ?) with forked or straight beard. R. Hound running r., legs straight or crossed, tail curled beneath or above, erect ears sometimes with chevrons above *BMC 66, M. 140-2, M. p. 137-8* 200 650

782A

782A Series Z-related. Skeletal hound r., perhaps copy of 782. R. Saltire standard or cross-crosslet design. *M. 143-4, M. p. 138-9*.. 125 450

783: various styles

783 'Vernus' group, Types 2b, 3b and 91. Degenerate head r., VER before, execution deteriorates in later issues. R. Standard. *M. 146-8, M. p. 140-6*.............. 65 165

784: various styles

784 'Saroaldo' Type 11. Bust r. becoming increasingly stylized R. Pseudo-legend SAROALDO(?) around standard enclosing FIT/RV legend .... *Extremely rare*
or saltire and pellets. *M. 151-3, M. p. 147-51*... 80 250

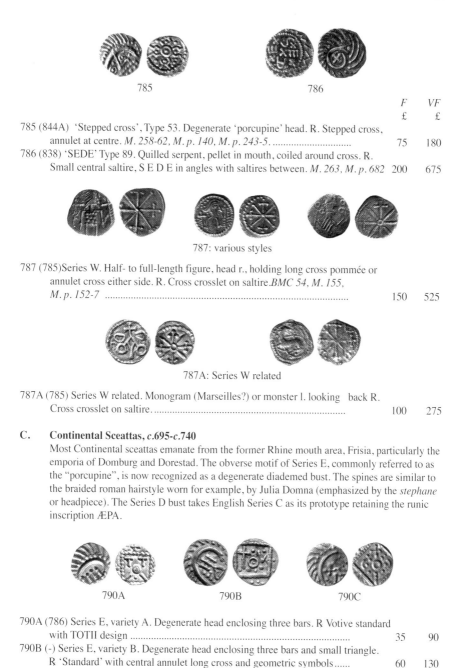

785   786

	F	VF
	£	£

785 (844A) 'Stepped cross', Type 53. Degenerate 'porcupine' head. R. Stepped cross, annulet at centre. *M. 258-62, M. p. 140, M. p. 243-5.* 75   180

786 (838) 'SEDE' Type 89. Quilled serpent, pellet in mouth, coiled around cross. R. Small central saltire, S E D E in angles with saltires between. *M. 263, M. p. 682* 200   675

787: various styles

787 (785) Series W. Half- to full-length figure, head r., holding long cross pommée or annulet cross either side. R. Cross crosslet on saltire.*BMC 54, M. 155, M. p. 152-7* 150   525

787A: Series W related

787A (785) Series W related. Monogram (Marseilles?) or monster l. looking   back R. Cross crosslet on saltire. 100   275

C.   Continental Sceattas, *c*.695-*c*.740

Most Continental sceattas emanate from the former Rhine mouth area, Frisia, particularly the emporia of Domburg and Dorestad. The obverse motif of Series E, commonly referred to as the "porcupine", is now recognized as a degenerate diademed bust. The spines are similar to the braided roman hairstyle worn for example, by Julia Domna (emphasized by the *stephane* or headpiece). The Series D bust takes English Series C as its prototype retaining the runic inscription ÆPA.

790A   790B   790C

790A (786) Series E, variety A. Degenerate head enclosing three bars. R Votive standard with TOTII design 35   90

790B (-) Series E, variety B. Degenerate head enclosing three bars and small triangle. R 'Standard' with central annulet long cross and geometric symbols...... 60   130

790C (-) Series E, variety C. Degenerate head enclosing three bars and small cross. R 'Standard' with central annulet, symmetrical geometric symbols. 60   130

790 *VICO*

	F	VF
	£	£

790V (788) — , Degenerate head enclosing bars. R. 'Standard' with letters possibly
reading VIC (*wic*, emporium) around central annulet. *M. p. 211-16*........   40   100

    790D   790E   790F

790D (786A) — , variety D. Degenerate head, with annulet at lower end, triangular head
    with pellet eye. R. 'Standard' with four pellets around central annulet.
    Dorestad. *M. 209-11*. (786)..   30   80
790E (-) — , variety E. Degenerate head, enclosing pellets, triangular head.
    R. 'Standard' with four lines and central annulet.   30   80
790F (-) — , variety F. Degenerate head in dolphin shape, with pellet outline,
    enclosing bars. R. 'Standard' with 3 or 4 saltires or crosses in corners and
    central annulet..   50   130

790, Series E, variety G1   with obverses G2, G4   and "G5"

790G (787) — , variety G1-4 (and G5), Degenerate head evolved into insect-like figure with
    triangular foreleg and sometimes pseudo-letters XAZO before. R. 'Standard'
    with four lines and central annulet. *M. 200-5, M. p. 216-19*   35   80
    "G5" has finely grained hair similar to type 10. R. Bishop's crook in standard with
    legend reading "VVILL…"

    790K   790L

790K (789) — , varieties K-L plumed bird, usually r. R. Standard with a variety of
    symmetrical geometric symbols. *M. 190-3, M. p.206-11*   50   135
791 (790) Later issues. Degenerate head. Innumerable varieties. R. 'Standard'.
    M. 214-53, M. p. 222-42...   30   75

    792   792 var.

792 (839) Series D, Type 2c. Bust r. (types with bust l. are possibly English
    and imitative), runic ÆPA before bust. R. Plain cross with pellets in angles,
    pseudo-letters around. *M. 158-80, M. p. 184-90*.   40   95

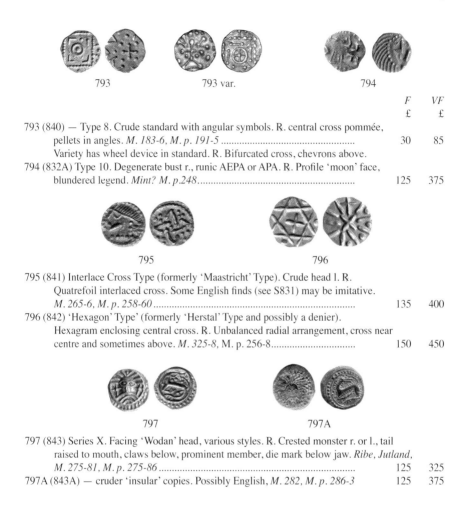

793   793 var.   794

	F £	*VF* £

793 (840) — Type 8. Crude standard with angular symbols. R. central cross pommée,
    pellets in angles. *M. 183-6, M. p. 191-5* 30 85
    Variety has wheel device in standard. R. Bifurcated cross, chevrons above.
794 (832A) Type 10. Degenerate bust r., runic AEPA or APA. R. Profile 'moon' face,
    blundered legend. *Mint? M. p.248.*.. 125 375

795   796

795 (841) Interlace Cross Type (formerly 'Maastricht' Type). Crude head l. R.
    Quatrefoil interlaced cross. Some English finds (see S831) may be imitative.
    M. 265-6, M. p. 258-60 .... 135 400
796 (842) 'Hexagon' Type' (formerly 'Herstal' Type and possibly a denier).
    Hexagram enclosing central cross. R. Unbalanced radial arrangement, cross near
    centre and sometimes above. *M. 325-8,* M. p. 256-8................................ 150 450

797   797A

797 (843) Series X. Facing 'Wodan' head, various styles. R. Crested monster r. or l., tail
    raised to mouth, claws below, prominent member, die mark below jaw. *Ribe, Jutland,*
    M. 275-81, M. p. 275-86 .... 125 325
797A (843A) — cruder 'insular' copies. Possibly English, *M. 282, M. p. 286-3*   125 375

D.   Secondary Sceattas, c.710-760

Die duplication is the exception in this coinage, with a substantial variation of execution and
fabric within each type. It is assumed that quality deteriorates over time and late issues may
be of more interest monetarily than aesthetically. This coinage was minted in all the main
regions of southern and eastern England. Some boundaries between Series remain indistinct
e.g. K and L, C and R.

800

800 (808) Series G, Type 3a. Diademed bust r., heavenward gaze, cross before.
    R. Standard with 3 or 4 saltires. *M. 267-70, M. p. 266-72* 75 200

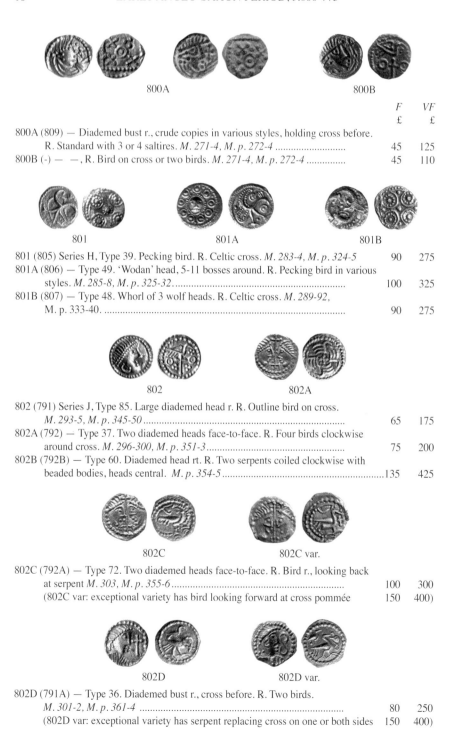

800A   800B

	F £	VF £

800A (809) — Diademed bust r., crude copies in various styles, holding cross before.
R. Standard with 3 or 4 saltires. *M. 271-4, M. p. 272-4* 45   125

800B (-) — —, R. Bird on cross or two birds. *M. 271-4, M. p. 272-4* 45   110

801   801A   801B

801 (805) Series H, Type 39. Pecking bird. R. Celtic cross. *M. 283-4, M. p. 324-5*   90   275

801A (806) — Type 49. 'Wodan' head, 5-11 bosses around. R. Pecking bird in various
styles. *M. 285-8, M. p. 325-32* 100   325

801B (807) — Type 48. Whorl of 3 wolf heads. R. Celtic cross. *M. 289-92,*
M. p. 333-40. 90   275

802   802A

802 (791) Series J, Type 85. Large diademed head r. R. Outline bird on cross.
M. 293-5, M. p. 345-50 65   175

802A (792) — Type 37. Two diademed heads face-to-face. R. Four birds clockwise
around cross. *M. 296-300, M. p. 351-3* 75   200

802B (792B) — Type 60. Diademed head rt. R. Two serpents coiled clockwise with
beaded bodies, heads central. *M. p. 354-5* 135   425

802C   802C var.

802C (792A) — Type 72. Two diademed heads face-to-face. R. Bird r., looking back
at serpent *M. 303, M. p. 355-6* 100   300

(802C var: exceptional variety has bird looking forward at cross pommée   150   400)

802D   802D var.

802D (791A) — Type 36. Diademed bust r., cross before. R. Two birds.
M. 301-2, M. p. 361-4 80   250

(802D var: exceptional variety has serpent replacing cross on one or both sides   150   400)

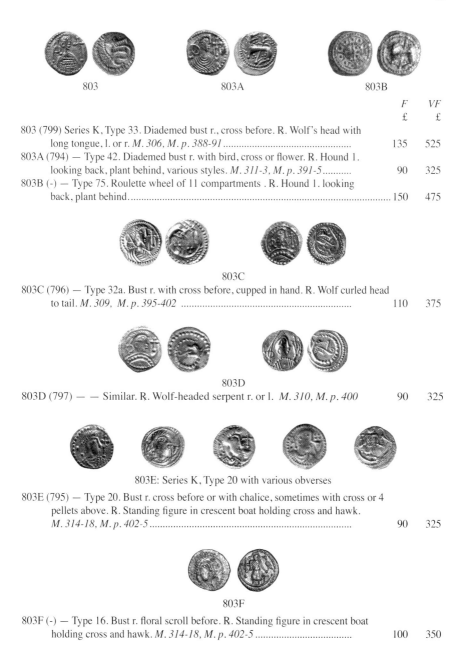

803   803A   803B

	F	VF
	£	£

803 (799) Series K, Type 33. Diademed bust r., cross before. R. Wolf's head with
  long tongue, l. or r. *M. 306, M. p. 388-91* 135 525

803A (794) — Type 42. Diademed bust r. with bird, cross or flower. R. Hound 1.
  looking back, plant behind, various styles. *M. 311-3, M. p. 391-5* 90 325

803B (-) — Type 75. Roulette wheel of 11 compartments . R. Hound 1. looking
  back, plant behind 150 475

803C

803C (796) — Type 32a. Bust r. with cross before, cupped in hand. R. Wolf curled head
  to tail. *M. 309, M. p. 395-402* 110 375

803D

803D (797) — — Similar. R. Wolf-headed serpent r. or l. *M. 310, M. p. 400* 90 325

803E: Series K, Type 20 with various obverses

803E (795) — Type 20. Bust r. cross before or with chalice, sometimes with cross or 4
  pellets above. R. Standing figure in crescent boat holding cross and hawk.
  M. 314-18, M. p. 402-5 .... 90 325

803F

803F (-) — Type 16. Bust r. floral scroll before. R. Standing figure in crescent boat
  holding cross and hawk. *M. 314-18, M. p. 402-5* 100 350

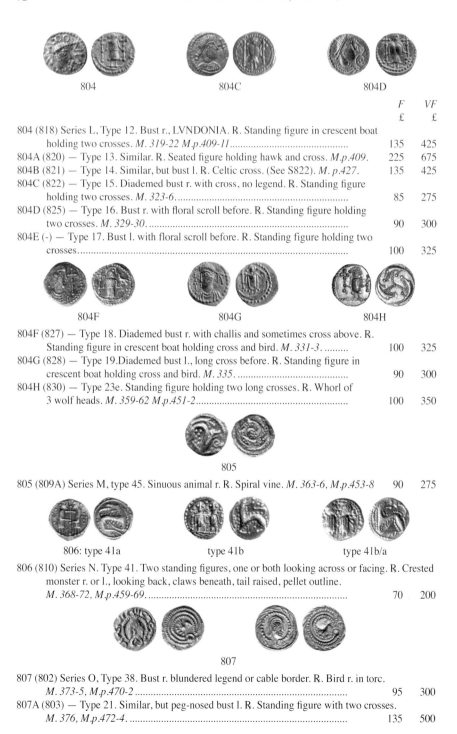

804   804C   804D

	F £	VF £

804 (818) Series L, Type 12. Bust r., LVNDONIA. R̃. Standing figure in crescent boat
    holding two crosses. *M. 319-22 M.p.409-11*... 135   425

804A (820) — Type 13. Similar. R̃. Seated figure holding hawk and cross. *M.p.409.* 225   675

804B (821) — Type 14. Similar, but bust l. R̃. Celtic cross. (See S822). *M. p.427.* 135   425

804C (822) — Type 15. Diademed bust r. with cross, no legend. R̃. Standing figure
    holding two crosses. *M. 323-6.*... 85   275

804D (825) — Type 16. Bust r. with floral scroll before. R̃. Standing figure holding
    two crosses. *M. 329-30.*... 90   300

804E (-) — Type 17. Bust l. with floral scroll before. R. Standing figure holding two
    crosses... 100   325

804F   804G   804H

804F (827) — Type 18. Diademed bust r. with challis and sometimes cross above. R̃.
    Standing figure in crescent boat holding cross and bird. *M. 331-3.* 100   325

804G (828) — Type 19.Diademed bust l., long cross before. R̃. Standing figure in
    crescent boat holding cross and bird. *M. 335.* 90   300

804H (830) — Type 23e. Standing figure holding two long crosses. R̃. Whorl of
    3 wolf heads. *M. 359-62 M.p.451-2*... 100   350

805

805 (809A) Series M, type 45. Sinuous animal r. R̃. Spiral vine. *M. 363-6, M.p.453-8*   90   275

806: type 41a   type 41b   type 41b/a

806 (810) Series N. Type 41. Two standing figures, one or both looking across or facing. R̃. Crested
    monster r. or l., looking back, claws beneath, tail raised, pellet outline.
    M. 368-72, M.p.459-69.... 70   200

807

807 (802) Series O, Type 38. Bust r. blundered legend or cable border. R̃. Bird r. in torc.
    M. 373-5, M.p.470-2 95   300

807A (803) — Type 21. Similar, but peg-nosed bust l. R̃. Standing figure with two crosses.
    M. 376, M.p.472-4. 135   500

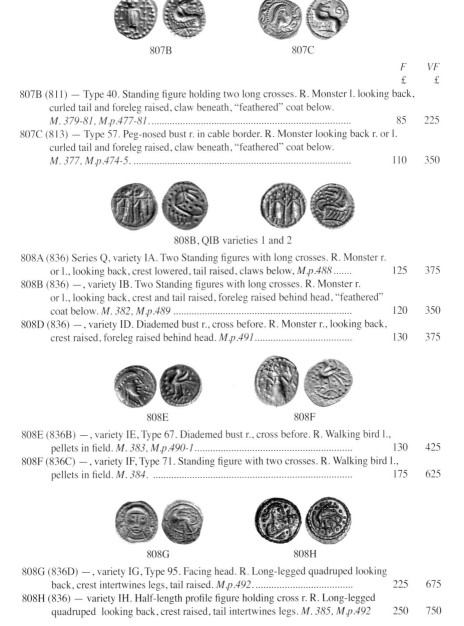

807B 807C

	F	VF
	£	£

807B (811) — Type 40. Standing figure holding two long crosses. R. Monster l. looking back, curled tail and foreleg raised, claw beneath, "feathered" coat below. *M. 379-81, M.p.477-81*.. 85 225

807C (813) — Type 57. Peg-nosed bust r. in cable border. R. Monster looking back r. or l. curled tail and foreleg raised, claw beneath, "feathered" coat below. *M. 377, M.p.474-5*. 110 350

808B, QIB varieties 1 and 2

808A (836) Series Q, variety IA. Two Standing figures with long crosses. R. Monster r. or l., looking back, crest lowered, tail raised, claws below, *M.p.488* 125 375

808B (836) —, variety IB. Two Standing figures with long crosses. R. Monster r. or l., looking back, crest and tail raised, foreleg raised behind head, "feathered" coat below. *M. 382, M.p.489* 120 350

808D (836) —, variety ID. Diademed bust r., cross before. R. Monster r., looking back, crest raised, foreleg raised behind head. *M.p.491*.................................... 130 375

808E 808F

808E (836B) —, variety IE, Type 67. Diademed bust r., cross before. R. Walking bird l., pellets in field. *M. 383, M.p.490-1*.. 130 425

808F (836C) —, variety IF, Type 71. Standing figure with two crosses. R. Walking bird l., pellets in field. *M. 384*. 175 625

808G 808H

808G (836D) —, variety IG, Type 95. Facing head. R. Long-legged quadruped looking back, crest intertwines legs, tail raised. *M.p.492*...................................... 225 675

808H (836) — variety IH. Half-length profile figure holding cross r. R. Long-legged quadruped looking back, crest raised, tail intertwines legs. *M. 385, M.p.492* 250 750

808X: various reverses

	F £	VF £

808X (836) —, variety IX. Series O, Type 40. Monster r., looking back, tail and crest raised, foreleg raised behind head. R. Elaborate beaded standard in beaded circle, outer linear border with annulets or standard, votive or beaded. *M.p.490* 125   400

     809A   809C   809D

809A (836) —, variety IIA. Quadruped l., tail intertwines legs. R. Bird l. cross over wing. *M.p.494* 125   325
809B (836) —, variety IIB. Quadruped r. tail intertwines legs. R. Bird l. cross over wing. *M.p.494* 125   300
809C (836) —, variety IIC. Quadruped l. tail intertwines legs. R. Bird l. cross below each wing. *M.p.494* 125   300
809D (836) —, variety IID. Quadruped r. or l. tail raised and crossed. R. Bird r. or l. crosses before and above. *M.p.495* 125   300

810A, QIIIA varieties

810A (836) —, variety IIIA. Quadruped l. triquetra tail loops up. R. Bird r. triquetra above. *M.p.496* 135   350
810B (836) —, variety IIIB. Quadruped r. triquetra tail erect. R. Bird l. triquetra above. *M. 386, M.p.496* 140   375
810C (836) —, variety IIIC. Quadruped r. tail erect. R. Bird r. *M. 387, M.p.496*   140   375

811A

811A (836A) — variety IV A-D Lion r. or l. R. Bird r. or l. *M.p.499* 125   350
811E (836A) — variety IV E Lion both sides. *M.p.501* 135   400

812 mules of Series R and Q

812 (832B) Series R and Q, Type 73. Crude radiate bust r. or l. blundered runes. R. Quadruped or bird r. *M. 388, M.p.496-8 & 518* 90   250

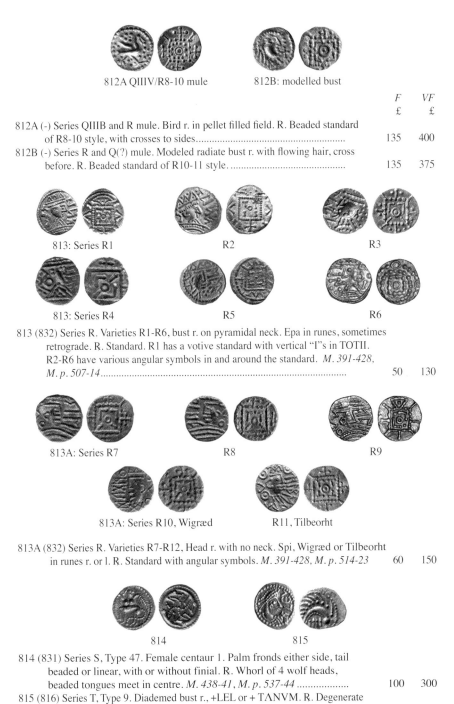

812A QIIIV/R8-10 mule   812B: modelled bust

	F	VF
	£	£

812A (-) Series QIIIB and R mule. Bird r. in pellet filled field. R. Beaded standard
of R8-10 style, with crosses to sides 135 400
812B (-) Series R and Q(?) mule. Modeled radiate bust r. with flowing hair, cross
before. R. Beaded standard of R10-11 style. 135 375

813: Series R1   R2   R3

813: Series R4   R5   R6

813 (832) Series R. Varieties R1-R6, bust r. on pyramidal neck. Epa in runes, sometimes
retrograde. R. Standard. R1 has a votive standard with vertical "I"s in TOTII.
R2-R6 have various angular symbols in and around the standard. *M. 391-428,*
M. p. 507-14 .... 50 130

813A: Series R7   R8   R9

813A: Series R10, Wigræd   R11, Tilbeorht

813A (832) Series R. Varieties R7-R12, Head r. with no neck. Spi, Wigræd or Tilbeorht
in runes r. or l. R. Standard with angular symbols. *M. 391-428, M. p. 514-23*   60 150

814   815

814 (831) Series S, Type 47. Female centaur l. Palm fronds either side, tail
beaded or linear, with or without finial. R. Whorl of 4 wolf heads,
beaded tongues meet in centre. *M. 438-41, M. p. 537-44* 100 300
815 (816) Series T, Type 9. Diademed bust r., +LEL or + TΛNVM. R. Degenerate
head l or r. *M. 442-4, M. p. 545-51* 120 350

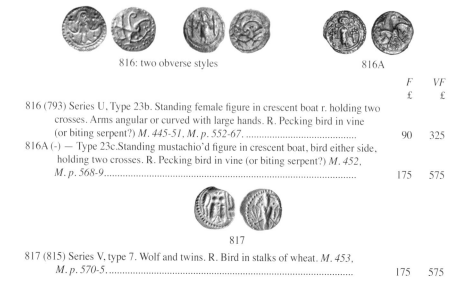

816: two obverse styles   816A

| | F | VF |
| | £ | £ |

816 (793) Series U, Type 23b. Standing female figure in crescent boat r. holding two
crosses. Arms angular or curved with large hands. R. Pecking bird in vine
(or biting serpent?) *M. 445-51, M. p. 552-67.*   90   325

816A (-) — Type 23c.Standing mustachio'd figure in crescent boat, bird either side,
holding two crosses. R. Pecking bird in vine (or biting serpent?) *M. 452,
M. p. 568-9*   175   575

817

817 (815) Series V, type 7. Wolf and twins. R. Bird in stalks of wheat. *M. 453,
M. p. 570-5.*   175   575

E.   Eclectic Sceattas, c.710-760

Included here are groups of types, related often by a common reverse motif (Triquetras,
Celtic cross, interlace, saltire, annulet cross groups and Type 70) that do not easily fit into the
main alphabetical classification, even though there may be some features in common with or
derived from the types therein. There are numerous 'mules' in this coinage, typically imitative
combinations of known obverse and reverse types not official paired. Only a few of these are
included.

820: C ARIP group, some varieties

820 (801) 'Carip' group. Bust r., CARIP, often blundered. R. include pecking bird,
wolf-serpent, or standing figure. *M. 336-40, M.p.416-21*   150   525

821: Triquetras group, some varieties

821 (804) 'Triquetras' group. Man and crosses, winged figure, facing bust, or pecking
bird. R. Interlaced cross with triquetra terminals, rosettes or pellets between.
M.p.422-5.   125   425

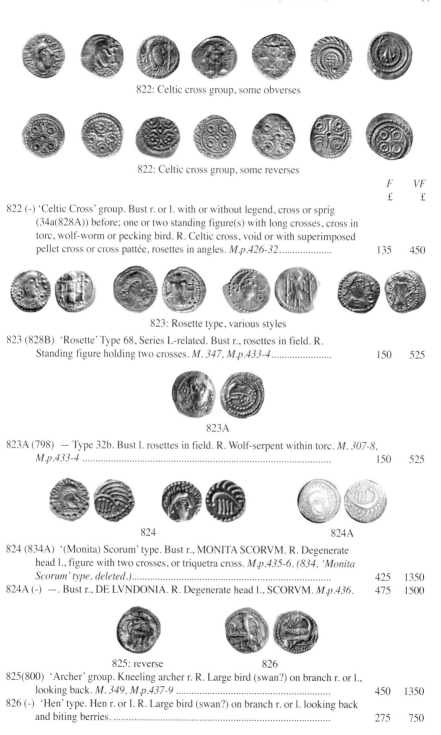

822: Celtic cross group, some obverses

822: Celtic cross group, some reverses

	F £	VF £

822 (-) 'Celtic Cross' group. Bust r. or l. with or without legend, cross or sprig (34a(828A)) before; one or two standing figure(s) with long crosses, cross in torc, wolf-worm or pecking bird. R. Celtic cross, void or with superimposed pellet cross or cross pattée, rosettes in angles. *M.p.426-32* .... 135　450

823: Rosette type, various styles

823 (828B) 'Rosette' Type 68, Series L-related. Bust r., rosettes in field. R. Standing figure holding two crosses. *M. 347, M.p.433-4* .... 150　525

823A

823A (798) — Type 32b. Bust l. rosettes in field. R. Wolf-serpent within torc. *M. 307-8, M.p.433-4* .... 150　525

824　　　　　　　824A

824 (834A) '(Monita) Scorum' type. Bust r., MONITA SCORVM. R. Degenerate head l., figure with two crosses, or triquetra cross. *M.p.435-6. (834, 'Monita Scorum' type, deleted.)* .... 425　1350

824A (-) —. Bust r., DE LVNDONIA. R. Degenerate head l., SCORVM. *M.p.436.* 475　1500

825: reverse　　　　826

825 (800) 'Archer' group. Kneeling archer r. R. Large bird (swan?) on branch r. or l., looking back. *M. 349, M.p.437-9* .... 450　1350

826 (-) 'Hen' type. Hen r. or l. R. Large bird (swan?) on branch r. or l. looking back and biting berries. .... 275　750

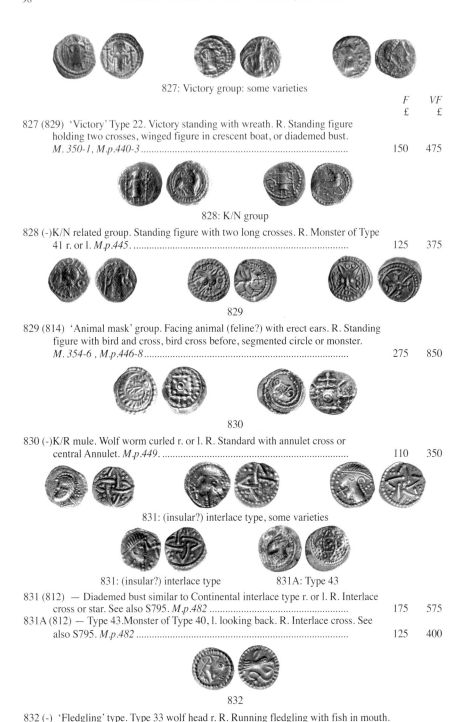

827: Victory group: some varieties

	F £	VF £

827 (829) 'Victory' Type 22. Victory standing with wreath. R. Standing figure
holding two crosses, winged figure in crescent boat, or diademed bust.
M. 350-1, M.p.440-3 150   475

828: K/N group

828 (-)K/N related group. Standing figure with two long crosses. R. Monster of Type
41 r. or l. *M.p.445.* 125   375

829

829 (814) 'Animal mask' group. Facing animal (feline?) with erect ears. R. Standing
figure with bird and cross, bird cross before, segmented circle or monster.
M. 354-6 , M.p.446-8 275   850

830

830 (-)K/R mule. Wolf worm curled r. or l. R. Standard with annulet cross or
central Annulet. *M.p.449.* 110   350

831: (insular?) interlace type, some varieties

831: (insular?) interlace type   831A: Type 43

831 (812) — Diademed bust similar to Continental interlace type r. or l. R. Interlace
cross or star. See also S795. *M.p.482* 175   575
831A (812) — Type 43.Monster of Type 40, l. looking back. R. Interlace cross. See
also S795. *M.p.482* 125   400

832

832 (-) 'Fledgling' type. Type 33 wolf head r. R. Running fledgling with fish in mouth.
Style degenerates to linear style. 275   750

833: Saltire group: some varieties

	F £	VF £
833 (833) 'Saltire Standard' types. Two standing figures or bust l. or r. R. Saltire and pellets in square. *M. 432-5, M.p.530-2*	90	225

833A: Saltire group, geometric reverses

833A (833) 'Saltire Standard' geometric types. Double croix ancrée or annulet cross. R. Saltire and pellets in square. *M. 432-5, M.p.530-2*	130	450

833A: Annulets group: some varieties

833B (833A) 'Annulet cross' types. Bust r. or l. with runic legend, 'Wodan' face, coiled serpent or saltire cross. R. Annulet cross, *M.p.534-6*	80	250

834: Type 70

834 (835) Type 70. Saltire-standard with geometric symbols both sides. Many varieties, typically base. R. Standard. *M. 436-7, M.p.532-4*	50	135

835: 'Wodan' head varieties

835 (844) Type 30. Facing 'Wodan' head various styles. R. Two standing figures, standard or Series N. type 41 monster r. *M. 429-31, M.p.527-30.*	150	500

836

836 (-) Monster in flight r. or l., looking back, tail erect. R. Swan-like bird r. or l., looking back, alternate with groups of pellets on limbs of central cross fourchée.	135	450

KINGS OF NORTHUMBRIA AND ARCHBISHOPS OF YORK

The issues associated with pre-Viking Northumbria encompass a late seventh-century emission of gold (see 762 & 762A), the following series of silver sceattas and the subsequent styca coinage. There are two special presentation issues, Eanred's broad penny and Wigmund's gold *solidus,* for neither of which is there yet evidence of monetary use within the kingdom.

The stycas developed in two phases, becoming a robust currency of small-denomination coins, which seem to have been of great practical use. Production must have ceased early in Osberht's reign, although the old money may have continued in circulation until the Viking capture of York in 867. The official styca coinage, however, does appear to have been overwhelmed by irregular issues, which may reflect a period of civil war during the years *c.* 843 to *c.* 855.

James Booth's classification of the silver sceat coinage of the eighth century is used here, with newly discovered types and variants added ('Sceattas in Northumbria', in Hill and Metcalf, *Sceattas in England and on the Continent, BAR* 128 (1984), pp.71-111, and 'Coinage and Northumbrian History: *c.*790-*c.*810, in D.M. Metcalf, *Coinage in Ninth Century Northumbria, BAR* 180 (1987), pp.57-90).

For the styca coinage of the ninth century Elizabeth Pirie provides an indispensable illustrated corpus of the known material in her *Coins of the Kingdom of Northumbria c.700-867,* 1996. Her classification is however over-complex for practical use, and several aspects of it, including her division of the coins of Aethelred II between his two reigns, have not been accepted by other scholars. The division here is that which is customarily adopted in volumes in the SCBI series. Moneyers' names are shown as they appear on the coinage.

846: Aldfrith   848: Aethelwald Moll

	F £	VF £
Æ **sceattas (a): Regal issues**		
846 **Aldfrith** (685-705). ALðFRIDVS in semi-uncial lettering around central boss.		
R. Lion(?) l. triple tail above	275	850
847 **Eadberht** (737-758). Small cross (mainly). R. Stylized stag, to l. or r.	90	275

847 Booth Class A   B   C

847A Class A: •EABERhTVΓ, around cross pattée. R. Animal r. with protruding tongue.	100	275
847B Class B: •ETBEREhTVΓ, around cross pattée. R. Animal l. without tongue.	100	275
847C Class C: •ETBEREhTVΓ, around tribrach. R. Animal l. with loop in tail enclosing a pellet	80	240

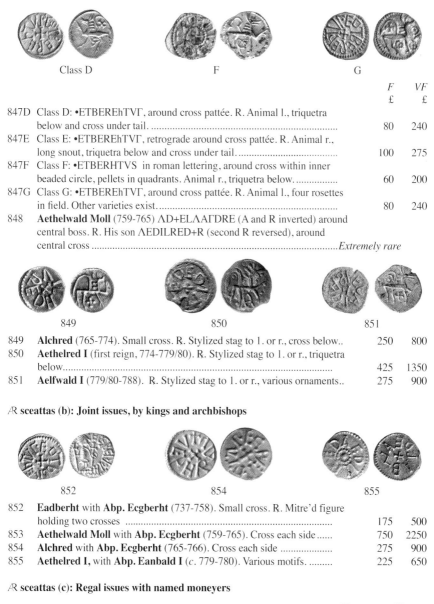

		Class D		F		G			

Class D   F   G

		F £	VF £
847D	Class D: •ETBEREhTVΓ, around cross pattée. R. Animal l., triquetra below and cross under tail.	80	240
847E	Class E: •ETBEREhTVΓ, retrograde around cross pattée. R. Animal r., long snout, triquetra below and cross under tail.	100	275
847F	Class F: •ETBERHTVS in roman lettering, around cross within inner beaded circle, pellets in quadrants. Animal r., triquetra below.	60	200
847G	Class G: •ETBEREhTVΓ, around cross pattée. R. Animal l., four rosettes in field. Other varieties exist.	80	240
848	**Aethelwald Moll** (759-765) ΛD+ELΛAΓDRE (A and R inverted) around central boss. R. His son ΛEDILRED+R (second R reversed), around central cross		*Extremely rare*

849   850   851

		F £	VF £
849	**Alchred** (765-774). Small cross. R. Stylized stag to l. or r., cross below..	250	800
850	**Aethelred I** (first reign, 774-779/80). R. Stylized stag to l. or r., triquetra below.	425	1350
851	**Aelfwald I** (779/80-788). R. Stylized stag to l. or r., various ornaments..	275	900

ΑR sceattas (b): Joint issues, by kings and archbishops

852   854   855

		F £	VF £
852	**Eadberht** with **Abp. Ecgberht** (737-758). Small cross. R. Mitre'd figure holding two crosses	175	500
853	**Aethelwald Moll** with **Abp. Ecgberht** (759-765). Cross each side	750	2250
854	**Alchred** with **Abp. Ecgberht** (765-766). Cross each side	275	900
855	**Aethelred I,** with **Abp. Eanbald I** (c. 779-780). Various motifs.	225	650

ΑR sceattas (c): Regal issues with named moneyers

856

		F £	VF £
856	**Aethelred I** (second reign, 789-796). R. CEOLBALD, CVDHEARD, HNIFVLA, TIDVVLF, central motifs vary	85	275

857   858

		F £	VF £
857	– Base metal. R. 'Shrine', "CVDCLS" (the moneyer Cuthgils)	325	1000
858	**Eardwulf** (first reign, 796-806). R. Small cross, CVDHEARD	750	2250

Special issues

863A

861A	**Eanred,** *c*. 830. Æ *penny*. Bust right. R. Cross, part moline part crosslet	2500	10500
863A	**Abp. Wigmund** (837-849/50). N *solidus*. Facing bust. R. Cross in wreath	27500	110000

Stycas (a): Issues in base silver, for kings and archbishop separately, *c*. 810- *c*. 830, with moneyers named

859

859	**Aelfwald II** (806-808). R. Small cross, CVDhEARD	250	750

860

860	**Eanred** (810-841 (total reign)). R. CVDhEARD, CYNVVLF, DAEGBERCT, EADVINI,EDILECH, HERREÐ, [HEARDVVLF, correctly VVLFHEARD], HVAETRED, TIDVINI, VILHEAH, VVLFHEARD, various central motifs	35	110

861

861	**Abp. Eanbald II** (796-835 (total tenure)). R. EODWVLF or EDILWEARD	50	165

Stycas (b): Issues in copper alloy, *c*. 830- *c*. 843/4, with moneyers named

862

		F £	VF £

862 **Eanred.** R. ALDATES, BADIGILS, BROD(E)R, FORDRED, FVLCNOD, MONNE, ODILO, W(D)IHTRED, VVLFRED, various central motifs — 25 70

865

865 **Aethelred II** (first reign, 841-843/4), R. ALGHERE, BRODER, COENRED, CVNEMVND, EANRED, FORDRED, HVNLAF, LEOFDEGN, MONNE, ODILO, VENDELBERHT, W(D)IHTRED, VVLFRED, VVLFSIG , various central motifs 20 60

866: Leofdegn's 'Special' motifs

866 – Leofdegn's 'Special' motifs, R. Hound 1., various elaborate cruciform central devices, LEOFDEGN 150 525

867 868 869

867 **Redwulf** (843/4). R. ALGHERE, BROTHER, COENRED, CVDBEREhT, EANRED, FORDRED, HVAETNOD, MONNE 30 100
868 **Aethelred II** (second reign 843/4-849/50), R. EANVVLF, EARDVVLF, FORDRED, MONNE, ODILO, VVLFRED 20 60
869 **Osberht** (849/50-867). R. EANVVLF, EDELHELM, MONNE, VINIBERHT, VVLFSIXT, VVLFRED 30 90

870 871

870 **Abp. Wigmund** (837-849/50). R. COENRED, EDELHELM, EDILVEARD, HVNLAF 20 60
871 **Abp. Wulfhere** (849/50-900). R. VVLFRED 45 150

Stycas (C): Irregular issues in copper alloy, (*c*.843/4-*c*.855), with moneyers' names

872 **Irregular Issues** (*c*.843/4-*c*.855). Various types; legends blundered..... 20 50

Further reading: *Pirie E.J.E. Coins of the Kingdom of Northumbria c.700-867. 1996*

In the kingdom of the Franks a reformed coinage of good quality *deniers* struck on broad flans had been introduced by Pepin in 755 and continued by his son Charlemagne and his descendants. A new coinage of *pennies* of similar size and weighing about 20 grains (1.3 gms) was introduced into England, probably by Offa, the powerful king of Mercia, about 755/780, though early pennies also exist of two little known kings of Kent, Heaberht and Ecgberht, of about the same period.

The silver penny (*Lat*. 'denarius', hence the *d*. of our £ *s*. *d*.) remained virtually the sole denomination of English coinage for almost five centuries, with the rare exception of occasional gold coins and somewhat less rare silver halfpence. The penny reached a weight of 24 grains, i.e., a 'pennyweight' during the reign of Alfred the Great. Silver pennies of this period normally bear the ruler's name, though not always his portrait, and the name of the moneyer responsible for their manufacture.

Pennies were issued by various rulers of the Heptarchy for the kingdoms of Kent, Mercia, East Anglia and Wessex by the Danish settlers in the Danelaw and the Hiberno-Norse kings of York, and also by the Archbishops of Canterbury and a Bishop of London. Under Eadgar, who became the sole ruler of England, a uniform coinage was instituted throughout the country, and it was he who set the pattern for the 'reformed' coinage of the later Anglo-Saxon and Norman period.

Halfpence were issued by most rulers from Alfred to Eadgar between 871-973 for S. England, and although all are rare today, it is probable that reasonable quantities were made.

Nos. 873-1387 are all silver pennies except where stated.

NB. Many pennies of the early part of this period have chipped flans and prices should be reduced accordingly.

KINGS OF KENT

		F £	VF £
873	**Heaberht** (*c*. 765). Monogram for REX. R. Five annulets, each containing a pellet, joined to form a cross	4500	17500
874	**Ecgberht** (*c*. 780). Similar. R. Varied..	1350	5250

875   877

875	**Eadberht Praen.** Type 1. (796-798). As illustration. R. Varied	1250	5000
875A	— Type 2. (*c*. 798). His name around, ꝥ in centre, R. Moneyer's name in angles of a tribrach	1100	4750
876	**Cuthred** (798-807). *Canterbury*. Various types without portrait	825	3000
877	— — Portrait. R. Cross and wedges or A..	850	3250

878   881

878	**Anonymous** (*c*. 822-823). *Canterbury*. As illustration or 'Baldred' style head	875	3500
879	**Baldred** (*c*. 823-825). *Canterbury*. diademed head r. R. DRUR CITS within inner circle	1250	5250
880	— Cross each side	850	3250
881	*Rochester*. Bust r. R. Cross moline or wheel design	950	4500

ARCHBISHOPS OF CANTERBURY

		F £	VF £

881A **Jaenberht** (765-792). New type (early). Under Ecgberht II of Kent (?). (before *c*. 780 ?) His name around small cross of pellets in centre. R. PONTIFEX in three lines 1350 6000

882 Under Offa of Mercia (*c*. 780-792) His name around central ornament or cross and wedges. R. OFFA REX in two lines 950 4500

883   885

883 — His name in three lines. R. OFFA or OFFA REX between the limbs of Celtic cross 950 4500

884 **Aethelheard** (el. 792, cons. 793, d. 805). With Offa as overlord. First issue (792-?), with title *Pontifex* 900 3500

886A   887

885 — Second issue (?-796), with title *Archiepiscopus* 850 3250

885A — Third issue (*c*. 796-798), with title *Archiepiscopus*. His name and AR around EP in centre. R. Moneyer's name, EADGAR or CIOLHARD..... 950 3750

886 — With Coenwulf as overlord. (798-800 ?) Fourth Issue. As last. R. King's name in the angles of a tribrach 950 3750

886A — Fifth issue (*c*. 798-805?). As last R. Coenwulf's name around Ⓜ in centre 800 3000

887 **Wulfred** (805-832). group I (805-*c*. 810). As illustration. R. Crosslet, alpha-omega.. 750 3250

888 — Group II (*c*. 810). As last. R. DOROVERNIA C monogram 725 3000

889 — Group III (pre- 823). Bust extends to edge of coin. R. As last 675 2750

890 — Groups IV and V (*c*. 822-823). Anonymous under Ecgberht. Moneyer's name in place of the Archbishop's. R. DOROBERNIA CIVITAS in three or five lines 725 3000

891 — Group VI (*c*. 823-825). Baldred type. Crude portrait. R. DRVR CITS in two lines... 950 4500

892 — Group VII (*c*. 832). Second monogram (Ecgberht) type. Crude portrait r., PLFRED. R. DORIB C. Monogram as 1035 .... 850 3500

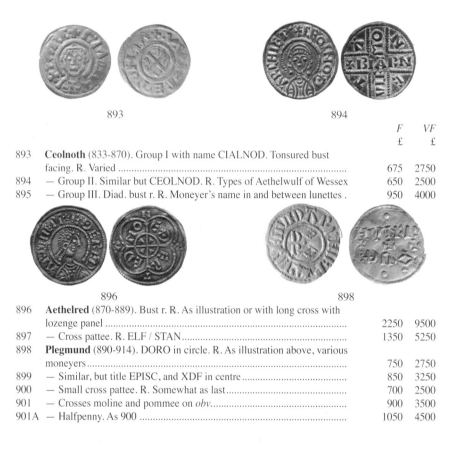

893   894

		F £	*VF* £

893   **Ceolnoth** (833-870). Group I with name CIALNOD. Tonsured bust
facing. R. Varied 675 2750
894   — Group II. Similar but CEOLNOD. R. Types of Aethelwulf of Wessex 650 2500
895   — Group III. Diad. bust r. R. Moneyer's name in and between lunettes . 950 4000

896   898

896   **Aethelred** (870-889). Bust r. R. As illustration or with long cross with
lozenge panel 2250 9500
897   — Cross pattee. R. ELF / STAN.. 1350 5250
898   **Plegmund** (890-914). DORO in circle. R. As illustration above, various
moneyers... 750 2750
899   — Similar, but title EPISC, and XDF in centre 850 3250
900   — Small cross pattee. R. Somewhat as last... 700 2500
901   — Crosses moline and pommee on *obv*.. 900 3500
901A — Halfpenny. As 900 .... 1050 4500

KINGS OF MERCIA

Until 825 Canterbury was the principal mint of the Kings of Mercia and some moneyers also struck
coins for the Kings of Kent and Archbishops of Canterbury.

GOLD

902   903

902   **Offa** (757-796). Gold *dinar*. Copy of Arabic dinar of Caliph Al Mansur,
dated 157 A.H. (A.D. 774), with OFFA REX added on *rev*...................... 135000 575000
903   Gold *penny*. Bust r., moneyer's name. R. Standing figure, moneyer's name 42500 175000

*A copy of a solidus with a diademed bust appears to read CIOLHEARD and is probably Mercian of
this or the following reign.*
For further information see: *The Coinage of Offa and his Contemporaries* by Derek Chick, 2010.

SILVER

904

905

		F £	VF £
904	Light Coinage. (*c*. 780?-792) *London and Canterbury*. Various types without portraits. Small flans..	675	2250
905	— (*c*. 780?-792) *London and Canterbury*. Various types with portraits. Small flans..	1100	4500

906

908

906	— East Anglia. Various types with portraits. R. Some with runic letters, small flans...	1250	5250
907	— — Various types without portraits. R. often with runic letters, small flans	750	2750
908	Heavy Coinage. (*c*. 792-796) *London, Canterbury and East Anglia*. Various types without portraits, large flans.	725	2500

909

912

909	**Cynethryth** (wife of Offa). Coins as light coinage of Offa. As illustration	3000	10500
910	— *O*. As *rev*. of last. R. EOBA on leaves of quatrefoil............................	1500	5250
911	**Eadberht** (Bishop of London, died 787/789). EADBERHT EP in three lines or ADBERHT in two lines within a beaded rectangle, EP below. R. Name of Offa..	1250	5000
912	**Coenwulf, King of Mercia** (796-821). Gold *penny* or *Mancus* of 30 pence. London, diademed bust of Coenwulf right, finely drawn with four horizontal lines on the shoulders	52500	210000
912A	Penny. Group I (796-805). *London*. Without portrait. His name in three lines. R. Varied	725	2750
913	— *Canterbury*. Name around as illus. below. R. Moneyer's name in two lines..	750	2850

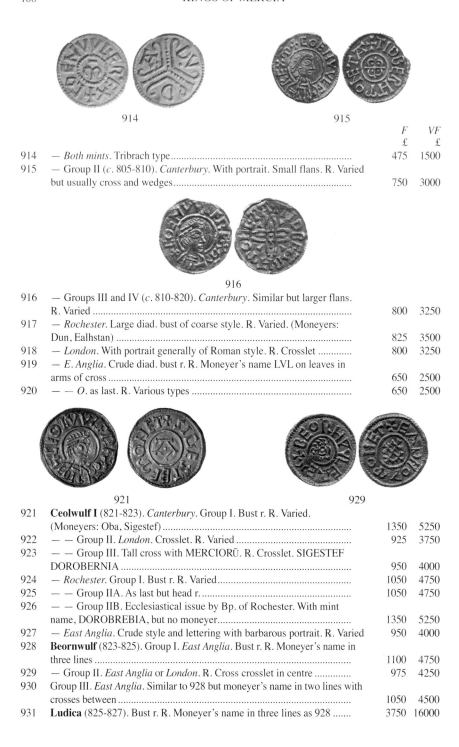

914   915

		F £	VF £

914 — *Both mints*. Tribrach type 475 1500

915 — Group II (*c.* 805-810). *Canterbury*. With portrait. Small flans. R. Varied
but usually cross and wedges 750 3000

916

916 — Groups III and IV (*c.* 810-820). *Canterbury*. Similar but larger flans.
R. Varied 800 3250

917 — *Rochester*. Large diad. bust of coarse style. R. Varied. (Moneyers:
Dun, Ealhstan) 825 3500

918 — *London*. With portrait generally of Roman style. R. Crosslet 800 3250

919 — *E. Anglia*. Crude diad. bust r. R. Moneyer's name LVL on leaves in
arms of cross 650 2500

920 — — *O.* as last. R. Various types 650 2500

921   929

921 **Ceolwulf I** (821-823). *Canterbury*. Group I. Bust r. R. Varied.
(Moneyers: Oba, Sigestef) 1350 5250

922 — — Group II. *London*. Crosslet. R. Varied 925 3750

923 — — Group III. Tall cross with MERCIORŪ. R. Crosslet. SIGESTEF
DOROBERNIA 950 4000

924 — *Rochester*. Group I. Bust r. R. Varied.. 1050 4750

925 — — Group IIA. As last but head r. 1050 4750

926 — — Group IIB. Ecclesiastical issue by Bp. of Rochester. With mint
name, DOROBREBIA, but no moneyer.. 1350 5250

927 — *East Anglia*. Crude style and lettering with barbarous portrait. R. Varied 950 4000

928 **Beornwulf** (823-825). Group I. *East Anglia*. Bust r. R. Moneyer's name in
three lines 1100 4750

929 — Group II. *East Anglia* or *London*. R. Cross crosslet in centre 975 4250

930 Group III. *East Anglia*. Similar to 928 but moneyer's name in two lines with
crosses between 1050 4500

931 **Ludica** (825-827). Bust r. R. Moneyer's name in three lines as 928 .... 3750 16000

932   933

		F	*VF*
		£	£
932	— Similar. R. Moneyer's name around cross crosslet in centre, as 929 ..	4000	17500
933	**Wiglaf,** first reign (827-829). *London*. Crude head r. R. Crosslet............	3250	13500

934   935

934	Second reign (830-840). *London*. Cross and pellets, or ⚔ R. Moneyer's name in three lines or between lunettes of pellets	2500	8500
935	**Berhtwulf** (840-852). Various types with bust..	950	4250
936	— without bust	975	4500
937	As before. R. IAETHELWLF REX. cross pommee over cross pattée (crude die copying on obverse of Aethelwulf of Wessex)	950	4250

938   939

938	**Burgred** (852-874). *B.M.C. type A*. Bust r. R. Moneyer's name in and between lunettes...	250	575
939	— — B. Similar but lunettes broken in centre of curve	475	1500

940   941

944

940	— — C. Similar but lunettes broken in angles...	265	625
941	— — D. Similar but legend divided by two lines with a crook at each end	260	600
942	— — E. As last, but m above and below...	675	2750
943	**Ceolwulf II** (874-*c*. 880). Bust r. R. Two emperors seated. Victory above	6750	27500
944	— R. Moneyer's name in angles of long cross with lozenge centre	1750	6500

KINGS OF EAST ANGLIA

945

		F £	VF £
945	**Beonna,** King of East Anglia, *c*. 758. Æ sceat. Pellet in centre, Runic inscription. R. EFE in Roman characters around saltire cross	850	3250
945A	— Similar. R. WILRED in runic around pellet or cross	950	3750
945B	— Similar. R. Interlace pattern (large flans)	1750	7500
945C	**Alberht** (749-?). Pellet in centre, AETHELBERT (runic) around R. Rosette in circle, TIAELRED (runic) around.	2750	10500
946	**Aethelberht** (d. 794). bust r. R. wolf and twins	7500	32500
947	**Eadwald** (*c*. 798). King's name in three lines. R. Moneyer's name in quatrefoil or around cross	1050	4500
947A	— King's name around cross or Ⓜ in centre. R. Moneyer's name in quartrefoil	1100	4750

948   951

948	**Aethelstan I** (*c*. 825-840). Bust r. or l. R. Crosslet or star	950	4000
949	Bust r. R. Moneyer's name in three or four lines	950	4000
950	Alpha or A. R. Varied	450	1650
951	*O*. and *rev*. Cross with or without wedges or pellets in angles	450	1650
952	— Similar, with king's name both sides	575	2000
952A	Name around ship in centre. R. Moneyer Eadgar, around cross of pellets or in two lines (Possibly the earliest of his coins.)	2750	12500

953   954

953	**Aethelweard** (*c*. 840-*c*. 855), A, Omega or cross and crescents. R. Cross with pellets or wedges	675	2750
954	**Edmund** (855-870). Alpha or A. R. Cross with pellets or wedges	350	1050
955	— *O*. Varied. R. Similar	350	1050

For the St. Edmund coins and the Danish issues struck in East Anglia bearing the name of Aethelred I, see Danish East Anglia.

	F £	VF £

Danish East Anglia, *c.* 885-915

956 **Aethelstan II** (878-890), originally named Guthrum? Cross pattee. R.
Moneyer's name in two lines.. 1350 5500
957 **Oswald** (unknown except from his coins). Alpha or A. R. Cross pattee.. 1750 7500
958 — Copy of Carolinigian 'temple' type. R Cross and pellets 2000 8000
959 **Aethelred I.** (*c.*870) As last, with name of Aethelred I. R. As last, or
cross-crosslet.. 1500 6500
959A — As 954 .... 1250 5250

960   962

960 **St. Edmund,** memorial coinage, Æ *penny,* type as illus. above, various
legends of good style 175 350
961 — Similar, but barbarous or semi-barbarous legends............................. 165 350
962 *Halfpenny.* Similar 525 1650
963 **St. Martin of Lincoln.** Sword dividing legend. R. Cross in voided cross.
LINCOI A CIVIT. 3250 12500
964 **Alfred.** (Viking imitations, usually of very barbarous workmanship.) of
lighter weight of approx. 1.3 grms. Bust r. R. *Londonia* monogram........ 1750 6250

965

965 — Similar, with moneyer's name (Aelfstan, Heawulf, Herewulf, Vinidat)
added... 2250 8000
966 — Small cross, as Alfred group II *(Br. 6),* various legends, some read
REX DORO 475 1400
967 — Similar. R. 'St. Edmund type' A in centre.. 750 3000
968 — Two emperors seated. R. As 964. (Previously attributed to Halfdene.) 3750 16500
969 *Halfpenny.* As 964 and 965.. 725 2750

970

970 — As 966 .... 475 1350

DANELAW, *c.* 898-915

971   974

975

		F £	VF £
971	**Alfred** (Imitations). ELFRED between ORSNA and FORDA. R. Moneyer's name in two lines (occasionally divided by horizontal long cross)	800	2750
972	— *Halfpenny.* Similar, of very crude appearance	725	2500
973	**Alfred/Plegmund.** *Obv.* ELFRED REX PLEGN	1350	5000
974	**Plegmund.** Danish copy of 900	650	2000
975	**Earl Sihtric.** Type as 971. SCELDFOR between GVNDI BERTVS. R SITRIC COMES in two lines	3500	13500

Viking Coinage of York?
References are to 'The Classification of Northumbrian Viking Coins in the Cuerdale hoard', by
C. S. S. Lyon and B. H. I. H. Stewart, in Numismatic Chronicle, 1964, p. 281 ff.

975A	**Guthfrith.** GU DE F. RE Small cross. R. Moneyer's name in two lines.	2500	9500
976	**Siefred.** C. SIEFRE DIIS REX in two lines. R. EBRAICE CIVITAS (or contractions), small cross. *L. & S. Ia, Ie, Ii*	425	1350
977	— Cross on steps between. R. As last. *L. & S. If, Ij*	550	1850
978	— Long cross. R. As last. *L. & S. Ik*	425	1350
979	SIEFREDVS REX, cross crosslet within legend. R. As last. *L. & S. Ih...*	375	1050

980   984

980	SIEVERT REX, cross crosslet to edge of coin. R. As last. *L. & S. Ic, Ig, Im*	400	1250
981	— Cross on steps between. R. As last. *L. & S. Il*	550	1850
982	— Patriarchal cross. R. DNS DS REX, small cross. *L. & S. Va*	425	1350
983	— — R. MIRABILIA FECIT, small cross. *L. & S. VIb*	525	1650
984	REX, at ends of cross crosslet. R. SIEFREDVS, small cross. *L. & S. IIIa, b*	400	1250
985	— Long cross. R. As last. *L. & S. IIIc*	375	1100
986	*Halfpenny.* Types as 977, *L. & S. Ib; 980, Ic; and 983, VIb*	750	2250

		F £	VF £
987	**Cnut.** CNVT REX, cross crosslet to edge of coin. R. EBRAICE CIVITAS, small cross. *L. & S. Io, Iq*	350	1050
988	— — R. CVNNETTI, small cross. *L. & S. IIc*	325	950
989	— Long cross. R. EBRAICE CIVITAS, small cross. *L. & S. Id, In, Ir*	225	625
990	— — R. CVNNETTI, small cross. *L. & S. IIa, IId*	185	425
991	— Patriarchal cross. R. EBRAICE CIVITAS, small cross. *L. & S. Ip, Is*	185	400
992	— — R.— *Karolus* monogram in centre. *L. & S . It*	750	2750

993   995

993	— — R. CVNNETTI, small cross. *L. & S. IIb, IIe*	175	375
994	*Halfpenny.* Types as 987, *L. & S. Iq; 989, Id; 991, Is; 992, Iu; 993, IIb and e*	650	1750
995	As 992, but CVNNETTI around *Karolus* monogram. *L. & S. IIf*	625	1650
996	**Cnut and/or Siefred.** CNVT REX, patriarchal cross. R. SIEFREDVS, small cross. *L. & S. IIId*	475	1350
997	— — R. DNS DS REX, small cross. *L. & S. Vc.*	525	1650

998

998	— — R. MIRABILIA FECIT. *L. & S. VId*	325	850
999	EBRAICE C, patriarchal cross. R. DNS DS REX, small cross. *L. & S. Vb*	425	1250

1000   1002

1000	— — R. MIRABILIA FECIT. *L. & S. VIc*	325	850
1001	DNS DS REX in two lines. R. ALVALDVS, small cross. *L. & S. IVa*	1350	4750
1002	DNS DS O REX, similar. R. MIRABILIA FECIT. *L. & S. VIa*	525	1650
1003	*Halfpenny.* As last. *L. & S. VIa*	700	2000
1004	**'Cnut'.** Name blundered around cross pattée with extended limbs. R. QVENTOVICI around small cross. *L. & S. VII*	675	1850
1005	*Halfpenny.* Similar. *L. & S. VII*	700	2000

York, early tenth century issues

1006   1009

	F £	*VF* £
1006 **St. Peter coinage.** Swordless type. Early issues. SCI PETRI MO in two lines. ℞. Cross pattee	300	850
1007 — similar. ℞. 'Karolus' monogram	875	3500
1008 *Halfpenny.* Similar. ℞. Cross pattee	700	2000
1009 **Regnald** (blundered types). RAIENALT, head to l. or r. ℞. EARICE CT, 'Karolus' monogram	3000	12500

1010

1010 — Open hand. ℞. Similar	1850	7250
1011 — Hammer. ℞. Bow and arrow	2500	9000
1012 Anonymous ℞. Sword	1650	6000

ENGLISH COINS OF THE HIBERNO-NORSE VIKINGS

Early period, *c*. 919-925

1013 **Sihtric** (921-927). SITRIC REX, sword. ℞. Cross, hammer or T	2650	9500
1014 **St. Peter coinage.** Sword type. Late issues SCI PETRI MO, sword and hammer. ℞. EBORACEI, cross and pellets	1050	3750

1015   1016

1015 — Similar. ℞. Voided hammer	950	3500
1016 — Similar. ℞. Solid hammer	1050	3750

St. Peter coins with blundered legends are rather cheaper.

		F £	VF £

Later period, 939-954 (after the battle of Brunanburh). Mostly struck at York.

1017 **Anlaf Guthfrithsson,** 939-941. Flower type. Small cross, ANLAF REX
TO D. Ɍ. Flower above moneyer's name 2500 10500

1018 — Circumscription type, with small cross each side, ANLAF CVNVNC,
M in field on reverse *(Derby)* 2250 9500

1018A— Two line type. ONLAF REX. Large letter both sides *(Lincoln?)* 2250 9500

1019

1019	— Raven type. As illustration, ANLAF CVNVNC..................................	1850	6500

1020 **Olaf Sihtricsson,** first reign, 941-944. Triquetra type, CVNVNC.
Ɍ. Danish standard.. 2000 8000

1021 — Circumscription type (a). Small cross each side, CVNVNC 1850 7250

1022 — Cross moline type, CVNVN C. Ɍ. Small cross 2000 8000

1023 — Two line type. Small cross. Ɍ. ONLAF REX. Ɍ. Name in two lines .. 1850 7250

1024 **Regnald Guthfrithsson,** 943-944. Triquetra type. As 1020. REGNALD
CVNVNC 2750 10500

1025 — Cross moline type. As 1022, but REGNALD CVNVNC 2750 10500

1026 **Sihtric Sihtricsson,** *c*. 942. Triquetra type. As 1020, SITRIC CVNVNC 2250 9500

1027 — Circumscription type. Small cross each side 2000 9000

1027A**Anonymous?** Two line type. Small cross ELTANGERHT. Ɍ.
RERNART in two lines 1350 3750

1028 **Eric Blood-axe,** first reign, 948. Two line type. Small cross, ERICVC REX
A; ERIC REX AL; or ERIC REX EFOR. Ɍ. Name in two lines 4250 13500

1029 **Olaf Sihtricsson,** second reign, 948-952. Circumscription type (b). Small
cross each side. ONLAF REX 1850 7250

1029A— Flower type. small cross ANLAF REX R. Flower above moneyer's
name.. 2250 9500

1029B— Two line type. Small cross, ONLAF REX. Ɍ. Moneyer's name in
two lines.. 1850 7500

1030 **Eric Blood-axe,** second reign, 952-954. Sword type. ERIC REX in two
lines, sword between. Ɍ. Small cross 4500 15000

Later, KINGS OF ALL ENGLAND FROM 959

All are silver pennies unless otherwise stated

BEORHTRIC, 786-802

Beorhtric was dependent on Offa of Mercia and married a daughter of Offa.

1031

		F £	VF £
1031	As illustration...	5250	20000
1032	Alpha and omega in centre. R. Omega in centre	4750	17500

ECGBERHT, 802-839

King of Wessex only, 802-825; then also of Kent, Sussex, Surrey, Essex and East Anglia, 825-839, and of Mercia also, 829-830.

1033	*Canterbury*. Group I. Diad. hd. r. within inner circle. R. Various.............	1350	5250
1034	— II. Non-portrait types. R. Various	925	3750

1035

1035	— III. Bust r. breaking inner circle. R. DORIB C	1200	4750
1036	*London*. Cross potent. R. LVN / DONIA / CIVIT	1500	6500
1037	— — R. REDMVND MONE around TA...	1100	4500
1038	*Rochester,* royal mint. Non-portrait types with king's name ECGBEO RHT	925	3750
1039	— — Portrait types, ECGBEORHT	1100	4750
1040	*Rochester,* bishop's mint. Bust r. R. SCS ANDREAS (APOSTOLVS)....	1350	5250
1041	*Winchester*. SAXON monogram or SAXONIORVM in three lines. R. Cross	925	3750

Son of Ecgberht; sub-King of Essex, Kent, Surrey and Sussex, 825-839; King of all southern England, 839-855; King of Essex, Kent and Sussex only, 855-858. No coins are known of his son Aethelbald who ruled over Wessex proper, 855-860.

1043   1045

		F £	VF £
1042	*Canterbury.* Phase I (839-c. 843). Head within inner circle. R. Various. *Br. 3*	725	2750
1043	— — Larger bust breaking inner circle. R. A. *Br. 1 and 2*	750	3000
1044	— — Cross and wedges. R. SAXONIORVM in three lines in centre. *Br. 10*	525	1650
1045	— — Similar, but OCCIDENTALIVM in place of moneyer. *Br. 11*	575	1750
1046	— Phase II (*c.* 843-848?). Cross and wedges. R. Various, but chiefly a form of cross or a large A. *Br. 4*	550	1650
1047	— — New portrait, somewhat as 1043. R. As last. *Br. 7*	725	2750
1048	— — Smaller portrait. R. As last, with *Chi/Rho* monogram. *Br. 7*	750	3000

1049   1051

1049	— Phase III (*c.* 848/851-*c.* 855). DORIB in centre. R. CANT mon. *Br. 5*	525	1650
1050	— — CANT mon. R. CAN M in angles of cross. *Br. 6*	675	2500
1051	— Phase IV (*c.* 855-859). Mostly Canterbury rarely Rochester. New neat style bust R. Large voided long cross. *Br. 8*	675	2400
1052	*Winchester.* SAXON mon. R. Cross and wedges. *Br. 9*	700	2750

Son of Aethelwulf; sub-King of Kent, Essex and Sussex, 858-860; King of all southern England,
860-865/6.

1053

	F	VF
	£	£
1053 Bust r., R large voided long cross. Mostly Canterbury, also known for Rochester	700	2500
1053A *O*. As 1053, R large cross pattée............................	1650	5000
1054 *O*. Similar, R. Cross fleury over floriate cross...........................	925	3750
1054A *O*. Similar, R. Moneyers name around beaded inner circle containing cross pattée	1750	5250

AETHELRED I, 865/866-871

Son of Aethelwulf; succeeded his brother Aethelberht.

1055

1055 As illustration, Wessex Lunettes, Canterbury, usually with bonnet.........	725	2500
1055A — —, London obv. dies in style as Burgred............................	750	2750
1056 Similar, but moneyer's name in four lines, Canterbury or Winchester	950	4000

For another coin with the name Aethelred see 959 under Viking coinages.
For further reading see: *Lyons & MacKay*, BNJ 2007

Brother and successor to Aethelred, Alfred had to contend with invading Danish armies for much of his reign. In 878 he and Guthrum the Dane divided the country, with Alfred holding all England south and west of Watling Street. Alfred occupied London in 886.

Types with portraits

	1057	1058

		F £	VF £
1057	As illustration, Wessex Lunettes, Canterbury, bust with bonnet. r. R. As Aethelred I. *Br. 1 (name often* AELBRED)	900	3250
1057A	— —, London obv. dies in style as Burgred	950	3500
1058	— R. Long cross with lozenge centre, as 944, *Br. 5*	2250	8500
1059	— R. Two seated figures, as 943. *Br. 2*	8500	32500
1060	— R. As Archbp. Aethered; cross within large quatrefoil. *Br. 3*	2750	10500

1061

1061	*London.* Bust. r. R. LONDONIA monogram	1850	7000
	Copies made of tin at the Wembley Exhibition are common		
1062	— R. Similar, but with moneyer's name (Tilewine) added	2000	7500
1063	— *Halfpenny.* Bust r. or rarely l. R. LONDONIA monogram as 1061	1050	3000
1064	*Gloucester.* R. Æ GLEAPA in angles of three limbed cross	4500	17500

Types without portraits

1065	King's name on limbs of cross, trefoils in angles. R. Moneyer's name in quatrefoil. *Br. 4.*	3500	12500

	1066	1069

1066	Cross pattée. R. Moneyer's name in two lines. *Br. 6*	475	1400
1067	— As last, but neater style, as Edw, the Elder	500	1500
1068	— *Halfpenny.* As 1066	475	1350
1069	*Canterbury.* As last but DORO added on *obv. Br. 6a*	525	1650
1070	*Exeter?* King name in four lines. R. EXA vertical	3500	13500
1071	*Winchester?* Similar to last, but PIN	3500	13500
1071A	*Oxford.* Elfred between OHSNA and FORDA. R. Moneyer's name in two lines (much commoner as a Viking Imitation - see 971)	875	3500
1072	'Offering penny'. Very large and heavy. AELFRED REX SAXORVM in four lines. R. ELIMO in two lines i.e. (*Elimosina,* alms)	12500	40000

For other pieces bearing the name of Alfred see under the Viking coinages.
For further reading see: Lyons & MacKay, The Lunettes Coinage of Alfred the Great BNJ 2008

Edward, the son of Alfred, aided by his sister Aethelflaed 'Lady of the Mericians', annexed all England south of the Humber and built many new fortified boroughs to protect the kingdom.

Rare types

1074   1078

		F	VF
		£	£
1073	*Br. 1. Bath?* R. BA	1850	8500
1074	— *2. Canterbury.* Cross moline in pommee. R. Moneyer's name	1350	5250
1075	— *3. Chester?* Small cross. R. Minster	2500	10500
1076	— *4.* — Small cross. R. Moneyer's name in single line	1050	4000
1077	— *5.* — R. Two stars	1650	7000
1078	— *6.* — R. Flower above central line, name below	1850	8500

1079   1081

1079	— *7.* — R. Floral design with name across field	1850	8500
1080	— *8.* — R. Bird holding twig	3250	13500
1081	— *9.* — R. Hand of Providence, several varieties	2500	10500
1082	— *10.* — R. City gate of Roman style	1750	8000

1083

1083	— *11.* — R. Anglo-Saxon burg	1650	6500

Ordinary types

1084   1087

1084	*Br. 12.* Bust l. R. Moneyer's name in two lines	850	3500
1086	— *12a.* Similar, but bust r. of crude style	1250	5250
1087	— *13.* Small cross. R. Similar (to 1084)	275	700
1087A	— — As last, but in *gold*	27500	95000
1088	**Halfpenny.** Similar to last	850	2750
1088A	— — R. Hand of Providence	1250	4500

Aethelstan, the eldest son of Edward, decreed that money should be coined only in a borough, that every borough should have one moneyer and that some of the more important boroughs should have more than one moneyer.

1089

		F	*VF*
		£	£
1089	**Main issues.** Small cross. R. Moneyer's name in two lines.....................	300	900
1090	Diad. bust r. R. As last	1100	4500
1091	— R. Small cross	1050	4250
1092	Small cross both sides..	375	1100

1093	1095

1093	— Similar, but mint name added	425	1200
1094	Crowned bust r. As illustration. R. Small cross	900	3500
1095	— Similar, but mint name added	925	3500
1096	**Local Issues.** *N. Mercian mints.* Star between two pellets. R. As 1089...	975	4000
1097	— Small cross. R. Floral ornaments above and below moneyer's name .	1050	4500
1098	— Rosette of pellets each side..	400	1200
1099	— Small cross one side, rosette on the other side	425	1350

1100	1104

1100	*N.E. mints.* Small cross. R. Tower over moneyer's name......................	1500	5500
1101	Similar, but mint name added	1650	6000
1102	— Bust in high relief r. or l. R. Small cross..	1400	5500
1103	— Bust r. in high relief. R. Cross-crosslet	1350	5250
1104	'Helmeted' bust or head r. R. As last or small cross	1250	5000
1104A	**Halfpenny**, small cross. R. Moneyer's name in two lines	850	2500

Eadmund, the brother of Aethelstan, extended his realm over the Norse kingdom of York.

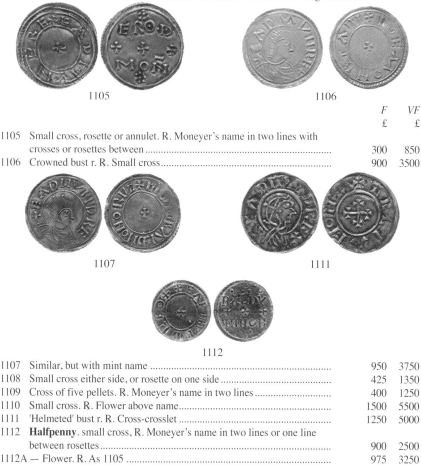

1105   1106

		F £	VF £
1105	Small cross, rosette or annulet. R. Moneyer's name in two lines with crosses or rosettes between	300	850
1106	Crowned bust r. R. Small cross	900	3500

1107   1111

1112

		F	VF
1107	Similar, but with mint name	950	3750
1108	Small cross either side, or rosette on one side	425	1350
1109	Cross of five pellets. R. Moneyer's name in two lines	400	1250
1110	Small cross. R. Flower above name	1500	5500
1111	'Helmeted' bust r. R. Cross-crosslet	1250	5000
1112	**Halfpenny**. small cross, R. Moneyer's name in two lines or one line between rosettes	900	2500
1112A	— Flower. R. As 1105	975	3250

EADRED, 946-955

Eadred was another of the sons of Edward. He lost the kingdom of York to Eric Bloodaxe.

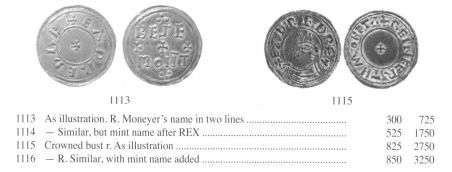

1113   1115

		F	VF
1113	As illustration. R. Moneyer's name in two lines	300	725
1114	— Similar, but mint name after REX	525	1750
1115	Crowned bust r. As illustration	825	2750
1116	— R. Similar, with mint name added	850	3250

		F	VF
		£	£
1117	Rosette. R. As 1113	425	1350
1118	Small cross. R. Rosette	425	1350
1119	— R. Flower enclosing moneyer's name. *B.M.C. II*	1500	5500
1120	**Halfpenny**. Similar to 1113	750	2250

HOWEL DDA, d. 949/950

Grandson of Rhodri Mawr, Howel succeeded to the kingdom of Dyfed *c*. 904, to Seisyllog *c*. 920 and became King of Gwynedd and all Wales, 942.

1121

| 1121 | HOPÆL REX, small cross or rosette. R. Moneyer's name in two lines . | 12500 | 42500 |

EADWIG, 955-959

Elder son of Eadmund, Eadwig lost Mercia and Northumbria to his brother Eadgar in 957.

1122   1123

1122	*Br. 1*. Type as illustration	625	1850
1123	— — Similar, but mint name in place of crosses	950	3000
1124	— 2. As 1122, but moneyer's name in one line	1250	4500
1125	— 3. Similar. R. Floral design	1750	6500
1126	— 4. Similar. R. Rosette or small cross	825	2500
1127	— 5. Bust r. R. Small cross	6500	22500

1128

1128	**Halfpenny**. Small cross. R. Flower above moneyer's name	1100	4000
1128A	— Similar. R. PIN (Winchester) across field	1350	4500
1128B	— Star. R. Moneyer's name in two lines	950	3000

King in Mercia and Northumbria from 957; King of all England 959-975.
It is now possible on the basis of the lettering to divide up the majority of Eadgar's coins into
issues from the following regions: N.E. England, N.W. England, York, East Anglia, Midlands, S.E.
England, Southern England, and S.W. England. (See 'Anglo-Saxon Coins', ed. R. H. M. Dolley.)

1129　　　　　　　　　　　　　　　　1135

1136

		F	*VF*
		£	£
1129	*Br 1*. Small cross. R. Moneyer's name in two lines, crosses between, trefoils top and bottom	225	575
1130	— — R. Similar, but rosettes top and bottom (a N.W. variety)	275	750
1131	— — R. Similar, but annulets between	275	750
1132	— — R. Similar, but mint name between (a late N.W. type)	450	1350
1133	— *2*. — R. Floral design	1250	4500
1134	— *4*. Small cross either side	240	600
1135	— — Similar, with mint name	375	1050
1136	— — Rosette either side	275	725
1137	— — Similar, with mint name	425	1250
1138	— *5*. Large bust to r. R. Small cross	975	3500
1139	— — Similar, with mint name	1100	4000
1140	**Halfpenny**. (8.5 grains.) *Br. 3*. Small cross. R. Flower above name	850	2750

1140A

1140A	— — R. Mint name around cross (Chichester, Wilton)	1250	4250
1140B	— Bust r. R. 'Londonia' monogram	950	3500

For Eadgar 'reform' issues see next page.

In 973 Eadgar introduced a new coinage. A royal portrait now became a regular feature and the reverses normally have a cruciform pattern with the name of the mint in addition to that of the moneyer. Most fortified towns of burghal status were allowed a mint, the number of moneyers varying according to their size and importance: some royal manors also had a mint and some moneyers were allowed to certain ecclesiastical authorities. In all some seventy mints were active about the middle of the 11th century (see list of mints pp. 137-138).

The control of the currency was retained firmly in the hands of the central government, unlike the situation in France and the Empire where feudal barons and bishops controlled their own coinage. Coinage types were changed at intervals to enable the Exchequer to raise revenue from new dies and periodic demonetization of old coin types helped to maintain the currency in a good state. No halfpence were minted during this period. During the latter part of this era, full pennies were sheared into 'halfpennies' and 'farthings'. They are far rarer than later 'cut' coins.

Further Reading: On the initial reform of the coinage under Eadgar see K. Jonsson, *The New Era: The Reformation of the Late Anglo-Saxon Coinage* (London: 1987). The nature and purpose of frequent periodic recoinages is explored by I. Stewart, '*Coinage and recoinage after Edgar's reform*', in *Studies in Late Anglo-Saxon Coinage*, ed. K. Jonsson (Stockholm: 1990), 455-85. References to individual types for mints and moneyers for much of the first half of the period may be found in K. Jonsson, *Viking Age Hoards and Late Anglo-Saxon Coins* (Stockholm: 1986).

Eadgar, 959-975 *(continued)*

1141

	F £	VF £
1141 **Penny**. Reform Small Cross type. Small diademed bust left. King's name 'Eadgar'. R. Small cross, name of moneyer and mint............................	1250	3500

EDWARD THE MARTYR, 975-978

The son of Eadgar by his first wife, Æthelflaed, Edward was murdered at Corfe in Dorset.

1142

| 1142 Sole type. As 1141, but reading 'Eadward'. .... | 1350 | 4500 |

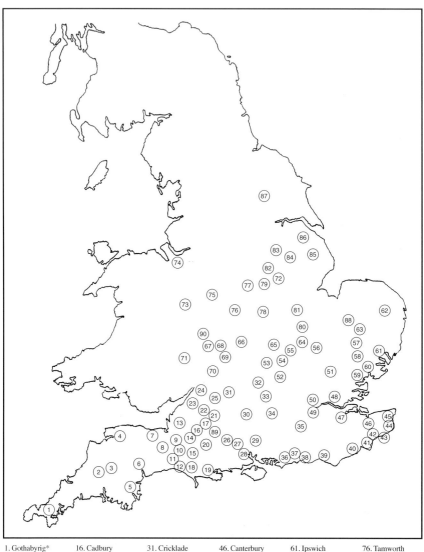

1. Gothabyrig*	16. Cadbury	31. Cricklade	46. Canterbury	61. Ipswich	76. Tamworth
2. Launceston	17. Bruton	32. Oxford	47. Rochester	62. Norwich	77. Derby
3. Lydford	18. Dorchester	33. Wallingford	48. Horndon	63. Thetford	78. Leicester
4. Barnstaple	19. Wareham	34. Reading	49. Southwark	64. Huntingdon	79. Nottingham
5. Totnes	20. Shaftesbury	35. Guildford	50. London	65. Northampton	80. Melton Mowbray
6. Exeter	21. Warminster	36. Chichester	51. Hertford	66. Warwick	81. Stamford
7. Watchet	22. Bath	37. Cissbury	52. Aylesbury	67. Worcester	82. Newark
8. Taunton	23. Bristol	38. Steyning	53. Buckingham	68. Pershore	83. Torksey
9. Langport	24. Berkeley	39. Lewes	54. Newport Pagnell	69. Winchcombe	84. Lincoln
10. Petherton	25. Malmesbury	40. Hastings	55. Bedford	70. Gloucester	85. Horncastle
11. Crewkerne	26. Wilton	41. Romney	56. Cambridge	71. Hereford	86. Caistor
12. Bridport	27. Salisbury	42. Lympne	57. Bury St Edmunds	72. Grantham*	87. York
13. Axbridge	28. Southampton	43. Hythe	58. Sudbury	73. Shrewsbury	88. Wilton. Norfolk*
14. Ilchester	29. Winchester	44. Dover	59. Maldon	74. Chester	89. Frome
15. Milborne Port	30. Bedwyn	45. Sandwich	60. Colchester	75. Stafford	90. Droitwich

*Possible location of uncertain mint

Son of Eadgar by his second wife Ælfthryth, Æthelred ascended the throne on the murder of his half-brother. He is known to posterity as 'The Unready' from 'Unrede', meaning 'without counsel', an epithet gained from the weakness of his royal government.During this reign England was subjected to Viking raids of increasing frequency and strength, and a large amount of tribute was paid in order to secure peace. Large hoards have been found in Scandinavia and the Baltic region and coins are often found peck-marked. There is a high degree of regional variation in the style of dies, particularly in Last Small Cross type, for which readers are advised to consult the following paper: C.S.S. Lyon, 'Die cutting styles in the Last Small Cross issue of c.1009-1017...', *BNJ* 68 (1998), 21-41.

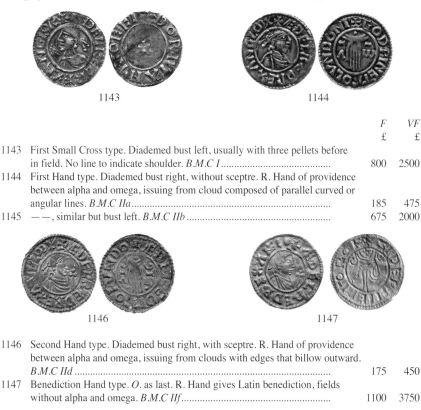

1143   1144

		F £	VF £
1143	First Small Cross type. Diademed bust left, usually with three pellets before in field. No line to indicate shoulder. *B.M.C I*	800	2500
1144	First Hand type. Diademed bust right, without sceptre. R. Hand of providence between alpha and omega, issuing from cloud composed of parallel curved or angular lines. *B.M.C IIa*	185	475
1145	— —, similar but bust left. *B.M.C IIb*	675	2000

1146   1147

1146	Second Hand type. Diademed bust right, with sceptre. R. Hand of providence between alpha and omega, issuing from clouds with edges that billow outward. *B.M.C IId*	175	450
1147	Benediction Hand type. *O.* as last. R. Hand gives Latin benediction, fields without alpha and omega. *B.M.C IIf*	1100	3750

1148   1150

1148	Crux type. Bare-headed bust left, with sceptre. R. Voided short cross with letters C, R, V, X, in angles. *B.M.C IIIa*	150	340
1149	Small Crux type. Reduced weight, small flans, sceptre inclined to bust such that the base penetrates drapery.	160	350
1150	Intermediate Small Cross type. RX at end of legend separate letters. *B.M.C I*	1350	4000

1151

1152

		F	VF
		£	£
1151	Long Cross type. Bare-headed bust left. R. Voided long cross. *B.M.C IVa*	150	340
1152	Helmet type. Armoured bust left in radiate helmet. *B.M.C VIII*...............	175	375
1153	As last but struck in gold.	35000	135000

1154

1156

		F	VF
1154	Last Small Cross type. Diademed bust left, RX at end of legend ligated together as one letter-form. *B.M.C I*	140	300
1154A	— —, similar but bust right..................................	325	850
1155	— —, similar but bust to edge of coin......................	625	1850
1156	Agnus Dei type. As illustration. *B.M.C X*...............	7250	22500

Son of King Swein Forkbeard of Denmark, Cnut was acclaimed king by the Danish fleet in England in 1014 but was forced to leave; Cnut returned and harried Wessex in 1015. Æthelred II died in 1016 and resistance to the Danes was continued by his son Eadmund Ironside, for whom no coins are known, but upon the latter's death in 1016 Cnut became undisputed king. The following year Cnut consolidated his position by marrying Emma of Normandy, the widow of Æthelred II.

There is a high degree of regional variation in the style of dies, particularly in Quatrefoil type, for which readers are advised to consult the following paper: M.A.S. Blackburn and C.S.S. Lyon, 'Regional die production in Cnut's Quatrefoil issue' in *Anglo-Saxon Monetary History*, ed. M.A.S. Blackburn (Leicester: 1986), 223-72. There is considerable weight fluctuation within and between the types.

Substantive types

1157

1158

1159

		F £	VF £
1157	Quatrefoil type (c.1017-23). Crowned bust left. *B.M.C VIII*	140	300
1158	Pointed Helmet type (1024-1030). *B.M.C XIV*	135	260
1159	Short Cross type (c.1029-1035/6). *B.M.C XVI*	125	250
1159A	— —, similar but sceptre replaced with a banner	750	2500

Posthumous type

1160	Jewel Cross type. BMC XX	575	2000

Type considered to have been struck under the auspices of his widow, Queen Emma of Normandy.

Harold was the illegitimate son of Cnut by Ælfgifu of Northampton and was appointed regent on behalf of his half-brother Harthacnut. Queen Emma of Normandy initially held Wessex for her son, Harthacnut, but by 1037 she had been driven from the country and Harold had been recognised as king throughout England. The principal issue was the Jewel Cross type which is also found in the name of Cnut and Harthacnut, cf. nos. 1160 and 1166.

1165

		F £	VF £
1162	Short Cross type (Autumn 1035). As 1159, but in the name of Harold. B.M.C. IIIa	950	3500
1163	Jewel Cross type (c.1036-38). B.M.C. I..	300	850
1164	Fleur-de-Lis type (1038-40). Armoured and diademed bust left. R. Voided long cross, trefoil of pellets in each angle. B.M.C. V	300	825
1165	— —, similar but fleur-de-lis between two pellets in each angle. B.M.C. V	275	750

HARTHACNUT, 1035-1042

Although Harthacnut was the only legitimate son of Cnut and his legitimate heir, the political situation in Denmark prevented him from leaving for England until 1040, by which time Harold had secured the kingdom. Harold's death allowed Harthacnut to reclaim England without bloodshed, but he himself died after two years of sole rule. The main variety of Harthacnut is Arm and Sceptre type from his sole reign. The Jewel Cross type from the early period is also found in the name of Cnut and Harold I, cf. nos. 1160 and 1163.

Early period (during regency) 1035–7

1166	Jewel Cross type. As 1163, but in the name of Harthacnut. Diademed bust left. B.M.C. I	1500	5500

1167   1168

1167	— —, similar but bust right. B.M.C I	1350	5000

Sole reign 1040–42

1168	Arm and Sceptre type. King's name given as 'Harthacnut'. Diademed bust left with sceptre in left hand, forearm visible across bust B.M.C. II	1250	4250

1169   1170

| 1169 | — —, Similar but king's name given as 'Cnut'. .... | 675 | 1850 |
| 1170 | **Danish types.** Types exist in the name of Harthacnut other than those listed above and are Scandinavian in origin. .... | 325 | 800 |

EDWARD THE CONFESSOR, 1042-1066

Son of Æthelred II and Emma of Normandy, Edward spent twenty-five years in Normandy before he was adopted into the household of his half-brother Harthacnut in 1040. On the death of Harthacnut, Edward was acclaimed king. He is known by the title 'The Confessor' owing to his piety and he was canonised after his death. There is considerable weight fluctuation within and between the types, which is often unaffected by the smallness of the flan, rather the coin might be thicker to compensate.

Further reading: P. Seaby, 'The sequence of Anglo-Saxon types 1030–1050', *BNJ* 28 (1955-7), 111–46; T. Talvio, 'The design of Edward the Confessor's coins', in *Studies in Late Anglo-Saxon Coinage*, ed. K. Jonsson (Stockholm: 1990), 489–99.

1171   1173

		F	VF
		£	£
1170A	Arm and Sceptre type (1042). *B.M.C. IIIa*	1250	4250
1171	Pacx type (1042–4). Diademed bust left. R. Voided long cross. *B.M.C. IV*	240	600
1172	— —, Similar but R. voided short cross. BMC V	250	650
1173	Radiate/Small Cross type (1044–6). *B.M.C. I*	150	350

1174   1175

| 1174 | Trefoil Quadrilateral type (1046–8). *B.M.C. III* .... | 150 | 350 |
| 1175 | Small flan type (1048–50). *B.M.C. II* .... | 135 | 300 |

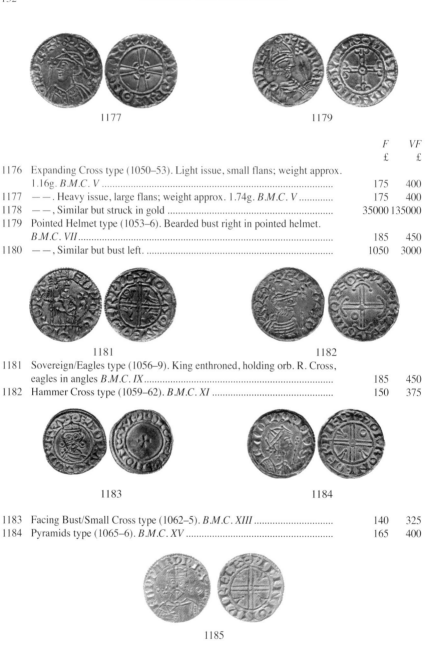

1177   1179

		F	*VF*
		£	£
1176	Expanding Cross type (1050–53). Light issue, small flans; weight approx. 1.16g. *B.M.C. V*	175	400
1177	——. Heavy issue, large flans; weight approx. 1.74g. *B.M.C. V*	175	400
1178	——, Similar but struck in gold	35000	135000
1179	Pointed Helmet type (1053–6). Bearded bust right in pointed helmet. *B.M.C. VII*	185	450
1180	——, Similar but bust left.	1050	3000

1181   1182

| 1181 | Sovereign/Eagles type (1056–9). King enthroned, holding orb. R. Cross, eagles in angles *B.M.C. IX* | 185 | 450 |
| 1182 | Hammer Cross type (1059–62). *B.M.C. XI* | 150 | 375 |

1183   1184

| 1183 | Facing Bust/Small Cross type (1062–5). *B.M.C. XIII* | 140 | 325 |
| 1184 | Pyramids type (1065–6). *B.M.C. XV* | 165 | 400 |

1185

| 1185 | Transitional Pyramids type (c.1065). *B.M.C. XIV* | 1850 | 5500 |

Most York coins of this reign have an annulet in one quarter of the reverse.

Harold was the son of Earl Godwine of Wessex, who had dominated the royal court, and was brother-in-law to Edward the Confessor. Harold successfully repulsed an invasion of Harald Hardrada of Norway, but was himself killed in the Battle of Hastings after a reign of ten months.

Further reading: H. Pagan, 'The coinage of Harold II', in *Studies in Late Anglo-Saxon Coinage*, ed. K. Jonsson (Stockholm: 1990), 177–205.

1186   1187

1186	Pax type. Crowned head left with sceptre. R. PAX across field. *B.M.C. I*	1200	2650
1187	— —, Similar but without sceptre. *B.M.C. Ia*	1350	3250
1188	— —, Similar but head right. *B.M.C. Ib*	2500	8500

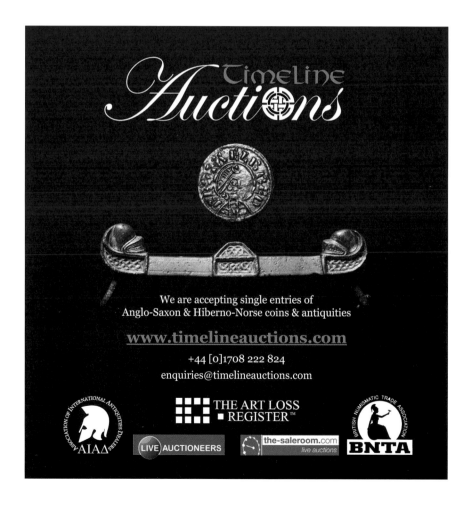

Cnut, Short Cross type (S.1159) - WULNOTH ON WINC:
moneyer Wulnoth   *mint* Winchester

William, Paxs type (S.1257) - LIFINC ON WINCE
moneyer Lifinc   *mint* Winchester

Old English special letters found on Anglo-Saxon and Norman coins:

Letter	Name	Modern Equivalent
Æ	Ash	E
Ð	Eth	Th
Ᵹ (P)	Wynn	W

In late Anglo-Saxon and Norman times coins were struck in the King's name at a large number of mints distributed in centres of population, and in times of emergency in places of refuge, across England and Wales. During the 10th century the use of a mint signature was sporadic but from the Reform type of Edgar the mint name is almost invariably given, usually in conjunction with that of the moneyer responsible, e.g. EDGAR ON BERCLE. At the peak, 71 mints struck the quatrefoil type of Cnut and 65 the PAXS type of William I and they provide a valuable insight into the economic and social structures of the period.

The output of the mints varied enormously and a dozen are exceptionally rare. Approximately 100,000 pennies survive, half of which emanate from the great centres of London, Canterbury, Lincoln, Winchester and York. At the other end of the scale a mint such as Rochester is known from about 500 coins, Derby from around 250, Guildford 100, Bedwyn 25, Horncastle 4 and Pershore 1. Many of these coins, particularly those from the great Scandinavian hoards, are in museum collections and are published in the Sylloge of Coins of the British Isles (SCBI) series.

There are too many type for mint combinations, over 1500 Saxon and 1000 Norman, to price each individually and our aim is to give an indication of value for the commonest Saxon and Norman type, in VF condition, for each of the 102 attested mints (excluding Baronial of Stephen's reign), and for a further 10 mints whose location or attribution is uncertain. The threshold VF price for a Norman coin (H1 B.M.C.15 £450) exceeds that for a Saxon coin (Cnut short cross £175) accounting for the difference in starting level. Prices for coins in lower grade would be less and there is a premium for the rarer types for each mint, but for many types, e.g. in the reigns of Harthacnut or Henry I, the value of the type itself far exceeds that of many of the constituent mints and a scarce mint is only worth a modest premium over a common one.

We also give the most characteristic mint signatures (often found abbreviated) and the reigns for which the mint is known. There are many pitfalls in identifying mints, not least that Saxon and Norman spelling is no more reliable than that of other ages and that late Saxon coins were widely imitated in Scandinavia. There is extensive literature and the specialist in this fascinating series can, for further details, consult J J North, English Hammered Coinage Vol.1.

Alf	—	Alfred the Great	Hd1	—	Harold I
EdE	—	Edward the Elder	HCn	—	Harthacnut
A'stn	—	Aethelstan	EdC	—	Edward the Confessor
Edm	—	Edmund	Hd2	—	Harold II
Edw	—	Edwig	W1	—	William I
Edg	—	Edgar	W2	—	William II
EdM	—	Edward the Martyr	H1	—	Henry I
Ae2	—	Aethelred	St	—	Stephen
Cn	—	Cnut			

Berkeley   Hastings

	SAXON VF £	NORMAN VF £
Axbridge (AXAN, ACXEPO) Edg, Ae2, Cn, HCn	2750	–
Aylesbury (AEGEL, AEEL), Ae2, Cn, EdC	2750	–
Barnstable (BARD, BEARDA) Edw, Edg, Ae2-Hd1, EdC, W1, H1	1250	1500
Bath (BADAN) EdE-A'stn, Edw-EdC, W1-St	400	900
Bedford (BEDAN, BEDEFOR) Edw-St	450	900
Bedwyn (BEDEPIN) EdC, W1	1750	4000
Berkeley (BEORC, BERCLE) EdC	7500	–
Bramber (BRAN) St	–	3000
Bridport (BRYDI, BRIPVT) A'stn, Ae2, Cn, HCn, EdC-W1	1250	1500
Bristol (BRICSTO, BRVCSTO) Ae2-St	450	700
Bruton (BRIVT) Ae2, Cn, HCn, EdC	2000	–
Buckingham (BVCIN) Edg, EdM-Hd1, HCn, EdC	3000	–
Bury St.Edmunds (EDMVN, S.EDM) EdC, W1, H1, St	1000	750
Cadbury (CADANBY) Ae2, Cn	5000	–
Caistor (CASTR, CESTR) EdM, Ae2, Cn	5000	–
Cambridge (GRANTE) Edg-St	300	900
Canterbury (DORO, CAENTPA, CNTL) Alf, A'stn, Edr, Edg-St	250	475
Cardiff (CIVRDI, CAIERDI) W1, H1, St, Mat	–	1250
Carlisle (CARD, EDEN) H1, St	–	1500
Castle Rising (RISINGE) St (type II-VII)	–	1750
Chester (LEIGE, LEGECE, CESTRE) A'stn, Edm, Edg-St	400	750
Chichester (CISSAN, CICEST) A'stn, Edg, Ae2-St	400	600
Christchurch (orig. Twynham) (TVEHAM, TPIN) W1, H1	–	3000
Cissbury (SIDESTEB, SIDMES) Ae2, Cn	2250	–
Colchester (COLN, COLECES) Ae2-St	350	650
Crewkerne (CRVCERN) Ae2, Cn, Hd1	3500	–
Cricklade (CROCGL, CRECCELAD, CRIC) Ae2-W2	1750	1500
Derby (DEORBY, DERBI) A'stn, Edm, Edg-St	1350	1250
Dorchester (DORCE, DORECES) Ae2-H1	900	1000
Dover (DOFERA, DOFRN) A'stn, Edg, Ae2-St	350	600
Droitwich (PICC, PICNEH) EdC, Hd2	3500	–
Dunwich (DVNE) St	–	1750
Durham (DVNE, DVRHAM, DVNHO) W1-St	–	2250
Exeter (EAXA, EAXCESTRE, IEXECE) Alf, A'stn, Edw-St	350	650
Frome (FRO) Cn, HCn, EdC	3500	–
Gloucester (GLEAP, GLEPECE, GLOPEC) Alf, A'stn, Edg-St	450	700
Grantham (GRANTHA, GRE) Ae2	6000	–
Guildford (GYLD, GILDEFRI) EdM-W2	1500	3000
Hastings (HAESTINGPOR, AESTI) Ae2-St	400	750
Hedon (HEDVN) St	–	4500
Hereford (HEREFOR, HRFRD) A'stn, Edg, Ae2-St	450	800
Hertford (HEORTF, HRTFI, RET) A'stn, Edw-EdC, W1-H1	400	1500
Horncastle (HORN) EdM, Ae2	6500	–
Horndon (HORNIDVNE) EdC	6500	–
Huntingdon (HVNTEN, HVTD) Edg, Ae2-St	400	1200
Hythe (HIÐEN, HIDI) EdC, W1, W2	3000	1500
Ilchester (GIFELCST, GIVELC, IVELCS) Edg, Ae2-St	750	1350
Ipswich (GIPESWIC, GYPES) Edg-St	400	700
Langport (LANCPORT, LAGEPOR) A'stn, Cn-EdC	2500	–
Launceston (LANSTF, LANSA, SANCTI STEFANI) Ae2, W1-H1	4000	2500
Leicester (LIHER, LEHRE, LEREC) A'stn, Edg, Ae2-St	450	900
Lewes (LAEPES, LEPEEI, LAPA) A'stn, Edg-St	400	750
Lincoln (LINCOLN, NICOLE) Edr, Edg-St	250	475
London (LVNDO, LVNDENE) Alf, A'stn, Edw-St	250	475
Lydford (LYDANFOR) Edg-EdC	500	–
Lympne (LIMENE, LIMNA) A'stn, Edg-Cn	900	–
Maldon (MAELDVN, MIEL) A'stn, Fdg, Ae2-Hd1, EdC-W2	500	1500
Malmesbury (MALD, MEALDMES, MELME) Edg, Ae2-W2	1750	2250
Marlborough (MAERLEBI) W1, W2	–	4000
Melton Mowbray (MEDELTV) Ae2, Cn	6500	–
Milborne Port (MYLE) Ae2, Cn, EdC	6000	–

	SAXON VF £	NORMAN VF £
Newark (NEWIR, NIWOR) Edg-Cn	5000	–
Newcastle (CAST) St	–	2250
Newport (NIPANPO, NIPEPORT) Edw, Edg, EdC	5000	–
Northampton (HAMTVN, HMTI, NORHAM) Edw, Edg-St	500	750
Norwich (NORDPIC) A'stn-Edr, Edg-St	250	500
Nottingham (SNOTING) A'stn, Ae2-St	1500	1500
Oxford (OXNA, OCXEN, OXENFO) Alf, A'stn, Edr-St	400	650
Pembroke (PEI, PAN, PAIN) H1, St	–	4000
Pershore (PERESC) EdC	7500	–
Petherton (PEDR, PEDI) Cn, EdC	6000	–
Pevensey (PEFNESE, PEVEN) W1-St	–	2500
Reading (READIN, REDN) EdC	5000	–
Rhuddlan (RVDILI) W1	–	3500
Rochester (ROFEC, ROFSC) A'stn, Edg-H1	500	1250
Romney (RVMED, RVMNE) Ae2-H1	500	900
Rye (RIE) St	–	3500
Salisbury (SEREB, SEARB, SALEB) Ae2-EdC, W1-St	400	600
Sandwich (SANDPI) EdC, W1-St	600	1000
Shaftesbury (SCEFTESB, CEFT, SAFTE) A'stn, Edg-St	600	800
Shrewsbury (SCROB, SCRVBS, SALOP) A'stn, Edg, Ae2-St	600	900
Southampton (HAMPIC, HAMTVN) A'stn, Edw-Cn	600	1000
Southwark (SVDBY, SVDGE, SVDPERC) Ae2-St	250	475
Stafford (STAFFO, STAEF) A'stn, Edg, Ae2-Hd1, EdC, W1-St	800	1250
Stamford (STANFORD) Edg-St	250	650
Steyning (STAENIG, STENIC) Cn-W2, St	350	700
Sudbury (SVDBI, SVBR) Ae2, Cn, EdC, W1-St	600	800
Swansea (SVENSEI) St	–	3000
Tamworth (TOMPEARÐ, TAMPRÐ) A'stn, Edg-Hd1, EdC, W1-St	1750	1500
Taunton (TANTVNE) Ae2-St	800	900
Thetford (ÐEOTFOR, DTF, TETFOR) Edg-St	250	500
Torksey (TVRC, TORC) EdM-Cn	4000	–
Totnes (DARENT, TOTANES, TOTNES) A'stn, Edw-HCn, W2, H1	600	1750
Wallingford (PELINGA, PALLIG) A'stn, Edm, Edg, Ae2-H1	450	650
Wareham (PERHAM, PERI) A'stn, Edg-St	600	1200
Warminster (PORIME) Ae2-Hd1, EdC	3000	–
Warwick (PAERINC, PERPIC, PAR) A'stn (?), Edg-St	800	1250
Watchet (PECED, PICEDI, WACET) Ae2-EdC, W1-St	1750	1750
Wilton (PILTVNE) Edg-St	350	650
Winchcombe (WENCLES, PINCEL, PINCL) Edg, Ae2, Cn, HCn-W1	1750	2000
Winchester (PINTONIA, PINCEST) Alf, A'stn, Edw-St	250	475
Worcester (PIGER, PIHREC, PIREC) EdM, Ae2-St	600	1000
York (EBORACI, EFORPIC, EVERWIC) A'stn, Edm, Edg-St	250	600

Mints of uncertain identification or location

"Brygin" (BRYGIN) Ae2	3500	–
"Dyr/Dernt" (DYR, DERNE, DERNT) EdC (East Anglia)	1500	–
"Weardburh" (PEARDBV) A'stn, Edg	4500	–
Abergavenny (?) (FVNI) W1	–	3000
Gothabyrig (GEODA, GODABYRI, IODA) Ae2-HCn	3000	–
Eye (?) (EI, EIE) St	–	3000
Peterborough (?) (BVRI) W1, St	–	3500
Richmond, Yorks (?) (R1) (type 1)	–	1750
St Davids (?) (DEVITVN) W1	–	3000
Wilton, Norfolk (?) (PILTV) Ae2 (LSC)	2500	–
Bamborough (BCI, CIB, OBCI) Henry of Northumberland	–	5500
Corbridge (COREB) Henry of Northumberland	–	5500

Aylesbury

Barnstaple

Cricklade

Dunwich

Exeter

Frome

Guildford

Horncastle

Ilchester

London

Milborne Port

Newark

Oxford

Pevensey

Rochester

Stafford

Torksey

Winchcombe

York

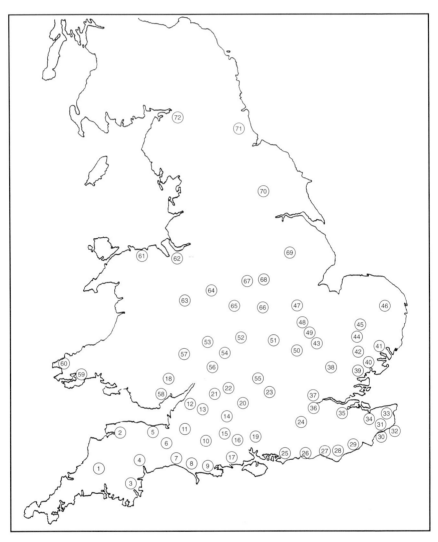

1. Launceston	13. Bath	25. Chichester	37. London	49. Huntingdon	61. Rhuddlan
2. Barnstaple	14. Marlborough	26. Steyning	38. Hertford	50. Bedford	62. Chester
3. Totnes	15. Wilton	27. Lewes	39. Maldon	51. Northampton	63. Shrewsbury
4. Exeter	16. Salisbury	28. Pevensey	40. Colchester	52. Warwick	64. Stafford
5. Watchet	17. Christchurch	29. Hastings	41. Ipswich	53. Worcester	65. Tamworth
6. Taunton	18. Abergavenny*	30. Romney	42. Sudbury	54. Winchcombe	66. Leicester
7. Bridport	19. Winchester	31. Hythe	43. Cambridge	55. Oxford	67. Derby
8. Dorchester	20. Bedwyn	32. Dover	44. Bury	56. Gloucester	68. Nottingham
9. Wareham	21. Malmesbury	33. Sandwich	45. Thetford	57. Hereford	69. Lincoln
10. Shaftesbury	22. Cricklade	34. Canterbury	46. Norwich	58. Cardiff	70. York
11. Ilchester	23. Wallingford	35. Rochester	47. Stamford	59. Pembroke	71. Durham
12. Bristol	24. Guildford	36. Southwark	48. Peterborough	60. St Davids*	72. Carlisle

Possible location of uncertain mint

William I maintained the Anglo-Saxon mint system and the practice of conducting frequent periodic recoinages by change of coin type. However, the twelfth-century witnessed a gradual transition from regional to centralised minting. Nearly seventy towns had moneyers operating under William I, but only thirty mint towns took part in the recoinage initiated by the Cross-and-Crosslets ('Tealby') coinage in 1158. Cut halfpennies and cut farthings were made during this period, but are scarce for all types up to BMC 13 of Henry I; cut coins are more frequently encountered for subsequent types.

Further reading: G.C. Brooke, *Catalogue of English Coins in the British Museum. The Norman Kings*, 2 volumes (London, 1916). (Abbr. BMC Norman Kings). I. Stewart, 'The English and Norman mints, c.600–1158', in *A New History of the Royal Mint*, ed. C.E. Challis (Cambridge, 1992), pp. 1–82.

WILLIAM I, 1066-1087

Duke William of Normandy claimed the throne of England on the death of his cousin Edward the Confessor. An important monetary reform occurred towards the close of the reign with the introduction of the *geld de moneta* assessed on boroughs. This may be seen as part of the raft of administrative reforms initiated by William I, which included the compilation of Domesday Book in 1086.

The date of the Paxs type is central to the absolute chronology of this and the subsequent reign. Currently evidence is equivocal on the matter. In BMC Norman Kings (London, 1916) it was designated the last type of the reign, an attribution maintained here, but some students regard it as having continued into the reign of William II or begun by him.

Further reading: D.M. Metcalf, 'Notes on the "PAXS" type of William I', *Yorkshire Numismatist* 1 (1988), 13–26. P.Grierson, 'Domesday Book, the geld de moneta and monetagium: a forgotten minting reform' *British Numismatic Journal* 55 (1985), 84–94.

1250   1251

		F £	VF £
1250	**Penny**. *B.M.C.* 1: Profile left type.	475	1350

1252   1253

| 1251 | *B.M.C.* 2: Bonnet type. | 275 | 750 |
| 1252 | *B.M.C.* 3: Canopy type | 500 | 1450 |

1254   1255

1253	*B.M.C.* 4: Two sceptres type.	350	900
1254	*B.M.C.* 5: Two stars type	275	700
1255	*B.M.C.* 6: Sword type.	450	1350

1256   1257

		F £	VF £
1256	*B.M.C.* 7: Profile right type (lead die struck examples exist from the Thames)	575	1750
1257	*B.M.C.* 8: Paxs type	250	550

WILLIAM II, 1087-1100

Second son of William I was killed while hunting in the New Forest. Five of the thirteen coin types in the name of 'William' have been assigned to the reign of William II, although it remains uncertain whether the Paxs type of his father continued into his reign.

1258   1259

		F	VF
1258	**Penny**. *B.M.C.* 1: Profile type.	900	3000
1259	*B.M.C.* 2: Cross in quatrefoil type.	800	2400

1260   1261

1260	*B.M.C.* 3: Voided cross type	800	2400
1261	*B.M.C.* 4: Cross pattée and fleury type......................	850	2500

1262

1262	*B.M.C.* 5: Cross fleury and piles type.......................	850	2500

Henry was the third son of William I. Administrative reforms and military action to secure Normandy dominated the king's work. After the death of his son in 1120 Henry sought to guarantee the throne for his daughter Matilda, widow of German Emperor Henry V.

The coin types continue to be numbered according to BMC Norman Kings (London, 1916), but the order 1, 2, 3, 4, 5, 6, 9, 7, 8, 11, 10, 12, 13, 14, 15 is now accepted as a working hypothesis for the reign. Greater uncertainty pertains to the chronology of the coin types. The reign coincided with a period of monetary crisis. Scepticism concerning the quality of coinage led to the testing of coins by the public, hindering their acceptance in circulation. In response the government ordered all coins mutilated at issue to force the acceptance of damaged coins. Thus, a few coins of type 6 and all of those of types 7–14 have an official edge incision or 'snick'. Round halfpennies were produced and as some are found snicked they can be dated to the period when official mutilation of the coinage was ordered. In 1124 there was a general purge of moneyers in England as the royal government attempted to restore confidence in the coinage.

Further reading: M.A.S. Blackburn, 'Coinage and currency under Henry I; A review', *Anglo-Norman Studies* 13 (1991), 49–81. M.M. Archibald and W.J. Conte, 'Five round halfpennies of Henry I. A further case for reappraisal of the chronology of types', *Spink's Numismatic Circular* 98 (1990), 232–6.

1263   1263A

		F	*VF*
		£	£
1263	**Penny**. *B.M.C.* 1: Annulets type	475	1500
1263A	*B.M.C.* 2: Profile/cross fleury type	400	1050

1264   1265

1264	*B.M.C.* 3: Paxs type	300	850
1265	*B.M.C.* 4: Annulets and piles type	400	1050

1266   1267

1266	*B.M.C.* 5: Voided cross and fleurs type....................................	750	2750
1267	*B.M.C.* 6: Pointing bust and stars type	1250	5000

1268

1268	*B.M.C.* 7: Facing bust/quatrefoil with piles type	300	850

1269

1270

		F £	VF £
1269	*B.M.C.* 8: Large profile/cross and annulets type...............................	1250	4500
1270	*B.M.C.* 9: Facing bust/cross in quatrefoil type	650	2000

1271

1272

1271	*B.M.C.* 10: Facing bust/cross fleury type	250	750
1272	*B.M.C.* 11: Double inscription type..	550	1750

1273

1274

1273	*B.M.C.* 12: Small profile/cross and annulets type	425	1200
1274	*B.M.C.* 13: Star in lozenge fleury type	425	1200

1275

1276

1275	*B.M.C.* 14: Pellets in quatrefoil type..	225	650
1276	*B.M.C.* 15: Quadrilateral on cross fleury type	150	450

1277

1277A

1277	*Round halfpenny*. Facing head. R. Cross potent with pellets in angles....	1650	5000
1277A	— —, As last but reverse from penny die of type 9.	2500	7500

Stephen of Blois seized the English throne on the death of his uncle, Henry I, despite his oath to support Matilda, with whom he contended for power during his reign.

Substantive types BMC 1 and BMC 7 were the only nation-wide issues, the latter introduced after the conclusion of the final political settlement in 1153. The other substantive types, BMC 2 and BMC 6, were confined to areas in the east of England under royal control. In western England coinage was issued by or on behalf of the Angevin party (q.v. below). In areas without access to new dies from London, coinage was produced from locally made dies and initially based on the designs of regular coins of BMC 1. Particular local types were produced in the midlands and the north, associated with prominent magnates, in the king's name or occasionally in the name of barons. Entries contain references to the article by Mack (M).

Further reading: R.P. Mack, 'Stephen and the Anarchy 1135-54', *British Numismatic Journal* 35 (1966), 38–112. M.A.S. Blackburn, 'Coinage and currency', in *The Anarchy of King Stephen's Reign*, ed. E. King (Oxford, 1994), 145–205.

Substantive royal issues

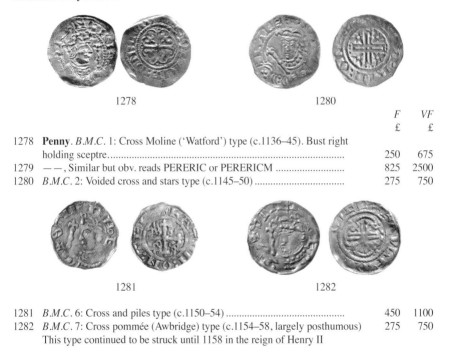

1278   1280

		F	VF
		£	£
1278	**Penny**. *B.M.C.* 1: Cross Moline ('Watford') type (c.1136–45). Bust right holding sceptre..	250	675
1279	— —, Similar but obv. reads PERERIC or PERERICM	825	2500
1280	*B.M.C.* 2: Voided cross and stars type (c.1145–50)	275	750

1281   1282

1281	*B.M.C.* 6: Cross and piles type (c.1150–54)	450	1100
1282	*B.M.C.* 7: Cross pommée (Awbridge) type (c.1154–58, largely posthumous) This type continued to be struck until 1158 in the reign of Henry II	275	750

The types designated BMC 3, 4 and 5 are non-substantive, listed as 1300–1302.

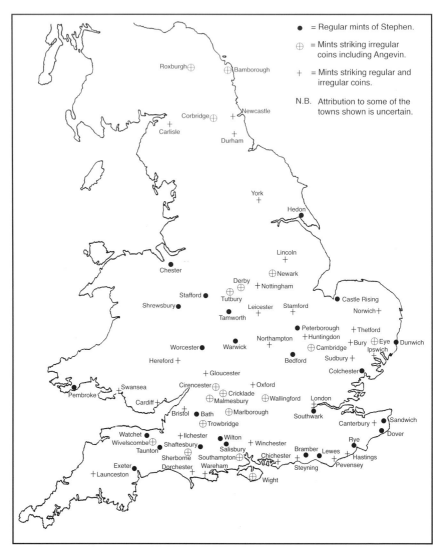

= Regular mints of Stephen.

⊕ = Mints striking irregular coins including Angevin.

+ = Mints striking regular and irregular coins.

N.B. Attribution to some of the towns shown is uncertain.

LOCAL AND IRREGULAR ISSUES OF THE CIVIL WAR

Coins struck from erased dies late 1130's to c.1145

The association of these coins with the Interdict of 1148 is erroneous. Some of the marks that disfigured the dies were probably cancellation marks, but the exigencies of the civil war required the re-employed of the dies. Other defacements may well be an overtly political statement.

	1283		1288		

		F	VF
		£	£
1283	As 1278, but obverse defaced with long cross. *East Anglian mints.* (M 137–47)	850	3000
1284	— —, but king's bust defaced with cross. *Nottingham (M 149)*	750	2250
1285	— —, but sceptre defaced with bar or cross. *Nottingham, Lincoln, Stamford.* (M 148, 150–54)	575	1500
1286	— —, but obverse legend erased. *Nottingham (M 157)*	625	1750
1286A	— —, but with defacement other than those noted above	475	1250

South Eastern variant

1287	As 1278, but king holds mace instead of sceptre. *Canterbury (M 158)*	975	3500

Eastern variants

1288	As 1278, but R. has roundels in centre, on cross limbs or in angles. *Suffolk mints (M 159–68)*	725	2000
1289	— —, but R. Plain cross, fleurs in angels. *Lincoln (M 169–73)*	725	2000
1290	— —, but R. Plain cross superimposed on cross moline *(M 174)*	675	1850
1290A	— —, but R. Quadrilateral over voided cross *(M 176)*	900	3000
1290B	— —, but cross penetrating legend to edge, fleurs inverted in angles. *Lincoln. (M 186–7)*	900	3000

Southern variants

	1291		1295		

1291	As 1278, but with large rosette of pellets at end of obverse legend *(M 184–5)*	675	1850
1292	— —, but with star at end of obverse legend *(M 187y)*	575	1500
1293	Bust r. or l., rosette in place of sceptre. R. As 1280, but solid cross. (M 181–3)	825	2500
1295	As 1278, but king wears collar of annulets. R. voided cross moline, annulet at centre. *Southampton. (M 207–212)*	375	1000

		F £	VF £

1296   As 1278, but reverse cross penetrates legend with fleur-de-lis tips.
       Leicester (M 177–8)   750   2250
1297   — —, but crude work. R. Voided cross, lis outward in angles. *Tutbury*
       (M 179)   750   2250

                          1298   1300
1298   — —, but crude work. R. Voided cross with martlets in angles. *Derby*
       (M 175)   2000   6500
1299   — —, but R. plain cross with T-cross in each angle *(M 180)*   875   2750
1300   *B.M.C.* 3: Facing bust. R. Cross pattée, fleurs inwards. *Northampton and*
       Huntingdon (?) (M 67–71)   1100   3750

                          1301   1302
1301   *B.M.C.* 4: Lozenge fleury type. *Lincoln or Nottingham (M 72–5)*   575   1600
1302   *B.M.C.* 5: Bust half-right. R. Lozenge in Cross Moline with fleurs. *Leicester*
       (M 76)   1250   4000
1303   As 1280, but obverse legend ROBERTVS. *(M 269)*   2500   8500

North-Eastern and Scottish Border variants
1304   As 1278, but star before sceptre. R. Anullets at tips of fleurs *(M 188)*   950   3000
1305   — —, but voided cross penetrating legend to edge *(M 189–92)*   975   3250
1306   — —, but crude style *(M 276–9, 281–2)*   575   1750
1307   — —, but R. Cross with cross pattée and crescent in angles *(M 288)*   1850   6000
       King David I of Scotland
1308   As 1305, but obverse legend DAVID REX *(M 280)*   1850   5500
       Earl Henry of Northumberland (son of King David I of Scotland)
1309   As 1278, but legend hENRIC ERL *(M 283–5)*   1850   5500
1310   — —, Similar but reverse cross fleury *(M 286–7)*   2000   6250
1311   As 1307, but obverse legend NENCI:COM *(M 289)*   1850   5500

York Issues: The Ornamented Group attributed to York (*c.*1150)
       King Stephen
1312   As 1278, but obverse inscription NSEPEFETI, NSEPINEI or STIEFNER.
       R. ornamental letters WISÐGNOTA *(M 215–6)*   1500   4500

1313   1315

	F £	VF £

1313 Flag type. As 1278, but lance with pennant before face, star right. R. As
  1278, letters and four ornaments in legend *(M 217)* 750 2750
1313A — —, Similar but with eight ornaments in reverse legend. *(M 217)* 850 3000
1314 As 1278, but legend STEIN and pellet lozenge for sceptre-head *(M 218)* 975 3500
1314A King standing facing, holding sceptre and standard with triple pennon. R.
  Cross pattée, crescents and quatrefoils in angles, ornaments in legend. ... 2750 8500
  King Stephen and Queen Matilda
1315 Two full-length standing figures holding sceptre. R. Legend of ornaments.
  (M 220) 3500 12500

1317   1320

Eustace Fitzjohn
1316 EVSTACIVS, knight standing with sword. R. Cross in quatrefoil,
  EBORACI EDTS or EBORACI TDEFL *(M 221-222)* 1750 5750
1317 — —, Similar but reverse legend ThOMHS FILIUS VLF *(M 223)* 1750 5750
1318 — —, Similar but reverse legend of ornaments and letters. *(M 224)* 1650 5250
1319 [EVSTA]CII. FII. IOANIS, lion passant right. R. Cross moline, ornaments in
  legend *(M 225)* 2750 8500
1320 EISTAOhIVS, lion rampant right. R. Cross fleury, ornaments in legend *(M 226)* 2500 8000
  William of Aumale, Earl of York
1320A WILLELMVS, Knight stg. r. holding sword. R. Cross in quatrefoil. As 1316 3000 10500

1322

Rodbert III de Stuteville
1321 ROBERTVS IESTV, knight holding sword on horse right. R. as 1314.
  (M 228) 4250 13500
1321A Type as 1312, but obverse legend RODBDS[T DE?] *(M 227)* 3000 9500
  Henry Murdac, Archbishop of York
1322 HENRICVS EPC, crowned bust, crosier and star before. R. similar to 1314
  but legend STEPHANVS REX *(M 229)* 2750 9000

Uncertain issues

		F	VF
		£	£
1323	Obv. as 1278. R̩. Cross pattée with annulets in angles *(M 272)*	675	1750
1324	Obv. as 1275 (Henry I, *B.M.C.* 14), but reverse as last *(M 274 extr)*	850	2500
1325	Other miscellaneous types/varieties	675	1500

THE ANGEVIN PARTY

Matilda was the daughter of Henry I and widow of German Emperor Henry V (d.1125) and had been designated heir to the English throne by her father. Matilda was Countess of Anjou by right of her second husband Geoffrey of Anjou. Matilda arrived in England in pursuit of her inheritance in 1139 and established an Angevin court at Bristol and controlled most of south-western England. Matilda's cause was championed by her half-brother, Henry I's illegitimate son, Robert, Earl of Gloucester.

The initial phase of coinage in Matilda's name copied the designs of Stephen's BMC 1 and are dated to the early 1140s. The second type was only discovered in the Coed-y-Wenallt hoard (1980). A group of coins invokes the names of past Norman kings 'William' and 'Henry' and the designs of Stephen BMC 1 and Henry I BMC 15. These coins were formally and erroneously attributed to Earl William of Gloucester and Duke Henry of Normandy. Coins of Earl William, and his father Earl Robert, of the Lion type are now known thanks to the discovery of the Box, Wiltshire hoard (1994). In addition to these great magnates a few minor barons placed their names on the coinage.

Further Reading: G. Boon, *Welsh Hoards 1979–81* (Cardiff, 1986). M.M. Archibald, 'The lion coinage of Robert Earl of Gloucester and William Earl of Gloucester', *British Numismatic Journal* 71 (2001), 71–86.

1326

Matilda (in England 1139–48)

1326	As 1278, but cruder style, legend MATILDI IMP or variant (M 230–40) *Bristol, Cardiff, Oxford and Wareham.*	1500	4000
1326A	— —, legend MATILDI IMP or IM.HE.MA. R̩. Cross pattée over fleury (Coed-y-Wenallt hoard) *Bristol and Cardiff.*	1600	4250
1326B	— —, as last but triple pellets at cross ends (Coed-y-Wenallt hoard). *Bristol and Cardiff.*	1600	4250
	Henry de Neubourg		
1326C	Similar type to 1326A but legend hENRICI dE NOVOB (Coed-y-Wenallt hoard) *Swansea*	1850	6500
	Anonymous issues in the name 'King Henry' and 'King William'		
1327	As 1278, but obverse legend hENRICVS or HENRICVS REX *(M 241–5)*	1250	3750
1327A	As 1295, but legend hENRIC *(M 246)*	1500	4250
1327B	As 1326A, but hENNENNVS	1600	4500
1328	Obv. as 1278. R̩. Cross crosslet in quatrefoil *(M 254)*	1600	4500
1329	— —, R̩. Quadrilateral on cross fleury *(M 248–53)*	1500	4250

1330   1331

		F £	VF £
1330	Facing bust and stars. R. Quadrilateral on cross botonnée *(M 255–8)*	1750	5000
1331	— —, Quadrilateral on voided cross botonnée *(M 259–61)*	1750	5000
1332	As 1329, but legend WILLEMVS or variant *(M 262)*	1500	4500
1333	As 1330, but legend WILLEMVS or variant *(M 263)*	1800	5500
1334	As 1331, but legend WILLEMVS or variant *(M 264–8)*	1800	5500

Earl Robert of Gloucester (1121/22–1147)

		F	VF
1334A	+ROB' COM' GLOC' (or variant), lion passant right. R. Cross fleury (Box hoard) .:	1750	5250

Earl William of Gloucester (1147-1183)

		F	VF
1334B	+WILLEMVS, lion passant right. R. Cross fleury (Box hoard)	1750	5250

Brian Fitzcount, Lord of Wallingford (?)

		F	VF
1335	As 1330, but legend B.R:C.I.T.B.R *(M 270)*	3500	10500

1336

Earl Patrick of Salisbury (?)

		F	VF
1336	Helmeted bust r. with sword, star behind. R. As 1329. *(M 271)*	3500	10500

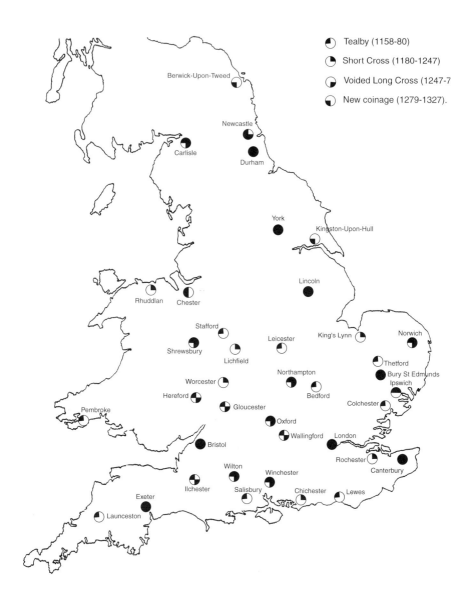

Tealby (1158-80)

Short Cross (1180-1247)

Voided Long Cross (1247-7

New coinage (1279-1327).

Berwick-Upon-Tweed

Newcastle

Carlisle

Durham

York

Kingston-Upon-Hull

Lincoln

Rhuddlan

Chester

Stafford

Shrewsbury

Lichfield

Leicester

King's Lynn

Norwich

Thetford

Northampton

Bury St Edmunds

Ipswich

Worcester

Hereford

Bedford

Colchester

Pembroke

Gloucester

Oxford

Wallingford

London

Bristol

Rochester

Wilton

Winchester

Canterbury

Ilchester

Salisbury

Chichester

Lewes

Exeter

Launceston

Moneyer table for the Cross and Crosslets (Tealby) coinage

From F £

London: Accard (CD), Alwin (ABCDF), Edmund (ACDE), Geffrei (ACE), Godefrei (ACDEF), Godwin (BDE), Hunfrei (AC), Iohan (ACDEF), Lefwine (BCEF), Martin (ABC), Pieres (ACEF), Pieres Mer. (ABD), Pieres Sal. (AEF), Ricard (ABCD), Rodbert (AC), Swetman (ABC), Wid (A), *110*

Canterbury: Alferg (A), Goldhavoc (ABCDEF), Goldeep (C), Lambrin (F), Raul (CDEF), Ricard (ABCDEF), Ricard Mr. (ABCDE), Rogier (ABCDEF), Rogier F. (A), Willem (C), Wiulf (ABCDEF), *110*

Bedford: Arfin (A), *Extremely Rare*

Bristol: Elaf (ACF), Rogier (ADEF), Tancard (ABD), *250*

Bury St Edmunds: Henri (BDE), Raul (F), Willem (A), *140*

Carlisle: Willem (ACDEF), *140*

Chester: Andreu (A), Willem (AD), *220*

Colchester: Alwin (AC), Pieres (CE), *250*

Durham: Cristien (C), Iohan (B), Walter (A), *180*

Exeter: Edwid (AC), Guncelin (AC), Rainir (BC), Ricard (A), Rogier (AD), *220*

Gloucester: Godwin (A), Nicol (A), Rodbert (A), Sawulf (A), *275*

Hereford: Driu (AC), Osburn (A), Stefne (A), [—]ward (A), *250*

Ilchester: Adam (CDF), Reinard (A), Ricard (A), Rocelin (A), *220*

Ipswich: Nicole (BCDEF), Robert (CEF), Turstain (CF), *110*

Launceston: Willem (A), *Extremely Rare*

Leicester: Ricard (A), Robert (A), *250*

Lewes: uncertain (F), *Extremely Rare*

Lincoln: Andreu (ABCDE), Godric (ABCD), Lanfram (ABCDF), Raulf (ABCDEF), Raven (ACF), Swein (ACD), *140*

Newcastle: Willem (ACDEF), *150*

Northampton: Ingeram (AC), Iosep (A), Pieres (A), Reimund (AC), Stefne (A), Waltier (AC), Warnier (AC), *180*

Norwich: Gilebert (ABF), Herbert (ACD), Herbert R (A)., Hugo (ACF), Nicol (AC), Picot (ABC), Reiner (AD), Ricard (A), *180*

Oxford: Adam (ADE), Aschetil (A), Rogier (A), *220*

Pembroke: Walter (A), *Extremely Rare*

Salisbury: Daniel (A), Levric (A), *220*

Shrewsbury: Warin (A), *Extremely Rare*

Stafford: Colbrand (AC), Willem (C), *275*

Thetford: Siwate (ACD), Turstain (ACD), Willem (ACDF), Willem Ma (A), Willem De (A), *140*

Wallingford: Fulke (A), *Extremely Rare*

Wilton: Anschetil (A), Lantier (A), Willem (A), *220*

Winchester: Herbert (AC), Hosbert (ACD), Ricard (AE), Willem (AC), *140*

York: Cudbert (A), Gerrard (A), Godwin (AD), Griffin (AD), Herbert (ACD), Hervi (A), Iordan (A), Norman (A), Willem (A), Wulfsi (A), *140*

Letters in brackets after moneyer's name indicate Class known to exist for the mint and moneyer combination

HENRY II, 1154-1189

Cross-and-crosslets ('Tealby') Coinage, 1158-1180

Coins of Stephen's last type continued to be minted until 1158. Then a new coinage bearing Henry's name replaced the currency of the previous reign which contained a high proportion of irregular and sub-standard pennies. The new Cross and Crosslets issue is more commonly referred to as the 'Tealby' coinage, as over 6000 of these pennies were discovered at Tealby, Lincolnshire, in 1807. Twenty nine mints were employed in this re-coinage, but once the re-minting had been completed not more than a dozen mints were kept open. The issue remained virtually unchanged for twenty-two years apart from minor variations in the king's portrait. The coins tend to be poorly struck on irregular flans.

Cut coins occur with varying degrees of frequency during this issue, according to the type and local area.

Further reading: *A Catalogue of English Coins in the British Museum. The Cross-and-Crosslet ("Tealby") Type of Henry II.* (London: 1951) by D.F. Allen.

1337   1338   1339

		F £	VF £
1337	Class A (1158-c.1163). No hair, no collar. Mantle falls from chin as two parallel lines between which is a line of pellets.	110	300
1338	Class B (c.1162-c.1163). Similar, but mantle of two folds which meet at chin (various compositions)	125	350
1339	Class C (c.1163-c.1167). Curl of hair at temple. Jewelled collar, mantle of many folds, field between sometimes jewelled, as is cuff	110	300

1340   1341   1342

		F	VF
1340	Class D (c.1167-c.1170). Jewelled collar continues down shoulder unbroken. Single curl of hair at temple, folds of mantle horizontal	110	300
1341	Class E (c.1170-c.1174). Similar to 1340. Jewelled collar only. Folds of mantle rise from hand to top of shoulder.	125	325
1342	Class F (c.1174-c.1180). Similar to 1341, but hair falls in long ringlets from temple.	110	300

The publishers acknowledge the work of the late Prof. Jeffrey Mass for re-organising and updating the short cross series.

'Short Cross' coinage of Henry II (1180-1189)

In 1180 a coinage of new type, known as the Short Cross coinage, replaced the Tealby issue. The new coinage is remarkable in that it covers not only the latter part of the reign of Henry II, but also the reigns of his sons Richard and John and on into the reign of his grandson Henry III, and the entire issue bears the name 'hɛNRICVS'. There are no English coins with the names of Richard or John. The Short Cross coins can be divided chronologically into various classes: ten mints were operating under Henry II and tables of mints, moneyers and classes are given for each reign.

1343   1344

1345

		F £	VF £
1343	Class 1a¹ - 1a³. Small face, square E, and/or C, and/or round M, irregular number of curls	150	500
1343A	Class 1a⁴ and 1a⁵. Small face, seriffed X, round E and C, square M, irregular number of curls	90	225
1344	1b. Fine portrait, curls 2 left and 5 right, stop before REX on most coins	75	200
1345	1c. Portrait less finely shaped, irregular number of curls, normally no stop before REX	65	175

RICHARD I, 1189-1199

Pennies of Short Cross type continued to be issued throughout the reign, all bearing the name hɛNRICVS. The coins of class 4, which have very crude portraits, continued to be issued in the early years of the next reign. The only coins bearing Richard's name are from his territories of Aquitaine and Poitou in western France.

1346   1347   1348A   1348C

1346	2. Chin whiskers made of small curls, no side whiskers, almost always 5 pearls to crown, frequently no collar, sometimes RE/X	135	400
1347	3. Large or small face, normally 7 pearls to crown, chin and side whiskers made up of small curls	110	275

	F	*VF*
	£	£
1348A 4a. Normally 7 pearls to crown, chin and side whiskers made up of small		
pellets, hair consisting of 2 or more non-parallel crescents left and right	90	225
1348B 4a* Same as last, but with reverse colon stops (instead of single pellets)	125	350
1348C 4b Normally 7 pearls to crown, chin and side whiskers made up of small		
pellets, single (or parallel) crescents as hair left and right, frequent		
malformed letters	80	200

JOHN, 1199-1216

'Short Cross' coinage *continued*. All with name hCNRICVS

The Short Cross coins of class 4 continued during the early years of John's reign, but in 1205 a re-coinage was initiated and new Short Cross coins of better style replaced the older issues. Coins of classes 5a and 5b were issued in the re-coinage in which sixteen mints were employed. Only ten of these mints were still working by the end of class 5. The only coins to bear John's name are the pennies, halfpence and farthings issues for Ireland.

1349   1350A   1350B

1351   1352   1353   1354

1349	4c. Reversed S, square face at bottom, 5 pearls to crown, normally single crescents as hair left and right	95	325
1350A	5a1 Reversed or regular S, irregular curved lines as hair (or circular curls containing no pellets), cross pattée as initial mark on reverse, *London and Canterbury* only...	225	675
1350B	5a2 Reversed S, circular curls left and right (2 or 3 each side) containing single pellets, cross pommée as initial mark on reverse	100	275
1350C	5a/5b or 5b/5a	75	185
1351	5b. Regular S, circular pelleted curls, cross pattée as initial mark on reverse	65	160
1352	5c. Slightly rounder portrait, letter X in the form of a St. Andrew's cross	65	160
1353	6a. Smaller portrait, with smaller letter X composed of thin strokes or, later, short wedges	60	150
1354	6b. Very tall lettering and long rectangular face	50	125

For further reading and an extensive listing of the English Short Cross Coinage see:
Sylloge of Coins of the British Isles. *The J. P. Mass Collection of English Short Cross Coins 1180-1247*

'Short Cross' coinage *continued* (1216-47)

The Short Cross coinage continued for a further thirty years during which time the style of portraiture and workmanship deteriorated. By the 1220s minting had been concentrated at London and Canterbury, one exception being the mint of the Abbot of Bury St. Edmunds.

Halfpenny and farthing dies are recorded early in this issue; a few halfpennies and now farthings have been discovered. See nos 1357 D-E.

| | 1355 | 1355A | 1355B |

| | F | VF |
| | £ | £ |

1355 6c. Lettering now shorter, face narrow and triangular (also issued in the reign of John) 55   150

1355A 6c. orn. Various letters now ornamental in design, curls 3/3 left and right   110   300

1355B 6x. Canterbury mint only, RE/X, curls 2/2, nostril pellets outside nose...   675   1500

1355C 6d. Face less distinct in shape, N's containing a pellet along the crossbar   110   275

| 1356A | 1356B | 1356C |

1356A 7a. Small compact face, letter A (rev. only) with top coming to a point under crossbar 35   110

1356B 7b. Letter A with square top, M appears as H (rev. only) 35   110

1356C 7c. Degraded portrait, letter A and M as in 7b, large lettering (rev. only)   30   100

| 1357A | 1357B | 1357C |

1357A 8a. New portrait; letter X in shape of curule; cross pattée as initial mark on reverse (early style), or cross pommée (late style) 110   325

1357B 8b. Degraded portrait, wedge-shaped X, cross pommée as initial mark .. 55   150

1357C 8c. Degraded portrait, cross pommée X, cross pommée as initial mark .. 55   150

1357D Round halfpenny in style of class 7, initial mark in shape of up-turned crescent, London mint only (dated to 1222) 2250   6500

1357E Round farthing in style of class 7, initial mark in shape of up-turned crescent, London mint only (dated to 1222) 2000   6000

Moneyer tables for the short cross coinage

Fine

Henry II:
London: Aimer (1a-b), Alain (1a-b), Alain V (1a-b), Alward (1b), Davi (1b-c),
Fil Aimer (1a-b), Gefrei (1c), Gilebert (1c), Godard (1b), Henri (1a-b),
Henri Pi (1a), Iefrei (1a-b), Iohan (1a-b), Osber (1b), Pieres (1a-c),
Pieres M (1a-b), Randvl (1a-b), Ravl (1b-c), Reinald (1a-b), Willelm (1a-b)　55
Carlisle: Alain (1b-c)　85
Exeter: Asketil (1a-b), Iordan (1a-b), Osber (1a-b), Ravl (1b), Ricard (1b-c),
Roger (1a-c)　75
Lincoln: Edmvnd (1b-c), Girard (1b), Hvgo (1b), Lefwine (1b-c), Rodbert (1b),
Walter (1b), Will. D.F. (1b), Willelm (1b-c)　65
Northampton: Filip (1a-b), Hvgo (1a-b), Ravl (1a-c), Reinald (1a-c), Simvn (1b),
Walter (1a-c), Willelm (1a-b)　55
Oxford: Asketil (1b), Iefrei (1b), Owein (1b-c), Ricard (1b-c), Rodbert (1b),
Rodbt. F. B. (1b), Sagar (1b)　70
Wilton: Osber (1a-b), Rodbert (1a-b), Iohan (1a)　75
Winchester: Adam (1a-c), Clement (1a-b), Gocelm (1a-c), Henri (1a),
Osber (1a-b), Reinier (1b), Rodbert (1a-b)　55
Worcester: Edrich (1b), Godwine (1b-c), Osber (1b-c), Oslac (1b)　75
York: Alain (1a-b), Efrard (1a-c), Gerard (1a-b), Hvgo (1a-c), Hunfrei (1a-b),
Isac (1a-b), Tvrkil (1a-c), Willelm (1a-b)　55

Richard I
London: Aimer (2-4a), Fvlke (4a-b), Henri (4a-b), Ravl (2), Ricard (2-4b),
Stivene (2-4b), Willelm (2-4b)　65
Canterbury: Goldwine (3-4b), Hernavd (4b), Hve (4b), Ioan (4b), Meinir (2-4b),
Reinald/Reinavd (2-4b), Roberd (2-4b), Samvel (4b), Simon (4b), Vlard (2-4b)　65
Carlisle: Alein (3-4b)　125
Durham: Adam (4a), Alein (4a-b), Pires (4b)　150
Exeter: Ricard (3)　135
Lichfield: Ioan (2)　2500
Lincoln: Edmvnd (2), Lefwine (2), Willelm (2)　100
Northampton: Giferei (4a), Roberd (3), Waltir (3)　110
Northampton or Norwich: Randvl (4a-b), Willelm (4a-b)　100
Shrewsbury: Ive (4a-b), Reinald/Reinavd (4a-b), Willem (4a)　175
Winchester: Adam (3), Gocelm (3), Osbern (3-4a), Pires (4a), Willelm (3-4a)　65
Worcester: Osbern (2)　250
York: Davi (4a-b), Efrard/Everard (2-4b), Hvgo/Hve (2-4a), Nicole (4a-b),
Tvrkil (2-4a)　65

John
London: Abel (5c-6b), Adam (5b-c), Beneit (5b-c), Fvlke (4c-5b), Henri (4c-5b/5a),
Ilger (5b-6b), Ravf (5c-6b), Rener (5a/b-5c), Ricard (4c-5b), Ricard B (5b-c),
Ricard T (5a/b-5b), Walter (5c-6b), Willelm (4c-5b), Willelm B (5a/b-5c),
Willelm L (5b-c), Willelm T (5b-c)　45
Canterbury: Goldwine (4c-5c), Hernavd/Arnavd (4c-5c), Hve (4c-5c), Iohan (4c-5c),
Iohan B (5b-c), Iohan M (5b-c), Roberd (4c-5c), Samvel (4c-5c), Simon (4c-5c)　45
Bury St Edmunds: Fvlke (5b-c)　90
Carlisle: Tomas (5b)　110
Chichester: Pieres (5b/a-5b), Ravf (5b/a-5b), Simon (5b/a-5b), Willelm (5b)　80
Durham: Pieres (5a-6a)　90
Exeter: Gileberd (5a-b), Iohan (5a-b), Ricard (5a-b)　75

Ipswich: Alisandre (5b-c), Iohan (5b-c)   60
Kings Lynn: Iohan (5b), Nicole (5b), Willelm (5b)   125
Lincoln: Alain (5a), Andrev (5a-5c), Hve (5a/b-5c), Iohan (5a), Ravf (5a/b-5b),
Ricard (5a-5b/a), Tomas (5a/b-5b)   45
Northampton: Adam (5b-c), Roberd (5b), Roberd T (5b)   60
Northampton or Norwich: Randvl (4c)   80
Norwich: Gifrei (5a/b-5c), Iohan (5a-c), Renald/Renavd (5a-c)   60
Oxford: Ailwine (5b), Henri (5b), Miles (5b)   70
Rochester: Alisandre (5b), Hvnfrei (5b)   90
Winchester: Adam (5a-c), Andrev (5b-c), Bartelme (5b-c), Henri (5a), Iohan (5a-c),
Lvkas (5b-c), Miles (5a-c), Ravf (5b-c), Ricard (5a-b)   45
York: Davi (4c-5b), Nicole (4c-5c), Renavd (5b), Tomas (5a/b-5b)   45

Henry III
London: Abel (6c-7a), Adam (7b-c), Elis (7a-b), Giffrei (7b-c), Ilger (6c-7b),
Ledvlf (7b-c), Nichole (7c-8c), Ravf (6c-7b), Ricard (7b), Terri (7a-b),
Walter (6b-c)   30
Canterbury: Arnold (6c/6x, 6x), Henri (6c-6c/d, 7a-c), Hivn/Ivn (6c-7b),
Iohan (6c-7c, 8b-c), Ioan Chic (7b-c), Ioan F. R. (7b-c), Nichole (7c, 8b-c),
Osmvnd (7b-c), Robert (6c, 7b-c), Robert Vi (7c), Roger (6c-7b),
Roger of R (7a-b), Salemvn (6x, 7a-b), Samvel (6c-d, 7a), Simon (6c-d, 7a-b),
Tomas (6d, 7a-b), Walter (6c-7a), Willem (7b-c, 8b-c), Willem Ta (7b-c)   30
Bury St Edmunds: Iohan (7c-8c), Norman (7a-b), Ravf (6c-d, 7a), Simvnd (7b-c),
Willelm (7a)   35
Durham: Pieres (7a)   80
Winchester: Henri (6c)   125
York: Iohan (6c), Peres (6c), Tomas (6c), Wilam (6c)   125

Irregular Local Issue
Rhuddlan (in chronological order)   95
Group I (c. 1180 – pre 1205) Halli, Tomas, Simond
Group II (c.1205 – 1215) Simond, Henricus

'Long Cross' coinage (1247-72)

By the middle of Henry's reign the coinage in circulation was in a poor state, being worn and clipped. In 1247 a fresh coinage was ordered, the new pennies having the reverse cross extended to the edge of the coin to help safeguard the coins against clipping. The earliest of these coins have no mint or moneyers' names. A number of provincial mints were opened for producing sufficient of the Long Cross coins, but these were closed again in 1250, only the royal mints of London and Canterbury and the ecclesiastical mints of Durham and Bury St. Edmunds remained open.

In 1257, following the introduction of new gold coinages by the Italian cities of Brindisi (1232), Florence (1252) and Genoa (1253), Henry III issued a gold coinage in England. This was a gold 'Penny' valued at 20 silver pence and twice the weight of the silver penny. The coinage was not a success, being undervalued, and it ceased to be minted after a few years; few coins have survived.

Cut halfpennies and farthings are common for this period, with a greater concentration in the early part. They are up to 100 times commoner than in late Anglo-Saxon times.

Without sceptre

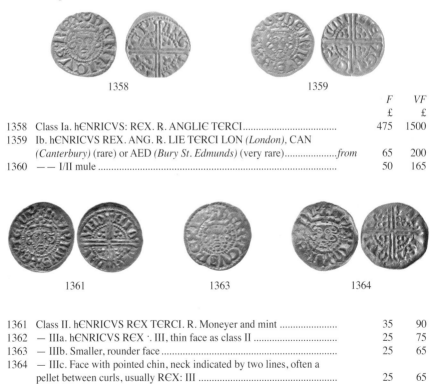

	1358		1359		

		F	VF
		£	£
1358	Class Ia. hENRICVS: REX. R̂. ANGLIE TERCI.......................	475	1500
1359	Ib. hENRICVS REX. ANG. R̂. LIE TERCI LON *(London)*, CAN		
	(Canterbury) (rare) or AED *(Bury St. Edmunds)* (very rare)......*from*	65	200
1360	— — I/II mule	50	165

| | 1361 | | 1363 | | 1364 |

1361	Class II. hENRICVS REX TERCI. R. Moneyer and mint	35	90
1362	— IIIa. hENRICVS REX ·. III, thin face as class II	25	75
1363	— IIIb. Smaller, rounder face	25	65
1364	— IIIc. Face with pointed chin, neck indicated by two lines, often a		
	pellet between curls, usually REX: III	25	65

For further reading see: The Brussels Hoard of 1908. The Long Cross Coinage of Henry III by Ron Churchill and Bob Thomas. Also - Mints and Moneyers During the Reign of Henry III by Ron Churchill.

With sceptre

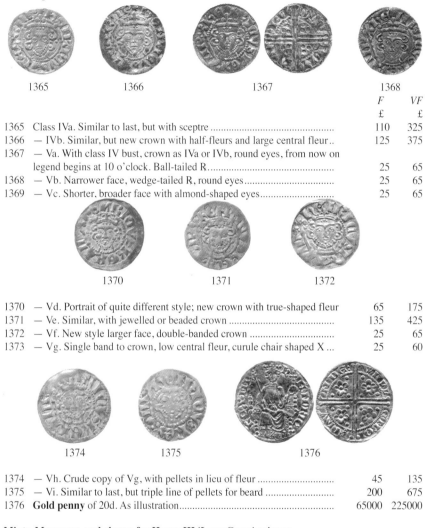

1365   1366   1367   1368

	F £	VF £
1365 Class IVa. Similar to last, but with sceptre	110	325
1366 — IVb. Similar, but new crown with half-fleurs and large central fleur ..	125	375
1367 — Va. With class IV bust, crown as IVa or IVb, round eyes, from now on legend begins at 10 o'clock. Ball-tailed R	25	65
1368 — Vb. Narrower face, wedge-tailed R, round eyes	25	65
1369 — Vc. Shorter, broader face with almond-shaped eyes	25	65

1370   1371   1372

1370 — Vd. Portrait of quite different style; new crown with true-shaped fleur	65	175
1371 — Ve. Similar, with jewelled or beaded crown	135	425
1372 — Vf. New style larger face, double-banded crown	25	65
1373 — Vg. Single band to crown, low central fleur, curule chair shaped X ...	25	60

1374   1375   1376

1374 — Vh. Crude copy of Vg, with pellets in lieu of fleur	45	135
1375 — Vi. Similar to last, but triple line of pellets for beard	200	675
1376 **Gold penny** of 20d. As illustration...	65000	225000

Mints, Moneyers, and classes for Henry III 'Long Cross' coinage

Fine

London: Davi or David (IIIc-Vf), Henri (IIIa-Vd, f, g), Ion, Ioh, Iohs or Iohan (Vc-g), Nicole (Ib/II mule, II-Vc), Renaud (Vg-i), Ricard (IIIc-Vg), Robert (Vg), Thomas (Vg), Walter (Vc-g), Willem (Vc-g and gold penny)   20

Bristol: Elis (IIIa, b, c), Henri (IIIb) , Iacob (IIIa, b, c), Roger (IIIa, b, c), Walter (IIIb, c)   25

Bury St. Edmunds: Ion or Iohs (II-Va, Vg, h, i), Randulf (Va-f), Renaud (Vg), Stephane (Vg)   25

Fine

Canterbury: Alein (Vg, h), Ambroci (Vg), Gilbert (II-Vd/c mule, Vf, g), Ion, Ioh,
Iohs, or Iohanes (IIIc-Vd, f, g), Nicole or Nichole (Ib/II mule, II-Vh), Ricard
(Vg, h), Robert (Vc-h), Roger (Vh), Walter (Vc-h), Willem or Willeme
(Ib/II mule, II-Vd, f, g)... 20

Carlisle: Adam (IIIa, b), Ion (IIIa, b), Robert (IIIa, b), Willem (IIIa, b)............. 50

Durham: Philip (IIIb), Ricard (V, b, c), Roger (Vg), Willem (Vg)...................... 70

Exeter: Ion (II-IIIc), Philip (II-IIIc), Robert (II-IIIc), Walter (II-IIIb)................. 30

Gloucester: Ion (II-IIIc), Lucas (II-IIIc), Ricard (II-IIIc), Roger (II-IIIc)........... 35

Hereford: Henri (IIIa, b), Ricard (IIIa, b, c), Roger (IIIa, b, c), Walter (IIIa, b, c) 40

Ilchester: Huge (IIIa, b, c), Ierveis (IIIa, b, c), Randulf (IIIa, b, c), Stephe
(IIIa, b, c) 70

Lincoln: Ion (II-IIIc), Ricard (II-IIIc), Walter (II-IIIc), Willem (II-IIIc)............. 25

Newcastle: Adam (IIIa, b), Henri (IIIa, b, c), Ion (IIIa, b, c), Roger (IIIa, b, c).. 25

Northampton: Lucas (II-IIIb), Philip (II-IIIc), Tomas (II-IIIc), Willem (II-IIIc) 25

Norwich: Huge (II-IIIc), Iacob (II-IIIc), Ion (II-IIIc), Willem (II-IIIc) 30

Oxford: Adam (II-IIIc), Gefrei (II-IIIc), Henri (II-IIIc), Willem (II-IIIc)........... 35

Shrewsbury: Lorens (IIIa, b, c), Nicole (IIIa, b, c), Peris (IIIa, b, c), Ricard (IIIa, b, c) 45

Wallingford: Alisandre (IIIa, b), Clement (IIIa, b), Ricard (IIIa, b), Robert (IIIa, b) 60

Wilton: Huge (IIIb, c), Ion (IIIa, b, c), Willem (IIIa, b, c) 35

Winchester: Huge (II-IIIc), Iordan (II-IIIc), Nicole (II-IIIc), Willem (II-IIIc) 25

York: Alain (II-IIIb), Ieremie (II-IIIb), Ion (II-IIIc), Rener (II-IIIc), Tomas (IIIb, c) 25

EDWARD I, 1272-1307

'Long Cross' coinage (1272-78). With name hЄNRICVS
The earliest group of Edward's Long Cross coins are of very crude style and known only of Durham
and Bury St. Edmunds. Then, for the last class of the type, pennies of much improved style were
issued at London, Durham and Bury, but in 1279 the Long Cross coinage was abandoned and a
completely new coinage substituted.

Cut halfpennies and farthings also occur for this issue, and within this context are not especially rare.

1377 1378

	F	VF
	£	£
1377 Class VI. Crude face with new realistic curls, Є and N ligate..................	25	80
1378 — VII. Similar, but of improved style, usually with Lombardic U..........	65	225

Mints, moneyers, and classes for Edward I 'Long Cross' coinage

London: Phelip (VII), Renaud (VII) ....*from*	40	
Bury St. Edmunds: Ioce (VII), Ion or Ioh (VI, VII) ....*from*	25	
Durham: Roberd (VI), Robert (VII) ....*from*	250	

New Coinage (from 1279).

A major re-coinage was embarked upon in 1279 which introduced new denominations. In addition to the penny, halfpence and farthings were also minted and, for the first time, a fourpenny piece called a 'Groat', wt. 89 grs., (from the French *Gros*).

The groats, though ultimately unsuccessful, were struck from more than thirty obverse dies and form an extensive series with affinities to the pence of classes 1c to 3g. The chronology of this series has now been definitively established (see Allen, M. The Durham Mint, pp. 172-179).

As mint administration was now very much centralized, the practice of including the moneyer's name in the coinage was abandoned (except for a few years at Bury St. Edmunds). Several provincial mints assisted with the re-coinage during 1279-81, then minting was again restricted to London, Canterbury, Durham and Bury.

The provincial mints were again employed for a subsidiary re-coinage in 1300 in order to remint lightweight coins and the many illegal *esterlings* (foreign copies of the English pennies, mainly from the Low Countries), which were usually of poorer quality than the English coins.

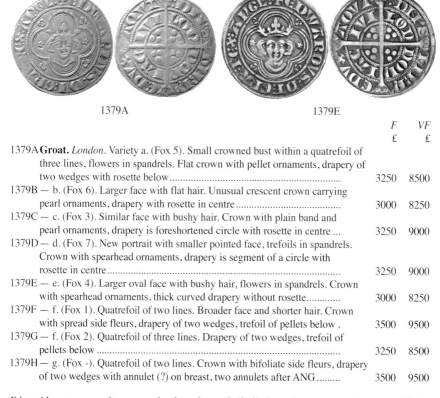

1379A   1379E

	F £	VF £
1379A **Groat.** *London.* Variety a. (Fox 5). Small crowned bust within a quatrefoil of three lines, flowers in spandrels. Flat crown with pellet ornaments, drapery of two wedges with rosette below	3250	8500
1379B — b. (Fox 6). Larger face with flat hair. Unusual crescent crown carrying pearl ornaments, drapery with rosette in centre	3000	8250
1379C — c. (Fox 3). Similar face with bushy hair. Crown with plain band and pearl ornaments, drapery is foreshortened circle with rosette in centre ...	3250	9000
1379D — d. (Fox 7). New portrait with smaller pointed face, trefoils in spandrels. Crown with spearhead ornaments, drapery is segment of a circle with rosette in centre	3250	9000
1379E — e. (Fox 4). Larger oval face with bushy hair, flowers in spandrels. Crown with spearhead ornaments, thick curved drapery without rosette	3000	8250
1379F — f. (Fox 1). Quatrefoil of two lines. Broader face and shorter hair. Crown with spread side fleurs, drapery of two wedges, trefoil of pellets below .	3500	9500
1379G — f. (Fox 2). Quatrefoil of three lines. Drapery of two wedges, trefoil of pellets below	3250	8500
1379H — g. (Fox -). Quatrefoil of two lines. Crown with bifoliate side fleurs, drapery of two wedges with annulet (?) on breast, two annulets after ANG	3500	9500

Edward I groats were often mounted as brooches and gilt. Such specimens are worth considerably less

1382   1383

	F £	VF £

1380 **Penny.** *London.* Class 1a. Crown with plain band, ЄDW RЄX; Lombardic
ᥒ on *obv;* pellet 'barred' S on rev. A with sloping top 275 900
1381 — 1b. — ЄD RЄX; no drapery on bust, Roman N 1250 4750
1382 — 1c. — ЄDW RЄX; Roman N, normal or reversed; small lettering 25 100
1383 — 1d. — ЄDW R;—; large lettering and face 25 90

1384   1385   1386

1384 — — — Annulet below bust 90 350
1385 — 2a. Crown with band shaped to ornaments; usually broken left petal
to central fleur portrait as 1d. N usually reversed 20 60
1386 — 2b. — tall bust; long neck; N reversed 20 60

1388

1387 — 3a. Crescent-shaped contraction marks; pearls in crown, drapery is
foreshortened circle with hook ends 25 85
1388 — 3b. — — drapery is segment of a circle, pearls in crown 25 80
1389 — 3c. — normal crown; drapery in one piece, hollowed in centre 20 60

1391   1392   1394

1390 — 3d. — — drapery in two pieces, broad face 20 60
1391 — 3e. — long narrow face (Northern mints) 20 65
1392 — 3f. — broad face, large nose, rougher work, late S first used............. 25 90
1393 — 3g. — Spread crown small neat bust, narrow face 20 60
1394 — 4a. Comma-shaped contraction mark, late S always used, C and Є open 25 65

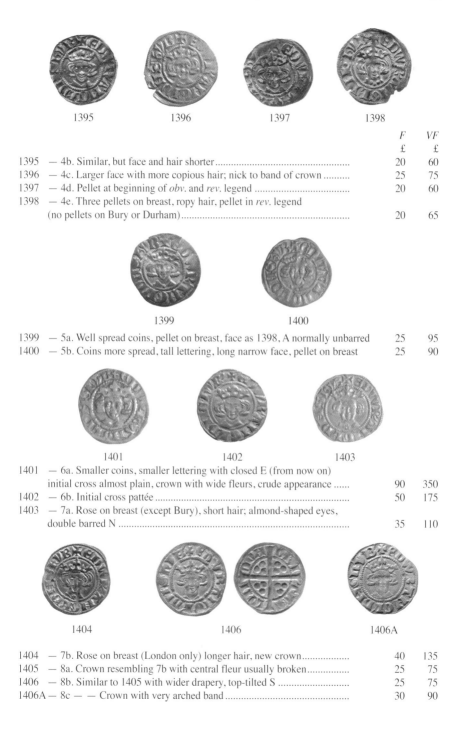

	1395	1396	1397	1398

		F	*VF*
		£	£
1395	— 4b. Similar, but face and hair shorter...................................	20	60
1396	— 4c. Larger face with more copious hair; nick to band of crown..........	25	75
1397	— 4d. Pellet at beginning of *obv*. and *rev*. legend..................................	20	60
1398	— 4e. Three pellets on breast, ropy hair, pellet in *rev*. legend (no pellets on Bury or Durham)...	20	65

	1399	1400

1399	— 5a. Well spread coins, pellet on breast, face as 1398, A normally unbarred	25	95
1400	— 5b. Coins more spread, tall lettering, long narrow face, pellet on breast	25	90

	1401	1402	1403

1401	— 6a. Smaller coins, smaller lettering with closed E (from now on) initial cross almost plain, crown with wide fleurs, crude appearance......	90	350
1402	— 6b. Initial cross pattée..	50	175
1403	— 7a. Rose on breast (except Bury), short hair; almond-shaped eyes, double barred N	35	110

	1404	1406	1406A

1404	— 7b. Rose on breast (London only) longer hair, new crown..................	40	135
1405	— 8a. Crown resembling 7b with central fleur usually broken.................	25	75
1406	— 8b. Similar to 1405 with wider drapery, top-tilted S	25	75
1406A	— 8c — — Crown with very arched band..	30	90

1407

	F £	VF £

1407 — 9a. Drapery of two wedges, pellet eyes, crown of 8a-b or new flatter
one; often star on breast 20 55

1408 — 9b. Small coins; Roman N, normal, un-barred, or usually of pot-hook
form; often star or (very rarely) pellet on breast. Some Durham coins are
from locally made dies... 20 55

1408A– 9c. Larger crude lettering with barred A and abbreviation marks.
(only found in combination with dies of 9b or 10ab, except Bury).......... 35 120

1409 - 10ab   1409B - 10ab

1409 — 10ab. ЄDWARD. Bifoliate crown (converted 9b or new taller one).
Narrow incurved lettering.. 20 45

1409A— 10ab. Similar with annulet on breast or a pellet each side of head
and on breast 70 200

1409B — 10ab. ЄDWAR (rarely ЄDWR). Similar to 1409. A few early coins
have the trifoliate crown of 9b.. 20 45

1410   1411

Crown 1   Crown 2   Crown 3   Crown 4   Crown 5

1410 — 10cf1. Crown 1 (Axe-shaped central fleur, wedge-shaped petals).
ЄDWA from now on. Stub-tailed. R.. 20 45

1411 — 10cf2. Crown 2 (Well-shaped central lis, no spearheads). Spreading hair. 20 45

1413   1414

		F £	VF £
1412	— 10cf3. Crown 3 (Left-hand arrowhead inclines to right). Early coins have the broken lettering of 10cf2; later have new lettering with round-backed Є.	20	45
1413	— 10cf4. Crown 4 (Neat with hooked petal to right-hand side fleur)	25	75
1414	— 10cf5. Crown 5 (taller and more spread, right-hand ornament inclines to left). Later coins are on smaller flans.	20	50

Some of the coins of class 10cf3 (c.1307-9), and all of the coins of classes 10cf4 and 10cf5 (c.1309-10), were struck in the reign of Edward II.

For a more detailed classification of Class 10, see 'Sylloge of British Coins, 39, The J. J. North Collection, Edwardian English Silver Coins 1279-1351', The Classification of Class 10, c. 1301-10, by C. Wood.

Prices are for full flan, well struck coins.

The prices for the above types are for London. For coins of the other mints see following pages; types are in brackets, prices are for the commonest type of each mint.

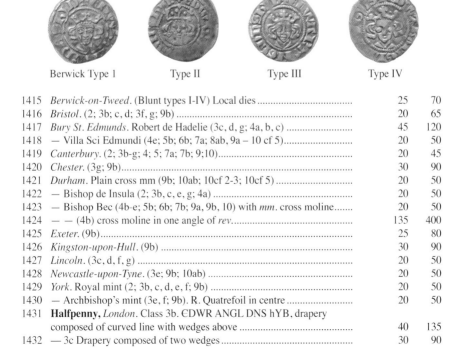

Berwick Type 1   Type II   Type III   Type IV

1415	*Berwick-on-Tweed*. (Blunt types I-IV) Local dies	25	70
1416	*Bristol*. (2; 3b; c, d; 3f, g; 9b)	20	65
1417	*Bury St. Edmunds*. Robert de Hadelie (3c, d, g; 4a, b, c)	45	120
1418	— Villa Sci Edmundi (4e; 5b; 6b; 7a; 8ab, 9a – 10 cf 5)	20	50
1419	*Canterbury*. (2; 3b-g; 4; 5; 7a; 7b; 9;10)	20	45
1420	*Chester*. (3g; 9b)	30	90
1421	*Durham*. Plain cross mm (9b; 10ab; 10cf 2-3; 10cf 5)	20	50
1422	— Bishop de Insula (2; 3b, c, e, g; 4a)	20	50
1423	— Bishop Bec (4b-e; 5b; 6b; 7b; 9a, 9b, 10) with *mm*. cross moline	20	50
1424	— — (4b) cross moline in one angle of *rev*.	135	400
1425	*Exeter*. (9b)	25	80
1426	*Kingston-upon-Hull*. (9b)	30	90
1427	*Lincoln*. (3c, d, f, g)	20	50
1428	*Newcastle-upon-Tyne*. (3e; 9b; 10ab)	20	50
1429	*York*. Royal mint (2; 3b, c, d, e, f; 9b)	20	50
1430	— Archbishop's mint (3e, f; 9b). R. Quatrefoil in centre	20	50
1431	**Halfpenny,** *London*. Class 3b. ЄDWR ANGL DNS hYB, drapery composed of curved line with wedges above	40	135
1432	— 3c Drapery composed of two wedges	30	90

1434A

	F £	*VF* £
1433 — 3g. New wide crown, thick-waisted S, drapery as 3b............................	25	80
1433A — — 4c. Narrower crown, drapery of two unequal wedges	30	110
1433B — — Similar, pellet before LON	45	140
1434 — 4e. Single-piece collar with (usually) three pellets on breast	50	160
1434A — 6. Small face with short hair, large coarse crown, closed Є	55	175
1435 — 7. Larger face with square jaw, open Є, usually double-barred N	45	135
1436 — 8. Similar, new crown with straight sides..	50	160
1437 — 10. ЄDWAR R ANGL DNS hYB, bifoliate or trifoliate crown, new waisted letters	30	100

The above prices are for London; halfpence of the mints given below were also struck.

	F	*VF*
1438 *Berwick-on-Tweed*. (Blunt types I, II and III)...........................	50	150
1439 *Bristol*. Class 3c, 3g, 4c	35	110
1440 *Lincoln*. Class 3c...	40	125
1441 *Newcastle*. Class 3e, single pellet in each angle of *rev.*............	55	150
1442 *York*. Class 3c-e..	35	110

1443A   1445

1443 **Farthing,** *London*. Class 1a. Base silver issue (6.65 grains), ЄDWARDVS RЄX. bifoliate crown with no intermediate jewels, inner circle. R. LONDONIЄNSIS, (rarely LONDRIЄNSIS), ...	60	200
1443A — 1c. Similar trifoliate crown	45	140
1444 — 2. Smaller face, trifoliate crown with intermediate jewels	30	110
1445 — 3c. New tapering face, wide at top, crown with curved band.............	30	110
1445A — 3de. Sterling silver issue (5.51 grains.) Є R ANGLIЄ bust (usually) to bottom of coin, no inner circle. R. LONDONIЄNSIS	35	120
1446 — 3g. Similar, new wide crown with curving side fleurs.	30	110
1446A — 4de. Similar to 3de. R. CIVITAS LONDON	45	160
1446B — 5. Similar, crude wide crown.	45	160
1447 — 6-7. New large face with wide cheeks, pellet or almond eyes............	35	125
1448 — 8. Similar, small rounded face, tall crude crown	35	125
1449 — 9a. Є R ANGL DN, small tapering face, (a variety has the face of class 6-7)...	40	150
1449A — 9b. Small ugly face, usually wide crown with outwards-sloping sides..	45	175
1450 — 10 ЄDWARDVS REX (-, A, AN or ANG,) large bust within inner circle. *Type 1450 often appears on oval flans.*	20	80

It is now thought that the order of London Farthings is class 4de, 6-7, 5, 9a, 8, 9b

1446   1452

	F	VF
	£	£
1451 *Berwick-on-Tweed*. (Blunt type I, IIIb)	125	400
1452 *Bristol*. Class 2, 3c, 3de	35	125
1453 *Lincoln*. Class 3de	40	135
1453A *Newcastle*. Class 3de, Ŗ NOVI CASTRI	225	750
1454 *York*. Class 2, 3c, 3de	40	135

For further information see: *Farthings and Halfpennies, Edward I and II*, P. and B R Withers, 2001

EDWARD II, 1307-27

The coinage of this reign differs only in minor details from that of Edward I. No groats were issued in the years *c*. 1282-1351.

1458 (12a)   1459 (13)   1460 (14)

1461 (15a)   1462 (15b)   1463 (15c)

		F	VF
1455	**Penny,** *London*. Class 11a. Broken spear-head or pearl on l. side of crown; long narrow face, straight-sided N; round back to C and Є	20	65
1456	— 11b. — Є with angular back (till 15b), N with well-marked serifs (late)	20	65
1457	— 11c. — — A of special form	45	135
1458	— 12a. Central fleur of crown formed of three wedges; thick cross mm	25	80
1458A	— 12b — Crown with diamond-shaped petals and cruciform central fleur; cross of four wedges mm	50	175
1458B	— 12c — Crown with heart-shaped petals; cross pattée mm	65	225
1459	— 13. Central fleur of crown as Greek double axe	25	70
1460	— 14. Crown with tall central fleur; large smiling face with leering eyes	20	65
1461	— 15a. Small flat crown with both spear-heads usually bent to l.; face of 14	25	80
1462	— 15b. — very similar, but smaller face	25	70
1463	— 15c. — large face, large Є	25	80

Berwick Type V   Type VI   Type VII

		F £	VF £
1464	*Berwick-on-Tweed*. (Blunt types V, VI and VII) Local dies except V......	30	85
1465	*Bury St. Edmunds*. (11; 12; 13; 14; 15)...	20	65
1466	*Canterbury*. (11; 12a; 13; 14; 15)	20	65
1467	*Durham*. King's Receiver (11a), *mm*. plain cross....................................	20	70
1468	— Bishop Bec. (11a), *mm*. cross moline	20	70
1469	— Bishop Kellawe (11; 12a; 13), crozier on *rev*.	20	70
1470	— Bishop Beaumont (13; 14; 15), *mm*. lion with lis................................	25	85
1471	*mm*. plain cross (11a, 14, 15c)	65	175

1472

1472	**Halfpenny,** *London*. Class 10-11, ЄDWARDVS REX (-, A, AN, ANG, ANGL or ANGLI,) bifoliate or trifoliate crown	45	175
1473	— *Berwick-on-Tweed*. (Blunt type V)	90	275

1474

1474	**Farthing,** *London*. Class 11, 13, ЄDWARDVS REX (-, A, AN, or AG), face with pellet eyes..	30	100
1475	— *Berwick-on-Tweed*. (Blunt type V)	100	375

During Edward's early years small quantities of silver coin were minted following the standard of the previous two reigns, but in 1335 halfpence and farthings were produced which were well below the .925 Sterling silver standard. In 1344 an impressive gold coinage was introduced comprising the Double Florin or Double Leopard valued at six shillings, and its half and quarter, the Leopard and the Helm. The design of the Florin was based on the contemporary gold of Philip de Valois of France.

The first gold coinage was not successful and it was replaced later the same year by a heavier coinage, the Noble, valued at 6s. 8d, i.e., 80 pence, half a mark or one third of a pound, together with its fractions. The Noble was lowered in weight in two stages over the next few years, being stabilized at 120 grains in 1351. With the signing of the Treaty of Bretigni in 1360 Edward's title to the Kingdom of France was omitted from the coinage, but it was resumed again in 1369.

In 1344 the silver coinage had been re-established at the old sterling standard, but the penny was reduced in weight to just over 20 grains and in 1351 to 18 grains. Groats were minted again in 1351 and were issued regularly henceforth until the reign of Elizabeth.

Subsequent to the treaty with France which gave England a cross-channel trading base at Calais, a mint was opened there in 1363 for minting gold and silver coins of English type. In addition to coins of the regular English mints, the Abbot of Reading also minted silver pence, halfpence and farthings with a scallop shell in one quarter of the reverse while coins from Berwick display one or two boar's or bear's heads.

There is evidence of re-use of dies at later periods, e.g. 3rd coinage halfpennies.

For further study of the English Hammered Gold Coinage see: Sylloge of Coins of the British Isles, 47, the Herbert Schneider Collection Volume One, by Peter Woodhead. 1996.

Mintmarks

6	1	2	3	74	4	5	7a

1334-51	Cross pattée (6)	1356	Crown (74)
1351-2	Cross 1 (1)	1356-61	Cross 3 (4)
1351-7	Crozier on cross end (76a, *Durham*)	1361-9	Cross potent (5)
1352-3	Cross 1 broken (2)	1369-77	Cross pattée (6)
1354-5	Cross 2 (3)		Plain cross (7a)

The figures in brackets refer to the plate of mintmarks in Appendix III.

GOLD

Third coinage, 1344-51, First period, 1344

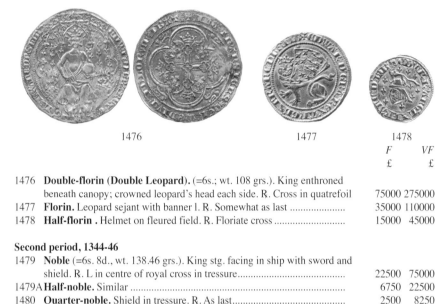

1476   1477   1478

F	*VF*
£	£

1476 **Double-florin (Double Leopard).** (=6s.; wt. 108 grs.). King enthroned
beneath canopy; crowned leopard's head each side. R. Cross in quatrefoil 75000 275000
1477 **Florin.** Leopard sejant with banner l. R. Somewhat as last 35000 110000
1478 **Half-florin .** Helmet on fleured field. R. Floriate cross 15000 45000

Second period, 1344-46
1479 **Noble** (=6s. 8d., wt. 138.46 grs.). King stg. facing in ship with sword and
shield. R. L in centre of royal cross in tressure....................................... 22500 75000
1479A **Half-noble.** Similar 6750 22500
1480 **Quarter-noble.** Shield in tressure. R. As last.. 2500   8250

1481

1482

Third period, 1346-51
1481 **Noble** (wt. 128.59 grs.). As 1479, but Є in centre; large letters 2500   9000
1482 **Half-noble.** Similar 2750   9500
1483 **Quarter-noble.** As 1480, but Є in centre 375   1050

Fourth coinage, 1351-77
Reference: L. A. Lawrence, *The Coinage of Edward III from 1351.*
Pre-treaty period, 1351-61. With French title.

		F	VF
		£	£
1484	**Noble** (wt. 120 grs.), series B (1351). Open Є and C, Roman M; *mm.* cross 1 (1)	1150	3750
1485	— — *rev.* of series A (1351). Round lettering, Lombardic M and N; closed inverted Є in centre	1250	4250
1486	C (1351-1352). Closed Є and C, Lombardic M; *mm.* cross 1 (1)	750	2400
1487	D (1352-1353). *O.* of series C. R. *Mm.* cross 1 broken (2)	1750	6000

1490   1498

1488	E (1354-1355). Broken letters, V often has a nick in r. limb; *mm.* cross 2 (3)	750	2250
1489	F (1356). *Mm.* crown (74)	1200	4000
1490	G (1356-1361). *Mm.* cross 3 (4). Many varieties	700	2100
1491	**Half-noble,** B. As noble with *rev.* of series A, but closed Є in centre not inverted	675	2250
1492	C. *O.* as noble. *Rev.* as last	750	2500
1493	E. As noble	1100	3500
1494	G. As noble. Many varieties	625	1850
1495	**Quarter-noble,** B. Pellet below shield. R. Closed Є in centre	350	850
1496	C. *O.* of series B. *Rev.* details as noble	425	1050
1497	E. *O.* as last. *Rev.* details as noble, pellet in centre	375	925
1498	G. *Mm.* cross 3 (4). Many varieties	325	725

Transitional treaty period, 1361. French title omitted, replaced by that of Aquitaine on the noble and (rarely) on the half-noble, but not on the quarter-noble; irregular sized letters; *mm.* cross potent (5).

1499

| 1499 | **Noble.** R. Pellets or annulets at corners of central panel | 975 | 3250 |

1504

		F £	VF £
1500	**Half-noble.** Similar	525	1500
1501	**Quarter-noble.** Similar. Many varieties. Pellet and rarely Є in centre....	300	625

Treaty period, 1361-69. Omits FRANC, new letters, usually curule-shaped X; *mm.* cross potent(5).

1502	**Noble.** *London.* Saltire or nothing before ЄDWARD	800	2400
1503	— Annulet before ЄDWARD (with, rarely, crescent on forecastle)........	750	2250
1504	*Calais.* C in centre of *rev.,* flag at stern of ship	850	2500
1505	— — without flag	850	2500

1506   1508

1506	**Half-noble.** *London.* Saltire before ЄDWARD	550	1500
1507	— Annulet before ЄDWARD	575	1600
1508	*Calais.* C in centre of *rev.,* flag at stern of ship	800	2500
1509	— — without flag..	850	2750
1510	**Quarter-noble.** *London.* As 1498. R. Lis in centre..............................	300	625
1511	— — annulet before ЄDWARD	300	625
1512	*Calais.* R. Annulet in centre...	325	700
1513	— — cross in circle over shield	325	750
1514	— R. Quatrefoil in centre; cross over shield	400	950
1515	— — crescent over shield...	425	975

Post-treaty period, 1369-1377. French title resumed.

1516	**Noble.** *London.* Annulet before ЄD. R. Treaty period die....................	1350	4250
1517	— — — crescent on forecastle...	950	2850
1518	— — post-treaty letters. R. Є and pellet in centre..............	850	2500
1519	— — — R. Є and saltire in centre..	975	3000
1520	*Calais.* Flag at stern. R. Є in centre..	900	2750

1521

		F £	VF £
1521	— — *Rev.* as 1518, with Є and pellet in centre	850	2500
1522	— As 1520, but without flag. R. Є in centre	900	2750
1523	**Half-noble.** *London. O.* Treaty die. *Rev.* as 1518	1650	5500
1524	*Calais.* Without AQT, flag at stern. R. Є in centre	1350	4500
1525	— — R. Treaty die with C in centre	1500	5000

SILVER

First coinage, 1327-35 (0.925 fineness)

1526   1530

1526	**Penny.** *London.* As Edw. II; Fox class XVd with Lombardic Ɲ's	275	850
1527	*Bury St. Edmunds.* Similar	350	1000
1528	*Canterbury; mm.* cross pattée with pellet centre	200	525
1529	— — three extra pellets in one quarter	175	500
1530	*Durham.* R. Small crown in centre	575	1500
1530A	*Reading.* R. Escallop in 2nd quarter	675	1750
1531	*York.* As 1526, but quatrefoil in centre of *rev;* three extra pellets in TAS quarter	165	450
1532	— — — pellet in each quarter of *mm*	165	450

1535   1537   1539

1534	— — — Roman N's on *obv.*	165	450
1535	*Berwick* (1333-1342, Blunt type VIII). Bear's head in one quarter of *rev.*	525	1500
1536	**Halfpenny.** *London.* Indistinguishable from EDWARD II (cf. 1472)	45	175
1537	*Berwick* (Bl. VIII). Bear's head in one or two quarters	85	250
1538	**Farthing.** *London.* Indistinguishable from those of EDWARD II (cf. 1474)	30	100
1539	*Berwick* (Bl. VIII). As 1537	75	225

1540   1542

		F £	*VF* £

Second coinage, 1335-43 (0.833 fineness)

1540 **Halfpenny.** *London.* ЄDWARDVS RЄX AN(G). Six-pointed star after
AN and before LON. Bifoliate or trifoliate crown. 25   80

1540A — — New tall crown. Star of eight or six points after ANG and DON
and before CIVI or none on rev. 25   85

1541 *Reading.* Escallop in one quarter, star before or after mint 200   650

1542 **Farthing.** *London.* A (N), six-pointed star after A (rarely omitted) and
before LON, flat crown... 25   80

1542A — ANG, star after ANG and before LON or after DON, tall crown........ 25   85

Third or florin coinage, 1344-51. Bust with bushy hair. (0.925 fine, 20 grs.)

1543   1544

Reverses: I. Lombardic **n** II. Roman N. III. Reversed N. IV. Reversed Double-barred N.

1543 **Penny.** Fox proposed 'Class XVI'. *London.* Class 1. ЄDW, Lombardic N. Rev. I.   20   95
1544 — — Class 2, ЄDWA, Lombardic N. Rev. I, II. 20   90
1545 — — Class 3. ЄDW. Roman N. Rev. I, II, III. 20   90
1546 — — Class 4. ЄDW. Reversed N. Rev. I, II, III, IV (doubtful) 20   90
1546A — Unusual types designated A to E. 35   125
1547 — Canterbury. Class 2. as 1544. Rev. I. 60   175
1548 — — Class 4. as 1546 Rev. I. 50   150
1549 *Durham,* Sede Vacante (possibly 1345 issues of Bishop Richard de Bury
or Bishop Hatfield). A, ЄDWR rev. No marks 35   120
1550 — — B, similar, ЄDWAR R... 40   135
1551 — Bp. Hatfield. C, similar, but pellet in centre of *rev.* 35   130
1552 — — — Crozier on *rev.*.. 40   130
1553 — — — — with pellet in centre of *rev.* 45   135
1554 — — D, ЄDWARDVS RЄX AI**n**, crozier on *rev.* 65   200

1555

1555 *Reading. obv.* as 1546. **R**. Escallop in one quarter................................... 175   650
1555A — — ЄDWARDVS RЄX A**n**G. Rev. as 1555...................................... 180   675
1556 *York. obv.* as 1546. **R**. Quatrefoil in centre 30   100

1557

1558

		F £	VF £
1557	**Halfpenny.** *London*. ЄDWARDVS RЄX	20	80
1558	— — ЄDWARDVS RЄX An.	20	80

1559

1561

1562

		F £	VF £
1559	— — as 1558 with pellet or small saltire each side of crown and/or in one reverse quarter	30	110
1560	— *Reading*. as 1557. Rev. Escallop in one quarter.	225	625
1561	— — as 1558. Rev. as 1560.	235	650
1562	**Farthing.** *London*. ЄDWARDVS RЄX	25	100
1562A	*Reading*. As S.1562. Rev. as 1560	250	800
1562B	— — ЄDWARDVS RЄX An. Rev. as 1560	275	850

Fourth coinage, 1351-77

Reference: L. A. Lawrence, *The Coinage of Edward III from 1351*.

A large variety of mules exist between styles and issue.

Pre-treaty period, 1351-61. With French title.

1563

1565

1567

		F £	VF £
1563	**Groat** (=4d., 72 grs.). *London,* series B (1351). Roman M, open C and Є; *mm*. cross 1	150	525
1564	— — — crown in each quarter	2500	8000
1565	— C (1351-2). Lombardic M, closed C and Є, R with wedge-shaped tail; *mm*. cross 1	45	200
1566	— D (1352-3). R with normal tail; *mm*. cross 1 or cross 1 broken (2)	50	225
1567	— E (1354-5). Broken letters, V often with nick in r. limb; *mm*. cross 2 (3)	40	160

		F £	VF £
1568	— — — lis on breast	50	240
1569	— F (1356). *Mm.* crown (74)..	60	240

1570   1572

1570	— G (1356-61). Usually with annulet in one quarter and sometimes under bust, *mm.* cross 3 (4). Many varieties	40	175
1571	*York*, series D. As London	185	650
1572	— E. As London	50	225

1573   1581

1573	**Halfgroat.** *London*, series B. As groat	80	275
1574	— C. As groat	30	120
1575	— D. As groat	40	135
1576	— E. As groat	35	125
1577	— F. As groat	40	135
1578	— G. As groat	35	125
1579	— — — annulet below bust	40	140
1580	*York*, series D. As groat..	70	250
1581	— E. As groat	45	150
1582	— — — lis on breast	65	225
1583	**Penny.** *London*. Series A (1351). Round letters, Lombardic m and n, annulet in each quarter; *mm.* cross pattee	80	275

1584   1585   1591

1584	— C. Details as groat, but annulet in each quarter	20	90
1585	— D. Details as groat, but annulet in each quarter	25	95
1586	— E. Sometimes annulet in each quarter................................	20	90
1587	— F. Details as groat..	25	95
1588	— G. Details as groat...	20	85
		F	VF

		£	£
1589	— — — annulet below bust	25	100
1590	— — — saltire in one quarter	35	135
1591	*Durham*, Bp. Hatfield. Series A. As 1583, but extra pellet in each quarter, VIL LA crozier DVRRℂM and VIL crozier LA DVRRℂM	70	275
1592	— C. Details as groat. R. Crozier, CIVITAS DVNℂLMIℂ	25	95
1593	— D — — —	25	100
1594	— E — — —	30	110
1595	— F — R. Crozier, CIVITAS DVRℂMℂ	25	100
1596	— G — — —	25	100
1597	— — — — — annulet below bust	30	110
1598	— — — — — saltire in one quarter	35	145
1599	— — — — — annulet on each shoulder	30	135
1600	— — — — — trefoil of pellets on breast	30	130
1601	— — — R. Crozier, CIVITAS DVRℂLMIℂ	45	165
1602	*York*, Royal Mint. Series D	30	110
1603	— — E	25	95
1604	— Archb. Thoresby. Series D. R. Quatrefoil in centre	30	120
1605	— — G —	25	100
1606	— — — annulet or saltire on breast	30	125

| 1607 | 1609 | 1609A |

1607	**Halfpenny.** *London*. Series E. ℂDWARDVS RℂX Aℿ	70	275
1608	— G, but with *obv*. of F (*mm*. crown). Annulet in one quarter	110	425
1609	**Farthing.** *London*. Series E. ℂDWARDVS RℂX	100	375
1609A	— — Series G. Annulet in one quarter	125	450

Transitional treaty period, 1361. French title omitted, irregular sized letters; *mm*. cross potent (5).

| 1610 | **Groat.** *London*. Annulet each side of crown .... | 575 | 2250 |

| 1611 | 1612 | 1615 |

1611	**Halfgroat.** Similar, but only seven arches to tressure	125	425
1612	**Penny,** *London*. Omits RℂX, annulet in two upper qtrs. of *mm*	75	275
1613	*York,* Archb. Thoresby. Similar, but quatrefoil enclosing pellet in centre of *rev*.	50	175
1614	*Durham*. Bp. Hatfield. Similar. R. Crozier, CIVITAS DORℂLMℂ	65	200
1615	**Halfpenny.** Two pellets over *mm*., ℂDWARDVS RℂX Aℿ	110	450

Treaty period, 1361-69. French title omitted, new letters, usually 'Treaty' X, rarely curule chair X
mm. cross potent (5).

		F £	*VF* £
1616	**Groat,** *London*. Many varieties	75	250
1617	— Annulet before CDWARD	80	275
1618	— Annulet on breast	135	525

1617   1618

1619	*Calais*. As last	150	475

1620

1620	**Halfgroat,** *London*. As groat	50	175
1621	— — Annulet before CDWARDVS	50	175
1622	— — Annulet on breast	60	200
1623	*Calais*. As last	110	325
1624	**Penny,** *London*. CDWARD ANGL R, etc	35	125
1625	— — — pellet before CDWARD	40	135
1626	*Calais*. R. VILLA CALCSIE	110	375
1627	*Durham*. R. CIVITAS DVNCLMIS	50	175
1628	— R. Crozier, CIVITAS DVRCMC	40	135
1629	*York*, Archb. Thoresby. Quatrefoil in centre of *rev.*, CDWARDVS DCI G RCX AN	40	135
1630	— — — CDWARDVS RCX ANGLI	30	110
1631	— — — — quatrefoil before CD and on breast	35	120
1632	— — — — annulet before CD	35	120
1633	— — — CDWARD ANGL R DNS HYB	40	135
1634	**Halfpenny.** CDWARDVS RCX AN, pellet stops	30	110

1635   1636

1635	— Pellet before CD, annulet stops	30	110
1636	**Farthing.** CDWARDVS RCX, pellet or no stops	150	525

Post-treaty period, 1369-77. French title resumed, X like St. Andrew's cross; *mm.* 5, 6, 7a.

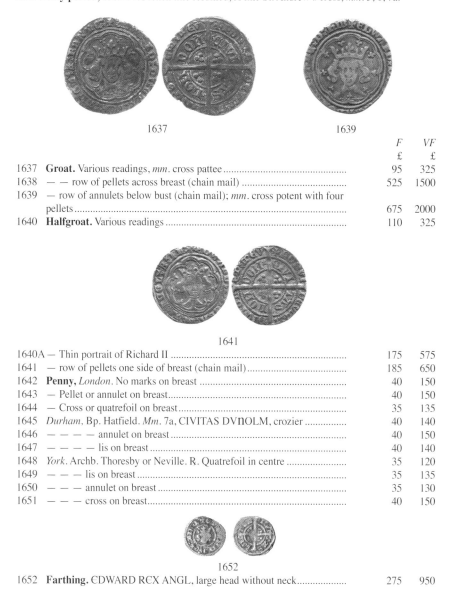

1637   1639

		F	VF
		£	£
1637	**Groat.** Various readings, *mm.* cross pattee	95	325
1638	— — row of pellets across breast (chain mail)	525	1500
1639	— row of annulets below bust (chain mail); *mm.* cross potent with four pellets	675	2000
1640	**Halfgroat.** Various readings	110	325

1641

1640A	— Thin portrait of Richard II	175	575
1641	— row of pellets one side of breast (chain mail)...................................	185	650
1642	**Penny,** *London.* No marks on breast	40	150
1643	— Pellet or annulet on breast...	40	150
1644	— Cross or quatrefoil on breast..	35	135
1645	*Durham,* Bp. Hatfield. *Mm.* 7a, CIVITAS DVΠOLM, crozier	40	140
1646	— — — — annulet on breast	40	150
1647	— — — — lis on breast	40	140
1648	*York.* Archb. Thoresby or Neville. R. Quatrefoil in centre	35	120
1649	— — — lis on breast...	35	135
1650	— — — annulet on breast	35	130
1651	— — — cross on breast...	40	150

1652

1652	**Farthing.** CDWARD RCX ANGL, large head without neck...................	275	950

For further reading see:
Halfpennies and Farthings of Edward III and Richard II. *Paul and Bente R. Withers, 2002.*

There was no change in the weight standard of the coinage during this reign and the coins evolve from early issues resembling those of Edward III to late issues similar to those of Henry IV.

There is no overall, systematic classification of the coins of Richard II but a coherent scheme for the gold coinage has been worked out and is published in the Schneider Sylloge (SCBI 47). This classification has been adopted here.

Reference: *Silver coinages of Richard II, Henry IV and V.* (B.N.J. 1959-60 and 1963).

Mintmark: cross pattée (6)

GOLD

		F £	VF £
1653	**Noble,** *London.* Style of Edw. III. IA. Lis over sail	1500	4500

1654   1658

1654	— IB. Annulet over sail	975	3000
1655	French title omitted. IIA. Crude style, saltire over sail. IIB. Fine style, trefoil over sail. IIC. Porcine style, no mark over sail	975	3000
1656	French title resumed. IIIA. Fine style, no marks	1050	3250
1657	— IIIB. Lis on rudder. IIIC. Trefoil by shield	1100	3500
1658	Henry IV style. IVA. Escallop on rudder. IVB. Crescent on rudder	1500	4500
1659	*Calais.* Style of Edw. III, IA, Edw. III lettering.......................................	2250	7500
1660	Style of Edw. III. IB. New lettering. Voided quatrefoil over sail	1200	3750

1661

1661	French title omitted. IIA. Crude style, no marks. IIB. Fine style, trefoil over sail. IIC. Porcine style, no marks...	1050	3250
1662	French title resumed. IIIA. Fine style, no marks	1100	3500
1663	— IIIB. Lion on rudder. IIIC. Two pellets by shield	1650	5000

	F	VF
	£	£

1664 **Half-noble,** *London*. With altered *obv.* of Edw. III. Usually muled with *rev.* or altered *rev.* of Edw. III 1350 4500

1665   1673

1665	Style of Edw. III. IB. No marks or saltire over sail	1100	4000
1666	French title omitted. IIA. New style, no marks	1250	4250
1667	French title resumed. IIIA. No marks. IIIB. Lion on rudder	1250	4250
1668	Henry IV style. IVB. Crescent on rudder	1650	5000
1669	*Calais*. Mule with *obv.* or *rev.* of Edw. III	2000	6500
1670	Style of Edw. III. IB. Quatrefoil over sail	1750	5500
1671	Late style. French title. IIIA. No marks. IIIB. Saltire by rudder	1650	5000
1672	**Quarter-noble,** *London*. IA. R in centre of *rev.*	475	1200
1673	IB Lis in centre of *rev.*	425	950
1674	— lis or cross over shield	450	1100

1675   1677

1675	IIIA. Pellet in centre of *rev.*	425	950
1676	IIIB. Trefoil of annulets over shield or trefoils in spandrels.....................	550	1350
1677	IVA. Escallop over shield	475	1200

SILVER

1680

1678	**Groat.** I. Style of Edw. III, F *(i.e. et)* before FRANC, etc.	500	1750
1679	II. New lettering, retrograde Z before FRANC, etc.................................	450	1650
1680	III. Bust with bushy hair, 'fishtail' serifs to letters	525	1850
1681	IV. New style bust and crown, crescent on breast	1500	6000

1682

	F	VF
	£	£
1682 **Halfgroat.** II. New lettering; with or without French title	275	850
1683 III. As 1680	300	950
1684 — — with *obv*. die of Edw. III (1640A)..	375	1250
1685 IV. As 1681, with or without crescent on breast	625	2000
1686 **Penny,** *London*. I Lettering as 1678, RICARDVS RЄX AПGLIЄ	165	575
1688 — II. As 1679, Z FRAПC lis on breast	175	600

1688   1692

1689 — III. As 1680, RICARD RЄX AnGLIЄ, fish-tail letters.......................	185	650
1690 *York*. I. Early style, usually with cross or lis on breast, quatrefoil in centre of *rev*	45	225
1691 — II. New bust and letters, no marks on breast......................................	45	225
1692 — Local dies. Pellet above each shoulder, cross on breast, REX AПGLIE or AПGILIE	50	250
1693 — — — RЄX DNS ЄB..	80	375
1694 — — — RЄX AПG FRAПC	75	350
1695 — III. As 1680, RЄX AПGL Z FRAПC (scallop after TAS)	75	325
1696 — IV. Very bushy hair, new letters, R. R in centre of quatrefoil	135	575
1697 *Durham*. Cross or lis on breast, DVПOLM...	110	450

1698   1699   1701   1704A

1698 **Halfpenny.** Early style. LONDON, saltire or annulet (rare) on breast	45	150
1699 Intermediate style. LOПDOП, no marks on breast	35	100
1700 Type III. Late style. Similar, but fishtail letters	35	110
1700A Type IV. Short, stubby lettering	40	125
1701 **Farthing.** Small bust and letters..	110	400
1703 Similar but no neck	110	400
1704 Rose in each angle of *rev*. instead of pellets	135	525
1704A Large head with broad face as Henry IV	150	575

For further reading see:
Halfpennies and Farthings of Edward III and Richard II. P. and B. R. Withers, 2002.

HENRY IV, 1399-1413

In 1412 the standard weights of the coinage were reduced, the noble by 12 grains and the penny by 3 grains, partly because there was a scarcity of bullion and partly to provide revenue for the king, as Parliament had not renewed the royal subsidies. As in France, the royal arms were altered, three fleur-de-lis taking the place of the four or more lis previously displayed.

Mintmark: cross pattée (6)

GOLD

Heavy coinage, 1399-1412

1706   1707

		F	VF
		£	£
1705	**Noble** (120 grs.), *London.* Old arms with four lis in French quarters; crescent or annulet on rudder	6750	25000
1706	— New arms with three lis; crescent, pellet or no marks on rudder	6250	22500
1707	*Calais.* Flag at stern, old arms; crown on or to l. of rudder	8500	32500

1709

1708	— — new arms; crown or saltire on rudder	7000	25000
1709	**Half-noble,** *London.* Old arms	6250	18500
1710	— new arms	5750	17500
1711	*Calais.* New arms	7000	22500
1712	**Quarter-noble,** *London.* Crescent over old arms	1350	4000
1713	— — — new arms	1200	3750
1714	*Calais.* New arms. R̥. *Mm.* crown	1750	5000

1715

	F £	VF £

Light coinage, 1412-13

1715 **Noble** (108 grs.). Trefoil, or trefoil and annulet, on side of ship. ℞. Trefoil
      in one quarter .... | 1750 | 5500 |

1716 **Half-noble.** Similar, but always with annulet .... | 2250 | 7500 |

1717

1717 **Quarter-noble.** Trefoils, or trefoils and annulets beside shield, lis above. ℞.
      Lis in centre .... | 750 | 2250 |

SILVER

Heavy coinage, 1399-1412

1718   **Halfgroat** (36 grs.). Star on breast .... | 1500 | 5250 |
1718A — Muled with Edw. III (1640A) *obv.* .... | 750 | 2500 |
1719   **Penny,** *London.* Similar, early bust with long neck .... | 850 | 3000 |
1720   — later bust with shorter neck, no star on breast .... | 850 | 3000 |

1722

1723

1725

1722 *York* Bust with broad face, round chin .... | 525 | 1350 |
1723 **Halfpenny.** Early small bust .... | 240 | 650 |
1724 — later large bust, with rounded shoulders, ... | 250 | 675 |
1725 **Farthing.** Face without neck .... | 850 | 2500 |

Light coinage, 1412-13

1726   1732

		F	VF
		£	£
1726	**Groat** (60 grs.). I. Pellet to l., annulet to r. of crown; altered die of Richard II	3000	9500
1727	New dies; II. Annulet to l., pellet to r. of crown, 8 or 10 arches to tressure	2750	9000
1728	— III. Similar but 9 arches to tressure	2500	7500
1729	**Halfgroat.** Pellet to l., annulet to r. of crown	1050	3250
1730	Annulet to l., pellet to r. of crown	950	2750
1731	**Penny,** *London.* Annulet and pellet by crown; trefoil on breast and before CIVI	800	2250
1732	— — annulet or slipped trefoil before LON	850	2500
1733	— Pellet and annulet by crown	850	2500
1734	*York.* Annulet on breast. R. Quatrefoil in centre	450	1100
1735	*Durham.* Trefoil on breast, DVnOLM	425	975

1737   1738

1737	**Halfpenny.** New dies; annulets by crown or neck, or no marks	250	750
1738	**Farthing.** Face, no bust; trefoil after RCX	750	2250

For further information see:
Halfpennies and Farthings of Henry IV, V and VI. P. and B. R. Withers, 2003.

There was no change of importance in the coinage of this reign. There was, however, a considerable development in the use of privy marks which distinguished various issues, except for the last issue of the reign when most marks were removed. The Calais mint, which had closed in 1411, did not re-open until just before the end of the reign. There is now some uncertainty as to whether types A and B of Henry V should be given to Henry IV.

Mintmarks

Cross pattee (4)   Pierced cross with   Pierced cross (18).
                    pellet centre (20)

GOLD

		F	VF
		£	£
1739	**Noble.** A. Quatrefoil over sail and in second quarter of *rev.* Short broad letters, no other marks..	1850	6500
1740	— B. Ordinary letters; similar, or with annulet on rudder......................	975	3000
1741	— C. Mullet by sword arm, annulet on rudder..	950	2750

1742   1744

1742	— — broken annulet on side of ship..	900	2500
1743	—D. Mullet and annulet by sword arm, trefoil by shield, broken annulet on ship..	975	3000
1744	— E. Mullet, or mullet and annulet by sword arm, trefoil by shield, pellet by sword point and in one quarter, annulet on side of ship......................	950	2750
1745	— — Similar, but trefoil on ship instead of by shield.............................	975	3000
1746	— F. Similar, but no pellet at sword point, trefoil in one quarter...........	1050	3250
1747	— G. No marks; annulet stops, except for mullet after first word...........	1500	5000
1748	**Half Noble.** B. As noble; Hen. IV *rev.* die.......................................	2000	7500
1749	— C. Broken annulet on ship, quatrefoil below sail................................	975	3000
1750	— — Mullet over shield, broken annulet on *rev.*	925	2750
1751	— F. Similar, but no annulet on ship, usually trefoil by shield	1200	3500
1752	— F/E. As last, but pellet in 1st and annulet in 2nd quarter....................	1350	4250

1753

1756

		F £	VF £
1753	— G. As noble, but quatrefoil over sail, mullet sometimes omitted after first word of *rev*...	1050	3250
1754	**Quarter Noble.** A. Lis over shield and in centre of *rev*. Short broad letters; quatrefoil and annulet beside shield, stars at corners of centre on *rev*......	725	1750
1755	— C. Ordinary letters; quatrefoil to l., quat. and mullet to r. of shield	425	950
1756	— — — annulet to l., mullet to r. of shield	375	750
1757	— F. Ordinary letters; trefoil to l., mullet to r. of shield	400	900
1758	— G. — no marks, except mullet after first word	400	900

SILVER

1759

1759	**Groat.** A. Short broad letters; 'emaciated' bust	1350	4250
1760	— — muled with Hen. IV *obv*..	1750	5500
1761	— — muled with Hen. IV *rev*	1500	4750

	1762B		1767		
1762	B. Ordinary letters; 'scowling' bust..			425	1350
1762A	— — mullet in centre of breast			475	1500
1762B	— — mullet to r. of breast			725	2250
1763	— — muled with Hen. IV			1100	3500
1764	C. Normal 'frowning' bust..			250	850
1765	— — mullet on r. shoulder			150	525
1766	— — R muled with Hen. IV..			675	1850
1767	G. Normal 'frowning' bust; no marks..			375	1250
1768	**Halfgroat.** A. As groat, but usually with annulet and pellet by crown			575	2000

		F	VF
		£	£
1769	B. Ordinary letters; no marks	375	1250
1770	— — muled with Hen. IV *obv.*	1050	3250
1771	C. Tall neck, broken annulet to l. of crown	125	400
1772	— — — mullet on r. shoulder	140	525

| 1774 | 1775 | 1788 |

1773	— — — mullet in centre of breast	120	375
1774	F. Annulet and trefoil by crown, mullet on breast	125	425
1775	G. New neat bust: no marks	120	400
1776	**Penny.** *London*. Altered Hen. IV *obv.* with mullet added to l. of crown ..	750	2250
1777	— A. Letters, bust and marks as 1768	275	900
1778	— C. Tall neck, mullet and broken annulet by crown	45	175
1779	— D. Similar, but whole annulet	45	180
1780	— F. Mullet and trefoil by crown	45	180
1781	— G. New neat bust, no marks, DI GRA	50	200
1782	*Durham*. C. As 1778 but quatrefoil at end of legend	45	175
1783	— D. As 1779	45	175
1784	— G. Similar, but new bust. R. Annulet in one qtr.	45	180
1785	*York*. C. As 1778, but quatrefoil in centre of *rev*.	35	135
1786	— D. Similar, but whole annulet by crown	40	135
1787	— E. As last, but pellet above mullet	50	200
1788	— F. Mullet and trefoil by crown	35	135
1789	— — Trefoil over mullet to l., annulet to r. of crown	45	175
1790	— G. Mullet and trefoil by crown (London dies)	40	160

| 1791 | 1796 | 1798 |

1791	— — Mullet and lis by crown, annulet in one qtr. (usually local dies)....	40	150
1792	**Halfpenny.** A. Emaciated bust, annulets by crown	175	575
1793	— altered dies of Hen. IV	225	750
1794	C. Ordinary bust, broken annulets by crown	30	100
1795	D. Annulets, sometimes broken, by hair	30	110
1796	F. Annulet and trefoil by crown	30	110
1797	G. New bust; no marks, (usually muled with Henry VI annulet *rev*.)	45	150
1797A	**Farthing.** *London*. B. Very large head	475	1500
1798	— G. Small face with neck	375	900
1798A	*Calais*. G. as 1798, VILLA CALIS	475	1500

For further information see:
Halfpennies and Farthings of Henry IV, V and VI. P and B. R. Withers, 2003.

The supply of gold began to dwindle early in the reign, which accounts for the rarity of gold after 1426. The Calais mint had reopened just before the death of Henry V and for some years a large amount of coin was struck there. It soon stopped minting gold; the mint was finally closed in 1440. A royal mint at York was opened for a short time in 1423/4.

Marks used to denote various issues become more prominent in this reign and can be used to date coins to within a year or so.

Reference: C. A. Whitton Heavy Coinage of Henry VI. (B.N.J. 1938-41).

Mintmarks

| 136 | 7a | 105 | 18 | 133 | 8 | 9 | 15 |

1422-7	Incurved pierced cross (136)	
1422-3	Lis (105, York)	
1422-60	Plain cross (7a, intermittently	
	Lis (105, on gold)	
1422-27	Pierced cross (18)	
1460	Lis (105, on rev. of some groats)	

1422-34	Cross pommée (133)
1427-34	Cross patonce (8)
	Cross fleury (9)
1434-35	Voided cross (15)
1435-60	Cross fleury (9)

For Restoration mintmarks see page 198.

GOLD

1799

Annulet issue, 1422-c.1430

		F	VF
		£	£
1799	**Noble.** *London.* Annulet by sword arm, and in one spandrel on *rev.;* trefoil stops on *obv.* with lis after hENRIC, annulets on *rev.*, with mullet after IhC	900	2500
1800	— Similar, but *obv.* from Henry V die	1750	6500
1801	— As 1799, but Flemish imitative coinage	750	2000

1802

| 1802 | *Calais.* As 1799, but flag at stern and C in centre of *rev* | 1050 | 3250 |

		F	VF
		£	£
1803	— — with h in centre of *rev.*	975	3000
1804	*York.* As London, but with lis over stern	1350	4250

1805

1805	**Half-noble.** *London.* As 1799	725	2000
1806	— Similar, but *obv.* from Henry V die	1250	3750
1807	*Calais.* As noble, with C in centre of *rev.*	1350	4000
1808	— — with h in centre of *rev.*	1250	3750
1809	*York.* As noble	1500	4500
1810	**Quarter-noble.** *London.* Lis over shield; *mm.* large lis	300	700
1811	— — — trefoil below shield	325	750
1812	— — — pellet below shield	325	750
1813	*Calais.* Three lis over shield; *mm.* large lis	475	1100

1814   1819

1814	— Similar but three lis around shield	375	900
1815	— As 1810, but much smaller *mm*	325	750
1816	*York.* Two lis over shield	375	900

Rosette-mascle issue, c.1430-31

1817	**Noble.** *London.* Lis by sword arm and in *rev.* field; stops, rosettes, or rosettes and mascles	1850	5750
1818	*Calais.* Similar, with flag at stern	2250	6500
1819	**Half-noble.** *London.* Lis in *rev.* field; stops, rosettes and mascles	2750	9000
1820	*Calais.* Similar, flag at stern; stops, rosettes	3250	10500
1821	**Quarter-noble.** *London.* As 1810; stops, as noble	1100	3250
1822	— without lis over shield	1250	3500
1823	*Calais.* Lis over shield, rosettes r. and l., and rosette stops	1250	3500

Pinecone-mascle issue, c.1431-2/3

1824

		F	VF
		£	£
1824	**Noble.** Stops, pinecones and mascles	1850	5750
1825	**Half-noble.** *O*. Rosette-mascle die. R. As last	3250	10500
1826	**Quarter-noble.** As 1810, but pinecone and mascle stops	1250	3750

1828

Leaf-mascle issue, c.1432/3-6

1827	**Noble.** Leaf in waves; stops, saltires with two mascles and one leaf	3500	13500
1828	**Half-noble.** (Fishpool hoard and Reigate hoard)	3250	12000
1829	**Quarter-noble.** As 1810; stops, saltire and mascle; leaf on inner circle of *rev.*	1350	4250

Leaf-trefoil issue, c.1436-8

1830	**Noble.** Stops, leaves and trefoils	3000	10000
1830A	**Half-noble.**	3500	12500
1831	**Quarter-noble.** Similar	1350	4250

Trefoil issue, 1438-43

1832	**Noble.** Trefoil to left of shield and in *rev.* legend	3250	10500

Leaf-pellet issue, 1445-54

1833	**Noble.** Annulet, lis and leaf below shield	3500	12500

Cross-pellet issue, 1454-61

1834	**Noble.** Mascle at end of *obv.* legend..	4250	15000

Muling exists in Henry VI coins spanning two or three issues. Full flan coins in the smaller denominations are difficult to find.

SILVER

Annulet issue, 1422-30

1835   1836

		F	VF
		£	£
1835	**Groat.** *London.* Annulet in two quarters of *rev.*	50	150
1836	*Calais.* Annulets at neck. R. Similar	40	135
1837	— — no annulets on *rev.*	65	250

1838

1838	*York.* Lis either side of neck. R. As 1835	1350	4000
1839	**Halfgroat.** *London.* As groat	40	150

1840   1843

1840	*Calais.* As 1836	30	100
1841	— — no annulets on *rev.*	40	140
1843	*York.* As groat	750	2500

1845

1844	**Penny.** *London.* Annulets in two qtrs.	30	110
1845	*Calais.* Annulets at neck. R. As above	30	100

		F	VF
		£	£
1847	*York*. As London, but lis at neck	750	2250
1848	**Halfpenny.** *London*. As penny	20	75
1849	*Calais*. Similar, but annulets at neck	20	75

1850

1852

		F	VF
1850	*York*. Similar, but lis at neck	450	1350
1851	**Farthing.** *London*. As penny, but *mm*. cross pommée	100	300
1852	*Calais*. Similar, but annulets at neck	135	450
1852A	*York*. Similar, but lis at neck	575	1500

Annulet-trefoil sub-issue

1854

1855

		F	VF
1854	**Groat.** *Calais*, as 1836 but trefoil to l. of crown, R trefoil after POSVI and only one annulet	80	275
1855	**Halfgroat.** *Calais,* similar, usually a mule with annulet issue.	55	185
1856	**Penny.** *Calais*. Similar, only one annulet on *rev*	80	275

Rosette-mascle issue, 1430-31. All with rosettes (early) or rosettes and mascles somewhere in the legends.

		F	VF
1858	**Groat.** *London*.	75	250

1859

1861

		F	VF
1859	*Calais*	50	150
1860	— mascle in two spandrels	60	175
1861	**Halfgroat.** *London*.	100	375

	1862	1870	1872

		F £	VF £
1862	*Calais*	35	110
1863	— mascle in two spandrels	40	135
1864	**Penny.** *London*	175	525
1865	*Calais*	35	110
1866	*York.* Archb. Kemp. Crosses by hair, no rosette	30	110
1867	— — Saltires by hair, no rosette	35	135
1868	— — Mullets by crown	30	120
1869	*Durham,* Bp. Langley. Large star to l. of crown, no rosette, DVΠOLMI	55	160
1870	**Halfpenny,** *London*	25	90
1871	*Calais*	25	85
1872	**Farthing,** *London*	175	525
1873	*Calais. Mm.* cross pommée	200	675

Pinecone-mascle issue, 1431-32/3. All with pinecones and mascles in legends.

	1874	1876	

1874	**Groat,** London	50	150
1875	*Calais*	45	145
1876	**Halfgroat,** *London*	65	175
1877	*Calais*	50	135
1878	**Penny,** *London*	50	175
1879	*Calais*	40	125
1880	*York,* Archb. Kemp. Mullet by crown, quatrefoil in centre of *rev.*	40	135
1881	— — rosette on breast, no quatrefoil	40	135
1882	— — mullet on breast, no quatrefoil	45	150
1883	*Durham,* Bp. Langley. DVΠOLMI	50	165

	1884		1886	

		F	VF
		£	£
1884	**Halfpenny,** *London*	20	75
1885	*Calais*	25	85
1886	**Farthing,** *London*	135	475
1887	*Calais. Mm.* cross pommée	175	625

Leaf-mascle issue, 1432/3-6. Usually with a mascle in the legend and a leaf somewhere in the design.

1888	**Groat.** *London.* Leaf below bust, all appear to read DONDON	475	1350
1889	— — *rev.* of last or next coinage	150	525

	1890		1892	

1890	*Calais.* Leaf below bust, and usually below MЄVM	125	425
1891	**Halfgroat.** *London.* Leaf under bust, pellet under TAS and DON	150	475
1892	*Calais.* Leaf below bust, and sometimes on *rev.*	135	425
1893	**Penny.** *London.* Leaf on breast, no stops on *rev.*	65	200
1894	*Calais.* Leaf on breast and below SIЄ	75	225
1895	**Halfpenny.** *London.* Leaf on breast and on *rev.*	35	100
1896	*Calais.* Leaf on breast and below SIЄ	75	225

	1897		1902	

Leaf-trefoil issue, 1436-8. Mostly with leaves and trefoil of pellets in the legends.

1897	**Groat.** *London.* Leaf on breast	85	240
1898	— without leaf on breast	85	240
1899	*Calais.* Leaf on breast	475	1350
1900	**Halfgroat.** *London.* Leaf on breast; *mm.* plain cross	70	225
1901	— *O. mm.* cross fleury; leaf on breast	65	200
1902	— — without leaf on breast	70	225
1902A	*Calais.* leaf on breast, mule with leaf mascle *rev.*	175	575

	F	VF
	£	£
1903 **Penny.** *London*. Leaf on breast..	75	250
1903A*Calais*. Similar	275	750
1904 *Durham*, Bp. Neville. Leaf on breast. R. Rings in centre, no stops, DVnOLM	125	375

1905   1907

1905 **Halfpenny.** *London*. Leaf on breast	20	90
1906 — without leaf on breast..	20	95
1906A*Calais*. leaf on breast, mule with leaf mascle rev.	100	325
1907 **Farthing.** *London*. Leaf on breast; stops, trefoil and saltire on *obv*........	125	400

Trefoil issue, 1438-43. Trefoil of pellets either side of neck and in legend, leaf on breast.

1910

1908 **Groat.** *London*. Sometimes a leaf before LON.......................................	85	275
1909 — Fleurs in spandrels, sometimes extra pellet in two qtrs.......................	90	300
1910 — Trefoils in place of fleurs at shoulders, none by neck, sometimes extra pellets	100	325
1911 *Calais*..	275	900

1911A   1912A

1911A**Halfgroat,** *London* Similar, but trefoil after DEUM and sometimes after POSUI Mule only with leaf trefoil *obv*.............................	150	475
1911B — *Calais Obv*. Similar to 1911, mule with leaf mascle *rev*......................	275	850
1912 **Halfpenny,** *London*	25	100
1912A**Farthing,** *London*	175	650

Trefoil pellet issue, 1443-5

1913

F	*VF*
£	£

1913 **Groat.** Trefoils by neck, pellets by crown, small leaf on breast; sometimes
extra pellet in two quarters 125   450

1915   1917

Leaf-pellet issue, 1445-54. Leaf on breast, pellet each side of crown, except where stated.

		F	*VF*
1914	**Groat.** ANGL; extra pellet in two quarters	65	225
1915	*Similar,* but ANGLI	65	225
1916	— — trefoil in *obv.* legend	85	300
1917	Leaf on neck, fleur on breast, R often extra pellet in two quarters	65	220
1918	As last, but two extra pellets by hair	275	1000
1919	**Halfgroat.** As 1914 *mm.* Cross patonce	90	300
1920	Similar, but *mm.* plain cross, some times no leaf on breast, no stops	75	250
1921	**Penny.** *London.* Usually extra pellets in two quarters	55	160
1922	— — pellets by crown omitted	55	175
1923	— — trefoil in legend	60	185
1924	*York,* Archb. Booth. R. Quatrefoil and pellet in centre	40	135
1925	— — two extra pellets by hair (local dies)	40	135
1926	*Durham,* Bp. Neville. Trefoil in *obv.* legend. R. Two rings in centre of cross	60	175

1928   1930

		F	*VF*
1927	— — Similar, but without trefoil...	60	175
1928	**Halfpenny.** Usually extra pellet in two quarters	20	75
1929	— *mm.* plain cross	20	75
1930	**Farthing.** As last	135	475

Unmarked issue, 1453-4

1931   1935

		F	VF
		£	£
1931	**Groat.** No marks on *obv.;* two extra pellets on *rev.*	625	1850
1932	— four extra pellets on *rev.*	750	2500
1933	**Halfgroat.** As 1931	350	1050

Cross-pellet issue, 1454-61

1934	**Groat.** Saltire either side of neck, pellets by crown, leaf and fleur on breast, extra pellets on *rev.*	725	2250
1935	Saltire on neck, no leaf, pellets by crown, usually mullets in legend; extra pellets on *rev.*	135	375
1936	— Similar, but mascles in place of mullets on *obv.*	145	400
1937	— — pellets by hair instead of by crown	200	675
1938	**Halfgroat.** Saltire on neck, pellets by crown and on *rev.*, mullets in legend	275	950

1940   1943   1944

1939	**Penny.** *London.* Saltire on neck, pellets by crown and on *rev.*, mascle(s), or mullet and mascle in legend	150	475
1940	*York,* Archb. Wm. Booth. Saltires by neck, usually leaf on breast, pellets by crown. R. Cross in quatrefoil in centre.	55	175
1941	*Durham,* Bp. Laurence Booth. Saltire and B or B only at neck, pellets by crown. R. Rings in centre	65	225
1942	**Halfpenny.** Saltires by neck, usually two extra pellets on *rev.*	35	125
1943	Similar, but saltire on neck, sometimes mullet after hЄnRIC	25	90
1944	**Farthing.** Saltire on neck, usually pellets by crown and on *rev.*, but known without either.	225	675

For further information see:
Halfpennies and Farthings of Henry IV, V and VI. P. and B. R. Withers, 2003.

Lis-pellet issue, 1456-61

1945

1945	**Groat.** Lis on neck; pellets by crown. R. Extra pellets	275	850

EDWARD IV, First Reign, 1461-70

In order to increase the supply of bullion to the mint the weight of the penny was reduced to 12 grains in 1464, and the current value of the noble was raised to 8s. 4d. Later, in 1465, a new gold coin was issued, the Ryal or 'Rose Noble', weighing 120 grains and having a value of 10s. However, as 6s. 8d. had become the standard professional fee the old noble was missed, and a new coin was issued to take its place, the Angel of 80 grains.

Royal mints were set up in Bristol, Coventry, Norwich and York to help with the recoinage. The Coventry and Norwich mints were not open for long, but the York and Bristol mints remained open until 1471 and 1472 respectively.

Reference: C. E. Blunt and C. A Whitton, The Coinage of Edward IV and Henry VI (Restored), B.N.J. 1945-7.

Mintmarks

105	9	7a	33	99	28	74	11

1461-4	Lis (105)	1467-70	Lis (105, *York*)	
	Cross fleury (9)	1467-8	Crown (74)	(often
	Plain cross (7a)		Sun (28)	combined)
1464-5	Rose (33 and 34)	1468-9	Crown (74)	(sometimes
1464-7	Pall (99, *Canterbury*)		Rose (33)	combined)
1465-6	Sun (28)	1469-70	Long cross	
1466-7	Crown (74)		fitchee (l.c.f) (11)	(often
			Sun (28)	combined)

GOLD

Heavy coinage, 1461-4

	F £	VF £

1946

1946	**Noble** (=6s. 8d., wt. 108 grs.). Normal type, but *obv.* legend commences at top left, lis below shield; *mm.*-/lis (Spink's sale May 1993)	4750	16000
1947	— Quatrefoil below sword arm; *mm.* rose/lis	5250	18000
1948	— R. Roses in two spandrels; *mm.* rose	6500	22500
1949	**Quarter-noble**	1750	5500

1950

	F	*VF*
	£	£

Light coinage, 1464-70

1950	**Ryal** or rose-noble (=10s., wt. 120 grs.), *London*. As illustration. Large fleurs in spandrels; *mm*. 33-74	750	2250
1951	— — Small trefoils in spandrels; *mm*. 74-11	750	2250

1952

1952	— Flemish imitative coinage (mostly 16th cent. on a large flan)	650	1500
1953	*Bristol*. B in waves, large fleurs; *mm*. sun, crown	1100	3250
1954	— — small fleurs in spandrels; *mm*. sun, crown	1200	3500
1955	*Coventry*. C in waves; *mm*. sun	1850	5750
1956	*Norwich*. Π in waves; *mm*. sun, rose	2000	6000
1957	*York*. Є in waves, large fleurs in spandrels, *mm*. sun, lis	1100	3250
1958	— — small fleurs, *mm*. sun. lis	1200	3500
1959	**Half-ryal.** *London*. As 1950	750	2000
1960	*Bristol*. B in waves; *mm*. sun, sun/crown	1500	4500
1961	*Coventry*. C in waves; *mm*. sun	5250	15000
1962	*Norwich*. Π in waves; *mm*. rose	4500	12500

1963   1965

		F £	VF £
1963	*York*. C in waves; *mm*. 28, 105, 33/105	750	2000
1963A	Similar but lis instead of C in waves (probably York)............................	975	3000
1964	**Quarter-ryal.** Shield in tressure of eight arcs, rose above. R. Somewhat as half ryal; *mm*. sun/rose	1350	4000
1965	Shield in quatrefoil. C above, rose on l., sun on r.; *mm*. 33/28-74/33	400	1100
1966	— — sun on l., rose on r.; *mm*. 74-11	425	1200

1967

1967	**Angel** (=6s. 8d., wt. 80 grs.). St. Michael spearing dragon. R. Ship, rays of sun at masthead, large rose and sun beside mast; *mm*.-/33	9000	30000
1968	— — small rose and sun at mast; *mm*.-/74	9500	32500

SILVER

1969   1972

Heavy coinage, 1461-4

1969	**Groat** (60 grs.). Group I, lis on neck, pellets by crown; *mm*. 9, 7a, 105, 9/105	165	475
1970	— Lis on breast, no pellets; *mm*. plain cross, 7a/105	175	525
1971	— — with pellets at crown; *mm*. plain cross..	200	575
1972	II, quatrefoils by neck, crescent on breast; *mm*. rose	165	500
1973	III, similar but trefoil on breast; *mm*. rose	150	475

1974   1979

	F £	VF £
1974 — — — eye in *rev.* inner legend, *mm.* rose	135	400
1975 — Similar, but no quatrefoils by bust	275	900
1976 — — Similar, but no trefoil on breast	200	600
1977 IV, annulets by neck, eye after TAS; *mm.* rose	375	1250
1978 **Halfgroat.** I, lis on breast, pellets by crown and extra pellets in two qtrs.; *mm.* 9, 7a	375	1500
1979 II, quatrefoils at neck, crescent on breast; *mm.* rose	300	900
1980 III, similar, but trefoil on breast, eye on rev.; *mm.* rose	250	650
1981 — Similar, but no mark on breast	250	650
1982 IV, annulets by neck, sometimes eye on *rev.; mm.* rose	275	800
1983 **Penny** (15 grs.), *London*. I, marks as 1978, but mascle after R꜀X; *mm.* plain cross	275	900
1984 II, quatrefoils by neck; *mm.* rose	200	625

1985   1991   1994

1985 III, similar, but eye after TAS; *mm.* rose	185	575
1986 IV, annulets by neck; *mm.* rose	200	600
1987 *York,* Archb. Booth. Quatrefoils by bust, voided quatrefoil in centre of *rev.; mm.* rose	120	325
1988 *Durham. O.* of Hen. VI. R. DVΠOLIΠ	120	325
1988A King's Receiver (1462-4). Local dies, mostly with rose in centre of rev.; *mm.* 7a, 33	30	120
1989 **Halfpenny.** I, as 1983, but no mascle	65	225
1990 II, quatrefoils by bust; *mm.* rose	40	135
1991 — saltires by bust; *mm.* rose	40	125
1992 III, no marks by bust; *mm.* rose	40	135
1992A —saltires by bust, eye after TAS, *mm.* rose	100	325
1993 IV, annulets by bust; *mm.* rose	40	135
1994 **Farthing.** I, pellets by crown, extra pellets on rev., with or without lis on breast	225	700
1994A II. saltires by bust; *mm.* rose	225	700
1994B III, no marks by bust; *mm.* rose	175	650

Light coinage, 1464-70. There is a great variety of groats and we give only a selection. Some have pellets in one quarter of the reverse, or trefoils over the crown; early coins have fleurs on the cusps of the tressure, then trefoils or no marks on the cusps, while the late coins have only trefoils.

		F £	VF £
1995	**Groat** (48 grs.), *London*. Annulets at neck, eye after TAS; *mm*. 33 (struck from heavy dies, IV)	110	400
1996	— — — Similar, but new dies, eye after TAS or DOn	125	450
1997	— Quatrefoils at neck, eye; rose (heavy dies, III)	100	325
1998	— — — Similar, but new dies, eye in *rev*. legend	100	325
1999	— No marks at neck, eye; *mm* rose	175	575

	2000 2002		
2000	— Quatrefoils at neck, no eye; *mm*. 33, 74, 28, 74/28, 74/33, 11/28	45	150
2001	— — — rose or quatrefoil on breast; *mm*. 33, 74/28	55	180
2002	— No marks at neck; *mm*. 28, 74, 11/28, 11	60	200
2003	— Trefoils or crosses at neck; *mm*. 11/33, 11/28, 11	55	175
2004	*Bristol*. B on breast, quatrefoils at neck; *mm*. 28/33, 28, 28/74, 74, 74/28	75	225
2005	— — trefoils at neck; *mm*. sun	90	350
2006	— — no marks at neck; *mm*. sun	175	575
2007	— Without B, quatrefoils at neck; *mm*. sun	150	525

Bristol is variously rendered as BRESTOLL, BRISTOLL, BRESTOW, BRISTOW.

2008	*Coventry*. C on breast, quatrefoils at neck, COVETRE; *mm*. 28/33, 28...	150	450
2009	— — Local dies, similar; *mm*. rose	185	575
2010	— — — as last, but no C or quatrefoils	185	575
2011	*Norwich*. n on breast, quatrefoils at neck, nORWIC or nORVIC, *mm*. 28/33, 28	135	375
2012	*York*. Є on breast, quatrefoils at neck; ЄBORACI; *mm*. 28, 105/74, 105, 105/28	65	225
2013	— Similar, but without Є on breast, *mm*. lis	135	475
2014	— C on breast, trefoils at neck; *mm*. 105/28, 105	75	275
2015	**Halfgroat.** *London*. Annulets by neck (heavy dies); *mm*. 33	225	750

2016

2016	— Quatrefoils by neck; *mm*. 33/-, 28/-, 74, 74/28	55	160
2017	— Saltires by neck; *mm*. 74, 74/28	65	180
2018	— Trefoils by neck; *mm*. 74, 74/28, 11/28	65	180
2019	— No marks by neck; *mm*. 11/28	90	275

		F £	*VF* £
2020	*Bristol.* Saltires or crosses by neck; *mm.* 33/28, 28, 74, 74/-	135	475
2021	— Quatrefoils by neck; *mm.* 28/-, 74, 74/-	125	425
2022	— Trefoils by neck; *mm.* crown	135	475
2023	— No marks by neck; *mm.* 74/28	150	500
2024	*Canterbury,* Archb. Bourchier (1464-7). Knot below bust; quatrefoils by neck; *mm.* 99/-, 99, 99/33, 99/28	45	150
2025	— — — quatrefoils omitted *mm.* 99	45	150
2026	— — — saltires by neck; *mm.* 99/-, 99/28	50	165
2026A	— — — trefoils by neck; *mm.* 99	50	175
2027	— — — wedges by hair and/or neck; *mm.* 99, 99/–, 99/33, 99/28	45	160
2028	— — As 2024 or 2025, but no knot	45	160
2029	— (1467-9). Quatrefoils by neck; *mm.* 74, 74/-	50	165
2030	— — Saltires by neck; *mm.* 74/-, 74	50	165
2031	— — Trefoils by neck; *mm.* 74, 74/-, 74/28, 33	45	150
2032	— No marks by neck; *mm.* sun	75	250
2033	*Coventry.* Crosses by neck; *mm.* sun	675	2000
2034	*Norwich.* Quatrefoils or saltires by neck; *mm.* sun	525	1500

2035   2063

2035	*York.* Quatrefoils by neck; *mm.* sun, lis, lis/-	75	275
2036	— Saltires by neck; *mm.* lis	70	250
2037	— Trefoils by neck; *mm.* lis, lis/-	80	300
2038	— Є on breast, quatrefoils by neck; *mm.* lis/-	75	275
2039	**Penny** (12 grs.), *London.* Annulets by neck (heavy dies); *mm.* rose	175	575
2040	— Quatrefoils by neck; *mm.* 74, sun. crown	60	200
2041	— Trefoil and quatrefoil by neck; *mm.* crown	60	200
2042	— Saltires by neck; *mm.* crown	60	200
2043	— Trefoils by neck; *mm.* crown, long cross fitchée	65	225
2044	— No marks by neck; *mm.* long cross fitchée	100	350
2045	*Bristol.* Crosses, quatrefoils or saltires by neck, BRISTOW; *mm.* crown	125	450
2046	— Quatrefoils by neck; BRI(trefoil)STOLL	135	500
2047	— Trefoil to r. of neck BRISTOLL	135	500
2048	*Canterbury,* Archb. Bourchier. Quatrefoils or saltires by neck, knot on breast; *mm.* pall	65	225
2049	— — Similar, but no marks by neck	65	225
2050	— — As 2048, but no knot	70	250
2051	— — Crosses by neck, no knot	70	225
2052	— Quatrefoils by neck; *mm.* crown	135	475
2053	— King's Receiver (1462-4). Local dies, mostly with rose in centre of rev.; *mm.* 7a, 33	30	120
2054	— *Durham,* Bp. Lawrence Booth (1465-70). B and D by neck, B on *rev.; mm.* 33	40	140
2055	— — Quatrefoil and B by neck; *mm.* sun	35	130
2056	— — B and quatrefoil by neck; *mm.* crown	40	140
2057	— — D and quatrefoil by neck; *mm.* crown	40	140
2058	— — Quatrefoils by neck; *mm.* crown	35	130
2059	— — Trefoils by neck; *mm.* crown	40	140
2060	— Lis by neck; *mm.* crown	35	130

		F £	VF £
2061	*York,* Sede Vacante (1464-5). Quatrefoils at neck, no quatrefoil in centre of *rev.; mm.* sun, rose	40	150
2062	— Archb. Neville (1465-70). Local dies, G and key by neck, quatrefoil on *rev.; mm.* sun, plain cross	30	120
2063	— — London-made dies, similar; *mm.* 28, 105, 11	35	140
2064	— — Similar, but no marks by neck; *mm.* large lis	40	150
2065	— — — Quatrefoils by neck; *mm.* large lis	40	150
2066	— — — Trefoils by neck; *mm.* large lis	35	140

2068   2077

		F £	VF £
2067	**Halfpenny,** *London.* Saltires by neck; *mm.* 34, 28, 74	25	100
2068	— Trefoils by neck; *mm.* 28, 74, 11	25	100
2069	— No marks by neck; *mm.* 11	35	135
2070	*Bristol.* Crosses by neck; *mm.* crown	90	325
2071	— Trefoils by neck; *mm.* crown	85	300
2072	*Canterbury.* Archb. Bourchier. No marks; *mm.* pall	65	200
2072A	— — — Trefoils by neck, *mm.* pall	65	200
2073	— Saltires by neck; *mm.* crown	60	175
2074	— — Trefoils by neck; *mm.* crown	60	175
2074A	*Norwich.* Quatrefoils by neck., *mm.* Sun	350	750
2074B	— — Trefoils by neck; *mm.* crown	475	950
2075	*York.* Royal mint. Saltires by neck; *mm.* lis/-, sun/-	45	140
2076	— — Trefoils by neck; *mm.* lis/-	40	130
2077	**Farthing,** *London.* ЄDWARD DI GRA RЄX, trefoils by neck, *mm.* crown	300	900

Full flan coins are difficult to find in the smaller denominations.

For further information see:
Halfpennies and Farthings of Edward IV to Henry VII. P. and B. R. Withers, 2004.

The coinage of this short restoration follows closely that of the previous reign. Only angel gold was issued, the ryal being discontinued. Many of the coins have the king's name reading hɛnRICV— another distinguishing feature is an R that looks like a B.

Mintmarks

Cross pattée (6)   Rose (33, Bristol)
Restoration cross (13)   Lis (105)
Trefoil (44 and 45)   Short cross fitchée (12)

GOLD

2078

		F £	*VF* £
2078	**Angel,** *London*. As illus. but no B; *mm*. -/6, 13, -/105, none	1500	4250
2079	*Bristol*. B in waves; *mm*. -/13, none	2750	7500
2080	**Half-angel,** *London*. As 2078; *mm*. -/6, -/13, -/105	4250	12500
2081	*Bristol*. B in waves; *mm*. -/13	5250	15000

SILVER

2082   2084   2087

2082	**Groat,** *London*. Usual type; *mm*. 6, 6/13, 6/105, 13, 13/6, 13/105, 13 /12	175	525
2083	*Bristol*. B on breast; *mm*. 13, 13/33, 13/44, 44, 44/13, 44/33, 44/12	325	950
2084	*York*. Є on breast; *mm*. lis, lis/sun	225	575
2085	**Halfgroat,** *London*. As 2082; *mm*. 13, 13/-	325	950
2086	*York*. Є on breast; *mm*. lis	425	1250
2087	**Penny,** *London*. Usual type; *mm*. 6, 13, 12	225	725
2087A	*Bristol*. Similar; *mm*. 12	375	1100
2088	*York*. G and key by neck; *mm*. lis	200	625
2089	**Halfpenny,** *London*. As 2087; *mm*. 12, 13,	175	525
2090	*Bristol*. Similar; *mm*. cross	250	750

The Angel and its half were the only gold denominations issued during this reign. The main types and weight standards remained the same as those of the light coinage of Edward's first reign. The use of the 'initial mark' as a mintmark to denote the date of issue was now firmly established.

Mintmarks

33	105	12	55	44	55	28	56	17

30	37	6	18	19	20	31	11	38

1471-83	Rose (33, *York & Durham*)	1473-7	Cross pattée (6)
	Lis (105, *York*)		Pierced cross 1 (18)
1471	Short cross fitchee (12)	1477-80	Pierced cross and
1471-2	Annulet (large, 55)		pellet (19)
	Trefoil (44)		Pierced cross 2 (18)
	Rose (33, *Bristol*)		Pierced cross, central
1471-3	Pansy (30, *Durham*)		pellet (20)
1472-3	Annulet (small, 55)		Rose (33, *Canterbury*)
	Sun (28, *Bristol*)	1480-3	Heraldic cinquefoil (31)
1473-7	Pellet in annulet (56)		Long cross fitchee
	Cross and four pellets (17)		(11, *Canterbury*)
	Cross in circle (37)	1483	Halved sun and rose (38)
			(Listed under Ed. IV/V.)

GOLD

2091   2093

		F	VF
		£	£
2091	**Angel.** *London.* Type as illus.; *mm.* 12, 55, 56, 17, 18, 19, 31	850	2250
2092	*Bristol.* B in waves; *mm.* small annulet	3500	10500
2093	**Half-angel.** As illus.; *mm.* 55, cross in circle, 19, 20/19, 31	725	2000
2094	King's name and title on rev.; *mm.* 12/-	800	2250
2095	King's name and the title both sides; *mm.* 55/-	950	2750

SILVER

2097

		F £	*VF* £
2096	**Groat,** *London.* Trefoils on cusps, no marks by bust; *mm.* 12-37	65	200
2097	— — roses by bust; *mm.* pellet in annulet..	110	375
2098	— Fleurs on cusps; no marks by bust; *mm.* 18-20...................................	65	200
2099	— — pellets by bust; *mm.* pierced cross	80	275
2100	— — rose on breast; *mm.* 31	65	200

2101   2107

2101	*Bristol.* B on breast no marks by bust; *mm.* 33, 33/55, 28/55, 55, 55/-, 28	200	575
2102	*York.* Є on breast no marks by bust; *mm.* lis...	175	525
2103	**Halfgroat,** *London.* As 2096; *mm.* 12-31	50	225
2104	*Bristol.* B on breast; *mm.* 33/12	250	750
2105	*Canterbury.* Archb. Bourchier. As 2103; *mm.* 33, 11, 11/31, 31	45	175
2106	— C on breast; *mm.* rose..	40	160
2107	— — Ŗ. C in centre; *mm.* rose..	40	160
2108	— — Ŗ. Rose in centre; *mm.* rose	40	160
2109	*York.* No. Є on breast; *mm.* lis	135	450
2110	**Penny,** *London.* No marks by bust; *mm.* 12-31	50	185
2111	*Bristol.* Similar; *mm.* rose...	150	525
2112	*Canterbury.* Archb. Bourchier. Similar; *mm.* 33, 11	65	225
2113	— C on breast; *mm.* rose..	75	250
2114	*Durham,* Bp. Booth (1471-6). No marks by neck; *mm.* 12, 44.................	30	100

2115   2116

2115	— — D in centre of *rev.;* B and trefoil by neck; *mm.* 44, 33, 56.............	30	100
2116	— — — two lis at neck; *mm.* rose..	30	110
2117	— — — crosses over crown, and on breast; *mm.* rose	30	110
2118	— — — crosses over crown, V under CIVI; *mm.* rose, pansy	35	110
2119	— — — B to l. of crown, V on breast and under CIVI............................	30	100

		F £	VF £
2120	— — As last but crosses at shoulders	30	100
2121	— — R. D in centre; *mm*. rose	30	110
2122	— Bp. Dudley (1476-83). V to r. of neck; as last	35	110

2123   2125   2131

2123	— — D and V by neck; as last, but *mm*. 31	30	100

Nos. 2117-2123 are from locally-made dies.

2124	*York,* Archb. Neville (1471-2). Quatrefoils by neck. R. Quatrefoil; *mm*. 12 (over lis)	45	165
2125	— — Similar, but G and key by neck; *mm*. 12 (over lis)	30	110
2126	— Neville suspended (1472-5). As last, but no quatrefoil in centre of *rev.*	35	135
2126A	— — no marks by bust, similar; *mm*. annulet	40	145
2127	— — No marks by neck, quatrefoil on *rev.; mm*. 55, cross in circle, 33..	30	110
2128	— — Similar but C and rose by neck; *mm*. rose	25	100
2129	— Archb. Neville restored (1475-6). As last, but G and rose	30	110
2130	— — Similar, but G and key by bust	25	100
2131	— Sede Vacante (1476). As 2127, but rose on breast; *mm*. rose	35	135
2132	— Archb. Lawrence Booth (1476-80). B and key by bust, quatrefoil on *rev.; mm*. 33, 31	25	100
2133	— Sede Vacante (1480). Similar, but no quatrefoil on rev.; *mm*. rose	35	120

2134   2140

2134	— Archb. Rotherham (1480-3). T and slanting key by neck, quatrefoil on *rev.; mm*. 33	30	110
2135	— — — Similar, but star on breast	40	135
2136	— — — Star on breast and to r. of crown	45	150
2137	**Halfpenny**, *London*. No marks by neck; *mm*. 12-31	20	80
2138	— Pellets at neck; *mm*. pierced cross	30	100
2139	*Canterbury* (Archbishop Bourchier). C on breast and in centre of *rev.; mm*. rose	75	225
2140	— C on breast only; *mm*. rose	70	200
2141	— Without C either side; *mm*. 11	70	200
2142	*Durham*, Bp. Booth. No marks by neck. R. DCRA̅ M, D in centre; *mm*. rose	150	450
2142A	— — Lis either side of neck. R. with or without D in centre	175	475
2142B	— — B to l. of crown, crosses at shoulders. R. with or without D. in centre; *mm*. rose	175	475
2143	— — — Bp. Dudley V to l. of neck; as last	150	450

Full flan coins are very difficult to find in the small denominations.

On 12th February, 1483, the prolific cinquefoil coinage of Edward IV came to an end and an indenture between the king and the new master of the mint, Bartholomew Reed, saw the introduction of the sun and rose mintmark.

Edward IV died on 9th April, 1483, but the sun and rose coinage continued, essentially unaltered, through the short reign of Edward V and into the reign of Richard III, ending with the indenture of 20th July, 1483, with Robert Brackenbury, who had been Richard's ducal treasurer, and the introduction of the boar's head mintmark.

New dies prepared after the accession of Richard III on 26th June, 1483, bear his name but coins of the sun and rose coinage struck under Edward IV and Edward V can only be distinguished by arranging the dies in sequence. This is possible for the angels (Schneider Sylloge, SCBI 47, p.41) but has not yet been achieved for the silver coinage.

Mintmark: Halved sun and rose.

GOLD

2144A

		F	*VF*
		£	£
2144	**Angel.** Type As 2091, reading EDWARD DEI GRA (Edward IV)	5500	15000
2144A	— Similar but reading EDWARD DI GRA (Edward V)	13500	35000
2145	**Half-angel.** As 2093 (probably Edward IV)...	4500	13500

SILVER

2146   2146A

2146	**Groat.** *London,* pellet below bust, reading EDWARD or EDVARD	1050	3500
2146A	— — No pellet below, reading EDWARD or EDWRD	950	3250
2147	**Penny.** *London* As 2110	975	3500
2148	**Halfpenny.** *London* As 2137	275	750

Richard's coinage follows the pattern of previous reigns. The portrait on the silver denominations remains stylised, though increasingly distinctive. It can be divided into three types according to mintmark. Type 1, the first sun and rose coinage, lasted 24 days to 20th July 1483. Type 2, the boar's head coinage, was issued until about June 1484. Type 3, the second sun and rose coinage, was struck until the end of the reign (Schneider Sylloge, SCBI 47, pp. 41-2).

It is evident that coin dies were stored in a 'loose-box' system which led to extensive muling between types. As an interim measure, after the indenture of 20th July, 1483, at least eleven existing sun and rose obverse dies, both gold and silver, were overpunched with the boar's head mark. The seven overpunched groat dies included four Edward IV/V dies, then still in use, and three dies of Richard III type 1.

Mintmarks

| SR1 | BH1 | BH2 | SR2 | SR3 | 105 | 33 |

Halved sun and rose, 1, 2 and 3.
Boar's head, 1 (62) 2 (63).
Lis (105, *Durham*)
Rose only (33).

GOLD

2150   2152

		F	VF
		£	£
2149	**Angel.** 1. Reading RICARD. R. R and rose by mast; *mm.* sun and rose 1	5250	15000
2150	— 2a. Reading EDWARD. R. E and rose or R and rose by mast; *mm.* boar's head 1 over sun and rose 1/sun and rose 1	9500	27500
2151	— 2b. Reading RICARD. R. R and rose by mast; mm. boar's head 1 over sun and rose 1/sun and rose 1, boar's head 1, boar's head 2 (often muled)	4250	12500
2152	— 3. Reading RICARD or RICAD; *mm.* sun and rose 2	3500	10500

2153

| 2153 | **Half-angel.** 2b. R. R and rose by mast; *mm.* boar's head 1 | 7500 | 22500 |

SILVER

2154   2155

	F £	VF £
2154 **Groat.** *London*. Reading RICARD 1. *mm*. sun and rose 1	675	1850
2155 — 2a. Reading EDWARD; *mm*. boar's head 1 over sun and rose 1/sun and rose 1	2000	5750

2156 - BH2   2158 - SR3

2156 — 2b. Reading RICARD; *mm*. boar's head 1 over sun and rose 1/sun and rose 1, boar's head 1, boar's head 2 (often muled)	850	2500
2157 — 3. *mm*. sun and rose 2, sun and rose 3	675	1800
2158 — — Pellet below bust, *mm*. sun and rose 2, sun and rose 3	725	2000
2159 *York*. 3. *mm*. sun and rose 2/-	2250	6500

2161   2164   2166

2160 **Halfgroat.** *London*. 2a. Reading EDWARD; *mm*. boar's head 1 over sun and rose 1/- (the *mm*. is indistinct)	2250	7500
2161 — 2b. Reading RICARD; *mm*. boar's head 2/-	1750	6250
2162 — 3. *mm*. sun and rose 2, sun and rose 2/-	1500	4750
2163 — — Pellet below bust; *mm*. sun and rose 2	1650	5500
2164 **Penny.** *London*. 2a. Reading EDWARD; *mm*. boar's head 1 over sun and rose 1/-	2000	6000
2165 — 2b. Reading RICARD; *mm*. boar's head 1/-	2500	7500
2166 *York*. Archb. Rotherham. T and upright key at neck. R. Quatrefoil in centre; *mm*. boar's head 1/-	375	1250
2167 — — *mm*. rose/-	350	1100
2168 — No marks at neck; *mm*. sun and rose 2/-	425	1350

2169   2171

2169 *Durham*. Bp. Sherwood. S on breast. R. D in centre; *mm*. lis/-................	300	900
2170 **Halfpenny.** *London*. 2b. No marks by neck; *mm*. boar's head 1/-	325	975
2171 — 3. *mm*. sun and rose 2/-	275	850
2171A**Farthing.** *London*. 3. *mm*. sun and rose 2/-...	1500	4500

HENRY VII, 1485-1509

For the first four years of his reign Henry's coins differ only in name and mintmark from those of his predecessors, but from 1489 radical changes were made in the coinage. On the Groat and subsequently on the lesser denominations the tradional open crown was replaced with an arched imperial crown. Though the pound sterling had been a denomination of account for centuries, a pound coin had never been minted. Now a magnificent gold pound was issued, and, from the design of the king enthroned in majesty, was called a 'Sovereign'. A small simplified version of the Sovereign portrait was at the same time introduced on the silver pence. The reverse of the gold 'Sovereign' had the royal arms set in the centre of a Tudor rose. A few years later the angel was restyled and St. Michael, who is depicted about to thrust Satan into the Pit with a cross-topped lance, is no longer a feathered figure but is clad in armour of Renaissance style. A gold ryal of ten shillings was also minted again for a brief period.

The other major innovation was the introduction of the shilling in the opening years of the 16th century. It is remarkable for the very fine profile portrait of the king which replaces the representational image of a monarch that had served on the coinage for the past couple of centuries. This new portrait was also used on groats and halfgroats but not on the smaller denominations.

Mintmarks

39	41	40	42	33	11	7a	123

105	76b	31	78	30	91	43	57

85	94	118	21	33	53

1485-7	Halved sun and rose (39)	1495-8	Pansy (30)
	Lis upon sun and rose (41)		Tun (123, *Canterbury*)
	Lis upon half rose (40)		Lis (105, York)
	Lis-rose dimidiated (42)	1498-9	Crowned leopard's head (91)
	Rose (33, *York*)		Lis issuant from rose (43)
1487	Lis (105)		Tun (123, *Canterbury*)
	Cross fitchée (11)	1499-1502	Anchor (57)
1487-8	Rose (33)	1502-4	Greyhound's head (85)
	Plain cross (7a, *Durham*)		Lis (105, profile issue only)
1488-9	No marks		Martlet (94, *York*)
1489-93	Cinquefoil (31)	1504-5	Cross-crosslet (21)
	Crozier (76b, *Durham*)	1504-9	Martlet (94, (*York, Canterbury*)
1492	Cross fitchée (11, gold only)		Rose (33, *York* and
1493-5	Escallop (78)		*Canterbury*)
	Dragon (118, gold only)	1505-9	Pheon (53)
	Lis (105, *Canterbury and York*)		
	Tun (123, *Canterbury*)		

GOLD

		F £	*VF* £
2172	**Sovereign** (20s; wt. 240 gr.). Group I. Large figure of king sitting on backless throne. ℞. Large shield crowned on large Tudor rose. *mm*. 31 ..	75000	300000
2173	— Group II. Somewhat similar but throne has narrow back, lis in background. ℞. Large Tudor rose bearing small shield. *mm*. -/11	65000	250000

2174

		F	*VF*
2174	— III. King on high-backed very ornamental throne, with greyhound and dragon on side pillars. ℞. Shield on Tudor rose; *mm*. dragon	32500	125000
2175	— IV. Similar but throne with high canopy breaking legend and broad seat, *mm*. 105/118, (also with no *obv*. i.c. *mm*. 105/118, very rare)	30000	110000
2176	— Narrow throne with a portcullis below the king's feet (like Henry VIII); *mm*. 105/21, 105/53	25000	90000
2177	**Double-sovereign** and **Treble-sovereign** from same dies as 2176. These piedforts were probably intended as presentation pieces *mm*. 105/21, 105/53	85000	350000

2178

		F	*VF*
2178	**Ryal** (10s.). As illustration: *mm*. -/11	30000	125000
2179	**Angel** (6s. 8d). I. Angel of old type with one foot on dragon. ℞. PϾR CRVCϾM. etc., *mm*. 39, 40, (also muled both ways)..............................	1500	4500
2179A	— With Irish title, and legend over angel head. mm. 33/-........................	1650	4750
2180	— — Name altered from RICARD? and h on *rev*. from R. mm. 41/39, 41/40, 41/-, 39/?	1750	5250

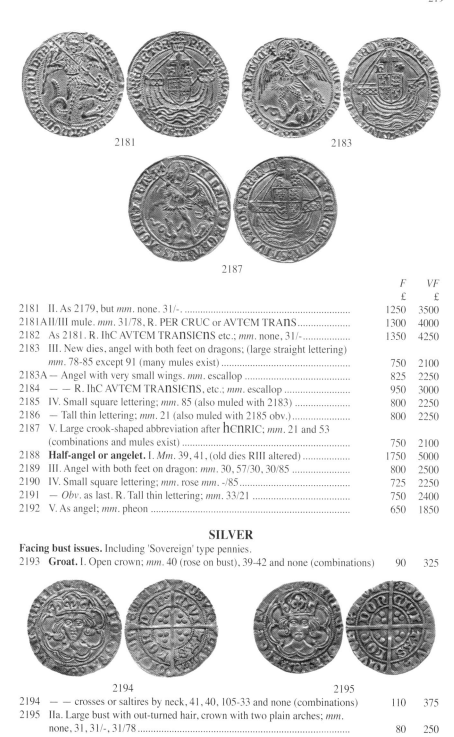

2181   2183

2187

		F	VF
		£	£
2181	II. As 2179, but *mm*. none. 31/-.	1250	3500
2181A	II/III mule. *mm*. 31/78, R. PER CRUC or AVTEM TRAns	1300	4000
2182	As 2181. R. IhC AVTEM TRAnSIEnS etc.; *mm*. none, 31/-	1350	4250
2183	III. New dies, angel with both feet on dragons; (large straight lettering) *mm*. 78-85 except 91 (many mules exist)	750	2100
2183A	— Angel with very small wings. *mm*. escallop	825	2250
2184	— — R. IhC AVTEM TRAnSIEnS, etc.; *mm*. escallop	950	3000
2185	IV. Small square lettering; *mm*. 85 (also muled with 2183)	800	2250
2186	— Tall thin lettering; *mm*. 21 (also muled with 2185 obv.)	800	2250
2187	V. Large crook-shaped abbreviation after hEnRIC; *mm*. 21 and 53 (combinations and mules exist)	750	2100
2188	**Half-angel or angelet.** I. *Mm*. 39, 41, (old dies RIII altered)	1750	5000
2189	III. Angel with both feet on dragon: *mm*. 30, 57/30, 30/85	800	2500
2190	IV. Small square lettering; *mm*. rose *mm*. -/85	725	2250
2191	— *Obv*. as last. R. Tall thin lettering; *mm*. 33/21	750	2400
2192	V. As angel; *mm*. pheon	650	1850

SILVER

Facing bust issues. Including 'Sovereign' type pennies.

2193	**Groat.** I. Open crown; *mm*. 40 (rose on bust), 39-42 and none (combinations)	90	325

2194   2195

2194	— — crosses or saltires by neck, 41, 40, 105-33 and none (combinations)	110	375
2195	IIa. Large bust with out-turned hair, crown with two plain arches; *mm*. none, 31, 31/-, 31/78	80	250

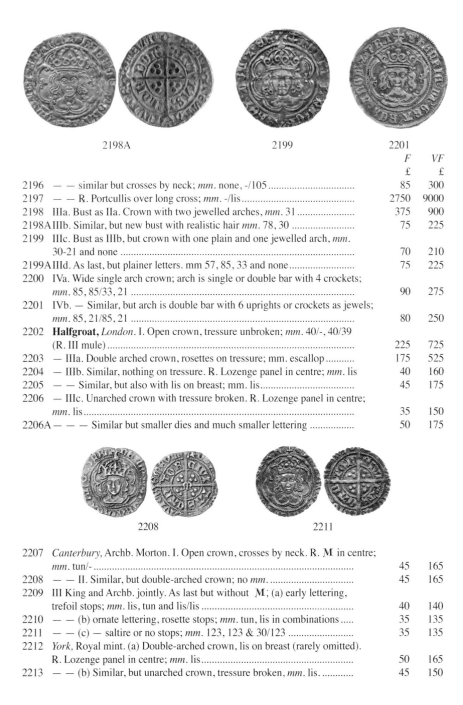

2198A   2199   2201

		F	VF
		£	£
2196	— — similar but crosses by neck; *mm*. none, -/105	85	300
2197	— — R. Portcullis over long cross; *mm*. -/lis	2750	9000
2198	IIIa. Bust as IIa. Crown with two jewelled arches, *mm*. 31	375	900
2198A	IIIb. Similar, but new bust with realistic hair *mm*. 78, 30	75	225
2199	IIIc. Bust as IIIb, but crown with one plain and one jewelled arch, *mm*.		
	30-21 and none	70	210
2199A	IIId. As last, but plainer letters. mm 57, 85, 33 and none	75	225
2200	IVa. Wide single arch crown; arch is single or double bar with 4 crockets;		
	mm. 85, 85/33, 21	90	275
2201	IVb. — Similar, but arch is double bar with 6 uprights or crockets as jewels;		
	mm. 85, 21/85, 21	80	250
2202	**Halfgroat,** *London*. I. Open crown, treasure unbroken; *mm*. 40/-, 40/39		
	(R. III mule)	225	725
2203	— IIIa. Double arched crown, rosettes on treasure; mm. escallop	175	525
2204	— IIIb. Similar, nothing on treasure. R. Lozenge panel in centre; *mm*. lis	40	160
2205	— — Similar, but also with lis on breast; mm. lis	45	175
2206	— IIIc. Unarched crown with treasure broken. R. Lozenge panel in centre;		
	mm. lis	35	150
2206A	— — — Similar but smaller dies and much smaller lettering	50	175

2208   2211

2207	*Canterbury,* Archb. Morton. I. Open crown, crosses by neck. R. M in centre;		
	mm. tun/-	45	165
2208	— — II. Similar, but double-arched crown; no *mm*.	45	165
2209	III King and Archb. jointly. As last but without M; (a) early lettering,		
	trefoil stops; *mm*. lis, tun and lis/lis	40	140
2210	— — (b) ornate lettering, rosette stops; *mm*. tun, lis in combinations	35	135
2211	— — (c) — saltire or no stops; *mm*. 123, 123 & 30/123	35	135
2212	*York,* Royal mint. (a) Double-arched crown, lis on breast (rarely omitted).		
	R. Lozenge panel in centre; *mm*. lis	50	165
2213	— — (b) Similar, but unarched crown, treasure broken, *mm*. lis.	45	150

	F	VF
	£	£
2214 — Archb. Savage. (a) Double-arched crown, keys at neck, no tressure; ornate lettering; *mm*. martlet	40	140
2215 — — (b) Similar, but fleured tressure, small square lettering; *mm*. martlet	45	150
2216 — — (c) As last, but tall thin lettering; *mm*. martlet	45	150
2217 — As last but no keys; *mm*. martlet	50	165

2221   2226

2218 **Penny.** Old type. London; *mm*. 40/-	175	575
2219 — — — crosses by bust, mm. small cross (obv.)	200	625
2220 — *Canterbury,* Archb. Morton. Open crown, *mm*. tun/- R. M in centre	200	575
2221 — — King and Archb. jointly, arched crown; *mm*. tun, tun/-	65	225
2222 — *Durham,* Bp. Sherwood. S on breast. R. D in centre; *mm*. 7a/-	55	175
2223 — *York,* Archb. Rotherham. With or without cross on breast, *mm*. 33/-, T and cross or key at neck. R. h in centre	40	150
2224 — — — T and trefoil at neck. R. Quatrefoil in centre and two extra pellets; *mm*. 39/-	40	140
2225 'Sovereign' type. *London*. Early lettering, no stops, no pillars to throne; no *mm*	100	350
2226 — — — single pillar on king's right side, trefoil stops; no *mm*. or 31/-..	40	135
2227 — — Ornate letters, rosette stops, single pillar; *mm*. lis (can be muled with above)	55	185
2228 — — saltire stops or none, two pillars; *mm*. none, -/30	40	135
2229 — — Similar, but small square lettering; no *mm*.	45	150
2230 — — Similar, but lettering as profile groats two double pillars; *mm*. 21, 53, none (sometimes on one side only)	40	135

2231   2233   2235

2231 — *Durham,* Bp. Sherwood. Crozier to r. of king, throne with one pillar. R. D and S beside shield	35	125
2232 — — Throne with two pillars, no crozier. R. As last	40	140
2233 — — Bp. Fox. Throne with one pillar. R. Mitre above shield, RD or DR at sides, no *mm*	30	110
2234 — — Similar, but two pillars	35	120
2235 *York,* Archb. Rotherham. Keys below shield; early lettering, trefoil stops, no pillars to throne, no *mm*.	35	120
2236 — — — single pillar	30	110
2237 — — — ornate lettering, rosette or no stops,	35	120
2238 — — — two pillars sometimes with crosses between legs of throne	35	110

2239   2244A   2245

2249   2250

		F	*VF*
		£	£
2239	**Halfpenny,** *London*. I. Open crown; *mm.* 40, 42	35	125
2240	— — — trefoils at neck; no *mm.*, rose	40	135
2241	— — — crosses at neck; *mm.* rose, cross fitchée.................	35	125
2242	— II. Double arched crown; *mm.* cinquefoil, none	30	85
2243	— — — saltires at neck; no *mm*	30	85
2244	— IIIa. Crown with single arch, ornate lettering; no *mm.*, pansy............	25	80
2244A	— IIIb. Similar but with rosette stops; *mm.* none, rose, lis	35	110
2245	— IIIc. Much smaller portrait; *mm.* pheon, lis, none	25	85
2246	*Canterbury*, Archb. Morton. I. Open crown, crosses by neck; R. M in centre	65	225
2247	— — II. Similar, but arched crown, saltires by bust; *mm.* profile eye (82)	65	225
2247A	— — — no marks at neck	60	200
2248	— III. King and Archb. Arched crown; *mm.* lis, none..............................	40	120
2249	*York*, Archb. Savage. Arched crown, key below bust to l or r. *mm.*		
	martlet	45	140
2250	**Farthing,** *London*. hꞓNRIC DI GRA RꞒX (A), arched crown	450	1250

*No.s 2239-49 have *mm.* on *obv.* only.

Profile issue

2251	Testoon (ls.). Type as groat. hꞓNRIC (VS); *mm.* lis................................	13500	30000
2252	— hꞓNRIC VII; *mm.* lis	15000	32500

2253   2254

2253	— hꞓNRIC SꞒPTIM; *mm.* lis	16500	35000
2254	**Groat,** *Tentative issue* (contemporary with full-face groats). Double band		
	to crown, hꞓNRIC VII; *mm.* none, 105/-, -/105: 105/85, 105, 85, 21	250	900
2255	— — — tressure on *obv.; mm.* cross-crosslet...........................	2750	8500
2256	— — hꞓNRIC (VS); *mm.* 105, -/105, 105/ 85, none	375	1350
2257	— — hꞓNRIC SꞒPTIM; *mm.* -/105.......................................	3000	9000

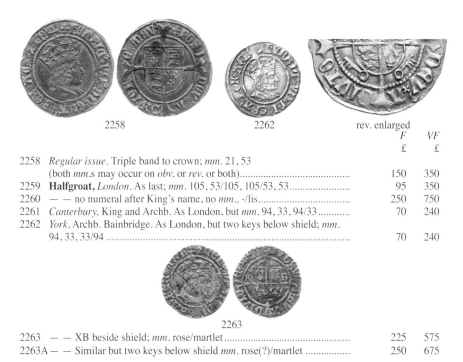

2258   2262   rev. enlarged

	F £	VF £
2258 *Regular issue*. Triple band to crown; *mm*. 21, 53 (both *mm*.s may occur on *obv.* or *rev.* or both)	150	350
2259 **Halfgroat,** *London*. As last; *mm*. 105, 53/105, 105/53, 53	95	350
2260 — — no numeral after King's name, no *mm*., -/lis	250	750
2261 *Canterbury,* King and Archb. As London, but *mm*. 94, 33, 94/33	70	240
2262 *York,* Archb. Bainbridge. As London, but two keys below shield; *mm*. 94, 33, 33/94	70	240

2263

2263 — — XB beside shield; *mm*. rose/martlet	225	575
2263A — — Similar but two keys below shield *mm*. rose(?)/martlet	250	675

Henry VIII is held in ill-regard by numismatists as being the author of the debasement of England's gold and silver coinage; but there were also other important numismatic innovations during his reign. For the first sixteen years the coinage closely followed the pattern of the previous issues, even to the extent of retaining the portrait of Henry VII on the larger silver coins.

In 1526, in an effort to prevent the drain of gold to continental Europe, the value of English gold was increased by 10%, the sovereign to 22s. 0d. and the angel to 7s. 4d., and a new coin valued at 4s. 6d.—the Crown of the Rose—was introduced as a competitor to the French *écu au soleil*. The new crown was not a success and within a few months it was replaced by the Crown of the Double Rose valued at 5s but made of gold of only 22 carat fineness, the first time gold had been minted below the standard 23c. At the same time the sovereign was again revalued to 22s. 6d. and the angel to 7s. 6d., with a new coin, the George Noble, valued at 6s. 8d. (one-third pound).

The royal cyphers on some of the gold crowns and half-crowns combine the initial of Henry with those of his queens: Katherine of Aragon, Anne Boleyn and Jane Seymour. The architect of this coinage reform was the chancellor, Cardinal Thomas Wolsey, who besides his other changes had minted at York a groat bearing his initials and cardinal's hat in addition to the other denominations normally authorized for the ecclesiastical mints.

When open debasement of the coinage began in 1544 to help finance Henry's wars, the right to coin of the archbishops of Canterbury and York and of the bishop of Durham was not confirmed. Instead, a second royal mint was opened in the Tower as in subsequent years were six others, at Southwark, York, Canterbury, Bristol, Dublin and Durham House in the Strand. Gold, which fell to 23c. in 1544, 22c. in 1545, and 20c. in 1546 was much less debased than silver which declined to 9oz 2dwt. in 1544, 6oz 2dwt. in 1545 and 4oz 2dwt. in 1546. At this last standard the blanched silver surface of the coins soon wore away to reveal the copper alloy beneath which earned for Henry the nickname 'Old Coppernose'.

Mintmarks

| 53 | 69 | 70 | 108 | 33 | 94 | 73 | 11 |

| 105 | 22 | 23 | 30 | 78 | 15 | 24 | 110 |

| 52 | 72a | 44 | 8 | 65a | 114 | 121 | 90 |

| 36 | 106 | 56 | S | E | 116 | 135 |

1509-26	Pheon (53)		1509-14	Martlet (94, *York*)
	Castle (69)		1509-23	Radiant star (22, *Durham & York*)
	Castle with H (70, gold)		1513-18	Crowned T (135, Tournai)
	Portcullis crowned (108)		1514-26	Star (23, *York & Durham*)
	Rose (33, *Canterbury*)			Pansy (30, *York*)
	Martlet (94, *Canterbury*)			Escallop (78, *York*)
	Pomegranate (73, but broader, *Cant.*)			Voided cross (15, *York*)
	Cross fitchée (11, *Cant.*)		1523-26	Spur rowel (24, *Durham*)
	Lis (105, *Canterbury, Durham*)			

1526-44   Rose (33)
           Lis (105)
           Sunburst 110)
           Arrow (52)
           Pheon (53)
           Lis (106)
           Star (23, *Durham*)
1526-9   Crescent (72a, *Durham*)
           Trefoil (44 variety,
           Durham)
           Flower of eight petals and
           circle centre (*Durham*)
1526-30   Cross (7a, sometimes
           slightly voided, *York*)
           Acorn (65a, *York*)

1526-32   Cross patonce (8, *Cant*.)
           T (114, *Canterbury*)
           Uncertain mark (121,
           Canterbury)
1529-44   Radiant star (22, *Durham*)
1530-44   Key (90, *York*)
1533-44   Catherine wheel (36,
           Canterbury)
1544-7   Lis (105 and 106)
           Pellet in annulet (56)
           S (Southwark)
           Є or E (Southwark)
1546-7   WS monogram (116, *Bristol*)

GOLD

First coinage, 1509-26

2265

		F	VF
		£	£
2264	**Sovereign** (20s.). Similar to last sov. of Hen. VII; *mm*. 108	12500	35000
2264A	**Ryal** (10s.) King in ship holding sword and shield. R. Similar to 1950, *mm*.-/108	*Extremely rare*	
2265	**Angel** (6s. 8d.). As Hen. VII, but hЄnRIC? VIII DI GRA RЄX, etc.; *mm*. 53, 69, 70, 70/69, 108, R. May omit h and rose, or rose only; *mm*. 69, 108	750	2200
2266	**Half-angel.** Similar (sometimes without VIII), *mm*. 69, 70, 108/33, 108	675	1850

Second coinage, 1526-44

2267

2267	**Sovereign** (22s. 6d.). As 2264, R. single or double tressure *mm*. 110, 105, 105/52	10000	30000
2268	**Angel** (7s. 6d.). As 2265, hЄnRIC VIII D(I) G(RA) R(ЄX) etc,; *mm*. 110, 105	1250	4500

		F	*VF*
		£	£
2269	**Half-angel.** Similar; *mm.* lis..	1350	5000

2270   2272

2270	**George-noble** (6s. 8d.). As illustration; *mm.* rose	9500	35000
2270A	— Similar, but more modern ship with three masts, without initials hR. R.		
	St. George brandishing sword behind head...	12500	42500
2271	**Half-George-noble.** Similar to 2270 *mm* rose, lis................................	8500	30000
2272	**Crown of the rose** (4s. 6d., 23 c. 3 ¹/₂ gr.). As illustration; *mm.* rose,		
	two legend varieties	7250	25000
2273	**Crown of the double-rose** (5s., 22 c). Double-rose crowned, hK (Henry and		
	Katherine of Aragon) both crowned in field. R. Shield crowned; *mm.* rose	750	2250

2274   2285

2274	— hK both sides; *mm.* rose/lis, lis, arrow	725	2250
2275*	— hK/hA or hA/hK; *mm.* arrow	2250	7500
2276*	— hR/hK or hI/hR; *mm.* arrow..	1250	3500
2277	— hA (Anne Boleyn); *mm.* arrow	2500	8000
2278	— hA/hR; *mm.* arrow	2250	7500
2279	— hI (Jane Seymour); *mm.* arrow...	800	2400
2280*	— hK/hI; *mm.* arrow	1250	3750
2281	— hR/hI; *mm.* arrow...	1050	3250
2282	— hR (Rex); *mm.* arrow	750	2400
2283	— — *mm.* pheon	1100	3500
2284	**Halfcrown.** Similar but king's name henric 8 on *rev.,* no initials; *mm.* rose	1350	4500
2285	— hK uncrowned on *obv.; mm.* rose	675	2000
2286	— hK uncrowned both sides; *mm.* rose/lis, lis, arrow..........................	675	2000
2287	— hI uncrowned both sides; *mm.* arrow	800	2250
2288	— hR uncrowned both sides; hIB RCX; *mm.* pheon	950	3000

*The hK initials may on later coins refer to Katherine Howard (Henry's fifth wife).

Third coinage, 1544-7

2291

	F	*VF*
	£	£

2289 **Sovereign,** I (20s., Wt. 200 gr., 23 c.). As illustration but king with larger face and larger design; *mm.* lis 32500 125000

2290 II (20s., wt. 200 or 192 grs., 23, 22 or 20 ct.). *Tower.* As illustration; *mm.* lis, pellet in annulet/lis 5250 18500

2291 — *Southwark.* Similar; *mm.* S, Є/S.. 5250 18500

2292 — — Similar but Є below shield; *mm.* S/Є 7500 25000

2293 — *Bristol.* As London but *mm.* WS/- 12500 35000

2294

2294 **Half-sovereign** (wt. 100 or 96 gr.), *Tower.* As illus.; *mm.* lis, pellet in annulet 950 3000

2295 — Similar, but with annulet on inner circle (either or both sides)........ 975 3250

2296 *Southwark. Mm.* S 975 3250

2297 — Є below shield; *mm.* S, Є, S/Є, Є/S, (known without sceptre; *mm.* S) 950 3000

2298 *Bristol.* Lombardic lettering; *mm.* WS, WS/- 1850 6500

2299 **Angel** (8s., 23 c). Annulet by angel's head and on ship, hЄnRIС' 8; *mm.* lis 750 2250

2300 — Similar, but annulet one side only or none................................... 825 2400

2301 **Half-angel.** Annulet on ship; *mm.* lis.. 675 1850

2302 — No annulet on ship; *mm.* lis.. 700 2000

2303

2304

2303 — Three annulets on ship; *mm.* lis.. 825 2500

2304 **Quarter-angel** Angel wears armour; *mm.* lis 750 2250

		F £	*VF* £
2304A—	Angel wears tunic; *mm.* lis	775	2350
2305	**Crown,** *London.* Similar to 2283, but hꞒnRIC' 8 ; Lombardic lettering; mm . 56	700	2250
2306	— without RVTILAnS; *mm.* 56......	750	2400
2307	— — — with annulet on inner circle	750	2400
2307A—	King's name omitted. DEI GRA both sides, *mm.* 56......	950	3000
2308	— *Southwark.* As 2306; *mm.* S, Ꞓ, E/S, C/-, E/Ꞓ	825	2500
2309	*Bristol.* hꞒnRIC VIII. ROSA etc. Ꞃ. D G, etc.; *mm.*-/WS	750	2250
2309A—	— with initials H R transposed on rev......	900	2750
2310	— Similar but hꞒnRIC(VS) 8 Ꞃ. DꞒI) G(RA); *mm.* -/WS, WS	800	2400
2311	**Halfcrown,** *London.* Similar to 2288; *mm.* 56, 56/-......	575	1400
2312	— — with annulet on inner circle *mm.* 56......	600	1500
2313	*Southwark.* As 2311; *mm.* S	675	1750
2314	— *O.* hꞒnRIC 8 ROSA SInꞒ SPIn. Ꞃ. DꞒI GRA, etc.; *mm.* Ꞓ	675	1750
2315	*Bristol. O.* RVTILAnS, etc. Ꞃ. hꞒnRIC 8; *mm.* WS/-......	750	2250

For other gold coins in Henry's name see page 221-2.

SILVER

First coinage, 1509-26

2316   2322

2316	**Groat.** Portrait of Hen. VII. *London mm.* 53, 69, 108, 108 over 135......	140	375
2317	— *Tournai; mm.* crowned T. Ꞃ. CIVITAS TORnACꞒn*......	850	3000
2318	**Halfgroat.** Portrait of Hen. VII. London; *mm.* 108, 108/-......	135	450
2319	— *Canterbury,* Archb. Warham. POSVI *rev.; mm.* rose......	150	525
2320	— — — WA above shield; *mm.* martlet......	110	325
2321	— — — WA beside shield; *mm.* cross fitchee......	110	325
2322	— — CIVITAS CAnTOR *rev.,* similar; *mm.* 73, 105, 11/105......	70	200
2323	— *York,* POSVI *rev.,* Archb. Bainbridge (1508-14). Keys below shield; *mm.* martlet......	80	250
2324	— — — XB beside shield no keys; *mm.* martlet......	80	250
2325	— — — Archb. Wolsey (1514-30). Keys and cardinal's hat below shield; *mm.* 94, 22......	175	525
2326	— — CIVITAS ꞒBORACI *rev.* Similar; *mm.* 22, 23, 30, 78, 15, 15/78..	75	225
2327	— — As last with TW beside shield; *mm.* voided cross......	110	325
2327A—	*Tournai.* As 2317......	850	2500

*Non-portrait groats and half-groats exist of this mint, captured during an invasion of France in 1513. (Restored to France in 1518.)

2328   2334   2336

		F	VF
		£	£
2328	**Penny,** 'Sovereign' type, *London; mm.* 69, 108 /-, 108/108	55	135
2329	— *Canterbury.* WA above shield; *mm.* martlet...	100	300
2330	— — — WA beside shield; *mm.* 73/-	75	225
2331	— *Durham,* Bp. Ruthall (1509-23). TD above shield; *mm.* lis.................	40	110
2332	— — — TD beside shield; above or below horizontal line *mm.* lis, radiant star	40	110
2333	— — Bp. Wolsey (1523-9). DW beside shield, cardinal's hat below; *mm.* spur rowel..	135	450
2334	**Halfpenny.** Facing bust, hЄnRIC DI GRA RЄX (AGL). *London; mm.* 69, 108/-	25	75
2335	— *Canterbury.* WA beside bust; *mm.* 73/-, 11	60	150
2335A	— *York.* Key below bust, *mm.* star, escallop...	75	200
2336	**Farthing.** *mm.* 108/-, hЄnRIC DI GRA RЄX, portcullis. R. CIVITAS LOnDON, rose in centre of long cross	275	750

Second coinage, 1526-44

2337D   2337E

		F	VF
2337	**Groat.** His own young portrait. *London;* Laker bust A, large renaissance-style bust, crown arch breaking inner circle. Roman/Roman lettering, roses in cross-ends; *mm.* rose	450	1500
2337A	— — Laker bust A1 but with Roman/Lombardic lettering, saltires in cross-ends; *mm.* rose	250	850
2337B	— —Laker bust A2 but withLombardic/Lombardic lettering, roses in cross-ends; *mm.* rose	325	1050
2337C	— — Laker bust A3 but with Lombardic/Lombardic lettering, saltires in cross-ends; *mm.* rose	200	575
2337D	— Laker bust B, smaller face with pointed nose, crown arch does not break inner circle. Lombardic lettering; *mm.* rose	120	425
2337E	— Laker bust D, larger squarer face with roman nose, fluffy hair, crown arch does not break inner circle. Lombardic lettering; *mm.* 33, 105, 110, 52, 53 (sometimes muled)...	95	260
2338	— — with Irish title HIB; reads hЄnRIC 8; *mm.* 53, 105, 53/105, 105/53,	275	900
2339	— *York,* Archb. Wolsey. TW beside shield, cardinal's hat below; *mm.* voided cross, acorn, muled (both ways)	110	350
2340	— — — omits TW; *mm.* voided cross	450	1500

2341   2343   2345

	F	VF
	£	£

2341 **Halfgroat.** *London;* type as groats, Lombardic lettering both sides.
      mm. rose to arrow or none (sometimes muled)... 70 / 185
2341A— — Mainly Roman letters on obv. or on both sides, *mm.* rose............. 125 / 475
2342 As 2341 with Irish title HIB; *mm.* pheon.. 375 / 1250
2343 — *Canterbury*, Archb. Warham (—1532). R. CIVITAS CAחTOR, WA
      beside shield; *mm.* 121, 121/-, 121/33, 8, 8/T, T.. 55 / 170
2344 — — — nothing by shield; *mm.* 121/-.. 75 / 225
2345 — — Archb. Cranmer (1533—). TC beside shield; *mm.* 36, 36/-........... 55 / 170
2346 — *York*, Archb. Wolsey (—1530). R. CIVITAS ЄBORACI, TW
      beside shield, hat below; *mm.* 15/-, 15.. 60 / 185
2347 — — Sede Vacante (1530/1). No marks; *mm.* key................................... 70 / 200
2348 — — Archb. Lee (1531-44). EL or LE beside shield; *mm.* key.............. 55 / 170
2349 **Penny.** 'Sovereign' type h . D . G . ROSA SIחЄ SPIחA, *London;*
      mm. rose to arrow (*obv.* only), *mm.* lis both sides.................................... 45 / 135

2349   2358   2362

2350 — *Canterbury*. WA beside shield; *mm.* 121/-, 8/-, T/-.............................. 75 / 225
2351 — — TC beside shield; *mm.* 36/-... 250 / 750
2352 — *Durham*, Bp. Wolsey (—1529). TW beside shield, hat below; *mm.* 23,
      23/44, 23/-, 72a/-, 44, 44/-, 72a/44 (muled with 2333 *obv.*, *mm.* 24/44).. 40 / 110
2353 — — Sede Vacante (1529-30). No marks; *mm.* 23/-, 22/-........................ 45 / 125
2354 — — Bp. Tunstall (1530—). CD beside shield; *mm.* 23, 23/-, 22/-, 22 ... 40 / 110
2355 — *York*. EL beside shield; *mm.* key/-.. 225 / 650
2356 **Halfpenny.** Facing bust, h D G ROSA SIЄ SPIA. *London;* sometimes
      annulet in centre of rev. *mm.* rose to arrow, arrow/- .... 30 / 100
2357 — *Canterbury*. WA beside bust; *mm.* 121/-, 8/-, T/-............................... 75 / 250
2358 — — TC beside bust; *mm.* 36/-.. 35 / 125
2359 — *York*. TW beside bust; *mm.* acorn/-.. 75 / 250
2359A— — —; key below bust... 85 / 275
2360 — — Sede Vacante. Key below bust; *mm.* 15/-... 60 / 175
2361 — — EL or LE beside bust; *mm.* key/-... 35 / 125
2362 **Farthing.** *O.* RVTILANS ROSA, portcullis; *mm.* 105/-, 110/-. R.
      DEO GRACIAS, long cross with pellet in each angle .... 350 / 800
2363 — — *mm.* arrow/- R. DEO GRACIAS, rose on long cross .... 375 / 950
2363A— *Canterbury*. O. Similar. R. Similar. *mm.* 36/- .... 900 / 2500

2364

	F	VF
	£	£

Third coinage, 1544-7 (Silver progressively debased. 9oz (2dwt), 6oz (2dwt) 4oz (2dwt)).

2364 **Testoon.** *Tower.* hℂnRIℂ'. VIII, etc. R. Crowned rose between crowned h
and R.POSVI, etc.; *mm.* lis, lis and 56, lis/two lis .... | 1100 | 6500 |
2365 — hℂnRIℂ 8, *mm.* 105 and 56, 105/56, 105 and 56/56, 56 .... | 750 | 4250 |
2366 — — annulet on inner circle of rev. or both sides; *mm.* pellet in annulet | 800 | 4500 |

2367

2367 — *Southwark.* As 2365. R. CIVITAS LONDON; *mm.* S, ℂ, S/ℂ, C/S .... | 800 | 4500 |
2368 — *Bristol. mm.*-/WS monogram. (Tower or local dies.) .... | 950 | 5500 |

2369 Bust 1   2374 Bust 2

2369 **Groat.** *Tower.* As ill. above, busts 1, 2, 3; *mm.* lis/-, lis .... | 110 | 475 |
2369A Bust 1, R. As second coinage; i.e. saltires in forks; *mm.* lis .... | 150 | 575 |
2370 Bust 2 or 3 annulet on inner circle, both sides or rev. only .... | 120 | 500 |
2371 *Southwark.* As 2367, busts 1, 2, 3, 4; no *mm.* or lis/-; S or S and ℂ or
ℂ in forks .... | 110 | 475 |
2372 *Bristol. Mm.*-/WS monogram, Bristol bust and Tower bust 2 or 3 .... | 120 | 525 |
2373 *Canterbury.* Busts 1, 2, (2 var); no *mm,* or lis/– .... | 110 | 475 |
2374 *York.* Busts 1 var., 2, 3, no *mm* .... | 110 | 475 |

		F	*VF*
		£	£
2375	**Halfgroat.** *Tower.* As 2365, bust 1; *mm.* lis, none	75	275
2376	*Southwark.* As 2367, bust 1; no *mm.*; S or Є and S in forks	110	350
2377	*Bristol. Mm.-*/WS monogram	80	300
2378	*Canterbury.* Bust 1; no *mm.*	60	210
2379	*York.* Bust 1; no *mm.*	75	275
2380	**Penny.** *Tower.* Facing bust; no *mm.* or lis/-	50	160
2381	*Southwark.* Facing bust; *mm.* S/-, Є/-, -/Є	90	275
2382	*Bristol.* Facing bust; no *mm.* (Tower dies or local but truncated at neck)	60	185

2388A

		F	*VF*
2383	*Canterbury.* Facing bust; no *mm.*	50	160
2384	*York.* Facing bust; no *mm.*	50	160
2385	**Halfpenny.** *Tower.* Facing bust; pellet in annulet in *rev.* centre,		
	no *mm.* or lis/-	60	175
2386	*Bristol.* Facing bust; no *mm.*	80	250
2387	*Canterbury.* Facing bust; no *mm.*, (some read H 8)	55	150
2388	*York.* Facing bust; no *mm.*	45	135
2388A	**Farthing** *obv.* Rose. R. Cross and pellets	850	2250

These coins were struck during the reign of Edward VI but bear the name and portrait of Henry VIII, except in the case of the half-sovereigns which bear the youthful head of Edward.

Mintmarks

56	105	52	K	E	116

66	115	33	122	t	94

GOLD

		F	VF
		£	£
2389	**Sovereign** (20 c), *London*. As no. 2290, but Roman lettering; *mm*. lis	7250	25000
2390	— *Bristol*. Similar but *mm*. WS	12500	37500

2391

2393

2391	**Half-sovereign.** As 2294, but with youthful portrait with sceptre. *Tower*; *mm*. 52, 105, 94 (various combinations)...	850	2500
2391A	— Similar but no sceptre; *mm*. 52, 52/56	875	2650
2392	— — — K below shield; *mm*.-/K, none,. E/-	900	2750
2393	— — — grapple below shield; *mm*. 122, none, 122/-, -/122.	950	3000
2394	— *Southwark*. Mm. E, E/-, -/E, Є /E. Usually Є or E (sometimes retrograde) below shield (sceptre omitted; *mm*. -/E)..	850	2500
2394A	— — — R. As 2296; *mm*.-/S..	925	2750

2395

		F	VF
		£	£
2395	**Crown.** Similar to 2305. *London; mm.* 52, 52/-, -/K, 122, 94, ...	700	2000
2396	— Similar but transposed legends without numeral; *mm.* -/arrow	750	2250
2396A	— As 2395, but omitting RVTILANS; *mm.* arrow	750	2250
2396B	Similar, but RVTILANS both sides; *mm.* arrow	950	3000
2397	— *Southwark.* Similar to 2396; *mm.* E	850	2750
2398	— — King's name on *obv.; mm.* E/-, -/E...................................	750	2250
2399	**Halfcrown.** Similar to 2311. *London; mm.* 52, K/-, 122/-, 94, -/52	650	1750
2399A	As last but E over h on *rev., mm.* 56/52.....................................	1100	3500
2399B	As 2399 but RVTILANS etc. on both sides, *mm.* arrow	850	2500
2400	— *Southwark. mm.* E, E/-, -/E	650	1750

SILVER

AR (4oz .333)

2401	**Testoon.** *Tower.* As 2365 with lozenge stops one side; -/56, 56..........	1850	9000

2403	2403 Bust 4	2403 Bust 6

Some of the Bristol testoons, groats and halfgroats with WS monogram were struck after the death of Henry VIII but cannot easily be distinguished from those struck during his reign.

2403	**Groat.** *Tower.* Busts 4, 5, 6 (and, rarely, 2). R. POSVI, etc.; *mm.* 105-94 and none (frequently muled)...	110	475
2404	— *Southwark.* Busts 4, 5, 6. R. CIVITAS LONDON; no *mm.* -/E; lis/-, -/lis, K/E; roses or crescents or S and Є in forks, or rarely annulets	95	425
2405	— *Durham House.* Bust 6. R. REDDE CVIQUE QVOD SVVM EST; *mm.* bow..	225	900
2406	— *Bristol. mm.* WS on *rev.* Bristol bust B, Tower bust 2 and 3	120	500
2407	— — *mm.* TC on *rev.* Similar, Bristol bust B	135	650
2408	— *Canterbury.* Busts 5, 6; no *mm.* or rose/-	95	425
2409	— *York.* Busts 4, 5, 6; no *mm.* or lis/-, -/lis...............................	95	425

		F	VF
		£	£
2410	**Halfgroat.** Bust 1. *Tower*. POSVI, etc.; *mm*. 52, 52/-, 52/K , -/K, 52/122, 122, -/122	90	325
2411	— *Southwark*. CIVITAS LONDON; *mm*. E, -/E, none, 52/E, K/E	60	200
2412	— *Durham House*. R. REDD, etc.; *mm*. bow, -/bow	375	1350
2413	— *Bristol*. *Mm*. WS on *rev*.	80	300
2414	— — *mm*. TC on *rev*.	90	325
2415	— *Canterbury*. No *mm*. or t/-, -/t,	55	200

2416

2416	— *York*. No *mm*., bust 1 and three quarter facing	65	250

2417   2421

2417	**Penny.** *Tower*. CIVITAS LONDON. Facing bust; *mm*. 52/-, -/52, -/K, 122/-, -/122, none	45	160
2418	— — three-quarter bust; no *mm*.	50	160
2419	— *Southwark*. As 2417; *mm*. E, -/E	55	175
2420	— *Durham House*. As groat but shorter legend; *mm*. -/bow	375	1250
2421	— *Bristol*. Facing busts, as 2382 but showing more body, no *mm*	75	250
2422	— *Canterbury*. Similar to 2417	50	160
2423	— — three-quarters facing bust; no *mm*	55	175
2424	— *York*. Facing bust; no *mm*	50	160
2425	— — three-quarters facing bust; no *mm*	60	175

2426   2428

2426	**Halfpenny.** *Tower*. 52?, none	40	125
2427	— *Canterbury*. No *mm*., sometimes reads H8	50	150
2428	— *York*. No *mm*.	45	135

Coinage in his own name

The 4 oz. 2.5dwt coins of Henry VIII and those issued under Edward in 1547 and 1548 caused much disquiet, yet at the same time government was prevented by continuing financial necessity from abandoning debasement. A stratagem was devised which entailed increasing the fineness of silver coins, thereby making them appear sound, while at the same time reducing their weight in proportion so that in practice they contained no more silver than hitherto. The first issue, ordered on 24 January 1549, at 8 oz.2 dwt. fine produced a shilling which, at 60 gr., was so light that it was rapidly discredited and had to be replaced in April by another at 6 oz. 2 dwt. Weighing 80 gr., these later shillings proved acceptable.

Between April and August 1551 the issue of silver coins was the worst ever – 3 oz. 2dwt. fine at 72s per lb. before retrenchment came in August, first by a 50% devaluation of base silver coin and then by the issue of a fine standard at 11oz. 1dwt. 'out of the fire'. This was the equivalent of 11oz.3dwt. commixture, and means that since sterling was only 11oz. 2dwt., this issue, which contained four new denominations – the crown, halfcrown, sixpence and threepence – was in effect the finest ever issued under the Tudors.

Some base 'pence' were struck in parallel with the fine silver, but at the devalued rate, they and the corresponding 'halfpence' were used as halfpence and farthings respectively.

The first dates on English coinage appear in this reign, first as Roman numerals and then on the fine issue crowns and halfcrowns of 1551-3, in Arabic numerals.

Mintmarks

| 66 | 52 | 35 | 115 | E | 53 | 122 |

| t | T | 111 | Y | 126 | 94 | 91A |

| 92 | 105 | y | 97 | 123 | 78 | 26 |

1547-8	Arrow (52)		
	E (Southwark)		
1548-50	Bow (66, *Durham House*)	1550	Martlet (94)
1549	Arrow (52)	1550	Leopard's head (91A)
	Grapple (122)	1550-1	Lion (92)
	Rose (35, *Canterbury*)		Lis (105, *Southwark*)
	TC monogram (115, *Bristol*)		Rose (33)
	Pheon (53)	1551	Y or y (117, *Southwark*)
	t or T (*Canterbury*)		Ostrich's head (97, gold only)
1549-50	Swan (111)	1551-3	Tun (123)
	Roman Y (*Southwark*)		Escallop (78)
1549-50	6 (126 gold only)	1552-3	Pierced mullet (26, *York*)

GOLD

First period, Apr. 1547-Jan. 1549

2430

		F	VF
		£	£
2429	**Half-sovereign** (20 c). As 2391, but reading EDWARD 6. Tower; *mm.* arrow	2500	9500
2430	— *Southwark* (Sometimes with E or ₵ below shield); *mm.* E................	2250	8000
2431	**Crown.** RVTILANS, etc., crowned rose between ER both crowned. R. EDWARD 6, etc., crowned shield between ER both crowned; *mm.* arrow, E over arrow/-	2250	9000
2431A	— *Obv.* as last. R. As 2305, *mm.* 52/56	2000	7500
2432	**Halfcrown.** Similar to 2431, but initials not crowned; *mm.* arrow	1750	5250

Second period, Jan. 1549-Apr. 1550

2433

2433	**Sovereign** (22 ct). As illustration; *mm.* arrow, –/arrow, Y, ...	5750	20000
2434	**Half-sovereign.** Uncrowned bust. *London.* TIMOR etc., MDXLIX on *obv. mm.* arrow	3750	13500

2435

| 2435 | — — SCVTVM, etc., as illustration; *mm.* arrow, **6,** Y............................ | 1850 | 6000 |

		F	VF
		£	£
2436	— *Durham House*. Uncrowned, 1/2 length bust with MDXLVIII at end of *obv*. legend; *mm*. bow; SCVTVM etc.	7500	25000
2437	— Normal, uncrowned bust. LVCERNA, etc., on *obv*.; *mm*. bow	6250	20000
2437A	— Normal, uncrowned bust. SCVTVM, etc. but with *rev*. as 2440, *mm*. bow	5500	17500

2438   2441

2438	— Crowned bust. *London*. EDWARD VI, etc. R. SCVTVM, etc.; *mm*. 52, 122, 111/52, 111, Y, 94	1750	5750
2439	— *Durham House*. Crowned, half-length bust; *mm*. bow	7500	25000
2440	— — King's name on *obv*. and *rev*.; *mm*. bow (mule of 2439/37)	8250	27500
2441	**Crown.** Uncrowned bust, as 2435; *mm*. 6, Y, 52/-, Y/-	2000	7250
2442	— Crowned bust, as 2438; *mm*. 52, 122, 111, Y (usually *obv*. only)	1850	6500
2443	**Halfcrown.** Uncrowned bust; R. As 2441, *mm*. arrow, Y, Y/-, 52/-	1750	6500
2444	— Crowned bust, as illus. above; *mm*. 52, 52/111, 111, 122, Y, Y/-	1350	4750
2445	— Similar, but king's name on *rev*., *mm*. 52, 122	1500	5000

Third period, 1550-3

| 2446 | **'Fine' sovereign** (30s.). King on throne; *mm*. 97, 123 | 35000 | 125000 |

2444   2448

2447	**Double sovereign.** From the same dies, *mm*. 97	95000	350000
2448	**Angel** (10s.). As illustration; *mm*. 97, 123	11000	37500
2449	**Half-angel.** Similar, *mm*. 97	12500	40000

2450

	F £	VF £
2450 **Sovereign**. (=20s.). Half-length figure of king r., crowned and holding sword and orb. R. Crowned shield with supporters; *mm*. y, tun	5250	16500

2451

2451 **Half-sovereign**. As illustration above; *mm*. y, tun	1750	5750
2452 **Crown**. Similar, but *rev*. SCVTVM etc., *mm*. y, tun	2000	6500
2453 **Halfcrown**. Similar, *mm*. tun, y..	2250	7000

*Small denominations often occur creased or straightened.

SILVER
First period, Apr. 1547-Jan. 1549

2455

2454 **Groat**. Crowned bust r. *Tower*. R. Shield over cross, POSVI, etc.; *mm*. arrow	850	3500
2455 — As last, but EDOARD 6, *mm*. arrow..	900	3750
2456 *Southwark*. *Obv*. as 2454. R. CIVITAS LONDON; *mm*.-/E or none, sometimes S in forks...	850	3500
2457 **Halfgroat**. *Tower*. *Obv*. as 2454; *mm*. arrow	675	2000
2458 *Southwark*. As 2456; *mm*. arrow, E on reverse only	575	1500

2459   2462

| | F | VF |
	£	£
2459 *Canterbury*. Similar. No *mm*., reads EDOARD or EDWARD (rare)	450	1350
2460 **Penny**. *Tower*. As halfgroat, but E.D.G. etc. R. CIVITAS LONDON; *mm*. arrow	475	1350
2461 *Southwark*. As last, but *mm*. -/E..	525	1500
2462 *Bristol*. Similar, but reads ED6DG or E6DG no *mm*...............................	450	1350
2463 **Halfpenny**. *Tower*. *O*. As 2460, *mm*. E (?). R. Cross and pellets	450	1500
2464 *Bristol*. Similar, no *mm*. but reads E6DG or EDG....................................	525	1750

Second period, Jan. 1549-Apr. 1550

At all mints except Bristol, the earliest shillings of 1549 were issued at only 60 grains but of 8 oz. 2 dwt standard. This weight and size were soon increased to 80 grains, (S.2466 onwards), but the fineness was reduced to 6 oz. 2 dwt so the silver content remained the same. Dies, mm G were prepared for a coinage of 80gr shillings at York, but were not used. Coins from the *mm* are found suitably overmarked, from other mints, S.2466-8. The shilling bust types are set out in *J. Bispham 'The Base Silver Shillings of Edward VI; BNJ 1985.*

Bust 1   2465A   Bust 2

60 gr; 8oz. 2 dwt.

	F	VF
2465 **Shilling**. *Tower*. Broad bust with large crown. *Obv.* TIMOR etc. MDXLIX. R. Small, oval garnished shield dividing ER. EDWARD VI etc., *mm*. 52, no *mm*, Bust 1; *mm*, –/52, Bust 2 (very rare)	275	1250
2465A *Southwark*. As last, Bust 1, *mm*. Y, EY/Y	250	1200
2465B *Canterbury*. As last, Bust 1, *mm*. -/rose..	325	1500

2465C

2465C *Durham House*. Bust with elaborate tunic and collar TIMOR etc. MDXLIX. R. Oval shield, very heavily garnished in different style. EDWARD VI etc., *mm*. bow (2469)   300   1350

80 gr; 6oz. 2 dwt.

Bust 3   Bust 4

Bust 5   2466C   2468

2472

		F £	VF £
2466	*Tower.* Tall, narrow bust with small crown. *Obv.* EDWARD VI etc. MDXLIX or MDL. R. As 2465 but TIMOR etc., Busts 3, 4 and 5, *mm.* 52-91a (frequently muled)	150	725
2466A	— *Obv.* as last, MDXLIX. R. Heavily garnished shield, Durham House style, Bust 3 *mm.* grapple..	425	1750
2466B	*Southwark.* As 2466, Busts 3, 4 and 5 *mm.* Y, Y/swan	145	700
2466C	— — — Bust 4; R. as 2466A. *mm.* Y..	425	1750
2467	*Bristol. Obv.* similar to 2466, Bust 3 or local die R. Shield with heavy curved garniture or as 2466, *mm.* TC, or TC over G	950	4500
2468	*Canterbury.* As 2466, Bust 3 and 4 *mm.* T, T/t, t/T, t...............................	175	850
2470	*Durham House.* Bust as 2465C. INIMICOS etc., no date. R. EDWARD etc.	185	950
2472	— Bust similar to 2466. EDWARD VI etc. R. INIMICOS etc.	175	850
2472A	— As last but legends transposed	325	1500
2472B	*Tower.* Elegant bust with extremely thin neck. Bust 6, R. As 2466, *mm.* martlet	475	2250
2472C	*Southwark.* As last, Bust 6, *mm.* Y...	275	1250

For coins of Edward VI countermarked, see p. 236

Third period, 1550-3

Very base issue (1551) 3oz. 2 dwt.

2473 Bust 6   2474   2476

	F	VF
	£	£
2473 **Shilling**, *Tower*. As 2472B. MDL or MDLI, *mm*. lion, rose, lion/rose	200	900
2473A *Southwark*. As last, *mm*. lis/Y, Y/lis, lis	200	900
2474 **Base Penny**. *London*. *O*. Rose. R. Shield; *mm*. escallop (*obv*.).........	55	225
2475 — — *York*. *Mm*. mullet (*obv*.) as illustration	50	200
2476 **Base Halfpenny**. As penny, but single rose	175	750

* The base penny and halfpenny were used as halfpenny and farthing respectively.

Fine silver issue, (1551-3) 11oz. 3 dwt.

2478

2478 **Crown**. King on horseback with date below horse. R. Shield on cross;
     mm. y. 1551; tun, 1551-3 (1553, wire line inner circle may be missing) .   950   2500

2479

2479 **Halfcrown**. Walking horse with plume; *mm*. y, 1551	625	2000
2480 Galloping horse without plume; *mm*. tun, 1551-3	675	2250

2482

2483   2484

		F	VF
		£	£
2481	Large walking horse without plume; *mm*. tun, 1553	1250	3750
2482	**Shilling**. Facing bust, rose l., value XII r. *mm*. y, tun (several bust varieties)	120	375
2483	**Sixpence**. *London*. Similar value VI, as illustration; *mm*. y/-, -/y, y, tun (bust varieties)	135	525
2484	*York*. As last, but rev. reads CIVITAS CBORACI; *mm*. mullet...............	200	900

2485   2486

| 2485 | **Threepence**. *London*. As sixpence, but value III; *mm*. tun .... | 175 | 850 |
| 2486 | *York*. As 2484, but III by bust .... | 475 | 1850 |

2487   2487A

| 2487 | **Penny**. 'Sovereign' type; *mm*. tun .... | 1350 | 4500 |
| 2487A | **Farthing**. *O*. Portcullis, R Cross and Pellets .... | 1250 | 4000 |

Mary brought English coins back to the sterling standard and struck all her gold coins at the traditional fineness of 0.995. The mintmarks usually appear at the end of the first or second word of the legends.

Pomegranate   Halved rose and castle

GOLD

2488

	F £	VF £
2488 **'Fine' Sovereign** (30s.). Queen enthroned. R. Shield on rose, MDLIII, MDLIIII and undated, *mm*. pomegranate, half-rose (or mule)	6500	22500

2489

2490

2489	**Ryal** (15s.). As illus, MDLIII. R̟. As 1950 but A DNO etc. *mm.* pomegranate/-	35000	125000
2490	**Angel** (10s.). Class I, annulet stops; *mm*. pomegranate	2000	6000
2490A	— Class II, pellet stops, *mm*. pomegranate (often muled with class I reverse)	2100	6250
2490B	— Class III, pellet stops, large Roman letters, *mm*. half-rose and castle .	2250	7000
2491	**Half-angel**. Similar; *mm*. pomegranate, pomegranate/-	5750	14500

246 MARY, 1553-54

SILVER

2492

	F	VF
	£	£

2492 **Groat**. Crowned bust l. Ɍ. VERITAS, etc.; *mm.* pomegranate,
pomegranate/- .... | 135 | 400

2493 **Halfgroat**. Similar .... | 675 | 2000

2494 **Penny**. Similar, but M. D. G. ROSA, etc. .... | 575 | 1850

2495

2495 — As last. Ɍ. CIVITAS LONDON; no *mm* .... | 575 | 1850

We are accepting
single entries and collections
of coins and antiquities
Sales commission from 0%

www.timelineauctions.com

+44 [0]1708 222 824
enquiries@timelineauctions.com

THE ART LOSS
■ REGISTER™

BNTA

The groats and smaller silver coins of this period have Mary's portrait only, but the shillings and sixpences show the bust of the queen's husband, Philip of Spain.

Mintmarks

Lis (105   Half-rose and castle

GOLD

2496A

			F	VF
			£	£
2496	**Angel**. As illustration; wire line inner circles, calm sea, *mm*. lis		5500	18500
2496A	— — New-style, large wings, wire line i.c.		5750	20000
2496B	— — As above but beaded i.c.		6250	21000
2497	**Half-angel**. Similar to 2496		13500	35000

SILVER

2497A

		F	VF
2497A	**Halfcrown (Pattern)**. As illustration. Bust of Philip r., crown above, date 1554 below. R. Bust of Mary l. crown and date 1554 above, without mark of value, no *mm*..	12500	35000
2498	**Shilling**. Busts face-to-face, full titles, undated, no *mm*.	425	1800
2499	— — — also without mark of value	475	2000

2500

		F	VF
		£	£
2500	− − 1554	425	1800
2501	− English titles only 1554, 1555	450	1850
2501A	− − undated..	575	2500
2502	− − without mark of value, 1554, 1555 (rare)	475	2000
2503	− − date below bust, 1554, 1555	4000	12500
2504	− − As last, but without ANG., 1555.................	4500	13500

2505   2506

		F	VF
2505	**Sixpence**. Similar. Full titles, 1554 (and undated?)..........................	425	1600
2506	− English titles only, 1555 (no *mm.*, rare), 1557 (*mm.* lis, rounder garnishing)	450	1650
2506A	− As last but heavy beaded i.c. on obv. 1555. (Irish 4d. obv. mule)	475	2000
2507	− − date below bust, 1554, 1557 (very rare)	1750	6500

2508   2510A

		F	VF
2508	**Groat**. Crowned bust of Mary 1. R. POSVIMVS etc. (several legend vars.); *mm*. lis	150	475
2509	**Halfgroat**. Similar, but POSVIM, *mm*. lis	450	1650
2510	**Penny**. Similar to 2495, but P. Z. M. etc.; *mm*. lis.................	425	1350
2510A	**Base penny**. Similar to 2495A, but P. Z. M . etc.; *mm*. halved rose and castle or castle/−, (used as a halfpenny).............................	65	225

Elizabeth's coinage is particularly interesting on account of the large number of different denominations issued. 'Crown' gold coins were again issued as well as the 'fine' gold denominations. In 1560 the base shillings of Edward VI's second and third coinages were called in and countermarked for recirculation at reduced values. Smaller debased coins were also devalued but not countermarked. The old debased groat became a three halfpence and other coins in proportion. The normal silver coinage was initially struck at 0.916 fineness as in the previous reign but between 1560 and 1577 and after 1582 the old sterling standard of 0.925 was restored. Between 1578 and 1582 the standard was slightly reduced and the weights were reduced by 1/32nd in 1601. Gold was similarly reduced slightly in quality 1578-82, and there was a slight weight reduction in 1601.

To help alleviate the shortage of small change, and to avoid the expense of minting an impossibly small silver farthing, a threefarthing piece was introduced to provide change if a penny was tendered for a farthing purchase. The sixpence, threepence, threehalfpence and threefarthings were marked with a rose behind the queen's head to distinguish them from the shilling, groat, half-groat and penny.

Coins of exceedingly fine workmanship were produced in a screw press introduced by Eloye Mestrelle, a French moneyer, in 1561. With parts of the machinery powered by a horse-drawn mill, the coins produced came to be known as 'mill money'. Despite the superior quality of the coins produced, the machinery was slow and inefficient compared to striking by hand. Mestrelle's dismissal was engineered in 1572 and six years later he was hanged for counterfeiting.

Mintmarks

1ST ISSUE	2ND ISSUE		3RD & 4TH ISSUES				
106	21	94	23	53	33	107	92
			74	71	77	65b	27

5TH ISSUE			6TH ISSUE				
7	14	113	60	54	79	72b	86

7TH ISSUE						
1	2	123	124	90	57	0

First Issue		Lis (106, milled)	1584-6	Escallop (79)
1558-60	Lis (106)	1569-71 Castle (71)	1587-9	Crescent (72b)
Second Issue		1572-3 Ermine (77)	1590-2	Hand (86)
1560-1	Cross crosslet (21)	1573-4 Acorn (65b)	1592-5	Tun (123)
	Martlet (94)	1573-8 Eglantine (27)	1594-6	Woolpack (124)
Third & Fourth Issue		Fifth Issue	1595-8	Key (90)
1560-6	Star (23, milled)	1578-9 Greek cross (7)	1598-1600	Anchor (57)
1561-5	Pheon (53)	1580-1 Latin cross (14)	1600	0
1565	Rose (33)	1582 Sword (113)	Seventh Issue	
1566	Portcullis (107)	Sixth Issue	1601-2	1
1566-7	Lion (92)	1582-3 Bell (60)	1602	2
1567-70	Coronet (74)	1582-4 A (54)		

N.B. *The dates for* mms *sometimes overlap. This is a result of using up old dies, onto which the new mark was punched.*

Hammered Coinage

GOLD

First to Fourth issues, 1559-78. ('Fine' gold of 0.994. 'Crown' gold of 0 .916 fineness. Sovereigns of 240 gr.). Mintmarks; lis to eglantine.

		F £	VF £
2511	**'Fine' Sovereign** (30 s.) Queen enthroned, tressure broken by throne, reads Z not ET, no chains to portcullis. R. Arms on rose; *mm*. lis............	7500	27500

2512

| 2512 | — — Similar but ET, chains on portcullis; *mm*. crosslet .... | 5750 | 17500 |

2513

2513	**Angel**. St. Michael. R. Ship. Wire line inner circles; *mm*. lis...................	1850	5500
2513A	— Similar, but beaded i.c. on *obv*., *mm*. lis	2000	6500
2514	— — Similar, but beaded inner circles; ship to r.; *mm*. 106, 21, 74, 27,...	1200	3250
2515	— — — Similar, but ship to l.; *mm*. 77-27	1250	3500
2516	**Half Angel**. As 2513, wire line inner circles; *mm*. lis	2250	6500
2516A	— As last, but beaded i.c.s, legend ends. Z.HIB	1350	4500
2517	— As 2514, beaded inner circles; *mm*. 106, 21, 74, 77-27	975	2850
2518	**Quarter Angel**. Similar; *mm*. 74, 77-27...	950	2850
2519	**Half Pound** (10 s.) Young crowned bust l. R. Arms. Wire line inner circles; *mm*. lis	5250	17500

2520

	F	VF
	£	£
2520 — Similar, but beaded inner circles; *mm*. 21, 33-107	1500	4500
2520A — — Smaller bust; *mm*. lion	1750	5250
2520B — — Broad bust, ear visible; *mm*. 92, 74, 71	1600	4750
2521 **Crown**. As 2519; *mm*. lis	2750	9000
2522 — Similar to 2520; *mm*. 21, 33-107	1250	3500
2522A — Similar to 2520B; *mm*. 74, 71, 92	1350	3750
2523 **Half Crown**. As 2519; *mm*. lis	2000	6500
2524 — Similar to 2520; *mm*. 21, 33-107 (2 busts)	1200	3250
2524A — Similar to 2520B; *mm*. 107-71	1250	3500
Fifth Issue, 1578-82 (`Fine' gold only of 0.992). *Mms* Greek cross,		
Latin cross and sword.		
2525 **Angel**. As 2514; *mm*. 7, 14, 113	1100	3200
2526 **Half Angel**. As 2517; *mm*. 7, 14, 113	975	2850
2527 — Similar, but without E and rose above ship; *mm*. latin cross	1200	3500
2528 **Quarter Angel**. As last; *mm*. 7, 14, 113	950	2850

Sixth Issue, 1583-1600 (`Fine' gold of 0.995, `crown' gold of 0.916; pound of 174.5 grs. wt.).
Mintmarks: bell to **O**.

2529

2529 **Sovereign** (30 s:). As 2512, but tressure not normally broken by back of		
throne; *mm*. 54-123	5250	16500

2530

	F	VF
	£	£

2530 **Ryal** (15 s.). Queen in ship. R. Similar to 1950; *mm*. 54-86 (*rev*. only) .. | 20000 | 60000

2531

2531 **Angel**. As 2514; *mm*. 60-123, 90-**O** .... | 1100 | 3200
2532 **Half Angel**. As 2517; *mm*. 60-86, 90-57 .... | 975 | 2850

2535

2533 **Quarter Angel**. As 2518; *mm*. 60-123, 90-57/– .... | 950 | 2750
2534 **Pound** (20 s.). Old bust l., with elaborate dress and profusion of hair; *mm*.,
           lion and tun/tun, 123-**O** .... | 3250 | 9000
2535 **Half Pound**. Similar; *mm*. tun... | 2250 | 7000
2535A — Similar but smaller bust with less hair; *mm*. 123-**O** .... | 2000 | 6500

2536

2536 **Crown**. Similar to 2534; *mm*. 123-90. **O** .... | 1850 | 5750
2537 **Half Crown**. Similar; *mm*. -/123, 123-0, **O** .... | 1650 | 4500

Seventh Issue, 1601-3 ('Fine' gold of 0.994, 'crown' gold of 0.916; Pound of 172 gr.). Mintmarks:
1 and **2**

		F	VF
		£	£
2538	**Angel**. As 2531; *mm*. **1, 2**	1650	5250
2539	**Pound**. As 2534; *mm*. **1, 2**	3500	10000
2540	**Half Pound**. As 2535A; *mm*. **1, 2**	3750	10500
2541	**Crown**. As 2536; *mm*. **1, 2**	3250	8500
2542	**Half Crown**. As 2537; *mm*. **1, 2**	2750	7250

Milled Coinage, 1561-70

2543

2543	**Half Pound**. Crowned bust l.; *mm*. star, lis	3250	9000
2544	**Crown**. Similar; *mm*. star, lis	2750	7500
2545	**Half Crown**. Similar; *mm*. star, lis	3500	10000

For further details on both Gold and Silver milled coinage, *see* D. G. Borden & I.D. Brown *'The milled coinage of Elizabeth I'*. BNJ 53, 1983

SILVER

Countermarked Edward VI base shillings (1560)

2546   2547

	Fair £	F £
2546 **Fourpence-halfpenny**. Edward VI 2nd period 6oz and 8oz shillings .... cmkd on obv. with a portcullis; *mm*. 66, –/33, 52, t, 111, Y and 122	1250	4500
2547 **Twopence-farthing**. Edward VI 3rd period 3 oz. shillings .... countermarked on obverse with a seated greyhound; *mm*. 92. 105, 35 and 87	1500	5250
N.B. *Occasionally the wrong countermark was used*		

First Issue, 1559-60 (.916 fine, shillings of 96 grs.)

2549   2551A

1A   1B   1D   2A   2B

	F £	VF £
2548 **Shilling**. Without rose or date. ELIZABET(H), wire line inner circles, pearls on bodice, busts 1A, and 1B; *mm*. lis.	475	2000
2549 — Similar, ELIZABETH, wire line and beaded inner circles, busts 1A, 1D, 2A and 2B; *mm*. lis	225	900

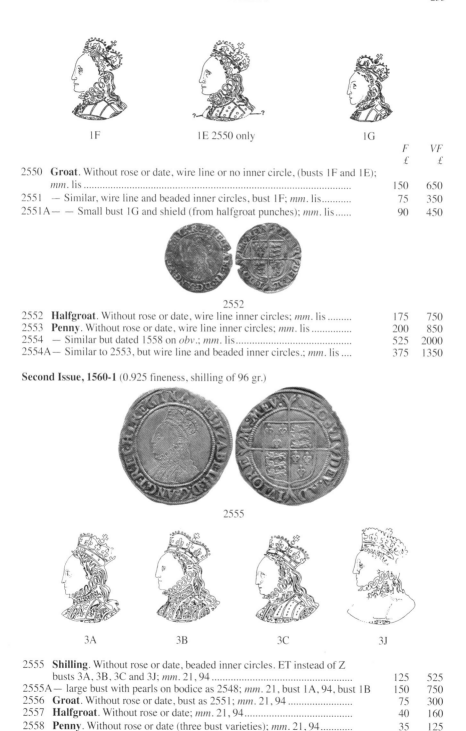

1F   1E 2550 only   1G

		F £	VF £

2550 **Groat**. Without rose or date, wire line or no inner circle, (busts 1F and 1E); *mm*. lis 150 650

2551 — Similar, wire line and beaded inner circles, bust 1F; *mm*. lis........... 75 350

2551A— — Small bust 1G and shield (from halfgroat punches); *mm*. lis...... 90 450

2552

2552 **Halfgroat**. Without rose or date, wire line inner circles; *mm*. lis 175 750

2553 **Penny**. Without rose or date, wire line inner circles; *mm*. lis 200 850

2554 — Similar but dated 1558 on *obv*.; *mm*. lis.. 525 2000

2554A— Similar to 2553, but wire line and beaded inner circles.; *mm*. lis 375 1350

Second Issue, 1560-1 (0.925 fineness, shilling of 96 gr.)

2555

3A   3B   3C   3J

2555 **Shilling**. Without rose or date, beaded inner circles. ET instead of Z
busts 3A, 3B, 3C and 3J; *mm*. 21, 94 .... 125 525

2555A— large bust with pearls on bodice as 2548; *mm*. 21, bust 1A, 94, bust 1B 150 750

2556 **Groat**. Without rose or date, bust as 2551; *mm*. 21, 94 .... 75 300

2557 **Halfgroat**. Without rose or date; *mm*. 21, 94...................................... 40 160

2558 **Penny**. Without rose or date (three bust varieties); *mm*. 21, 94........... 35 125

Third and Fourth Issues, 1561-77 (Same fineness and weight as last)

2559 2561 2561B

	F	VF
	£	£

2559 **Sixpence**. With rose and date, large flan (inner beaded circle 19mm), large bust 3D with hair swept back, 1561; *mm*. pheon 150 625
2560 — Similar, small bust 1F, 1561; *mm*. pheon 80 350

3D 2559 only   1F 2560   3E 2561B only

2562   4B 2562

2561 — Smaller flan (inner beaded circle 17.5mm). Small bust 1F, 1561-6; *mm*. 53-107   65   240
2561B — Similar, very large bust 3E, 1563-5; *mm*. pheon 100 475
2562 — Intermediate bust 4B, ear shows, 1566-73; *mm*. 92-77 .... 65 240
2562A — Similar, without date; *mm*. lion, coronet, ermine................................ 675 2000

2563   5A 2563

2563 — Larger bust 5A, 1573-7; *mm*. 77-27.. 60 225

		F	*VF*
		£	£
2564	**Threepence**. With rose and date 1561, large flan (inner circle 15mm.); *mm.* pheon	45	200
2565	— smaller flan (inner circle 14mm.). Regular bust, 1561-7; *mm.* 53-92 .	40	175
2566	— taller bust, ear shows, 1567-77; *mm.* 74-27	40	175
2566A	— Similar, without rose, 1568; *mm.* coronet	325	900

	2567 2571		
2567	**Halfgroat**. Without rose or date; *mm.* 107-71	55	200
2568	**Threehalfpence**. With rose and date 1561, large flan (inner circle 12.5mm.)		
	mm. pheon	60	200
2569	— — Smaller flan (inner circle 10.5-11.5mm.); 1561-2, 1564-78; *mm.* 53-27	45	175
2570	**Penny**. Without rose or date; *mm.* 33-71, 65b, 27	35	125
2571	**Threefarthings**. With rose and date 1561-2, 1564, 1567, 1568, 1572-7;		
	mm. 53, 74, 77-27	75	225

Fifth Issue, 1578-82 (0.921 fineness, "shilling" of 95.6 gr.)

	2572 2573		
2572	**Sixpence**. As 2563, 1578-82; *mm.* 7-113..	60	225
2573	**Threepence**. As 2566, 1578-82; *mm.* 7-113..	35	150
2574	**Threehalfpence**. As 2569, 1578-9, 1581-2; *mm.* 7-113...........................	45	175
2575	**Penny**. As 2570; *mm.* 7-113	35	125
2576	**Threefarthings**. As 2571, 1578-9, 1581-2; *mm.* 7-113........................	75	225

Sixth Issue, 1582-1600 (0.925 fineness, shilling of 96 gr.)

	2577		
2577	**Shilling**. Without rose or date, ELIZAB; busts 3B and 6A ear concealed, *mm.*		
	60-72b. Bust 6B. Ear shows, *mm.* 79-**0** (mules occur)	110	450

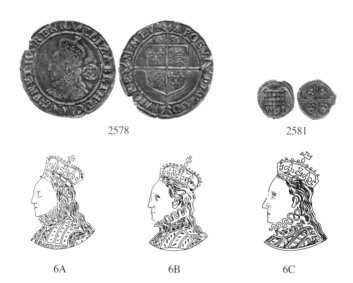

2578   2581

6A   6B   6C

		F £	VF £

2578 **Sixpence**. As 2572, ELIZABETH, 1582, 1583 *mm*. bell 65 240

2578A — Similar, ELIZAB, 1582-1589; *mm*. 60-72b... 60 225

2578B — Similar, but bust 6C 1589-1600, *mm*. 72b-**0**...................................... 60 225

2579 **Halfgroat**. Without rose or date, two pellets behind bust. R. CIVITAS
LONDON; *mm*. 60-**0** (*mm*. bell sometimes without pellets or with ··/II). 30 85

2580 **Penny**. Without rose or date. R. CIVITAS LONDON; *mm*. 60-**0**; 90-**0**
on obv only 35 125

2581 **Halfpenny**. Portcullis. R. Cross and pellets; *mm*. none, 54-**0** 30 90

Seventh Issue, 1601-2 (0.925 fineness, shilling of 92.9 gr.)

2582

2582 **Crown**. As illustration, *mm*. **1** 1500 4000

2582A – Similar, *mm*. **2** 3500 10500

2583   2588

		F	VF
		£	£
2583	**Halfcrown**. As illustration, *mm*. **1**	1100	2750
2583A	Similar, *mm*. **2**	3500	12500
2584	**Shilling**. As 2577; bust 6B *mm*. **1, 2**	125	450
2585	**Sixpence**. As 2578B, 1601-2; *mm*. **1, 2**	65	250
2586	**Halfgroat**. As 2579, *mm*. **1, 2**	30	85
2587	**Penny**. As 2580, *mm*. **1, 2**	35	125
2588	**Halfpenny**. As 2581, *mm*. **1, 2**	30	90

Milled coinage

2589	**Shilling**. Without rose or date; *mm*. star. Plain dress, large size (over 31 *mm*.)	750	2500
2590	— decorated dress, large size	375	1350
2591	— — intermediate size (30-31 *mm*.)	300	900
2592	— — small size (under 30 *mm*.)	275	800

2593   2594

2593	**Sixpence**. Small bust, large rose. ℞. Cross fourchee, 1561 *mm*. star	135	450
2594	Tall narrow bust with plain dress, large rose, 1561-2; *mm*. star	125	425

2595   2596

2595	— similar, but decorated dress, 1562	125	425
2596	Large broad bust, elaborately decorated dress, small rose, 1562; *mm*. star	125	425
2597	— — cross pattée on *rev*., 1562, 64 *mm*. star	135	450

2599

	F	VF
	£	£
2598 — similar, pellet border, 1562-4	135	450
2598A Bust with low ruff, raised rim, 1564, 1566 (both overdates)	150	500
2599 Small bust, 1567-8, ℞. As 2593; *mm*. lis	125	425

2600   2601

2600	Large crude bust breaking legend; 1570, *mm*. lis; 1571/0, *mm*. castle (over lis)	325	1250
2601	**Groat**. As illustration	150	625
2602	**Threepence**. With rose, small bust with plain dress, 1561	175	650
2603	Tall narrow decorated bust with medium rose, 1562	135	475
2604	Broad bust with very small rose, 1562	140	525
2605	Cross pattee on *rev*., 1563, 1564/3	225	750

2606

2606	**Halfgroat**. As groat	175	575
2607	**Threefarthings**. E . D . G . ROSA, etc., with rose. ℞. CIVITAS LONDON, shield with 1563 above	3250	7500

Further reading:
The Hammered Silver Coins produced at the Tower Mint during the reign of Elizabeth I.
I. D. Brown, C. H. Comber and W. Wilkinson. 2006

Portcullis money

Trade coins of 8, 4, 2, and 1 Testerns were coined at the Tower Mint in 1600/1 for the first voyage of the incorporated 'Company of Merchants of London Trading into the East Indies'. The coins bear the royal arms on the obverse and a portcullis on the reverse and have the *mm*. **O**. They were struck to the weights of the equivalent Spanish silver 8, 4, 2 and 1 reales.

2607A

	F	VF
	£	£
2607A Eight testerns	4250	12500

2607B

| 2607B Four testerns .... | 1750 | 5250 |

2607C

2607D

| 2607C Two testerns... | 1350 | 3750 |
| 2607D One testern... | 1100 | 2750 |

THE HOUSE OF STUART, THE COMMONWEALTH, AND THE HOUSE OF ORANGE, 1603-1714

JAMES I, 1603-25

With the accession of James VI of Scotland to the English throne, the royal titles and coat of arms are altered on the coinage; on the latter the Scottish rampant lion and the Irish harp now appear in the second and third quarters. In 1604 the weight of the gold pound was reduced and the new coin became known as the 'Unite'. Fine gold of 0·979 and crown gold of 0·916 fineness were both issued, and a gold four-shilling piece was struck 1604-19. In 1612 all the gold coins had their values raised by 10%; but in 1619 the Unite was replaced by a new, lighter 20s. piece, the 'Laurel', and a lighter rose-ryal, spur-ryal and angel were minted.

In 1613 the king granted Lord Harington a licence to coin farthings of copper as a result of repeated public demands for a low value coinage; this was later taken over by the Duke of Lennox. Towards the end of the reign coins made from silver sent to the mint from the Welsh mines had the Prince of Wales's plumes inserted over the royal arms.

Mintmarks

| 125 | 105 | 33 | 79 | 84 | 74 | 90 |

| 60 | 25 | 71 | 45 | 32 | 123 | 132 |

| 72b | 7a | 16 | 24 | 125 | 105 | 46 |

First coinage
1603-4   Thistle (125)
1604-5   Lis (105)

Second coinage
1604-5   Lis (105)
1605-6   Rose (33)
1606-7   Escallop (79)
1607   Grapes (84)
1607-9   Coronet (74)

1609-10   Key (90)
1610-11   Bell (60)
1611-12   Mullet (25)
1612-13   Tower (71)
1613   Trefoil (45)
1613-15   Cinquefoil (32)
1615-16   Tun (123)
1616-17   Book on lectern (132)
1617-18   Crescent (72b, gold)

1618-19   Plain cross (7a)
1619   Saltire cross (16, gold)

Third coinage
1619-20   Spur rowel (24)
1620-1   Rose (33)
1621-3   Thistle (125)
1623-4   Lis (105)
1624   Trefoil (46)

GOLD

First coinage, 1603-4 (Obverse legend reads D' . G' . ANG : SCO : etc.)

		F	VF
		£	£
2608	**Sovereign** (20s.). King crowned r., half-length, first bust with plain armour. R. EXVRGAT, etc.; *mm*. thistle	2400	9500
2609	— second bust with decorated armour; *mm*. thistle, lis	2500	10000

2610   2611

2610	**Half-sovereign.** Crowned bust r. R. EXVRGAT, etc.; *mm*. thistle	4500	17500
2611	**Crown.** Similar. R. TVEATVR, etc.; *mm*. 125, 105/125	2250	7500
2612	**Halfcrown.** Similar; *mm*. thistle, lis	900	3000

N.B. *The Quarter-Angel of this coinage is considered to be a pattern (possibly a later strike), although coin weights are known.*

Second coinage, 1604-19 (Obverse legend reads D' G' MAG : BRIT : etc.)

2613

2613	**Rose-ryal** (30s., 33s. from 1612). King enthroned. R. Shield on rose; *mm*. 33-90, 25-132	2750	9500

2614

		F £	VF £
2614	**Spur ryal** (15s., 16s. 6d. from 1612). King in ship; *mm*. 33, 79, 74, 25-32, 132	7500	27500
2615	**Angel** (10s., 11s. from 1612). Old type but larger shield; *mm*. 33-74, 60-16	1750	5250
2616	— — pierced for use as touch-piece	950	2500
2617	**Half-angel** (5s., 5s. 6d. from 1612). Similar; *mm*. 71-132, 7a, 16	3250	10500
2618	**Unite** (20s., 22s. from 1612). Half-length second bust r. R. FACIAM etc.; *mm*. lis or rose	750	2000

2619

2619	— fourth bust; *mm*. rose to cinquefoil.....................................	700	1650
2620	— fifth bust; *mm*. cinquefoil to saltire...................................	700	1650
2621	**Double-crown**. Third bust r. R. HENRICVS, etc.; *mm*. lis or rose	500	1250

2623

2622	Fourth bust; *mm*. rose to bell	450	1100
2623	Fifth bust; *mm*. key, mullet to saltire	425	1100

2624   2627

		F £	VF £
2624	**Britain crown**. First bust r.; *mm*. lis to coronet	300	675
2625	Third bust; *mm*. key to cinquefoil..	300	675
2626	Fifth bust; *mm*. cinquefoil to saltire......................................	275	650
2627	**Thistle crown** (4s.). As illus.; *mm*. lis to plain cross	275	700
2628	— IR on only one side or absent both sides; *mm*. 79, 74, 71-123	285	725
2629	**Halfcrown**. I' D' G' ROSA SINE SPINA. First bust; *mm*. lis to key	250	550
2630	Third bust; *mm*. key to trefoil, trefoil/tower..	250	550
2631	Fifth bust; *mm*. cinquefoil to plain cross	240	525

Third coinage, 1619-25

2632	**Rose-ryal** (30s.; 196.5 grs.). King enthroned. R. XXX above shield; lis, lion and rose emblems around; *mm*. 24, 125, 105	3500	10500
2633	Similar but plain back to throne; *mm*. trefoil..	3750	12000

2634

2634	**Spur-ryal** (15s.). As illus. R. Somewhat like 2614, but lis are also crowned. *mm*. 24-125, 46	7500	27500

2635

2635	**Angel** (10s.) of new type; *mm*. 24-46	2250	6500
2636	— pierced for use as touch-piece...	975	2500

2637   2638

		F	*VF*
		£	£
2637	**Laurel** (20s.; 140.5 gr.). First (large) laur, bust l.; *mm.* 24, 24/-	1050	3250
2638	Second, medium, square headed bust, `SS' tie ends; *mm.* 24, 33	675	1850
2638A	Third, small rounded head, ties wider apart; *mm.* 33, 125........................	650	1650
2638B	Fourth head, very small ties; *mm.* 105, 46...................................	625	1600
2638C	Fourth head variety, tie ends form a bracket to value; *mm.* lis	650	1650

2639
| 2639 | Fifth, small rather crude bust; *mm.* trefoil .... | 2750 | 8500 |

2641A   2642A

2640	**Half-laurel.** First bust; *mm.* spur rowel..	550	1500
2641	— As 2638A; *mm.* rose...	575	1750
2641A	— As 2638B; *mm.* 33-46, 105/-..	500	1350
2642	**Quarter-laurel.** Bust with two loose tie ends; *mm.* 24-105...................	275	700
2642A	Bust as 2638C; *mm.* 105, 46, 105/46..	260	675
2642B	As last but beaded, i.c. on *rev.* or both sides; *mm.* 105, 46......................	275	700

Rev. mm. on ¹/₂ *and* ¹/₄ *laurels normally follows REGNA.*

SILVER

2644

<table>
<tr><td></td><td></td><td align="right">F
£</td><td align="right">VF
£</td></tr>
</table>

First coinage, 1603-4

		F £	VF £
2643	**Crown**. King on horseback. R. EXVRGAT, etc., shield; *mm*. thistle, lis.	1050	3500
2644	**Halfcrown**. Similar	900	4500

2646

2645	**Shilling**. First bust, square-cut beard. R. EXVRGAT, etc.; *mm*. thistle ...	110	475
2645A	— transitional bust, nape of neck shows above broad collar, crown similar to first bust, shoulder armour as second bust, *mm*. thistle	150	750
2646	— Second bust, beard appears to merge with collar; *mm*. thistle, lis	85	300
2647	**Sixpence**. First bust; 1603; *mm*. thistle	80	375

2648	2649	2650

2648	Second bust; 1603-4; *mm*. thistle, lis	55	275
2649	**Halfgroat**. First bust, II behind head; *mm*. thistle, lis	30	110
2650	**Penny**. First bust I behind head; *mm*. thistle	65	275
2650A	— Second bust; *mm*. thistle, lis	25	80

2651

2651	**Halfpenny**. As illustration; *mm*. thistle, lis	20	70

Second coinage, 1604-19

2652

		F £	*VF* £
2652	**Crown**. King on horseback. R. QVAE DEVS, etc. *rev.* stops; *mm.* 105-84	800	2500
2653	**Halfcrown**. Similar; *mm.* 105-79	1050	4250
2654	**Shilling**. Third bust, beard cut square and stands out (*cf.* illus. 2657); *mm.* lis, rose ...	75	285
2655	— Fourth bust, armour plainer (*cf.* 2658); *mm.* 33-74, 90 over 74, or 60 over 74	75	285

2656

2656	— Fifth bust, similar, but hair longer; single-arched crown, *mm.* 74; higher double-arched crown, *mm.* 74 (rare), 90-7a	80	300

2657   2658

2657	**Sixpence**. Third bust; 1604-6; *mm.* lis, rose, escallop	60	240
2658	— Fourth bust; 1605-16; *mm.* rose to book, 90/60, 25/60	65	250
2658A	— Fifth bust, 1618; *mm.* plain cross	900	3000

2659

		F £	*VF* £
2659	**Halfgroat**. As illus. but larger crown on *obv*.; *mm*. lis to coronet............	20	65
2660	— — Similar, but smaller crown on *obv*.; *mm*. coronet to plain cross......	20	65
2660A	As before, but TVEATVR legend both sides; *mm*. plain cross over book	30	100
2661	**Penny**. As halfgroat but no crowns; *mm*. 105-32,7a and none, -/84, 32/-	20	65
2662	— As before but TVEATVR legend both sides; *mm*. mullet...................	30	90
2663	**Halfpenny**. Rose, R Thistle (with *mm*.) 105-25, 32; all *mm*s on *rev*. only	15	60

Third coinage, 1619-25

2664	**Crown**. As 2652, with plain or grass ground line, colon stops on *obv*., no stops on *rev*.; *mm*. 33-46	700	1750

2665

2665	— — plume over shield; *mm*. 125-46	850	2500

2667

2666	**Halfcrown**. As 2664 with plain or grass ground line; all have bird-headed harp; *mm*. 33-46..	225	650
2666A	— — Similar but no ground line; *mm*. rose..	575	1750

2668   2669

		F	VF
		£	£
2667	— — Plume over shield; groundline *mm*. 125-46	350	1350
2668	**Shilling**. Sixth (large) bust, hair longer and very curly; *mm*. 24-46	90	350
2669	— — plume over shield; *mm*. 125-46	200	750

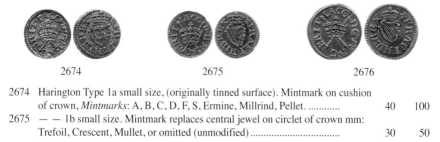

2670   2672   2673

2670	**Sixpence**. Sixth bust; 1621-4; *mm*. 33-46; 1621/0, *mm*. rose	70	275
2671	**Halfgroat**. As 2660 but no stops on *rev*.; *mm*. 24-46 and none, 105 and 46, 46/- *mm*. 24 with *rev*. stops known	20	50
2671A	Similar but no inner circles; *mm*. lis, trefoil over lis	20	65
2672	**Penny**. As illus.; *mm*. 24, 105, two pellets, none, trefoil,	15	50
2672A	— Similar but without inner circles on one or both sides; *mm*. lis, two pellets	15	50
2673	**Halfpenny**. As 2663, but no *mm*.	15	45

COPPER

For further details see Tim Everson, *The Galata Guide to the Farthing Tokens of James I and Charles I*

Farthings

2674   2675   2676

| 2674 | Harington Type 1a small size, (originally tinned surface). Mintmark on cushion of crown, *Mintmarks*: A, B, C, D, F, S, Ermine, Millrind, Pellet. | 40 | 100 |
| 2675 | — — 1b small size. Mintmark replaces central jewel on circlet of crown mm: Trefoil, Crescent, Mullet, or omitted (unmodified) | 30 | 50 |

	F	VF
	£	£
2675A — — 1c small size. Mintmark below crown, *mm*: :<	40	100
2676 — — 2 normal size. Mintmark on reverse only, *mm*: Cinquefoil, Cross saltire, Lis, Mullet, Trefoil	20	40
2676A — — 3, large crown and harp, mintmark on reverse only, *mm* Martlet ...	30	70
2677 Lennox Type 1, mintmark on reverse only; *mm*: Bell, Tower	35	70

2678	2679	2680

	F	VF
2678 — — 2, mintmark both sides, *mm*: Flower, Fusil	10	30
2679 — — 3, mintmark on obverse only, *mm*: Annulet, Coronet, Cross flory fitchée, Cross patée fourchée, Dagger, Eagle's head, Fusil, Key (horizontal), Lion passant, Quatrefoil, Rose (double), Roundel, Thistlehead, Trefoil, Tun, Turtle, Woolpack	10	30
2679A Contemporary counterfeits of Lennox Type 3, *mm*: A, Annulet, Coronet, Crescent, Cross (plain or patée), Dagger, Fusil, Key, Mascle, Roundel, Star (pierced), Stirrup, Trefoil, Triangle, Triangle with pellet below, Tun	10	25
2680 — — 4, as 3 but with larger, 9 jewel, crowns, *mm*: A, Dagger, Fusil, Lion rampant, Lis (three), Mascle, Stirrup, Trefoil, Triangle	10	30
2680A Contemporary forgeries of Lennox Type 4, *mm* A, Annulet, Dagger, Fusil, Lis, Mascle, Pellets (four), Tun,	10	25
2681 — — 5, oval flan, legend starts at bottom left, *mm* Cross patée	60	120

Lennox Type 5, the oval farthings, were issued for use in Ireland

Numismatically, this reign is one of the most interesting. Some outstanding machine-made coins were produced by Nicholas Briot, a French die-sinker, but they could not be struck at sufficient speed to supplant hand-hammering methods, and the weights often had to be adjusted by blank filing. In 1637 a branch mint was set up at Aberystwyth to coin silver extracted from the Welsh mines and dies supplied from Tower Mint. After the king's final breach with Parliament the parliamentary government continued to issue coins at London with Charles's name and portrait until the king's trial and execution. The coinage of copper farthings continued to be manufactured privately under licences held first by the Duchess of Richmond and, lastly, by Lord Maltravers. Parliament took control of the Token House in 1643, and production ceased the following year.

During the Civil War coins were struck at a number of towns to supply coinage for those areas of the country under Royalist control. Many of these coins have an abbreviated form of the 'Declaration' made at Wellington, Shropshire, Sept., 1642, in which Charles promised to uphold the Protestant Religion, the Laws of England and the Liberty of Parliament. Amongst the more spectacular pieces are the gold triple unites and the silver pounds and half-pounds struck at Shrewsbury and Oxford, and the emergency coins, some made from odd-shaped pieces of silver plate during the sieges of Newark, Scarborough, Carlisle and Pontefract.

Mintmarks

| 105 | 10 | 96 | 71 | 57 | 88 | 101 | 35 |

| 87 | 107 | 60 | 70 | 123 | 57 | 119a | 23 |

| 119b | 98 | 112 | 81 | 120 | 109 |

Tower Mint under Charles I

1625	Lis (105)	1633-4	Portcullis (107)
1625-6	Cross Calvary (10)	1634-5	Bell (60)
1626-7	Negro's head (96)	1635-6	Crown (75)
1627-8	Castle (71)	1636-8	Tun (123)
1628-9	Anchor (57)	1638-9	Anchor (57)
1629-30	Heart (88)	1639-40	Triangle (119a)
1630-1	Plume (101)	1640-1	Star (23)
1631-2	Rose (35)	1641-3	Triangle in circle
1632-3	Harp (87)		(119b)

Tower Mint under Parliament

1643-4	P in brackets (98)
1644-5	R in brackets (112)
1645	Eye (81)
1645-6	Sun (120)
1646-8	Sceptre (109)

Mint mark no. 57 maybe upright, inverted, or horizontal to left or right.

| 59 | B | 58*var* | 58 |

Briot's Mint

1631-2	Flower and B (59)	1638-9	Anchor (57)
1632	**B**		Anchor and B (58)
			(B upright or on side)
			Anchor and Mullet (58v)

61	104	35	92	103	6	65b	71
89	91*var*	131	84	94*var*	64	93	34
102	67	127	128	129	25	83	100
	134	71	A	B	75		

Provincial Mints

1638-42	Book (61, *Aberystwyth*)
1642	Plume (104, *Shrewsbury*)
	Pellets or pellet (*Shrewsbury*)
1642-3	Rose (35, *Truro*)
	Bugle (134, *Truro*)
1642-4	Lion (92, *York*)
1642-6	Plume (103, *Oxford*)
	Pellet or pellets (*Oxford*)
	Lis (105, *Oxford*)
1643	Cross pattee (6, *Bristol*)
	Acorn (65b, *Bristol*)
	Castle (71, *Worcester* or *Shrewsbury*)
	Helmet (89, *Worcester* and *Shrewsbury*)
1643-4	Leopard's head (91 *var. Worcester*)
	Two lions (131, *Worcester*)
	Lis (105, *Worcs.* or *Shrews.*)
	Bunch of grapes (84, *Worcs.* or *Shrews.*)
	Bird (94 var., *Worcs.* or *Shrews.*)
1643-4	Boar's head (64 *Worcs.* or *Shrews.*)
	Lion rampant (93, *Worcs.* or *Shrews.*)
	Rosette (34, *Worcs.* or *Shrews.*)
1643-5	Plume (102, *Bristol*)
	Br. (67, *Bristol*)
	Pellets (*Bristol*)
	Rose (35, *Exeter*)
	Rosette (34, *Oxford*)
1643-6	Floriated cross (127, *Oxford*)
1644	Cross pattee (6, *Oxford*)
	Lozenge (128, *Oxford*)
	Billet (129, *Oxford*)
	Mullet (25, *Oxford*)
1644-5	Gerb (83, *Chester*)
	Pear (100, *Worcester*)
	Lis (105, *Hereford?*)
	Castle (71, *Exeter*)
1645-6	Plume (102, *Ashby, Bridgnorth*)
1645	A (*Ashby*)
1646	B (*Bridgnorth*)
1648-9	Crown (75, *Aberystwyth Furnace*)

Tower mint, under the King (1625-42), and under Parliament (1642-9)

Tower Gold

For bust varieties on Tower Mint Gold see H. Schneider BNJ 1955-61

Numbers in brackets following each entry refer to numbers employed in previous editions of this catalogue

	F	VF
	£	£
2682 **Angel**. St. Michael slaying dragon, no mark of value. R. Three masted ship, royal arms on mainsail; mm. lis, cross calvary	4500	13500
2682A — — — pierced for use as touch-piece (2683)	1500	4500
2683 — X in field to right of St. Michael; m.m. negro's head, castle, anchor, heart, castle and negro's head/castle, anchor and castle/anchor (2684)	3000	9500
2683A — — — pierced for use as touch-piece (2685)	975	3000
2684 — X in field to left of St. Michael; mm. negro's head, heart, rose, harp, portcullis, bell, crown, tun, anchor, triangle, star, triangle-in-circle (2686)	2750	8500

2684A   2685

	F	VF
2684A — — — pierced for use as touch-piece (2687)	925	2750
2685 **Unite**. Group A, first bust, in coronation robes, bust 1, high double-arched crown. R. Square-topped shield, plain or elaborate garnishing; mm. lis (2688, 2688A)	750	1850
2686 — — bust 1a, flatter single-arched crown; mm. lis, cross calvary (2689, 2689A)	750	1850
2687 Group B, second bust, in ruff, armour and mantle. R. Square-topped shield; m.m. cross calvary, negro's head, castle, anchor, heart (2690)	725	1800

2688

	F	VF
2688 — — more elongated bust, usually dividing legend, mm. anchor, heart, plume (2690A)	725	1800
2689 — — — anchor below bust; mm. (2691)	2000	6500
2689A Group B/C mule. R. Oval shield with CR at sides; mm. plume (2691A)	975	3250
2690 Group C, third bust, shorter with heavier armour. R. Oval shield with CR at sides; mm. plume, rose (2692)	800	2000
2691 Group D, fourth bust, with falling lace collar, bust 4, large bust with jewelled crown.R. Oval shield with CR at sides; mm. harp, portcullis (2693)	700	1750

	F £	VF £
2692 — — bust 5, smaller bust, unjewelled crown; mm. portcullis, bell, crown, tun, anchor, triangle, star (2693A)	700	1750
2693 — — — (under Parliament); mm. (P), (P)/- (2710)	1350	4500
2694 Group F, sixth 'Briot's' bust, with stellate lace collar. R. Oval shield with CR at sides, mm. triangle, star, triangle-in-circle (2694)	825	2250
2695 — — (under Parliament); mm. (P), (R) (2711)	1500	4750

2696

| 2696 Group G, (under Parliament), seventh bust, smaller collar; mm. eye, sun, sceptre (2712).. | 1650 | 5000 |

2697

| 2697 **Double-crown**. Group A, first bust, in coronation robes, bust 1, high double-arched crown, both arches jewelled. R. Square-topped shield; mm. lis (2696) | 625 | 1750 |
| 2698 — — bust 1a, flatter crown, outer arch only jewelled; m.m. lis, cross calvary (2696A) .... | 525 | 1500 |

2699

2699 Group B, second bust, in ruff, armour and mantle, bust 2. R. Square-topped shield; mm. cross calvary, negro's head, castle, anchor (2697)................	475	1250
2700 — — busts 3-4, more elongated bust, usually dividing legend; mm. anchor, heart, plume (2697A)	475	1250
2701 Group C, third bust, bust 5. R. Oval shield with CR at sides; mm. plume, rose (2698)...	525	1500
2702 Group D, fourth bust, with falling lace collar, bust 6, large bust with jewelled crown. R. Oval shield with CR at sides; mm. harp, crown (2699)	500	1350

		F	VF
		£	£
2703	— — bust 7, smaller head, inner or both arches of crown unjewelled; mm. harp, portcullis, bell, crown, tun, anchor (2699A-C)	475	1250
2703A	— — — Group Da, (under Parliament), re-cut Group D bust punches; m.m. eye (2713)	1100	3500
2704	Group E, fifth bust, 'Aberystwyth' bust, bust 8, double-arched crown. R. Oval shield with CR at sides; m.m. anchor (2700)	850	2500
2705	— — bust 9, smaller 'Aberystwyth' bust, single-arched crown; m.m. anchor, triangle (2700A)	750	2250
2705A	— — — Group Ea, (under Parliament), re-cut bust 9; m.m. sun, sceptre (2714)	1050	3250
2706	Group F, sixth 'Briot's' bust, with stellate lace collar, bust 10. R. Oval shield with CR at sides; mm. triangle, star, triangle-in-circle (2701)	525	1500
2707	— — (under Parliament); mm. (P), (R) (2715)	750	2250
2708	Group H, (under Parliament), bust 11, dumpy crude bust, single flat-arched crown; mm. sun (2716)	1350	4000

2710   2715

2709	**Crown**. Group A, first bust, in coronation robes, bust 1 var, tall narrow bust, double-arched crown. R. Square-topped shield; mm. lis (2703)	300	700
2710	— bust 1, broader, less angular bust; m.m. lis, cross calvary (2703A)	325	750
2711	Group B, second bust, in ruff, armour and mantle, bust 2. R. Square-topped shield; mm. cross calvary, negro's head, castle (2704)	275	650
2712	— — bust 3, narrower; more elongated bust; m.m. anchor, heart, plume (2704A)	275	650
2713	— — — anchor below bust; mm. anchor (2704B)	675	1750
2713A	Group B/C mule. R. Oval shield with CR at sides; mm. plume, rose (2705)	300	725
2714	Group C, third bust, bust 4. R. Oval shield with CR at sides; mm. plume (2706)	375	950
2715	Group D, fourth bust, with falling lace collar, busts 5, 7. R. Oval shield with CR at sides; m.m. harp, -/harp, portcullis, portcullis/bell, bell, crown, tun, anchor, triangle, star/triangle, star, triangle-in-circle (2707)	250	575
2716	— — (under Parliament), bust 5, jewelled crown; m.m. (P), (R), eye, sun (2717)	350	850
2716A	— — (under Parliament), bust 6, unjewelled crown; m.m. eye, sun, sceptre (2717A)	400	950
2717	Group E, fifth bust, small 'Aberystwyth' bust, bust 8. R. Oval shield with CR at sides; mm. anchor (2708)	475	1250
2721C	— Group F, sixth 'Briot's' bust, bust 9, only known as Briot/hammered mule (see 2721C below)	1350	4500

	F £	VF £

Nicholas Briot's coinage, 1631-2

2718   **Angel**. Type somewhat as Tower but smaller and neater; *mm*. -/B .... | 12500 | 35000

2719

2719	**Unite**. As illustration. R. FLORENT etc.; *mm*. flower and B/B	5000	14500
2720	**Double-crown**. Similar but X. R. CVLTORES, etc. *mm*. flower and B/B	2750	7500
2720A	Similar but King's crown unjewelled: *mm*. flower and B/B, B	2850	8000
2721	**Crown**. Similar; *mm*. B	5750	17500

Briot's Hammered issue, 1638-9

2721A	**Unite**. Briot's (sixth) bust, large lace collar. R. FLORENT etc., Briot's square-topped shield dividing crowned C R; *mm*. anchor........................	7250	25000
2721B	**Double-crown**. Briot's bust, similar. R. CVLTORES etc., square-topped shield dividing crowned C R; *mm*. anchor..	2500	7500
2721C	**Crown**. Briot's bust, similar. R. CVLTORES etc., oval shield dividing crowned C R (a Briot hammered issue/Tower mule); *mm*. anchor...........	1350	4500

Provincial issues and coinage of the English Civil War 1638-49
Chester mint, 1644

| 2722 | **Unite**. As Tower. Somewhat like a crude Tower sixth bust. R. Crowned, oval shield, crowned CR, *mm*. plume .... | 32500 | 95000 |

Shrewsbury mint, 1642 (See also 2749)

| 2723 | **Triple unite**, 1642. Half-length figure l holding sword and olive-branch; *mm*.: R. EXVRGAT, etc., around RELIG PROT, etc., in two wavy lines. III and three plumes above, date below .... | 75000 | 225000 |

Oxford mint, 1642-6

2724	**Triple unite**. As last, but *mm*. plume, tall narrow bust, 1642..................	16500	47500
2725	Similar, 1643	22500	70000
2725A	Large bust of fine style. King holds short olive branch; *mm*. small lis	47500	175000
2726	As last, but taller bust, with scarf behind shoulder, 1643, *mm*. plume	17500	52500

2727

		F	VF
		£	£
2727	Similar, but without scarf, longer olive branch, 1643	16500	47500
2728	Similar, but OXON below 1643, rosette stops	25000	75000
2729	Smaller size, olive branch varies, bust size varies, 1644 OXON	17500	52500
2730	— Obv. as 2729, 1644 / OX	18500	60000
2731	**Unite**. Tall thin bust. R. 'Declaration' in two wavy lines, 1642; *no mm*...	3250	9500
2732	— R. 'Declaration' in three lines on continuous scroll, 1642-3	3250	9500
2733	Tall, well-proportioned bust. R. Similar, 1643, no *mm*	3750	12500
2734	Shorter bust, king's elbow not visible. R. Similar, 1643; *mm*. plume/-	3000	8000

2735

2735	Similar but longer olive branch curving to l. 1644 / OX; *mm*. plume	3000	8250
2735A	Similar, but dumpy bust breaking lower i.c., small flan	3000	8500
2736	Tall bust to edge of coin. R. Similar, 1643	7250	22500
2737	As 2734. R. 'Declaration' in three straight lines, 1644 / OX (as shilling *rev*. S2971)	6500	17500
2738	Similar to 2734, but smaller size; small bust, low olive branch. 1645	4000	12500
2739	— R. Single plume above 'Declaration', 1645-6 / OX; *mm*. plume, rosette, none	3500	10000
2740	**Half-unite**. 'Declaration' in three straight lines, 1642	3250	9500
2741	'Declaration' on scroll; *mm*. plume; 1642-3	3000	9000

2742

		F	VF
		£	£
2742	Bust to bottom of coin, 1643; Oxford plumes	2000	6500
2743	— 1644 / OX. Three Shrewsbury plumes (neater work)........................	3250	10000

Bristol mint, 1643-5
2744	Unite. Somewhat as 2734; Two busts known. *mm*. Br. or Br/ plumelet.;		
	1645	30000	95000
2745	Half-unite. Similar 1645	13500	37500

Truro mint, 1642–3
| 2745A | Half-Unite. Crowned bust l. (similar to Tower 4th bust). R. | | |
| | CVLT, etc., crowned shield... | 13500 | 37500 |

Exeter mint, 1643–5
2746	Unite. *obv*. sim. to early Oxford bust. R. FLORENT, etc., crowned oval		
	shield between crowned CR, *mm*. rose......................................	35000	110000
2747	— R. CVLTORES, etc., similar but no CR	35000	110000

Worcester mint, 1643-4
| 2748 | Unite. Crude bust R. FLORENT, etc., double annulet stops, crowned oval | | |
| | shield, lion's paws on either side of garniture, no *mm*............... | 32500 | 95000 |

Salopia (Shrewsbury) mint, 1644
| 2749 | Unite. *Obv*. bust in armour. R. Cr. shield, crowned CR. *mm*. lis/- .... | 32500 | 100000 |

Colchester besieged, 1648
| 2750 | Ten Shillings Gateway of castle between CR; below OBS COL 16 S/X 48. | | |
| | Uniface – now considered a later concoction .... | | |

Pontefract besieged, 1648-9. After the death of Charles I, in the name of Charles II
2751	Unite. DVM : SPIRO : SPERO around CR crowned. CAROLVS :		
	SECVИDVS : 16 48, castle, OBS on l., PC above.	75000	250000
2752	Unite. CAROL : II, etc., around HANC : DEVS, etc. R. POST : MORTEM,		
	etc.,around castle. *Octagonal*..	75000	250000

SILVER
Tower mint, under the King (1625-42), and under Parliament (1642-9)
2753	Crown. Group I, first horseman, type 1a, king on horseback left, horse		
	caparisoned with plume on head and crupper. R. Square-topped shield over		
	long cross fourchee; mm. lis, cross calvary..	650	2000
2754	— — 1b. R. Plume above shield, no cross fourchee; mm. lis, cross		
	calvary, castle..	950	3500
2755	Group II, second horseman, type 2a, smaller horse, plume on head only,		
	cross on housing. R. Oval shield over cross fourchee, CR above; mm. harp	600	1750
2756	— — 2b1. R. Plume between CR above shield, no cross fourchee; mm.		
	plume, rose..	750	2500
2757	— — 2b2. R. Plume between CR, cross fourchee; mm. harp	800	2750

2758

	F	VF
	£	£

2758   Group III, third horseman, type 3a, horse without caparisons, sword upright.
R. Oval shield without CR; mm. bell, crown, tun, anchor, triangle, star..   600   1750

2759   — — 3b. R. Plume above shield; mm. portcullis, crown, tun   625   1850

2760   'Briot's' horseman with groundline, lozenge stops on obverse; mm. triangle
in circle   3500   12500

2761   Group IV, (under Parliament), fourth horseman, type 4, foreshortened horse
R. Oval shield; mm. (P), (R), eye, sun (2838)   600   1750

2762   Group V, (under Parliament), fifth horseman, type 5, tall spirited horse;
mm. sun (2839)   750   2500

2763

2763   **Halfcrown.** Group I, first horseman, type 1a1, horse caparisoned with plume
on head and crupper, rose on housings, ground-line. R. Square-topped shield
over long cross fourchee; mm. lis (2761)   350   1350

2764   — — 1a2. No rose on housings, no ground-line; mm. lis, cross calvary (2762)   225   800

2765   — — — ground-line; mm. lis (2762A)   375   1500

2766   — — — 1a3. No rose on housings, no ground-line. R. No long cross, heavy or light
garnishing to shield; mm. cross calvary*, negro's head, castle (2763-2763B)   200   700

2767   — — — 1b. R. Plume above shield, heavy or light garnishing; mm. lis, cross
calvary*, negro's head, castle, anchor (2765, 2765A)   675   2250

2768   Group II, second horseman, type 2/1b, plume on horse's head only, rose on
housings. R. Plume over shield; mm. heart, plume (2766)   1100   3500

2769   — — 2a. Smaller horse, cross on housings. R. Oval shield with CR above
(CR divided by rose (very rare), lis over rose (rare), or lis); mm. plume,
rose, plume/rose (2767)   90   350

2770   — — — 2b. R. Plume between CR above shield; mm. plume, rose (2768)   250   850

2771

	F £	VF £
2771 — — 2c. R. Oval draped shield with CR at sides; mm. harp, portcullis, portcullis/harp (2769)	85	275
2772 — — — 2d. R. Plume above shield; mm. harp (2770)	1250	4500

2776   2779

2773	Group III, third horseman, type 3a1, no caparisons on horse, scarf flying from king's waist. R. Oval garnished shield; mm. bell, bell/crown, crown, tun, triangle (2771)	75	250
2774	— — — 3b. R. Plume above shield; mm. portcullis, bell, crown, tun (2772)	135	575
2775	— — 3a2. King wears cloak flying from shoulder. R. Oval garnished shield; mm. tun, anchor, triangle, star, triangle-in-circle (2773)	70	250
2776	— — — — rough ground under horse; mm. triangle, star (2774)	65	240
2777	— — horseman of finer style, short busy tail, cloak like arrowhead behind shoulder, no ground below; mm. triangle, star (2773 var.)	110	425
2778	— — 3a3, (under Parliament), no ground, cruder workmanship; mm. (P), (R), eye, sun (2840)	50	175
2779	Group IV, fourth horseman, type 4, foreshortened horse. R. Oval garnished shield; mm. star, triangle in circle (2775)	65	200
2779A	— — (under Parliament); mm. (P) (2841)	135	575
2780	Group V, (under Parliament), fifth horseman, type 5, tall spirited horse. R. Oval garnished shield; mm. sun, sceptre (2842)	75	250

Light weight half crowns (204 grains) exist of No. 2766 and 2767, mm. cross calvary

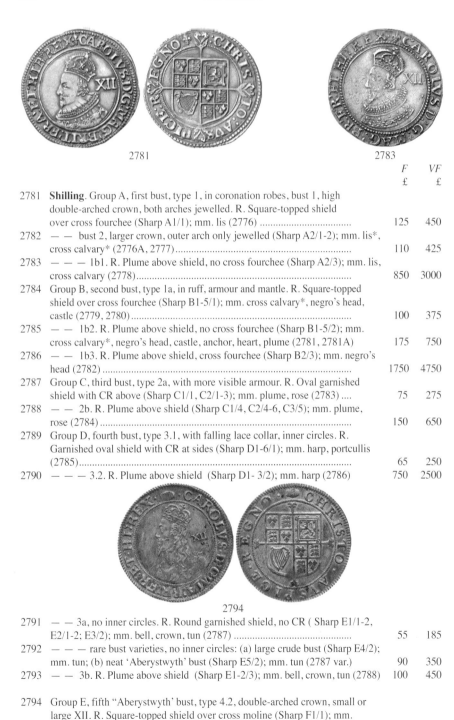

2781   2783

		F	VF
		£	£
2781	**Shilling**. Group A, first bust, type 1, in coronation robes, bust 1, high double-arched crown, both arches jewelled. R. Square-topped shield over cross fourchee (Sharp A1/1); mm. lis (2776)	125	450
2782	— — bust 2, larger crown, outer arch only jewelled (Sharp A2/1-2); mm. lis*, cross calvary* (2776A, 2777)	110	425
2783	— — — 1b1. R. Plume above shield, no cross fourchee (Sharp A2/3); mm. lis, cross calvary (2778)	850	3000
2784	Group B, second bust, type 1a, in ruff, armour and mantle. R. Square-topped shield over cross fourchee (Sharp B1-5/1); mm. cross calvary*, negro's head, castle (2779, 2780)	100	375
2785	— — 1b2. R. Plume above shield, no cross fourchee (Sharp B1-5/2); mm. cross calvary*, negro's head, castle, anchor, heart, plume (2781, 2781A)	175	750
2786	— — 1b3. R. Plume above shield, cross fourchee (Sharp B2/3); mm. negro's head (2782)	1750	4750
2787	Group C, third bust, type 2a, with more visible armour. R. Oval garnished shield with CR above (Sharp C1/1, C2/1-3); mm. plume, rose (2783)	75	275
2788	— — 2b. R. Plume above shield (Sharp C1/4, C2/4-6, C3/5); mm. plume, rose (2784)	150	650
2789	Group D, fourth bust, type 3.1, with falling lace collar, inner circles. R. Garnished oval shield with CR at sides (Sharp D1-6/1); mm. harp, portcullis (2785)	65	250
2790	— — — 3.2. R. Plume above shield (Sharp D1- 3/2); mm. harp (2786)	750	2500

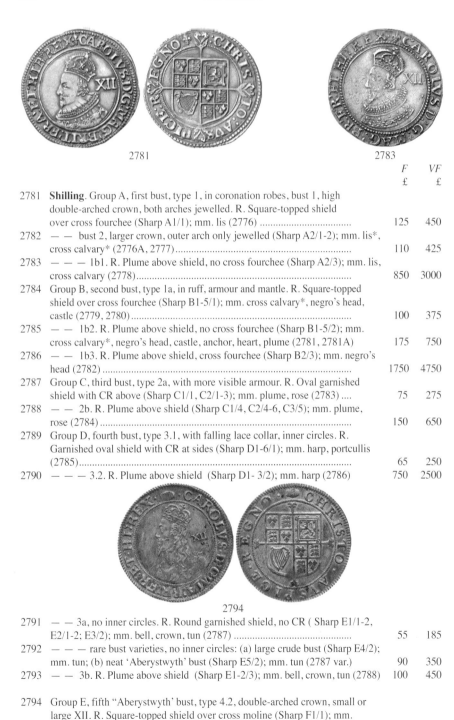

2794

		F	VF
2791	— — 3a, no inner circles. R. Round garnished shield, no CR (Sharp E1/1-2, E2/1-2; E3/2); mm. bell, crown, tun (2787)	55	185
2792	— — — rare bust varieties, no inner circles: (a) large crude bust (Sharp E4/2); mm. tun; (b) neat 'Aberystwyth' bust (Sharp E5/2); mm. tun (2787 var.)	90	350
2793	— — 3b. R. Plume above shield (Sharp E1-2/3); mm. bell, crown, tun (2788)	100	450
2794	Group E, fifth "Aberystwyth' bust, type 4.2, double-arched crown, small or large XII. R. Square-topped shield over cross moline (Sharp F1/1); mm. tun, anchor (2791)	65	275

		F	VF
		£	£

2795 — — 4.1, larger bust, single-arched crown, small or large XII (Sharp F2/1);
mm. tun, anchor (2789) 70 300

2796 — — 4.3, smaller bust, single-arched crown, large XII (Sharp F3/1-2);
mm. tun, anchor, triangle (2792) 55 225

2797   2800

2797 — — 4.1var., larger bust with rounded shoulder, large XII (Sharp F5/1-2);
mm. anchor, triangle (2790) 55 225

2798 — — rare bust varieties : (a) small 'Aberystwyth' bust, double-arched
crown (Sharp F4/1); mm. anchor (to right); (b) small 'Briot's' bust, with
stellate lace collar, single-arched crown (Sharp F6/1-2); mm. triangle;
(c) small 'Aberystwyth' bust, single-arched crown (Sharp F7/2); mm.
triangle-in-circle (2790 var.) 125 525

2803   2804

2799 Group F, sixth large 'Briot's' bust, type 4.4, with stellate lace collar,
double-arched crown. R. Square-topped shield over cross moline (Sharp G
1/1-2); mm. triangle, star, triangle-in-circle (2793) 40 150

2800 — — — (under Parliament) (Sharp G1-2/2); mm. (P), (R), eye, sun (2843) 40 150

2801 — — 4.4 var., (under Parliament), small thin bust, 'nick' below truncation
(Sharp G3/2); mm. sun (2843A) 250 850

2802 Group G, (under Parliament), seventh bust, type 4.5, tall coarse narrow bust.
R. Square-topped shield over cross moline (Sharp H1/1); mm. sun, sceptre
(2844).. 60 250

2803 — — 4.6, shorter slim better proportioned bust (Sharp H2/2); mm. sceptre
(2845).. 60 250

2804 — — — short broad bust (Sharp H3/2); mm. sceptre (2845A) 75 350

*Light weight shillings (81.75 grains) exist of No. 2782, mm. lis, cross calvary over lis; No. 2784,
mm. cross calvary; and No. 2785 mm. cross calvary*
See Sharp BNJ 1977 for bust varieties.

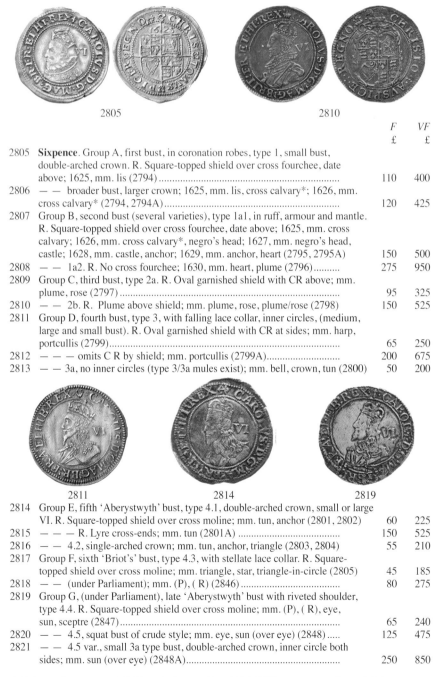

2805   2810

	F £	VF £
2805 **Sixpence**. Group A, first bust, in coronation robes, type 1, small bust, double-arched crown. R. Square-topped shield over cross fourchee, date above; 1625, mm. lis (2794)	110	400
2806 — — broader bust, larger crown; 1625, mm. lis, cross calvary*; 1626, mm. cross calvary* (2794, 2794A)	120	425
2807 Group B, second bust (several varieties), type 1a1, in ruff, armour and mantle. R. Square-topped shield over cross fourchee, date above; 1625, mm. cross calvary; 1626, mm. cross calvary*, negro's head; 1627, mm. negro's head, castle; 1628, mm. castle, anchor; 1629, mm. anchor, heart (2795, 2795A)	150	500
2808 — — 1a2. R. No cross fourchee; 1630, mm. heart, plume (2796)	275	950
2809 Group C, third bust, type 2a. R. Oval garnished shield with CR above; mm. plume, rose (2797)	95	325
2810 — — 2b. R. Plume above shield; mm. plume, rose, plume/rose (2798)	150	525
2811 Group D, fourth bust, type 3, with falling lace collar, inner circles, (medium, large and small bust). R. Oval garnished shield with CR at sides; mm. harp, portcullis (2799)	65	250
2812 — — — omits C R by shield; mm. portcullis (2799A)	200	675
2813 — — 3a, no inner circles (type 3/3a mules exist); mm. bell, crown, tun (2800)	50	200

2811   2814   2819

2814 Group E, fifth 'Aberystwyth' bust, type 4.1, double-arched crown, small or large VI. R. Square-topped shield over cross moline; mm. tun, anchor (2801, 2802)	60	225
2815 — — — R. Lyre cross-ends; mm. tun (2801A)	150	525
2816 — — 4.2, single-arched crown; mm. tun, anchor, triangle (2803, 2804)	55	210
2817 Group F, sixth 'Briot's' bust, type 4.3, with stellate lace collar. R. Square-topped shield over cross moline; mm. triangle, star, triangle-in-circle (2805)	45	185
2818 — — (under Parliament); mm. (P), (R) (2846)	80	275
2819 Group G, (under Parliament), late 'Aberystwyth' bust with riveted shoulder, type 4.4. R. Square-topped shield over cross moline; mm. (P), (R), eye, sun, sceptre (2847)	65	240
2820 — — 4.5, squat bust of crude style; mm. eye, sun (over eye) (2848)	125	475
2821 — — 4.5 var., small 3a type bust, double-arched crown, inner circle both sides; mm. sun (over eye) (2848A)	250	850

* Light weight sixpences (40.85 grains) exist of No. 2806, 1625, mm. cross calvary, 1626, mm. cross calvary; and No. 2807, 1626, mm. cross calvary

2822   2824   2832

		F £	VF £

2822 **Halfgroat**. Group A, without bust, crowned rose each side, type 1, inner
circles on one or both sides;mm. lis, lis/-, cross calvary, castle, none (2806) ... 25 90

2823 — — 1a, without inner circles; mm. negro's head, castle, anchor, heart,
plume (2807)... 25 90

2824 Group B, second bust, type 2a, in ruff and mantle. R. Oval shield; mm.
plume, rose (2808) 25 100

2825 — — 2b. R. plume above shield; mm. plume, plume/-, rose (2809) 35 150

2826 Group C, third bust, more armour, crown breaks inner circle; mm. plume,
rose (2809A) 25 100

2827 — — R. Plume above shield; mm. plume (2809B)................................. 35 150

2828 Group D, fourth bust, type 3.1, no inner circles. R. Oval shield dividing
C R; mm. harp, portcullis crown (2810).. 20 75

2829 — — — — 3.2-4, inner circle on one or both sides; mm. harp, portcullis,
../harp (2811-13) 20 75

2830 — — — 3.5-6. R. Oval shield, no C R, no inner circle or obv. only; mm. harp,
portcullis (2814-15) 25 85

2831 — — 3a1. R. Rounder shield, no inner circles; mm. bell, crown, tun, anchor,
triangle (2816) 20 75

2832 — — 3a2-3, inner circles on obverse or both sides; mm. anchor, triangle, star,
triangle-in-circle (2817-18) 25 80

2833 — — — (under Parliament), type 3a3, inner circles both sides; mm. (P)/triangle-
in-circle, (P), (R), eye, sun, sceptre (2849).. 20 75

2834 Group E, fifth 'Aberystwyth' bust, types 3a4-5, no inner circles or on reverse
only; mm. anchor (2819-20) 40 135

2835 — — 3a6, very small bust (from penny puncheon), no inner circles; mm.
anchor (2821)... 50 150

2836 Group G, (under Parliament), seventh bust, type 3a7, older bust with pointed
beard; mm. eye, sun, sceptre (2850) 20 75

2837 **Penny**. Group A, without bust, rose each side, type 1, inner circles; mm.
lis, negro's head, one or two pellets (2822) 20 70

2838 — — 1a, no inner circles; mm. lis, anchor, one or two pellets (2823).... 20 70

2839 — — 1b, inner circle on reverse; mm. negro's head/two pellets (2824). 40 125

2840 Group B, second bust, type 2, in ruff and mantle. R. Oval shield, inner
circles; mm. plume, plume/rose, rose (2825) 30 100

2841 — — 2.1, no inner circles; mm. plume, rose (2826) 30 100

2842 Group C, third bust, type 2a1, more armour visible, no inner circles;
mm. plume, plume/rose, rose (2827)... 25 95

2843 — — 2a2-4, inner circles on obverse, both sides or reverse; mm. plume,
rose (2828-30)... 25 95

2845   2851

		F £	*VF* £
2844	Group D, fourth bust, type 3.1, with falling lace collar. R. CR by shield, no inner circles; mm. harp, one or two pellets (2831)	20	65
2845	— — — 3.2, no C R by shield, no inner circles; mm. harp, portcullis, pellets, none (2832)	20	65
2846	— — — — 3.3-4, inner circles on obverse or reverse; mm. harp, two pellets (2833-34)	20	70
2847	— — 3a1, shield almost round with scroll garniture, no inner circles; mm. bell, triangle, one to four pellets, none (2835)	20	60
2848	— — 3a1 var., inner circle on one or both sides; mm. triangle/two pellets (2835A)	25	85
2849	Group E, fifth 'Aberystwyth' bust, type 3a3, inner circle on obverse or none; mm. triangle, anchor, one or two pellets, none (2836)	20	70
2850	Group G, (under Parliament), seventh bust, type 3a2, older bust, inner circle on obverse only; mm. one or two pellets (2851)	25	75
2851	**Halfpenny**. Rose each side, no legend or mm (2837)	15	50

NICHOLAS BRIOT'S COINAGE, 1631-9

First milled issue, 1631-2

2852	**Crown**. King on horseback. R. Crowned shield between CR crowned; *mm*. flower and B / B	900	2250

2853

2853	**Halfcrown**. Similar	575	1500
2854	**Shilling**. Briot's early bust with falling lace collar. R. Square-topped shield over long cross fourchee; R. Legend starts at top or bottom (extr. rare) *mm*. flower and B/B, B	425	950

2855

2855	**Sixpence**. Similar, but VI behind bust; *mm*. flower and B/B, flower and B/-	175	475

2856   2856A

	F £	VF £

2856 **Halfgroat**. Briot's bust, B below, II behind. R. IVSTITIA, etc., square-topped shield over long cross fourchee 65 175

2856A Pattern halfgroat. Uncrowned bust in ruff r. R. crowned, interlocked Cs. (North 2687). (Included because of its relatively regular appearance.) ... 60 150

2857 **Penny**. Similar, but I behind bust, B below bust; position of legend may vary 65 185

Second milled issue, 1638-9

2859

2858 **Halfcrown**. As 2853, but *mm*. anchor and B 475 1250

2859 **Shilling**. Briot's late bust, the falling lace collar is plain with broad lace border, no scarf. R. As 2854 but cross only to inner circle; *mm*. anchor and B, anchor or muled 185 525

2860 **Sixpence**. Similar, but VI; *mm*. anchor, anchor and mullet/anchor 85 240

The last two often exhibit flan reduction marks.

Hammered issue, 1638-9

2861 **Halfcrown**. King on Briot's style horse with ground line. R. Square-topped shield; *mm*. anchor, triangle over anchor. Also muled with Tower *rev* 450 1250

2862 **Shilling**. Briot's first hammered issue, Sim. to 2859; R. Square-topped shield over short cross fleury, contraction stops on *obv*., pellet stops *rev. mm*. anchor 750 2500

2862A — Briot's second hammered issue. As 2862 but lozenge stops both sides. *mm*. anchor, triangle over anchor or triangle 275 900

2862B Tower, Group E, obv. type 4.1 var. (S.2797) above R. as Briot's 1st or 2nd hammered issue; mm. Δ over anchor... 375 1250

2862C Tower, Group F, obv. type 4.4 (S.2799 above) R. as Briot's 2nd hammered issue; mm Δ/Δ over anchor. 225 750

YORK, 1643-4. *Mm. Lion*

2867

		F	VF
		£	£
2863	**Halfcrown**. 1. Ground-line below horse. ℞. Square-topped shield between CR	575	1750
2864	— 2. — ℞. Oval shield as Tower 3a, groundline grass or dotted	475	1600
2865	— 3. No ground-line. ℞. Similar	475	1600
2866	— 4. As last, but EBOR below horse with head held low. Base metal, often very base (*These pieces are contemporary forgeries*)....................	100	300
2867	— 5. Tall horse, mane in front of chest, EBOR below. ℞. Crowned square-topped shield between CR, floral spray in legend	350	1050

2868

| | | F | VF |
| | | £ | £ |

2868   — 6. As last, but shield is oval, garnished (*rev.* detail variations)............   325   850

2869   — 7. Similar, but horse's tail shows between legs. R. Shield as last, but with lion's skin garniture, no CR or floral spray   300   825

2870   2872

2870 **Shilling**. 1. Bust in scalloped lace collar similar to 3¹. R. EBOR above square-topped shield over cross fleury..   250   750

2871   — 2. Similar, but bust in plain armour, mantle; coarse work   275   800

2872   — 3. Similar R. EBOR below oval shield   275   800

2873   — 4. — Similar, but crowned oval shield (*obv.* finer style)....................   235   650

2874   — 5. — As last, but lion's skin garniture   240   675

2875 **Sixpence**. *Obv.* Sim. to 2870. Crowned oval shield   325   900

2876   2877

2876   — — Crowned CR at sides   300   725

2877 **Threepence**. As type 1 shilling, but III behind bust. R. As 2870............   65   175

ABERYSTWYTH, 1638/9-42. *Mm.* book.

Plume 1=with coronet and band. Plume 2=with coronet only

2878

		F £	VF £
2878	**Halfcrown**. Horseman similar to 2773, but plume 2 behind. R. Oval garnished shield with large plume above. *Obv.* plume 2, *rev.* plume 1.....	1000	4000
2879	— Similar to 2774, plume 1 behind King, ground below horse. *Obv.* squat plume 1, *rev.* plume 1	1050	4250
2880	As 2773 but more spirited horse, no ground. FRAN ET HIB, plume 2/1	950	3750

2881

2881	**Shilling**. Bust with large square lace collar, plume 2 before, small XII. R. As Tower 3b...	525	1750
2882	— inner circle on *rev.*	475	1500
2883	As 2881, but large plume 1 or 2, large XII, inner circles, large or .... small shield	500	1500

2884

2884	As last, but small narrow head, square lace collar, large or square plume	525	1600
2885	Small Briot style face, small crown, plume 2, large shield	575	1850
2885A	**Sixpence**. *Obv.* as Tower bust 3a, plume before. R. as 2889; inner circles both sides, *mm.* book (*obv.* only)..	525	1500

2886

		F	VF
		£	£
2886	Somewhat as 2881, but double-arched crown, small VI; no inner circles	325	1050
2887	Similar to 2886, but single arched crown, plume 2, inner circle *obv*. Large VI	350	1100
2888	Similar, but with inner circles both sides..	350	1100
2889	— — *Rev*. with small squat-shaped plume above, sometimes no *rev. mm*.	325	1050
2890	Bust as the first Oxford sixpence; with crown cutting inner circle	475	1350

2891   2894

2891	**Groat**. Large bust, lace collar, no armour on shoulder. Crown breaks or touches inner circle. R. Shield, plume 1 or 2...	75	225
2892	— Similar, armour on shoulder, shorter collar. R. Similar	85	240
2893	— Smaller, neater bust well within circle. R. Similar	75	225
2894	**Threepence**. Small bust, plume 2 before. R. Shield, plume 1 or 2 above, *obv*. legend variations...	55	175
2895	— Similar, but crown cuts i.c. squat pl. on *obv*., R. Pl. 2, *obv*. legend variations..	60	185
2900	**Halfgroat**. Bust as Tower type 3. R. Large plume. No inner circles, *mm*. pellet/book,book	65	225
2900A	Bust as 2886. R. As last, no inner circle	55	175

2901   2903   2907

2901	Bust with round lace collar; single arch crown, inner circles, colon stops	50	160
2902	After Briot's bust, square lace collar: inner circles...................................	50	160
2903	**Penny**. As 2901; CARO; no inner circles	75	275
2904	As 2901; CARO; inner circles	70	250
2905	As last but reads CAROLVS; inner circles..	80	300

		F £	VF £
2906	*Obv.* similar to 2890, tall narrow bust, crown touches inner circle	85	325
2907	**Halfpenny**. No legend. *O.* Rose. R. Plume	225	750

ABERYSTWYTH-FURNACE, 1648/9. *Mm.* crown

2908	**Halfcrown**. King on horseback. R. Sim. to 2878....................	1350	6500
2909	**Shilling**. Aberystwyth type, but *mm.* crown	3750	12500
2910	**Sixpence**. Similar	2000	5250

2911   2913

2911	**Groat**. Similar	250	750
2912	**Threepence**. Similar...	300	900
2913	**Halfgroat**. Similar. R. Large plume	375	1050
2914	**Penny**. Similar..	850	2500

UNCERTAIN MINTS

2915

2915	**Halfcrown**. As illustration, (Hereford?) dated 1645 or undated	2500	8500
2915A	**Halfcrown**. (Compton House) Scarf with long sash ends. CH (Chirk castle?) below horse. R. Oval shield 1644	3750	10500
2915B	— — R. Crowned oval shield, lion paws	3250	9500

SHREWSBURY, 1642. Plume without band used as *mm.* or in field.

2917	**Pound**. King on horseback, plume behind, from the puncheon of Tower grp. 3 crowns. R. Declaration between two straight lines, XX and three Shrewsbury plumes above, 1642 below; *mm.* pellets, pellets/-	3250	9000
2918	Similar, but Shrewsbury horse walking over pile of arms; no *mm.*, pellets	3000	8500
2919	As last, but cannon amongst arms and only single plume and XX above Declaration, no *mm.*...	5250	15000
2920	**Half-pound**. As 2917, but X; *mm.* pellets	1850	5000
2921	Similar, but only two plumes on *rev.*; *mm.*, pellets...................................	2750	7500
2922	Shrewsbury horseman with ground-line, three plumes on *rev.*; *mm.*, none, pellets/-	1650	4500
2923	— with cannon and arms or arms below horse; *mm.* pellets/-	1750	4750

	F	*VF*
	£	£
2924 — no cannon in arms, no plume in *obv*. field; *mm*. plume/pellets, plume/-	1350	3250
2925 **Crown**. Aberystwyth horseman from the puncheon of a Tower halfcrown no ground line	16500	52500

2926

2926 Shrewsbury horseman with ground-line; *mm*. -/pellets, pellets/-, none ...	1100	3250
2927 **Halfcrown**. *O*. From Aberystwyth die; (S2880); *mm*. book. R. Single plume above Declaration, 1642	2750	9500
2928 Sim. to Aberystwyth die, fat plume behind. R. Three plumes above Declaration; *mm*. pellets, pellets/-	950	3000
2929 Shrewsbury horseman, no ground line. R. As 2927, single plume, no *mm*.	1100	3500
2929A — — R. As 2933	950	3000

2930

2930 — R. 2: plume; 6, above Declaration	1750	6500
2931 — with ground-line. R. Similar	1750	6500
2932 — — R. As 2927, single plume	1100	3500
2933 — — R. Three plumes above Declaration; *mm*. none or pellets	925	2750
2933A — — R. Aberystwyth die, plume over shield; *mm*. -/book	3250	10500
2934 As 2933 but no plume behind king; *mm*. plume/pellets	775	2250
2935 **Shilling**. *O*. From Aberystwyth die; S2885 *mm*. book. R. Declaration type	1850	6000
2936 *O*. From Shrewsbury die. R. Similar	3250	9500

OXFORD, 1642-6. *Mm.* usually plume with band, except on the smaller denominations when it is lis or pellets. There were so many dies used at this mint that we can give only a selection of the more easily identifiable varieties.

For many years Oxford Halfcrowns and Shillings have been catalogued according to Morrieson obverse die varieties. In many cases, these are very small and difficult to identify. We have, therefore, simplified the obverse classification and used the available space to expand the listing of the more interesting reverse varieties.

2943

		F	*VF*
		£	£
2937	**Pound**. Large horseman over arms, no exergual line, fine workmanship. R. Three Shrewsbury plumes and XX above Declaration, 1642 below; *mm.* plume/pellets	5250	17500
2938	— Similar, but three Oxford plumes, 1643; *mm.* as last	4500	13500
2939	Shrewsbury horseman trampling on arms, exergual line. R. As last, 1642	3000	9000
2940	— — cannon amongst arms, 1642-3; *mm.* similar	2750	7500
2941	— as last but exergue is chequered, 1642; *mm.* similar	3750	12500
2942	Briot's horseman, 1643; *mm.* similar	6250	17500
2943	*O*. As 2937. R. Declaration in cartouche, single large plume above, 1644 OX below	11500	35000
2944	**Half-pound**. Shrewsbury horseman over arms, Oxford plume behind. R. Shrewsbury die, 1642; mm. plume/-	1500	3500
2945	— R. Three Oxford plumes above, 1642; mm. plume/-	1350	3250
2945A	— — 1643; *mm.* plume/-	1350	3250
2946	**Crown**. Shrewsbury die with groundline. R. Three Oxford plumes, 1642; no mm.	1100	3250
2946A	— — 1643; no *mm.*	1100	3250
2947	Oxford horseman, grass below. R. Three Oxford plumes, 1643; *mm.* plume/-	1250	3500

2948

		F £	VF £

2948 Rawlins' crown. King riding over a view of the city. R. Floral scrolls
above and below Declaration, date in script, 1644 OXON; *mm.*
floriated cross/- *(Electrotypes and copies of this coin are common)* 27500 95000

2949 **Halfcrown.** *O.* Shrewsbury die with groundline, plume behind. R.
Oxford die, declaration in two lines, three Oxford plumes above,
1642 below; no *mm.* 825 2500

2950 — no plume behind. R. as last, 1642; *mm.* plume/- 575 1650

2951 Shrewsbury horseman with groundline, Oxford plume behind. R.
Shrewsbury die, 1642; *mm.* plume/- 550 1450

2952 — R. Three Oxford plumes, 1642; *mm.* plume/- 325 850

2953 — — without groundline, 1642; *mm.* plume/- 325 850

2954   2955

2954 Oxford horseman without groundline, 1643; *mm.* plume/- 310 825

2954A — — R. Shrewsbury die, 1642; *mm.* plume/- or no *mm.* 550 1450

2955 — with groundline. R. Three Oxford plumes, 1643; *mm.* plume/- 325 850

2956 Briot horseman, grassy, rocky or uneven ground. R. Three Oxford plumes,
1643; *mm.* plume/-, plume & rosette/- 285 750

2957 — — 1643 OX; *mm.* plume/rosette, rosette 300 775

2961   2965A

		F £	VF £
2958	— — 1644 OX; *mm.* plume/-	300	775
2958A	— — lozenges by OX, 1644 OX; *mm.* plume/-	325	850
2959	— — 1645 OX; *mm.* plume/-, plume/rosette	310	800
2959A	— — pellets by date, 1645 OX; *mm.* plume/-	335	900
2960	— — 1646 OX; *mm.* plume/-	325	850
2961	— — pellets or annulets by plumes and date, 1646 OX; *mm.* plume/- ...	335	900
2962	— R. Large central plume and two Oxford plumes, 1643; *mm.* plume/-	310	825
2963	— — 1643 OX; *mm.* plume/-, rosette/-, plume & rosette/rosette, plume & rosette/-	300	775
2964	— — rosettes by OX, 1643 OX; *mm.* rosette/-, plume & rosette/-	335	900
2965	— — plain, pellets or lozenges by plumes and/or OX, 1644 OX; *mm.* plume/- plume/rosette, rosette	285	750
2965A	— — date in script, 1644 OX; *mm.* plume/-	300	775
2966	— — rosettes by plumes and date, 1644 OX; *mm.* plume & rosette/rosette	525	1350
2967	— — small plumes by date, 1644 OX; *mm.* plume & rosette/-, rosette ..	675	1750
2968	— R. Large central plume and two small Shrewsbury plumes, lozenges in field, date in script, 1644 OX; *mm.* plume/rosette	675	1750
2969	— — small plumes by date, pellets by OX, 1644 OX; *mm.* plume/-	700	1850
2970	**Shilling.** *O.* Shrewsbury die. R. Declaration in three lines, three Oxford plumes above, 1642; *mm.* plume/-..	1500	4500

2971

2971	Oxford bust (small). R. Three Oxford plumes, 1642; *mm.* Oxford plume/-,	300	950
2972	Oxford bust (small or large). R. Three Oxford plumes, 1643; *mm.* Oxford plume/-, Oxford plume/rosette	325	1050
2972A	— — pellets by date, 1644; *mm.* plume/-	425	1250
2972B	— — 1644 OX; mm. plume/rosette	425	1250
2973	— R. Oxford and two Shrewsbury plumes, lozenges by date, 1644 OX; *mm.* plume/-	475	1500
2974	— R. Three Shrewsbury plumes, 1643; *mm.* plume/-	400	1200

	F £	VF £
2975 Fine Oxford bust. R. Three Oxford plumes, lozenges in field, 1644 OX; *mm.* Shrewsbury plume/-	375	1100
2975A — — large date in script, 1644 OX; *mm.* plume/-	400	1200
2976 — 1645 OX; *mm.* plume/-	2250	6000
2976A — R. Oxford and two Shrewsbury plumes, 1644 OX; *mm.* plume/-	475	1500
2977 — R. Three Shrewsbury plumes, 1644 OX; *mm.* plume/-	400	1200
2978 — — annulets or pellets at date, 1646; *mm.* plume/floriated cross, plume/-	425	1250

2979

2979 Rawlins' die. Fine bust with R. on truncation. R. Three Oxford plumes, rosettes or lozenges by plumes, lozenges by date, 1644 OX; *mm.* Shrewsbury plume/rosette, Shrewsbury plume/-	1050	3500
2979A — — pellets by date, no OX, 1644; *mm.* plume/-	1250	3750
2979B — R. Oxford and two Shrewsbury plumes, 1644 OX; *mm.* plume/-	1350	4000

2980A

2980 **Sixpence.** O. Aberystwyth die R. Three Oxford plumes, 1642; *mm.* book/-	375	1100
2980A — — 1643; *mm.* book/-	350	975
2981 — R. Three Shrewsbury plumes, 1643; *mm.* book/-	325	950
2982 — R. Shrewsbury plume and two lis, 1644 OX (groat rev. die); *mm.* book/-	750	2000
2983 **Groat.** O. Aberystwyth die. R. Shrewsbury plume and two lis, 1644 OX; *mm.* book/-	325	900
2984 — R. Three Shrewsbury plumes, 1644 OX; mm. book/-	350	950

2985

2985 Oxford bust within inner circle. R. As 2983, 1644 OX; mm. floriated cross/-	225	675

		2987	2990		

		F	VF
		£	£
2985A	— R. Three Shrewsbury plumes, 1644 OX; *mm*. floriated cross/-	350	950
2985B	— R. Single plume, 2 scrolls and OX monogram over Decl, 1645; *mm*. floriated cross/-	375	1100
2986	Large bust to top of coin. R. As 2983, 1644 OX; *mm*. lis/-	325	900
2987	Large bust to bottom of coin. R. As 2983, 1644 OX; no *mm*.	325	900
2988	— R. Single plume, 2 scrolls and OX monogram over Decl, 1645; no *mm*.	240	700
2989	Rawlins' die, no inner circle, R on shoulder. R. As 2983, 1644 OX; no *mm*.	475	1350
2990	— R. Single plume, Declaration in cartouche, 1645; no *mm*.	350	950
2991	— — 1646/5; no mm.	325	900
2992	**Threepence.** *O*. Aberystwyth die. R. Three lis over Declaration, 1644 OX; *mm*. book/-	200	575
2993	Rawlins; die, R below shoulder. R. Aberystwyth die, oval shield; *mm*. lis/book	200	575
2994	— R. Three lis over Declaration, 1644; *mm*. lis/-	135	400

2994	3000

2995	Crown breaks inner circle, no R. R. Three lis, 1646/4; *mm*. lis/-	150	450
2996	**Halfgroat.** Small bust, beaded or wireline inner circle. R. Large plume in field; *mm*. mullet/lis, lis, -/lis, plain cross/-, plain cross/lis	135	375
2997	— R. Three lis over Delcration, 1644 OX; *mm*. lis	150	450
2998	**Penny.** *O*. Aberystwyth die, CARO. R. Small plume in field; *mm*. book/-	165	500
2999	Aberystwyth die, CAROLVS; R. Large plume; *mm*. book/-	175	525
3000	Rawlins' die, CARO. R. Small plume; *mm*. lis/mullet, lis/-	225	750
3001	Broad bust, CAROL. R. Small plume; *mm*. lis...............................	225	750
3002	— R. Three lis over Declaration, 1644; *mm*. lis	850	2500

BRISTOL MINT, 1643-5. *Mm*. usually plume or Br., except on small denominations

3003	**Halfcrown.** *O*. Oxford die with or without ground-line. R. Declaration, three Bristol plumes above, 1643 below, *mm*. plume/- or plume/cross....	575	1500
3004	— Obv. as above. R as above, but *mm*. Br. 1643...............................	650	1750
3005	King wears unusual flat crown, *obv*. *mm*. acorn? between four pellets. R. As 3003, 1643	575	1500
3006	— Obv. as above. R as 3004, *mm*. Br., 1643-4	525	1350
3007	Shrewsbury plume behind king. R. As last..	450	1200
3008	— Obv. as above. R as 3004 but Br below date instead of as *mm* . 1644	475	1250

3009

		F	VF
		£	£
3009	— Obv. as 3007 but Br below horse. R as above but 1644-5	450	1200
3010	— Obv. as above. R as 3004, *mm*. Br. and Br. below date, 1644-5	475	1250
3011	**Shilling**. *O*. Oxford die. R. Declaration, 1643, 3 crude plumes above, no *mm*.	675	2000

3012   3014

3012	— — R Similar, but *mm*. Br., 1643-4, less crude plumes	525	1500
3013	—Obv. Coarse bust. R. As 3011, no *mm*., 1643	1050	3500
3014	— — Coarse bust, R. as 3012, *mm*. Br, but 1644	575	1750

3016A   3017

3015	Obv. Bust of good style, plumelet before face. R. As 3012 *mm*. Br. but 1644-5	475	1350
3016	— — R.as 3012, 1644, but Br below date instead of *mm*.	525	1500
3016A	— — R as 3012, 1644 but plume and plumelet either side	475	1350
3017	—Obv. Taller bust with high crown, no plumelets before, *mm*. Br. on its side. R As 3016 Br.below 1644-5	575	1650
3018	—Obv. As 3017 but no *mm*. R as above but *mm*. Br., no Br. below 1644-5	600	1750
3018A	— — R as above but plume and plumelets, 1645	750	2500
3019	**Sixpence**. Small bust, nothing before. R. Declaration surrounded by CHRISTO etc., 1643; *mm*. ./Br..	625	1750

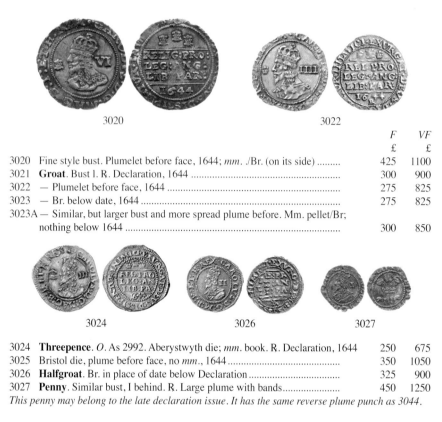

3020   3022

		F	VF
		£	£
3020	Fine style bust. Plumelet before face, 1644; *mm.* ./Br. (on its side)	425	1100
3021	**Groat**. Bust l. R. Declaration, 1644	300	900
3022	— Plumelet before face, 1644	275	825
3023	— Br. below date, 1644	275	825
3023A	— Similar, but larger bust and more spread plume before. Mm. pellet/Br; nothing below 1644	300	850

          3024   3026   3027

3024	**Threepence**. *O.* As 2992. Aberystwyth die; *mm.* book. R. Declaration, 1644	250	675
3025	Bristol die, plume before face, no *mm.*, 1644	350	1050
3026	**Halfgroat**. Br. in place of date below Declaration	325	900
3027	**Penny**. Similar bust, I behind. R. Large plume with bands	450	1250

This penny may belong to the late declaration issue. It has the same reverse plume punch as 3044.

LATE 'DECLARATION' ISSUES, 1645-6

After Bristol surrendered on 11 September 1645, many of the Royalist garrison returned unsearched to Oxford and the Bristol moneyers appear to have continued work, using altered Bristol dies and others of similar type bearing the marks A, B and plume. Ashby de la Zouch was reinforced from Oxford in September 1645 and, following its fall on 28 February 1645/6, Royalist forces marched to Bridgnorth-on-Severn, holding out until 26 April 1646. Mr Boon suggested (cf. SCBI 33, p. xli) that Ashby and Bridgnorth are plausible mint sites and the most likely candidates for the A and B marked issues, if these do indeed represent fixed mint locations.

ASHBY DE LA ZOUCH, 1645

3028	**Halfcrown**. Horseman of Bristol type, A below. R. Altered Bristol die. A (over Br) below date, 1645; *mm.* plume/A (over Br)	3250	10500
3029	- - R. A below date (new die), 1645; *mm.* plume/A	3250	10500
3030	- - R. Nothing below date 1645; *mm.* plume/A	2750	9000
3031	**Shilling**. Crowned bust left. R. Declaration type, A below date, 1645; mm. plume/A	1500	4500

3032

		F £	VF £
3032	- plumelet before face, 1645; *mm*. plume/A	1650	5500
3033	**Sixpence.** Bust of Bristol style, plumelet before face. R. Declaration type, 1645; *mm*. A (on its side)/-	1050	3000
3034	**Groat**. Similar, plumelet before face, 1645; *mm*. A (on its side)/-	975	2750
3035	**Threepence.** Similar, plumelet before face. R. Single plumelet above Declaration, 1645; no *mm*.	675	2000

BRIDGNORTH-ON-SEVERN, 1646

3036	**Halfcrown**. Horseman of Bristol type, A below (same die as 3028-30). R. Scroll above Declaration, B below, 1646; *mm*. plume/A	3750	12500
3036A	- - R. Nothing below date, 1646; *mm*. plume/-	2750	9000

3037

3037	- plumelet (over A) below horse (same die as 3028-30 recut). R. Nothing below date, 1646; *mm*. plume, plume/-	1500	4500
3038	- - plumelet below date, 1646; *mm*. plume	1500	4500
3039	**Shilling.** Crowned bust left, plumelet before face (same die as 3032). R. Scroll above Declaration, 1646; *mm*. plume/plumelet	725	2250
3039A	- Bristol obverse die, nothing before face. R. Scroll above Declaration, 1646; *mm*. Br/-	975	2750
3040	- - plume before face (altered die of 3039A), 1646; *mm*. plumelet (over Br)/-	725	2250

3041   3042

		F	VF
		£	£
3041	**Sixpence.** Crowned bust left, plume before face. R. Scroll above Declaration, 1646; *mm*. B/-	325	900
3042	**Groat.** Similar, plumelet before face, 1646; *mm*. plumelet, plumelet/-	275	725
3043	**Threepence.** Similar, plumelet before face. R. Single plume above Declaration, 1646; *mm*. plumelet/-	275	675
3044	**Halfgroat.** Crowned bust left, II behind. R. Large plume with bands dividing date, 1646; no *mm*	525	1200

3045   3047

TRURO, 1642-3. *Mm*. rose except where stated

3045	**Crown.** King on horseback, head in profile, sash flies out in two ends. R. CHRISTO, etc., round garnished shield	475	975
3046	**Halfcrown.** King on walking horse, groundline below, R. Oblong shield, CR above, *mm*. bugle/–	3500	10500
3047	Galloping horse, king holds baton. R. Oblong shield, CR at sides	3500	10500
3048	Walking horse, king holds sword. R. Similar	1100	3750
3049	— R. Similar, but CR above	1100	4000
3050	Galloping horse, king holds sword. R. Similar, but CR at sides	1350	5000
3051	— R. Similar, but CR above	1500	5250
3052	Trotting horse. R. Similar, but CR at sides	1050	3500
3053	**Shilling.** Small bust of good style. R. Oblong shield	4250	12500

EXETER, 1643-6. Undated or dated 1644-5 *Mm*. rose except where stated

3054	**Half-pound.** King on horseback, face towards viewer, sash in large bow. R. CHRISTO, etc., round garnished shield. Struck from crown dies of 3055 on a thick flan	5250	15000
3055	**Crown.** King on horseback, sash in large bow. R. Round garnished shield	525	1250

		F	*VF*
		£	£
3056	— Shield garnished with twelve even scrolls	575	1500
3057	As 3055, R̃ Date divided by *mm*. 16 rose 44	550	1350
3058	— R̃ Date to l. of *mm*. 1644	525	1250
3059	— *mm*: rose/Ex, 1645	550	1350
3060	King's sash flies out in two ends; *mm*. castle/rose, 1645	625	1650
3061	— *mm*. castle/Ex, 1645	525	1300
3062	— *mm*. castle, 1645	475	1100
3063	**Halfcrown**. King on horseback, sash tied in bow. R. Oblong shield CR at sides	950	3250
3064	— R. Round shield with eight even scrolls	450	1100

3065

3065	— R. Round shield with five short and two long scrolls	400	850
3066	— R. Oval shield with angular garnish of triple lines	825	2500

3067

3067	Briot's horseman with lumpy ground. R. As 3064	500	1350
3068	— R. As 3065	475	1250
3069	— R. As 3066	825	2500
3070	— R. As 3065, date to l. of *mm*. 1644	550	1500

3071

3071	King on spirited horse galloping over arms. R. Oval garnished shield, 1642 in cartouche below	5750	17500

		F	VF
		£	£

3072 — R. As 3070, date to 1. of *mm*. 1644-5 .... 7250 20000
3073 — R. *mm*. castle, 1645 .... 7500 22500
3074 Short portly king, leaning backwards on ill-proportioned horse, 1644, 16 rose 44 .... 1650 5000
3075 Horse with twisted tail, sash flies out in two ends R. As 3064 .... 650 1750

3076

3076— R. As 3070, date divided by *mm*. 16 rose 44, or date to 1. of *mm*. 1644-5 575 1600
3077 — R. *mm*. castle, 1645 .... 650 1750
3078 — R. *mm*. Ex, 1645 .... 600 1650
3079 — R. Declaration type; *mm*. Ex. 1644-5 .... 3750 12500
3080 — R. Similar, Ex also below declaration, 1644 .... 3500 11000
3081 **Shilling.** Large Oxford style bust. R. Round shield with eight even scrolls 1250 3750
3082 — R. Oval shield with CR at sides 1750 5500
3083 Normal bust with lank hair. R. As 3081 .... 750 2250
3083A— R. As 3082 .... 1500 5250
3084 — R. Round shield with six scrolls 575 1650

3085

3085 — R. Similar, date 1644, 45 to left of rose *mm*. 16 rose 44 (rare), 1644 to right of rose (very rare).. 525 1400
3086 — R. Declaration type, 1645 .... 2250 7000

3087A

3087 **Sixpence.** Similar to 3085, large bust and letters 1644 rose.................... 325 1000
3087A — Smaller bust and letters from punches used on 3088, small or large VI, 16 rose 44 .... 350 1050

	F	VF
	£	£

3088 **Groat**. Somewhat similar but 1644 at beginning of *obv.* legend.............. | 185 | 525 |

	3089		3090		3092	
3089	**Threepence**. Similar. R. Square shield, 1644 above...............................				175	475
3090	**Halfgroat**. Similar, but II. R. Oval shield, 1644				325	850
3091	— R. Large rose, 1644..				350	900
3092	**Penny**. As last but I behind head..				375	950

WORCESTER, 1644-45

3093 **Halfcrown**. King on horseback l., W below; *mm.* two lions. R. Declaration
       type 1644 altered from 1643 Bristol die; *mm.* pellets.............................. | 1750 | 5250 |
3094 — R. Square-topped shield; *mm.* helmet, castle .... | 1200 | 3750 |
3095 — R. Oval shield; *mm.* helmet.. | 1350 | 4000 |

3096

3096	Similar but grass indicated; *mm.* castle. R. Square-topped shield; *mm.* helmet or pellets..	975	3250
3097	— R. Oval draped shield, lis or lions in legend......................................	1050	3500
3098	— R. Oval shield CR at sides, roses in legend	1050	3500
3099	— R. FLORENT etc., oval garnished shield with lion's paws each side .	1200	3750
3100	Tall king, no W or *mm.* R. Oval shield, lis, roses, lions or stars in legend	975	3250
3101	— R. Square-topped shield; *mm.* helmet	1050	3500
3102	— R. FLORENT, etc., oval shield; no *mm.*..	1200	3750
3103	Briot type horse, sword slopes forward, ground-line. R. Oval shield, roses in legend; *mm.* 91v, 105, none (combinations)..	1200	3750
3104	— Similar, but CR at sides, 91v/-...	1350	4000
3105	Dumpy, portly king, crude horse. R. As 3100; *mm.* 91v, 105, none	1050	3500

3106

		F £	VF £
3106	Thin king and horse. R. Oval shield, stars in legend; *mm*. 91v, none......	975	3250

WORCESTER OR SALOPIA (SHREWSBURY), 1643-4

3107	**Shilling**. Bust of king l., adequately rendered. R. Square-topped shield; *mm*. castle	2250	7500
3108	— R. CR above shield; *mm*. helmet and lion	2250	7500
3109	— R. Oval shield; *mm*. lion, pear	2000	6500
3110	— Bust a somewhat crude copy of last (two varieties); *mm*. bird, lis. R. Square-topped shield with lion's paws above and at sides; *mm*. boar's head, helmet...	2250	7000

3108

3111	— — CR above	2000	6500
3112	— R. Oval shield, lis in legend; *mm*. lis	1850	5500
3113	— R. Round shield; *mm*. lis, 3 lis	1750	5000
3114	Bust r.; *mm*. pear/-, pear/lis. R. draped oval shield with or without CR. (Halfcrown reverse dies)..	3750	12500
3115	**Sixpence**. As 3110; *mm*. castle, castle/boar's hd	2000	6000

3116   3117

3116	**Groat**. As 3112; *mm*. lis/helmet, rose/helmet..	750	2000
3117	**Threepence**. Similar; *mm*. lis	425	975
3118	**Halfgroat**. Similar; *mm*. lis (*O*.) various (R.)	475	1050

	F	*VF*
	£	£

SALOPIA (SHREWSBURY), 1644

3119 **Halfcrown**. King on horseback l. SA below; *mm*. lis. R. (*mm*. lis, helmet,
lion rampant, none). Cr. oval shield; CHRISTO etc. *mm*. helmet 4750 15000

3120 — R. FLORENT, etc., crowned oval shield, no *mm*. 4750 15000

3121 — SA erased or replaced by large pellet or cannon ball; *mm*. lis in legend,
helmet. R. As 3119.. 2500 8500

3122 Tall horse with mane blown forward, nothing below; *mm*. lis. R.
Large round shield with crude garniture; *mm*. helmet.............................. 1050 3500

3123 — R. Uncrowned square-topped shield with lion's paw above and at sides;
mm. helmet.. 1350 4000

3124 — R. Small crowned oval shield; *mm*. various 975 3250

3125

3125 — R. As 3120	1200	3750
3126 Finer work with little or no mane before horse. R. Cr. round or oval shield	1200	3750
3127 Grass beneath horse. R. Similar; *mm*. lis or rose	1500	4500
3128 Ground below horse. R. As 3120..	2000	6500

HARTLEBURY CASTLE (WORCS.), 1646

3129

3129 **Halfcrown**. *O. Mm*. pear. R. HC (Hartlebury Castle) in garniture below
shield; *mm*. three pears 1650 4500

CHESTER, 1644

3130

	F £	VF £
3130 **Halfcrown**. As illus. R. Oval shield; *mm.* three gerbs and sword	1050	3500
3131 — Similar, but without plume or CHST; R. Cr. oval shield with lion skin; *mm.* prostrate gerb; -/cinquefoil, ⁻/⦂	1050	3500
3132 — R. Crowned square-topped shield with CR at sides both crowned *rev.*; *mm.* cinquefoil (these dies were later crudely recut)	1650	5250
3133 As 3130, but without plume or CHST. R. Declaration type, 1644 *rev.*; *mm.* plume	1500	5000
3133A**Shilling**. Bust l. R. Oval garnished shield; *mm.* ∴ (obv. only)	3000	9500
3133B — R. Square-topped shield; *mm.* as last	3000	9500
3133C — R . Shield over long cross	2750	9000
3134 **Threepence**. R. Square-topped shield; *mm.*-/ prostrate gerb	975	3250

WELSH MARCHES? 1644

3135

3135 **Halfcrown**. Crude horseman, l. R. Declaration of Bristol style divided by a dotted line, 3 plumes above, 1644 below	1100	3500

CARLISLE, 1644-5

3137   3139

		F £	VF £
3136	**Three shillings**. Large crown above C R between rosettes III. S below. rev. OBS . CARL / . 1645, rosette below	13500	32500
3137	Similar but :- OBS :/-: CARL :./.1645, rosette above and below	12500	30000
3138	**Shilling**. Large crown above C R between trefoil of pellets, XII below. *rev.* as 3137	8500	17500
3139	R. Legend and date in two lines..	9000	18500

Note. *(3136-39) Round or Octagonal pieces exist.*

NEWARK, 1645-6

3140   3142

		F £	VF £
3140	**Halfcrown**. Large crown between CR ; below, XXX. *rev.* OBS / NEWARK / 1645	950	2400
3140A	— Similar 1646..	925	2250
3141	**Shilling**. Similar but crude flat shaped crown, NEWARKE, 1645	900	2500
3142	Similar but normal arched crown, 1645	750	1750
3143	— NEWARK, 1645 or 1646...	725	1650

3144   3146

		F £	VF £
3144	**Ninepence**. As halfcrown but IX, 1645 or 1646	675	1600
3145	— NEWARKE, 1645	725	1700
3146	**Sixpence**. As halfcrown but VI, 1646	800	1850

PONTEFRACT, June 1648-March 1648-9. Before execution of Charles I

3147 **Two shillings** (lozenge shaped). DVM : SPIRO : SPERO around CR
      crowned. R. Castle surrounded by OBS, PC, sword and 1648 .... | 7500 | 22500

3148

| 3148 | **Shilling** (lozenge shaped, octagonal or round). Similar .... | 2000 | 5500 |
| 3149 | — Similar but XII on r. dividing PC .... | 2000 | 5500 |

After the execution of Charles I (30 Jan. 1648/9), in the name of Charles II

3150

3150 **Shilling** (octagonal). *O*. As last. R. CAROLVS : SECV И DVS : 1648, castle
      gateway with flag dividing PC, OBS on l., cannon   protrudes on r. | 2100 | 5750

3151 CAROL : II : etc., around HANC : DE / VS : DEDIT 1648. R. POST :
      MORTEM : PATRIS : PRO : FILIO around gateway etc. as last .... | 2250 | 6000

SCARBOROUGH, July 1644-July 1645

3156

3165

3169

		VF
Type I. Large Castle with gateway to left, SC and value Vs below		
3152	**Crown.** (various weights)	75000
Type II. Small Castle with gateway, no SC, value punched on flan		
3153	**Five shillings and eightpence.**	52500
3154	**Crown.** Similar...	75000
3155	**Three shillings.** Similar	40000
3156	**Two shillings and tenpence.** Similar	40000
3157	**Two shillings and sevenpence.** Similar	40000
3158	**Halfcrown.** Similar	55000
3159	**Two shillings and fourpence.** Similar	40000
3161	**One shilling and ninepence.** Struck from a different punch	35000
3162	**One shilling and sixpence.** Similar to 3159..........................	35000
3163	**One shilling and fourpence.** Similar	35000
3164	**One shilling and threepence.** Similar..................................	35000
3165	**Shilling.** Similar	45000
3166	**Sixpence.** Similar	32500
3167	**Groat.** Similar	27500

VF

Type III. Castle gateway with two turrets, value punched below

3168	**Two shillings and twopence**	20000
3169	**Two shillings.** Castle punched twice.....................	20000
3170	**One shilling and sixpence.** Similar to 3168.........................	17500
3171	**One shilling and fourpence.** Similar	17500
3172	**One shilling and threepence.** Similar.....................	17500
3173	**One shilling and twopence.** Similar	16000
3174	**One shilling and one penny.** Similar.....................	16000
3175	**Shilling.** Similar.....................	20000
3176	**Elevenpence.** Similar.....................	15000
3177	**Tenpence.** Similar.....................	15000
3178	**Ninepence.** Similar.....................	15000
3178A	**Eightpence.** Similar.....................	13500
3179	**Sevenpence.** Similar.....................	13500
3180	**Sixpence.** Similar	17500

COPPER

For further details see Tim Everson, *The Galata Guide to the Farthing Tokens of James I and Charles I*

Farthings

3182

3183

		F	*VF*
		£	£
3181	Richmond 1a, colon stops, CARO over IACO, five jewel crowns on obverse, mm on obverse only; *mm*: Coronet, Crescent with mullet.	20	50
3182	— — 1b, colon stops, CARO over IACO, nine jewel crowns on obverse, *mm*: Dagger, Mascle	20	50
3183	— — 2 CARO, colon stops, *mm* on obverse only, *mm*: Lombardic A, Lombardic A with pellet below, Annulet, Annulet with pellet within, Bell, Book, Castle, Cinquefoil, Crescent (large and small), Cross (pellets in angles), Cross calvary, Cross patée, Cross patée fitchée, Cross patonce, Cross patonce in saltire, Cross saltire, Dagger, Ermine, Estoile (pierced), Eye, Fish hook, Fleece, Fusil, Fusils (two), Halberd, Harp, Heart, Horseshoe, Key (vertical), Leaf, Lion passant, Lis (large), Lis (demi), Lis (three), Martlet, Mascle with pellet within, Nautilus, Pike-head, Rose (single), Shield, Star, Tower, Trefoil, Tun, Woolpack, Woolpack over Crescent.	10	30
3183A	— — CARA farthings (Contemporary forgeries manufactured from official punches. Usually F for E in REX), mm on obverse only; *mm*: Annulet, Coronet, Cross patée fourchée, Dagger, Fusil, Key, Mascle, Trefoil, Tun	150	300
3183B	— — Contemporary forgeries of Richmond Type 2, mm: Lombardic A, Annulet, Annulet with saltire within, Barbell and pellets, Cross (pellets in angles), Cross patée, Cross patonce, Cross patonce in saltire, Cross saltire, Dagger, Fusil, Heart, Horseshoe, Key (horizontal), Lis (large), Lis, Lis demi, Lis (three), Lis (two), Mascle, Mascle with pellet within, Rose, Star, Thistlehead, Tower, Triangle, Triangle (inverted), Tun.........................	5	15

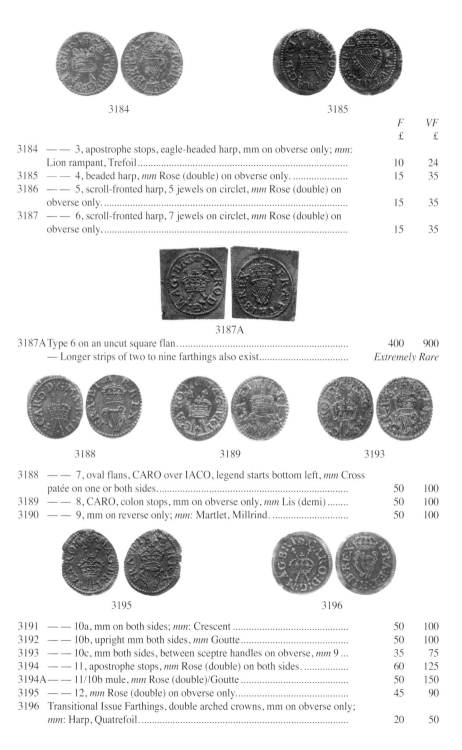

3184   3185

	F £	VF £
3184 — — 3, apostrophe stops, eagle-headed harp, mm on obverse only; *mm*: Lion rampant, Trefoil	10	24
3185 — — 4, beaded harp, *mm* Rose (double) on obverse only.	15	35
3186 — — 5, scroll-fronted harp, 5 jewels on circlet, *mm* Rose (double) on obverse only.	15	35
3187 — — 6, scroll-fronted harp, 7 jewels on circlet, *mm* Rose (double) on obverse only.	15	35

3187A

3187A Type 6 on an uncut square flan.	400	900
— Longer strips of two to nine farthings also exist	*Extremely Rare*	

3188   3189   3193

3188 — — 7, oval flans, CARO over IACO, legend starts bottom left, *mm* Cross patée on one or both sides.	50	100
3189 — — 8, CARO, colon stops, mm on obverse only, *mm* Lis (demi)	50	100
3190 — — 9, mm on reverse only; *mm*: Martlet, Millrind.	50	100

3195   3196

3191 — — 10a, mm on both sides; *mm*: Crescent	50	100
3192 — — 10b, upright mm both sides, *mm* Goutte	50	100
3193 — — 10c, mm both sides, between sceptre handles on obverse, *mm* 9	35	75
3194 — — 11, apostrophe stops, *mm* Rose (double) on both sides.	60	125
3194A — — 11/10b mule, *mm* Rose (double)/Goutte	50	150
3195 — — 12, *mm* Rose (double) on obverse only	45	90
3196 Transitional Issue Farthings, double arched crowns, mm on obverse only; *mm*: Harp, Quatrefoil.	20	50

	F £	VF £
3197 Maltravers Type 1, inner circles, mm on obverse only; *mm*: Rose (double), Woolpack	50	100
3197A Counterfeits of Maltravers Type 1, *mm*: Bell, Lis, Tun, Woolpack	15	35
3198 — — 2, mm both sides; *mm*: Bell, Lis (large), Lis (small), Martlet, Rose (double), Woolpack.................	15	35
3198A Counterfeits of Maltravers Type 2, *mm*: Bell, Cross patée, Harp, Lis (small), Mascle, Star, Woolpack	15	35

3199   3200

3199 — — 3, different mm on each side; *mm*: Woolpack/Rose (double), Martlet/ Bell, Woolpack/Portcullis, Lis/Portcullis, Harp/Bell, Harp/Billet............	15	35
3199A Counterfeits of Maltravers Type 3, *mm*: Bell/Cross patée fitchée, Bell/ Woolpack, Cross patée fitchée/Bell, Tun/Bell, Woolpack/Lis.................	15	35
3200 Maltravers Oval Type 4, no inner circles, legend starts bottom left, mm Lis (large) on both sides.............	75	150

Richmond Types 7 to 12 and Maltravers Type 4, 3188 to 3195 and 3200, the oval farthings, were issued for use in Ireland.

3201   3202   3203

(There is frequent muling between types in the Rose Farthing sequence)

3201 Rose Type 1, large double-arched crowns, sceptres within inner Circle, BRIT, mm on obv. or rev. or both; *mm*: Lis, Martlet	45	90
3202 — — 2, similar but small crowns and sceptres just cross inner circle, BRIT, mm on obverse only or both sides, *mm* Lis	30	75
3203 — — 3, similar but crowns with pointed sides and sceptres almost to outer circle, BRIT, *mm* Lis, Cross patée, Mullet, Crescent...............	15	35

3204   3206   3207

3204 - - Mules of Type 3 with Types 4a and 4b, *mm* Lis, Mullet, Crescent.	15	35
3205 - - 4a Single arched crowns, Long legends with CAROLVS, MAG, FRAN and HIB, *mm*: Lis, Mullet, Crescent.	10	25
3206 — — 4b Single arched crowns, Short legends with CAROLV, MA, FRA and HI, *mm*: Mullet, Crescent...................	10	25
3206A Counterfeits of Rose type 4, *mm* Crescent...............	20	45
3207 — — 5, sceptres below crown, *mm* Mullet on both sides	35	75

The Rose farthings were also authorised for use in Ireland but do not seem to have reached there.

The coins struck during the Commonwealth have inscriptions in English instead of Latin which was considered to savour too much of popery. St. George's cross and the Irish harp take the place of the royal arms. The silver halfpenny was issued for the last time. Coins with *mm.* anchor were struck during the protectorship of Richard Cromwell.

Mintmarks

1649-57 Sun   1658-60 Anchor

GOLD

3208

	F £	*VF* £		*F* £	*VF* £
3208 Unite. As illustration; *mm.* sun,					
1649	2650	7500	1654	2400	6000
1650	2500	6500	1655	3500	10500
1651	2250	5500	1656	2750	8000
1652	2500	6500	1657	2650	7500
1653	2250	5500			
3209 Similar, *mm.* anchor,					
1658	10000	25000	1660	8500	22500
3210 Double-crown. Similar; but X; *mm.* sun,					
1649	1750	5500	1654	1500	5000
1650	1500	4750	1655	2500	7500
1651	1350	4250	1656	3000	8500
1652	1500	5000	1657	2500	7500
1653	1350	4250			
3211 Similar, *mm.* anchor, 1660				4750	13500

3212

	F £	VF £		F £	VF £
3212 Crown. Similar, but V; *mm*. sun,					
1649	1350	4000	1654	1350	4000
1650	1250	3750	1655	1750	6000
1651	1250	3750	1656	1750	6000
1652	1100	3500	1657	1650	5500
1653	1100	3500			
3213 Similar *mm*. anchor,					
1658	3250	9500	1660	3500	10500

3215
(Blondeau's Pattern Halfcrown)

SILVER

	F £	VF £		F £	VF £
3214 Crown. Same type; *mm*. sun,					
1649	3000	8500	1653	950	2250
1651	1500	3500	1654	1050	2500
1652	1050	2500	1656	1000	2400
3215 Halfcrown. Similar; *mm*. sun,					
1649	625	1750	1654	300	800
1651	325	850	1655	1250	3250
1652	325	850	1656	275	650
1653	275	625	1657	1850	4500
3216 Similar, *mm*. anchor					
1658	1500	3250	1660	1500	3250
1659	3750	9500			

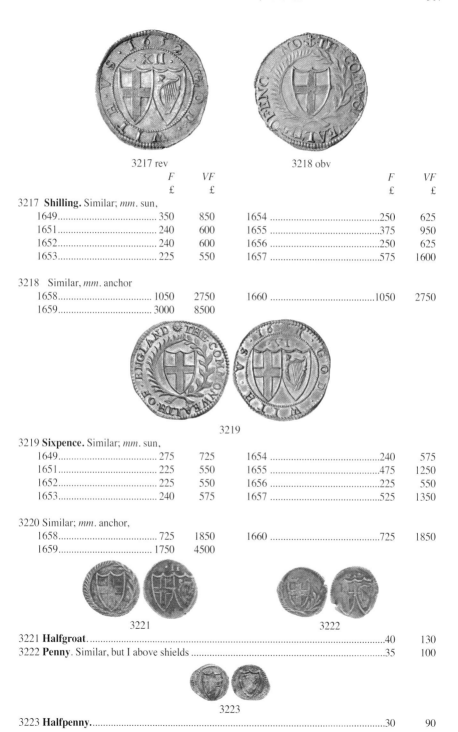

3217 rev   3218 obv

	F	VF		F	VF
	£	£		£	£

3217 Shilling. Similar; *mm.* sun,

	F	VF		F	VF
1649	350	850	1654	250	625
1651	240	600	1655	375	950
1652	240	600	1656	250	625
1653	225	550	1657	575	1600

3218 Similar, *mm.* anchor

	F	VF		F	VF
1658	1050	2750	1660	1050	2750
1659	3000	8500			

3219

3219 Sixpence. Similar; *mm.* sun,

	F	VF		F	VF
1649	275	725	1654	240	575
1651	225	550	1655	475	1250
1652	225	550	1656	225	550
1653	240	575	1657	525	1350

3220 Similar; *mm.* anchor,

	F	VF		F	VF
1658	725	1850	1660	725	1850
1659	1750	4500			

3221   3222

		F	VF
3221 Halfgroat.		40	130
3222 Penny. Similar, but I above shields		35	100

3223

		F	VF
3223 Halfpenny.		30	90

Oliver Cromwell, 'the Great Emancipator' was born on 25th April 1599 in Huntingdon. He married Elizabeth Bourchier in August 1620 and had nine children seven of whom survived infancy. The Protectorate was established on 16th December 1653, with work on the production of portrait coins authorised in 1655. Although often referred to as patterns, there is in fact nothing to suggest that the portrait coins of Oliver Cromwell were not *intended* for circulation. Authorised in 1656, the first full production came in 1657 and was followed by a second more plentiful one before Cromwell's death on 3rd September 1658. All coins were machine made, struck from dies by Thomas Simon (1618-1665) in the presses of the Frenchman, Pierre Blondeau. Later, some of Simon's puncheons were sold in the Low Countries and an imitation Crown was made there. Other Dutch dies were prepared and some found their way back to the Mint, where in 1738 it was decided to strike a set of Cromwell's coins. Shillings and Sixpences were struck from the Dutch dies, and Crowns from new dies prepared by John Tanner. Dutch and Tanner Halfbroads were also made. Oliver was succeeded as Lord Protector by his son Richard for whom no coins were struck.

GOLD

	F £	VF £	EF £
3224　Fifty shillings. Laur. head l. ℞. Crowned Shield of the Protectorate, die axis ↑↓ 1656 from the same dies as the Broad	15000	37500	110000

Lettered edge PROTECTOR · LITERIS · LITERÆ · NUMMIS · CORONA · ET · SALUS

3225
1656 gold Broad

3225　Broad. of Twenty Shillings. Laur. head l. ℞. Crowned Shield of the Protectorate, but grained edge die axis ↑↓ 1656.	4750	10500	25000

SILVER

3226
1658 Crown 8 over 7 - Die flawed drapery

3226	**Crown.** Dr. bust l. ℞. Crowned shield, 1658/7. Lettered edge ↑↓	1650	3250	6500
3226A	**Crown.** Dutch copy, similar with A Ͷ G legend 1658	1750	3750	9000
3226B	**Crown.** Tanner's copy (struck 1738) dated 1658	1750	3750	9000

		F £	VF £	EF £
3227	**Halfcrown.** Dr. bust l. R. Crowned shield 1656 HI type legend, lettered edge, die axis ↑↓	2500	5500	13500

3227A
1658 Halfcrown with HIB obverse legend

3227A Halfcrown. Similar,1658 HIB type legend, lettered edge, die axis ↑↓	1250	2250	5250

3228	3230
1658 Shilling	Copper Farthing

3228	**Shilling.** Dr. bust l. R. Crowned shield, grained edge, 1658 die axis ↑↓	750	1500	3750
3229	**Sixpence.** Similar 1658 die axis ↑↓		*Extremely rare*	

COPPER

3230	**Farthing.** Dr. bust l. R. CHARITIE AND CHANGE, shield ↑↓ ..	3000	6500	—

There are also other reverse types for this coin, and an obverse with mullet on top.

For the first two years after the Restoration the same denominations, apart from the silver crown, were struck as were issued during the Commonwealth although the threepence and fourpence were soon added. Then, early in 1663, the ancient hand hammering process was finally superceded by the machinery of Blondeau.

For the emergency issues struck in the name of Charles II in 1648/9, see the siege pieces of Pontefract listed under Charles I, nos. 3150-1.

Hammered coinage, 1660-2

Mintmark: Crown.

GOLD

3301

3302   3303

	F	VF
	£	£

First issue. Without mark of value; *mm.* crown on *obv.* only

3301	**Unite** (20s.). Type as illustration	2250	6500
3302	**Double-crown.** As illustration	1500	4500
3303	**Crown.** Similar	1750	5250

3304

Second issue. With mark of value; *mm.* crown on *obv.* only

3304	**Unite.** Type as illustration	1750	5000
3305	**Double-crown.** As illustration	1350	4000
3306	**Crown.** Similar	2250	6500

SILVER

3307

		F	VF
		£	£

First issue. Without inner circles or mark of value; *mm*. crown on *obv.* only

3307   **Halfcrown**. Crowned bust, as 3308..   1500   5000

3308   3309

			F	VF
3308	**Shilling**. Similar. (Also known with smaller harp on reverse.)		500	1650
3309	**Sixpence**. Similar		375	1100
3310	**Twopence**. Similar		55	150
3311	**Penny**. Similar		40	120
3312	As last, but without mintmark		50	135

3313   3316

Second issue. Without inner circles, but with mark of value; *mm*. crown on *obv.* only

			F	VF
3313	**Halfcrown**. Crowned bust		1350	4500
3314	**Shilling**. Similar		750	2250
3315	**Sixpence**. Similar		1500	4500
3316	**Twopence**. Similar, but mm. on obv. only		90	300

	F £	VF £
3317 Similar, but mm. both sides (machine made)	30	100
3318 Bust to edge of coin, legend starts at bottom l. (machine made, single arch crown)	25	90
3319 **Penny**. As 3317	30	90
3320 As 3318 (single arch crown)	25	80

3321   3326

Third issue. With inner circles and mark of value; *mm.* crown on both sides

	F £	VF £
3321 **Halfcrown**. Crowned bust to i.c. (and rarely to edge of coin)	225	750
3322 **Shilling**. Similar, rarely *mm.* crown on *obv.* only. (Also known with smaller harp on reverse.)	175	600
3323 **Sixpence**. Similar	135	475
3324 **Fourpence**. Similar	40	125
3325 **Threepence**. Similar	25	90
3326 **Twopence**. Similar	20	70
3327 **Penny**. Similar	20	70

Grading of Early and Later Milled Coinage

Milled coinage refers to coins that are struck by dies worked in a mechanical coining press. The early period is defined from the time of the successful installation of Peter Blondeau's hand powered machinery at the mint, initiated to strike the first portrait coins of Oliver Cromwell in 1656. The early period continuing until the advent of Matthew Boulton's steam powered presses from 1790. The coinage of this early period is therefore cruder in its execution than the latter. When pricing coins of the early peiod, we only attribute grades as high as extremely fine, and as high as uncirculated for the latter period. Most coins that occur of the early period in superior grades than those stated, in particular copper coins retaining full original lustre, will command considerably higher prices, due to their rarity. We suggest the following definitions for grades of preservation:

Milled Coinage Conditions

Proof   A very carefully struck coin from specially prepared dies, to give a superior definition to the design, with mirror-like fields. Occurs occasionally in the Early Milled Coinage, more frequently in the latter period. Some issues struck to a matt finish for Edward VII.

FDC   *Fleur-de-coin*. Absolutely flawless, untouched, without wear, scratches, marks or hairlines. Generally applied to proofs.

UNC   *Uncirculated*. A coin in as new condition as issued by the Mint, retaining full lustre or brilliance but, owing to modern mass-production methods of manufacture and storage, not necessarily perfect.

EF   *Extremely Fine*. A coin that exhibits very little sign of circulation, with only minimal marks or faint wear, which are only evident upon very close scrutiny.

VF   *Very Fine*. A coin that exhibits some wear on the raised surfaces of the design, but really has only had limited circulation.

F   *Fine*. A coin that exhibits considerable wear to the raised surfaces of the design, either through circulation, or damage perhaps due to faulty striking

Fair   *Fair*. A coin that exhibits wear, with the main features still distinguishable, and the legends, date and inscriptions still readable.

Poor   *Poor*. A coin that exhibits considerable wear, certainly with milled coinage of no value to a collector unless it is an extremely rare date or variety.

Examples of Condition Grading

Early Milled

Gold Nʹ   Silver ÆR   Copper Æ

Extremely Fine

Gold Aʋ   Silver ÆR   Copper Æ

Very Fine

Fine

George III
fifth bust Guinea

James II
Second bust Crown

George II
old head Halfpenny

Later Milled

Gold Aʋ   Silver ÆR   Copper Æ

Uncirculated

Gold A⁄   Silver Æ   Copper Æ

Extremely Fine

Very Fine

Fine

*Victoria
Jubilee head Half-Sovereign*

*George IV
laureate bust Crown*

*Victoria
Young head Farthing*

Charles II was born at St James Palace on 29th May 1630. He spent a long exile in France and returned after the fall of the Protectorate in 1660. The Restoration commenced and he married Catherine of Braganza, but he bore no legitimate successor. Charles II died on 6th February 1685.

Early in 1663, the ancient hand hammering process was finally superceded by the machinery of Blondeau. John and Joseph Roettier, two brothers, engraved the dies with a safeguard against clipping, the larger coins were made with the edge inscribed DECVS ET TVTAMEN and the regnal year. The medium-sized coins were given a grained edge.

The new gold coins were current for 100s., 40s., 20s. and 10s., and they came to be called 'Guineas' as the gold from which some of them were made was imported from Guinea by the Africa Company (whose badge was the Elephant and Castle). It was not until some years later that the Guinea increased in value to 21s. and more. The Africa Co. badge is also found on some silver and so is the plume symbol indicating silver from the Welsh mines. The four smallest silver denominations, though known today as 'Maundy Money', were actually issued for general circulation: at this period the silver penny was probably the only coin distributed at the Royal Maundy ceremonies. Though never part of the original agreement, smaller coins were eventually also struck by machinery.

A good regal copper coinage was issued for the first time in 1672, but later in the reign, farthings were struck in tin (with a copper plug) in order to help the Cornish tin industry.

Engravers and designers: John Roettier (1631-1700), Thomas Simon (1618-1665)

GOLD

3328
1672 First bust type Five-Guineas

Milled coinage

	F £	VF £	EF £		F £	VF £	EF £

3328　Five Guineas. First laur. bust r., pointed trun., regnal year on edge in words, die axis ↑↓
　　　(e.g. 1669=VICESIMO PRIMO), R. Crowned cruciform shields, sceptres in angles

	F	VF	EF		F	VF	EF
1668 VICESIMO	3000	6750	20000	1671 – TERTIO	3000	7000	22000
1668 V. PRIMO	3250	7000	22500	1672 – QVARTO ....:...	2750	6500	20000
1669 – PRIMO	2750	6500	20000	1673 – QVINTO	2750	6500	20000
1670 – SECVNDO..	2750	6500	20000	1674 – SEXTO	3500	7250	24000
1670 – Similar proof *FDC* –		–	125000				

3328A Five Guineas. First bust. Similar hair of different style. Shorter ties

	F	VF	EF		F	VF	EF
1675 V. SEPTIMO ..	3000	7000	22000	1677 – NONO...........	2750	6500	20000
1676 – SEPTIMO ...	2750	6500	20000	1678/7– TRICESIMO..	2750	6500	20000
1676 – OCTAVO.....	3000	7000	22500				

3329　Five Guineas. First bust with elephant below, similar die axis ↑↓

	F	VF	EF		F	VF	EF
1668 VICESIMO ...	2650	6250	18500	1675 V. SEPTIMO.....	3250	7250	24000
1669 – PRIMO	3250	7250	24000	1677/5– NONO...........	3750	7500	26500

3330

1676 Five-Guineas with elephant and castle provenance mark

	F	VF	EF		F	VF	EF
	£	£	£		£	£	£

3330 Five Guineas. First bust with elephant and castle below, similar die axis ↑↓

1675 – SEPTIMO ... 3750	7750	30000	1677 – NONO...........3250	7250	24000
1676 – OCTAVO..... 3000	7000	22500	1678/7– TRICESIMO..3250	7250	24000

3331 Five Guineas. Second laur. bust r., rounded trun. similar die axis ↑↓

1678/7 TRICESIMO. 2750	6500	20000	1682 T. QVARTO 2650	6250	18500
1679 – PRIMO........ 2650	6250	18500	1683 – QVINTO........2650	6250	18500
1680 – SECVNDO.. 2750	6500	20000	1683/2 – QVINTO.......2750	6500	19000
1681 – TERTIO....... 2750	6500	20000	1684 – SEXTO 2650	6250	18500

3332 Five Guineas. Second laur. bust r., with elephant and castle below, similar die axis ↑↓

1680 T. SECVNDO 3250	7250	24000	1683 T. QVINTO.......3000	7000	22500
1681 – TERTIO....... 3000	7000	22500	1684 – SEXTO 2750	6500	20000
1682 – QVARTO..... 2750	6500	20000			

3333

1664 First bust type Two Guineas

3333 Two Guineas. First laur. bust r., pointed trun. R. Crowned cruciform shields, sceptres in angles, die axis ↑↓

1664 1650	4000	9500	1671 2000	5000	13500
1665	*Extremely rare*		1673	*Extremely rare*	
1669	*Extremely rare*				

3334

1664 Two Guineas with elephant only below

3334 Two Guineas. First bust with elephant below, similar die axis ↑↓

1664...1500 3500 8250

3335
1675 Two Guineas - second bust

3339
1663 Guinea first bust, elephant below

	F £	VF £	EF £		F £	VF £	EF £

3335 Two Guineas. Second laur. bust r., rounded trun, similar die axis ↑↓

1675	1650	4000	9000	1680	1750	4750	12000
1676	1650	4000	9000	1681	1600	3750	8750
1677	1600	3750	8750	1682	1500	3500	8500
1678/7	1500	3500	8500	1683	1500	3500	8500
1679	1600	3750	8750	1684	1600	3750	8750

Overstruck dates are listed only if commoner than the normal date or if no normal date is known.

3336 Two Guineas. Second bust with elephant and castle below, similar die axis ↑↓

1676	1750	4250	9500	1682	1750	4250	9500
1677		*Extremely rare*		1683	1850	4750	12000
1678	1750	4250	9500	1684	1750	4500	10500

3337 Two Guineas. Second bust with elephant only below, die axis ↑↓ 1678 ... *Extremely rare*

3337A Broad of 20s. Laur. and dr. bust r. R. Crowned shield of arms (approx. 3400 issued),
die axis ↑↓ 1662 . 1350   3000   8500

3338 Guinea. First laur. bust r., R. Crowned cruciform shields, die axis
↑↓ 1663 3500   11000   37500

3339 Guinea. First bust with elephant below, similar die axis ↑↓ 1663 2750   8500   27500

3340 Guinea. Second laur. bust r.,similar die axis ↑↓

| 1663 | 3500 | 10000 | 35000 | 1664 | 2250 | 6750 | 22500 |

3341
1664 Guinea second bust elephant below

3342
1666 Guinea - third bust

3341 Guinea. Second bust with elephant below, similar die axis ↑↓ 1664 ..3500   10000   35000

3342 Guinea. Third laur. bust r. similar die axis ↑↓

1664	950	3250	12000	1669	900	2650	10500
1665	900	2650	10500	1670	900	2650	10500
1666	900	2650	10500	1671	900	2650	10500
1667	900	2650	10500	1672	950	3250	12000
1668	875	2400	10000	1673	950	3250	12000

3343 Guinea. Third laur. bust r., with elephant below, similar die axis ↑↓

| 1664 | 1650 | 5000 | 17500 | 1668 | | *Extremely rare* | |
| 1665 | 11650 | 5000 | 17500 | | | | |

3344
Fourth bust

3345
Fourth bust - elephant below

	F	VF	EF		F	VF	EF
	£	£	£		£	£	£

3344 Guinea. Fourth laur. bust r., rounded trun. similar die axis ↑↓

1672	775	2250	7250	1679	675	2000	6750
1673	750	2100	7000	1679 ' O' over' o' on it's side and			
1674	775	2250	7250	R of FRA over A	850	2250	—
1675	775	2250	7250	1680	675	2000	6750
1675 CRAOLVS error	2500	—	—	1680 8 over 7 and O over			
1676	675	2000	6750	inv. 9 or 6 in date		*Extremely rare*	
1676/4	1000	—	—	1681	750	2100	7000
1677	675	2000	6750	1682	750	2100	7000
1677 GRATIR error		*Extremely rare*		1682 rev.@90° axis	800	2250	7250
1677 CAROLVS error	750	2250	7000	1683	675	2000	6750
1678	675	2000	6750	1684	750	2100	7000

3345 Guinea. Fourth laur. bust r., with elephant and castle below, similar die axis ↑↓

1674		*Extremely rare*		1679	875	2750	10500
1675	875	2750	10500	1680	875	2750	10500
1676	850	2600	10000	1681	875	2750	10500
1677	850	2600	10000	1682	875	2750	10500
1677	2500	—	—	1683	850	2600	10000
1677 GRATIR error		*Extremely rare*		1684	875	2750	10500
1678	850	2600	10000				

3346 Guinea. — — with elephant below bust, similar die axis ↑↓

1677/5		*Extremely rare*		1678	3250	10500	—

3347
1669 Half-Guinea, first bust

3347 Half-Guinea. First laur. bust r., pointed trun.R. Crowned cruciform shields, sceptres in angles die axis ↑↓

1669	425	1200	3750	1671	525	1450	5000
1670	400	1100	3500	1672	450	1200	3750

3348 - 1684 Half-Guinea, second bust

	F	VF	EF		F	VF	EF
	£	£	£		£	£	£

3348 Half-Guinea. Second laur. bust r., rounded trun. similar die axis ↑↓

	F	VF	EF		F	VF	EF
1672	425	1100	3500	1678/7	400	1050	3500
1673	450	1200	3750	1679	400	1050	3500
1674	475	1300	4250	1680	425	1100	3750
1675	425	1200	3750	1681	425	1100	3750
1676	400	1100	3500	1682	400	1050	3500
1676/4	425	1200	3750	1683	400	1050	3500
1677	425	1100	3750	1684	400	1050	3500
1678	425	1100	3750				

3349 Half-Guinea. Second bust with elephant and castle below, similar die axis ↑↓

	F	VF	EF		F	VF	EF
1676	675	1700	5500	1681	675	1700	5500
1677	650	1650	5250	1682	650	1650	5250
1678/7	650	1650	5250	1683		*Extremely rare*	
1680	675	1700	5500	1684	650	1650	5250

SILVER

3350 - 1662 Crown, first type, rose below bust

3350 Crown. First dr. bust r., rose below, numerous varieties in length and style of hair ties. R.
Crowned cruciform shields, interlinked C's in angles edge undated,
die axis ↑↓ 1662 225   750   5250

3350A Crown. — — Similar, die axis ↑↑ 1662...275   900   —

3350B Crown. — striped cloak to drapery, 1662 similar die axis ↑↓ 300   950   —

3350C Crown. — — II of legend at 12 o'clock, similar die axis ↑↓ 1662..1750   —   —

3351 Crown. — — edge dated, similar die axis ↑↓ or ↑↑ 1662.................225   750   5250

3352 Crown. — legend re-arranged no rose, edge dated, similar die
axis ↑↓ 1662 250   900   5750

3353 Crown. — — edge not dated, similar die axis ↑↓ 1662 250   850   5500

3354 Crown. — — shields altered, 1663, similar regnal year on edge in
Roman figures ANNO REGNI XV die axis ↑↓ 225   750   5250

1663 no stops on reverse 240   800   5000

1663 edge not dated, as 3350 ....*Extremely rare*

3354A

	F	VF	EF			F	VF	EF
	£	£	£			£	£	£

3354A Pattern 'Petition' Crown, 1663 by Thomas Simon. Laur. Bust r. of fine style in high relief, *Simon* below, edge inscription of Simon's 'petition': THOMAS SIMON. MOST. HVMBLY. PRAYS. YOVR MAJESTY etc., etc... 15000 57500 225000

3354B Pattern 'Reddite' Crown, 1663, by Thomas Simon, struck from the same dies, edge inscription: REDDITE. QVAE. CESARIS etc., etc. 12500 45000 175000

3355 Crown. Second dr. bust r. smaller than first bust and with curving tie to wreath. Regnal year on edge in Roman figures (e.g. 1664 = XVI), die axis ↑↓

1664 edge XVI 210	750	4250	1665 XVII 1100	3000	—
1664 Proof *FDC* .... —	—	40000	1666 XVIII.................... 275	900	4750
1665 XVI................ 1350	—	—	1666 XVIII RE·X 325	950	5000
1665/4 XVII 1250	3250	—	1667 XVIII.................. 3250	—	—

3356 Crown. Second bust elephant below, similar, die axis ↑↓

1666 XVIII 750	2400	15000	1666 XVIII RE·X 800	2500	—

3357
1668 Crown - second bust

3357 Crown. Second bust, similar, Regnal year on edge in words (e.g. 1667= DECIMO NONO) die axis ↑↓

1667 D. NONO 210	700	4500	1669 V· PRIMO..............325	1000	—
1667 — AN.· REG.·... 210	700	4500	1669/8 V· PRIMO..........375	1200	—
1668 VICESIMO 200	650	4250	1670 V. SECVNDO 200	650	4250
1668 — error edge			1670/69 V. SECVND......275	850	4500
inverted..................... 350	—	—	1671 V· TERTIO 200	650	4250
1668/7 VICESIMO 225	700	4500	1671 — T/R in ET 325	950	—
1668/5 VICESIMO	*Extremely rare*		1671 — ET over FR 350	1050	—

3358
Third bust Crown

	F	VF	EF		F	VF	EF
	£	£	£		£	£	£

3358 Crown. Third dr. bust r. much larger and broader than second bust, tie nearly straight. From end of tie to top of nose is 20mm. R.Similar die axis ↑↓

	F	VF	EF		F	VF	EF
1671 V. TERTIO.......	200	650	4000	1675 — EGNI error 575		1850	—
1671 V. QVARTO.......450		1350	—	1676 V. OCTAVO 200		650	4000
1672 V. QVARTO.....	200	650	4000	1676 OCCTAVO 210		675	4250
1673 V. QVARTO		Extremely rare		1677 V. NONO...............200		650	4000
1673 V. QVINTO	200	650	4000	1677/6 V. NONO............200		650	4000
1673 B/R in BR	250	800	—	1678/7 TRICESIMO 275		850	4750
1673/2 V. QVINTO ... 225		700	4250	1679 T. PRIMO..............200		650	4000
1674 V. SEXTO..............		Extremely rare		1680/79 T. SECVNDO.......240		750	4750
1675/3 V. SEPTIMO . 625		2000	—	1680 T. SECVNDO 225		725	4500
1675 — 675		2250	—				

3359
Fourth bust Crown

3359 Crown. Fourth dr. bust r. still larger, with older features and more pointed nose. From end of tie to tip of nose is 21mm. R.Similar die axis ↑↓

	F	VF	EF		F	VF	EF
1679 T. PRIMO 210		675	3750	1682/1 T. QVARTO 210		675	3750
1679 HIBR·EX.......... 375		1350	—	1682 T. QVARTO...........240		750	4000
1680 T. SECVNDO... 210		675	3750	1682/1 QVRRTO error 225		700	3850
1680/79 T. SECVNDO .250		800	4500	1683 T. QVINTO 325		1050	6500
1681 T. TERTIO 210		675	3750	1684 T. SEXTO..............275		900	4750

3360 Crown.— elephant and castle below bust, die axis ↑↓

	F	VF	EF
1681 T. TERTIO 3500		9000	—

3361 - First bust Halfcrown   3362 - Second bust Halfcrown

	F	VF	EF		F	VF	EF
	£	£	£		£	£	£

3361 Halfcrown. First dr. bust r. R. Crowned cruciform shields, interlinked C's in angles, regnal year on edge in Roman figures die axis ↑↓

1663 XV 200 1000 4000
1663 XV V/S in CAROLVS 300 1100 4250
1663 XV A/T in GRATIA...300 1100 4250
1663 XV no stops on obverse 325 1200 4500

3362 Halfcrown. Second dr. bust r., similar die axis ↑↓ 1664 XVI 350 1250 5250

3363 Halfcrown. Third dr. bust r., similar die axis ↑↓ 1666/4 XVIII ....950 3250 —

3364 - Third bust, elephant below Halfcrown

3364 Halfcrown. Third bust elephant below, die axis ↑↓ 1666 XVIII..............850 3000 —

3365 - 1670 Halfcrown, third bust   MRG for MAG var

3365 Halfcrown. Third dr. bust r. regnal date on edge in words (eg. 1667=DECIMO NONO) ↑↓

1667/4 D. NONO 3500	—	—	1670 V. SECVNDO 150	625	3000
1668/4 VICESIMO 350	1350	—	1670 – MRG for MAG..... 275	950	—
1669/4 V. PRIMO......... 275	950	—	1670 V/S CAROLVS 250	850	—
1669 V. PRIMO............ 350	1350	—	1670 E/R in ET 250	875	—
1669 — R/I in PRIMO .375	1450	—			

3366
1671 Halfcrown third bust variety

	F	VF	EF		F	VF	EF
	£	£	£		£	£	£

3366   Halfcrown. Third bust variety r. R. Similar die axis ↑↓

	F	VF	EF		F	VF	EF
1671 V. TERTIO..........160		625	3000	1672 V. TERTIO...................*Extremely rare*			
1671 A/R in MAG........250		850	—	1672 V. QVARTO..........160		625	3000
1671/0 V. TERTIO.......185		675	3250				

3367
Fourth bust Halfcrown

3367   Halfcrown. Fourth dr. bust r. R. Similar die axis ↑↓

1672 V. QVARTO..........150	550	3000	1678 TRICESIMO.........200	825	6500
1673 V. QVINTO..........150	550	3000	1679 T. PRIMO.............140	525	2750
1673 —A/R in FRA 185	675	—	1679 — DECNS error 200	750	—
1673 — B/R in BR........185	675	—	1679 — DNCVS error.....160	600	—
1673 — FR/M in FRA...185	675	—	1679 — PRICESIMO 150	575	3000
1674 V. SEXTO.............175	675	3250	1680 T. SECVNDO........140	550	2750
1674/3 V. SEXTO..........225	750	—	1680 T. SECVNDO error ..175	600	3000
1675 V. SEPTIMO 150	550	3000	1681 T. TERTIO.............185	675	3250
1675 — Retrograde 1 175	650	3250	1681/0 — 275	850	—
1676 V. OCTAVO..........140	500	2750	1682 T. QVARTO...........140	550	2750
1676 R/T in BR 250	825	—	1682/79 T. QVARTO 250	800	—
1676 — Retrograde 1 150	550	3000	1683 T. QVINTO 140	550	2750
1676 F/H in FRA...........185	700	—	1684/3 T. SEXTO 275	850	—
1677 V. NONO 140	525	2750			
1677 F/H in FRA...........185	700	—			

3369 - Plume in centre

	F	VF	EF			F	VF	EF
	£	£	£			£	£	£

3368 Halfcrown. Fourth bust plume below, R. Similar die axis ↑↓

1673 V. QVINTO 6500   17500   —   1683 T. QVINTO 7500   20000   —

3369 Halfcrown.— plume below bust and in centre of *rev.*, die axis ↑↓

1673 V. QVINTO 8500   22500   —

3370 - Elephant and Castle below bust

3370 Halfcrown.— elephant and castle below bust, die axis ↑↓

1681 T. TERTIO 3500   9500   27500

SHILLINGS

First bust   First bust variety   Second bust   Third bust

First bust   First bust variety   First and first bust   Second bust
                                          variety, double top leaf   single top leaf

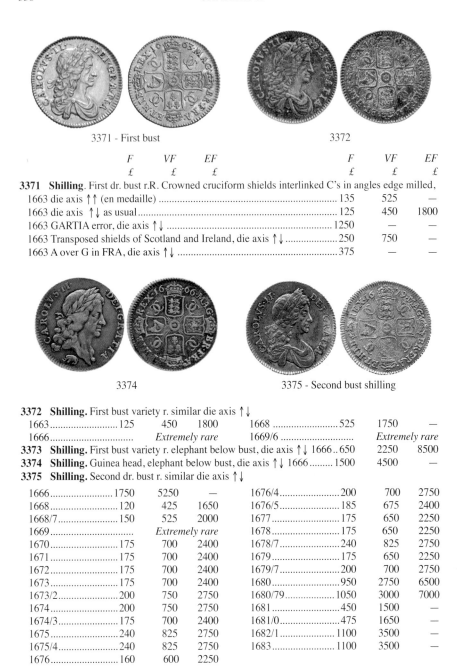

3371 - First bust   3372

	F £	VF £	EF £		F £	VF £	EF £

3371 Shilling. First dr. bust r.R. Crowned cruciform shields interlinked C's in angles edge milled,

	F	VF	EF
1663 die axis ↑↑ (en medaille)	135	525	—
1663 die axis ↑↓ as usual	125	450	1800
1663 GARTIA error, die axis ↑↓	1250	—	—
1663 Transposed shields of Scotland and Ireland, die axis ↑↓	250	750	—
1663 A over G in FRA, die axis ↑↓	375	—	—

3374   3375 - Second bust shilling

3372 Shilling. First bust variety r. similar die axis ↑↓

	F	VF	EF			VF	EF
1663	125	450	1800	1668	525	1750	—
1666		*Extremely rare*		1669/6		*Extremely rare*	

3373 Shilling. First bust variety r. elephant below bust, die axis ↑↓ 1666..650   2250   8500

3374 Shilling. Guinea head, elephant below bust, die axis ↑↓ 1666 1500   4500   —

3375 Shilling. Second dr. bust r. similar die axis ↑↓

	F	VF	EF			F	VF	EF
1666	1750	5250	—	1676/4	200	700	2750
1668	120	425	1650	1676/5	185	675	2400
1668/7	150	525	2000	1677	175	650	2250
1669		*Extremely rare*		1678	175	650	2250
1670	175	700	2400	1678/7	240	825	2750
1671	175	700	2400	1679	175	650	2250
1672	175	700	2400	1679/7	200	700	2750
1673	175	700	2400	1680	950	2750	6500
1673/2	200	750	2750	1680/79	1050	3000	7000
1674	200	750	2750	1681	450	1500	—
1674/3	175	700	2400	1681/0	475	1650	—
1675	240	825	2750	1682/1	1100	3500	—
1675/4	240	825	2750	1683	1100	3500	—
1676	160	600	2250				

The 1668 shilling is also known with large 6's in the date

3376 - Plume both sides shilling of 1671

	F £	VF £	EF £		F £	VF £	EF £

3376 Shilling. Second Bust — plume below bust and in centre of *rev.* similar die axis ↑↓

1671	400	1250	3750	1676	450	1450	4250
1673	425	1350	4000	1679	425	1350	4000
1674	400	1250	3750	1680/79	1100	3000	7000
1675	425	1350	4000				

3378
1679 Shilling - plume on obverse only

3377 Shilling. — Plume *rev.* only, similar die axis ↑↓ 1674 850   2750   6500
3377A — — bust var. lower tie turns down .... *Extremely rare*
3378 Shilling. — Plume *obv.* only similar die axis ↑↓
1677 900   2850   6750   1679 850   2750   6500
3379 Shilling. — elephant and castle below bust, die axis ↑↓ 1681/0 2750   9000   —

3380
Third bust Shilling

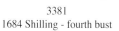
3381
1684 Shilling - fourth bust

3380 Shilling. Third dr. (large) bust r. similar die axis ↑↓
1674 475   1650   5000   1675/3 375   1200   3750

3381 Shilling. Fourth dr. (large) bust r., older features, similar die axis ↑↓
1683 225   750   2400   1684 225   750   2400

3382
1677 Sixpence

	F £	VF £	EF £		F £	VF £	EF £

3382 Sixpence. Dr. bust r. R. Crowned cruciform shields, interlinked C's in angles die axis ↑↓

1674	75	250	700	1679	110	325	875
1675	80	275	750	1680	85	275	800
1675/4	80	275	750	1681	75	250	700
1676	90	300	850	1682	95	350	900
1676/5	90	300	850	1682/1	90	300	850
1677	75	250	700	1683	75	250	700
1678/7	80	275	750	1684	80	260	750

3383   3384 -
Undated Fourpence   1678 Fourpence

3383 Fourpence. Undated. Crowned dr. bust l. to edge of coin, value
behind. R. Shield, die axis ↑↓ 20   50   120

3384 Fourpence. Dated. Dr. bust r. R. Crowned four interlinked Cs quartered emblems die axis ↑↓

1670	20	45	135	1678	18	40	110
1671	18	40	120	1678/6	18	40	100
1672/1	18	40	120	1678/7	18	40	100
1673	18	40	110	1679	10	25	75
1674	18	40	110	1680	12	30	100
1674/4 sideways	20	40	150	1681	15	32	90
1674 7 over 6	18	40	100	1681 B/R in HIB	18	38	150
1675	18	40	110	1681/0	15	32	115
1675/4	18	45	120	1682	18	40	95
1676	18	40	110	1682/1	18	40	115
1676 7 over 6	18	45	120	1683	18	40	115
1676/5	18	45	120	1684	20	40	120
1677	15	32	100	1684/3	20	40	110

3386 - 1678 Threepence

	F £	VF £	EF £		F £	VF £	EF £
3385 Threepence. Undated. As 3383, die axis ↑↓ 14						35	110
3386 Threepence. Dated. Dr. bust r. R. Crowned three interlinked C's, die axis ↑↓							
1670 12		28	95	1678 12		25	110
1671 11		22	85	1678 on 4d flan 12		25	115
1671 GRⱯTIA 18		38	150	1679 11		20	65
1671 GRⱯTIA 12		28	100	1679 O/A in CAROLVS 15		38	150
1672/1 11		22	85	1680 12		25	90
1673 11		22	85	1681 12		25	90
1674 12		25	95	1681/0 12		30	100
1675 15		30	100	1682 15		30	110
1676 11		22	95	1682/1 15		32	95
1676/5 12		28	100	1683 15		30	110
1676 ERA for FRA 12		38	160	1684 15		30	115
1677 15		30	105	1684/3 15		32	95

3388 - 1678 Twopence

	F £	VF £	EF £		F £	VF £	EF £
3387 Twopence. Undated. As 3383 (double arch crown) die axis ↑↓ 10						28	75
3388 Twopence. Dated. Dr. bust r. R. Crowned pair of linked C's, die axis ↑↓							
1668 die axis ↑↑ 15		30	100	1678/6 13		28	100
1670 10		22	75	1679 10		22	70
1671 10		22	75	1679 HIB over FRA 13		38	150
1672/1 10		22	75	1680 10		22	75
1672/1 GRⱯTIⱯ 13		38	165	1680/79 13		28	85
1673 13		28	90	1681 10		22	80
1674 10		22	75	1682/1 13		28	90
1675 12		25	90	1682/1 ERA for FRA 13		38	150
1676 10		22	85	1683 10		22	80
1677 13		28	85	1683/2 13		28	80
1678 12		28	100	1684 13		28	85

3390 - 1678 Penny

	F	VF	EF		F	VF	EF
	£	£	£		£	£	£

3389 Penny. Undated. As 3383 (double arch crown) die axis ↑↓ .... 10 | | | | 33 | 110 |

3390 Penny. Dated. Dr. bust r. R. Crowned C die axis ↑↓

1670	12	25	105	1678	22	50	145
1671	12	25	105	1678 RATIA error	12	35	150
1672/1	12	25	105	1679	22	50	145
1673	12	25	105	1680	12	25	105
1674	14	30	120	1680 on 2d flan		*Extremely rare*	
1674 ƆRATIA error	18	38	150	1681	22	55	165
1675	12	25	105	1682	20	45	130
1675 ƆRATIA error	18	35	150	1682/1	18	40	145
1676	20	45	140	1682 ERA for FRA	18	40	150
1676 ƆRATIA error	15	35	175	1683/1	13	30	105
1677	12	25	105	1684	22	50	145
1677 ƆRATIA error	15	35	175	1684/3	22	50	150

3391 Maundy Set. Undated. The four coins .... 90 | | | | 200 | 520 |

3392 Maundy Set. Dated. The four denominations. Uniform dates

1670	90	250	600	1678	100	260	750
1671	80	200	550	1679	80	220	600
1672	85	230	580	1680	75	190	580
1673	70	200	550	1681	90	260	650
1674	80	210	580	1682	80	220	660
1675	80	220	580	1683	80	200	680
1676	90	240	640	1684	90	250	700
1677	80	220	620				

COPPER AND TIN

3393 - 1675 Halfpenny

	F £	VF £	EF £		F £	VF £	EF £
3393 Copper **Halfpenny** Cuir. bust l. R. Britannia seated l. date in ex., die axis ↑↓							
1672	60	350	1400	1673 no rev. stop	90	500	—
1672 CRAOLVS error		*Extremely rare*		1675	60	350	1400
1673	50	330	1200	1675 no stops on obv.	90	500	—
1673 CRAOLVS error	190	—	—	1675/3	165	600	—
1673 no stops on obv.		*Extremely rare*					

3394
1672 Farthing

3394 Copper **Farthing.** Cuir. bust l. R. Britannia sealed l. date in ex., die axis ↑↓

	F	VF	EF		F	VF	EF
1672	45	265	825	1673 BRITINNIA error	225	—	—
1672 Rev.				1673 no stops on obv.	165	—	—
loose drapery	65	325	1000	1673 no rev. stop	165	—	—
1672 no stops on obv.	65	325	1000	1674	55	300	900
1672 RO/OL on obv.	90	450	—	1675	50	275	825
1672 die axis ↑↑	65	325	1000	1675 no stop after			
1673	50	275	825	CAROLVS	165	—	—
1673 CAROLA error	130	500	—	1679	55	300	900
1673 O/sideways O	75	325	1100	1679 no rev. stop	65	325	1100

3395 - Tin Farthing

Prices for tin coinage based on corrosion free examples, and in the top grades with some lustre

3395 Tin **Farthing.** Somewhat similar, but with copper plug, edge inscribed NUMMORVM FAMVLVS, and date on edge only die axis ↑↓

		F	VF	EF
1684	various varieties of edge	55	250	900	3600
1685			*Extremely rare*	

James II, brother of Charles II, was born on 14th October 1633, he married Anne Hyde with whom he produced 8 children. He lost control of his reign when the loyalist Tories moved against him over his many Catholic appointments. Parliament invited his protestant daughter Mary with husband William of Orange to be joint rulers. James II abdicated and died in exile in France.

During this reign the dies continued to be engraved by John Roettier (1631-1700), the only major difference in the silver coinage being the ommission of the interlinked C's in the angles of the shields on the reverses. The only provenance marked silver coin of this reign is the extremely rare plume on reverse 1685 Shilling. The elephant and castle provenance mark continues to appear on some of the gold coins of this reign. Tin halfpence and farthings provided the only base metal coinage during this short reign. All genuine tin coins of this period have a copper plug.

GOLD

	F £	VF £	EF £		F £	VF £	EF £

3396 Five Guineas. First laur. bust l., R. Crowned cruciform shields sceptres misplaced in angles smaller crowns date on edge in words (e.g. 1686 = SECVNDO)
die axis ↑↓ 1686 SECVNDO 3500 7500 26000

3397 Five Guineas. First laur bust l. R. similar bust sceptres normal. die axis ↑↓
1687 TERTIO ....3250 7250 22500 1688 QVARTO.......3250 7250 22500

3397A
1687 Five Guineas, second bust

3397A Five Guineas. Second laur. bust l. R. similar die axis ↑↓
1687 TERTIO ....3000 6750 20000 1688 QVARTO.......3000 6750 20000

3398
1687 Five Guineas, first bust, elephant and castle below

3398 Five Guineas. First laur. bust l. Elephant and castle below R. Similar die axis ↑↓
1687 TERTIO ....3250 7000 22500 1688 QVARTO.......3500 7250 24000

3399 - Two Guineas

	F	*VF*	*EF*		*F*	*VF*	*EF*
	£	£	£		£	£	£

3399 Two Guineas. Laur. bust l. R. Crowned cruciform shields, sceptres in angles, edge milled, die axis ↑↓

1687	2250	5250	14000	1688/7	2400	5500	15000

3400 Guinea. First laur. bust l. R. Crowned cruciform shields, sceptres in angles, edge milled, die axis ↑↓

1685	750	2500	8250	1686 B/I in HIB	Extremely rare
1686	750	2500	8250	1686/5 second 6 over S	Extremely rare

3401 Guinea. First bust elephant and castle below R. similar die axis ↑↓

1685	850	3000	10500	1686	1350	—	—

3402   3403

1688 Guinea, second bust

3402 Guinea. Second laur. bust l. R. similar die axis ↑↓

1686	725	2400	7500	1687/6	750	2500	7750
1687	725	2400	7500	1688	675	2250	7250

3404

3403 Guinea. Second bust elephant and castle below R. similar die axis ↑↓

1686	825	2750	9500	1688	800	2650	9250
1687	800	2650	9250				

3404 Half-Guinea. Laur. bust l. R. Crowned cruciform shields sceptres in angles, edge milled die axis ↑↓

1686	475	1050	3500	1687	475	1050	3500
1686 OBV/BVS	525	1100	3750	1688	475	1050	3500

3405 Half-Guinea. Laur bust with elephant and castle below, R. similar die axis ↑↓

1686	750	2250	7000

SILVER

3406
1686 Crown, first bust

| | *F* | *VF* | *EF* | | *F* | *VF* | *EF* |
| | £ | £ | £ | | £ | £ | £ |

3406 Crown. First dr. bust, l. regnal year on edge in words (e.g. 1686 = SECVNDO) die axis ↑↓

1686 SECVNDO 325   1050   5000

1686 — No stops on obverse 375   1250   5500

3407
1687 Crown, second bust

3407 Crown. Second dr. bust l. narrower than first bust. R. Crowned cruciform shields edge inscribed in raised letters

    die axis ↑↓

| 1687 TERTIO .... 240 | 750 | 3250 | 1688/7 QVARTO ...... 300 | 900 | 3500 |
| 1688 QVARTO .... 275 | 800 | 3250 | | | |

	3408			1st bust	2nd bust	
	1686 Halfcrown, first bust			Halfcrown hair ties		
	F	VF	EF	F	VF	EF
	£	£	£	£	£	£

3408 Halfcrown. First laur and dr. bust, l. regnal year on edge in words
(e.g. 1685 = PRIMO) die axis ↑↓

1685 PRIMO	225	625	3000	1686 TERTIO	225	650	3000
1686 SECVNDO	210	600	2850	1687 TERTIO	225	625	2850
1686/5 —	240	700	3250	1687/6 —	275	750	3250
1686 TERTIO V over S or B				1687 — 6 over 8	300	900	—
in JACOBVS	240	700	3250	1687 A/R in GRATIA	275	750	3250

3409 Halfcrown. Second laur and dr. bust l. R. Crowned cruciform shields
edge inscribed in raised letters die axis ↑↓

| 1687 TERTIO | 225 | 650 | 3000 | 1688 QVARTO | 225 | 650 | 3000 |

3410
1687 Shilling

3410 Shilling. Laur and Dr. bust l. R. Crowned cruciform shields die axis ↑↓

1685	225	575	2250	1687	240	650	2650
1685 no stops on rev.	250	675	2750	1687 G/A in MAG	250	675	2750
1686	225	600	2500	1687/6	225	625	2500
1686/5	275	700	2750	1687/6 G/A in MAG	240	650	2650
1686 V/S in JACOBVS	240	650	2650	1688	250	675	2750
1686 G/A in MAG	250	675	2750	1688/7	240	650	2650

3411 Shilling. Similar, plume in centre of *rev.*, die axis ↑↓ 1685 .... 7500 — —

3412
1686 Sixpence, early shileds, indented tops

3412 Sixpence. Laur and dr. bust l. R. Early type crowned cruciform shields die axis ↑↓

| 1686 | 140 | 425 | 975 | 1687/6 | 160 | 475 | 1250 |
| 1687 | 160 | 475 | 1250 | | | | |

3413
1687 Sixpence, later shields

	F £	VF £	EF £		F £	VF £	EF £
3413 Sixpence. Similar R. Late type shields die axis ↑↓							
1687 150	450	1000		1687 Later/early shields . 160	475	1250	
1687/6 185	500	1300		1688 150	450	1000	

3414	3415	3416	3417
Fourpence	Threepence	Twopence	Penny

3414 Fourpence. Laur. head l. R. IIII Crowned die axis ↑↓

1686 18	30	100	1688 22	45	140
1686 Date over crown 18	30	110	1688 1 over 8 25	55	150
1687/6 15	25	90	1688/7 22	45	130
1687 8 over 7 18	30	110			

3415 Threepence. Laur. head l. R. III Crowned die axis-↑↓

1685 12	30	95	1687 12	32	100
1685 Groat flan 35	80	150	1687/6 12	32	100
1686 12	35	100	1688 22	50	145
1686 4d obv. die 18	40	120	1688/7 25	55	140

3416 Twopence. Laur. head l. R. II Crowned die axis ↑↓

1686 15	32	90	1687 ERA for FRA 25	45	140
1686 IΛCOBVS 18	35	100	1688 18	40	130
1687 15	32	90	1688/7 18	40	120

3417 Penny. Laur. head l. R. I Crowned die axis ↑↓

1685 18	30	100	1687/8 22	40	120
1686 18	35	100	1688 22	45	130
1687 18	35	100	1688/7 22	45	120
1687/6 18	35	100			

3418 Maundy Set. As last four. Uniform dates

1686 100	280	500	1688 160	325	700
1687 100	280	500			

TIN

3419 Tin Halfpenny

	Fair £	F £	VF £	EF £

Prices for tin coinage based on corrosion free examples, and in the top grades with some lustre

3419 Halfpenny. Laur. and dr. bust r. R. Britannia seated l. date on edge die axis ↑↓

		Fair	F	VF	EF
1685	various varieties of edge	100	250	775	3850
1686		110	275	825	4200
1687		90	300	775	3850

3420
Cuirassed bust Tin Farthing

3420 Farthing. Laur. and Cuir. bust r. R. Britannia seated l. date on edge die axis ↑↓

		Fair	F	VF	EF
1684				*Extremely rare*	
1685	various varieties of edge	65	195	700	3000
1686	two varieties of edge	80	225	775	3250
1687				*Extremely rare*	

3421 Farthing. Dr. bust r.; date on edge, 1687 various varieties of edge ↑↓

	Fair	F	VF	EF
	100	250	875	3750

Mary Stuart was born on 30 April 1662, and married William of Orange as part of Charles II's foreign policy. She eventually became William's loyal servant but bore him no children. The Bill and the Claim of Rights were both passed in 1689 and forbade the Royal and Prerogative rights of Monarchs. Mary died from smallpox on 28 December 1694.

Due to the poor state of the silver coinage, much of it worn hammered coin, the Guinea, which was valued at 21s. 6d. at the beginning of the reign, circulated for as much as 30s. by 1694. The elephant and elephant and castle provenance marks continue on some gold coin. The tin Halfpennies and Farthings were replaced by copper coins in 1694. The rampant Lion of Nassau is now placed as an inescutcheon on the centre of the royal arms. The WM monogram appears in the angles of the silver coins of this reign.

Engravers and designers: George Bower (d.1689), Henry Harris (d.1704), John Roettier (1631-1700), James Roettier (1663-1698), Norbert Roettier (b.1665)

GOLD

3422
Five Guineas

	F	VF	EF		F	VF	EF
	£	£	£		£	£	£

3422 Five Guineas. Conjoined busts r. regnal year on edge in words (e.g. 1691 = TERTIO) ↑↓

	F	VF	EF		F	VF	EF
1691 TERTIO	2750	6250	18500	1693 QVINTO	2750	6250	18500
1692 QVARTO	2850	6500	18500	1694/2 SEXTO	3000	6750	20000
1692 QVINTO	3250	8000	22500	1694 SEXTO	2850	6500	19000

3423
Elephant and castle below busts

3423 Five Guineas. Conjoined busts, elephant and castle below, R. Crowned shield of arms die axis ↑↓

	F	VF	EF		F	VF	EF
1691 TERTIO	2850	6250	19000	1694/2 SEXTO	3000	6750	21000
1692 QVARTO	2850	6250	19000	1694 SEXTO	2850	6500	20000
1693 QVINTO	2850	6500	20000				

3424
1694 Two Guineas

	F £	VF £	EF £		F £	VF £	EF £

3424 Two Guineas. Conjoined busts r. R. Crowned shield of arms, Lion of Nassau at centre
die axis ↑↓

1693	1650	4250	11000	1694/3	1650	4000	10500

3425 Two Guineas. Conjoined busts, elephant and castle below, R. similar die axis ↑↓

| 1691 | | *Extremely rare* | | 1694/3 | 1750 | 4500 | 12500 |
| 1693 | 2000 | 5000 | 13500 | | | | |

3426
1689 Guinea

3427
1689 Elephant and castle below busts

3426 Guinea. Conjoined busts r. R. Crowned shield of arms Lion of Nassau at centre die axis ↑↓

1689 Early slanting harp				1690 FT for ET exists.....			
with base of harp in line				1690 D of DEI over G exists			
with X of REX	—	—	7500	1690 GVLIFLMVS	725	2400	8250
1689 Later upright harp				1691	700	2250	8000
with base of harp in line				1692	700	2250	8000
with R of REX	650	2000	7500	1693	700	2250	8000
1689 MVS over EL exists				1694	700	2250	8000
1690	700	2250	8000	1694/3	700	2250	8000

3427 Guinea. Conjoined busts elephant and castle below R. Similar die axis ↑↓

1689	675	2100	7500	1692	725	2400	8250
1689 G of REGINA over E		*Extremely rare*		1693	850	2750	10000
1690	850	2750	10000	1694	725	2400	8250
1691	725	2400	8250	1694/3	750	2500	8500

3428 Guinea. Conjoined busts elephant only below, R. Similar die axis ↑↓

| 1692 | 900 | 2750 | 9750 | 1693 | 1100 | 3250 | 10500 |

Overstruck dates are listed only if commoner than the normal date or if no normal date is known.

3429
1689 Half-Guniea, first busts, first shield

3430
1690 Half-Guinea, second busts, second shield

	F £	VF £	EF £		F £	VF £	EF £

3429 Half-Guinea. First busts r. R. First Crowned shield of arms die axis ↑↓
1689 575   1400   3750

3430 Half-Guinea. Second busts r. R. Second Crowned shield of arms die axis ↑↓

1690	550	1350	3500	1693		*Extremely rare*	
1691	550	1350	3500	1693/2	600	1450	4000
1692	575	1400	3750	1694	550	1350	3500

3431 Half-Guinea. Second busts elephant and castle below, R. Second shield of arms die axis ↑↓

| 1691 | 600 | 1600 | 4000 | 1692 | 600 | 1600 | 4000 |

3432 Half-Guinea. Second busts elephant only below, R. Second shield of arms die axis ↑↓
1692.........................750   1750   5500

SILVER

3433
Crown

3433 Crown. Conjoined busts r. regnal year on edge in words (e.g. 1691 = TERTIO) die axis ↑↓

1691 TERTIO	550	1600	5250	1692 QVARTO	550	1600	5250
1691 I/E in legend	625	1750	5750	1692/ɀ QVARTO	575	1650	5500
1691 TERTTIO	625	1750	5750	1692/ɀ QVINTO	550	1600	5250

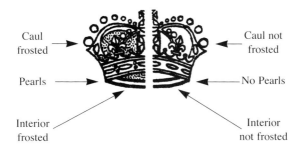

Caul frosted → ← Caul not frosted

Pearls → ← No Pearls

Interior frosted ↗ ↖ Interior not frosted

3434
1689 Halfcrown - first reverse

3435
1689 Halfcrown - second reverse

	F	VF	EF		F	VF	EF
	£	£	£		£	£	£

3434 Halfcrown. First busts, r. R. First crowned shield, 1689 PRIMO R. Crown with caul and interior frosted, with pearls edge inscribed die axis ↑↓ 130 375 1700

1689— 2nd L/M in GVLIELMVS 135 400 1800

1689 — 1st V/A in GVLIELMVS, only caul frosted 135 400 1800

1689 — — interior also frosted, no pearls 135 400 1800

1689 Caul only frosted, pearls 130 375 1700

1689 — no pearls 135 400 1800

1689 No frosting, pearls 130 375 1700

1689 No stops on obverse 250 700 2250

1689 FRA for FR 185 600 2100

3435 Halfcrown. First busts r. R. Second crowned shield die axis ↑↓

1689 PRIMO R. Caul and interior frosted with pearls	110	375	1700	1689 no frosting, pearls	110	375	1700
1689 — — no pearls	120	400	1800	1689 no frosting, no pearls	110	375	1700
1689 Caul only frosted pearls	110	375	1700	1690 SECVNDO —	175	500	2000
1689 interior frosted, no pearls.................	120	400	1800	1690 — GRETIA error with second V of GVLIELMVS struck over S	550	1400	4000
1689 Caul only frosted, no pearls.....................	120	400	1800	1690 TERTIO.................	185	550	2100
				1690 TERTIO.................	185	550	2100

3436

Halfcrown, second busts, third reverse

	F	VF	EF			F	VF	EF
	£	£	£			£	£	£

3436 Halfcrown. Second busts r. ℞. Crowned cruciform shields, WM monogram in angles die axis ↑↓

	F	VF	EF		F	VF	EF
1691 TERTIO	150	475	2000	1692 QVINTO 250	725	2250
1692 QVARTO	150	475	2000	1693 QVINTO 150	450	1850
1692 R/G in REGINA also				1693 3/inverted 3 175	525	2100
showing H/B in HI....	200	525	2100	1693 inverted 3 225	725	2250

3437 - Shilling   3438 - Sixpence

3437 Shilling. Conjoined busts r. ℞. Crowned cruciform shields, WM monogram in angles die axis ↑↓

1692	200	550	2250	1693 9/0	225	650	2400
1692 inverted 1	225	650	2400	1693	200	550	2250
1692 RE/ET on R	250	750	—				
1692 A of GRATIA							
over T and T over I	225	750	—				

3438 Sixpence. Conjoined busts r. ℞. Crowned cruciform shields, WM monogram in angles die axis ↑↓

1693	135	400	975	1694	150	450	1100
1693 inverted 3	200	550	1350				

3439 - Groat, first busts

3439 Fourpence. First busts, r. no tie to wreath. ℞. Crowned 4 die axis ↑↓

1689 GV below bust	15	30	80	1690	20	50	110
1689 G below bust	15	30	80	1690 6 over 5	20	55	120
1689 stop befor G	15	30	80	1691	20	45	130
1689 berries in wreath	15	30	80	1691/0	20	40	120
1689 GVLEELMVS	65	190	–	1694	20	60	160
1689 I over first E in GVLEELMVS							
corrected die for above	65	190	–				

3440
Groat, Second busts

	F	VF	EF		F	VF	EF
	£	£	£		£	£	£

3440 Fourpence. Second busts r. tie to wreath. R. Crowned 4 die axis ↑↓

1692	30	70	180	1693/2	35	85	280
1692/1	25	60	165	1694	30	70	200
1692 MAR•IA		*Extremely rare*		1694 small lettering	30	70	200
1693	35	85	280				

3441 Threepence. First busts, r. no tie to wreath. R. Crowned 3 die axis ↑↓

1689	15	30	75	1690 6 over 5	20	50	105
1689 No stops on rev.	20	40	110	1690 Large lettering	20	50	105
1689 LMV over MVS	20	40	110	1690 9 over 6	20	50	105
1689 Hyphen stops on rev.	20	40	100	1691	100	220	450
1690	20	50	105				

3442 Threepence. Second busts, r. tie to wreath R. Crowned 3 die axis ↑↓

1691	40	130	220	1693 GV below bust	20	55	130
1692 G below bust	25	65	135	1694 G below bust	20	55	130
1692 GV below bust	25	65	135	1694 — MΛRIΛ error	24	60	170
1692 GVL below bust	25	65	135	1694 GV below bust	20	55	130
1693 G below bust	20	55	130	1694 GVL below bust	20	55	130
1693/2 G below bust	20	55	130				

3443 Twopence. Conjoined busts r. R. Crowned 2 die axis ↑↓

1689	18	40	90	1694/3	18	42	115
1691	18	40	100	1694/3 no stop after DG	18	42	115
1692	20	45	120	1694 MARLA error	35	65	275
1693	15	42	100	1694 HI for HIB	20	42	110
1693/2	18	42	115	1694 GVLI below bust	20	42	110
1693 GV below bust	18	42	115	1694 GVL below bust	20	42	110
1694	20	45	110				

3444 - Penny   3445 - Legend intruded

3444 Penny. Legend continuous over busts, R. Crowned 1 die axis ↑↓

| 1689 | 220 | 380 | 700 | 1689 MΛRIΛ | 230 | 380 | 725 |
| 1689 GVIELMVS error | 240 | 450 | 900 | | | | |

3445 Penny. Legend broken by busts, R. Crowned 1 die axis ↑↓

1690	28	55	125	1694 date spread	22	50	120
1691/0	35	60	120	1694 no stops on obv	22	55	125
1692	45	85	190	1694 HI for HIB	28	60	190
1692/1	35	80	180	1694 — 9/6	25	55	135
1693	35	60	130				

3446 - Maundy Set

	F £	VF £	EF £		F £	VF £	EF £

3446 Maundy Set. The four denominations. Uniform dates

1689	350	700	1250	1693	180	420	950
1691	175	400	900	1694	145	350	850
1692	160	380	875				

TIN AND COPPER

3447
Tin Halfpenny first busts

	Fair £	F £	VF £	EF £

Prices for tin coinage based on corrosion free examples, and in the top grades with some lustre

3447 Tin **Halfpenny.** Small dr. busts r.; date on edge ↑↓ 1689 ....925 1800 — —

— — — obv. with star stops 1689 .... *Extremely rare*

3448
Tin Halfpenny cuirassed busts

3448 Tin **Halfpenny.** — Large cuir. busts r.; R. Britannia seated L. date only on edge, die axis ↑↓

1690 various edge varieties 80 190 800 3250

3449 Tin **Halfpenny.** Similar date in ex. and on edge die axis ↑↓

1691 various edge varieties 70 175 700 2750

1691 in ex. 1692 on edge .... *Extremely rare*

1692 ....70 175 700 2750

3450 Tin **Farthing.** Small dr. busts r. R. Britannia seated l. die axis ↑↓

1689 ....275 700 2250 —

1689, in ex. 1690 on edge .... *Extremely rare*

3451
Tin Farthing

	Fair	F £	VF £	EF £
3451 Tin **Farthing.** Large cuir. busts r. R. Britannia seated l.die axis ↑↓				
1690, in ex. 1689 on edge		*Extremely rare*		
1690 various edge varieties	55	175	700	3000
1691 various edge varieties	55	175	700	3000
1692	70	190	750	3000

3452
1694 Halfpenny

3452 Copper **Halfpenny,** Conjoined busts r. R. Britannia die axis ↑↓				
1694		85	275	1150
1694 GVLIEMVS error		225	600	–
1694 MVRIA error		275	650	–
1694 MΛRIΛ error		165	525	–
1694 BRITΛNNI/Λ		195	550	–
1694 no rev. stop		165	525	–
1694 GVLEELMVS		275	625	–

3453
1694 Farthing

3453 Copper **Farthing**, Conjoined busts r. R. Britannia die axis ↑↓				
1694		75	275	1000
1694 MΛRIΛ error		200	500	–
1694 no stop after MΛRIΛ		120	415	–
1694 — BRITΛNNIΛ		140	415	–
1694 no stop on rev.		120	350	–
1694 no stop on obv.		120	350	–
1694 GVLIELMS, BRITΛNNIΛ errors		250	525	–
1694 BRITΛNNIΛ		155	475	–
1694 Broad heavier flan 25.5mm		225	500	–

William of Orange was born on 4th November 1650. He married Mary Stuart under Charles II's foreign policy and was invited to England by Parliament, where he proceeded to supress the Jacobite rebellion. The Bank of England was founded during this reign, and William ruled alone and without issue after Mary's death until his own demise on 8th March 1702 following a serious fall from his horse.

In 1696 a great re-coinage was undertaken to replace the hammered silver that made up most of the coinage in circulation, much of it being clipped and badly worn. Branch mints were set up at Bristol, Chester, Exeter, Norwich and York to help with the re-coinage. For a short time before they were finally demonetized, unclipped hammered coins were allowed to circulate freely provided they were officially pierced in the centre. Silver coins with roses between the coats of arms were made from silver obtained from the West of England mines. The elephant and castle provenance mark continues on some guineas and half-guineas.

Engravers and designers: Samuel Bull (d.c.1720), John Croker (1670-1740), Henry Harris (d.1704), John Roettier (1663-1698).

GOLD

3454
1699 Five Guineas, first bust

	F £	VF £	EF £		F £	VF £	EF £
3454 Five Guineas. First laur. bust r. regnal year on edge in words (e.g. 1699 = UNDECIMO) ↑↓							
1699 UNDECIMO	3000	6750	24000	1700 DVODECIMO	3000	6750	24000

3455
Elephant and castle below first bust

3455 Five Guineas. First bust elephant and castle below, 1699 UNDECIMO......3250   7500   25000

3456
1701 Five Guineas 'Fine Work'

	F	VF	EF			F	VF	EF
	£	£	£			£	£	£

3456 Five Guineas. Second laur. bust r. ('fine work'), R. Crowned cruciform shields Plain or ornamental sceptres DECIMO TERTIO die axis ↑↓ 1701* 2850   6250   20000

3457
'Fine work' Two Guineas

3457 Two Guineas. ('fine work'), Laur. bust r. similar die axis ↑↓ 1701 1850   4250   11000

3458
1695 Guinea, first bust

3458 Guinea. First laur. bust r. R. Crowned cruciform shields, sceptres in angles die axis ↑↓
1695 large and small   1696 600   2250   7000
lis in French arms 575   2000   6250   1697 600   2250   7000

3459 Guinea. First bust elephant and castle below R. Similar die axis ↑↓
1695 1050   3250   12000   1696 .... *Extremely rare*

* Beware of low grade counterfeits

3460
Second bust

3463
Ornamental sceptres

| | F £ | VF £ | EF £ | | F £ | VF £ | EF £ |

3460 Guinea. Second laur. bust r. R. Similar with human-headed harp in Irish arms. die axis ↑↓
1697 ....625 2000 6500   1700 large or small lions
1698 ....600 1850 6000   in arms......................600   1850   6000
1699 ....625 2000 6500

3461 Guinea. Second bust elephant and castle below. R. Similar die axis ↑↓
1697 ....1350 4500 −   1699 .... *Extremely rare*
1698 ....1200 4000 12000   1700 ....1250 4250 −

3462 Guinea. Second laur. bust. r. R. Similar with Human headed harp. Large lettering and
large date, die axis ↑↓ 1698..625 2000 6250

3463 Guinea. — R. Narrow crowns, plain or ornamented sceptres, axis ↑↓ 1701.........600 1850 6000

3464 Guinea. Second bust elephant and castle below, die axis ↑↓ 1701 .... *Extremely rare*

3465 Guinea. Third laur. bust r. ('fine work'), R. Similar die axis ↑↓1701........950 3250 10500

3466
1695 Half-Guniea, early harp

3468
Later harp

3466 Half-Guinea. Laur. bust r. R. With early harp, die axis ↑↓ 1695 ....325 850 2500

3467 Half-Guinea. Laur. bust elephant and castle below. R. With early harp, die axis ↑↓
1695 ....600 1650 5000   1696 ....475 1350 3750

3468 Half-Guinea. Laur. bust r. R. Crowned cruciform shields, sceptres in angles with late harp, die axis ↑↓
1697 ....575 1600 4750   1700 ....350 950 3250
1698 ....325 850 2500   1701 ....325 875 2600
1699 .... *Extremely rare*

3469 Half-Guinea. Laur. bust elephant and castle below, die axis ↑↓ 1698 ....500 1500 4250

SILVER

First harp

3470
Crown - first bust - round collar

	F £	VF £	EF £		F £	VF £	EF £

3470 Crown. First dr. bust, r. with curved breast plate or drapery. ℞.First harp, regnal year on edge in words (e.g. 1696 = OCTAVO) ↑↓

	F	VF	EF		F	VF	EF
1695 SEPTIMO......... 100		350	1650	1696 G/D IN GRA 200		600	2400
1695 SEPTIMO cinquefoils				1696 — no stops........ 200		575	2250
for crosses on edge 225		575	—	1696/5.........................200		575	—
1695 OCTAVO 100		350	1750	1696 GEI for DEI.......350		1000	—
1695 TVTA·EN error 225		575	—	1696 — no stops........ 375		1100	—
1695 plain edge proof *FDC* £10500				1696 plain edge proof *FDC* £12000			
1696 OCTAVO 95		325	1650				
1696 No stops on							
obverse 225		625	2500				

Second harp

3471
1696 Crown, second bust - hair across breast

3471 Crown. Second dr. bust r. with two locks of hair across the bust and no hair below the truncation. ℞. Second harp (hair across breast), 1696 (two varieties) die axis ↑↓
OCTAVO .... *Each unique*

3472
Third bust, straight breastplate

	F	VF	EF
	£	£	£

3472 Crown. Third dr. bust, r. Easily distinguished by the straight breast plate or drapery. Ŗ. First harp, die axis ↑↓ 1696 OCTAVO 100 350 1650

1696 TRICESIMO .... *Extremely rare*

1696 plain edge proof *FDC* £10500

3473 Crown. Similar, Ŗ. Second harp, die axis ↑↓ 1697 NONO 1250 4250 18500

Third harp

3474
1700 Crown, third bust variety

3474 Crown. Third bust variety r. of same general style but dies have been recut and hair varied a little. Tie is slightly longer and thinner than normal third bust. Ŗ. Third harp with scroll front and back, ↑↓ 1700 DVODECIMO 110 375 1850

1700 DECIMO. TERTIO.. 135 425 2000

3475 Halfcrown. First bust r. Ŗ. Small shields, 1696 die axis ↑↓ OCTAVO 80 275 1500

— — 1696 DECⱯS error 90 325 1600

3476 Halfcrown. B (*Bristol*) below First bust, die axis ↑↓ 1696 OCTAVO....... 90 350 1650

— 1696 B Similar proof *FDC* £15000

3477
Chester Mint

3478
Exeter Mint

3477 Halfcrown. C (*Chester*) below first bust, die axis ↑↓ 1696 OCTAVO 200 650 2250

3478 Halfcrown. E (*Exeter*) below first bust, die axis ↑↓ 1696 OCTAVO 200 625 2250

	F	VF	EF
	£	£	£
3479 Halfcrown. N (*Norwich*) below first bust, die axis ↑↓ 1696 OCTAVO	175	575	2000
3480 Halfcrown. y (*York*) below first bust, die axis ↑↓ 1696 OCTAVO	175	575	2000

3480
1696 Halfcrown - York Mint

3481
1696 Halfcrown, large shield
reverse with early harp

	F	VF	EF
3481 Halfcrown. First bust r. R. Large shield, early harp, die axis ↑↓ 1696 OCTAVO	75	275	1500
1696 Proof plain edge	—	—	10000
3482 Halfcrown. — B (*Bristol*) below bust, die axis ↑↓ 1696 OCTAVO	100	375	1600
3483 Halfcrown. — C (*Chester*) below bust, die axis ↑↓ 1696 OCTAVO	200	625	2250
3484 Halfcrown. — E (*Exeter*) below bust, die axis ↑↓ 1696 OCTAVO	150	525	1850
3485 Halfcrown. — N (*Norwich*) below bust, die axis ↑↓ 1696 OCTAVO	275	1100	—
3486 Halfcrown. — y (*York*) below bust, die axis ↑↓ 1696 OCTAVO	110	425	1750
— — die axis ↑↓ 1696 y (*York*), Scots Arms at date		*Extremely rare*	
— die axis ↑↓ y over E 1696	250	850	—

3487
Large shields, ordinary harp

	F	VF	EF		F	VF	EF
	£	£	£		£	£	£
3487 Halfcrown. First bust r. R. Large shields, ordinary harp die axis ↑↓							
1696 OCTAVO	175	575	2000	1697 G/A in MAG	375	—	—
1697 NONO	75	275	1350	1697/6 —	150	500	1850
1697 — GRR for GRA		*Extremely rare*		1697 Proof plain edge *FDC* £9500			
3488 Halfcrown. — B (*Bristol*) below first bust, die axis ↑↓ 1697 NONO					85	350	1500
1697 proof on thick flan *FDC*						*Extremely rare*	
1697 — no stops on reverse					135	525	1850

3489
Chester Mint Halfcrown, large shields

	F £	VF £	EF £		F £	VF £	EF £

3489 Halfcrown. — C *(Chester)* below first bust, similar die axis ↑↓
1696 OCTAVO 175   575   2250   1697 NONO 135   525   1850

3490
Exeter Mint Halfcrown, large shields

3490 Halfcrown. — E *(Exeter)* below first bust, similar die axis ↑↓
1696 OCTAVO 120   475   1750   1697 NONO 80   300   1350
1696 NONO 375   —   —   1697 E over C or B
1697 OCTAVO 375   —   —   under bust 200   700   —

3491
Norwich Mint Halfcrown, large shields

3491 Halfcrown. — N *(Norwich)* below first bust, similar die axis ↑↓
1696 OCTAVO 375   1100   —   1697 NONO 125   525   1850
1697 OCTAVO 250   850   —   1697 — Scots Arms at date *Fair* £900
3492 Halfcrown. — — y *(York)* below first bust, similar die axis ↑↓
1697 NONO 85   325   1350   1697 OCTAVO 325   —   —
3493 Halfcrown. Second dr. bust r. (hair across breast), die axis ↑↓ 1696 OCTAVO   *Unique*

3494
1700 Halfcrown, modified large shields

	F £	VF £	EF £		F £	VF £	EF £

3494 Halfcrown. First dr. bust R. Modified large shields die axis ↑↓

	F	VF	EF		F	VF	EF
1698 OCTAVO	375	950	—	1699 — Lion of			
1698 DECIMO	70	225	1100	Nassau inverted	575	1200	—
1698/7 —	250	800	—	1700 DVODECIMO	85	225	1100
1698 UNDECIMO	350	950	—	1700 D. TERTIO	90	275	1200
1699 UNDECIMO	150	475	1750	1700 — DECVS error	90	275	1200
1699 — Inverted A's for				1701 D. TERTIO	85	225	1100
V's on edge	200	575	—	1701 — no stops			
1699 — Scots Arms at				on reverse	120	400	1500
date	800	—	—				

3495
1701 Halfcrown, elephant and castle below bust

3495 Halfcrown. – elephant and castle below bust, die axis ↑↓
1701 D. TERTIO 2500   6000   —

3496
1701 Halfcrown, plumes on reverse

3496 Halfcrown. – R. Plumes in angles, die axis ↑↓ 1701 D. TERTIO 250   800   4500

SHILLINGS

First bust
This bust is distinctive in having the hair turned outwards above and below the crown of the head

Third bust
This is rather like the first bust but the hair at the back all turns downwards and inwards

Third bust variety,
tie thicker, more hair below bust, more aquiline profile and coarser features

3498
Bristol Mint

3499
1696 Chester Mint Shilling

	F £	VF £	EF £		F £	VF £	EF £
3497 **Shilling.** First dr. bust r. R. Crowned cruciform shields edge milled die axis ↑↓							
1695	40	110	550	1696 2nd L over M	125	425	—
1695 E of ET over H	50	150	675	1696-1669 error date	750	2000	—
1696	35	90	450	1697	35	85	450
1696/5 and GVLICLMVS		*Scarce variety*		1697 plain edge proof in copper			*Unique*
1696 no stops on reverse	100	350	—	1697 E/A in DEI	150	475	—
1696 MAB for MAG error	525	—	—	1697 GRI for GRA error	250	675	2500
1696 GVLIEMVS error	475	—	—	1697 Arms of Scot/Ireland transposed	575	—	—
1696 GVLIELMᐯS error	90	275	—	1697 Irish Arms at date	675	—	—
1696 GᐯLIELMVS error	110	375	—	1697 no stops on reverse	110	375	—
1696 GVLELMVS	475	—	—	1697 GVLELMVS error	475	—	—
				1697 GVLIELMᐯS error	90	325	—
				1697 L/M in legend	125	425	—

3498 **Shilling.** Similar B (*Bristol*) below bust die axis ↑↓

	F	VF	EF		F	VF	EF
1696	55	200	850	1696 small x in REX		*Scarce variety*	
1696 GᐯLIELMVS error and large G in MAG		*Scarce variety*		1697	65	225	875

3499 **Shilling.** Similar C (*Chester*) below bust die axis ↑↓

	F	VF	EF		F	VF	EF
1696	80	250	950	1696 thick flan proof *FDC*		*Extremely rare*	
1696 R/V in GRA	110	350	1250	1697	80	250	950

3500

	F £	VF £	EF £		F £	VF £	EF £

3500 Shilling. Similar E (*Exeter*) below bust die axis ↑↓
1696 80   250   950   1697 80   275   1000
1697 E over N ....   *Extremely rare*
3501 Shilling. Similar N (*Norwich*) below bust die axis ↑↓
1696 90   325   1200   1697 90   325   1200
1697 no stops on obv.......   *Extremely rare*
3502 Shilling. Similar y (*York*) below bust die axis ↑↓
1696 70   220   850   1697 Arms of Scotland/Ireland
Also known with no stop after GVLIELMVS   transposed 900   —   —
1697 70   220   850
1697 Arms of France/Ireland
        transposed 900   —   —
3503 Shilling. Similar Y (*York*) below bust die axis ↑↓
1696 85   275   1000   1697 125   425   —
1697 Y over Λ 325   950   —
3504 Shilling. Second dr. bust r. (hair across breast), similar die axis ↑↓ 1696   *Unique**

3505 - Third bust   3507 - Chester Mint

3505 Shilling. Third dr. bust r., similar die axis ↑↓ 1697....................................35   110   525
3506 Shilling. Similar B (*Bristol*) below bust, die axis ↑↓ 1697 85   325   1100
3507 Shilling. Similar C (*Chester*) below bust die axis ↑↓
1696 125   375   1350   1697 no stops on reverse. 100   325   1100
1697 small or large   1697 Arms of Scotland
        lettering 75   240   900   at date ....*Extremely rare*
1697 FR.A error 100   325   1100
3508 Shilling. Similar E (*Exeter*) below bust, die axis ↑↓
1696 2000   —   —   1697 90   300   1000
3509 Shilling. Similar N (*Norwich*) below bust, die axis ↑↓ 1697 125   400   1350
3510 Shilling. Similar y (*York*) below bust die axis ↑↓
1696 ....*Extremely rare*   1697 80   250   950
3511 Shilling. Third bust variety r. similar die axis ↑↓
1697 GΛLIELMVS ....   1697 GVLIELMΛS error... 135   400   —
        error.....................135   400   —   1698 75   250   950
1697 40   125   525   1698 plain edge proof *FDC* £5750

	F	VF	EF		F	VF	EF
	£	£	£		£	£	£
3512 **Shilling.** Similar B *(Bristol)* below bust, die axis ↑↓ 1697 85					325	1200
3513 **Shilling.** Similar C *(Chester)* below bust, die axis ↑↓ 1697 125					400	1350
3514 **Shilling.** Similar R. Plumes in angles, die axis ↑↓ 1698 175					600	2000

Third bust   Fourth bust   Fifth bust

3515   3516
Fourth bust   Fifth bust

3515 **Shilling** Fourth dr. bust ('flaming hair') r. similar die axis ↑↓
1698 150   575   1750   1699 135   525   1650
1698 No stops on reverse ..*Extremely rare*   1699 plain edge proof *FDC* £6750
1698 plain edge proof *FDC* £6500

3516 **Shilling.** Fifth dr. bust (hair high) r. similar die axis ↑↓
1699 125   400   1350   1700 no stop after DEI.. 120   475   —
1699 Plain edge proof ....*Extremely rare*   1700 Tall O's no stops
1700 35   110   450   on reverse 45   150   600
1700 no stops on rev, also   1701 small or large lions.. 80   300   1100
     with larger O's ....*Scarce variety*   1701 DEI/GRA 275   —   —
1700 Circular small
     O's in date 35   110   450

3517
1701 Shilling, plumes on reverse

3517 **Shilling.** Similar R. Plumes in angles die axis ↑↓
1699 165   525   1750   1701 165   525   1750

3518
1699 Shilling, roses on reverse

3520
First bust Sixpence, French arms at date

	F £	VF £	EF £			F £	VF £	EF £
3518	**Shilling.** Similar R. Roses in angles, die axis ↑↓ 1699 200						675	2250
3519	**Shilling.** Similar plume below bust, die axis ↑↓ 1700 2250						8500	—

SIXPENCES

First bust   Third bust   Early harp.   Later harp,
                                    large crown.   small crown.

3520 Sixpence. First dr. bust r. R. Crowned cruciform shields, large crowns, edge milled, early
harp, die axis ↑↓

1695 30	80	250	1696 Scots Arms		
1696 25	65	185	at date............450	—	—
1696 Heavy flan 750	—	—	1696/5 45	110	450
1696 French Arms			1696 no stops on		
at date..............475	—	—	obverse 60	175	550
1696 GVLIELMⱯS....45	135	475	1696 DFI for DEI.....135	—	—

3521 Sixpence. Similar B *(Bristol)* below bust, die axis ↑↓ 1696 ....30 90 325
  — — 1696 B over E 50 125 475
3522 Sixpence. Similar C *(Chester)* below bust, die axis ↑↓ 1696...............35 95 350

3523

3525
1696 York Mint sixpence,
early harp, first bust

3523 Sixpence. Similar E *(Exeter)* below bust, die axis ↑↓ 1696..................50 135 450
3524 Sixpence. Similar N *(Norwich)* below bust, die axis ↑↓ 1696..............50 135 450
3525 Sixpence. Similar y *(York)* below bust, die axis ↑↓ 1696 ....30 90 325

	F £	VF £	EF £		F £	VF £	EF £
3526 Sixpence. Similar Y *(York)* below bust, die axis ↑↓ 1696 35					100	350	
— — — 1696 no stops on obverse 65					150	475	
3527 Sixpence. Similar R. Later harp, large crowns, die axis ↑↓ 1696 65					150	475	
— — — 1696 no stops on obverse 90					250	—	

3528 Sixpence. — — — B *(Bristol)* below bust, similar die axis ↑↓

1696 75	175	500	1697 50	125	400
1696 no stops on obv. 90	225	625			

3529 Sixpence. — — — C *(Chester)* below bust, similar die axis ↑↓ 1697 110   275   675

3530 Sixpence. — — — E *(Exeter)* below bust, similar die axis ↑↓ 1697 ...65   150   475

3531 Sixpence. — — R. small crowns, similar die axis ↑↓

1696 65	150	475	1697 Arms of France/Ireland
1697 30	80	300	transposed ....350 — —
1697 GVLIELMΛS 65	175	—	

3532
Bristol Mint Sixpence, small crowns

3532 Sixpence. — — — B *(Bristol)* below bust, similar die axis ↑↓

1696 75	175	525	1697 35	85	300
1696 no stops on O. 110	275	675	1697 B over E 50	125	400

3533 Sixpence. — — — C *(Chester)* below bust, similar die axis ↑↓

1696 90	250	575	1697 Irish shield		
1697 40	110	350	at date 375	950	—
			1697 Plain edge 150	375	950

3534 Sixpence. — — — E *(Exeter)* below bust, similar die axis ↑↓

1697 50	125	425	1697 E over B 110	275	750

3535 Sixpence. — — — N *(Norwich)* below bust, similar die axis ↑↓

1696 90	250	575	1697 45	110	350
1697 GVLIEMVS 150	450	—			

3536 Sixpence. — — — y *(York)* below bust, similar die axis ↑↓

1697 45	110	375	1697 Irish shield at date .250	675	—

3537
Second bust Sixpence

3538
Sixpence, third bust,
later harp, large crowns

	F	VF	EF		F	VF	EF
	£	£	£		£	£	£

3537 Sixpence. Second dr. bust r. R. Similar die axis ↑↓

1696	275	750	1750	1696 GVLELMVS	325	850	2000
1697 GVLIELMⱯS	200	575	1600	1697	150	475	1450
1697 G/I in GRA	175	525	1500	1697 GR/DE in GRA	200	575	1650
1697 GVLIEMVS	200	575	1600				

3537A Sixpence. Third dr. bust, r. early harp, large crowns. E *(Exeter)* below
   bust, 1696 750   2250   —

3537B Sixpence. — — — Y *(York)* below bust, similar die axis ↑↓ 1696 375   950   —

3538 Sixpence. Third dr. bust, r., R. Later harp, large crowns, similar die axis ↑↓

1697 GVLIEIMVS	35	85	300	1699	85	225	525
1697	25	70	250	1700	35	80	325
1697 GⱯLIELMVS	40	90	325	1701	60	150	475
1698	40	100	350				

3539 Sixpence. — — B *(Bristol)* below bust, similar die axis ↑↓

1697	55	140	450	1697 IRA for FRA	100	250	—

3540
Chester Mint Sixpence, third bust

3540 Sixpence. — — C *(Chester)* below bust, similar die axis ↑↓ 1697 90   240   575

3541 Sixpence. — — E *(Exeter)* below bust, similar die axis ↑↓ 1697 110   275   650

3542 Sixpence. Third dr. bust, r. R. Small crowns, similar die axis ↑↓

1697	35	80	275	1697 G/D in GRA	125	300	750
1697 D/F in DEI	125	300	750				

3543 Sixpence. — — C *(Chester)* below bust, similar die axis ↑↓ 1697 80   200   525

3544 Sixpence. — — E *(Exeter)* below bust, similar die axis ↑↓ 1697 75   175   475

3545
York Mint Sixpence - Y provenance mark

3547
Sixpence, roses on reverse

	F	VF	EF		F	VF	EF
	£	£	£		£	£	£

3545 Sixpence.— — Y *(York)* below bust, similar die axis ↑↓ 1697............60 | 135 | 400

3546 Sixpence.— — R. Plumes in angles, similar die axis ↑↓
1698 ....80 | 200 | 525 | 1699 ....80 | 200 | 525

3547 Sixpence.— R. Roses in angles, similar die axis ↑↓
1699 ....100 | 250 | 650 | 1699 GѴLIELMVS . 125 | 300 | —

3548
1700 Sixpence, plume below bust

3549
1699 Groat or Fourpence

3548 Sixpence.— plume below bust, R. Similar die axis ↑↓ 1700..............ß | — | —

3549 Fourpence. Laur. and dr. bust r. R. 4 Crowned die axis ↑↓
1697 .... *Unique* | 1700 ....25 | 50 | 165
1698 ....28 | 60 | 190 | 1701 ....30 | 65 | 190
1699 ....25 | 50 | 145 | 1702 ....20 | 40 | 90

3550 Threepence. Laur. and dr. bust r. R. 3 Crowned die axis ↑↓
1698 ....20 | 40 | 110 | 1701 GBA for GRA ...24 | 45 | 140
1699 ....25 | 50 | 125 | 1701 small lettering ...20 | 40 | 110
1700 ....22 | 45 | 125 | 1701 large lettering ....20 | 40 | 110

3551 Twopence. Laur. and dr. bust r. R. Crown to edge of coin, large figure 2 die axis ↑↓
1698 ....25 | 50 | 135

3551A Twopence. Laur. and dr. bust r. R Crown within inner circle of legend, smaller figure 2, die axis ↑↓
1698 ....25 | 45 | 125 | 1700 ....18 | 30 | 95
1699 ....18 | 30 | 95 | 1701 ....18 | 30 | 95

3552 Penny. Laur. and dr. bust r. R. 1 Crowned die axis ↑↓
1698 ....20 | 40 | 125 | 1699 ....40 | 80 | 225
1698 IRA for FRA error 25 | 45 | 110 | 1700 ....35 | 70 | 165
1698 HI.BREX error... 25 | 45 | 110 | 1701 ....20 | 40 | 105

3553 - 1701 Maundy Set

	F £	VF £	EF £		F £	VF £	EF £
3553 Maundy Set. The four denominations. Uniform dates							
1698 120	220	725	1700 155	340	775
1699 170	380	850	1701 120	280	700

COPPER

3554 - Halfpenny

3554 Halfpenny. First issue. Laur. and cuir. bust r. R. Britannia with r. hand raised die axis ↑↓

1695 50	210	1150	1697 38	175	950
1695 BRITANNIΛ error 225	—	—	1697 all stops omitted 250	—	—
1695 no stop on rev. 70	275	—	1697 I/E in TERTIVS......250	—	—
1695 no stops on obv......70	275	—	1697 GVLILMVS,		
1696 40	175	1000	no rev. stop 330	—	—
1696 GVLIEMVS,			1697 no stop		
no rev. stop 325	—	—	after TERTIVS 55	275	—
1696 TERTVS error.......300	—	—	1698 50	210	1150

3555 Halfpenny. Second issue. Laur. and cuir. bust r. R. Britannia Date in legend die axis ↑↓

1698 Stop after date 38	200	1050	1699 GVLIEMVS error.......250	—	—
1699 no stop after date 32	165	1000	1699 BRITAN IA error.......250	—	—
1699 BRITANNIΛ error 250	—	—			

3556 Halfpenny. Third issue. Laur. and cuir. bust r. R. Britannia with r. hand on knee die axis ↑↓

1699 38	175	950	1700 BRITΛNNIΛ error 45	175	950
1699 stop after date....... 250	—	—	1700 — no stop after 50	195	1000
1699 BRITANNIΛ error 110	380	—	1700 BRIVANNIA error ..... *Extremely rare*		
1699 GVILELMVS error ...300	—	—	1700 GVLIELMS 110	350	—
1699 TERTVS error...... 300	—	—	1700 GVLIEEMVS 70	250	1200
1699 — no rev. stop...... 165	—	—	1700 TER TIVS 50	195	1000
1699 no stops on obv. 95	380	—	1700 I/V in TERTIVS 250	—	—
1699 no stop after...............			1701 45	175	950
GVLIELMVS 95	325	—	1701 BRITANNIA 55	225	1050
1700 38	175	950	1701 — no stops on obv. 250	—	—
1700 no stops on obv. ... 110	350	—	1701 — inverted A's		
1700 no stop after			for V's 65	250	1050
GVLIELMVS 110	350	—			

3557
1696 Farthing date in exergue

3558
1699 Farthing date in legend

	F	VF	EF		F	VF	EF
	£	£	£		£	£	£

3557 Farthing. First issue Laur. and cuir. bust r. R. Britannia l. die axis ↑↓

1695 45	250	950		1698 225	625	—
1695 GVLIELMV error . 225	—	—		1698 B/G on rev. 350	—	—
1696 40	210	900		1699 40	240	900
1697 35	175	825		1699 GVLILEMVS• 195	450	—
1697 GVLIELMS error 275	—	—		1700 35	155	775
1697 TERTIV error.......275	—	—		1700 RRITANNIA 250	—	—

3558 Farthing. Second issue. Laur. and cuir. bust r. R. Britannia date at end of legend die axis ↑↓

1698 Stop after date 50	275	1000	1699 — No stop before or after *Extremely rare*		
1699 no stop after date 55	300	1050	1699 BRITANNIΛ 250	—	—
1699 no stop after GVLIELMVS 140	—	—	1699 BRITANNIΛ 250	—	—

Anne, the second daughter of James II, was born on 6th February 1665 and as a protestant succeeded to the throne on William III's death. Anne married Prince George of Denmark and produced 17 children, sadly none surviving to succeed to the throne. Anne died on 1st August 1714.

The Act of Union of 1707, which effected the unification of the ancient kingdoms of England and Scotland into a single realm, resulted in a change in the royal arms—on the Post-Union coinage the English lions and Scottish lion are emblazoned per pale on the top and bottom shields. After the Union the rose in the centre of the reverse of the gold coins is replaced by the Garter star.

Following a successful Anglo-Dutch expedition against Spain, bullion seized in Vigo Bay was sent to be minted into coin, and the coins made from this metal had the word VIGO placed below the Queen's bust. The elephant and castle provenance mark continues on some guineas in the Post-Union period.

Engravers and designers: Samuel Bull (d.c1720), Joseph Cave (d.c1760), James Clerk, John Croker (1670-1741), Godfrey Kneller (1646-1723)

GOLD

3560
1705 Pre-Union Five Guineas

Before Union with Scotland. The shields on the reverse are Pre-Union type.

	F	VF	EF		F	VF	EF
	£	£	£		£	£	£

3560 Five Guineas. Dr. bust l, regnal year on edge in words (e.g. 1705 = QVARTO) die axis ↑↓
1705 QVARTO 4750   12000   37500   1706 QVINTO 4500   11000   35000
3561 Five Guineas. Similar VIGO below bust, die axis ↑↓ 1703 (Three varieties)
SECVNDO 32500   90000   225000

3562   3563
1705 Pre-Union Guinea   1703 VIGO Guinea

3562 Guinea. Dr. bust l. R. Crowned cruciform shields sceptres in angles die axis ↑↓
1702 1000   3500   10500   1705 1100   3750   11000
1702 proof *FDC* ....   *Extremely rare*   1706 1100   3750   11000
1702 plain edge proof.............*Extremely rare*   1707 1100   3750   11000
3563 Guinea. Similar with VIGO below bust, die axis ↑↓ 1703 12500   32500   75000

3564
Pre-Union Half-Guinea

3565
VIGO Half-Guinea

	F	VF	EF		F	VF	EF
	£	£	£		£	£	£

3564 Half-Guinea. Dr bust l. R. Crowned cruciform shields sceptres in angles die axis ↑↓
1702 750   2250   6500   1705 700   2000   6000
3565 Half-Guinea. Similar with VIGO below bust, 1703 4500   12500   27500

3566
1706 Post-Union Five Guineas

After Union with Scotland. The shields on the reverse are changed to Post-Union type die axis ↑↓
3566 Five Guineas. Dr. bust l., regnal year on edge in words 1706 QVINTO 3250   6750   21000

3567
1709 - Narrow shields

3568
1711 - Broad shields

3567 Five Guineas. Similar R. Narrower shields, tall narrow crowns, larger rev. lettering, die axis ↑↓
1709 OCTAVO 3500   7000   22500
3568 Five Guineas. New bust l. R. Broader shields edge inscribed die axis ↑↓
1711 DECIMO........3500   7000   22500   1714/3 D. TERTIO.......3750   7250   23500
1713 DVODECIMO 3500   7000   22500   1714 D. TERTIO..........3750   7500   24000

3569 - 1713 Two Guineas

	F	VF	EF			F	VF	EF
	£	£	£			£	£	£

3569 Two Guineas. Dr. bust l.R. Crowned cruciform shields sceptres in angles edge milled die axis ↑↓

1709	 1600	3500	9000	1713	 1500	3250	8500
1711	 1500	3250	8500	1714/3	 1650	3750	9500

3570 Guinea. First dr. bust l. R. Crowned cruciform shields sceptres in angles edge milled die axis ↑↓

1707	 675	2850	8500	1708	 675	2850	8500

3571	3574
1708 Guinea, first bust, elephant and castle below	1713 Guinea, third bust

3571 Guinea. First dr. bust l. elephant and castle below, R. Similar die axis ↑↓

1707	 850	3500	10500	1708	....	*Extremely rare*

3572 Guinea. Second dr. bust l. R. Similar die axis ↑↓

1707	 550	2400	7250	1712	 625	1500	4250
1708	 525	2100	6750	1713/1	 575	1350	4000
1709	 525	2100	6750	1713	 550	1250	3750
1710	 625	1500	4250	1714	 575	1350	4000
1711	 625	1500	4250	1714 GRATIA	 550	1250	3750

3573 Guinea. Second bust elephant and castle below R. Similar die axis ↑↓

1708	 800	3250	9500	1709	 725	2850	8500

3574* Guinea. Third dr. bust l. R. Similar die axis ↑↓

1710	 650	1500	4250	1713	 575	1250	3750
1711	 650	1500	4250	1714	 575	1250	3750
1712	 650	1500	4250	1714 GRATIA	 600	1350	4000
1713/1	 600	1350	4000				

3575 - 1710 Half-Guinea

3575 Half-Guinea. Dr. bust l. R. Crowned cruciform shields, sceptres in angles, edge milled die axis ↑↓

1707	 350	800	2400	1711	 325	725	2250
1708	 375	850	2500	1712	 350	800	2400
1709	 350	800	2400	1713	 325	725	2250
1710	 325	725	2250	1714	 325	725	2250

* *If there exists any difference between the 2nd and 3rd busts, it is miniscule.*

SILVER

3576
1703 VIGO Crown

	F	VF	EF		F	VF	EF
	£	£	£		£	£	£

Before Union with Scotland. The shields on the reverse are Pre-Union type.

3576 Crown. VIGO below dr. bust, l., regnal year on edge in words (e.g. 1703 = TERTIO) die axis↑↓

1703 TERTIO 375   1250   5000

3577
1705 Crown, plumes on reverse

3578
1707 Pre-Union crown, roses and plumes

3577 Crown. Dr bust l. R. Plumes in angles, die axis ↑↓ 1705 QVINTO .. 475   1750   5750

3578 Crown. R. Similar Crowned cruciform shields Roses and plumes in angles die axis ↑↓

1706 QVINTO 275   675   2500   1707 SEXTO 250   600   2250

3579
1703 Halfcrown, plain below bust

3579 Halfcrown . Dr. bust l. R. Similar Regnal year on edge in words die axis ↑↓

1703 TERTIO 675   1750   7500

3580
1703 VIGO Halfcrown

	F	VF	EF			F	VF	EF
	£	£	£			£	£	£
3580	**Halfcrown.** Similar VIGO below bust, die axis ↑↓ 1703 TERTIO					175	500	1850

3581
Halfcrown, plumes on reverse

3581 Halfcrown. Dr. bust l. R. Plumes in angles, similar die axis ↑↓

1704 TERTIO	185	700	3000	1705 QVINTO	200	750	3000

3582	3583
Halfcrown, Pre-Union,	Shilling
roses and plumes	

3582 Halfcrown. Dr. bust l. R. Roses and plumes in angles, similar die axis ↑↓

1706 QVINTO	135	400	1500	1707 SEXTO............	125	375	1400

First bust   Second bust

3583 Shilling. First dr. bust l. R. Similar die axis ↑↓ 1702 90   300   1000

		F	VF	EF			F	VF	EF
		£	£	£			£	£	£

3584 **Shilling.** Similar R. Plumes in angles, die axis ↑↓ 1702 90   375   1350

3585 **Shilling.** First dr. bust VIGO below , die axis ↑↓

1702 85   300   900   1702 :ANNA 135   450   1500

3586
1703 VIGO Shilling

3587
'Plain' Shilling

3586 **Shilling.** Second dr. bust, l. VIGO below R. Similar, die axis ↑↓ 1703 80   275   850

3587 **Shilling.** Similar R. Crowned cruciform shields, angles plain, die axis ↑↓

1704 425   1250   −   1705 200   625   1750

3588 **Shilling.** Second dr. bust l. R. Plumes in angles die axis ↑↓

1704 135   500   1500   1705 100   375   1100

3589 **Shilling.** Second dr. bust l. R. Roses and plumes in angles die axis ↑↓

1705 100   375   1100   1707 125   425   1350

3590 **Sixpence.** Dr. bust l. VIGO below dr. bust, l. die axis ↑↓ 1703.................35   110   375

3591 **Sixpence.** Dr bust l., R. Angles plain, die axis ↑↓ 1705 55   175   525

3592 **Sixpence.** Similar R. Early shields, plumes in angles, die axis ↑↓ 1705 40   135   475

3593
1705 Plumes Sixpence

Early Shield

Late Shield

3593 **Sixpence.** Similar R. Late shields, plumes in angles, die axis ↑↓1705 50   150   525

3594 **Sixpence.** Similar R. Crowned cruciform shields Roses and plumes in angles die axis ↑↓

1705 45   140   500   1707 45   140   500

3595
Groat or fourpence, first bust

3595 **Fourpence.** First dr. bust l. small face, curls at back of head point downwards.

R Small crown above the figure 4 die axis ↑↓

1703 20   50   150   1704 15   30   75

3595C
Groat or Fourpence, second bust

	F	VF	EF		F	VF	EF
	£	£	£		£	£	£

3595A Fourpence. Second dr. bust l. larger face, curls at back of head point upwards die axis ↑↓

	F	VF	EF		F	VF	EF
1705	40	95	200	1709	15	32	85
1706	15	30	85	1710	13	28	70
1708	18	38	95				

3595B –Fourpence. Similar R Large crown with pearls on arch, larger serifs on the figure 4 die axis ↑↓

1710	13	28	80	1713	15	30	80

3595C Fourpence. Second dr. bust l., but with re-engraved hair R. Crowned 4 die axis ↑↓

1710	12	25	80	1713	15	30	85

3596 Threepence. First dr. bust l., broader, tie riband pointing outwards. R. Crowned 3 die axis ↑↓

1703 7 above crown	18	45	130	1703 7 not above crown	18	45	130

3596A Threepence. Second dr. bust l., taller and narrow, tie riband pointing inwards die axis ↑↓

1704	18	40	100	1706	15	35	105
1705	18	45	130				

3596B
Threepence, third bust

3596B Threepence. Third larger more finely engraved dr. bust l. R. Crowned 3, die axis ↑↓

	F	VF	EF		F	VF	EF
1707	15	30	75	1710	12	28	85
1708	15	35	105	1713	15	35	100
1708/7	15	35	105	1713 mule with 4d obv.			
1709	15	35	105	die	20	42	150

3597 Twopence. First dr. bust l., as fourpence, R. Crown to edge of coin, small figure 2 die axis ↑↓

1703	22	50	130	1705	25	55	135
1704	20	40	80	1706	20	40	95
1704 No stops on obv.	22	50	110	1707	20	40	80

3597A Twopence. Second dr. bust l., as fourpence, R Crown within inner circle of legend, large figure 2 die axis ↑↓

1708	20	40	85	1710	18	35	80
1709	25	50	115	1713	20	40	80

3598 Penny. Dr. bust l. R. Crowned 1 die axis ↑↓

1703	25	50	125	1709	20	40	90
1705	22	45	105	1710	60	120	230
1706	22	45	105	1713/0	30	55	135
1708	200	300	450				

3599
1713 Maundy Set

	F £	VF £	EF £		F £	VF £	EF £

3599 Maundy Set. The four denominations. Uniform dates

1703	125	280	700	1709	120	240	600
1705	135	285	700	1710	140	290	700
1706	110	220	600	1713	110	220	600
1708	280	420	900				

After Union with Scotland

The shields on the reverse are changed to the Post-Union types. The Edinburgh coins have been included here as they are now coins of Great Britain.

3600 Crown. Second dr. bust, l. E (Edinburgh) below, R. Crowned
cruciform shields regnal year on edge in words, die axis ↑↓
(e.g. 1708 = SEPTIMO)

1707 SEXTO	200	525	2000	1708 SEPTIMO	200	575	2250
1707 SEPTIMO	1500	—	—	1708/7 SEPTIMO	210	600	2400

3601
Crown, second bust, plain reverse

3601 Crown. Second dr. bust l. R. Crowned cruciform shields, angles plain die axis ↑↓

1707 SEPTIMO	185	525	2000	1708 SEPTIMO	185	525	2000

3602 Crown. Similar R. Plumes in angles, die axis ↑↓

1708 SEPTIMO	185	525	2000	1708 — BR for BRI			*Extremely rare*

3603
1713 Crown, third bust, roses and plumes

	F	VF	EF		F	VF	EF
	£	£	£		£	£	£
3603 **Crown.** Third dr. bust. l. R. Roses and plumes, 1713 DVODECIMO	200	550	2250				

3604
1708 Halfcrown, Post-Union

3604 **Halfcrown.** Dr. bust R. Plain, regnal year on edge in words (e.g. 1709 = OCTAVO), die axis ↑↓

1707 SEPTIMO 95	325	1350	1709 OCTAVO 95	325	1350
1707 no stops on reverse ..150	525	—	1713 DVODECIMO 100	350	1400
1708 SEPTIMO 95	325	1350			

3605

3605 **Halfcrown.** Dr. bust E below R. Crowned cruciform shields die axis ↑↓

1707 SEXTO 95	500	1300	1708 SEPTIMO 95	300	1300
1707 SEPTIMO 475	2250	7500	1709 OCTAVO 275	950	—

3606
1708 Halfcrown, plumes on reverse

3607
1714 Halfcrown, roses and plumes

	F	VF	EF		F	VF	EF
	£	£	£		£	£	£

3606 **Halfcrown.** Similar R. Plumes in angles, die axis ↑↓ 1708 SEPTIMO .. 110   375   1750

3607 **Halfcrown.** Similar R. Roses and plumes in angles die axis ↑↓

1710 NONO 95	300	1300	1714 D. TERTIO 95	300	1300
1712 UNDECIMO 90	285	1250	1714/3 D. TERTIO 110	350	1400
1713 DVODECIMO 90	285	1250			

3608
1707 Edinburgh Mint Shilling, second bust

3609
1708 E* Shilling

3608 **Shilling.** Second dr. bust, l. E *(Edinburgh)* below, R. Crowned cruciform shields die axis ↑↓

1707 110	400	1350	1707 Plain edge proof *FDC* £8000		
1707 no stops on			1708 175	575	1850
reverse 275	800	—			

3609 **Shilling.** Similar E* *(Edinburgh)* below bust die axis ↑↓

1707 125	450	1500	1708/7 325	—	—
1708 125	450	1500	1708 no rays to garter star ...... *Extremely rare*		

3609A Shilling. Similar E* *(Edinburgh)* local dies die axis↑↓

1707 275	850	—	1708 300	900	—

Third bust   Fourth bust

3610
Shilling, third bust

3611
Shilling, plumes on reverse

	F £	VF £	EF £		F £	VF £	EF £

3610 Shilling Third dr. bust. l. R. Crowned cruciform shields, angles Plain, die axis ↑↓

| 1707 | 30 | 120 | 525 | 1709 | 30 | 110 | 475 |
| 1708 | 30 | 110 | 475 | 1711 | 90 | 275 | 950 |

3611 Shilling. Third dr. bust. l. R. Plumes in angles die axis ↑↓

| 1707 | 90 | 275 | 950 | 1708 | 90 | 275 | 950 |

3612 Shilling. Third dr. bust. E below R. angles plain die axis ↑↓

| 1707 | 90 | 275 | 950 | 1708/7 | 125 | 350 | 1100 |
| 1708 | 100 | 300 | 1000 | | | | |

3613 Shilling. Second dr. bust l. R. Roses and plumes, die axis ↑↓ 1708 ... 135   450   1350

3614
1708 Shilling, roses and plumes

3614 Shilling. Third dr. bust l. R. Crowned cruciform shields Roses and plumes die axis ↑↓

| 1708 | 100 | 325 | 950 | 1710 | 100 | 300 | 900 |

3615   3620   3623

Edinburgh bust – E* Shilling Edinburgh Mint Sixpence   1707 Sixpence, plumes on reverse

	F	VF	EF		F	VF	EF
	£	£	£		£	£	£

3615 Shilling. 'Edinburgh' bust, E* below, R. Crowned cruciform shields die axis ↑↓

1707 525   –   –   1709 150   500   1500

1708 200   650   1750

3616 Shilling. — E below, R. Similar die axis ↑↓ 1709 375   1250   –

3617 Shilling. Fourth dr. bust. l. R. Roses and plumes die axis ↑↓

1710 80   250   850   1713/2 80   250   850

1710 plain edge proof *FDC*   *Extremely rare*   1714 65   185   700

1712 70   200   725   1714/3 85   250   850

3618 Shilling. Similar, R. angles plain, die axis ↑↓

1711 30   110   475   1711 plain edge proof *FDC*   *Extremely rare*

3619 Sixpence. Normal dr. bust. l. R. angles plain die axis ↑↓

1707 40   125   425   1711 25   70   240

1707 BR. FRA error .. 475   –   –   1711 Large Lis 30   80   275

1708 45   140   475

3620 Sixpence. Normal dr. bust E *(Edinburgh)* below R. Similar die axis ↑↓

1707 45   125   425   1708/7 75   200   625

1707 Proof FDC £5000   1708 60   160   475

3621 Sixpence. Normal dr. bust E* *(Edinburgh)* below, R. Similar die axis ↑↓

1708 60   175   550   1708/7 75   200   625

3622 Sixpence. 'Edinburgh' bust, l. E* below, R. Similar die axis ↑↓ 1708 .. 70   185   575

3623 Sixpence. Normal dr. bust. l. R. Plumes in angles die axis ↑↓

1707 40   125   400   1708 45   135   450

3624 Sixpence. Similar R. Roses and plumes in angles, die axis ↑↓ 1710 ... 55   160   500

COPPER

3625

1714 Pattern Farthing

3625 Farthing. Dr. bust l. R. Britannia 1714 pattern only, die axis ↑↓ 325   600   1250

GEORGE I, 1714-27

George I was born on 28th May 1660 son of Ernest, Elector of Hanover and Sophia grandaughter of James I, and inherited the English Throne on a technicality, Parliament considered him a better alternative than James Edward Stuart – Anne's half-brother. He was however, thoroughly German, did not want to learn English and spent over half his reign in Germany. He brought two mistresses with him to England while his wife ironically languished in a German prison on a charge of adultery. His reign created a government that could run independently of the King. The office of Prime Minister was created in 1721. He also kept England out of war for his entire reign, and he died on 11 June 1727.

The coins of the first of the Hanoverian kings have the arms of the Duchy of Brunswick and Luneberg on one of the four shields, the object in the centre of the shield being the Crown of Charlemagne. The King's German titles also appear, in abbreviated form, and name him 'Duke of Brunswick and Luneberg. Arch-treasurer of the Holy Roman Empire, and Elector', and on the Guinea of 1714, 'Prince Elector'. A Quarter-Guinea was struck for the first time in 1718, but it was of an inconvenient size, and the issue was discontinued. The elephant and castle provenance mark continues on some guineas and half-guineas, but today are rarely seen.

Silver coined from bullion supplied to the mint by the South Sea Company in 1723 shows the Company's initials S.S.C.; similarly Welsh Copper Company bullion has the letters W.C.C. below the King's bust; and plumes and an interlinked CC in the reverse angles. Roses and plumes together on the reverse indicate silver supplied by the Company for Smelting Pit Coale and Sea Coale.

Engravers and Designers: Samuel Bull (d.c.1720), John Croker (1670-1741), John Rudulf Ochs Snr, (1673-c.1748), Norbert Roettier (b.1665)

Prime Minister: Sir Robert Walpole (1676 – 1745) –Whig, 1721-42

GOLD

3626
1717 Five Guineas

	F	VF	EF		F	VF	EF
	£	£	£		£	£	£

3626 Five Guineas. Laur. head r. regnal year on edge in words (e.g. 1717 = TERTIO) die axis↑↓

	F	VF	EF		F	VF	EF
1716 SECVNDO	3750	8500	27500	1720 SEXTO	4000	9000	30000
1717 TERTIO	4000	9000	30000	1726 D. TERTIO	3750	8500	27500
Variety O for D on edge exits				Variety Ʌ for N on edge exists			

3627
Two Guineas

	F £	VF £	EF £		F £	VF £	EF £

3627 Two Guineas. Laur. head r. R. Crowned cruciform shields, sceptres in angles, edge milled, die axis ↑↓

1717	1350	2750	7250	1720/17	1500	2850	7500
1720	1350	2750	7250	1726	1250	2600	7000

3628
1714 'Prince Elector' Guinea

3630
Third bust

3631
Fourth bust

3628 Guinea. First laur. head r. R. Legend ends ET PR . EL (Prince Elector), die axis ↑↓

1714	1350	3500	9500

3629 Guinea. Second laur. head, r. tie with two ends, R. Crowned cruciform shields, sceptres in angles normal legend ↑↓ 1715 650   1500   4250

3630 Guinea. Third laur. head, r. no hair below truncation R. Similar die axis ↑↓

1715	550	1300	3750	1716	575	1400	4000

3631 Guinea. Fourth laur. head, r. tie with loop at one end R. Similar die axis ↑↓

1716	575	1300	3750	1720 large or small			
1717	600	1400	4000	20 in date	575	1400	4000
1718		*Extremely rare*		1721	575	1400	4000
1718/7		*Extremely rare*		1722	550	1350	3850
1719	550	1350	3850	1722/0	575	1400	4000
1719/6		*Extremely rare*		1723	575	1400	4000

3632 Guinea. Fourth Laur. head, elephant and castle below R. Similar die axis ↑↓

1721		*Extremely rare*		1722		*Extremely rare*	

3633
Guinea, fifth bust

	F £	VF £	EF £		F £	VF £	EF £

3633 Guinea. Fifth (older) laur. head, r. tie with two ends R. Similar die axis ↑↓

	F	VF	EF		F	VF	EF
1723	550	1350	3850	1725	550	1350	3850
1723 II for H in TH	700	1700	—	1725 large 5 in date	700	1700	—
1724	550	1350	3850	1726	500	1250	3750
1724 R/I in				1727	650	1500	4500
GEORGIVS	700	1700	—				

3634 Guinea. Fifth laur. head, elephant and castle below, die axis ↑↓ 1726 .... 1750 4750 16500

3635 Half-Guinea. First laur. head r. R. Crowned cruciform shields, sceptres in angles die axis ↑↓

	F	VF	EF		F	VF	EF
1715	625	1500	4250	1721			*Extremely rare*
1717	350	750	2750	1722	350	750	2750
1718	325	700	2500	1722/0	375	775	2850
1718/7	350	725	2650	1723	375	800	3000
1719	325	700	2500	1724	400	850	3250
1720	350	750	2750				

3636 Half-Guinea. First laur. head elephant and castle below, die axis ↑↓ 1721 *Extremely rare*

3637
Half-Guinea, second bust

3638
Quarter Guinea

3637 Half-Guinea. Second (older) laur. head r. R. Crowned cruciform shields, sceptres in angles die axis ↑↓

	F	VF	EF		F	VF	EF
1725	300	675	2500	1727	350	750	2750
1726	325	700	2500				

3638 Quarter-Guinea. Laur. head R. Similar die axis ↑↓ 1718 .... 150 275 550

SILVER

3639A - 1726 Crown - small roses and plumes

	F	VF	EF		F	VF	EF
	£	£	£		£	£	£

3639 Crown. Laur and dr. bust r. R. Roses and plumes in angles, regnal year on edge in words
(e.g. 1716 = SECVNDO) die axis ↑↓

| 1716 SECVNDO | 525 | 1250 | 3750 | 1720/18 SEXTO | 525 | 1250 | 3750 |
| 1718/6 QUINTO | 550 | 1350 | 4000 | | | | |

3639A Crown. Similar R. small roses and plumes in angles

| 1720 SEXTO | 625 | 1500 | 5000 | 1726 D. TERTIO | 550 | 1350 | 4000 |

3640 Crown. Similar R. SSC (South Sea Company) in angles, die axis ↑↓

| 1723 DECIMO | | | | | 525 | 1250 | 3750 |

3641 - 1715 Pattern Halfcrown

3641 Halfcrown. Laur and dr. bust r. R. Angles plain (pattern only), die axis ↑↓ 1715 *FDC* £11000

3642 - Halfcrown, roses and plumes

3642 Halfcrown. — R. Roses and plumes in angles, regnal year on edge in words
(e.g. 1717 = TIRTIO)

1715 SECVNDO	300	800	3000	1717 TIRTIO	300	800	3000
1715 Edge wording out...				1720/17 SEXTO	300	800	3000
of order	350	950	3500	1720 SEXTO	325	900	3250
1715 Plain edge	500	1650	—				

3643 - 1723 SSC Halfcrown

	F	VF	EF		F	VF	EF
	£	£	£		£	£	£

3643 Halfcrown. Similar R. SSC in angles, die axis ↑↓1723 DECIMO 300   750   2750

3644 - 1726 Halfcrown small roses and plumes

3644 Halfcrown. — R. Small roses and plumes, die axis ↑↓ 1726 D.TERTIO ...3750   10500   22500

3645		3646
Shilling, roses and plumes		1721 Shilling, plain reverse

3645 Shilling. First laur. and dr. bust. r. R. Roses and plumes in angles, die axis ↑↓

1715	80	240	850	1721	150	475	1450
1716	150	475	1450	1721/0	100	350	1200
1717	125	450	1350	1721/19	125	450	1350
1718	75	225	750	1721/18 plumes and			
1719	125	425	1350	roses error	375	1500	—
1720	110	375	1250	1722	100	375	1250
1720/18	200	625	1750	1723	125	450	1350

3646 Shilling. First laur. and dr. bust r. R. angles plain (i.e. no marks either side) die axis ↑↓

1720	30	120	575	1721	125	450	1350
1720 large O	40	125	600	1721 O of GEORGIVS over zero			

LETTERING ERRORS:
3645 1716 V of GEORGIVS over L   1720 Large O in date
      1717 Large lettering on obverse

3647   3649
1723 SSC Shilling, first bust   1727 Shilling, second bust

	F	VF	EF		F	VF	EF
	£	£	£		£	£	£

3647 Shilling. First laur. and dr. bust r. ℞. SSC in angles, die axis ↑↓

1723	30	75	300	1723 C/SS in 3rd			
1723 French Arms at				quarter	35	100	350
date	150	425	1250				

LETTERING VARIETIES:

B·RVN on Rev., Large N in BRVN and stop between E.T. after BRVN.

3648 Shilling. Second dr. bust, r. bow to tie. ℞. Similar, die axis ↑↓ 1723 ... 35 ... 110 ... 425

3649 Shilling. Similar ℞. Roses and plumes in angles die axis ↑↓

1723	100	350	1100	1726 no stops on obv.	650	1750	—
1724	110	375	1200	1727	525	1350	—
1725	100	350	1100	1727 no stops on obv exists			
1725 no stops on obv.	110	375	1200	1727 no stops on rev	450	1250	—
1725 no stops on rev	120	400	1250				

3650 - 1726 WCC Shilling

3650 Shilling. Second laur. and dr. bust r. W.C.C. (Welsh Copper Company) below bust die axis ↑↓

| 1723 | 650 | 1650 | 4750 | 1725 | 675 | 1750 | 5000 |
| 1724 | 650 | 1650 | 4750 | 1726 | 675 | 1750 | 5000 |

3651 Sixpence. Laur. and dr. bust r. ℞. Roses and plumes in angles, die axis ↑↓

| 1717 | 90 | 250 | 675 | 1720/17 | 90 | 250 | 675 |
| 1717 Plain edge | | *Extremely rare* | | | | | |

3652 - 1723 SSC Sixpence   3653 - 1726 Sixpence,
                                        small roses and plumes

3652 Sixpence. Laur. and dr. bust r. ℞. SSC in angles, die axis ↑↓

| 1723 | 25 | 80 | 300 | 1723 larger lettering ... 30 | 80 | 325 |

3653 Sixpence. Similar ℞. Small roses and plumes, die axis ↑↓ 1726 .... 85 ... 250 ... 650

	F £	VF £	EF £		F £	VF £	EF £

3654 Fourpence. Laur. and dr. bust r. ℞. Crowned 4, die axis ↑↓

| 1717 | ....15 | 40 | 100 | 1723 | ....20 | 50 | 140 |
| 1721 | ....15 | 40 | 100 | 1727 | ....22 | 55 | 150 |

3655 Threepence. Laur. and dr. bust r. ℞. Crowned 3, die axis ↑↓

| 1717 | ....20 | 45 | 95 | 1723 | ....20 | 50 | 140 |
| 1721 | ....25 | 45 | 95 | 1727 small lettering ......20 | | 50 | 125 |

3656 Twopence. Laur. and dr. bust r. ℞. Crowned 2, die axis ↑↓

1717	12	32	65	1726	12	25	60
1721	12	25	60	1727 small lettering 15		32	85
1723	15	40	110				

3657 Penny. Laur. and dr. bust r. ℞. Crowned 1, die axis ↑↓

1716	12	32	65	1723	15	30	80
1718	12	32	65	1725	12	32	65
1720	12	32	65	1726	15	40	70
1720 HIPEX error 20		85	130	1727 BRI·FR................20		50	110

3658

3658 Maundy Set. As last four. Uniform dates

| 1723 | ....120 | 250 | 750 | 1727 | ....110 | 240 | 650 |

COPPER

3659

3659 Halfpenny. 'Dump' issue obv. legend continuous over bust, plain edge, die axis ↑↓

1717	40	250	800	1718 no stops on obv.... 165		500	—
1717 no stops on obv.110		525	—	1719	1000	—	—
1718	35	225	725	1719 grained edge 1000		—	—
1718 R/B on rev. 55		250	900	*(1719 is an extremely rare date, perhaps only 2*			
				or 3 known to exist of each type)			

3660

	F £	VF £	EF £		F £	VF £	EF £

3660 Halfpenny. Second issue, second obverse, plain left shoulder strap, less hair to the right of tie knot, R. Britannia plain edge, die axis ↑↓

1719	45	210	900	1722	35	155	700
1719 grained edge	1000	—	—	1722 ∀ for V on obv.	110	500	—
1720	35	175	825	1723	35	155	750
1721	35	165	725	1723 Thin Flan		*Extremely rare*	
1721 stop after date	45	200	800	1723 no stop on rev.	110	525	—
1721/0	45	200	800	1724	35	155	700

3660A Halfpenny. Second issue, second obverse, ornate shoulder straps, die axis ↑↓

1719	45	195	900

3661   3662

3661 Farthing. 'Dump' issue, Similar die axis ↑↓

1717	220	675	1250	1718		*Unique*	

3662 Farthing. Second issue laur. and cuir. bust r. R. Britannia, date in ex. die axis ↑↓

1719 small letters	65	330	775	1720 obv. large letters	85	350	—
1719 no stop on rev.	75	380	—	1721	30	135	650
1719 large lettering				1721/0	45	165	675
on obv.	35	165	650	1721 stop after date	40	165	625
1719 — no stops on				1722	35	155	625
obv.	75	410	—	1722 obv. large letters	45	210	725
1719 — no stops on rev	95	450	—	1723 R/≍ in REX	110	330	900
1719 last A/I on rev.	85	350	—	1723	35	165	600
1720	35	165	600	1724	35	165	625
1720 milled edge	165	500	1150				

George II was born on 30 October 1683 and was raised in Hanover, but upon his succession to the throne as George I's only child, he adapted himself to English society. His passions were the military, music and his wife – Caroline of Anspach, though he despised his eldest son Frederick as his own father despised him. George declared war on Spain in 1739 and he was the last King to have personally led his troops at the battle of Dettingen on 17 June 1743. Upon his death on 25 October 1760 the throne passed to his grandson George as Frederick had already died.

Silver was coined only spasmodically by the Mint during this reign; and no copper was struck after 1754. Gold coins made from bullion supplied by the East India Company bear the Company's E.I.C. initials. Some of the treasure seized by Admiral Anson during his circumnavigation of the globe, 1740-4, and by other privateers, was made into coin, which had the word LIMA below the king's bust to celebrate the expedition's successful harassment of the Spanish Colonies in the New World. Hammered gold was finally demonetized in 1733.

Engravers and designers: John Croker (1670-1741), John Rudolf Ochs Snr (1673-1748) and jnr (1704-88), Johann Sigismund Tanner (c.1706-75)

Prime Ministers: Sir Robert Walpole (1676-1745) Whig, 1721-43; Spencer Compton (1673-1743) Whig 1742-3; Henry Pelham (c.1695-1754) Whig 1743-54; William Cavendish (1720-1764) Whig 1756-7; Thomas Pelham-Holles (1693-1768) Whig 1754-6; 1757-62.

GOLD

3663A
1741 Five Guineas - revised shield

	F £	VF £	EF £		F £	VF £	EF £

3663 Five Guineas. Young laur. head l. R. Crowned shield of arms, die axis ↑↓ regnal year on edge in words (e.g. 1729 = TERTIO)

	F £	VF £	EF £		F £	VF £	EF £
1729 TERTIO	2750	5750	18500	1729 Plain edge proof *FDC* £65000			

3663A Five Guineas. Similar R. Revised shield garnish die axis ↑↓

	F £	VF £	EF £		F £	VF £	EF £
1731 QVARTO	3250	6750	25000	1738 DVODECIMO	2850	6000	20000
1731 QVARTO proof *FDC* £70000				1741/38 D. QVARTO	2750	5750	18500
1735 NONO	3250	6750	25000	1741 D. QVARTO	2650	5750	18000

3664 Five Guineas. Young laur. head, E.I.C. (East India Company) below, die axis ↑↓

	F £	VF £	EF £
1729 TERTIO	2500	5500	15000

3665

1746 LIMA Five Guineas

	F	*VF*	*EF*			*F*	*VF*	*EF*
	£	£	£			£	£	£

3665　Five Guineas. Old laur. head, l. LIMA below, ↑↓1746 D. NONO... 2750　　5750　16000

3666　Five Guineas. Old laur. head plain below, R. Crowned shield, edge inscribed die axis ↑↓
1748 V. SECVNDO 2750　　5750　16000　　1753 V. SEXTO ..... 2750　　5750　16500

3667　Two Guineas. Young laur. head l. R Crowned shield with rounded arches, die axis ↑↓
1733 Proof *FDC* £32500　　　　　　　　1734/3 .... 1650　　4000　10500

3667A

1735 Two Guineas - new reverse

3667A Two Guineas. – R. Crown with pointed arches, new type of shield garnishing die axis ↑↓
1735 .... 1100　　2250　6250

3667B Two Guineas. Repositioned legend on obverse R. Similar
1738*........................ 850　　1350　3250　　1739 .... 850　　1400　3500

3668

1740 Two Guineas - Intermediate head

3668　Two Guineas. Intermediate laur. head l. R. Crowned shield of arms die axis ↑↓
1739*........................ 825　　1350　3250　　1740 .... 850　　1400　3500
1740/39.................... 875　　1500　3750

3669　Two Guineas. Old laur. head l. R. Crowned shield of arms die axis ↑↓ ..
1748 .... 900　　1600　4250　　1753 .... 950　　1650　5000

*Beware recent forgeries.

Overstruck dates are listed only if commoner than normal date or if no normal date is known.

	F £	VF £	EF £		F £	VF £	EF £

3670 Guinea. First young laur. head, l. small lettering, die axis ↑↓ 1727 ... 950   2750   8500

3671   3676
1727 Guinea - small reverse shield

3671 Guinea. Similar larger lettering, smaller shield, die axis ↑↓
1727 1000   3000   9000   1728 1000   3000   9000

3672 Guinea. Second (narrower) young laur. head l. die axis ↑↓
1729 Proof *FDC* £16500   1731 625   1700   4750
1730 700   1850   5500   1732 650   1800   5250

3673 Guinea. Second young laur. head, E.I.C. below R. Crowned shield of arms die axis ↑↓
1729 1200   3500   10500   1732 1000   3000   9000
1731 1100   3250   10000

3674 Guinea. Second young laur. head l. larger lettering R. Crowned shield of arms die axis ↑↓
1732 625   1750   5000   1736 550   1500   4250
1733 550   1450   4000   1737 575   1650   4500
1734 550   1450   4000   1738 575   1650   4500
1735 550   1500   4250

3675 Guinea. − − E.I.C. below, die axis ↑↓ 1732 1000   3000   9000
Note: All 1739-45 Guineas read GEORGIUS

3676 Guinea. Intermediate laur. head l. r. Crowned shield of arms die axis ↑↓
1739 550   1450   3750   1741/39 775   2400   6750
1740 575   1500   4000   1743 775   2400   6750

3677 Guinea. Similar E.I.C. below, R. Similar die axis ↑↓ 1739 1000   3000   9000

3678 Guinea. Similar larger lettering on *obv*., GEORGIUS die axis ↑↓
1745 (also exists with small S in date) 550   1450   3750

3678A   3679
1746 Guinea - GEORGIVS legend   LIMA below bust Guinea

3678A Guinea. Similar as last but reads GEORGIVS die axis ↑↓
1746 575   1500   4000

3679 Guinea. Intermediate laur. head LIMA below, GEORGIUS die
axis ↑↓ 1745 1500   4500   12000

3680
Old head Guinea

	F	VF	EF		F	VF	EF
	£	£	£		£	£	£

3680 Guinea. Old laur. head l. R. Crowned shield of arms die axis ↑↓

1747	475	1150	3500	1753	475	1150	3500
1748	475	1150	3500	1755	475	1150	3500
1749	475	1150	3500	1756	450	1100	3250
1750	475	1150	3500	1758	425	975	2750
1751	450	1100	3250	1759	375	950	2650
1752	450	1100	3250	1760	375	950	2750

3681 Half-Guinea. Young laur. head. l. R First shield of arms, die axis ↑↓

1728	550	1400	3750	1729	525	1350	3500

1728 Proof *FDC* £9000

3681A
1731 Half-Guinea - modified shield

3681A Half-Guinea. Young laur. head l. R. Modified garnished shield die axis ↑↓

1730	425	1050	3250	1736	350	875	2750
1731	325	850	2650	1737	400	950	3000
1732	350	875	2750	1738	325	800	2500
1734	325	850	2650	1739	325	850	2650

3682 Half-Guinea. Young laur. head l. E.I.C. below R. Similar die axis ↑↓

1729	625	1600	4500	1732	....	*Extremely rare*	
1730	750	2000	5750	1739	....	*Extremely rare*	
1731	....	*Extremely rare*					

3683A
Half-guinea - GEORGIVS legend

3683 Half-Guinea. Intermediate laur. head l. R. Similar die axis ↑↓

1740	300	750	2500	1745	325	850	2650
1743	....	*Extremely rare*					

3683A Half-Guinea. Similar, but reads GEORGIVS, die axis ↑↓ 1746 275   625   2000

3684
LIMA Half-Guinea

3685
Half-Guinea, old head

	F £	VF £	EF £		F £	VF £	EF £

3684 Half-Guinea. Intermediate laur. head LIMA below, die axis ↑↓ 1745 1050 2750 6500
3685 Half-Guinea. Old laur. head l. R. Similar die axis ↑↓

	F	VF	EF		F	VF	EF
1747	325	725	2250	1753	275	625	2000
1748	325	725	2250	1755	260	575	1850
1749	350	750	2400	1756	250	550	1750
1750	325	725	2250	1758	260	575	1850
1751	300	700	2100	1759	250	550	1750
1751/0	325	725	2250	1759/8	260	575	1850
1752	275	625	2000	1760	250	550	1750

SILVER

3686
Crown, young head

3686 Crown. Young laur. and dr. bust. l. R. Crowned cruciform shields Roses and plumes in angles, regnal year on edge in words (e.g. 1736 = NONO), die axis ↑↓

1732 SEXTO	350	850	2750	1735 OCTAVO	325	825	2600
1732 Proof, plain edge *FDC* £11000				1736 NONO	325	825	2600
1734 SEPTIMO	425	1100	3500				

3687
3687 Crown. Similar R. Roses in angles die axis ↑↓

1739 DVODECIMO	300	800	2400	1741 D. QVARTO	300	750	2250

3688
Crown, old head

	F	VF	EF		F	VF	EF
	£	£	£		£	£	£

3688 Crown. Old laur. and dr. bust l. ℞. Crowned cruciform shields Roses in angles, die axis ↑↓
1743 D. SEPTIMO 325   725   2100

3689 Crown. — LIMA below, die axis ↑↓ 1746 D. NONO............................325   725   2100

3690
Plain reverse

3691
1731 Pattern Halfcrown

3690 Crown. Old laur. and dr. bust l. ℞. angles Plain (i.e. no marks either side) die axis ↑↓
1746 Proof only, VICESIMO *FDC* £8000
1750 V. QVARTO 300   800   2400   1751 V. QVARTO 350   825   2600

3691 Halfcrown. Young dr. bust l. ℞. angles plain (pattern only), 1731 *FDC* £5500

3692
1736 Halfcrown, roses and plumes

3693
1741 Halfcrown, roses on reverse

	F	VF	EF		F	VF	EF
	£	£	£		£	£	£

3692 Halfcrown. Young laur. and dr. bust l. Ŗ. Roses and plumes, regnal year on edge in words (e.g. 1732 = SEXTO), die axis ↑↓

1731 QVINTO	150	400	1450	1735 OCTAVO	165	450	1750
1732 SEXTO	150	400	1450	1736 NONO	165	450	1750
1734 SEPTIMO	165	450	1750

3693 Halfcrown. Young laur. and dr. bust l. Ŗ. Roses in angles die axis ↑↓

1739 DVODECIMO	140	350	1450	1741 Large *obv.* letters	150	375	1500
1741 D. QVARTO	140	350	1450	1741/39 D. QVARTO	165	425	1600

3694 Halfcrown. Old dr. bust. l. GEORGIUS Ŗ. Roses in angles die axis ↑↓

1743 D. SEPTIMO	110	275	1100	1745/3 D. NONO	120	300	1250
1745 D. NONO	110	275	1100

3695 Halfcrown. Old laur. and dr. bust LIMA below die axis ↑↓

1745 D. NONO	70	175	625	1745/3	85	225	850

3695A Halfcrown. Old laur. and dr. bust as last LIMA below but reads GEORGIVS die axis ↑↓

1746 D. NONO	65	165	600	1746/5 D. NONO	75	185	650

3696
1751 Halfcrown

3697
1727 Plumes Shilling

3696 Halfcrown. Old laur. and dr. bust l. Ŗ. Plain angles die axis ↑↓

1746 proof only VICESIMO *FDC* £3500   1751 V. QVARTO 250 600 2250
1750 V. QVARTO 200   525   2000

3697 Shilling. Young laur. dr. bust. l. R. Plumes in angles, die axis ↑↓

1727	125	475	1500	1731	135	500	1600

3698
Shilling, young bust, small letters

3699
Young bust Shilling, large letters

	F £	VF £	EF £		F £	VF £	EF £

3698 Shilling. Young laur. and dr. bust l. R. Roses and plumes in angles, die axis ↑↓

1727	65	240	950	1731	70	250	1000
1728	80	275	1100	1732	80	275	1100
1729	80	275	1100				

3699 Shilling. Young laur. and dr. bust l. R. Plain, die axis ↑↓ 1728 85   275   1000

3700 - Shilling, plain reverse   3701 - Shilling, roses reverse

3700 Shilling. Similar larger lettering. R. Roses and plumes in angles die axis ↑↓

1734	60	210	850	1737	60	210	850
1735	65	225	900	1737 known with GRΛTIΛ error			
1736	60	210	850	1737 with 3/5 exists			
1736/5	65	225	900				

3701 Shilling. Young laur. and dr. bust l. R. Roses in angles die axis ↑↓

1739 size of garter				1739 smaller garter star	75	240	750
varies	50	200	625	1741	50	200	625
1739/7	110	375	1250	1741/39	110	375	1250

3702
Shilling, old bust, roses

3703
LIMA Shilling

3702 Shilling. Old laur. and dr. bust, l. R. Roses in angles die axis ↑↓

1743	35	120	475	1745/3	50	175	650
1743/1	50	175	650	1747 only known with GEORGIVS			
1745	45	150	600	on obv	40	135	575

3703 Shilling. Old laur. and dr. bust LIMA below die axis ↑↓

| 1745 only known with GEORGIVS | | | | 1746 | 85 | 275 | 900 |
| on obv | 30 | 110 | 525 | 1746/5 | 85 | 275 | 900 |

N.B. In and after 1746 the 'U' was changed to 'V' on old Head Shillings.

3704
1758 Shilling

	F	VF	EF		F	VF	EF
	£	£	£		£	£	£

3704 **Shilling.** Old laur. and dr. bust R. plain angles die axis ↑↓

1746 Proof only *FDC* £2250				1750/7	45	150	575
1750	40	135	550	1751	110	325	1000
1750/6	45	150	575	1758 also known with small			
1750 Wide O	45	150	575	58 in date	20	45	200

3705	3706	3707
1728 Sixpence, young bust	1728 Sixpence, plumes on reverse	1728 Sixpence, roses and plumes

3705 **Sixpence.** Young laur. and dr. bust. l. R. Angles plain, die axis ↑↓ 1728...50 175 550
1728 Proof *FDC* £3500

3706 **Sixpence.** Similar R. Plumes in angles die axis ↑↓ 1728 45 150 525

3707 **Sixpence.** Young laur. and dr. bust l. R. Roses and plumes in angles die axis ↑↓

1728	30	125	425	1735	35	135	450
1731	30	125	425	1735/4	45	150	475
1732	30	125	425	1736	40	135	450
1734	35	135	450				

3708	3709
Sixpence, roses	Sixpence, old bust, roses

3708 **Sixpence.** Young laur. and dr. bust l., R. Roses in angles, die axis ↑↓

| 1739 | 30 | 120 | 375 | 1741 | 30 | 125 | 400 |
| 1739 O/R in legend | 40 | 135 | 450 | | | | |

3709 **Sixpence.** Old laur. and dr. bust. l. R. Roses in angles die axis ↑↓

| 1743 | 25 | 100 | 325 | 1745/3 | 30 | 100 | 350 |
| 1745 | 25 | 90 | 325 | | | | |

	F	VF	EF		F	VF	EF
	£	£	£		£	£	£

3710 Sixpence. Old laur. and dr. bust LIMA below bust R. angle plain die axis ↑↓
1745 30   90   325
3710A Sixpence. Similar as last but reads GEORGIVS die axis ↑↓
1746 20   75   300   1746/5 35   120   375

3711
Proof Sixpence

3711 Sixpence. Old laur. and dr. bust l. R. angles plain die axis ↑↓
1746 *proof only FDC* £1650
1750 25   80   300   1758 10   25   100
1751 30   90   325   1758 ÐEI error 20   40   150
1757 10   25   100   1758/7 15   35   135
3712 Fourpence. Young laur. and dr. bust l. R. Small dome-shaped crown without pearls on arch, figure 4
1729 22   48   120   1731 20   45   110
3712A Fourpence. Similar R. Double arched crown with pearls, large figure 4, die axis ↑↓
1732 22   48   120   1740 18   35   100
1735 22   48   125   1743 35   80   250
1737 22   48   125   1743/0 35   80   250
1739 20   45   110   1746 15   30   85
                                                      1760 22   45   130
3713 Threepence. Young laur. and dr. bust l. R. Crowned 3, pearls on arch, die axis ↑↓
1729 18   38   90
3713A Threepence. Similar R. Ornate arch die axis ↑↓
1731 Smaller lettering   18   38   90   1731 18   38   90
3713B Threepence. Similar R. Double arched crown with pearls, die axis ↑↓
1732 18   38   85   1743 Large lettering ... 15   30   80
1732 with stop over head 18   38   85   1743 Small lettering ... 15   30   80
1735 18   38   90   1743 — stop over head 18   35   85
1737 15   35   80   1746 12   25   75
1739 15   30   80   1746/3 14   30   75
1740 15   30   80   1760 18   38   85
3714 Twopence. Young laur. and dr. bust l. R. Small crown and figure 2, die axis ↑↓
1729 10   25   70   1731 10   25   65
3714A Twopence. Young laur. and dr. bust l. R. Large crown and figure 2 die axis ↑↓
1732 15   25   70   1743/0 15   28   70
1735 15   25   65   1746 12   22   60
1737 15   25   70   1756 12   25   50
1739 15   25   70   1759 12   25   45
1740 22   35   90   1760 18   30   75
1743 15   28   70
3715 Penny. Young laur. and dr. bust l. head. R. Date over small crown and figure 1, die axis ↑↓
1729 12   25   70   1731 12   25   70

	F £	VF £	EF £		F £	VF £	EF £

3715A Penny. Young laur. and dr. bust l. R. Large crown dividing date die axis ↑↓

	F	VF	EF		F	VF	EF
1732 12	25	65		1753/2 10	25	45
1735 15	30	60		1753 10	25	50
1737 15	30	65		1754 10	25	50
1739 12	25	60		1755 10	25	50
1740 12	25	60		1756 10	25	50
1743 10	22	60		1757 10	25	50
1746 10	20	60		1757 GRATIA: 12	35	70
1746/3 12	32	65		1758 10	25	50
1750 10	20	40		1759 10	25	50
1752 10	20	40		1760 18	30	75
1752/0 10	30	60					

3716

3716 Maundy Set. The four denominations. Uniform dates

	F	VF	EF		F	VF	EF
1729 85	200	480		1739 75	180	425
1731 85	200	480		1740 80	185	430
1732 75	180	430		1743 100	210	500
1735 80	180	430		1746 70	150	400
1737 75	180	430		1760 85	200	480

COPPER

3717

3717 Halfpenny. Young laur. and cuir. bust l. R. Britannia, date in ex. die axis ↑↓

	F	VF	EF		F	VF	EF
1729 17	100	380		1733 13	90	370
1729 rev. no stop 22	110	410		1734 13	90	370
1730 13	100	360		1734 R/O on obv 22	145	450
1730 GEOGIVS error .22	150	470		1734/3 33	210	—
1730 stop after date 22	110	380		1734 no stops on obv. 33	210	—
1730 no stop after				1735 13	90	370
REX on obv........28	160	470		1736 17	110	400
1731 13	90	360		1736/0 22	130	450
1731 rev. no stop 22	150	440		1737 17	100	400
1732 13	100	360		1738 11	75	370
1732 rev. no stop 22	150	440		1738 V/S on obv 22	145	450
				1739 13	75	370

	F	VF	EF		F	VF	EF
	£	£	£		£	£	£

3718 Halfpenny. Old laur. and cuir. bust l., GEORGIUS R. Britannia, date in ex. die axis ↑↓

1740	11	80	330	1743	11	80	330
1742	11	80	330	1744	11	80	330
1742/0	22	130	425	1745	11	80	330

3719

1746 Halfpenny

3719 Halfpenny. Old laur. and cuir. bust l. GEORGIVS, R. Britannia, date in ex. die axis ↑↓

1746	11	65	330	1751	11	65	330
1747	11	70	365	1752	11	65	330
1748	11	70	365	1753	11	65	330
1749	11	70	330	1754	11	70	365
1750	11	70	365				

3720

3720 Farthing. Young laur. and cuir. bust l. R. Britannia, date in ex. die axis ↑↓

1730	13	70	330	1735 3 over 5	22	130	425
1731	13	70	330	1736	13	70	330
1732	17	75	365	1736 triple tie ribands	33	130	425
1732/1	22	110	385	1737 small date	11	65	300
1733	13	70	330	1737 large date	11	65	300
1734	17	75	365	1739	11	65	300
1734 no stop on obv.	33	120	385	1739/5	—	100	300
1735	11	65	300				

3721 Farthing. Old laur. and cuir. bust. GEORGIUS R. Britannia, date in ex. die axis ↑↓

1741	17	80	300	1744	11	65	275

3722 Farthing. Similar R. Britannia, date in ex. die axis ↑↓

1746	9	65	240	1750	17	75	275
1746 V over U	100	250	—	1754	6	45	135
1749	17	75	275	1754/0	28	13	300

George III, grandson of George II was born on 4 June 1738. He married Charlotte of Mecklenburg and they had nine sons and six daughters. The French Revolution and the American War of Independence both happened in his long reign, the longest yet of any King. The naval battle of Trafalgar and the Battle of Waterloo also took place during his reign. Later in his reign, he was affected by what seems to be the mental disease porphyria, and the future George IV was appointed as regent. George III died at Windsor Castle on 29 January 1820.

During the second half of the 18th century very little silver or copper was minted. In 1797 Matthew Boulton's 'cartwheels', the first copper Pennies and Twopences, demonstrated the improvement gleaned from the application of steam power to the coining press.

During the Napoleonic Wars bank notes came into general use when the issue of Guineas was stopped between 1799 and 1813, but gold 7s. pieces, Third-Guineas; were minted to relieve the shortage of smaller money. As an emergency measure Spanish 'Dollars' were put into circulation for a short period after being countermarked, and in 1804 Spanish Eight Reales were overstruck and issued as Bank of England Dollars.

The transition to a 'token' silver coinage began in 1811 when the Bank of England had 3s and 1s. 6d. tokens made for general circulation. Private issues of token money in the years 1788-95 and 1811-15 helped to alleviate the shortage of regal coinage. A change over to a gold standard and a regular 'token' silver coinage came in 1816 when the Mint, which was moved from its old quarters in the Tower of London to a new site on Tower Hill, began a complete re-coinage. The Guinea was replaced by a 20s. Sovereign, and silver coins were made which had an intrinsic value lower than their face value. The St. George design used on the Sovereign and Crown was the work of Benedetto Pistrucci.

Engravers and Designers:– Conrad Heinrich Kuchler (c.1740-1810), Nathaniel Marchant (1739-1816), John Rudulf Ochs Jnr. (1704-88), Lewis Pingo (1743-1830), Thomas Pingo (d.1776) Benedetto Pistrucci (1784-1855), Johann Sigismond Tanner (c.1706-75), Thomas Wyon (1792-1817), William Wyon (1795-1851), Richard Yeo (d.1779).

GOLD

Early Coinages

3723
1770 Pattern Five Guineas

3723 Five Guineas. Pattern only, young long haired bust r. R. crowned shield of arms, die axis ↑↑ (en medaille)
1770 *FDC* £190,000   1773 *FDC* £180,000
3723A Five Guineas. Pattern only, young bust right, hair extends under bust similar
1777 *FDC* £165,000

3724
1768 Pattern Two Guineas

3724A
1777 Pattern Two Guineas

3724   Two Guineas. Pattern only, young long haired bust r. R. crowned shield of arms, die axis ↑↑
(en medaille)
1768 *FDC* £40,000   1773 *FDC* £37,500
3724A Two Guineas. Pattern only, thinner young bust right, hair extends under bust similar
1777 *FDC* £35,000
There are six different bust varieties for 3723 and 3724, for further details see Wilson & Rasmussen

3725   3726
1761 Guinea first head, two leaf wreath   1763 Guinea second head

	F	VF	EF		F	VF	EF
	£	£	£		£	£	£
3725 Guinea. First laur. head r., 1761 (varieties with two or three leaves at top							
of wreath). R. Crowned shield of arms die axis ↑↓ 1700			4250		8000		
3726 Guinea. Second laur. head r. R. Crowned shield of arms die axis ↑↓							
1763 1300	3750	7500		1764 no stop			
1764 1300	3250	7000		over head........ 2250	4750	9500	

*Plain edge patterns exist of 1761 Guinea by John Tanner and 1763 by Richard Yeo. Both are
extremely rare and trade too infrequently to price.*

3727	3728	3729
Guinea, third head	Guinea, fourth head	Guinea, fifth head, 'spade' type

	F	VF	EF		F	VF	EF
	£	£	£		£	£	£

3727 Guinea. Third laur. head r. R. Crowned shield of arms die axis ↑↓

1765	400	675	1650	1770	950	1850	4000
1766	400	700	1750	1771	400	625	1500
1767	500	900	2100	1772	400	625	1500
1768	400	675	1650	1773	400	625	1500
1769	425	725	1900	1773 first 7 over 1	425	1000	—

3728 Guinea. Fourth laur. head r. Crowned shield of arms die axis ↑↓

1774	400	575	1150	1779 9/7 error *exists*			
1774 Proof *FDC* £8000				1781	400	600	1200
1775	400	600	1200	1782	400	600	1200
1776	400	750	1550	1783	400	625	1300
1777	500	600	1250	1784	400	600	1200
1778	500	950	2350	1785	400	600	1200
1778 E over C in REX *exists*				1786	400	600	1200
1779	400	750	1500				

3729 Guinea. Fifth laur. head r. R. 'Spade'-shaped shield, die axis ↑↑

1787	350	475	975	1794	350	525	1000
1787 Proof *FDC* £7250				1795		350	525	1000
1788	350	525	1000	1796	350	650	1250
1788 second 8/7 *exists*				1797	350	625	1200
1789	350	550	1050	1798*	350	450	900
1790	350	575	1100	1798/2 error *exists*			
1791	350	525	1000	1798/7	350	650	1400
1792	350	525	1000	1799	400	700	1600
1793	350	550	1050	* *Beware counterfeits*			

3730	3731
1813 Guinea "Military type"	Half-Guinea, first head

3730 Guinea. Sixth laur. head. r. R. Shield in Garter, known as the Military guinea, die axis ↑↑

1813	750	1850	3800

3731 Half-Guinea. First laur. head r. R. Crowned shield of arms die axis ↑↓

1762	675	1750	4200	1763	750	2150	5000

Note: All figure 1's are Roman style I's for Guineas from 1781-1799.

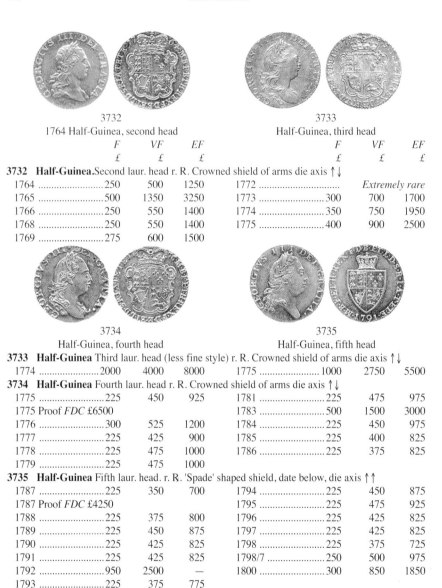

3732
1764 Half-Guinea, second head

3733
Half-Guinea, third head

	F	VF	EF		F	VF	EF
	£	£	£		£	£	£

3732 Half-Guinea. Second laur. head r. R. Crowned shield of arms die axis ↑↓

1764	250	500	1250	1772		*Extremely rare*	
1765	500	1350	3250	1773	300	700	1700
1766	250	550	1400	1774	350	750	1950
1768	250	550	1400	1775	400	900	2500
1769	275	600	1500				

3734
Half-Guinea, fourth head

3735
Half-Guinea, fifth head

3733 Half-Guinea Third laur. head (less fine style) r. R. Crowned shield of arms die axis ↑↓

1774	2000	4000	8000	1775	1000	2750	5500

3734 Half-Guinea Fourth laur. head r. R. Crowned shield of arms die axis ↑↓

1775	225	450	925	1781	225	475	975
1775 Proof *FDC* £6500				1783	500	1500	3000
1776	300	525	1200	1784	225	450	975
1777	225	425	900	1785	225	400	825
1778	225	475	1000	1786	225	375	825
1779	225	475	1000				

3735 Half-Guinea Fifth laur. head. r. R. 'Spade' shaped shield, date below, die axis ↑↑

1787	225	350	700	1794	225	450	875
1787 Proof *FDC* £4250				1795	225	475	925
1788	225	375	800	1796	225	425	825
1789	225	450	875	1797	225	425	825
1790	225	425	825	1798	225	375	725
1791	225	425	825	1798/7	250	500	975
1792	950	2500	—	1800	300	850	1850
1793	225	375	775				

3736
Half-Guinea, sixth head

3736 Half-Guinea Sixth laur. head. r. R. Shield in Garter, date below die axis ↑↑

1801	225	325	650	1803	225	350	700
1802	225	350	700				

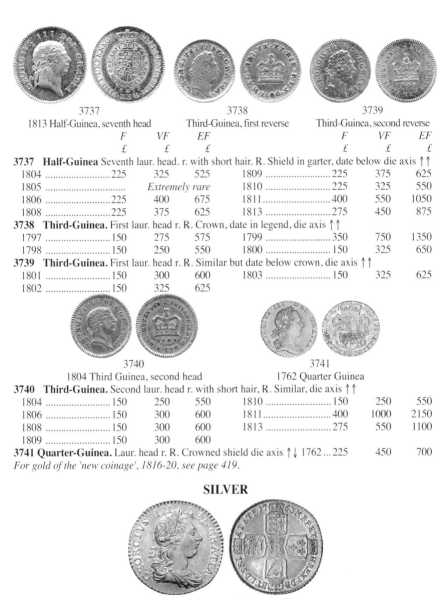

	3737				3738			3739	
	1813 Half-Guinea, seventh head				Third-Guinea, first reverse			Third-Guinea, second reverse	

	F	VF	EF		F	VF	EF
	£	£	£		£	£	£

3737 Half-Guinea Seventh laur. head. r. with short hair. ℞. Shield in garter, date below die axis ↑↑

1804	225	325	525	1809	225	375	625
1805	....	*Extremely rare*		1810	225	325	550
1806	225	400	675	1811	400	550	1050
1808	225	375	625	1813	275	450	875

3738 Third-Guinea. First laur. head r. ℞. Crown, date in legend, die axis ↑↑

1797	150	275	575	1799	350	750	1350
1798	150	250	550	1800	150	325	650

3739 Third-Guinea. First laur. head r. ℞. Similar but date below crown, die axis ↑↑

1801	150	300	600	1803	150	325	625
1802	150	325	625				

3740	3741
1804 Third Guinea, second head	1762 Quarter Guinea

3740 Third-Guinea. Second laur. head r. with short hair, ℞. Similar, die axis ↑↑

1804	150	250	550	1810	150	250	550
1806	150	300	600	1811	400	1000	2150
1808	150	300	600	1813	275	550	1100
1809	150	300	600				

3741 Quarter-Guinea. Laur. head r. ℞. Crowned shield die axis ↑↓ 1762 ... 225   450   700

For gold of the 'new coinage', 1816-20, see page 419.

SILVER

3742 - 1763 Northumberland shilling

3742 Shilling. Young laur. and dr. bust, r. known as the 'Northumberland' shilling, die axis ↑↓

1763* 425   850   1750

Plain edge patterns exist for 1764 and 1778. Both are extremely rare.

3743 Shilling. Older laur. and dr. bust, ℞. No semée of hearts in Hanoverian shield, die axis ↑↑

1787 30   60   150

1787 Proof *FDC* ....   *Extremely rare*

1787 plain edge proof *FDC* £1000

1787 plain edge pattern by Pingo, border of dots at perimeter *FDC* £850

*Beware, low grade counterfeits exist

	F	VF	EF		F	VF	EF
	£	£	£		£	£	£

3744 **Shilling.** — No stop over head, die axis ↑↑ 1787 40   80   250

3745
1781 No stops at date Shilling

3745 **Shilling.** — No stops at date, die axis ↑↑ 1787 55   135   350
3745A **Shilling.** — No stops on *obv.*, die axis ↑↑ 1787...............................375   850 1950
3746 **Shilling.** — R. With semée of hearts, die axis ↑↑ 1787.........................30   60   140
    1787 1/1 retrograde 55   135   350
    1787 plain edge proof *FDC (Also known on large 27mm flan.)* £1000

           Hanoverian Arms

No semée of hearts   With semée of hearts   3747 - 1798 Shilling

3747 **Shilling.** No stop over head, 1798: known as the 'Dorrien and Magens' shilling *UNC* £22,500
3748 **Sixpence.** Laur. and dr. bust r. R. Without semée of hearts, die axis ↑↑
    1787 18   45   110   1787 Proof *FDC*.............*Extremely rare*
3749 **Sixpence.** Similar R. With semée of hearts, die axis ↑↑ 1787 18   45   110

3749   3750
1787 Sixpence, with hearts   1772 Fourpence

3750 **Fourpence.** Young laur. and dr. bust r. R. Crowned 4, die axis ↑↓

1763	15	30	75	1772/0	10	30	90
1763 Proof *FDC of highest rarity*				1776	15	30	75
1765	200	375	900	1780	15	30	75
1766	15	30	75	1784	18	35	80
1770	12	30	55	1786	20	40	95
1772	18	35	80				

3751	3753	3755
'Wire Money' Fourpence	Young bust Threepence	Older bust Threepence

	F	VF	EF		F	VF	EF
	£	£	£		£	£	£

3751 Fourpence. Older laur. and dr. bust. ℞. Thin 4 ('Wire Money'), die axis ↑↑

| 1792 | ....20 | 55 | 110 | | | | |

3752 Fourpence. Older laur. and dr. bust r. ℞. Normal Crowned 4, die axis ↑↑

| 1795 | .... 10 | 30 | 75 | 1800 | .... 8 | 25 | 65 |

3753 Threepence. Young laur. dr. bust r. ℞. Crowned 3, die axis ↑↓

1762	8	18	50	1772 small III	12	30	75
1763	8	18	50	1772 very large III	 10	25	65
1763 Proof *FDC of highest rarity*				1780	12	25	70
1765	225	425	950	1784	12	30	70
1766	 12	30	70	1786	 10	25	65
1770	 12	30	65				

3754 Threepence. Older laur. dr. bust. r. ℞. Thin 3 ('Wire Money'), die axis ↑↑

| 1792 | ....20 | 60 | 130 | | | | |

3755 Threepence. Older laur. and dr. bust r. ℞. Normal Crowned 3, die axis ↑↑

| 1795 | .... 12 | 30 | 65 | 1800 | .... 10 | 25 | 45 |

3756 Twopence. Young laur. and dr. bust r. ℞. Crowned 2, die axis ↑↓

1763	 18	35	60	1776	 14	35	80
1763 Proof *FDC of highest rarity*				1780	 12	22	60
1765	 100	375	525	1784	 10	22	60
1766	 10	22	45	1786	 10	20	55
1772	 10	22	45	1786 large obv. lettering . 6		20	55
1772 second 7/6	8	30	65				

3756
Young bust Twopence

3757 Twopence. Older laur. and dr. bust. r. ℞. Thin 2 ('Wire Money'), die axis ↑↑

| 1792 | .... 20 | 55 | 100 | | | | |

3758 Twopence. Older laur. and dr. bust r. ℞. Normal Crowned 2, die axis ↑↑

| 1795 | ....8 | 18 | 45 | 1800 | ....7 | 20 | 50 |

3759 Penny. Young laur. and dr. bust r. ℞. Crowned 1, die axis ↑↓

1763	 15	25	60	1779	 10	22	60
1763 Proof *FDC*	....................*Extremely rare*			1780	 12	25	70
1766	 12	22	60	1781	 12	22	60
1770	 10	18	60	1784	 12	20	50
1770	 10	22	60	1786	 10	18	45
1776	 10	18	60				

3760 Penny. Older laur. and dr. bust. r. ℞. Thin 1 ('Wire Money'), die axis ↑↑

| 1792 | .... 12 | 35 | 65 | | | | |

	F	VF	EF		F	VF	EF
	£	£	£		£	£	£

3761 Penny. Older laur. and dr. bust r. ℞. Normal Crowned 1, die axis ↑↑

1795 7   20   50   1800 7   20   55

3762 Maundy Set. Young laur. and dr. bust. r. Uniform dates

1763 110	250	500	1780 ....110 250	475
1763 Proof set *FDC* £10000			1784 110	250	475
1766 110	250	475	1786 110	250	475
1772 110	250	475			

3763 Maundy Set. — Older laur. and dr. bust. r. ℞. Thin numerals ('Wire Money'),

1792 200   450   750

3764 Maundy Set. Older laur. and dr. bust r. ℞. Normal numerals. Uniform dates

1795 100   225   450   1800 100   225   425

Emergency Issue, die axis ↑↑

3765 Dollar. Pillar type (current for 4s 9d). Spanish American 8 Reales, oval countermark with head of George III.

Mexico City Mint — m̊ mint mark in reverse legend 1100   2500   —

Bolivia, Potosi Mint – PTS monogram in reverse legend 1400   3250   —

Peru, Lima Mint – LIMÆ monogram in reverse legend 1500   3500   —

two initials of mint master

denomination

mint mark

3765A
Peru Mint Portrait type Dollar with oval countermark

3765A Dollar. Portrait type, oval countermark.

Mexico City Mint — m̊ mint mark in reverse legend 150   375   800

Bolivia, Potosi Mint — PTS monogram in reverse legend 200   650   1250

Chile, Santiago Mint — s̊ mint mark in reverse legend 675   1750   —

Guatemala Mint — NG mint mark in reverse legend.........................675   1750   —

Spain, Madrid Mint mint mark in reverse left field............................400   1250   2500

Spain, Seville Mint mint mark in reverse left field 400   1250   2500

Peru, Lima Mint — LIMÆ monogram in reverse legend 250   700   1350

3765B Dollar. — Oval countermark on silver French Ecu of crown size 3500   8500   —

3765C Dollar. — Oval countermark on USA Dollar...   *Of highest rarity*

3765D Dollar. — Oval countermark on silver Italian crown size coins ....   *Of highest rarity*

mint mark S   Mint Master
                               Initials
3766   3766B
Seville Mint Portrait Dollar with octagonal countermark

	F £	VF £	EF £
3766 Dollar octagonal countermarks with head of George III			
Mexico City Mint — m̥	400	800	1850
Bolivia, Potosi Mint — PTS monogram	850	1750	3750
Guatamala Mint — NG	1200	2750	—
Peru, Lima Mint — LIME monogram	550	1250	3000
Spain, Madrid Mint M to left of reverse shield	1000	2200	—
Spain, Seville Mint S to left of reverse shield	1100	2500	—
3766A Dollar. — Octagonal countermark on French Ecu or Italian Scudi	*Of highest rarity*		
3766B Dollar. — Octagonal countermark on USA Dollar	12500	30000	—

3767
Half-Dollar with oval countermark, Madrid Mint

3767 Half-Dollar. With similar oval countermark of George III,			
Bolivia, Potosi Mint — PTS monogram	350	750	1350
Chile, Santiago Mint — s̥ mint mark	500	950	—
Spain, Madrid Mint — Crowned M to left of shield	200	450	900
Spain, Seville Mint — Crowned S to left of shield	200	450	900
3767A Half Dollar. With Octagonal countermark. Similar *from*	600	1100	—

Bank of England Issue

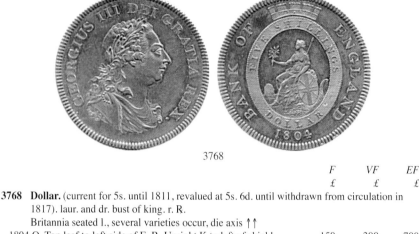

3768

	F £	VF £	EF £

3768 Dollar. (current for 5s. until 1811, revalued at 5s. 6d. until withdrawn from circulation in 1817). laur. and dr. bust of king. r. ℞.
Britannia seated l., several varieties occur, die axis ↑↑

	F	VF	EF
1804 O. Top leaf to left side of E, R. Upright K to left of shield	150	300	700
1804 — — no stops in CHK on truncation	185	400	850
1804 O. Top leaf to centre of E R. Similar	175	350	775
1804 — — no stop after REX	150	300	725
1804 — R. K inverted and incuse	200	475	950
1804 O. Top leaf to right side of E, R. normal K		*Extremely rare*	
1804 — R. K inverted to left of shield	200	450	900

Various 1804 Proof striking of varieties above *FDC from* £1250 to £3000
These dollars were re-struck from Spanish-American 8-Reales until at least 1811. Dollars that still show dates and Mint marks of original coin beneath are worth up to 25% more.

3769
1811 Three Shillings, first bust

3770
Three Shillings, second head

3769 Three Shillings. Dr and laur. bust in armour r. ℞. BANK / TOKEN / 3 SHILL. / date (in oak wreath), die axis ↑↑

1811	25	75	250	1812	25	80	275

1811 Proof *FDC* £1100

3770 Three Shillings. — Laureate head r. Top leaf between I/G ℞. As before but wreath of oak and olive, die axis ↑↑

1812	25	75	250	1813	25	80	300
1812 Proof *FDC* £1100				1814	25	80	300
1812 Proof in gold *FDC*		*Extremely rare*		1815	25	80	300
1812 Proof in platinum *FDC*		*Extremely rare*		1816*	375	750	2000

*Beware of counterfeits

3771
Eighteenpence, first bust

3772
Eighteenpence, second head

	F	VF	EF		F	VF	EF
	£	£	£		£	£	£

3771 Eighteenpence. Dr. and laur. bust r. in armour ℞ BANK/TOKEN/Is. 6D./date (in oak wreath) ↑↑

1811 15   40   200   1812 20   45   225

1811 Proof *FDC* £950

3772 Eighteenpence. Laureate head r. die axis ↑↑

1812 15   40   200   1813 Platinum proof *FDC of the highest rarity*

1812 Proof *FDC* £950   1814 15   45   225

1812 Platinum proof *FDC of the highest rarity*   1815 15   45   225

1812 Proof ℞. Small letters *FDC* £2500   1816 15   45   225

1813 15   45   200

3773
1812 Pattern Ninepence, 9D type

3773 Ninepence. Similar, Laur. head 1812, ℞. 9D type (pattern only) die axis ↑↑ *FDC* £1700

3773A Ninepence. — — 1812, ℞. 9 pence type (pattern only) die axis ↑↑ FDC £3000

COPPER

First Issue — Tower Mint, London

3774

3775

Rev. C, leaves point between A and N

	F	VF	EF		F	VF	EF
	£	£	£		£	£	£

3774 Halfpenny. Laur. and Cuir. bust r. R. Britannia l. date in ex., die axis ↑↓

	F	VF	EF		F	VF	EF
1770 15		65	350	1772 ball below			
1770 Proof die axis ↑↑ *FDC* £1600				spear blade 10		55	275
1770 Proof in silver *FDC*		*Extremely rare*		1772 no incuse			
1770 no stop on rev. 20		75	425	hair coil 12		60	325
1771 12		55	325	1772 — no stop on rev.... 20		75	375
1771 no stop on rev. 20		75	400	1773 15		65	350
1771 ball below				1773 no stop after REX 22		75	425
spear blade 12		55	300	1773 no stop on rev. 22		75	425
1772 incuse hair coil				1774 different obv.			
on rev. 12		60	350	profile 20		90	475
1772 GEORIVS error 40		125	475	1775 — 13		80	475

3775 Farthing. Laur. and cuir. bust r. R. Britannia l. date in ex., die axis ↑↓

	F	VF	EF		F	VF	EF
1771 Rev A. leaf to r.of N.20		75	350	1773 no stop after REX . 28		85	400
1771 Rev B. leaf to N....20		65	325	1774 13		60	275
1771 Rev C....................20		65	300	1775 13		60	300
1771 1st 7/1 30		185	575	1775 struck en			
1773 12		55	275	medaille ↑↑ 28		85	375
1773 no stop on rev........15		75	375	1775 GEORGIVS......... 40		250	750

Note: 1771 varieties refer to the direction the top leaf of olive branch points in Britannia's hand

Second Issue—Soho Mint. Birmingham 'Cartwheel' coinage, die axis ↑↓

3776

3776 Twopence. Legends incuse on raised rim,

1797 Copper proof *FDC* £1700	1797	40	175	600
1797 Bronzed proof *FDC* £1500	1797 Gold proof *FDC* ....*Extremely rare*			
1797 Silver proof *FDC*..........*Extremely rare*	1797 Gilt copper *FDC* £2500			

Prices for UNCIRUCALTED copper coins are no longer quoted. Truly uncirculated copper coins of this period are too seldom traded on the market to fix a meaningful price. As a guide a truly uncirulated coin with full lustre or bloom should fetch 3-4 times the EF price.

3777

		VF	EF		F	VF	EF
		£	£		£	£	£
3777	**Penny.** 1797. Similar, 10 leaves in wreath on obv.				12	75	400
	1797 11 leaves in wreath on obv.				20	100	550
	1797 Gilt copper proof *FDC* £1650						
	1797 Copper proof *FDC* £1150						
	1797 Bronzed proof *FDC* £1000						
	1797 Silver proof *FDC* .... *Extremely rare*						
	1797 Gold proof *FDC* .... *Extremely rare*						

Halfpence and Farthings of this issue are patterns.

Third Issue—Soho Mint, Birmingham, die axis ↑↓

3778   3779

3778 Halfpenny. Laur. and dr. bust r., R. Britannia l. date below

1799 Ship on rev. with			1799 Ship with		
5 incuse gunports	10	85	plain hull	15	120
1799 Ship with 6			1799 — raised line		
relief gunports	12	110	on hull	15	120
1799 Ship with 9 relief			1799 Copper proof *FDC* £550		
gunports	15	125	1799 Bronzed proof *FDC* £500		
....			1799 Gilt copper proof *FDC* £925		

3779 Farthing. Laur. and dr. bust r. date below R. Britannia l.

1799 Obv. with 3 berries			1799 Obv. with 4 berries		
in wreath	8	70	in wreath	8	80
1799 Copper *FDC* £400			1799 Gold proof *FDC of the highest rarity*		
1799 Bronzed proof *FDC* £375			1799 Silver proof *FDC Extremely rare*		
1799 Copper gilt proof *FDC* £675					

Fourth Issue—Soho Mint, Birmingham, die axis ↑↓

3780

	VF £	EF £		VF £	EF £

3780   Penny. Shorter haired, laur. and dr. bust r. date below. R. Britannia l. date below

1806 incuse hair curl by tie knot 10	85	1807 Copper proof *FDC* £650

1806 incuse hair curl
  by tie knot 10   85
1806 no incuse hair curl.............. 15   110
1806 Copper proof *FDC* £550
1806 Bronzed proof *FDC* £500
1806 Gilt copper proof *FDC* £850
1806 Silver proof *FDC* £4750
1807 15   110

1807 Copper proof *FDC* £650
1807 Bronzed proof *FDC* £600
1807 Gilt copper proof *FDC* £950
1807 Silver proof *FDC* ....*Extremely rare*
1807 Gold proof *FDC* ....*Extremely rare*
1807 Platinum proof *FDC* ....*Extremely rare*
1808 Proof *FDC*................................*Unique*

3781   3782

3781   Halfpenny. Shorter haired laur. and dr. bust r. date below, R. Britannia l.

1806 rev. no berries...................... 8   55
1806 rev. 3 berries...................... 10   85
1806 Copper proof *FDC* £400
1806 Bronzed proof *FDC* £375
1806 Gilt proof *FDC* £650
1806 Silver proof *FDC* ....*Extremely rare*

1807 10   80
1807 Copper proof *FDC* £400
1807 Bronzed proof *FDC* £350
1807 Gilt copper *FDC* £600
1807 Silver proof *FDC* £3500
1807 Gold proof *FDC* ....*Extremely rare*

3782   Farthing. Shorter haired laur. and dr. bust r. date below, R. Britannia l.

1806 K. on tr. 10   95
1806 incuse dot on tr...................... 35   150
1806 Copper proof *FDC* £400
1806 Bronzed proof *FDC* £350
1806 Gilt copper proof *FDC* £600
1806 Silver proof *FDC* ....*Extremely rare*
1806 Gold proof *FDC*..............*Extremely rare*

1807 12   100
1807 Copper proof *FDC* £450
1807 Bronzed proof *FDC* £400
1807 Gilt copper proof *FDC* £650
1807 Silver proof *FDC* ....*Extremely rare*
1807 Gold proof *FDC* ....*Extremely rare*

Prices for UNCIRUCALTED copper coins are no longer quoted. Truly uncirculated copper coins of this period are too seldom traded on the market to fix a meaningful price. As a guide a truly unciruclated coin with full lustre or bloom should fetch 3-4 times the EF price.

Last or new coinage, 1816-20
The year 1816 is a landmark in the history of our coinage. For some years at the beginning of the 19th century Mint production was virtually confined to small gold denominations, regular full production being resumed only after the Mint had been moved from the Tower of London to a new site on Tower Hill. Steam powered minting machinery made by Boulton and Watt replaced the old hand-operated presses and these produced coins which were technically much superior to the older milled coins.

In 1816 for the first time British silver coins were produced with an intrinsic value somewhat below their face value, the first official token coinage. The old Guinea was replaced by a Sovereign of twenty shillings in 1817, the standard of 22 carat (0.916) fineness still being retained.

Mint Master or Engraver's and/or designer's initials:
B.P. (Benedetto Pistrucci 1784-1855)   WWP (William Wellesley Pole)

GOLD

3783

3783 Five Pounds. 1820 LX (Pattern only) laur. head r. date below R. St George and dragon, edge inscribed die axis ↑↓ *FDC* £165000
1820 Similar plain edge proof *FDC (*only two struck) *Of highest rarity*

3784

3784   Two Pounds. 1820 LX (Pattern only) laur. head r. date below R. St George and dragon, edge inscribed die axis ↑↓ *FDC* £30000
1820 Similar plain edge proof *FDC   Extremely rare*

3785   3785A

	F	VF	EF	UNC		F	VF	EF	UNC
	£	£	£	£		£	£	£	£

3785 Sovereign. laur. head r. coarse hair, legend type A (Descending colon after BRITANNIAR,
no space between REX and F:D:). R. St. George and dragon, die axis ↑↓

1817	500	875	2000	3250	1818	875	1750	4250	7500
1817 Proof *FDC* £20000					1819	50000	100000	225000	—
1817 ↑↑ die axis .1000	—	—	—					

3785A Sovereign. Similar legend type B (Ascending colon after BRITANNIAR, space between
REX and F:D:) ↑↓

1818	775	1500	4000	7000	1818 Proof *FDC* £23500

3785B Sovereign. laur head r. hair with tighter curls, legend type A. R. Similar die axis ↑↓

1818	....	*Extremely rare*

3785C
Large date, open 2 variety

3785C Sovereign. Similar legend type B. (as above) die axis ↑↓

1818	....	*Extremely rare*	1820	short date height, alignment			
1820	Roman I in date .	*Extremely rare*		varies 475	850	2000	3500
1820	open 2, alignment of date		1820	closed 2 alignment of date			
	varies 450	800	2000	3250		varies 500	1000	2250	3250
1820	thin date, smaller 0 Proof *FDC* £17500						

The above 1820 entries are the main variations, there do exist other subtle differences which are
merely sub-varieties and therefore are not included.

3786
1817 Half-Sovereign

3786 Half-Sovereign. laur head r. date below R̩. Crowned shield, edge milled die axis ↑↓

1817	200	375	650	1100	1818 Proof *FDC* £8500			
1817 Proof *FDC* £6500					1818	275	450	750	1300
1818/7	425	850	1900	—	1820	225	400	700	1200

SILVER

3787
1818 George III Crown

	F	VF	EF	UNC		F	VF	EF	UNC
	£	£	£	£		£	£	£	£

3787 Crown. Laur. head r. R̨. Pistrucci's St. George and dragon within Garter edge inscribed, die axis ↑↓

		F	VF	EF	UNC
1818, edge LVIII		50	125	600	1200
1818	LVIII error edge inscription		*Extremely rare*		
1818	LVIII Proof *FDC*		*Extremely rare*		
1818	LIX	50	125	650	1250
1818	LIX TUTΛMEN error	85	350	–	–
1819	LIX	45	110	550	1100
1819	LIX no stops on edge	70	225	750	1650
1819	LIX R. Thicker ruled garter	65	135	675	–
1819/8	LIX	75	275	825	–
1819	LX	55	135	600	1200
1819	LX no stop after TUTAMEN	65	150	700	–
1820	LX	50	125	600	1200
1820	LX R. S/T in SOIT	70	225	800	–
1820/19	LX	85	325	900	–

3788
1817 Halfcrown, large bust

3788 Halfcrown. Large laur. bust or 'bull' head r. date below R. Crowned garter and shield die axis ↑↑

	F	VF	EF	UNC		F	VF	EF	UNC
1816	40	95	425	650	1817 E/R in DEI		*Extremely rare*		
1816 Proof *FDC* £3750					1817 S/I in PENSE	65	275	750	–
1816 Plain edge proof *FDC* £4000					1817 Proof *FDC* £3750				
1817	35	90	400	600	1817 Plain edge proof *FDC* £4000				
1817 D/T in DEI	75	350	850	–					

3789
1817 Halfcrown, small head

	F	VF	EF	UNC		F	VF	EF	UNC
	£	£	£	£		£	£	£	£

3789 Halfcrown. Small laur. head r. date below, ℞. Crowned garter and shield die axis ↑↑

1817*......................40	100	325	650	1818 Proof *FDC* £4250
1817 Proof *FDC* £3750				1819 Proof *FDC* £4250
1817 Plain edge proof *FDC* £4000				1819 ....40 100 425 675
1817 Reversed s's in garter *Extremely rare*				1819/8 .... *Extremely rare*
1818 Reversed s's in garter *Extremely rare*				1820 ....50 120 500 800
1818*......................50 125 475 775				1820 Proof *FDC* £3750
				1820 Plain edge proof *FDC* £3750

3790
1819 Shilling

3790   Shilling. laur. head r. date below ℞. Crowned Shield in Garter edge milled, die axis ↑↑

1816 ....12 25 80 150	1818 ....30 70 215 475
1816 Proof *FDC* £1100	1818 High 8 ....35 80 240 500
1816 Plain edge proof *FDC* £1250	1819/8 ....20 40 140 350
1816 Proof in gold *FDC* *Extremely rare*	1819 ....18 35 100 190
1817 ....15 25 90 165	1819 9/6 exists
1817 RRITT flaw ...25 40 160 350	1820 ....18 35 100 190
1817 Plain edge proof *FDC* £1100	1820 I/S in HONI 40 80 275 525
1817 GEOE error....75 225 600 1100	1820 Proof *FDC* £1250
1817 E over R in GEOR *exists*	

* Beware recent low grade forgeries

3791
1817 Sixpence

	F	VF	EF	UNC		F	VF	EF	UNC
	£	£	£	£		£	£	£	£

3791 Sixpence. laur head r. date below Ṛ. Crowned Shield in Garter edge milled, die axis ↑↑

1816	10	18	65	130	1819/8	18	30	95	175
1816 Proof plain edge *FDC* £950					1819	15	25	90	150
1816 Proof in gold *FDC*		*Extremely rare*			1819 small 8	15	25	80	145
1817	12	20	75	140	1820	15	25	80	140
1817 Proof plain edge *FDC* £950					1820 inverted 1	90	325	650	—
1817 Proof milled edge *FDC* £1250					1820 I/S in HONI	85	300	575	—
1818	15	25	85	160	1820 obv. no colons	125	400	750	—
1818 Proof milled edge *FDC* £1350					1820 milled edge Proof *FDC* £1200				

3792

3792 Maundy Set. (4d., 3d., 2d. and 1d.) laur. head, date below die axis ↑↑

1817		90	180	375	1820	90	180	375
1818		90	180	375				
3793 — Fourpence. 1817, 1818, 1820	*from*				15	30	65	100
3794 — Threepence. 1817, 1818, 1820	*from*				12	25	55	80
3795 — Twopence. 1817, 1818, 1820	*from*				12	20	35	65
3796 — Penny. 1817, 1818, 1820	*from*				10	18	35	65

Maundy pennies are always the most requested oddment, it is the smallest coin in the set and is therefore the easiest to lose. Penny collectors also dictate supply and demand for this coin.

George IV, eldest son of George III, was born on 12 August 1762 and was almost a complete opposite to his father. He was very extravagant and lived in the height of luxury. He especially influenced fashion of the time which became known as the 'Regency' style. He had numerous mistresses, and had an arranged marriage with Caroline of Brunswick. She later moved to Italy with their only daughter, but returned to claim her place as Queen upon George's accession. George banned her from ever being crowned, and he died without ever conceiving a son on 26 June 1830, when his younger brother William ascended the throne.

The Mint resumed the coinage of copper farthings in 1821, and pennies and halfpennies in 1825. A gold Two Pound piece was first issued for general circulation in 1823. A full cased proof set of the new bare head coinage was issued in limited quantities in 1826.

Engraver's and/or designer's initials on the coins:
B. P. (Benedetto Pistrucci)   W.W. P. (William Wellesley Pole) – Master of the Mint
J. B. M. (Jean Baptiste Merlen)

Engravers and Designers:– Francis Legett Chantrey (1781-1842) Jean Baptiste Merlen (1769-c.1850) Benedetto Pistrucci (1784-1855) William Wyon (1795-1851)

GOLD

3797

3797 Five Pounds. 1826 Bare head l. date below ℞. Crowned shield and mantle, inscribed edge, die axis ↑↓   Proof *FDC* £25000
1826 Piedfort proof *FDC* ....   *Extremely rare*

3798

	VF	EF	UNC
	£	£	£

3798 Two Pounds. 1823 Proof *FDC* £8000
1823 Proof no JBM below truncation *FDC* ....   *Extremely rare*
1823 Large bare head. l. ℞. St. George, inscribed edge ↑↓ .... | 1000 | 2150 | 3500 |

3799

3799 Two Pounds. Bare head l. date below R. Crowned shield and mantle inscribed edge
   die axis ↑↓
   1824 Proof *FDC*   *Extremely rare*   1826. Piedfort proof *FDC*   *Extremely rare*
   1825 Proof plain edge *FDC* £13500   1826. Proof *FDC* £8000

3801
Sovereign, second type

	F	VF	EF	UNC		F	VF	EF	UNC
	£	£	£	£		£	£	£	£

3800 Sovereign. Laur. head. l. R. St. George and dragon date in ex., die axis ↑↓

	F	VF	EF	UNC		F	VF	EF	UNC
1821	475	750	1750	2500	1823	950	3000	7000	—
1821 Proof *FDC* £5750					1824	550	925	2000	2750
1822*	500	800	2000	3000	1825	750	2250	5000	8000

3801 Sovereign. Bare head. date below l. R. Crowned shield, die axis ↑↓

	F	VF	EF	UNC		F	VF	EF	UNC
1825	450	750	1500	2750	1827*	500	800	1750	3000
1825 Proof 7 heart semée *FDC* £9000					1828	6000	13500	25000	—
1825 Plain edge proof *FDC* £9500					1829	525	850	2000	3200
1826	475	775	1600	2750	1830	525	850	2000	3200
1826 Proof *FDC* £4750					1830 die axis ↑↑			*Extremely rare*	

3803
Half-Sovereign, second reverse

3802 Half-Sovereign. Laur. head. l. R. Ornately garnished Crowned shield. die axis ↑↓

	F	VF	EF	UNC
1821	650	1650	3500	5000
1821 Proof *FDC* £5500				

3803 Half-Sovereign. Laur. head l. R. Plain Crowned shield die axis ↑↓

	F	VF	EF	UNC		F	VF	EF	UNC
1823	200	300	750	1200	1825	200	275	650	1000
1824	200	350	700	1100					

*Beware counterfeits

3804 -1825 Half Sovereign, bare head

	F	VF	EF	UNC		F	VF	EF	UNC
	£	£	£	£		£	£	£	£

3804 Half-Sovereign. Bare head. date below l. R. Crowned garnished shield die axis ↑↓

1826	200	375	675	1000	1827	200	400	700	1100
1826 Proof *FDC* £2500					1828	200	400	700	1100

3804A Half-Sovereign. Similar with extra tuft of hair to l. ear, much heavier border, die axis ↑↓

1826	200	325	575	950	1827	200	350	625	975
1826 Proof *FDC* £2250					1828	200	350	625	975

SILVER

WWP →   ← B.P.

3805 - 1821 Laureate bust Crown

3805   Crown. Laur. head. l. R. St. George, date in exergue, B.P. to upper right, tiny WWP under
lance, die axis ↑↓

1821*, edge	SECUNDO	60	175	800	1750
1821	SECUNDO WWP inverted under lance	95	475	1100	2750
1821	SECUNDO Proof *FDC* £4500				
1821	SECUNDO Proof in copper *FDC* £5500				
1821	TERTIO Proof *FDC* £5750				
1822	SECUNDO	70	250	975	2500
1822	TERTIO	65	225	900	2000

3806 - 1826 Proof Crown, bare head

3806 Crown. Bare head. l. R. Shield with crest inscribed edge, die axis ↑↓

1825 Proof *FDC* £16000	1826 Proof *FDC* £8250

* Beware of recent counterfeits in high grade

3807   3807

Halfcrown, lightly garnished shield,   Heavy garnishing, right thistle leaf closer,
right thistle leaf further from stem   more parallel to its stem

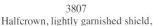
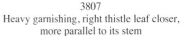

	F	VF	EF	UNC		F	VF	EF	UNC
	£	£	£	£		£	£	£	£

3807 Halfcrown. Laur. head. l. R. Crowned Garnished shield, die axis ↑↓

1820	30	95	375	675	1821 Heavier shield garnishing				
1820 Proof *FDC* £2200						45	100	475	950
1820 Plain edge proof *FDC* £2500					1823 —	950	3000	11500	—
1821	30	95	375	675					

3808   3809

Halfcrown, second reverse   1826 Halfcrown, bare head, third reverse

3808 Halfcrown. Laur. head l. R. Crowned Shield in garter and collar die axis ↑↓

| 1823 | 35 | 100 | 450 | 875 | 1824 | 45 | 120 | 525 | 975 |
| 1823 Proof *FDC* £4500 | | | | | 1824 Proof *FDC* £5000 | | | | |

3809 Halfcrown. Bare head. date below l. R. Crowned Shield with crest die axis ↑↓

1824		*Extremely rare*			1826	40	95	350	750
1824 Proof *FDC*		*Extremely rare*			1826 Proof *FDC* £1600				
1825	35	85	325	675	1828	120	275	900	2200
1825 Proof *FDC* £2200					1829	85	175	525	975
1825 Plain edge proof *FDC* £2500									

3810 - First reverse   3811 - Second reverse

3810 Shilling. Laur. head. l. R. Crowned garnished shield, die axis ↑↓

| 1821 | 15 | 65 | 220 | 525 | 1821 Milled edge Proof *FDC* £1250 | | | | |

3811 Shilling. Laur. head l. R. Crowned shield in Garter die axis ↑↓

1823	50	125	350	875	1825	18	65	275	625
1823 Proof *FDC* £3000					1825 Milled edge Proof *FDC* £3000				
1824	10	55	250	600	1825/3		*Extremely rare*		
1824 Milled edge Proof *FDC* £3000									

3812 - Third reverse

	F	VF	EF	UNC		F	VF	EF	UNC
	£	£	£	£		£	£	£	£

3812 Shilling. Bare head l. date below R. Lion on crown die axis ↑↓

1825	10	55	175	450	1826/2	....	*Extremely rare*		
1825 Roman I	150	450	1100	2200	1827	50	130	450	950
1825 Milled edge Proof *FDC* £1000					1829	30	75	350	800
1826	8	40	125	375	1829 Milled edge Proof *FDC* £2750				
1826 Proof *FDC* £675									

3813 - First reverse   3814 - Second reverse   3815 -Third reverse

3813 Sixpence. Laur. head. l. R. Crowned Garnished shield, die axis ↑↓

| 1821 | ....10 | 35 | 165 | 450 | 1821 BBITANNIAR. | 100 | 350 | 950 | — |
| 1821 Proof *FDC* £825 | | | | | | | | | |

3814 Sixpence. Laur. head l. R. Crowned Shield in Garter die axis ↑↓

1824	10	35	200	475	1825 Proof *FDC* £1350				
1824 Proof *FDC* £1350					1826	40	120	350	775
1825	10	30	190	450	1826 Proof *FDC* £2000				

3815 Sixpence. Bare head. l. with or without tuft of hair to l. of ear date below R. Lion on crown die axis ↑↓

1826	10	35	120	425	1828	15	65	250	625
1826 Proof *FDC* £600					1829	15	40	175	475
1827	60	150	325	775	1829 Proof *FDC* £1450				

3816 - 1822 Maundy Set

	EF	FDC		EF	FDC
	£	£		£	£

3816 Maundy Set. (4d., 3d., 2d. and 1d.) laur head l. die axis ↑↓

1822	....	195	425	1827	....	165	375
1822 Proof set *FDC*		*Extremely rare*		1828	....	165	375
1823	....	165	375	1828 Proof set *FDC*		*Extremely rare*	
1824	....	195	425	1829	....	165	375
1825	....	165	375	1830	....	165	375
1826	....	165	375				

3817	**Maundy Fourpence.** 1822-30 ....*from*	20	55
3818	**— Threepence.** small head, 1822 ....*from*	40	85
3819	**— Threepence.** normal head, 1823-30 ....*from*	18	50
3820	**— Twopence.** 1822-30 ....*from*	18	45
3821	**— Penny.** 1822-30..*from*	25	55

See note on p. 423 (under 3796)

COPPER

3822 - First Issue Farthing

	F	VF	EF	UNC		F	VF	EF	UNC
	£	£	£	£		£	£	£	£

First Issue, 1821-6. Obv. reads GEORGIUS IIII

3822 Farthing. Laur. and dr. bust l. R. Britannia r. date in ex. die axis ↑↓

1821 3	15	80	160	1823 — I for 1 in date ... 25	90	300	—
1822 leaf ribs incuse 2	12	70	145	1825 — 3	15	80	165
1822 — inv. A's legend . 30	100	350	—	1825 — D/U in DEI 20	85	300	—
1822 leaf ribs raised 2	12	70	145	1825 leaf ribs raised 5	18	85	175
1822 Proof *FDC* £950				1825 gold proof *FDC*	*Extremely rare*		
1822 Proof die axis ↑↑ *FDC* £1250				1826 — 5	20	90	200
1823 — 3	15	80	155	1826 R/E in GRATIA 20	80	275	—

See 3825 for Second Issue farthings of 1826 which have die axis ↑↑

3823 - 1826 Penny - plain saltire

Second issue, 1825-30. Obv. reads GEORGIUS IV

3823 Penny. Laur. head. l. R. Britannia, with shield bearing saltire of arms die axis ↑↑

1825 12	55	300	800	1826-Proof *FDC* £575			
1825 Proof *FDC* £1450				1826 thick line on			
1826 plain saltire				saltire 15	70	325	900
on rev. 10	50	250	700	1826-Proof *FDC* £550			
1826 Proof *FDC* £650				1827 plain saltire .. 225	875	3500	13500
1826 thin line on							
saltire 10	55	300	800				

3824 - 1827 Halfpenny   3825 - 1830 Farthing

	F	VF	EF	UNC		F	VF	EF	UNC
	£	£	£	£		£	£	£	£

3824 Halfpenny. die axis ↑↑ Laur. head. l. R. Britannia, with shield bearing saltire of arms

	F	VF	EF	UNC		F	VF	EF	UNC
1825 12		45	225	400	1826 rev. raised line				
1826 rev. two incuse					on saltire........ 10		35	190	375
lines on saltire ..8		20	140	325	1827 rev. two incuse lines				
1826 Proof *FDC* £475					on saltire 10		25	165	350

3825 Farthing. die axis ↑↑ Laur. head. l. R. Britannia, with shield bearing saltire of arms

	F	VF	EF	UNC		F	VF	EF	UNC
1826 2		10	75	160	1828 2		10	80	170
1826 Proof *FDC* £375					1829 3		15	90	250
1826 Roman I 20		60	375	675	1830 2		10	80	170
1827 3		10	85	185					

3826 - 1828 Half-Farthing   3827 - 1827 Third-Farthing

3826 Half-Farthing. (for use in Ceylon). Laur. head. l. date below R.Britannia die axis ↑↑

	F	VF	EF	UNC		F	VF	EF	UNC
1828 rev. helmet intrudes					1830 rev. helmet to				
legend.............12		30	150	350	base of legend 25		75	325	—
1828 rev. helmet to base					1830 rev. helmet intrudes				
of legend 12		35	175	450	legend............12		35	165	425

3827 Third-Farthing. (for use in Malta). Laur. head. l. date below R.Britannia die axis ↑↑

	F	VF	EF	UNC
1827		15	85	250
1827 Proof *FDC* £550				

Copper coins graded in this catalogue as UNC have full mint lustre.

PS1 Proof Set, new issue, 1826. Five pounds to Farthing (11 coins) *FDC* £52500

William IV was born on 21 August 1765, and ascended the throne on his elder brother's death. From c.1791-1811 while Duke of Clarence, he was cohabiting with the actress Dorothea Jordan (1762-1816) who bore him ten illegitimate children. After the death of George IV's daughter, William was forced into a legitimate marriage with Adelaide of Saxe-Coburg and Meinigen. She bore him two daughters who both died in childhood. His reign was most notable for the introduction of the Reform bill and abolition of slavery. William was the last King of Hanover, and died on 20 June 1837 when the throne passed to his niece Victoria.

In order to prevent confusion between the Sixpence and Half-Sovereign the size of the latter was reduced in 1834, although the weight remained the same. The smaller gold piece was not acceptable to the public and in the following year it was made to the normal size. In 1836 the silver Groat was again issued for general circulation: it is the only British silver coin which has a seated Britannia as the type and was revised upon the suggestion of Mr Joseph Hume thus rendering the nickname "Joey". Crowns were not struck during this reign for general circulation; but proofs or patterns of this denomination were made and are greatly sought after. Silver Threepences and Three-Halfpence were minted for use in the Colonies.

Engraver's and/or designer's initials on the coins:
   W. W. (William Wyon)
Engravers and Designers:– Francis Legett Chantry (1781-1842) Jean Baptiste Merlen (1769-c.1850) William Wyon (1795-1851).

<h2 style="text-align:center">GOLD</h2>

3828	3829B
1831 Proof Two Pounds	Second bust with broad ear top

	F	VF	EF	UNC			F	VF	EF	UNC
	£	£	£	£			£	£	£	£

3828 Two Pounds. bare head r. R. crowned shield and mantle, date below, edge plain. die axis ↑↓
   1831 (proof only) *FDC* £9750

3829 Sovereign. First bust. r. top of ear narrow and rounded, nose to 2nd N of BRITANNIAR, fine obv. beading. R. Crowned shield. Die axis ↑↓

1831	650	1000	2700	4250	1832	800	1500	3500	6000
					1832 Proof *FDC* £16000				

3829A Sovereign. Similar, WW without stops die axis ↑↓

1831	1000	2000	3750	6500

3829B Sovereign. Second bust. r. top of ear broad and flat, nose to 2nd I in BRITANNIAR, coarser obv. beading.↑↓

1830 plain edge proof *FDC* £14000	1836	475	900	2000	3250
1831 ....5750 11000 — —	1836 N of ANNO struck				
1831 Proof plain edge *FDC* £5250	in shield......4250	10000	19500	—
1832* 475 750 1900 3000	1837	475	900	2000	3250
1833 ....500 950 2150 3500	1837 Tailed 8........550	975	2100	—
1835 ....500 950 2250 4000					

* Beware of counterfeits

3830
1834 Half-sovereign

3831
Large size Half-Sovereign

	F	VF	EF	UNC		F	VF	EF	UNC
	£	£	£	£		£	£	£	£

3830 Half-Sovereign. Small size (17.9mm), bare head r.R. Crowned shield and mantle. die axis ↑↓

1831 Proof plain edge *FDC* £3250	1834	....	350	700	1350	2200

1831 Proof milled edge *FDC* £7500

3831 Half-Sovereign. Large size (19.4mm), bare head r.R. Crowned shield and mantle.die axis ↑↓

1835	225	475	925	1500	1837	225	475	1000	1600
1836	275	500	1100	1650					

3832 Half-Sovereign. *Obv.* struck from Sixpence die (19.4mm) in error,

1836	1750	3500	7000	—

SILVER

3833 - 1831 Crown. W.W. on truncation

	F	VF	EF	UNC		F	VF	EF	UNC
	£	£	£	£		£	£	£	£

3833 Crown. R. Shield on mantle, 1831 Proof only W.W. on trun. struck ↑↓ *FDC* £15000

   1831 Proof struck in gold *FDC* £160000

   1831 Bare head r. W. WYON on trun. struck ↑↑ en medaille (medal die axis) *FDC* £20000

   1831 Bare head r. similar die axis ↑↓ *FDC* £19500

   1834 Bare head r. W.W. on trun. struck die axis ↑↓ *FDC* £32000

WW script

WW block

3834

3834 Halfcrown. Bare head.WW in script on trun. R. Shield on mantle, die axis ↑↓

						F	VF	EF	UNC
1831 Plain edge proof *FDC* £2200					1835	40	140	525	1250
1831 Milled edge proof *FDC* £2450					1836/5	50	140	750	1350
1834	30	85	425	825	1836	30	85	425	875
1834 Plain edge proof *FDC* £3500					1836 Proof *FDC* £2750				
1834 Milled edge proof *FDC* £2000					1837	50	190	675	1450

3834A

3834A Halfcrown. Bare head r. block WW on trun. R. Similar. die axis ↑↓

   1831 Proof *FDC* £2000

   1834 50   185   700   1450

3835 - 1831 Shilling   3836 - 1834 Sixpence

	F	VF	EF	UNC		F	VF	EF	UNC
	£	£	£	£		£	£	£	£

3835 Shilling. Bare head r. ℞. Value in wreath, date below. die axis ↑↓

1831 Plain edge Proof *FDC* £925	1835 Proof *FDC Extremely rare*
1831 Milled edge proof *FDC* £2900	1836 ....20 50 300 675
1834 ....15 50 275 625	1836 Proof *FDC Extremely rare*
1834 Milled edge Proof *FDC* £1850	1837 ....28 80 350 800
1835 ....20 55 300 650	1837 Proof *FDC* £2250

3836 Sixpence. Bare head r. ℞. Value in wreath, date below. die axis ↑↓

1831 ....15 30 160 400	1835 Proof *FDC Extremely rare*
— Proof *FDC* die axis ↑↓ or ↑↑ £550	1836 ....25 50 325 575
1831 Proof milled edge *FDC* £875	1836 Proof *FDC Extremely rare*
1834 ....15 30 185 400	1837 ....30 65 325 575
1834 large date 20 40 220 450	1837 Proof *FDC Extremely rare*
1834 Proof *FDC* £1050	1837 B/RRITANNIAR ....*Extremely rare*
1835 ....15 30 160 400	

3837 - 1836 Groat   3839 - 1835 Three-Halfpence

3837 Groat. Bare head r. ℞. Britannia seated, date in ex. die axis ↑↑

1836 ....5 20 80 140	1837 ....10 25 95 175
1836 Proof *FDC* £850	1837 Type 2 obv. 'more wiry hair' *values as above*
1836 Plain edge proof *FDC* £800	1837 Proof *FDC* £950
1836 Proof in gold *FDC* £12500	1837 Plain edge proof *FDC* £1100

3838 Threepence. Obverse 1, small head, low hair (for use in the West Indies). As Maundy
threepence but with a dull surface, ↑↓

| 1834 13   28   115   275 | 1836 8   20   95   250 |
| 1835 8   20   85   225 | 1837 15   30   125   250 |

3838A — Obverse 2, large head, high hair

| 1834 10   25   95   250 | 1836 7   15   65   150 |
| 1835 9   20   80   195 | 1837? may not exist |

3839 Three-Halfpence (for Colonial use). Bare head r. ℞. Value, Crowned in wreath, die axis ↑↓

1834 ....5 15 60 110	1836 ....7 22 65 130
1835/4 ....6 20 65 130	1837 ....15 40 145 375
1835 unconfirmed without 5/4	1837 Proof *FDC* £1000

3840 - 1831 Maundy Set

	EF	FDC		EF	FDC
	£	£		£	£
3840 Maundy Set (4d., 3d., 2d. and 1d.). Bare head r. Die axis ↑↓					
1831	195	450	1834	150	400
— Proof *FDC* £700			1835	150	400
1831 Proof struck in gold *FDC* £21000			1836	195	425
1832	165	425	1837	195	425
1833	150	400			
3841 — **Fourpence**, 1831-7...*from*				18	40
3842 — **Threepence**, 1831-7..*from*				30	60
3843 — **Twopence**, 1831-7...*from*				15	40
3844 — **Penny**, 1831-7..*from*				25	45

See note on p. 423 (under 3796)

COPPER

3845 - 1837 Penny

	F	VF	EF		F	VF	EF
	£	£	£		£	£	£
3845 Penny. Bare head r. No initials on trun. date below. R. Britannia r. die axis ↑↑							
1831	18	70	450	1834	20	85	550
1831 Proof *FDC* ↑↓ £725				1837	60	195	975
1831 Proof *FDC* ↑↑ £775							
3846 Penny. Bare head r. date below. incuse initials on trun. R. Britannia r. die axis ↑↑							
1831 W.W on trun	125	475	—	1831 .W.W on trun	35	115	475

3847 - 1831 Halfpenny   3848 - 1831 Farthing

3847 Halfpenny. Bare head r. date below. R. Britannia r. die axis ↑↑							
1831	12	35	150	1834	15	40	165
1831 Proof *FDC* ↑↓ £475				1837	10	30	135
1831 Proof *FDC* ↑↑ £575							

438

| | F | VF | EF | | F | VF | EF |
| | £ | £ | £ | | £ | £ | £ |

3848 **Farthing.** Bare head r. date below. R. Britannia r. die axis ↑↑

1831 rev. incuse line				1835 die axis ↑↓	10	30	135
on saltire............	3	15	95	1835 die axis ↑↑	3	15	90
1831 Proof *FDC* ↑↓ £450				1835 rev. incuse line			
1831 Proof *FDC* ↑↑ £500				on saltire............	3	18	95
1834 incuse saltire	3	15	95	1836 rev. raised line			
1834 rev. raised line				on saltire............	3	15	90
on saltire............	5	18	110	1837 —	3	18	95

3849 - 1837 Half-Farthing   3850 - 1835 Third-Farthing

3849 **Half-Farthing** (for use in Ceylon). Bare head r. date below. R. Britannia r. die axis ↑↑

1837 65   225   550

3850 **Third-Farthing** (for use in Malta). Bare head r. date below. R. Britannia r. die axis ↑↑

1835 10   30   160

1835 Proof *FDC* £825

Copper coins graded in this catalogue as UNC have full mint lustre

PS2 Proof set. Coronation, 1831. Two pounds to farthing (14 coins). *FDC* £41000

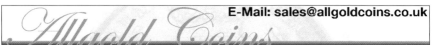

Victoria was born on 24 May 1819, and enjoyed the longest reign of any Monarch so far. She marrried the German, Prince Albert with whom she enjoyed 17 years of Marriage. Upon Albert's death she became the 'Widow of Windsor' descending into a 25 year period of mourning. She skillfully avoided conflict with other European powers, and produced connections with many Royal houses all over Europe. The Great Exhibition of 1851 was a sign of the power of the largest Empire in the world. Victoria died on 22 January 1901 at the age of 81.

In 1849, as a first step towards decimalization, a silver Florin (¹/₁₀th pound) was introduced, but the coins of 1849 omitted the usual *Dei Gratia* and these so-called 'Godless' Florins were replaced in 1851 by the 'Gothic' issue. The Halfcrown was temporarily discontinued but was minted again from 1874 onwards. Between 1863 and 1880 reverse dies of the gold and silver coins were numbered in the course of Mint experiments into the wear of dies. The exception was the Florin where the die number is on the obverse below the bust.

The gold and silver coins were redesigned for the Queen's Golden Jubilee in 1887. The Double-Florin which was then issued was abandoned after only four years; the Jubilee Sixpence of 1887, known as the 'withdrawn' type, was changed to avoid confusion with the Half-Sovereign. Gold and silver were again redesigned in 1893 with an older portrait of the Queen, but the 'old head' was not used on the bronze coinage until 1895. The heavy copper Penny had been replaced by the lighter bronze 'bun' Penny in 1860. In 1874-6 and 1881-2 some of the bronze was made by Heaton in Birmingham, and these have a letter H below the date. From 1897 Farthings were issued with a dark surface.

Early Sovereigns had a shield-type reverse, but Pistrucci's St. George design was used again from 1871. In order to increase the output of gold coinage, branches of the Royal Mint were set up in Australia at Sydney and Melbourne and, later, at Perth for coining gold of imperial type.

Engraver's and/or designer's initials on the coins:

W. W. (William Wyon 1795-1851)   T. B. (Thomas Brock 1847-1922)
L. C. W. (Leonard Charles Wyon 1826-91)   B. P. (Benedetto Pistrucci, 1784-1855)
J. E. B. (Joseph Edgar Boehm 1834-90)

Engravers and Designers: George William De Saulle, (1862-1903) William Dyce (1806-64), Jean Baptiste Merlen (1769-c.1850) Edward Poynter (1836-1919)

GOLD

Young Head Coinage, 1838-87

3851
1839 Five Pounds - DIRIGIT reverse

3851 Five Pounds. 1839. Young filleted bust l. plain rear fillet R. 'Una and the lion' (proof only)
DIRIGIT legend, inscribed edge, die axis ↑↑   *FDC* £55,000
– 1839 Similar – DIRIGIT legend, struck on thick flan   *FDC* £75,000
– 1839 Similar – DIRIGIT legend, plain edge die axis ↑↑   *FDC* £54,000
– 1839 –13 leaves to rear fillet, R. DIRIGE legend–proof   *FDC* £48,500
– 1839 Similar – DIRIGE legend edge plain proof   *FDC* £50,500
– 1839 –9 leaves to rear fillet, DIRIGE legend   *FDC* £48,500
– 1839 Similar – DIRIGE legend edge plain   *FDC* £51,500
– 1839 Similar – DIRIGIT legend edge plain proof   *FDC* £55,000

Truly FDC 1839 Five Pound coins are hardly ever seen.

3852
Sovereign - first smaller young head

3852C
Second large head

	F £	VF £	EF £	UNC £		F £	VF £	EF £	UNC £

3852 Sovereign. First (small) young head. l. date below. R. First shield. London mint, die axis ↑↓

	F	VF	EF	UNC		F	VF	EF	UNC
1838	750	1400	2950	5000	1843/2 or Ϲ	450	700	1350	2750
1838 Proof *FDC*	*Extremely rare*				1844 wider date	350	525	950	1550
1838 Plain edge proof *FDC* £16500					1844 closer date	390	575	1100	1850
1839	1000	1950	3500	7000	1844 first 4/Ϧ	650	1500	—	—
1839 die axis ↑↓ Proof *FDC* £5750					1845 4/Ϧ	750	1500	2250	—
1839 die axis ↑↑ Proof *FDC* £6250					1845 wider date	325	500	900	1500
1839 Milled edge proof *FDC* £15000					1845 closer date	375	625	975	1750
1841	4000	9500	20000	—	1845 Roman I	725	1400	—	—
1841 GRΛTIΛ	4000	9500	20000	—	1846	325	500	900	1500
1842	375	550	950	1550	1846 4/Ϧ	750	1500	—	—
1842 Open 2	650	1250	—	—	1846 Roman I	675	1250	—	—
1842 GRΛTIΛ	650	1500	—	—	1847	325	500	900	1500
1843	350	525	900	1450	1847 Roman I	700	1450	—	—
1843 Roman I	675	1250	—	—	1848	1000	2000	6000	—

3852A Sovereign. Similar R similar but leaves of the wreath arranged differently with tops of leaves closer to crown.

1838	4500	9000	22500	—

3852B Sovereign. Similar narrower shield. Considerably modified floral emblems, different leaf arrangement ↑↓

1843	4500	9500	20000	—

3852C Sovereign. Second (large) head. l. W W still in relief. date below R. Shield with repositioned legend die axis ↑↓

	F	VF	EF	UNC		F	VF	EF	UNC
1848	325	425	875	1800	1852	BV	400	800	1500
1849	325	425	875	1800	1853	BV	400	750	1200
1849 Roman I	675	1250	—	—	1853 F over E				
1850	350	500	925	1600	in DEF	750	1650	—	—
1850 Roman I	675	1250	—	—	1853 ∀ICTORIA	1250	—	—	—
1850 ∀ICTORIA	1250	—	—	—	1854	400	700	1300	3000
1850 8/5	*Extremely rare*				1855	350	625	975	—
1851	BV	400	650	1150	1872	BV	400	600	1000
1852 Roman I	675	1250	—	—					

BV= Bullion value only (if gold price over £1,000 an ounce)
NB Truly UNCIRCULATED Victorian sovereigns without any surface marks or hairlines are very rarely seen.

3852D
WW Incuse on truncation

3852E
Extra line in ribbon - 'Ansell' named
after Royal Mint Chemist G.F. Ansell

	F	VF	EF	UNC		F	VF	EF	UNC
	£	£	£	£		£	£	£	£

3852D Sovereign. Similar — WW incuse on trun. die axis ↑↓

	F	VF	EF	UNC		F	VF	EF	UNC
1853	325	600	975	2250	1860	BV	300	475	900
1853 Roman I	675	1250	—	—	1860 large 0	BV	400	600	1100
1853 Proof *FDC* £15000					1861	BV	375	550	1000
1854	BV	400	700	1250	1861 Roman I	500	750	1450	3000
1854 C over					1861 C over rotated C in				
rotated C	750	1650	—	—	obv. leg	750	1650	—	—
1855 Roman I	650	1450	—	—	1861 T over V in				
1855	BV	400	700	1250	VICTORIA	400	750	—	—
1856	BV	400	700	1250	1861 F/V in DEF				
1857	BV	400	700	1250	narrow date	500	1250	—	—
1857 ∀ICTORIA	1250	—	—	—	1861 E over				
1857/5				*Variety exists*	rotated E	750	1650	—	—
1858 small date	BV	400	700	1250	1862 R/E in BRIT	750	1650		
1858 large date	BV	425	750	1350	1862 Roman I	500	975	—	—
1858 8/7	750	—	—	—	1862 wide date	BV	375	550	1200
1859	BV	400	700	1250	1862 R/Я in				
1860 O over C in					VICTORIA	1250	2850	—	—
obv. leg	400	1000	—	—	1862 F/∀ in DEF	500	1250	—	—
1860 Roman I	650	1450	—	—	1862 narrow date	BV	375	575	1100
1860 ∀ICTORIA	1250	2750	—	—	1863	BV	375	550	1050
1860 DEI GRA∧	650	1500	—	—	1863 Roman I	500	975	—	—

3852E Sovereign. Similar — As 3852D 'Ansell' ribbon. Additional raised line on the lower part of the ribbon ↑↓

	F	VF	EF	UNC
1859	750	1700	7000	12500

3852F Sovereign. Similar — As 3852D with die number 827 on trun. die axis ↑↓

	F	VF	EF	UNC
1863	4000	9000	16000	—

3853 - Die number location

3853 Sovereign. Similar As 3852D R. die number in space below wreath, above floral emblem, die axis ↑↓

	F	VF	EF	UNC		F	VF	EF	UNC
1863	BV	375	550	1000	1866/5 DIE 17 only	350	500	750	—
1864	BV	375	550	1000	1868	BV	375	525	1000
1865	BV	375	575	1050	1869	BV	375	525	1000
1866	BV	375	550	1000	1870	BV	400	600	1150

3853A Sovereign. Similar — As 3853 with die number 827 on trun. R. die number is always no. 22 die axis ↑↓

	F	VF	EF	UNC
1863	3500	7000	14000	—

3853B Sovereign. Similar — WW in relief on trun. R. die number below wreath, above floral emblem die axis ↑↓

	F	VF	EF	UNC		F	VF	EF	UNC
1870	BV	400	550	1100	1873	BV	400	575	1150
1871	BV	350	475	950	1874	2000	4250	9500	—
1872	BV	350	475	950					

BV= Bullion value only (if gold price over £1,000 an ounce)

3854 - 'M' Melbourne Mint mark   3855 - 'S' Sydney Mint mark

	F	VF	EF	UNC			F	VF	EF	UNC
	£	£	£	£			£	£	£	£

3854 Sovereign. Second (large) head. l. WW in relief date below Ŗ. M below wreath for Melbourne Mint, Australia ↑↓

		F	VF	UNC				F	VF	UNC
1872 M	BV	350	500	1350		1883 M	BV	350	775	2500
1872/1 M	375	550	1250	3950		1884 M	BV	350	500	1100
1874 M	BV	350	550	1900		1885 M	BV	350	500	1100
1880 M	650	1650	3750	9500		1886 M	1900	4500	6750	17500

3854A Sovereign. Third young head. Similar but different hair arrangement.

		F	VF	UNC				F	VF	UNC
1881 M	BV	350	525	2200		1887 M	600	1400	4000	10000
1882 M	BV	350	500	1350						

3855 Sovereign. Similar — As 3854. Ŗ. with S below wreath for Sydney Mint, Australia die axis ↑↓

		F	VF	UNC				F	VF	UNC
1871 S	BV	350	500	1300		1880 S VICTORIA	750	3000	5500	12500
1872 S	BV	350	575	1650		1881 S	BV	350	575	1750
1873 S	BV	350	550	1650		1882 S	BV	350	550	1300
1875 S	BV	350	550	1650		1883 S	BV	350	525	1050
1877 S	BV	350	525	1300		1884 S	BV	350	525	1050
1878 S	BV	350	525	1300		1885 S	BV	350	500	1000
1879 S	BV	350	525	1300		1886 S	BV	350	500	1000
1880 S	BV	350	575	1650		1887 S	BV	350	575	1750

3855A Sovereign. Second (large) head WW incuse on trun. date below Ŗ. with S below wreath for Sydney Mint die axis ↑↓

		F	VF	EF	UNC
1871 S	BV	350	475	2100	

Note: The prices for Australian mint sovereigns are led by current trends in the Australian numismatic market place. Being very condition conscious, it is truly UNC coins which command the highest price, any detraction from a true UNC coin should be taken at the EF guide price. The exchange rate of the Pound Sterling versus Australian Dollar also has an influence on price fluctuation.

3856A - Horse with long tail, small BP in exergue

3856 Sovereign. First young head. l. WW buried in narrow trun. Ŗ. St. George. London mint. Horse with short tail. Large BP and date in ex. die axis ↑↓

	F	VF	EF	UNC
1871	—	BV	375	700

1871 Proof milled edge*FDC* £14500   1871 Plain edge proof *FDC* £9000

3856A Sovereign. — — As 3856 Ŗ. Horse with long tail. Small BP and date in ex.die axis ↑↓

	F	VF	EF	UNC			F	VF	EF	UNC
1871	—	BV	350	750		1876	—	BV	350	750
						1878	—	BV	350	750
1871 Proof *FDC* plain edge £9250										
1872	—	BV	350	750		1879	550	1250	4250	—
1873	—	BV	350	750		1880	—	BV	350	750
1874	—	BV	350	750						

3856B Sovereign. — — As 3856 Ŗ. Horse with short tail, small BP and date in ex.die axis ↑↓

	F	VF	EF	UNC			F	VF	EF	UNC
1880	—	BV	350	750		1884	—	BV	350	750
1880 Second 8/7	BV	350	450	850		1885	—	BV	350	750

BV= Bullion value only. At the time of going to press the spot price for gold was £1092 per oz.

	F	VF	EF	UNC		F	VF	EF	UNC
	£	£	£	£		£	£	£	£

3856C Sovereign. — — As 3856 R. Horse with short tail, date but no BP in ex.die axis ↑↓

1880 .... BV	300	425	600	1880 Second 8/7 ....BV	325	425	625

3856D Sovereign. Second head. l. WW complete, on broad trun. R. Horse with long tail, small BP and date in ex.die axis ↑↓

1880 Second 8/7 .....BV	325	425	600	1880 .... BV	325	400	550

3856E Sovereign. — — As 3856D R. Horse with short tail. Date but no BP in ex. die axis ↑↓

1880 ....BV	325	425	600

3856F Sovereign. — — As 3856E R. Horse with short tail, small BP and date in ex. die axis ↑↓

1880 .... BV	325	425	575	1885 ....BV	325	400	550
1884 .... BV	325	425	575	1887 Proof *FDC* £25000			

3857
Melbourne Mint, WW buried in truncation

3857 Sovereign. — — First head. l. WW buried in trun. M below head for Melbourne Mint, Australia. R. Horse with long tail, small BP and date in ex. die axis ↑↓

1872 M .... BV	350	1250	4000	1877 M ....BV	325	400	1200
1873 M .... BV	325	400	1500	1878 M ....BV	325	400	1200
1874 M .... BV	325	400	1500	1879 M ....BV	325	400	1000
1875 M .... BV	325	400	1200	1880 M ....BV	325	400	1100
1876 M .... BV	325	400	1200	1881 M ....BV	325	400	1100

3857A Sovereign. — — As 3857 R. horse with short tail, date but no BP in ex die axis ↑↓

1881 M .... BV	325	400	1100	1883 M ....BV	325	400	1800
1882 M .... BV	325	350	950	1885 M ....BV	325	375	1500

3857B Sovereign. First head l. WW buried in trun. M below head for Melbourne Mint, Australia R. Horse with short tail, small BP and date in ex. die axis ↑↓

1882 M .... BV	325	400	950	1884 M ....BV	325	400	800
1883 M .... BV	325	400	950	1885 M ....BV	325	400	1200

3857C Sovereign. — — Second head. l. WW complete on broad truncation. R. Horse with short tail, small BP in ex.

1882 M .... BV	325	400	1250	1885 M ....BV	325	400	800
1883 M .... BV	325	400	900	1886 M ....BV	325	400	800
1884 M .... BV	325	400	650	1887 M ....BV	325	400	950

3857D Sovereign. First head. l. WW buried in trun. M below R. Horse with medium tail, small BP

1879 M .... BV	325	400	1500	1881 M ....BV	325	400	1750
1880 M .... BV	325	400	1500	1882 M ....BV	—	—	—

3857E Sovereign. Second head. l. WW complete on trun. M below R. Horse with short tail, no BP in ex.

1884 M ....*Extremely rare*	1885 M ....BV	325	400	1100

3858 Sovereign First head. l. WW buried in narrow trun. S below head for Sydney Mint, Australia, R. Horse with short tail, large BP and date in ex. die axis ↑↓

1871 S ....BV	325	950	3250

3858A Sovereign. — — As 3858 R. Horse with long tail, small BP and date in ex. die axis ↑↓

1871 S .... BV	325	1100	3600	1875 S ....BV	325	400	1500
1872 S .... BV	325	400	1700	1876 S ....BV	325	400	1500
1873 S .... BV	325	400	2650	1879 S ....BV	325	1250	3450
1874 S .... BV	325	400	2100	1880 S ....BV	325	400	1500

BV= Bullion value only. At the time of going to press the spot price for gold was £1092 per oz.

3859 - Type A1   3859A - Type A2

	F	VF	EF	UNC		F	VF	EF	UNC
	£	£	£	£		£	£	£	£

3858B Sovereign. First head. As 3858 R. Horse with short tail, date but no BP in ex. die axis ↑↓

| 1880 S | BV | 325 | 475 | 1800 | 1881 S | BV | 325 | 400 | 1400 |

3858C Sovereign. Second head. l. WW complete on broad trun. R.
Horse with long tail, small BP and date in ex. die axis ↑↓

| 1880 S | | | | BV | 325 | 450 | 1500 |

3858D Sovereign. — — As 3858C R. Horse with short tail, date but no BP in ex. die axis ↑↓

| 1881 S | BV | 325 | 400 | 1200 | 1882 S | BV | 325 | 450 | 800 |

3858E Sovereign. — — As 3858D R. Horse with short tail small BP and date in ex. die axis ↑↓

1882 S	BV	325	400	800	1885 S	BV	325	450	800
1883 S	BV	325	475	1800	1886 S	BV	325	450	800
1884 S	BV	325	400	950	1887 S	BV	325	450	800

3858F Sovereign. Second head. Horse with long tail, no BP in ex.

| 1880 S | | | | |

3859 Half-Sovereign. Type A1. First (smallest) young head. date below l. R. First shield, die axis ↑↓

1838	185	325	800	1450	1849	175	300	725	1100
1839 die axis ↑↓ or ↑↑ Proof only FDC £3250					1850	250	550	1500	—
1839 Milled edge proof FDC Extremely rare					1851	175	300	625	1050
1841	200	325	900	1650	1852	175	300	650	1100
1842	175	300	650	1100	1853	175	300	625	1000
1843	175	325	750	1250	1853 Proof small date FDC £8000				
1844	175	325	650	1100	1853 Proof large date FDC £11500				
1845	300	750	2250	—	1855	175	300	650	1100
1846	175	325	650	1100	1856	175	300	625	1050
1847	175	325	650	1100	1856/5	225	350	750	1200
1848 Close date	175	325	650	1100	1857	175	300	650	1100
1848/7	250	500	975	1850	1858	175	300	650	1100
1848 Wide date	200	325	825	1500					

3859A Half-Sovereign. Type A2, Second (larger) young head. date below. R. First shield die axis ↑↓

1858	175	300	525	950	1861	175	300	600	900
1859	175	300	525	950	1862	750	2000	7000	—
1860	175	300	500	900	1863	175	300	475	850

3860	3860D	3860E	3860F
Die number location	Type A3	Type A4	Type A5

3860 Half-Sovereign. Type A2, second head, date below R. die number below shield, die axis ↑↓

1863	175	250	675	1100	1867	BV	200	500	875
1864	BV	200	500	875	1869	BV	200	500	875
1865	BV	200	500	875	1870	BV	175	475	750
1866	BV	200	500	875	1871	BV	175	475	750

BV= Bullion value only. At the time of going to press the spot price for gold was £1092 per oz.

	F	VF	EF	UNC		F	VF	EF	UNC
	£	£	£	£		£	£	£	£

3860A Half-Sovereign. Second head, date below R. Re-engraved shield legend and rosettes closer to border, coarse boarder teeth both sides, with die number below shield die axis ↑↓

1870 275   600   1250   —   1871 225   500   1100   —

3860B Half-Sovereign. Second head, date below R. As last but with normal border teeth and no die number below shield die axis ↑↓

1871 300   675   1600   —

3860C Half-Sovereign. Second head, date below obv. with repositioned legend, nose now points to T in VICTORIA. R Similar to last but with die number below shield die axis ↑↓

1871 300   800   1500   —   1872 225   500   1100   —

3860D Half-Sovereign. Type A3, Third (larger still) young head l, date below. R. As 3860A, with die number below shield die axis ↑↓

1872 .... BV	185	425	800	1875 ....BV	175	400	700
1873 .... BV	185	425	800	1876 ....BV	175	400	700
1874 .... BV	200	425	850	1877 ....BV	175	400	700

3860E - Half Sovereign   3861 - Type A5

3860E Half-Sovereign. Type A4. Fourth young head l. hair ribbon now narrow, date below. R. As last with die number below shield die axis ↑↓

1876 .... BV	175	400	700	1878 ....BV	175	400	700
1877 .... BV	175	400	700	1879 175	225	575	1000

3860F Half-Sovereign. Type A5. Fifth young head l. in very low relief, date below. R. As last with die number below shield die axis ↑↓

1880 175   225   575   1100

3860G Half-Sovereign. Type A4. Fourth young head, without die number below shield.

1876 .... *Extremely rare*

3861 Half-Sovereign. Fifth head, date below. R. Cross on crown buried in border. Legend and rosettes very close to heavy border, no die number below shield die axis ↑↓

1880 .... BV	185	425	750	1885 ....BV	175	400	600
1883 .... BV	175	400	600	1885/3 175	275	750	1250
1884 .... BV	175	400	600				

3862 Half-Sovereign. Type A2, Second (larger) young head l. nose points between T and O. Date below R. First crowned shield cross clear of border with S below shield for Sydney Mint, Australia, die axis ↑↓

1871 S 175   225 1350 15000   1871 S Proof ....*Extremely rare*

3862A Half-Sovereign. Similar obv. with repositioned legend, nose now points to T in VICTORIA. Date below R Re-engraved shield cross touches border, S below shield die axis ↑↓

1872 S 175   225 1350 15000

3862B Half-Sovereign. Type A3. Third (larger still) young head l. I of DEI points to rear fillet. Date below R. As last die axis ↑↓

1875 S 175   225 1350 15000

3862C Half-Sovereign. Type A4. Fourth young head l. front hair fillet now narrow. R. As last, die axis ↑↓

1879 S 175   225 1100 13000

3862D Half-Sovereign. Type A5. Fifth young head l. in low relief wider tr. no front ear lobe. Date below R as last. die axis ↑↓

1880 S 175	200	1350	22500	1882 S ....*Extremely rare*
1880 S Proof..........................*Extremely rare*				1883 S 175 250 850 18000
1881 S 175	375	1950	26000	

* Beware recent forgeries

BV= Bullion value only. At the time of going to press the spot price for gold was £1092 per oz.

	F	VF	EF	UNC		F	VF	EF	UNC
	£	£	£	£		£	£	£	£

3862E Half-Sovereign. Fifth head, date below R. Cross on crown buried in border. Legend and rosettes very close to heavy border, S below shield die axis ↑↓

1880 S 175	225	650	20000	1883 S Proof ....*Extremely rare*
1881 S 175	250	1500	19000	1886 S 175 225 1150 10000
1882 S 225	700	4000	24000	1887 S 175 225 1150 8000
1883 S 175	225	1150	9000	

3863 Half-Sovereign. Type A3. Third (larger still) young head l. Date below R. Re-engraved shield with M below shield for Melbourne Mint, Australia die axis ↑↓

1873 M 175   225   1850 15000   1877 M 175   285   3500 16750

3863A Half-Sovereign. Type A4, fourth young head l. hair ribbon now narrow. R. As last die axis ↑↓

1877 M 175   225   1250 15000   1882 M 175   225   2750 17000

3863B Half-Sovereign. Type A5. Fifth young head l. in low relief.Date below R. As last die axis ↑↓

1881 M 175	775	8000	22250	1885 M 200 750 6000 19000
1882 M 175	225	1250	8250	1886 M 175 600 8000 20000
1884 M 175	350	5000	18000	1886 M Proof ....*Extremely rare*
1884 M Proof ....*Extremely rare*				1887 M 175 2000 12000 28000

Jubilee Coinage, 1887-93, die axis ↑↑

3864 - 1887 Five Pounds

3864* Five Pounds. Jubilee bust l. R. St. George date in ex. 1887 1750   2000   2500   3250
— Proof *FDC* £5000
— Proof no B.P. in exergue £5750
3864A* Five Pounds. Jubilee bust l. R. St George, S on ground for Sydney Mint, Australia
1887 S ....   *Extremely rare*
3865* Two Pounds. Jubilee bust l. R. St George die axis ↑↑ 1887 700   900   1150   1500
1887 Proof *FDC* £1950
1887 Proof no BP in exergue FDC *Extremely rare*
3865A* Two Pounds. R. St George, S on ground for Sydney Mint, Australia ↑↑
1887 S ....   *Extremely rare*

3866 - 1887 Sovereign

3866* Sovereign. Normal JEB (angled J) designer's initials fully on trun. R. St. George. die axis ↑↑

1887............................	BV	350	475	1890		350	500	700
1888............................	BV	325	550					

* Beware recent forgeries
BV= Bullion value only. At the time of going to press the spot price for gold was £1092 per oz.

	VF	EF	UNC		F	VF	EF	UNC
	£	£	£		£	£	£	£

3866A Sovereign. Similar with tiny JEB (hooked J) designer's initials at base of truncation die axis ↑↑
1887 350   750   110   —

3866B Sovereign. Similar repositioned legend. G: of D:G: now closer to crown. Normal JEB (angled J)
    designer's initials at base of trun. ↑↑
1887 Proof *FDC* £1750 ....   1890 .... BV   350   475
1888 .... BV   350   500   1891 600   1200   —   —
1889 .... BV   350   475

3866C Sovereign. Similar obv. as last. R. Horse with longer tail die axis ↑↑
1891 .... BV   350   475   1892 .... BV   350   475
1891 Proof *FDC* £17500

3867
"M' Melbourne Mint on groundline above 8's in date

3867 Sovereign. Similar with small spread JEB (angled J) designer's initials fully on trun. R. M on
ground for Melbourne Mint, Australia, die axis ↑↑
1887 M .... BV   400   825

3867A Sovereign. Similar with normal JEB designer's initials on trun. (angled J) die axis ↑↑
1887 M .... BV   400   550
1888 M 475   1250   2800
1889 M 300   800   2400
1890 M .... *Extremely rare*

3867B Sovereign. Similar repositioned legend. G: of D: G: now closer to crown. Normal JEB (angled J)
    initials at base of trun. die axis ↑↑
1887 M .... BV   400   600   1889 M .... BV   400   550
1888 M .... BV   400   550   1890M .... BV   400   550
1888 Proof *FDC* .... *Extremely rare*   1891M .... BV   450   1250

3867C Sovereign. Similar obv. as last. R. Horse with longer tail die axis ↑↑
1891 M .... BV   475   2000   1893M .... BV   400   850
1892 M .... BV   400   500

3868 Sovereign. First legend with normal JEB (hooked J) initials in arc on trun. R. S on ground for
    Sydney Mint, Australia die axis ↑↑
1887 S 475   1850   6500   1889S .... BV   400   900
1888 S .... BV   400   800   1890S 300   600   1900

3868A Sovereign. Similar with small spread JEB designer's initials straight on trun.(hooked J) die
axis ↑↑
1887 S .... BV   475   3250
1887 S Proof.. *Extremely rare*
1888 S .... BV   400   1250
1889 S .... *Extremely rare*

3868B Sovereign. Similar repositioned legend. G: of D:G: now closer to crown. Normal JEB (angled J)
initials on trun. die axis ↑↑
1888 S .... BV   400   450   1890S .... BV   400   700
1889 S .... BV   400   600

3868C Sovereign. Similar obv. as last. R. Horse with longer tail die axis ↑↑
1891 S .... BV   400   500   1893S .... BV   400   650
1892 S .... BV   400   625

BV= Bullion value only. At the time of going to press the spot price for gold was £1092 per oz.

	3869					3869D		
higher shield, cross blends into border					Plain trun., lower shield, cross clear of border			

	F	VF	EF	UNC		F	VF	EF	UNC
	£	£	£	£		£	£	£	£

3869 Half-Sovereign. Similar obv. normal JEB designer's initials. on trun. Ŗ. High shield die axis ↑↑

| 1887 | BV | 150 | 225 | 325 | 1890 | BV | 200 | 475 | — |

— Proof *FDC* £950

3869A Half-Sovereign. Similar small close JEB intitials. on trun. Ŗ. High shield die axis ↑↑

| 1887 | BV | 175 | 425 | — |

3869B Half-Sovereign. Similar normal JEB initials. on trun. Ŗ. Lower shield, date therefore spread apart, complete cross at top, die axis ↑↑

| 1890 | BV | 175 | 425 | — | 1892 | BV | 175 | 425 | — |

3869C Half-Sovereign. Similar no JEB initials on trun. Ŗ. High Shield die axis ↑↑

| 1887 | BV | 175 | 425 | — | 1891 | BV | 175 | 425 | — |
| 1890 | BV | 240 | 350 | — | 1892 | BV | 175 | 425 | — |

3869D Half-Sovereign. Jubilee bust 1. Ŗ. Lower shield, date therefore spread apart die axis ↑↑

| 1890 | BV | 240 | 350 | 1892 | BV | 240 | 350 |
| 1891 | BV | 275 | 375 | 1893 | BV | 275 | 375 |

3870

3870 Half-Sovereign. Similar small very spread JEB initials on trun. Ŗ. High shield, M below for Melbourne Mint, Australia, die axis ↑↑

| 1887 M | 165 | 200 | 400 | 2500 | 1887 M Proof | *Extremely rare* |

3870A Half-Sovereign. Similar small close JEB initials on trun. Ŗ. As last die axis ↑↑

| 1887 M | 165 | 225 | 450...2150 | 1887 M Proof | *Extremely rare* |

3870B Half-Sovereign. Similar normal JEB initials on trun. Ŗ. Lower shield, date therefore spread part die axis ↑↑

| 1893 M | 165 | 250 | 600 | 3500 |

3871 Half-Sovereign. Similar small very spread JEB initials on trun. (hooked J) Ŗ. High shield S below for Sydney Mint, Australia ↑↑

| 1887 S | 165 | 200 | 475 | 2150 |

3871A Half-Sovereign. Similar small close JEB initials on trun. Ŗ As last. die axis ↑↑

| 1887 S | 165 | 200 | 350 | 1750 | 1887 S Proof | *Extremely rare* |

3871B Half-Sovereign. Jubilee bust 1. Normal JEB initials on trun. Ŗ. Lower shield, date therefore spread apart, S below for Sydney Mint, Australia die axis ↑↑

| 1889 S | 165 | 250 | 1975 | 8250 |

3871C Half-Sovereign. Jubilee bust 1. Normal JEB initials on trun. Ŗ. High shield, S below for Sydney Mint, Australia die axis ↑↑

| 1891 S | 165 | 300 | 1400 | 6250 |

3871D Half-Sovereign. Jubilee bust 1. No JEB initials on trun. Ŗ. As last die axis ↑↑

| 1891 S | 165 | 250 | 800 | 5250 |

BV= Bullion value only. At the time of going to press the spot price for gold was £1092 per oz.

Old Head coinage, 1893-1901, die axis ↑↑

3872
1893 Five Pounds

	F	*VF*	*EF*	*UNC*
	£	£	£	£

3872* Five Pounds. Old veiled bust l. R. St. George and dragon, date and BP in ex.

1893..1950   2500   3500   4750
1893 Proof *FDC* £6000

3873   3874
1893 Two Pounds   1893 Sovereign

3873* Two Pounds. Old veiled bust l. R. St. George and dragon, date and BP in ex. die axis ↑↑

1893..750   950   1500   2000
1893 Proof *FDC* £2750

	EF	*UNC*		*EF*	*UNC*
	£	£		£	£

3874 Sovereign. Old veiled bust l. R. St. George, London Mint die axis ↑↑

1893	BV	400	1898	BV	400
1893 Proof *FDC* £1950			1899	BV	400
1894	BV	400	1900	BV	400
1895	BV	400	1901	BV	400
1896	BV	400			

3875 Sovereign. Similar R. St. George. M on ground for Melbourne Mint, Australia die axis ↑↑

1893 M	BV	500	1898 M	BV	450
1894 M	BV	450	1899 M	BV	425
1895 M	BV	450	1900 M	BV	425
1896 M	BV	425	1901 M	BV	425
1897 M	BV	425			

* Beware recent forgeries
BV= Bullion value only. At the time of going to press the spot price for gold was £1092 per oz.
NB Truly UNCIRCULATED old bust sovereigns are very scarce. Any surface defects will cause the
value to drop significantly.

3876
Perth Mint mark

	F	VF	EF	UNC		F	VF	EF	UNC
	£	£	£	£		£	£	£	£

3876 Sovereign. Similar — P on ground for Perth Mint, Australia die axis ↑↑

1899 P	BV	300	500	2650	1901 P	BV	300	500	
1900 P	BV	300	500						

3877 Sovereign. Similar — S on ground for Sydney Mint, Australia die axis ↑↑

1893 S	BV	450		1898 S	BV	300	500
1894 S	BV	450		1899 S	BV	450	
1895 S	BV	450		1900 S	BV	450	
1896 S	BV	300	500	1901 S	BV	450	
1897 S	BV	300	500				

3878
1893 Half -Sovereign

3878 Half-Sovereign. Old veiled bust 1.R. St. George. Date in ex. (no B.P. on this issue in exergue) London Mint die axis ↑↑

1893	BV	165	300	1897	BV	165	300
— Proof *FDC* £1150				1898	BV	165	300
1894	BV	165	300	1899	BV	165	300
1895	BV	165	300	1900	BV	165	300
1896	BV	165	300	1901	BV	165	300

3879 Half-Sovereign. Similar — M on ground for Melbourne Mint, Australia die axis ↑↑

1893 M			*Extremely rare*		1900 M	165	250	750	3250
1896 M	165	250	475	3750	1900 M Proof			*Extremely rare*	
1899 M	165	250	700	4000	1896 M Proof			*Extremely rare*	
1899 M Proof			*Extremely rare*						

3880 Half-Sovereign. Similar — P on ground for Perth Mint, Australia die axis ↑↑

1899 P		Proof only *unique*		1900 P	200	300	850	6500

3881 Half-Sovereign. Similar — S on ground for Sydney Mint, Australia die axis ↑↑

1893 S	165	250	600	2750	1897 S	165	250	500	3250
1893 S Proof			*Extremely rare*		1900 S	165	300	425	1950

BV= Bullion value only. At the time of going to press the spot price for gold was £1092 per oz.
NB Truly UNCIRCULATED old bust sovereigns are very scarce. Any surface defects will cause the value to drop significantly.

SILVER

Young head coinage, die axis ↑↓

Edge Stops

Cinquefoil

Star

3882 - 1844 Crown

	F	VF	EF	UNC		F	VF	EF	UNC
	£	£	£	£		£	£	£	£

†**3882 Crown.** Young head. l. R. Crowned shield, regnal year on edge in Roman figures (eg 1847 = XI)

	F	VF	EF	UNC
1839 Proof only *FDC* £11000				
1844 Star stops	70	250	1650	3750
1844 Cinquefoil stops	150	500	2750	4750
1844 Mistruck edge lettering	175	550	3000	–
1845 Star stops	75	300	1900	4000
1845 Cinquefoil stops	75	300	1650	3750
1847 XI Cinquefoil stops	150	450	2500	4250

3883

1847 Gothic Crown

3883*Crown. 'Gothic' type, bust 1. R. Crowned cruciform Shields, emblems in angles. inscribed edge, mdcccxlvii=1847 Undecimo on edge die axis ↑↓ 750   1150   2250   3500

1847 Septimo on edge of highest rarity.   1847 Proof, Plain edge die axis ↑↑ *FDC* £6000

1847 Proof in gold plain edge *FDC* of highest rarity   1847 Proof in white metal plain edge *FDC* £12500

3884 Crown. Similar mdccccliii=1853. Septimo on edge die axis ↑↑ Proof *FDC* £15000

1853 plain edge proof *FDC* £25000

3885 Halfcrown. Type A[1]. Young head l. with one ornate and one plain fillet binding hair. WW in relief on trun. R. Crowned shield of arms, edge milled. Die axis ↑↓

1839 Milled edge Proof *FDC Extremely rare*   1839 Proof plain edge *FDC* £2750

3886 Halfcrown. Type A[2] Similar, but two ornate fillets binding hair.die axis ↑↓

1839 Proof only *FDC* £4000

3886A Halfcrown. Type A[2/3] Similar, Two plain fillets, WW relief, die axis ↑↓ plain edge

1839 Proof *FDC* £5000

*Beware of recent forgeries.

†The Victorian young head Crowns are notoriously hard to drade. A truly UNC coin must show all design elements clearly excepially on hair fillets and the reverse shield. All facial features and hair must also be present.

	F	VF	EF	UNC		F	VF	EF	UNC
	£	£	£	£		£	£	£	£

3887 Halfcrown. Type A³. Similar two plain fillets. WW incuse on trun. die axis ↑↓

| 1839 | 1000 | 3250 | 7500 | — | 1839 Milled edge Proof *FDC* £4000 | | | | |
| 1839 Plain edge Proof *FDC* £4500 | | | | | 1840 | 70 | 225 | 850 | 1850 |

3888 Halfcrown. Type A⁴. Similar but no initials on trun. die axis ↑↓

1841	950	1950	4500	7000	1849 large date	75	250	925	1800
1842	60	175	800	1650	1849/7		*Extremely rare*		
1843	150	475	1500	3000	1849 small date	125	375	1050	2150
1844	55	165	750	1500	1850	75	350	950	1950
1844 not in edge collar		*Extremely rare*			1850 Proof *FDC* £9000				
1845	55	165	750	1500	1853 Proof *FDC* £4000				
1845 5/3		*Extremely rare*			1862 Proof *FDC* £9500				
1846	55	165	750	1500	1862 Plain edge Proof *FDC* £7500				
1848/6	225	600	1650	3250	1864 Proof *FDC* £8000				
1848/7		*Extremely rare*			1864 Plain edge Proof *FDC* £7500				
1848	225	650	1750	3750					

3889
Type A5 Halfcrown

3890
1849 'Godless' Florin

3889 Halfcrown. Similar Type A⁵. As last but design of inferior workmanship R. Crowned shield
die axis ↑↓

1874	25	70	325	750	1881	22	70	325	800
1874 Proof *FDC* £5500					1881 Proof *FDC* £5750				
1875	25	70	300	775	1881 Plain edge proof *FDC* £7500				
1875 Proof *FDC* £5000					1882	25	75	350	825
1876	25	75	325	800	1883	15	60	250	700
1876/5	35	85	475	1000	1883 Plain edge proof *FDC* £7500				
1877	25	70	325	800	1884	20	70	325	800
1878	30	70	325	800	1885	20	70	325	800
1878 Proof *FDC* £5750					1885 Proof *FDC* £5750				
1879	30	75	400	875	1886	20	70	325	800
1879 Proof *FDC* £56250					1886 Plain edge proof *FDC* £6500				
1880	22	70	325	800	1887	25	80	350	825
1880 Proof *FDC* £6250					1887 Proof *FDC* £6000				

3890 Florin. 'Godless' type A (i.e. without D.G.), WW behind bust within linear circle, die axis ↑↓

| 1848 Plain edge (Pattern) *FDC* £1750 | | | | | 1849 WW obliterated | 50 | 95 | 375 | 700 |
| 1848 Milled edge ↑↑ or ↑↓ Proof *FDC* £3250 | | | | | 1849 | 25 | 65 | 250 | 475 |

3891 Florin. 'Gothic' type B¹. Reads brit:, WW below bust, date at end of obverse legend in gothic
numerals (1851 to 1863) Crowned cruciform Shields, emblems in angles, edge milled. die axis ↑↓

mdcccli Proof only *FDC* £17000					mdccclvii Proof *FDC* £4250				
mdccclii	20	50	275	650	mdccclviii	20	50	300	725
mdccclii Proof *FDC* £3500					mdccclviii Proof *FDC* £4250				
mdccclii, ii/i	25	60	300	725	mdccclix	20	50	300	725
mdcccliii	20	50	275	700	mdccclx	25	50	325	750
mdcccliii Proof *FDC* £4000					mdccclxii	225	600	1500	3000
mdcccliv	750	1650	4750	—	mdccclxii Plain edge Proof *FDC* £5750				
mdccclv	30	85	275	750	mdccclxiii	750	1750	3250	4750
mdccclvi	30	85	275	750	mdccclxiii Plain edge Proof *FDC* £6000				
mdccclvii	25	60	300	725					

3891   3893

1853 Florin Type B1

	F	VF	EF	UNC		F	VF	EF	UNC
	£	£	£	£		£	£	£	£

3892 Florin. Type B². Similar as last but die number below bust (1864 to 1867) die axis ↑↓

mdccclxiv 25	70	350	725		mdccclxv 45	120	500	900
mdccclxiv heavy flan 325	700	1500	3500		mdccclxvi...............40	90	375	750
mdccclxiv heavy flan Proof *FDC* £6500					mdccclxvii...............35	80	375	750
mdccclxvii Proof *FDC* £4250								

3893 Florin. Type B³. Similar reads britt:, die number below bust (1868 to 1879) die axis

mdccclxviii...............35	100	425	900		mdccclxxiii...............25	60	250	650
mdccclxix...............30	90	425	850		mdccclxxiii Proof *FDC* £3750			
mdccclxix Proof *FDC* £4750					mdccclxxiv............30	75	375	750
mdccclxx 25	65	325	750		mdccclxxiv iv/iii 40	90	325	850
mdccclxx Proof *FDC* £4750					mdccclxxv 25	60	300	725
mdccclxxi...............25	65	325	750		mdccclxxvi............25	60	300	325
mdccclxxi Proof *FDC* £4250					mdccclxxvii............30	60	300	750
mdccclxxii...............20	50	250	650		mdccclxxix................		*Extremely rare*	

3894 Florin. Type B⁴. Similar as last but with border of 48 arcs and no WW below bust die axis ↑↓
1877 mdccclxxvii .... *Extremely rare*

3895 Florin. Type B⁵. Similar but border of 42 arcs (1867, 1877 and 1878) die axis ↑↓

mdccclxvii 2750	—	—	—		mdccclxxviii...........25	60	300	675
mdccclxxvii.............30	70	375	800		mdccclxxviii Proof *FDC*		*Extremely rare*	

3896 Florin. Type B⁵/⁶. Similar as last but no die number below bust (1877, 1879) die axis ↑↓

mdccclxxvii...........125	275	625	1350		mdccclxxix..........120	300	750	1500

3897 Florin. Type B⁶. Similar reads britt:, WW; Border of 48 arcs (1879) die axis ↑↓
mdccclxxviii ....*Known to exist*
mdccclxxix ....25 | 60 | 300 | 700

3898 Florin. Type B⁷. Similar as last but no WW, Border of 38 arcs (1879) die axis ↑↓
mdccclxxix ....25 | 60 | 300 | 700
mdccclxxix Proof *FDC* £4750

3899 Florin. Type B³/₈. Similar as next but younger portrait (1880) die axis ↑↓
mdccclxxx .... *Extremely rare*

3900 Florin. Type B⁸. Similar but border of 34 arcs (1880 to 1887) die axis ↑↓

mdccclxxx...............20	50	300	650		mdccclxxxiii Proof *FDC* £3250			
mdccclxxx Proof *FDC* £4250					mdccclxxxiv...........20	50	300	625
mdccclxxxi...............20	50	300	650		mdccclxxxv 25	60	300	625
mdccclxxxi Proof *FDC* £4000					mdccclxxxv Proof *FDC* £4250			
mdccclxxxi/xxri 35	90	350	750		mdccclxxxvi...........20	45	300	625
mdccclxxxiii............20	50	300	650		mdccclxxxvi Proof *FDC* £4500			

3901 Florin. Type B⁹. Similar but border of 46 arcs die axis ↑↓
1887 mdccclxxxvii...35 | 75 | 400 | 800
mdccclxxxvii Proof *FDC* .... *Extremely rare*

3902 Shilling. Type A¹. First head l., WW on trun.Ŗ. crowned mark of value within wreath, date
below, die axis ↑↓

1838.........................20	60	300	600		1839 50	115	400	800
1838 Proof *FDC* £3200					1839 Proof *FDC* £1850			

3903 Shilling Type A². Second head, l. WW on trun. (proof only), 1839 die axis ↑↑ *FDC* £900

3904 - Type A3 Shilling

	F	VF	EF	UNC		F	VF	EF	UNC
	£	£	£	£		£	£	£	£

3904 Shilling Type A³. Second head, l. no initials on trun. R. Similar die axis ↑↓

	F	VF	EF	UNC		F	VF	EF	UNC
1839	25	60	300	550	1852	15	35	250	475
1839 Proof plain edge *FDC* £850					1853	15	30	225	475
1839 Proof plain edge en medaille ↑↑ *FDC* £2000					1853 Milled edge Proof *FDC* £1350				
1839 Proof milled edge *FDC Extremely rare*					1854	225	575	1600	3250
1840	30	85	350	625	1854/1	275	800	2750	—
1840 Proof *FDC* £3250					1855	15	30	200	475
1841	65	80	375	650	1856	15	30	200	475
1842	25	55	250	525	1857	15	30	200	475
1842 Proof *FDC* £3250					1857 REG F: Ɔ:error	195	550	1500	—
1843	30	75	350	650	1858	15	30	200	475
1844	25	50	250	525	1859	15	30	200	475
1845	35	65	300	575	1859 9/8 *exists*				
1846	25	50	250	525	1859 Proof *FDC* £3750				
1848 over 6	75	225	775	1350	1860	18	40	250	550
1849	30	60	275	575	1861	18	40	250	550
1850	750	1500	3750	—	1861 D/B in FD	125	300	750	—
1850/49	825	1750	4000	—	1862	50	80	325	625
1851	60	150	550	1200	1863	100	225	500	1100
1851 Proof *FDC* £4250					1863/1	120	300	800	—

3905 Shilling Type A⁴. Similar as last, R. Die number above date die axis ↑↓

	F	VF	EF	UNC		F	VF	EF	UNC
1864	15	35	185	475	1866 BBITANNIAR	70	275	875	—
1865	15	35	185	475	1867	20	40	175	475
1866	15	35	185	475					

3906 Shilling Type A⁵. Third head, l. R. Similar no die number above date die axis ↑↓

	F	VF	EF	UNC		F	VF	EF	UNC
1867 Proof £3750					1879	225	500	1150	2000
1867 Proof plain edge £4000					1879 Proof, milled edge, *FDC* £3500				

3906A - Type A6 Shilling
Die number location above date

3906A Shilling Type A⁶. Third head, l. R. Similar die number above date die axis ↑↓

	F	VF	EF	UNC		F	VF	EF	UNC
1867	175	450	1350	2750	1873	12	25	185	475
1868	15	30	185	475	1874	12	25	185	475
1869	25	45	275	525	1875	12	25	185	475
1870	20	40	250	500	1876	18	35	200	500
1871	15	25	185	475	1877	12	25	185	475
1871 Plain edge proof *FDC* £3500					1878	25	45	275	550
1871 Milled edge proof *FDC* £3250					1878 Milled edge Proof *FDC* £3500				
1872	15	25	185	475	1879 uncertain to exist as normal coin or proof?				

	F	VF	EF	UNC		F	VF	EF	UNC
	£	£	£	£		£	£	£	£

3907 Shilling Type A[7]. Fourth head, l. R. Similar no die number above date die axis ↑↓

	F	VF	EF	UNC		F	VF	EF	UNC
1879	12	25	175	400	1883 plain edge Proof *FDC* £4000				
1879 Proof *FDC* £3500					1884	12	25	150	300
1880	12	25	150	350	1884 Proof *FDC* £3000				
1880 Proof plain edge £3250					1885	12	20	135	275
1880 Proof milled edge £2750					1885 Proof *FDC* £3000				
1881	12	25	150	300	1886	12	20	135	275
1881 Proof plain edge £3500					1886 Proof *FDC* £3000				
1881 Proof milled edge £2500					1887	15	30	175	375
1882	15	40	200	375	1887 Proof *FDC* £2500				
1883	12	25	150	300					

3907A Shilling. Type A7. Fourth head, R. Similar die number above date die axis ↑↓

	F	VF	EF	UNC		F	VF	EF	UNC
1878	12	25	150	300	1879	15	40	200	375
1878 Milled edge Proof *FDC* £3000									

3908
Type A1 Sixpence

3908 Sixpence. Type A[1]. First head l. R. Crowned mark of value within wreath, date below die axis ↑↓

	F	VF	EF	UNC		F	VF	EF	UNC
1838	15	30	150	400	1851	12	25	150	425
1838 Proof *FDC* £1850					1852	10	25	150	400
1839	15	30	150	400	1853	10	25	145	350
1839 Proof *FDC* £800					1853 Proof *FDC* £950				
1840	15	30	150	425	1854	165	450	950	2250
1841	18	35	175	475	1855	10	25	150	425
1842	15	30	150	425	1855/3	15	30	165	450
1843	15	30	150	425	1855 Proof *FDC*		*Extremely rare*		
1844 Small 44	12	25	150	425	1856	10	25	150	425
1844 Large 44	18	35	175	450	1857	10	25	150	425
1845	12	25	150	425	1858	10	25	150	425
1846	12	25	150	450	1858 Proof *FDC*		*Extremely rare*		
1847 An example in fair condition sold at DNW,					1859	10	25	150	425
29/9/10, lot 1773 for £850 + premium					1859/8	12	25	150	425
1848	50	125	575	1300	1860	12	25	150	425
1848/6 or 7	50	125	550	1200	1862	95	225	650	1350
1850	12	25	150	425	1863	70	150	450	1000
1850/3	18	35	200	375	1866		*Extremely rare*		

3909
Die number location above date

3912
Type 'A5' Sixpence

3909 Sixpence. Type A[2]. First head, R. Similar die number above date die axis ↑↓

	F	VF	EF	UNC		F	VF	EF	UNC
1864	10	25	150	425	1866	10	20	150	425
1865	10	25	165	400					

	F	VF	EF	UNC		F	VF	EF	UNC
	£	£	£	£		£	£	£	£

3910 Sixpence. Type A³. Second head, l. R. Similar die number above date die axis ↑↓

1867......................12	25	150	450	1873......................10	20	130	350
1867 Proof *FDC* £2250				1874......................10	20	130	350
1868......................12	25	150	450	1875......................10	20	130	350
1869......................12	25	185	500	1876......................12	25	150	475
1869 Proof *FDC* £2500				1877......................10	20	130	350
1870......................12	25	185	500	1878......................10	20	130	350
1870 plain edge Proof *FDC* £2500				1878 DRITANNIAR 150	400	950	—
1871......................10	20	130	375	1878 Proof *FDC* £2000			
1871 plain edge Proof *FDC* £2500				1878/7....................40	175	700	—
1872......................10	20	130	375	1879......................12	25	150	425

3911 Sixpence. Type A⁴. Second head, l. R. Similar No die number die axis ↑↓

1871......................10	20	130	400	1879 milled edge Proof *FDC* £2000
1871 Proof *FDC* £1850				1879 plain edge Proof *FDC* £2500
1877......................10	20	130	375	1880......................10	20	135	300
1879......................10	20	130	375	

3912 Sixpence. Type A⁵. Third head l. R. Similar die axis ↑↓

1880......................10	18	100	225	1883 plain edge Proof *FDC Extremely rare*
1880 Proof *FDC* £2250				1884......................10	18	95	200
1881......................10	18	95	200	1885......................10	18	95	200
1881 plain edge Proof *FDC Extremely rare*				1885 Proof *FDC* £2000
1881 milled edge Proof *FDC Extremely rare*				1886......................10	18	95	200
1882......................15	35	145	400	1886 Proof *FDC* £2000
1883......................10	18	95	200	1887......................10	18	85	200
1883 Small R legend 18	40	160	400	1887 Proof *FDC* £1750

3913 Groat (4d.). Young head l.R. Britannia seated r. date in ex, edge milled, die axis ↑↑

1837 Plain edge Proof £12000				1846...................... 10	20	80	190
1837 Milled edge Proof £10000				1847/6 (or 8) 35	125	425	800
1838.........................8	15	75	175	1848/6 15	40	110	225
1838 plain edge Proof *FDC* £1100				1848.........................8	18	80	175
1838 Milled edge Proof £1000				1848/7/6 15	35	135	375
1838/∞ 10	25	90	200	1849.........................7	18	80	175
1839.........................9	18	75	200	1849/8 10	20	90	190
1839 die axis ↑↑ Proof plain edge *FDC* £500				1851......................25	90	325	700
1839 die axis ↑↓ Proof plain edge *FDC* £550				1852......................45	140	450	950
1840.........................9	18	75	175	1853......................100	250	750	1600
1840 small round o...12	22	80	200	1853 Proof *FDC* milled edge £1000
1841.........................12	28	125	275	1853 Proof *FDC* plain edge £1100
1842......................10	20	80	200	1854.........................8	18	75	175
1842 Proof *FDC* £1200				1855.........................8	18	75	175
1842/1 12	22	85	250	1855/3 12	30	80	175
1843......................10	20	80	190	1857 Milled or plain edge proof *FDC* £1650
1843 4 over 5 15	28	90	275	1857 Plain edge pattern £2000
1844.........................9	18	85	190	1862 Plain or milled edge Proof *FDC* £2000
1845......................10	20	80	190	1862 Plain edge pattern *FDC* £2750

	F	VF	EF	UNC		F	VF	EF	UNC
	£	£	£	£		£	£	£	£

3914 Threepence. Type A[1]. First bust, young head, high relief, ear fully visible. Dei axis ↑↓
R Crowned 3; as Maundy threepence but with a less prooflike surface.

	F	VF	EF	UNC		F	VF	EF	UNC
1838*...................... 10		30	85	200	1851 reads 1551 £550				
1838 BRITANNIAB ...		*Extremely rare*			1851 5 over 8 18		45	165	300
1839*...................... 15		45	120	250	1852*.................... 60		200	575	875
1839 Proof (see Maundy)					1853 30		100	270	475
1840*...................... 12		38	95	250	1854 10		25	95	225
1841*...................... 13		42	110	250	1855 12		40	110	250
1842*...................... 15		45	130	275	1856 10		25	95	200
1843*...................... 10		30	85	200	1857 10		35	100	250
1844*...................... 12		40	100	200	1858 10		20	80	200
1845...................... 10		20	70	175	1858 BRITANNIAB ..		*Extremely rare*		
1846...................... 35		110	290	525	1858/6 18		40	175	—
1847*...................... 50		175	350	850	1858/5 15		35	135	—
1848*...................... 45		150	375	800	1859 10		20	80	200
1849...................... 12		45	115	250	1860 10		35	100	250
1850...................... 10		22	70	150	1861 10		20	80	200
1851...................... 10		30	90	225					

*Issued for Colonial use only.

3914A - Type A2   3914C - Type A4

3914A Threepence. Type A[2]. First bust variety, slightly older portrait with aquiline nose ↑↓

	F	VF	EF	UNC		F	VF	EF	UNC
1859...................... 10		20	80	175	1865 10		22	100	200
1860...................... 10		20	80	175	1866 10		20	80	175
1861...................... 10		20	80	175	1867 10		20	80	175
1862...................... 15		30	90	175	1868 10		20	80	175
1863...................... 18		40	100	200	1868 RRITANNIAR ..		*Extremely rare*		
1864...................... 10		20	80	175					

3914B Threepence. Type A[3]. Second Bust, slightly larger, lower relief, mouth fuller,
nose more pronounced, rounded truncation die axis ↑↓

	F	VF	EF	UNC
1867 10		30	100	225

3914C Threepence. Type A[4]. Obv. as last. R. Tie ribbon further from tooth border, cross on
crown nearer to tooth border die axis ↑↓

	F	VF	EF	UNC		F	VF	EF	UNC
1866		*Extremely rare*			1874 7		18	55	115
1867...................... 10		35	90	200	1875 7		18	55	115
1868...................... 10		35	90	200	1876 7		18	55	115
1869...................... 15		35	100	275	1877 8		20	65	125
1870...................... 8		20	75	150	1878 8		20	65	125
1871...................... 10		25	80	175	1879 8		20	65	125
1872...................... 10		25	80	175	1879 Proof *FDC*........		*Extremely rare*		
1873...................... 6		18	55	125	1884 6		10	55	100

3914D Threepence. Type A[5]. Third bust, older features, mouth closed, hair strands
leading from 'bun' vary, die axis ↑↓

	F	VF	EF	UNC		F	VF	EF	UNC
1880...................... 6		15	60	115	1885 5		10	45	100
1881...................... 5		10	45	100	1885 Proof *FDC*.........		*Extremely rare*		
1882...................... 7		15	70	175	1886 5		10	45	100
1883...................... 5		10	45	100	1887 6		15	60	115

3914E Twopence. Young head 1. R Date divided by a crowned 2 within a wreath, die axis ↑↓

	F	VF	EF	UNC		F	VF	EF	UNC
1838...................... 5		12	30	75	1848 7		15	40	85

3915 - Three-Halfpence

	F	VF	EF	UNC		F	VF	EF	UNC
	£	£	£	£		£	£	£	£

3915 Three-Halfpence. (for Colonial use).Young head 1. R. Crowned value and date, die axis ↑↓

1838	7	15	50	125	1843 Proof *FDC*			*Extremely rare*	
1838 Proof *FDC* £750.					1843/34	7	20	75	165
1839	6	12	45	110	1843/34 Proof *FDC*			*Extremely rare*	
1840	10	25	90	200	1860	8	20	75	175
1841	6	18	55	135	1862	8	20	75	175
1842	6	18	55	135	1862 Proof *FDC* £1000				
1843	6	10	40	110	1870 Proof only £1250				

3916 - 1880 Maundy Set

3916 Maundy Set. (4d., 3d., 2d. and 1.) Young head 1., die axis ↑↓

	EF	UNC		EF	UNC
1838	225	550	1864	150	375
1838 Proof *FDC* £1350			1865	150	375
1838 Proof in gold *FDC* £22500			1866	140	360
1839	200	525	1867	140	360
1839 Proof die axis ↑↑ *FDC* £775			1867 Proof set *FDC* £1250		
1840	250	575	1868	140	360
1841	300	675	1869	150	400
1842	250	525	1870	140	360
1843	200	500	1871	125	320
1844	230	575	1871 Proof set *FDC* £1250		
1845	200	475	1872	125	320
1846	300	700	1873	125	320
1847	300	625	1874	125	320
1848	300	625	1875	125	320
1849	250	575	1876	125	320
1850	180	525	1877	125	320
1851	180	500	1878	135	350
1852	175	350	775	1878 Proof set *FDC* £1250	
1853	235	600	1879	125	320
1853 Proof *FDC* £975			1880	125	320
1854	185	500	1881	125	320
1855	200	500	1881 Proof set *FDC* £1250		
1856	150	375	1882	125	320
1857	200	450	1882 Proof set *FDC* £1250		
1858	150	350	1883	125	320
1859	150	350	1884	125	320
1860	150	350	1885	125	320
1861	165	350	1886	125	320
1862	180	425	1887	135	350
1863	180	425			

				from	EF	UNC
3917 — **Fourpence**, 1838-87				*from*	15	35
3918 — **Threepence**, 1838-87				*from*	20	55
3919 — **Twopence**, 1838-87				*from*	12	35
3920 — **Penny**, 1838-87				*from*	15	40

Maundy Sets in good quality original cases are worth approximately £20 more than the prices quoted.
Refer to footnote after 3796.

Jubilee Coinage 1887-93, die axis ↑↑

3921
1887 Crown

	F	VF	EF	UNC		F	VF	EF	UNC
	£	£	£	£		£	£	£	£

3921 Crown. Jubilee bust l. R. St. George and dragon,date in ex, edge milled, die axis ↑↑

1887	30	45	95	200	1889	30	45	115	300
1887 Proof *FDC* £1200					1890	30	55	150	350
1888 narrow date	30	50	150	325	1891	30	65	185	425
1888 wide date	120	300	625	1000	1892	40	70	235	500

3922 Double-Florin (4s.).Jubilee bust l. R. (As Florin) Crowned cruciform shields. Sceptre in
angles. Roman I in date, die axis ↑↑

1887	25	45	85	175
1887 Proof *FDC* £750				

3923
1887 Double-Florin
Arabic 1 in date

3924
1887 Halfcrown

3923 Double-Florin Jubilee bust l. R. Similar but Arabic 1 in date, die axis ↑↑

1887	25	40	80	150	1889	25	45	95	200
1887 Proof *FDC* £600					1889 inverted 1 for I in				
1888	25	45	90	200	VICTORIA	50	90	300	625
1888 inverted 1 for I in					1890	25	55	115	250
VICTORIA	45	85	225	600					

3924 Halfcrown. Jubilee bust l. R. Crowned shield in garter and collar, die axis ↑↑

1887	18	25	45	100	1890	20	35	110	220
1887 Proof *FDC* £350					1891	20	35	125	325
1888	20	30	85	200	1892	20	40	135	250
1889	20	35	85	200					

3925
1890 Florin reverse

	F	VF	EF	UNC		F	VF	EF	UNC
	£	£	£	£		£	£	£	£

3925 Florin. Jubilee bust l. ℞. Crowned cruciform shields, sceptres in angles, die axis ↑↑

	F	VF	EF	UNC		F	VF	EF	UNC
1887	12	20	40	85	1890	18	50	200	500
1887 Proof *FDC* £275					1891	35	85	350	700
1888 obverse die of 1887	20	50	110	215	1892	40	95	400	825
1888	15	35	70	150	1892 Proof *FDC* £8500				
1889	15	40	95	200					

3926
small head Shilling

3926 Shilling. Small Jubilee head. ℞. Crowned shield in Garter, die axis ↑↑

	F	VF	EF	UNC		F	VF	EF	UNC
1887	8	15	25	55	1888/7	10	20	55	125
1887 Proof *FDC* £200					1889	55	135	475	875

3927 Shilling. Large Jubilee head. ℞. Similar as before, die axis ↑↑

	F	VF	EF	UNC		F	VF	EF	UNC
1889	10	18	60	125	1891	15	25	80	165
1889 Proof *FDC* £1650					1891 Proof *FDC* £1850				
1890	12	22	70	150	1892	15	25	80	165

3928
1887 'withdrawn type' Sixpence

3928 Sixpence. JEB designer's initials below trun. ℞. Shield in Garter (withdrawn type), die axis ↑↑

	F	VF	EF	UNC		F	VF	EF	UNC
1887	7	12	20	40	1887 JEB on trun.	30	75	160	375
1887 Proof *FDC* £150					1887 R/V in				
					VICTORIA	25	55	135	275

		3929				3930		
		Crowned value Sixpence				1888 Groat		

F	VF	EF	UNC		F	VF	EF	UNC
£	£	£	£		£	£	£	£

3929 Sixpence. ℞. Jubilee bust 1. Crowned, value in wreath, die axis ↑↑

1887...................7	12	20	50	1890 10	20	45	110
1887 Proof *FDC* £975				1890 Proof *FDC*........	*Extremely rare*		
1888...................9	18	35	100	1891 12	25	50	120
1888 Proof *FDC* £1500				1892 14	30	55	135
1889...................9	18	35	100	1893 500	1000	3000	5500

3930 Groat (for use in British Guiana). Jubilee Bust 1. ℞. Britannia seated r. date in axis, die axis ↑↑

1888 Milled edge Proof *FDC* £1000				1888 15	40	80	185

3931 Threepence. As Maundy but less prooflike surface, die axis ↑↑

1887...................... —	4	10	25	1890 4	7	15	40
1887 Proof *FDC* £120				1891 4	7	18	45
1888...................5	8	20	50	1892 5	8	20	50
1889...................4	7	15	40	1893 25	70	175	400

3932
1889 Maundy Set

	EF	FDC			EF	FDC
	£	£			£	£

3932 Maundy Set. (4d., 3d., 2d. and 1d.) Jubilee bust 1.die axis ↑↑

1888...	125	225	1890		125	225
1888 Proof set *FDC* ....*Extremely rare*			1891		125	225
1889...	125	225	1892		125	225

			EF	FDC
3933 — Fourpence, 1888-92 ....*from*			15	35
3934 — Threepence, 1888-92 ....*from*			20	40
3935 — Twopence, 1888-92 ....*from*			12	30
3936 — Penny, 1888-92...*from*			18	40

Maundy Sets in the original undamaged cases are worth approximately £15 more than the prices quoted.
See footnote after 3796.

Old Head Coinage 1893-1901, die axis ↑↑

3937

1893 Old Head Crown

	F	VF	EF	UNC
	£	£	£	£

3937 Crown. Old veiled bust l. R. St. George. date in ex. Regnal date on edge, die axis ↑↑

	F	VF	EF	UNC
1893 edge LVI	22	35	195	400
1893 Proof *FDC* £1350				
1893 LVII	35	95	450	800
1894 LVII	22	50	300	650
1894 LVIII	22	50	300	650
1895 LVIII	22	45	250	600
1895 LIX	22	45	225	575
1896 LIX	25	75	400	750
1896 LX	22	50	250	600
1897 LX	22	45	225	550
1897 LXI	22	45	225	550
1898 LXI	35	95	500	900
1898 LXII	22	45	300	625
1899 LXII	22	45	225	600
1899 LXIII	22	45	265	650
1900 LXIII	22	45	225	600
1900 LXIV	22	45	200	550

3938

Halfcrown

	F	VF	EF	UNC		F	VF	EF	UNC
	£	£	£	£		£	£	£	£

3938 Halfcrown. Old veiled bust l. R. Shield in collar, edge milled, die axis ↑↑

	F	VF	EF	UNC		F	VF	EF	UNC
1893	15	35	65	150	1897	15	35	75	175
1893 Proof *FDC* £650					1898	18	45	100	250
1894	18	50	150	350	1899	18	40	90	225
1895	15	45	125	275	1900	18	35	75	175
1896	15	45	125	275	1901	18	35	80	200

3938A Small reverse design with long border teeth

	F	VF	EF	UNC
1896	20	45	165	315

3939
Old Head Florin

	F	VF	EF	UNC		F	VF	EF	UNC
	£	£	£	£		£	£	£	£

3939 Florin. Old veiled bust l. R. Three shields within garter, die axis ↑↑

	F	VF	EF	UNC		F	VF	EF	UNC
1893	12	25	65	135	1897	12	25	70	150
1893 Milled edge Proof *FDC* £400					1898	12	30	85	200
1894	15	35	125	300	1899	12	25	80	175
1895	14	30	95	225	1900	12	25	70	150
1896	14	30	95	225	1901	12	25	75	165

3940A
1901 Shilling

3941
1897 Sixpence

3940 Shilling. Old veiled bust l. R. Three shields within Garter, small rose, die axis ↑↑

	F	VF	EF	UNC		F	VF	EF	UNC
1893	12	25	55	110	1894	12	25	70	150
1893 small lettering	12	20	50	100	1895	15	30	80	175
1893 Proof *FDC* £250					1896	12	25	70	150

3940A Shilling. Old veiled bust l. R. Second reverse, larger rose, die axis ↑↑

	F	VF	EF	UNC		F	VF	EF	UNC
1895	12	20	60	125	1899	12	20	60	125
1896	12	18	55	120	1900	12	18	55	120
1897	12	18	50	110	1901	12	18	55	120
1898	12	18	55	120					

3941 Sixpence. Old veiled bust l. R. Value in wreath, die axis ↑↑

	F	VF	EF	UNC		F	VF	EF	UNC
1893	9	15	35	95	1897	10	20	40	85
1893 Proof *FDC* £185					1898	10	20	45	95
1894	12	20	50	125	1899	10	20	45	95
1895	10	20	45	100	1900	10	20	45	95
1896	10	20	45	95	1901	9	15	40	85

3942 Threepence. Old veiled bust l. R. Crowned 3. As Maundy but less prooflike surface, die axis ↑↑

	F	VF	EF	UNC		F	VF	EF	UNC
1893	4	7	15	55	1897	4	7	15	40
1893 Proof *FDC* £125					1898	4	7	15	45
1894	4	8	22	65	1899	4	7	15	45
1895	4	8	20	55	1900	4	7	12	40
1896	4	7	20	55	1901	4	7	15	40

3943
1901 Maundy Set

	EF	FDC		EF	FDC
	£	£		£	£

3943 Maundy Set. (4d., 3d., 2d. and 1d.) Old veiled bust l., die axis ↑↑

1893	110	160	1898	115	165
1894	115	180	1899	115	165
1895	115	165	1900	115	165
1896	115	165	1901	115	160
1897	115	165			

3944 — **Fourpence.** 1893-1901	*from*	10	25
3945 — **Threepence.** 1893-1901	*from*	18	35
3946 — **Twopence.** 1893-1901	*from*	10	25
3947 — **Penny.** 1893-1901	*from*	18	35

Maundy Sets in the original undamaged cases are worth approximately £15 more than the prices quoted. See footnote after 3796.

COPPER AND BRONZE

Young Head Copper Coinage, 1838-60, die axis ↑↑

3948
Penny
Rev. with ornamental trident prongs (OT)

	F	VF	EF	UNC		F	VF	EF	UNC
	£	£	£	£		£	£	£	£

3948 Penny. Young head l. date below R̩. Britannia seated r.

1839 Bronzed proof *FDC* £1600					1845 OT	16	40	275	775
1841 Rev. OT	15	60	275	850	1846 OT	12	30	225	675
1841 Proof *FDC* £2000					1846 OT colon close .				
1841 Silver Proof *FDC* £5750					to DEF	16	35	250	725
1841 OT. no colon					1847 — —	10	25	200	550
after REG	6	25	150	475	1847 OT DEF—:...	10	25	200	550
1843 OT. —	75	275	1750	4000	1848/7 OT	6	25	200	575
1843 OT REG:	85	400	2250	4250	1848 OT	6	25	200	575
1844 OT	12	25	200	575	1848/6 OT	25	140	675	—
1844 Proof *FDC* £2500					1849 OT	225	600	2250	4000

Copper coins graded in this catalogue as UNC have full mint lustre.

	F	VF	EF	UNC		F	VF	EF	UNC
	£	£	£	£		£	£	£	£

3948 Penny. (Continued)

	F	VF	EF	UNC		F	VF	EF	UNC
1851 OT 20	30	225	750		1856 Proof *FDC* £2500				
1851 OT DEF:.........15	25	200	675		1856 OT DEF—:.....115	400	1150	2750	
1853 OT DEF—:.......6	15	135	425		1857 OT DEF—:.......10	20	150	500	
1853 Proof *FDC* £1850					1857 PT DEF: 6	15	140	475	
1853 Plain trident, (PT)					1858 OT DEF—:.........6	12	125	400	
DEF: 18	35	165	575		1858/7 — — 6	15	140	475	
1854 PT 6	15	135	425		1858/2 10	30	140	475	
1854/3 PT 15	65	250	675		1858 no ww on trun 6	18	140	475	
1854 OT DEF—:.....10	20	140	450		1859 7	20	150	500	
1855 OT — 6	15	140	425		1859 Proof *FDC* £3000				
1855 PT DEF: 6	15	150	425		1860/59 600	1500	3750	6000	
1856 PT DEF: 115	300	800	2500						

3949
1845 Halfpenny

3949 Halfpenny. Young head l. date below R. Britannia seated r., die axis ↑↑   1853 Rev. incuse dots

	F	VF	EF	UNC		F	VF	EF	UNC
1838...........................8	18	90	300		1852 Rev. normal shield .12	25	110	325	
1839 Bronzed proof FDC £450					1853 dots on shield........5	10	55	150	
1841 6	15	80	250		1853 — Proof FDC £700				
1841 — Proof FDC £1250					1853/2 — 18	45	165	375	
1841 Silver proof FDC		*Extremely rare*			1854 — 5	10	60	150	
1843 30	55	225	700		1855 — 5	10	60	165	
1844 15	40	175	350		1856 — 6	16	80	250	
1845 200	450	1600	—		1857 — 5	15	70	185	
1846 15	40	175	350		1857 Rev. normal				
1847 15	40	175	350		shield 5	12	65	175	
1848 30	75	225	550		1858 — 6	12	70	200	
1848/7 15	35	175	350		1858/7 — 6	12	70	200	
1851 6	18	90	300		1858/6 — 6	12	70	200	
1851 Rev. incuse dots ..					1859 — 6	12	70	200	
on shield 6	20	100	325		1859/8 — 12	22	110	325	
1852 Similar..............10	20	95	300		1860* — 1400	3500	7000	11000	

Overstruck dates are listed only if commoner than normal date, or if no normal date is known.

*These 1860 large copper pieces are not to be confused with the smaller and commoner bronze issue with date on reverse (nos. 3954, 3956 and 3958).

Copper coins graded in this catalogue as UNC have full mint lustre.

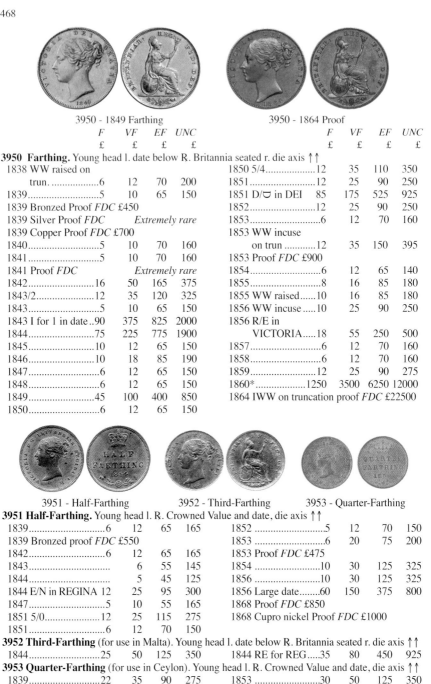

3950 - 1849 Farthing   3950 - 1864 Proof

	F	VF	EF	UNC
	£	£	£	£

3950 Farthing. Young head l. date below Ŗ. Britannia seated r. die axis ↑↑

	F	VF	EF	UNC		F	VF	EF	UNC
1838 WW raised on trun. 6	12	70	200	1850 5/4..................12	35	110	350
1839..........................5	10	65	150	1851..........................12	25	90	250
1839 Bronzed Proof *FDC* £450				1851 D/Ʊ in DEI	85	175	525	925
1839 Silver Proof *FDC*		*Extremely rare*		1852..........................12	25	90	250
1839 Copper Proof *FDC* £700				1853..........................6	12	70	160
1840..........................5	10	70	160	1853 WW incuse on trun 12	35	150	395
1841..........................5	10	70	160	1853 Proof *FDC* £900			
1841 Proof *FDC*		*Extremely rare*		1854..........................6	12	65	140
1842........................16	50	165	375	1855..........................8	16	85	180
1843/2.....................12	35	120	325	1855 WW raised......10	16	85	180
1843..........................5	10	65	150	1856 WW incuse 10	25	90	250
1843 I for 1 in date ..90	375	825	2000	1856 R/E in VICTORIA.....18	55	250	500
1844........................75	225	775	1900	1857..........................6	12	70	160
1845........................10	12	65	150	1858..........................6	12	70	160
1846........................10	18	85	190	1859........................12	25	90	275
1847..........................6	12	65	150	1860*..................1250	3500	6250	12000
1848..........................6	12	65	150	1864 IWW on truncation proof *FDC* £22500			
1849........................45	100	400	850				
1850..........................6	12	65	150				

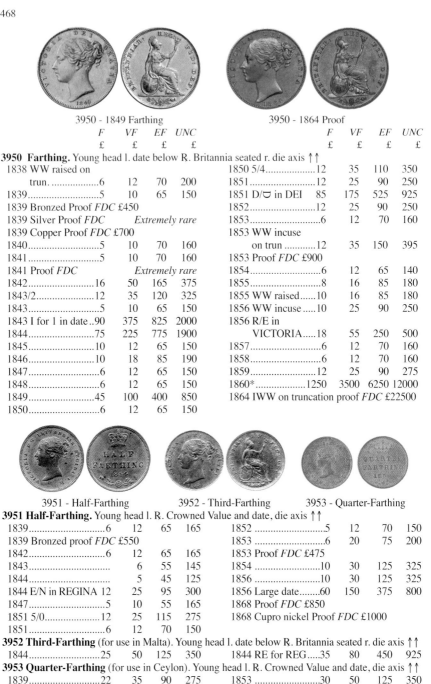

3951 - Half-Farthing   3952 - Third-Farthing   3953 - Quarter-Farthing

3951 Half-Farthing. Young head l. Ŗ. Crowned Value and date, die axis ↑↑

	F	VF	EF	UNC		F	VF	EF	UNC
1839..........................6	12	65	165	1852 5	12	70	150
1839 Bronzed proof *FDC* £550				1853 6	20	75	200
1842..........................6	12	65	165	1853 Proof *FDC* £475			
1843..........................	6	55	145	1854 10	30	125	325
1844..........................	5	45	125	1856 10	30	125	325
1844 E/N in REGINA 12	25	95	300	1856 Large date........60	150	375	800
1847..........................5	10	55	165	1868 Proof *FDC* £850			
1851 5/0...................12	25	115	275	1868 Cupro nickel Proof *FDC* £1000			
1851..........................6	12	70	150				

3952 Third-Farthing (for use in Malta). Young head l. date below Ŗ. Britannia seated r. die axis ↑↑

	F	VF	EF	UNC		F	VF	EF	UNC
1844........................25	50	125	350	1844 RE for REG.....35	80	450	925

3953 Quarter-Farthing (for use in Ceylon). Young head l. Ŗ. Crowned Value and date, die axis ↑↑

	F	VF	EF	UNC		F	VF	EF	UNC
1839........................22	35	90	275	1853 30	50	125	350
1851........................20	30	85	250	1853 Proof *FDC* £1000			
1852........................20	30	80	200	1868 Proof *FDC* £850			
1852 Proof *FDC* £1100				1868 Cupro-nickel Proof *FDC* £1100			

Copper coins graded in this catalogue as UNC have full mint lustre.

*These 1860 large copper pieces are not to be confused with the smaller and commoner bronze issue with date on reverse (nos. 3954, 3956 and 3958).

Bronze Coinage, "Bun Head" Issue, 1860-95, die axis ↑↑

When studying an example of the bronze coinage, if the minutiae of the variety is not evident due to wear from circulation, then the coin will not be of any individual significance. Proofs exist of most years and are generally extremely rare for all denominations.

3954 The Bronze Penny. The bronze coinage is the most complicated of the milled series from the point of view of the large number of different varieties of obverse and reverse and their combinations. Below are set out illustrations with explanations of all the varieties. The obverse and reverse types listed below reflect those as listed originally by C W Peck in his British Museum Catalogue of Copper, Tin and Bronze Coinage 1558-1958, and later in "The Bronze Coinage of Great Britain" by Michael J Freeman which gives much fuller and detailed explanations of the types. Reference can also be compared to "The British Bronze Penny" by Michael Gouby.

OBVERSES

Obverse 1 (1860) - laureate and draped bust facing left, hair tied in bun, wreath of 15 leaves and 4 berries, L C WYON raised on base of bust, **beaded border** and thin linear circle.

Obverse 1* (1860) - laureate and draped bust facing left, hair tied in bun, **more bulging lowered eye with more rounded forehead**, wreath of **15 leaves and 4 berries**, which are weaker in part, L C WYON raised on base of bust, **beaded border** and thin linear circle.

Obverse 3 (1860-61) - laureate and draped bust facing left, hair tied in bun, **complete rose to drapery**, wreath of 15 leaves and 4 berries, **two leaves have incuse outlines**, L C WYON raised on base of bust **nearly touches border**, toothed border and thin linear circle both sides.

Obverse 2 (1860-62) - laureate and draped bust facing left, hair tied in bun, wreath of 15 leaves and 4 berries, **L C WYON** raised **lower on base of bust** and clear of border, **toothed border** and thin linear circle both sides.

Obverse 4 (1860-61) - laureate and draped bust facing left, hair tied in bun, **finer hair strands at nape of neck**, wreath of 15 leaves and 4 berries, two leaves have incuse outlines, **L C WYON below bust, nearly touches border, toothed border of shorter teeth**, and thin linear circle both sides.

OBVERSES (*continued*)

Obverse 5 (1860-61) - laureate and draped bust facing left, hair tied in bun, **finer hair strands at nape of neck**, wreath of 15 leaves and 4 berries, **leaf veins incuse**, two leaves have incuse outlines, **no signature below bust**, toothed border and thin linear circle both sides.

Obverse 7 (1874) - laureate and draped bust facing left, hair tied in bun, finer hair strands at nape of neck, **wreath of 17 leaves, leaf veins raised, 6 berries**, no signature, toothed border and thin linear circle both sides.

Obverse 6 (1860-74) - laureate and draped bust facing left, hair tied in bun, finer hair strands at nape of neck, **wreath of 16 leaves, leaf veins raised, no signature**, toothed border and thin linear circle both sides. There is a **prominent flaw** on the **top stop of the colon after D at the end of the legend**.

Obverse 8 (1874-79) - laureate and draped bust facing left, hair tied in bun, with **close thicker ties to ribbons**, wreath of 17 leaves, leaf veins raised, 6 berries, no signature, toothed border and thin linear circle both sides.

Obverse 9 (1879-81) - laureate and draped bust facing left, hair tied in bun, with close thicker ties, wreath of 17 leaves, **double leaf veins incuse**, 6 berries, no signature, toothed border and thin linear circle both sides.

OBVERSES (*continued*)

Obverse 10 (1880-81) - laureate and draped bust facing left, hair tied in bun, with close thicker ties, **wreath of 15 leaves, leaf veins raised and recessed**, **4 berries**, no signature, toothed border and thin linear circle both sides.

Obverse 12 (1881-94) - laureate and draped bust facing left, hair tied in bun, with close thicker ties, **no curls at nape of neck**, nose more hooked, wreath of 15 leaves, leaf veins raised, 4 berries, no signature, **toothed border, more numerous teeth**, and thin linear circle both sides, weak on obverse, **larger lettering**.

Obverse 11 (1881-83) - laureate and draped bust facing left, more **hooked nose**, hair tied in bun, with close thicker ties, nose more hooked, wreath of 15 leaves, **leaf veins raised**, 4 berries, no signature, toothed border and thin linear circle both sides, **weak circle on obverse**.

Obverse 13 (1889) - laureate and draped bust facing left, hair tied in bun, with close thicker ties, no curls at nape of neck, nose more hooked, **wreath of 14 leaves, leaf veins raised**, no signature, toothed border and thin linear circle both sides, larger lettering.

REVERSES

Reverse A (1860) - Britannia seated right on rocks with shield and trident, **crosses on shield outlined with double raised lines**, L.C.W. incuse below shield, date below in exergue, lighthouse with 4 windows to left, ship sailing to right, **beaded border** and linear circle.

Reverse C (1860) - Britannia seated right on rocks with shield and trident, **crosses on shield outlined with wider spaced thinner double raised lines, thumb touches St. George Cross**, L.C.W. incuse below shield, date below in exergue, lighthouse with 4 windows to left, rocks touch linear circle, ship sailing to right, **beaded border** and linear circle.

Reverse B (1860) - Britannia with **one incuse hemline**, seated right on rocks with shield and trident, **crosses on shield outlined with treble incuse lines**, L.C.W. incuse below shield, date below in exergue, lighthouse with 4 windows to left, ship sailing to right, **beaded border** and linear circle.

Reverse D (1860-61) - Britannia seated right on rocks with shield and trident, crosses on shield outlined with wider spaced thinner double raised lines, thumb touches St. George Cross, L.C.W. incuse below shield, date below in exergue, lighthouse with 4 windows to left, rocks touch linear circle, ship sailing to right, **toothed border**.

REVERSES *(continued)*

Reverse E (1860) - Britannia seated right on rocks with **thick rimmed shield and trident**, crosses on shield outlined with wider spaced thinner double raised lines, thumb touches St. George Cross, **L.C.W. incuse below foot**, date below in exergue, lighthouse with **sharper masonry** to left, **rocks touch linear circle**, ship sailing to right, toothed border.

Reverse G (1861-75) - Britannia seated right on rocks with **convex shield and trident**, no signature, date below in exergue, bell-topped lighthouse to left, **lamp area depicted with five vertical lines, no rocks to left, sea crosses linear circle**, ship sailing to right, toothed border.

Reverse F (1861) - Britannia seated right on rocks with thick rimmed shield and trident, **incuse lines on breastplate**, crosses on shield outlined with wider spaced thinner double raised lines, thumb touches St. George Cross, **no L.C.W. extra rocks**, date below in exergue, **lighthouse with rounded top** and sharp masonry, **three horizontal lines** between masonry and top, rocks touch linear circle, ship sailing to right, toothed border.

Reverse H (1874-75, 1877) - Britannia seated right on rocks, **smaller head, thinner neck**, with convex shield and trident, no signature, **narrow date** below in exergue, **tall thin lighthouse** to left with **6 windows, lamp area of four vertical lines**, close date numerals, **tiny rock to left, sea touches linear circle**, ship sailing to right, toothed border.

REVERSES (*continued*)

Reverse I (1874) - Britannia seated right on rocks with convex shield and trident, **thick trident shaft**, no signature, **narrow date** below in exergue, **thicker lighthouse** to left with **4 windows**, lamp area of four vertical lines, close date numerals, tiny rock to left, sea touches linear circle, ship sailing to right, toothed border.

Reverse L (1880) - Britannia seated right on rocks with shield and trident, **extra feather to helmet plume, trident with three rings above hand**, date below in exergue, lighthouse with **cluster of rocks to left**, ship sailing to right, toothed border.

Reverse J (1875-81) - **larger Britannia** seated right on rocks with shield and trident, **left leg more visible**, **wider date** below in deeper exergue, lighthouse to left, ship sailing to right, **sea does not meet linear circle either side**, toothed border.

Reverse M (1881-82) - larger Britannia seated right on rocks with shield and trident, **flatter shield heraldically coloured**, date and **H below in exergue**, lighthouse to left with faint masonry, ship sailing to right, **sea does not meet linear circle**, toothed border.

Reverse K (1876, 1879) - Britannia with **larger head** seated right on rocks with convex shield and trident, **thicker helmet**, no signature, **narrow date** and in exergue, **tall thin lighthouse** to left, tiny rock to left, **sea touches linear circle**, ship sailing to right, toothed border.

REVERSES (*continued*)

Reverse O (1882 - proof only) – **larger Britannia** seated right on rocks with shield and trident, flatter shield heraldically coloured, date and **H in exergue**, lighthouse to left with faint masonry, ship sailing to right, **sea meets linear circle**, toothed border with more teeth.

Reverse N (1881-94) - **thinner Britannia** seated right on rocks with shield and thinner trident, **helmet plume ends in a single strand**, shield heraldically coloured with different thickness crosses, date in exergue, thinner lighthouse to left, ship sailing to right, sea meets linear circle, toothed border with more teeth.

Beaded border

Toothed border

Shield outlined with double raised lines

Shield outlined with treble incuse lines

Normal nose

More hooked nose

3954

	F	VF	EF	UNC		F	VF	EF	UNC
	£	£	£	£		£	£	£	£

3954 Penny. Laur. bust l. Ʀ. Britannia seated r. date in ex. lighthouse l. ship to r., die axis ↑↑

	F	VF	EF	UNC		F	VF	EF	UNC
1860 obv 1, rev A 75	150	575	1600		1864 Upper serif 25	125	875	3350
1860 obv 1, rev B 20	60	325	1000		1864 Crosslet 4 30	175	1000	3850
1860 obv 1*, rev A .175	475	1250	2350		1865 obv 6, rev G.........10	25	200	825
1860 obv 1, rev C 70	135	600	2000		1865/3 obv 6, rev G 50	150	575	1600
1860 obv 1*, rev C .135	475	1100	2200		1866 obv 6, rev G...........5	20	115	550
1860 obv 1, rev D ..450	850	2300	3850		1867 obv 6, rev G........10	35	225	1000
1860 obv 2, rev B .475	875	2600	4250		1868 obv 6, rev G........15	45	275	1050
1860 obv 2, rev D.......5	20	80	350		1869 obv 6, rev G.......125	450	1750	4250
1860 — heavy flan. 2500	—	—	—		1870 obv 6, rev G.........12	30	175	700
1860 N/Z in ONE, 2+D 95	300	775	1750		1871 obv 6, rev G.........45	175	800	2000
1860 obv 3, rev D.......5	20	90	400		1872 obv 6, rev G...........5	20	95	475
1860 obv 3, rev E ... 150	375	925	2000		1873 obv 6, rev G...........5	20	95	475
1860 obv 4, rev D 4	15	90	500		1874 obv 6, rev G...........5	20	135	675
1860 obv 5, rev D..... 10	50	235	800		1874 obv 7, rev G.........10	40	150	550
1860 obv 6, rev D.....40	150	425	950		1874 obv 8, rev G.........25	60	200	850
1860 obv 6, rev G...500	1200	2600	—		1874 obv 8 rev H..........20	55	175	800
1861 obv 2, rev D.....80	200	500	1300		1874 obv 6, rev H.........35	90	400	925
1861 obv 2, rev F ... 135	275	900	1850		1874 obv 7, rev H.........10	40	150	550
1861 obv 2, rev G.....35	125	375	1000		1875 obv 8, rev G.........20	65	275	625
1861 obv 3, rev D ..300	600	1550	2850		1875 obv 8, rev H...........4	15	80	400
1861 obv 4, rev D.......4	20	95	500		1875 obv 8, rev J 5	20	95	450
1861 — — heavy flan...2500	—	—	—		1877 obv 8, rev J 4	15	90	400
1861 obv 4, rev F ... 125	350	1150	2850		1877 obv 8, rev H.....2000	—	—	—
1861 obv 4, rev G.....45	200	575	1750		1878 obv 8, rev J 4	20	120	650
1861 obv 5, rev D.......4	15	90	475		1879 obv 8, rev J 10	25	150	800
1861 obv 5, rev F ... 900	—	—	—		1879 obv 9, rev J 3	10	80	300
1861 obv 5, rev G... 125	400	1150	2350		1879 obv 9, rev K.........30	100	375	1400
1861 obv 6, rev D 4	15	90	350		1880 obv 9, rev J 4	20	150	550
1861 — — — 6 over 8 500	2000	—	—		1880 obv 9, rev L...........4	20	150	550
1861 obv 6, rev F ..200	600	1550	—		1881 obv 9, rev J 4	20	125	650
1861 obv 6, rev G.......4	15	90	400		1881 obv 10, rev J 35	100	375	950
1861 — 8 over 6.....500	2000	—	—		1881 obv 11, rev J 65	175	575	1250
1862 obv 2, rev G...550	1350	2850	3650		1882† obv 11, rev N. 1000	3350	—	—
1862 obv 6, rev G.......4	15	90	350		1883 obv 12, rev N.........4	15	90	375
1862 — 8 over 6.....650	2000	—	—		1883 obv 11, rev N.........4	15	90	425
1862 — Halfpenny					1884 obv 12, rev N.........4	10	80	275
numerals 950	2950	4500	—		1885 obv 12, rev N.........4	10	80	275
1863 obv 6, rev G.......4	15	90	350		1886 obv 12, rev N.........4	12	80	300
1863 Die number below 1350	3850	—	—		1887 obv 12, rev N.........4	10	80	275
1863 slender 3 1100	2650	—	—		1888 obv 12, rev N.........4	12	80	300
1863/1 obv 6, rev G 1000	2600	—	—		1889 obv 12, rev N.........5	18	100	475

† not to be confused with Heaton Mint - H - the mint letter is the first device to disappear on worn specimens
Bronze coins graded in this catalogue as UNC have full mint lustre

autumn

	F £	VF £	EF £	UNC £		F £	VF £	EF £	UNC £

3954 Penny. (Continued)

	F	VF	EF	UNC		F	VF	EF	UNC
1889 obv 13, rev N..........4	10	70	275		1893 obv 12, rev N..........4	10	60	275
1890 obv 12, rev N..........4	10	70	275		1893 obv 12, rev N 3			
1891 obv 12, rev N..........4	10	65	275		over 2 600	—	—	—
1892 obv 12, rev N..........4	10	70	275		1894 obv 12, rev N..........4	18	95	350

3955 Penny. Similar R. Britannia, H Mint mark below date – (struck by Ralph Heaton & Sons, Birmingham)

	F	VF	EF	UNC		F	VF	EF	UNC
1874 H obv 6, rev G 8	25	125	475		1876 H obv 8, rev K 4	20	95	375
1874 H obv 6, rev H....12	35	175	575		1876 H obv 8, rev J........12	35	175	575
1874 H obv 6, rev I ...200	1000	2300	—		1881 H obv 11, rev M.....5	20	90	425
1874 H obv 7, rev G....12	35	150	525		1881 H obv 9, rev M 475	1250	2600	—
1874 H obv 7, rev H......8	25	125	450		1882 H obv12, rev M .. 12	30	150	650
1874 H obv 7, rev I ...175	480	2100	—		1882 H obv 12, rev N 4	15	80	300
1875 H obv 8, rev J 40	120	1050	2350		1882/1 H obv 11, rev M 12	30	125	850

3955
H Mint mark location

3956
1860 Halfpenny Beaded border

3956 Halfpenny. Laur. bust l. R. Britannia seated r. date in ex. lighthouse l. ship to r., die axis ↑↑

	F	VF	EF	UNC		F	VF	EF	UNC
1860 Beaded border 2	8	55	175		1861 — R. no hemline			
1860 no tie to wreath....8	18	110	400		to drapery 4	15	100	375
1860 Toothed border ...3	12	100	325		1861 — R. door on ...			
1860 round top light house	18	110	400		lighthouse.........2	8	80	250
1860 5 berries in					1861 HALP error .300	800	—	—
wreath.................5	15	100	375		1861 6 over 8 275	750	—	—
1860 — 15 leaves,					1862 1	6	70	200
4 berries..............3	12	95	300		1862 Die letter to left of lighthouse			
1860 — rounded					A................600	1400	2500	3750
lighthouse...........4	15	120	375		B................900	2000	—	—
1860 — Double incuse .					C.............1000	2500	—	—
leaf veins 5	16	110	400		1863 small 3.............2	8	95	325
1860 — 16 leaves					1863 large 3.............2	8	95	300
wreath..............12	35	165	525		1864 3	12	100	375
1860 TB/BBmule 700	1400	2600	—		1865 4	16	135	575
1861 5 berries in					1865/3....................50	125	375	1100
wreath..............12	35	150	475		1866 3	12	100	375
1861 15 leaves in					1867 3	16	110	475
wreath.................8	22	110	425		1868 2	12	100	400
1861 — R. no hemline .					1869 30	90	475	1350
to drapery 12	35	150	475		1870 3	10	95	350
1861 — R. Door on					1871 30	100	475	1350
lighthouse...........5	16	110	425		1872 3	10	90	275
1861 4 leaves double					1873 3	12	100	350
incuse veins 3	12	90	300		1873 R. hemline to			
1861 16 leaves wreath ..5	16	110	425		drapery 3	12	100	375
1861 — R. LCW incuse					1874 7	28	175	600
on rock..............12	35	150	475		1874 narrow date.... 16	65	400	900

Bronze coins graded in this catalogue as UNC have full mint lustre

	F £	VF £	EF £	UNC £		F £	VF £	EF £	UNC £

3956 Halfpenny.

1874 older features	8	30	175	600	1885	2	6	80	225
1875	2	8	90	275	1886	2	6	80	225
1877	2	8	90	275	1887	2	6	80	225
1878	6	25	150	550	1888	2	6	80	225
1878 wide date	100	200	500	1050	1889	2	6	80	225
1879	2	8	80	225	1889/8	30	65	250	550
1880	3	10	90	275	1890	2	6	70	200
1881	3	10	90	275	1891	2	6	70	200
1883	2	10	90	275	1892	3	8	90	275
1883 rose for brooch obv.	30	70	175	350	1893	2	6	80	225
1884	2	6	80	225	1894	3	9	90	275

3957 Halfpenny. Similar R. Britannia, H Mint mark below date (struck by Ralph Heaton & Sons, Birmingham)

1874 H	2	7	90	275	1881 H	2	7	90	275
1875 H	3	8	95	300	1882 H	2	7	90	275
1876 H	2	7	90	275					

3958
1860 Farthing

3960
1868 Third-Farthing

3958 Farthing. Laur bust l. R. Britannia seated r. date in ex. lighthouse l. ship to r. die axis ↑↑

1860 Beaded border		5	45	130	1875 small date	12	30	175	500
1860 Toothed border		8	55	150	1875 —older features	10	25	120	375
1860 — 5 berries		5	50	135	1877 Proof only £8000				
1860 TB/BB mule	175	475	1000	—	1878		5	40	130
1861 5 berries		5	50	135	1879 large 9		6	45	135
1861 4 berries		5	55	150	1879 normal 9		5	40	120
1862		5	55	135	1880		6	55	150
1862 large 8	60	190	400	—	1881		5	40	130
1863	25	55	300	625	1883	2	12	65	175
1864 4 no serif		8	60	160	1884		4	35	90
1864 4 with serif		10	65	175	1885		4	35	90
1865		5	50	135	1886		4	35	90
1865/2		12	60	190	1887		5	45	120
1866		5	45	135	1888		5	40	110
1867		5	55	150	1890		5	40	110
1868		6	55	150	1891		4	35	100
1869		12	65	190	1892	2	12	65	190
1872		5	50	135	1893		4	35	100
1873		4	50	135	1894		5	35	115
1875 large date	5	12	65	200	1895	10	30	110	325

Bronze coins graded in this catalogue as UNC have full mint lustre

	F	VF	EF	UNC		F	VF	EF	UNC
	£	£	£	£		£	£	£	£

3959 Farthing. Similar R. Britannia. H Mint mark below date (struck by Ralph Heaton & Sons, Birmingham)

	F	VF	EF	UNC		F	VF	EF	UNC
1874 H older features 5		12	65	165	1876 H large 6........10		35	100	235
1874 H,G over sideways					1876 H normal 6.....5		12	65	175
◡ on obv..............150		350	850	—	1881 H......................2		8	45	130
1875 H younger features .85		250	475	975	1882 H......................2		8	50	130
1875 H older features......4			35	120					

3960 Third-Farthing (for use in Malta). Laur. head l. R. Crowned date and Value die axis ↑↑

	F	VF	EF	UNC		F	VF	EF	UNC
1866...............................1		6	35	100	1881 2		8	40	110
1868...............................1		6	35	95	1884 1		6	35	100
1876...............................2		8	40	110	1885 1		6	35	100
1878...............................1		6	35	100					

Old Head Issue, 1885-1901, die axis ↑↑

Proofs exist of most years and are generally extremely rare for all denominations

3961
1897 Penny

	VF	EF	UNC		VF	EF	UNC
	£	£	£		£	£	£

3961 Penny. Old veiled bust l. R. Britannia seated r. date in ex., die axis ↑↑

	VF	EF	UNC		VF	EF	UNC
1895...........................	3	35	100	1898	10	45	110
1896...........................	5	40	90	1899	5	40	95
1897...........................	5	40	90	1900	8	35	80
1897 O'NE flawed	100	500	1500	1901	3	25	60

3961 'Normal Tide'	3961A 'Low Tide'
Horizon is level with folds in robe	Horizon is level with hem line of robe

3961A Penny. Similar As last but 'Low tide' and 'P' 2mm from trident, 1895...50   100   425   1400
3961B Penny. Similar, higher tide level above two folds of robe, 1897......25   75   400   1250
3962 Halfpenny. Old veiled bust l. R. Britannia seated r. date in ex., die axis ↑↑

	F	VF	EF		F	VF	EF
1895...........................	5	15	75	1898	5	15	75
1896...........................	4	12	70	1899	4	12	70
1897...........................	4	12	70	1900	4	12	65
1897 Higher tide level.	8	18	75	1901	2	10	55

	VF £	EF £	UNC £		VF £	EF £	UNC £

3963 Farthing. Old veiled bust l. R. Britannia seated r. date in ex. Bright finish, die axis ↑↑

| 1895 | 2 | 10 | 45 | 1897 | 5 | 15 | 50 |
| 1896 | 3 | 12 | 50 | | | | |

3962 - Old Head Halfpenny   3964 - Old Head Farthing

3964 Farthing. Similar Dark finish, die axis ↑↑

1897	2	10	40	1899	3	12	40
1897 Higher tide level.	5	16	50	1900	2	10	35
1898	3	12	40	1901		6	30

Proof Sets

PS3 Young head, **1839.** 'Una and the Lion' Five Pounds, and Sovereign to Farthing (15 coins) *FDC* £80000

PS4 — **1853.** Sovereign to Half-Farthing, including Gothic type Crown (16 coins) *FDC* £60000

PS5 Jubilee head. Golden Jubilee, **1887.** Five pounds to Threepence (11 coins)*FDC* £15000

PS6 — — **1887.** Crown to Threepence (7 coins) *FDC* £2850

PS7 Old head, **1893.** Five Pounds to Threepence (10 coins) *FDC* £18500

PS8 — — **1893.** Crown to Threepence (6 coins) *FDC* £3250

† *NB Truly 'FDC' proof sets are hardly ever encountered. Component coins showing any surface marks, hairlines or nicks will be worth less than the prices quoted above.*

EDWARD VII, 1901-10

'Edward the Peacemaker' was born on 9 November 1841, and married Princess Alexandra of Denmark. He indulged himself in every decadent luxury, while his wife tried to ignore his extra-marital activities. Edward travelled extensively and was crucial in negotiating alliances with Russia and France. Edward VII died on 6 May 1910.

Five Pound pieces, Two Pound pieces and Crowns were only issued in 1902. A branch of the Royal Mint was opened in Canada at Ottawa and coined Sovereigns of imperial type from 1908.

Unlike the coins in most other proof sets, the proofs issued for the Coronation in 1902 have a matt surface in place of the more usual brilliant finish.

Designer's initials: De S. (G. W. De Saulles 1862-1903)
B. P. (Benedetto Pistrucci, d. 1855)

Engravers and Designers: WHJ Blakemore, George William De Saulles (1862-1903), Benedetto Pistrucci (1784-1855)

GOLD

Die axis: ↑↑

3966 - Matt Proof Five Pounds 1902

	VF	EF	UNC		F	VF	EF	UNC
	£	£	£		£	£	£	£

3965 **Five Pounds.** Bare head r. R. St. George and dragon, date in ex.
1902 .... 1800 2250 2750 3750
3966 **Five Pounds.** Similar Proof. 1902. *Matt surface FDC* £2750
3966A **Five Pounds.** Similar Proof 1902S. S on ground for Sydney Mint, Australia   *Extremely rare*

3967 - 1902 Two Pounds   3969 - 1902 Sovereign

3967 **Two Pounds.** Bare head r. R. St George and dragon, date in ex.
1902.. 750 950 1250 1750
3968 **Two Pounds.** Similar Proof. 1902. *Matt surface FDC* £1500
3968A Two Pounds. Similar Proof 1902S. S on ground for Sydney Mint, Australia   *Extremely rare*
3969 **Sovereign.** Bare head r. R . St. George and dragon, date in ex. London mint, die axis ↑↑

1902 Matt proof *FDC* £500				1906	—	BV	375
1902...........................	—	BV	325	1907	—	BV	375
1903...........................	—	BV	375	1908	—	BV	375
1904...........................	—	BV	375	1909	—	BV	375
1905...........................	—	BV	375	1910	—	BV	375

3970 Sovereign. Similar R. C on ground for Ottawa Mint, Canada
1908 C (Satin proof only) *FDC* £7000   1909 C Satin finish
1909 C .... 325 475 850   specimen *FDC* ....*Extremely rare*
                                                                    1910 C........................ 300 450 750

BV= Bullion value only. At the time of going to press the spot price for gold was £1092 per oz.

| | *EF* | *UNC* | | *EF* | *UNC* |
| | £ | £ | | £ | £ |

3971 Sovereign. Similar R. St. George M on ground for Melbourne Mint, Australia, die axis ↑↑

1902 M .... BV	400	1906 M .... BV	425
1902 M Proof ....*Extremely rare*		1907 M .... BV	425
1903 M .... BV	425	1908 M .... BV	425
1904 M .... BV	425	1909 M .... BV	425
1904 M Proof ....*Extremely rare*		1910 M .... BV	425
1905 M .... BV	425	1910 M Proof ....*Extremely rare*	

3972 Sovereign. Similar R. P on ground for Perth Mint, Australia die axis ↑↑

1902 P............................... BV	425	1907 P................................... BV	400
1903 P............................... BV	450	1908 P................................... BV	400
1904 P............................... BV	450	1909 P................................... BV	400
1905 P............................... BV	400	1910 P................................... BV	425
1906 P............................... BV	400		

3973 Sovereign. Similar R. S on ground for Sydney Mint, Australia die axis ↑↑

1902 S .... BV	400	1906 S	400
1902 S Proof...........................*Extremely rare*		1907 S	400
1903 S .... BV	400	1908 S	400
1904 S .... BV	400	1909 S	400
1905 S .... BV	400	1910 S	400

3974A - 1902 Half-Sovereign, no BP in exergue

| | *F* | *VF* | *EF* | *UNC* | | *F* | *VF* | *EF* | *UNC* |
| | £ | £ | £ | £ | | £ | £ | £ | £ |

3974 A Half-Sovereign. Bare head r. R. St. George. London Mint no BP in exergue, die axis ↑↑

| 1902 Matt proof *FDC* £450 | | | | 1903...............................BV | 165 | 225 |
| 1902................................BV | 165 | 225 | 1904...............................BV | 165 | 225 |

3974 B Half-Sovereign. R. Similar with BP in exergue

1904 ....BV	165	225	1908 ....BV	165	225
1905 ....BV	165	225	1909 ....BV	165	225
1906...............................BV	165	225	1910...............................BV	165	225
1907 ....BV	165	225			

3975 Half-Sovereign. Similar R. M on ground for Melbourne Mint, Australia, die axis ↑↑

| 1906 M ....165 | 400 | 1500 | 4000 | 1908 M ....BV | 165 | 275 | 950 |
| 1907 M ....BV | 165 | 250 | 1500 | 1909 M ....BV | 165 | 300 | 1300 |

3976 A Half-Sovereign. — P on ground for Perth Mint, Australia R. no BP in exergue, die axis ↑↑

| 1904 P..................165 | 300 | 1950 | 9500 | | | | |

3976 B Half-Sovereign. Similar R. P on ground for Perth Mint, Australia R. with BP in exergue, die axis ↑↑

| 1904 P.......................................*Extremely rare* | | | | 1909 P..................165 | 300 | 1000 | 4500 |
| 1908 P..................165 | 300 | 1950 | 8500 | | | | |

3977 A Half-Sovereign. Similar R. S on ground for Sydney Mint, Australia R. No BP in exergue, die axis ↑↑

| 1902 S ....BV | 165 | 250 | 750 | 1903 S ....BV | 165 | 200 | 1250 |
| 1902 S Proof............................*Extremely rare* | | | | | | | |

3977 B Half-Sovereign. — S on ground for Sydney Mint, Australia R. with BP in exergue, die axis ↑↑

| 1906 S ....BV | 165 | 850 | 1910 S ....BV | 150 | 500 |
| 1908 S ....BV | 165 | 525 | | | |

BV= Bullion value only. At the time of going to press the spot price for gold was £1092 per oz.

SILVER

3978
1902 Crown

| F | VF | EF | UNC | | F | VF | EF | UNC |

3978 Crown. Bare head r. R. St. George and dragon date in ex. die axis ↑↑

1902.........................80   140   240   375   1902 error edge inscription.... *Extremely rare*

3979 Crown. Similar Matt proof *FDC* £325

3980   3981
1904 Halfcrown   Florin

3980 Halfcrown. Bare head r. R. Crowned Shield in Garter, die axis ↑↑

1902......................... 20	45	110	250	1906........................ 20	65	325	950
1902 Matt proof *FDC* £225				1907........................ 20	60	300	900
1903*.................. 200	625	2500	5000	1908........................ 25	60	500	1250
1904*.................... 70	325	1000	2750	1909........................ 20	55	400	1000
1905*.................. 600	1750	5000	10000	1910........................ 20	45	275	700

3981 Florin. Bare head r. R. Britannia standing on ship's bow die axis ↑↑

1902...................... 10	25	75	135	1906........................ 15	35	175	500
1902 Matt proof *FDC* £150				1907........................ 15	45	200	525
1903...................... 15	35	175	450	1908........................ 20	55	335	775
1904...................... 20	50	250	575	1909........................ 20	55	315	725
1905...................... 70	200	800	1750	1910........................ 15	30	135	375

*Beware of recent forgeries.

3982
1902 Shilling

3983
1902 Sixpence

	F	VF	EF	UNC		F	VF	EF	UNC
	£	£	£	£		£	£	£	£

3982 Shilling. Bare head r. R. Lion passant on crown die axis ↑↑

	F	VF	EF	UNC		F	VF	EF	UNC
1902	8	16	65	110	1906	8	15	80	250
1902 Matt proof *FDC* £115					1907	8	15	85	275
1903	10	25	175	475	1908	15	30	190	525
1904	10	20	150	425	1909	15	30	190	525
1905	125	350	1350	2750	1910	8	15	75	150

3983 Sixpence. Bare head r. R. Value in wreath die axis ↑↑

	F	VF	EF	UNC		F	VF	EF	UNC
1902	8	15	55	90	1906	7	15	60	130
1902 Matt proof *FDC* £95					1907	8	15	65	135
1903	7	15	60	135	1908	8	16	70	150
1904	10	30	125	300	1909	7	15	65	130
1905	8	25	90	225	1910	7	10	50	90

3984 Threepence. As Maundy but dull finish die axis ↑↑

	F	VF	EF	UNC		F	VF	EF	UNC
1902	4	7	15	35	1906	5	10	40	110
1902 Matt proof *FDC* £35					1907	5	10	30	60
1903	5	10	30	60	1908	4	7	15	50
1904	6	12	40	110	1909	5	10	30	60
1905	5	10	30	85	1910	4	7	15	50

3985
1903 Maundy Set

	EF	FDC		EF	FDC
	£	£		£	£

3985 Maundy Set (4d., 3d., 2d. and 1d.) Bare head r. die axis ↑↑

	EF	FDC		EF	FDC
1902	100	165	1906	100	165
1902 Matt proof *FDC* £175			1907	100	165
1903	100	165	1908	100	165
1904	100	165	1909	150	250
1905	100	165	1910	150	250

	EF	FDC
	£	£
3986 — **Fourpence.** 1902-10 ....*from*	10	25
3987 — **Threepence.** 1902-10 ....*from*	12	25
3988 — **Twopence.** 1902-10 ....*from*	10	25
3989 — **Penny.** 1902-10 ....*from*	15	30

Maundy sets in the original undamaged cases are worth approximately £15 more than the prices quoted.
See foontnote after 3796.

BRONZE

3990
1902 Penny

3990 Normal Tide

'3990A 'Low Tide'

	VG	F	VF	EF	UNC		VG	F	VF	EF	UNC
	£	£	£	£	£		£	£	£	£	£

3990 Penny. Bare head r. R. Britannia seated r. date in ex. die axis ↑↑

	VG	F	VF	EF	UNC		VG	F	VF	EF	UNC
1902....................			2	20	65	1906....................		6	30	110	
1903 Normal 3 ...			4	25	95	1907....................		3	35	120	
1903 Open 3 ...60	120	400	—	—		1908....................		6	30	110	
1904....................			10	55	150	1909....................		8	35	120	
1905....................			8	50	135	1910....................		4	25	100	

3990A Penny. Similar R. As last but 'Low tide', 1902 10   50   175   325

3991
Halfpenny

	VF	EF	UNC		F	VF	EF	UNC
	£	£	£		£	£	£	£

3991 Halfpenny. Bare head r. R̶. Britannia seated r. date in ex. die axis ↑↑

1902	2	18	55	1907		2	20	85
1903	4	20	80	1908		2	20	85
1904	4	28	120	1909		4	25	95
1905	4	25	95	1910		4	20	85
1906	4	25	90					

3991A Halfpenny. Similar R. As last but 'Low tide', 1902......................20   85   175   425

3992
Farthing

3993
1902 Third-Farthing

3992 Farthing. Bare head r. R. Britannia seated r. date in ex. Dark finish die axis ↑↑

1902	1	10	35	1907	2	12	40
1903	2	12	40	1908	2	12	40
1904	4	18	40	1909	2	12	40
1905	2	12	40	1910	4	25	50
1906	2	12	40				

3993 Third-Farthing (for use in Malta) Bare head r. R. Crowned date and value die axis ↑↑.
1902 8   25   60
No proofs of the bronze coins were issued in 1902

Proof Sets
PS9   Coronation, **1902.** Five Pounds to Maundy Penny, matt surface, (13 coins) *FDC*   £5500
PS10 — 1902. Sovereign to Maundy Penny, matt surface, (11 coins)...................*FDC*   £2150

† *NB Truly 'FDC' proof sets are hardly ever encountered. Component coins showing any surface marks, hairlines or nicks will be worth less than the prices quoted above.*

George V, the second son of Edward VII, was born on 3 June 1865 and married Mary of Teck who bore him five sons and a daughter. He was King through World War I and visited the front on several occassions. He suffered a fall breaking his pelvis on one of these visits, an injury that would pain him for the rest of his life. He watched the Empire divide; Ireland, Canada, Australia, New Zealand and India all went through changes. He died on 20th January 1936 only months after his Silver Jubilee.

Paper money issued by the Treasury during the First World War replaced gold for internal use after 1915 but the branch mints in Australia and South Africa (the main Commonwealth gold producing countries) continued striking Sovereigns until 1930-2. Owing to the steep rise in the price of silver in 1919/20 the issue of standard (.925) silver was discontinued and coins of .500 silver were minted.

In 1912, 1918 and 1919 some Pennies were made under contract by private mints in Birmingham. In 1918, as Half-Sovereigns were no longer being minted, Farthings were again issued with the ordinary bright bronze finish. Crown pieces had not been issued for general circulation but they were struck in small numbers about Christmas time for people to give as presents in the years 1927-36, and in 1935 a special commemorative Crown was issued in celebration of the Silver Jubilee.

As George V died on 20 January, it is likely that all coins dated 1936 were struck during the reign of Edward VIII.

Engravers and Designers:– George Kuger Gray (1880-1943), Bertram MacKennal (1863-1931), Benedetto Pistrucci (1784-1855) Percy Metcalfe (1895-1970)

Designer's initials:

B. M. (Bertram Mackennal)   P. M. (Percy Metcalfe)
K. G. (G. Kruger Gray)   B. P. (Benedetto Pistrucci; d. 1855)

Die axis: ↑↑

GOLD

£

3994 Five Pounds.* Bare head l. R. St. George and dragon, date in ex., 1911 (Proof only).....4000
3995 Two Pounds.* Bare head l. R. St. George and dragon, date in ex., 1911 (Proof only).....1750

3996

	VF	EF	UNC		VF	EF	UNC
	£	£	£		£	£	£

3996 Sovereign. Bare head l. R. St. George and dragon. London Mint die axis: ↑↑

	VF	EF	UNC		VF	EF	UNC
1911	BV	BV	425	1914	BV	BV	375
1911 Proof *FDC* £850				1915	BV	BV	375
1911 Matt Proof *FDC* of highest rarity				1916	BV	350	600
1912	BV	BV	375	1917*	5000	13500	—
1913	BV	BV	375	1925	BV	BV	350

Forgeries exist of these and of most other dates and mints.

BV= Bullion value only. At the time of going to press the spot price for gold was £1092 per oz.

	F	VF	EF	UNC		F	VF	EF	UNC
	£	£	£	£		£	£	£	£

3997 Sovereign. Bare head l. R. St George, C on ground for the Ottawa Mint, Canada die axis: ↑↑

1911 C ....BV	300	500	1917 C ....BV	300	425
1913 C 425	1350	—	1918 C ....BV	300	425
1914 C 300	750	—	1919 C ....BV	300	425
1916 C* 6000	13500	—			

* Beware of recent forgeries

3997
Canada 'c' Mint mark

3998 Sovereign. Similar R. I on ground for Bombay Mint, India 1918 ....BV   325   475

3999 Sovereign. Similar R. M on ground for Melbourne Mint, Australia die axis: ↑↑

1911 M .... BV	375	1920 M 1450	2750	4000	6250
1912 M .... BV	375	1921 M 5000	8500	12000	19500
1913 M .... BV	375	1922 M 4000	6000	9000	16000
1914 M .... BV	375	1923 M .... BV	325	400
1915 M .... BV	375	1924 M .... BV	325	400
1916 M .... BV	375	1925 M ....BV	375
1917 M .... BV	375	1926 M .... BV	325	400
1918 M .... BV	375	1928 M 950	1500	2150	3500
1919 M 325	425				

4000 Sovereign. Similar small bare head l. die axis: ↑↑

1929 M 650	1200	2150	3750	1930 M	BV	250	350
1929 M Proof *FDC* ....*Extremely rare*	1931 M 350	450	550	750

4000	4001
1930 M Sovereign, small head	Perth Mint Sovereign

4001 Sovereign. Similar R. P on ground for Perth Mint, Australia die axis: ↑↑

1911 P.........................BV	325	1920 P.........................BV	325
1912 P.........................BV	325	1921 P.........................BV	325
1913 P.........................BV	325	1922 P.........................BV	325
1914 P.........................BV	325	1923 P.........................BV	325
1915 P.........................BV	325	1924 P............. —	BV	325	400
1916 P.........................BV	325	1925 P...........BV	275	450	600
1917 P.........................BV	325	1926 P...........550	975	1650	3500
1918 P.........................BV	325	1927 P...........BV	275	475	650
1919 P.........................BV	325	1928 P............. —	BV	325	400

BV= Bullion value only. At the time of going to press the spot price for gold was £1092 per oz.

	VF	EF	UNC		F	VF	EF	UNC
	£	£	£		£	£	£	£

4002 Sovereign. Similar — small bare head l. die axis: ↑↑

| 1929 P | BV | 325 | 400 | 1931 P | BV | 325 |
| 1930 P | BV | 325 | 400 | | | |

4003 Sovereign. Similar R. S on ground for Sydney Mint, Australia die axis: ↑↑

1911 S	BV	325	1919 S			BV	375
1912 S	BV	325	†1920 S			*Of highest rarity*
1913 S	BV	325	1921 S	675	1000	1850	2500
1914 S	BV	325	1922 S	7500	12750	19500	27500
1915 S	BV	325	1923 S	5000	8750	14500	20000
1916 S	BV	325	1924 S	600	1200	1650	2750
1917 S	BV	325	1925 S			BV	375
1918 S	BV	325	1926 S	8500	16500	25000	32500

4004 Sovereign. Similar R. SA on ground for Pretoria Mint, South Africa die axis: ↑↑

1923 SA	2000	4000	7500	1926 SA	BV	325
1923 SA Proof *FDC* £1250				1927 SA	BV	325
1924 SA	3000	6000	—	1928 SA	BV	325
1925 SA	BV	325			

4005 Sovereign. Similar — small head die axis: ↑↑

| 1929 SA | BV | 325 | 1931 SA | BV | 325 |
| 1930 SA | BV | 325 | 1932 SA | BV | 325 |

† *An example of the proof 1920 S sold in an overseas auction in 2009 for the equivalent of £415,000*

4003
1921 Sydney 's' Sovereign

4006
1914 Half-sovereign

4006 Half-Sovereign. Bare head l. R. St. George and dragon date in ex. London Mint die axis: ↑↑

1911	BV	165	225	1913	BV	165	225
1911 Proof *FDC* £550				1914	BV	165	225
1911 Matt Proof *FDC of highest rarity*				1915	BV	165	225
1912	BV	165	225			

4007 Half-Sovereign. Similar R. M on ground for Melbourne Mint, Australia die axis: ↑↑

| 1915 M | | BV | BV | 225 |

4008 Half-Sovereign. Similar R. P on ground for Perth Mint, Australia die axis: ↑↑

| 1911 P | BV | 165 | 350 | 1918 P | 300 | 750 | 3000 | 4250 |
| 1915 P | BV | 150 | 325 | | | |

4009 Half-Sovereign. Similar R. S on ground for Sydney Mint, Australia die axis: ↑↑

1911 S	BV	BV	175	1915 S	BV	BV	175
1912 S	BV	BV	175	1916 S	BV	BV	175
1914 S	BV	BV	175			

4010 Half-Sovereign. Similar R. SA on ground for Pretoria Mint, South Africa die axis: ↑↑

| 1923 SA Proof *FDC* £975 | | | 1926 SA | BV | BV | 185 |
| 1925 SA | BV | BV | 185 | | | |

BV= Bullion value only. At the time of going to press the spot price for gold was £1092 per oz.

SILVER

First Coinage. Sterling silver (.925 fine)

4011
1911 Halfcrown

	F	VF	EF	UNC		F	VF	EF	UNC
	£	£	£	£		£	£	£	£

4011 Halfcrown. Bare head l. R. Crowned shield in Garter die axis: ↑↑

	F	VF	EF	UNC		F	VF	EF	UNC
1911	10	30	85	225	1915	10	15	40	90
1911 Proof *FDC* £250					1916	10	15	40	90
1912	10	30	75	200	1917	10	20	60	135
1913	10	35	85	250	1918	10	15	45	110
1914	10	15	45	100	1919	10	20	55	135

4012
1912 Florin

4013
1911 Proof

4012 Florin. Bare head l. R. Crowned Cruciform shields sceptres in angles die axis: ↑↑

	F	VF	EF	UNC		F	VF	EF	UNC
1911	8	15	60	145	1915	8	25	65	175
1911 Proof *FDC* £165					1916	8	15	50	95
1912	8	20	70	200	1917	8	18	55	120
1913	10	30	85	220	1918	8	15	45	95
1914	8	15	50	100	1919	8	18	55	125

4013 Shilling. Bare head l. R. Lion passant on crown, within circle die axis: ↑↑

	F	VF	EF	UNC		F	VF	EF	UNC
1911	5	12	40	80	1915		4	35	80
1911 Proof *FDC* £110					1916		4	35	80
1912	5	15	45	100	1917		5	40	110
1913	8	20	75	200	1918		4	35	80
1914	5	12	40	85	1919	4	10	45	95

4014
1911 Sixpence

| | F | VF | EF | UNC | | F | VF | EF | UNC |
| | £ | £ | £ | £ | | £ | £ | £ | £ |

4014 Sixpence. Bare head l. R. Lion passant on crown, within circle die axis: ↑↑

1911	3	10	30	60	1916	3	10	30	60
1911 Proof *FDC* £85					1917	6	18	55	150
1912	5	12	40	75	1918	3	10	30	60
1913	6	15	45	80	1919	5	12	35	70
1914	3	10	30	60	1920	6	15	45	85
1915	3	10	30	70					

4015 Threepence. As Maundy but dull finish die axis: ↑↑

1911	3	7	28	1916	3	7	22
1911 Proof *FDC* £45				1917	3	7	22
1912	3	7	28	1918	3	7	22
1913	3	7	28	1919	3	7	22
1914	3	7	28	1920	4	10	32
1915	3	7	32				

4016
1915 Maundy Set

| | EF | FDC | | EF | FDC |
| | £ | £ | | £ | £ |

4016 Maundy Set (4d., 3d., 2d. and 1d.) die axis: ↑↑

1911	115	180	1916	115	180
1911 Proof *FDC* £180			1917	115	180
1912	115	180	1918	115	180
1913	115	180	1919	115	180
1914	115	180	1920	145	215
1915	115	180			

4017 — Fourpence. 1911-20	*from*	12	30
4018 — Threepence. 1911-20	*from*	15	32
4019 — Twopence. 1911-20	*from*	10	25
4020 — Penny. 1911-20	*from*	12	30

See footnote after 3796

Second Coinage. Debased silver (.500 fine). Types as before.

	F	VF	EF	UNC		F	VF	EF	UNC
	£	£	£	£		£	£	£	£

4021 Halfcrown. Deeply engraved. Bare head l. R. Crowned shield in garter die axis: ↑↑

| 1920 | .....5 | 15 | 60 | 175 |

4021A — recut shallow portrait

1920	8	20	75	200	1924 Specimen Finish	...........*Extremely rare*			
1921	5	15	60	150	1925	30	80	375	975
1922	5	12	60	150	1926	5	20	85	185
1923	4	8	40	85	1926 No colon				
1924	5	12	60	150	after OMN	.20	50	175	375

4022 Florin. Deeply engraved. Bare head l. R. Crowned cruciform shields, sceptres in angles die axis: ↑↑

| 1920 | .....5 | 15 | 60 | 150 |

4022A — recut shallow portrait

1920	7	20	75	165	1924	4	15	65	140
1921	4	10	55	110	1924 Specimen Finish	...........*Extremely rare*			
1922	4	8	50	95	1925	30	60	275	625
1922 Proof in gold *FDC of highest rarity*					1926	4	15	65	135
1923	4	8	40	85					

4023 Shilling. Deeply engraved. Bare head l. R. Lion passant on crown within circle die axis: ↑↑

| 1920 | .....5 | 15 | 45 | 90 | 1921 nose to S | ....15 | 35 | 90 | 215 |

4023A — recut shallow portrait

1920	6	20	65	150	1924	3	12	55	90
1921 nose to SV	...5	20	65	150	1925	5	15	65	150
1922	3	6	45	85	1926	3	10	35	80
1923	2	5	35	80					

Note: 1923 and 1924 Shillings exist struck in nickel

4024 Sixpence. Bare head l. R. Lion passant on crown within circle die axis: ↑↑

1920	3	7	30	80	1924	2	4	20	60
1921	2	4	25	75	1924 Specimen Finish *FDC* £2500				
1922	2	5	25	75	1924 Proof in gold *FDC* £25000				
1923	3	6	30	85	1925	2	4	30	65

4025 - George V Sixpence   4026 - Threepence

4025 Sixpence. Similar new beading and broader rim die axis: ↑↑

| 1925 | .....2 | 4 | 30 | 55 | 1926 | ....2 | 4 | 30 | 55 |

4026 Threepence. Bare head l. R. Crowned 3 die axis: ↑↑

1920		2	5	25	1924 Proof in gold *FDC* £12500				
1921		2	5	25	1925	................BV	2	22	70
1922		3	20	85	1926	2	8	45	140
1924 Specimen Finish	...........*Extremely rare*								

			EF	FDC				EF	FDC
			£	£				£	£

4027 Maundy Set. (4d., 3d., 2d. and 1d.) die axis: ↑↑

1921	....		110	185	1925	....		110	185
1922	....		110	185	1926	....		110	185
1923	....		110	185	1927	....		110	185
1924	....		110	185					

4028 — **Fourpence.** 1921-7	....................................*from*	18	35
4029 — **Threepence.** 1921-7	....................................*from*	15	30
4030 — **Twopence.** 1921-7	....................................*from*	12	25
4031 — **Penny.** 1921-7	....................................*from*	18	35

2nd coinage
BM more central on tr.

3rd coinage
Modified Effigy
BM to right of tr.

Third Coinage. As before but modified effigy, with details of head more clearly defined. The BM on truncation is nearer to the back of the neck and without stops; beading is more pronounced.

	F £	VF £	EF £	UNC £		F £	VF £	EF £	UNC £

4032 Halfcrown. Modified effigy l. R. Crowned Shield in Garter die axis: ↑↑

| 1926 | 6 | 25 | 85 | 220 | 1927 Proof in gold *FDC of highest rarity* |
| 1927 | 5 | 10 | 45 | 100 |

4033 Shilling. Modified effigy l. R. Lion passant on crown, within circle die axis: ↑↑

| 1926 | 3 | 4 | 30 | 60 | 1927 | 3 | 7 | 40 | 70 |

4034 Sixpence. Modified effigy l. R. Lion passant on crown, within circle die axis: ↑↑

| 1926 | | 5 | 20 | 45 | 1927 | 3 | 5 | 25 | 50 |

4035 Threepence. Modified effigy l. R. Crowned 3 die axis: ↑↑

| 1926 | | | | | | | 2 | 15 | 50 |

Fourth Coinage. New types, 1927-36

4036
1927 'Wreath' Crown proof

4036 Crown. Modified Bare head l. R. Crown and date in wreath die axis: ↑↑

1927 –15,030 struck Proof only† *FDC* £300				1931 –4056 struck ..110	250	475	725
1927 Matt Proof *FDC of highest rarity*				1932 –2395 struck . 180	350	750	1050
1928* –9034 struck 100	200	400	700	1933* –7132 struck 100	200	425	700
1929 –4994 struck ..115	250	500	800	1934 –932 struck . 1500	2500	4000	5500
1930 -4847 struck .. 100	225	450	750	1936 –2473 struck . 175	350	775	1100

†*N.B. Proofs of other dates from 1927 also exist, but are extremely rare as they were for V.I.P. issue*
* *Beware recent counterfeits*

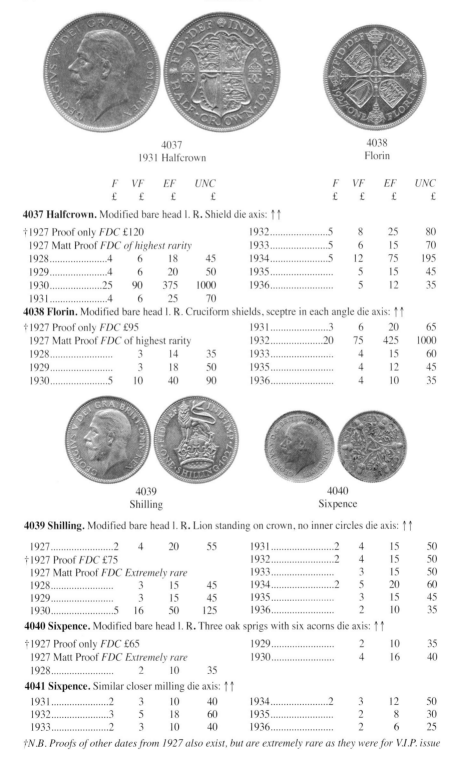

4037
1931 Halfcrown

4038
Florin

	F £	VF £	EF £	UNC £		F £	VF £	EF £	UNC £

4037 Halfcrown. Modified bare head l. R. Shield die axis: ↑↑

†1927 Proof only *FDC* £120					1932	5	8	25	80
1927 Matt Proof *FDC of highest rarity*					1933	5	6	15	70
1928	4	6	18	45	1934	5	12	75	195
1929	4	6	20	50	1935		5	15	45
1930	25	90	375	1000	1936		5	12	35
1931	4	6	25	70					

4038 Florin. Modified bare head l. R. Cruciform shields, sceptre in each angle die axis: ↑↑

†1927 Proof only *FDC* £95					1931	3	6	20	65
1927 Matt Proof *FDC of highest rarity*					1932	20	75	425	1000
1928		3	14	35	1933		4	15	60
1929		3	18	50	1935		4	12	45
1930	5	10	40	90	1936		4	10	35

4039
Shilling

4040
Sixpence

4039 Shilling. Modified bare head l. R. Lion standing on crown, no inner circles die axis: ↑↑

1927	2	4	20	55	1931	2	4	15	50
†1927 Proof *FDC* £75					1932	2	4	15	50
1927 Matt Proof *FDC Extremely rare*					1933		3	15	50
1928		3	15	45	1934	2	5	20	60
1929		3	15	45	1935		3	15	45
1930	5	16	50	125	1936		2	10	35

4040 Sixpence. Modified bare head l. R. Three oak sprigs with six acorns die axis: ↑↑

†1927 Proof only *FDC* £65					1929		2	10	35
1927 Matt Proof *FDC Extremely rare*					1930		4	16	40
1928		2	10	35					

4041 Sixpence. Similar closer milling die axis: ↑↑

1931	2	3	10	40	1934	2	3	12	50
1932	3	5	18	60	1935		2	8	30
1933	2	3	10	40	1936		2	6	25

†N.B. Proofs of other dates from 1927 also exist, but are extremely rare as they were for V.I.P. issue

BRONZE

4042	4043
Threepence	George V Maundy Set

	F	VF	EF	UNC		F	VF	EF	UNC
	£	£	£	£		£	£	£	£

4042 Threepence. Modified Bare head l. R. Three oak sprigs with three acorns die axis: ↑↑

	F	VF	EF	UNC		F	VF	EF	UNC
†1927 Proof only *FDC* £55					1932			2	20
1927 Matt Proof *FDC of highest rarity*					1933			2	20
1928		2	3	15	55	1934		2	18
1930		3	8	20	65	1935		2	20
1931				2	20	1936		2	15

	EF	FDC		EF	FDC
	£	£		£	£
4043 Maundy Set. As earlier sets die axis: ↑↑			1933	125	190
1928	110	185	1934	125	190
1929	110	185	1935	125	190
1930	140	200	1936	135	265
1931	110	185			
1932	110	185			

The 1936 Maundy was distributed by King Edward VIII

		EF	FDC
4044 — Fourpence. 1928-36 ....*from*	12	30
4045 — Threepence. 1928-36 ....*from*	12	30
4046 — Twopence. 1928-36 ....*from*	12	30
4047 — Penny. 1928-36 ....*from*	18	35

Silver Jubilee Commemorative issue, die axis: ↑↑

4048
1935 'Jubilee' Crown

	VF	EF	UNC
	£	£	£
4048 Crown. 1935. R. St. George, incuse lettering on edge –714,769 struck ..	20	30	45
1935 — error edge		*Extremely rare*	
4049 Crown. Similar Specimen striking issued in box			75

4050 Crown. Similar raised lettering on edge 2,500 struck. Proof (.925 Æ) *FDC* £625
    — error edge inscription Proof *FDC* £3350
    — Proof in gold –28 struck £32500

†*N.B. Proofs of other dates from 1927 also exist, but are extremely rare as they were for V.I.P. issue*

BRONZE

4052
1912 H Penny

H Mint mark location – 4052

KN Mint mark location
as above – 4053

	F	VF	EF	UNC			F	VF	EF	UNC
	£	£	£	£			£	£	£	£

4051 Penny. Bare head l. R. Britannia seated right die axis: ↑↑

1911	2	18	65		1919	3	25	70
1912	3	28	75		1920	3	28	80
1913	5	30	90		1921	3	25	70
1914	3	25	70		1922	5	35	125
1915	3	28	75		1922 Rev. of 1927	.2500	7500	—	—
1916	3	25	70		1922 Specimen finish..		*Extremely rare*	
1917	3	25	70		1926	6	40	130
1918	3	25	70					

4052 Penny. Bare head l. R. Britannia, H (Heaton Mint, Birmingham, Ltd.) to l. of date die axis: ↑↑

1912 H	2	18	125	350		1919 H	3	25	350	1100
1918 H	4	30	300	750						

4053 Penny. Bare head l. R. Britannia KN (King's Norton Metal Co.) to l. of date die axis: ↑↑

1918 KN	5	75	425	1350		1919 KN	8	95	950	2400

4054 Penny. Modified effigy l. R. as 4051

1926	40	325	1500	3750

4054A Penny. Modified effigy. R. Britannia seated r. Shorter index finger date in ex. die axis ↑↑

1922	*Of the highest rarity*		1927	2	18	55
1926	*Of the highest rarity*					

4055 Penny. Small bare head l. R. Britannia Seated r. date in ex. die axis: ↑↑

1928	2	18	50		1933		*Extremely rare*	
1929	2	18	60		1934	4	30	80
1930	5	30	80		1935	2	10	45
1931	3	25	65		1936	1	8	30
1932	5	40	175					

4056 Halfpenny. Bare head l. R. Britannia Seated r. date in ex. die axis: ↑↑

1911	1	10	50		1919	2	12	55
1912	2	12	55		1920	3	15	65
1913	2	12	55		1921	2	12	55
1914	2	14	60		1922	4	25	90
1915	2	15	65		1923	2	12	55
1916	2	15	65		1924	2	12	55
1917	2	12	55		1924 Specimen finish..		*Extremely rare*	
1918	2	12	55		1925	2	12	55

†N.B. Proofs of other dates from 1927also exist, but are extremely rare as they were for V.I.P. issue

	VF £	EF £	UNC £		VF £	EF £	UNC £

4057 Halfpenny. Modified effigy l. R. Britannia Seated r. date in ex. die axis: ↑↑

1925	4	20	75	1927	2	10	50
1926	2	12	55				

4056
Halfpenny

4058
Small head

4058 Halfpenny. Small bare head l. R. Britannia Seated r. date in ex. die axis: ↑↑

1928	1	8	45	1933	1	8	45
1929	1	8	45	1934	1	14	50
1930	4	15	50	1935	1	8	45
1931	1	8	45	1936	1	7	30
1932	1	8	45				

4059
Farthing

4062
Third-Farthing

4059 Farthing. Bare head l. R. Britannia Seated r. date in ex. Dark finish die axis: ↑↑

1911	4	22	1915		5	28
1912	3	20	1916		3	20
1913	3	20	1917		3	20
1914	3	20	1918		10	45

4060 Farthing. Similar Bright finish, die axis: ↑↑ 1918-25 ... 5 22

4061 Farthing. Modified effigy l. R. Britannia Seated r. date in ex. die axis: ↑↑

1926	2	18	1932		2	18
1927	2	18	1933		2	18
1928	2	18	1934		2	20
1929	2	18	1935		5	32
1930	3	25	1936		2	18
1931	2	18				

4062 Third-Farthing (for use in Malta). Bare head l. R. Crowned date and Value die axis: ↑↑

1913	5	25	55

Proof Sets

PS11 Coronation, **1911.** Five pounds to Maundy Penny (12 coins) ...... *FDC* £7500
PS12 — **1911.** Sovereign to Maundy Penny (10 coins) ...... *FDC* £2200
PS13 — **1911.** Half crown to Maundy Penny (8 coins) ...... *FDC* £900
PS14 New type, **1927.** Wreath type Crown to Threepence (6 coins) ...... *FDC* £700

† *NB Truly 'FDC' proof sets are hardly ever encountered. Component coins showing any surface marks, hairlines or nicks will be worth less than the prices quoted above.*

Succeeded his father on 20 January 1936. Abdicated 10 December. Edward VIII was born 23 June 1894, and was very popular as Prince of Wales. He ruled only for a short time before announcing his intended marriage to the American divorcee Wallis Simpson; a potential religious and political scandal. Edward was not a traditionalist, as evidenced on the proposed coinage, where he insisted against all advice on having his effigy face the same way as his father's, instead of opposite. He abdicated in favour of his brother, and became Edward, Duke of Windsor, marrying Mrs Simpson in France, where they lived in exile. He governed the Bahamas from 1940-45 and died on 28 May 1972.

No coins of Edward VIII were issued for currency within the United Kingdom bearing his name and portrait. The Mint had commenced work on a new coinage prior to the Abdication, and various patterns were made. No Proof Sets were issued for sale and only a small number of sets were struck.

Coins bearing Edward's name, but not his portrait, were issued for the colonial territories of British East Africa, British West Africa, Fiji and New Guinea. The projected U.K. coins were to include a Shilling of essentially `Scottish' type and a nickel brass Threepence with twelve sides which might supplement and possibly supersede the inconveniently small silver Threepence.

Engravers and Designers:– George Kruger Gray (1880-1943), Thomas Humphrey Paget (1893-1974), Benedicto Pistucci (1784-1855) Frances Madge Kitchener, Percy Metcalfe (1895-1970), H Wilson Parker (1896-1980)

Designer's initials: H. P. (T. Humphrey Paget)   B.P. (Benedetto Pistrucci, d. 1855)
K. G. (G. Kruger Gray)   M. K. (Madge Kitchener)
W. P. (H. Wilson Parker)

Die axis ↑↑

GOLD

4063
Edward VIII Proof Five Pounds

4063 Proof Set
Gold, Five Pounds, Two Pounds and Sovereign, Silver Crown, Halfcrown, Florin, Scottish Shilling, Sixpence and Threepence, Brass Threepence, Penny, Halfpenny and Farthing, 1937 *FDC. Only one complete set known.*

FDC
£

Five Pounds, Bare head 1. R St George and dragon, date in ex 450000
Two Pounds, Bare head 1. R St George and dragon, date in ex 200000
Sovereign, Bare head 1. R. St George and dragon date in ex 325000
Crown, Bare head 1. R. Crowned Shield of arms and supporters........................ 175000
Halfcrown, Bare head 1. R. Quartered Standard of arms 95000
Florin, Bare head 1. R. Crowned rose and emblems 75000
Shilling, Bare head 1. R. Lion seated facing on crown 45000
Sixpence, Bare head 1. R. Six interlinked rings... 37500
Threepence, Bare head 1. R. three interlinked rings 30000

4064A

4064A Nickel brass. Threepence, 1937 Bare head 1. R. Thrift plant below 45000
        Bronze. Penny, 1937 65000
        Halfpenny, 1937... 35000
        Farthing, 1937... 30000

Note: Matt proofs exist of most denominations

Pattern

Edward VIII Brass Threepence

UNC
£

4064B Nickel brass dodecagonal Threepence, 1937. Bare head 1. R. Thrift plant of more
        naturalistic style than the modified proof coin. A small number of these coins were
        produced of differing thickness for experimental purposes and a few did get into
        circulation... 45000

George VI was born on 14 December 1895 and never expected to be King. He suffered ill-health through much of his life and had a stammer. He married Elizabeth Bowes Lyon and together they became very popular especially through the ravages of World War II, when Buckingham Palace was bombed. The war took its toll on George, and ever a heavy smoker he succumbed to lung cancer on 6th February 1952. Elizabeth, known after his death as 'Queen Elizabeth the Queen Mother', lived on to the age of 101 dying on 30 March 2002.

Though they were at first issued concurrently, the twelve-sided nickel-brass Threepence superseded the small silver Threepence in 1942. Those dated 1943-4 were not issued for circulation in the U.K. In addition to the usual English 'lion' Shilling, a Shilling of Scottish type was issued concurrently. This depicts the Scottish lion and crown flanked by the shield of St. Andrew and a thistle. In 1947, as silver was needed to repay the bullion lent by the U.S.A. during the war, silver coins were replaced by coins of the same type and weight made of cupro-nickel. In 1949, after India had attained independence, the title IND:IMP (Indiae Imperator) was dropped from the coinage. Commemorative Crown pieces were issued for the Coronation and the 1951 Festival of Britain.

Engravers and Designers:– Frances Madge Kitchener, George Kruger Gray (1880-1943), Percy Metcalfe (1895-1970) Thomas Humphrey Paget (1893-1974), H Wilson Parker (1896-1980), Benedetto Pistrucci (1784-1855)

Designer's initials: K. G. (G. Kruger Gray)   B. P. (Benedetto Pistrucci, d. 1855)
                      H. P. (T. Humphrey Paget)   W. P. (Wilson Parker)

Die axis ↑↑

GOLD

4074
1937 Proof Five Pounds

4076
1937 Proof Sovereign

	FDC £
4074 Five Pounds. Bare head l. R. St. George, 1937. Proof plain edge only (5001 struck)..	2150
4074-4077 Proof Struck to Matt finish *FDC of highest rarity*	
4075 Two Pounds. Similar, 1937. Proof plain edge only (5001 struck)	1250
4076 Sovereign. Similar, 1937. Proof plain edge only (5001 struck)	2000
4077 Half-Sovereign. Similar, 1937. Proof plain edge only (5001 struck)	650

SILVER

First coinage. Silver, .500 fine, with title IND:IMP

4078
1937 Crown

	VF £	EF £	UNC £
4078 Crown. Coronation commemorative, 1937. R. Arms and supporters	15	30	45

4079 Crown. Similar 1937 Proof *FDC* £85
Similar 1937 Frosted 'VIP' Proof £975
— 1937 Matt Proof *FDC of highest rarity*

4080
Halfcrown

4081
1937 Florin

	EF £	UNC £		EF £	UNC £

4080 Halfcrown. Bare head l. R. Shield die axis: ↑↑

	EF	UNC		EF	UNC
1937	5	25	1941	5	25
1937 Proof *FDC* £30			1942	5	20
1937 Matt Proof *FDC of highest rarity*			1943	5	25
1938	10	50	1944	5	20
1939	5	25	1945	5	20
1940	8	30	1946	5	20

4081 Florin. Bare head l. R. Crowned rose, etc. die axis: ↑↑

	EF	UNC		EF	UNC
1937	4	20	1941	4	20
1937 Proof *FDC* £25			1942	4	20
1937 Matt Proof *FDC of highest rarity*			1943	4	20
1938	8	45	1944	4	20
1939	4	20	1945	4	15
1940	5	25	1946	4	15

4082
1942 'English' Shilling

4083
1945 'Scottish' Shilling

4082 Shilling. 'English' reverse. Bare head l. R. Lion standing on large crown die axis: ↑↑

	EF	UNC		EF	UNC
1937	3	20	1941	3	20
1937 Proof *FDC* £22			1942	3	20
1937 Matt Proof *FDC of highest rarity*			1943	3	20
1938	8	45	1944	3	20
1939	3	20	1945	3	15
1940	5	25	1946	3	15

	EF	UNC		VF	EF	UNC
	£	£		£	£	£

4083 Shilling. 'Scottish' reverse. Bare head l. R. Lion seated facing on crown die axis: ↑↑

	EF	UNC		VF	EF	UNC
1937	3	15	1941		4	25
1937 Proof *FDC* £22			1942		4	25
1937 Matt Proof *FDC of highest rarity*			1943		3	20
1938	8	40	1944		3	20
1939	3	20	1945		3	15
1940	5	25	1946		3	15

4084
1945 Sixpence

4085
1944 Threepence

4084 Sixpence. Bare head l. R. GRI crowned die axis: ↑↑

	EF	UNC			EF	UNC
1937	2	15	1941		2	20
1937 Proof *FDC* £18			1942		2	15
1937 Matt Proof *FDC of highest rarity*			1943		2	15
1938	6	25	1944		2	15
1939	2	20	1945		2	15
1940	5	25	1946		2	15

4085 Threepence. Bare head l. R. Shield on rose die axis: ↑↑

	EF	UNC		VF	EF	UNC
1937	2	15	1941		4	25
1937 Proof *FDC* £15			1942*	8	20	40
1937 Matt Proof *FDC of highest rarity*			1943*	8	25	50
1938	2	15	1944*	15	35	100
1939	6	30	1945*		*Extremely rare*	
1940	5	25	* *issued for Colonial use only*			

4086
1937 Maundy Set

	EF	FDC		EF	FDC
	£	£		£	£

4086 Maundy Set. Silver, .500 fine. Uniform dates die axis: ↑↑

	EF	FDC		EF	FDC
1937	95	140	1941	110	185
1937 Proof *FDC* £140			1942	110	185
1937 Matt Proof *FDC of highest rarity*			1943	110	185
1938	110	185	1944	110	185
1939	110	185	1945	110	185
1940	125	200	1946	110	185

	EF £	FDC £		EF £	FDC £

4087 — **Fourpence.** 1937-46 .... *from* — 20
4088 — **Threepence.** 1937-46 .... *from* — 22
4089 — **Twopence.** 1937-46 .... *from* — 20
4090 — **Penny.** 1937-46 .... *from* — 28

Second coinage. Silver, .925 fine, with title IND:IMP (Maundy only)
4091 Maundy Set (4d., 3d., 2d. and 1d.). Uniform dates die axis: ↑↑

1947	110	185	1948	110	185

4092 — **Fourpence,** 1947-8 20
4093 — **Threepence,** 1947-8 22
4094 — **Twopence,** 1947-8 20
4095 — **Penny,** 1947-8 28

Third coinage. Silver, .925 fine, but omitting IND:IMP. (Maundy only)
4096 Maundy Set (4d., 3d., 2d. and 1d.). Uniform dates die axis: ↑↑

1949	110	185	1951	125	200
1950	125	200	1952	150	225

1951 Matt Proof *FDC Extremely rare*   1952 Proof in copper *FDC Extremely rare*

The 1952 Maundy was distributed by Queen Elizabeth II.

4097 — **Fourpence,** 1949-52 .... *from* — 20
4098 — **Threepence,** 1949-52 .... *from* — 22
4099 — **Twopence,** 1949-52 .... *from* — 20
4100 — **Penny,** 1949-52 .... *from* — 28

See footnote re Maundy Pennies after 3796.

CUPRO-NICKEL

Second coinage. Types as first (silver) coinage, IND:IMP.

	EF £	UNC £		EF £	UNC £

4101 Halfcrown. Bare head l. R. Shield die axis: ↑↑

1947	2	12	1948	2	10

4102 Florin. Bare head l. R. Crowned rose die axis: ↑↑

1947	2	12	1948	2	12

4103 Shilling. 'English' reverse. Bare head l. die axis: ↑↑

1947	2	12	1948	2	12

4104 Shilling. 'Scottish' reverse. Bare head l. die axis: ↑↑

1947	2	12	1948	2	12

4105 Sixpence. Bare head l. R. GRI crowned die axis: ↑↑

1947	2	10	1948	2	10

Third coinage. Types as before but title IND:IMP. omitted

4106
1949 Halfcrown

	VF £	EF £	UNC £		VF £	EF £	UNC £

4106 Halfcrown. Bare head l. R. Shield die axis: ↑↑

1949............................		3	25	1951 Proof *FDC* £35			
1950............................		8	35	1951 Matt Proof *FDC* £2750			
1950 Proof *FDC* £40				1952................................			*Unique*
1950 Matt Proof *FDC of highest rarity*				1952 Proof *FDC* £70000			
1951............................	1	8	35				

4107 Florin. Bare head l. R. Crowned rose die axis: ↑↑

1949............................		5	30	1951		8	35
1950............................		8	30	1951 Proof *FDC* £35			
1950 Proof *FDC* £30				1951 Matt Proof *FDC* £2000			
1950 Matt Proof *FDC of highest rarity*							

4108 Shilling. 'English' reverse. Bare head l. die axis: ↑↑

1949............................		5	30	1951 Proof *FDC* £25			
1950............................		8	30	1951 Matt Proof *FDC* £1750			
1950 Proof *FDC* £30				1952 Proof *FDC* £25000			
1951............................		6	30				

4109 Shilling. 'Scottish' reverse. Bare head l. die axis: ↑↑

1949............................		5	30	1951............................		6	30
1950............................		8	30	1951 Proof *FDC* £25			
1950 Proof *FDC* £30				1951 Matt Proof *FDC* £1750			
1950 Matt Proof *FDC Extremely rare*							

4110
1952 Sixpence

4110 Sixpence. Bare head l. R. Crowned cypher die axis: ↑↑

1949............................		1	12	1951............................		5	20
1950............................		3	15	1951 Proof *FDC* £20			
1950 Proof *FDC* £22				1951 Matt Proof *FDC* £1500			
1950 Matt Proof *FDC Extremely rare*				1952......................5		40	125

Festival of Britain issue die axis: ↑↑

4111
Festival of Britain Crown

	EF	UNC
	£	£
4111 Crown. Bare head l. R. St. George and dragon, date in ex, 1951. *Proof-like*	5	20
Similar — 1951 Frosted 'VIP' Proof £850		
Similar — 1951 Matt Proof *FDC* £4000		
Similar — 1951 Plain edge Proof *FDC* £1000		

NICKEL BRASS

First issue, with title IND:IMP.

4112	4113
1941 Brass Threepence	Second issue obverse

	VF	EF	UNC		VF	EF	UNC
	£	£	£		£	£	£
4112 Threepence (dodecagonal). Bare head l. R. Thrift plant die axis: ↑↑							
1937..............................		2	12	1942..............................		2	12
1937 Proof *FDC* £20				1943..............................		2	12
1937 Matt Proof *FDC of highest rarity*				1944..............................		2	15
1938..............................		6	28	1945..............................		5	20
1939..............................		10	50	1946	30	250	850
1940..............................		6	30	1948..............................		10	65
1941..............................		3	15				

Second issue, omitting IND:IMP.

4113 Threepence. Bare head l. R. Similar die axis: ↑↑

1949	30	200	650	1951..............................3		30	150
1950		25	135	1951 Proof *FDC* £50			
1950 Proof *FDC* £45				1951 Matt Proof *FDC* £1000			
1950 Matt Proof *FDC of highest rarity*				1952..............................		5	25

BRONZE

First issue, with title IND:IMP.

4114
1938 Penny

	EF £	UNC £		EF £	UNC £
4114 Penny. Bare head l. R. Britannia Seated r. date in ex die axis: ↑↑					
1937............................		10	1944 —........................	6	35
1937 Proof *FDC* £25			1945 —........................	5	28
1938............................	1	15	1946 —........................	2	12
1939............................	4	20	1947 —.................................		10
1940............................	10	60	1948 —.................................		10
1940 Double exergue line	4	25	1946 ONE' die flaw 75		225

4115
1937 Halfpenny

4116
1943 Farthing

4115 Halfpenny. Bare head l. R. Ship sailing l. date below die axis: ↑↑

	EF	UNC		EF	UNC
1937....................................		10	1943....................................		10
1937 Proof *FDC* £18			1944....................................		10
1938............................	1	15	1945............................	1	12
1939............................	3	28	1946............................	3	22
1940............................	3	28	1947............................	1	12
1941....................................		12	1948............................	1	12
1942....................................		10			

4116 Farthing. Bare head l. R. Wren l. date above die axis: ↑↑

	EF			EF
1937.........................	8	1943....................................		8
1937 Proof *FDC* £15		1944....................................		8
1938.........................	15	1945....................................		8
1939.........................	8	1946....................................		8
1940.........................	8	1947....................................		8
1941.........................	8	1948....................................		8
1942.........................	8			

	VF £	EF £	UNC £		VF £	EF £	UNC £

4117 Penny. Bare head l. R. Britannia Seated r. date in ex. die axis: ↑↑

1949..			10	1951.......................	10	35	60
1950.......................6		20	75	1951 Proof *FDC* £50			
1950 Proof *FDC* £35				1951 Matt Proof *FDC* £2500			
1950 Matt Proof *FDC* ....*Extremely rare*				1952 Proof only *FDC Unique*			

4118
Second issue Halfpenny

4119
Second issue Farthing

4118 Halfpenny. Bare head l. R. Ship Sailing l. date below die axis: ↑↑

1949..............................		4	20	1951..............................		5	30
1950..............................		3	15	1951 Proof *FDC* £18			
1950 Proof *FDC* £15				1951 Matt Proof *FDC* £1000			
1950 Matt Proof *FDC* *Extremely rare*				1952..............................		1	12

4119 Farthing. Bare head l. R. Wren l. date above die axis: ↑↑

1949..			8	1951..			10
1950..			8	1951 Proof *FDC* £18			
1950 Proof *FDC* £15				1951 Matt Proof *FDC* £950			
1950 Matt Proof *FDC* .*Extremely rare*				1952..			8

The coins dated 1952 were issued during the reign of Elizabeth II.

Proof Sets

PS15 Coronation, **1937.** Five pounds to Half-sovereign (4 coins) ....*FDC*   £6000
PS16 — **1937.** Crown to Farthing, including Maundy Set (15 coins)....................*FDC*   £425
PS17 Mid-Century, **1950.** Halfcrown to Farthing (9 coins) ....*FDC*   £200
PS18 Festival of Britain, **1951.** Crown to Farthing (10 coins) ....*FDC*   £250

Elizabeth II was born on 21 April 1926. Our current Monarch has lived a long and glorious reign celebrating her Golden Jubilee in 2002. She married Philip a distant cousin in 1947 and has four children, Charles, Anne, Andrew and Edward. Significantly she is the first Monarch to pay taxes and her coinage has been an interesting one with the change to decimal coinage and the numerous bust changes since 1953.

The earliest coins of this reign have the title BRITT:OMN, but in 1954 this was omitted from the Queen's titles owing to the changing status of so many Commonwealth territories. The minting of 'English' and 'Scottish' shillings was continued. A Coronation commemorative crown was issued in 1953, another crown was struck on the occasion of the 1960 British Exhibition in New York and a third was issued in honour of Sir Winston Churchill in 1965. A very small number of proof gold coins were struck in 1953 for the national museum collections, but between 1957 and 1968 gold sovereigns were minted again in quantity for sale in the international bullion market and to counteract the activities of counterfeiters.

Owing to inflation the farthing had now become practically valueless; production of these coins ceased after 1956 and the coins were demonetized at the end of 1960. In 1965 it was decided to change to a decimal system of coinage in the year 1971. As part of the transition to decimal coinage the halfpenny was demonetized in August 1969 and the halfcrown in January 1970. (See also introduction to Decimal Coinage.

Designer's initials:

A. V. (Avril Vaughan)
B. P. (Benedetto Pistrucci, 1784-1855)
B. R. (Bruce Rushin)
C.D. (Clive Duncan)
C. T. (Cecil Thomas)
D. C. (David Cornell)
E. F. (Edgar Fuller)
G. L. (Gilbert Ledward)
I. R. B. (Ian Rank-Broadley)
J. B. (James Butler)
J. M. (Jeffrey Matthews)
J. M. M. (John Mills)
M. B. (Matthew Bonaccorsi)

M. G. (Mary Gillick)
M. M. D. (Mary Milner Dickens)
M. N. (Michael Noakes)
M. R. (Michael Rizzello)
N. S. (Norman Sillman)
P. N. (Philip Nathan)
R. D. (Ron Dutton)
R. D. M. (Raphael David Maklouf)
R. E. (Robert Elderton)
r. e. (Robert Evans)
R. L. (Robert Lowe)
T. N. (Timothy Noad)
W. G. (William Gardner)
W. P. (Wilson Parker 1896-1980)

Other designers whose initials do not appear on the coins:
Christopher Ironside (1913-1992)
Arnold Machin (1911-1999)
David Wynne
Professor Richard Guyatt
Eric Sewell
Oscar Nemon

Leslie Durbin
Derek Gorringe
Bernard Sindall
Tom Phillips
Edwina Ellis
David Gentleman
Matthew Dent

PRE-DECIMAL ISSUES
Die axis ↑↑

GOLD

First coinage, with title BRITT.OMN, 1953. *Proof only. Originally produced for institutional collecting.*

4120 Five Pounds. Young laur. head r. R. St. George 1953 .... *of the highest rarity*
4121 Two Pounds. Young laur. head r. R. St. George 1953 .... *of the highest rarity*
4122 Sovereign. Young laur. head r. R. St. George 1953 .... *of the highest rarity*
4123 Half-Sovereign. Young laur. head r. R. St. George 1953 .... *of the highest rarity*

Second issue, BRITT.OMN omitted

4125
1958 Sovereign

	EF	UNC		EF	UNC
	£	£		£	£

4124 Sovereign. Young laur head r. R. St. George, fine graining on edge

1957...BV   300
1957 Proof *FDC* £9500

4125 Sovereign. Similar, but coarser graining on edge

1958............................BV	300	1963 Proof *FDC* £9750		
1958 Proof *FDC* £9750		1964............................BV	300
1959............................BV	300	1965............................BV	300
1959 Proof *FDC* £9750		1966............................BV	300
1962............................BV	300	1967............................BV	300
1963............................BV	300	1968............................BV	300

SILVER

The Queen's Maundy are now the only coins struck regularly in silver.
The location of the Maundy ceremony is given for each year.

First issue, with title BRITT:OMN:

4126
Maundy Set

	EF	FDC		EF	FDC
	£	£		£	£

4126 Maundy Set (4d., 3d., 2d. and 1d.), 1953. *St Paul's Cathedral* 500   900
1953 Proof struck in gold *FDC Extremely rare*
1953 Proof struck in nickel bronze *FDC Extremely rare*
1953 Matt Proof *FDC Extremely rare*
4127 — Fourpence. 1953   200
4128 — Threepence. 1953...   175
4129 — Twopence. 1953...   175
4130 — Penny. 1953   350

Second issue, with BRITT:OMN: omitted

4131 Maundy Set (4d., 3d., 2d. and 1d.). Uniform dates

1954 *Westminster* 110	185	1956 *Westminster* 110	185
1955 *Southwark*............................110	185	1957 *St. Albans* 110	185

BV= Bullion value only. At the time of going to press the spot price for gold was £1092 per oz.

	EF	FDC		EF	FDC
	£	£		£	£

4131 Maundy Set

1958 *Westminster* 110	185	1965 Canterbury...........110	185
1959 *Windsor* 110	185	1966 Westminster.......110	185
1960 *Westminster* 110	185	1967 Durham..............110	185
1961 *Rochester*............110	185	1968 Westminster.......110	185
1962 *Westminster* 110	200	1969 Selby.................110	185
1963 *Chelmsford* 110	185	1970 Westminster.......110	185
1964 Westminster.........110	185		

4132 — Fourpence. 1954-70 ....*from*   20
4133 — Threepence. 1954-70 ....*from*   25
4134 — Twopence. 1954-70 ....*from*   20
4135 — Penny. 1954-70...*from*   30
See footnote after 3796

CUPRO-NICKEL

First issue, 1953, with title BRITT.OMN.

4136 - 1953 Coronation Crown

	EF	UNC	Proof FDC
	£	£	£

4136 Crown. Queen on horseback. R. Crown in centre of emblematical cross,
shield of Arms in each angle, 1953 .... 4 | 8 | 35
Similar 1953 Frosted 'VIP' proof £750
Similar 1953 Matt Proof *FDC* £3750

4137 - 1953 Halfcrown   4138 - 1953 Florin

4137 Halfcrown. First obverse die, I of DEI points to a space between beads .   5   2500
4137A Halfcrown. Second obverse die, I of DEI points to a bead, with title
BRITT:OMN: Young laur. head r. R. Arms, 1953   5   20
Similar 1953 Matt Proof *FDC* £2000
4138 Florin. Young laur. head r. R. Double rose, 1953.....................................   4   12
Similar 1953 Matt Proof *FDC* £1750

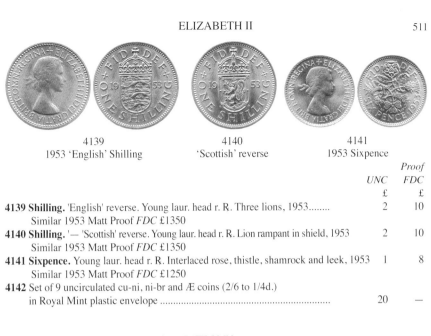

4139
1953 'English' Shilling

4140
'Scottish' reverse

4141
1953 Sixpence

		UNC £	Proof FDC £
4139 Shilling. 'English' reverse. Young laur. head r. R. Three lions, 1953........		2	10
Similar 1953 Matt Proof *FDC* £1350			
4140 Shilling. '— 'Scottish' reverse. Young laur. head r. R. Lion rampant in shield, 1953		2	10
Similar 1953 Matt Proof *FDC* £1350			
4141 Sixpence. Young laur. head r. R. Interlaced rose, thistle, shamrock and leek, 1953		1	8
Similar 1953 Matt Proof *FDC* £1250			
4142 Set of 9 uncirculated cu-ni, ni-br and Æ coins (2/6 to 1/4d.)			
in Royal Mint plastic envelope		20	—

Second issue, similar types but omitting BRITT.OMN.

4143
1960 Crown

4144
1965 Churchill Crown

		EF £	UNC £
4143 Crown, 1960. Young laur. head r. R. As 4136		5	12
— — Similar, from polished dies (New York Exhibition issue)		10	35
— — 'VIP' *Proof,* frosted design *FDC* £650			
4144 Crown, Churchill commemorative, 1965. As illustration. R. Bust of Sir Winston			
Churchill r.			2
— — Similar, "Satin-Finish". VIP *Specimen*			1500

	EF £	UNC £		EF £	UNC £		EF £	UNC £
4145 Halfcrown. Young laur. head r. R. As 4137								
1954......................8		45	1960......................		20	1965......................		6
1955......................		12	1961		6	1966......................		3
1956......................		18	1961 Polished die..		20	1967......................		3
1957......................		8	1962......................		6	1970 Proof *FDC* £12		
1958......................8		40	1963......................		6			
1959......................8		45	1964......................		8			

4146
1957 Florin

	EF	UNC		UNC
	£	£		£

4146 Florin. Young laur. head r. R. As 4138

1954	8	50	1962	5
1955		12	1963	4
1956		12	1964	4
1957	8	50	1965	4
1958	10	50	1966	3
1959	10	60	1967	3
1960		12	1970 Proof *FDC* £8	
1961		12		

4147 Shilling. 'English' reverse. Young laur. head r. R. As 4139

1954	6	1961	3
1955	6	1962	2
1956	12	1963	2
1957	5	1964	2
1958	8	65	1965	2
1959	5	1966	2
1960	8	1970 Proof *FDC* £8	

4148 Shilling. 'Scottish' reverse. Young laur. head r. R. As 4140

1954	6	1961	20
1955	8	1962	5
1956	12	1963	2
1957	5	35	1964	2
1958	4	1965	2
1959	10	90	1966	2
1960	8	1970 Proof *FDC* £8	

4149 Sixpence. Young laur. head r. R. As 4141

1954	8	1962	2
1955	4	1963	2
1956	5	1964	2
1957	4	1965	1
1958	10	1966	1
1959	3	1967	1
1960	7	1970 Proof *FDC* £7	
1961	6		

NICKEL BRASS

First issue, with title BRITT.OMN.

4152   4153
1953 Brass Threepence   Second issue

	UNC		UNC
	£		£
4152 Threepence (dodecagonal). Young laur. head r. R. Crowned portcullis, 1953	5		
— Proof *FDC* £12 Similar 1953 Matt Proof *FDC* £1100			

Second issue (omitting BRIT.OMN)
4153 Threepence Similar type

1954..	8	1962..	2
1955..	10	1963..	2
1956..	10	1964..	2
1957..	6	1965..	2
1958..	15	1966..	1
1959..	6	1967..	1
1960..	7	1970 Proof *FDC* £6	
1961..	3		

BRONZE

First issue, with title BRITT.OMN.

4154   4155   4156
1953 Penny   1953 Halfpenny   1953 Farthing

	VF	EF	UNC	Proof FDC
	£	£	£	£
4154 Penny. Young laur. head r. R. Britannia (only issued with Royal Mint set in plastic envelope)				
1953 Beaded border 1		3	12	25
1953 Toothed border *FDC* £2500				
Similar 1953 Matt Proof *FDC* £2500				
4155 Halfpenny. Young laur. head r. R. Ship, 1953..			3	12
Similar 1953 Matt Proof *FDC* £950				
4156 Farthing. Young laur. head r. R. Wren, 1953			2	10
Similar 1953 Matt Proof *FDC* £850				

ELIZABETH II

	UNC £		*EF* £	*UNC* £

Second issue, omitting BRITT.OMN.

4157 Penny. Young laur. head r. R. Britannia (1954-60 *not issued*)

1954	65000	1965	1
1961	3	1966	1
1962	1	1967	1
1963	1	1970 Proof *FDC* £7	
1964	1		

4158 Halfpenny. Young laur. head r. R. Ship (1961 *not issued*)

1954	8	1960	1
1954 larger border teeth	10	1962	1
1955	6	1963	1
1956	8	1964	1
1957	4	1965	1
1957 calm sea	40	1966	1
1958	3	1967	1
1959	2	1970 Proof *FDC* £4	

4159 Farthing. Young laur. head r. R. Wren

1954	6	1956 3	10
1955	6		

Proof Sets

PS19 Coronation, **1953.** Crown to Farthing (10 coins) .... *FDC* 150

PS20 'Last Sterling', **1970.** Halfcrown to Halfpenny plus medallion .... *FDC* 35

PRE-DECIMAL PROOF SETS

All prices quoted assume coins are in their original case. Issued by the Royal Mint in official case from 1887 onwards, but earlier sets were issued privately by the engraver. All pieces have a superior finish to that of the current coins.

		No. of coins	FDC £
PS1	**George IV, 1826.** New issue, Five Pounds to Farthing	(11)	55000
PS2	**William IV, 1831.** Coronation, Two Pounds to Farthing	(14)	41500
PS3	**Victoria, 1839.** Young head. "Una and the Lion" Five Pounds and Sovereign to Farthing	(15)	82500
PS4	— **1853.** Sovereign to Half-Farthing, including Gothic type Crown	(16)	62500
PS5	— **1887.** Jubilee bust for Golden Jubilee, Five Pounds to Threepence	(11)	15000
PS6	— **1887.** Silver Crown to Threepence	(7)	3000
PS7	— **1893.** Old bust, Five Pounds to Threepence	(10)	17500
PS8	— **1893.** Silver Crown to Threepence	(6)	3500
PS9	**Edward VII, 1902.** Coronation, Five Pounds to Maundy Penny. Matt finish to surfaces	(13)	6500
PS10	— **1902.** Sovereign to Maundy Penny. Matt finish	(11)	2150
PS11	**George V, 1911.** Coronation, Five Pounds to Maundy Penny	(12)	7500
PS12	— **1911.** Sovereign to Maundy Penny	(10)	2200
PS13	— **1911.** Silver Halfcrown to Maundy Penny	(8)	900
PS14	— **1927.** New Coinage. Wreath type Crown to Threepence	(6)	700
PS15	**George VI, 1937.** Coronation. Five Pounds to Half-Sovereign	(4)	6000
PS16	— **1937.** Coronation. Crown to Farthing, including Maundy Set	(15)	425
PS17	— **1950.** Mid-Century, Halfcrown to Farthing	(9)	200
PS18	— **1951.** Festival of Britain, Crown to Farthing	(10)	250
PS19	**Elizabeth II, 1953.** Coronation. Crown to Farthing	(10)	150
PS20	— **1970.** "Last Sterling" set. Halfcrown to Halfpenny plus medallion	(8)	35

The decision to adopt decimal currency was announced in March 1966 following the recommendation of the Halsbury Committee of Enquiry which had been appointed in 1961. The date for the introduction of the new system was 15 February 1971 and it was evident that the Royal Mint facilities which had been located on Tower Hill for more than 150 years would be unable to strike the significant quantities of coins required on that site. The Government therefore decided to build a new mint at Llantrisant in South Wales.

The new system provided for three smaller bronze coins with the denominations of a half new penny, one new penny and two new pence, and very large numbers were struck and stock piled for D-Day. The cupro-nickel five and ten new pence denominations with the same specifications as the shilling and florin were introduced in 1968 and circulated along side the former denominations. A further change was the introduction in 1969 of a 50 new pence coin to replace the ten shilling banknote.

In 1982 and 1983 two more new coins were introduced; the 20 pence which helped to reduce demand for five and ten pence pieces, and the first circulating non-precious metal £1 coin which replaced the bank note of the same value.1982 also saw the removal of the word "NEW" from all denominations from half penny to fifty pence.

Increasing raw material costs, and inflation also play a part in the development of a modern coinage system and smaller 5 and 10 pence coins were introduced in 1990 and 1992 respectively. A further change in 1992 was the use of copper plated steel for the one and two pence bronze coins. The plated steel coins are magnetic unlike the solid bronze alloy. Further changes were made in 1997 when the fifty pence coin was reduced in size and a bimetallic circulating £2 was also introduced to reduce demand for the one pound value.

In 2008, 40 years after the introduction of the first of the decimal coin designs, a completely new series was issued. After an open competition that attracted more than 4,000 entries, designs by a young graphic designer, Matthew Dent, were selected, and represent a somewhat radical approach that uses elements of the shield of the Royal Arms for the denominations of 50 pence to 1 pence. The £1 shows the complete shield. Interestingly none of the coins show the value in numerical form.

The Mint offered sets of the new designs in various metals and qualities, and also gave collectors an opportunity to acquire the last issues of the original series. These, together with various commemorative issues, present collectors with a significant and varied range, and illustrate the importance of the sales of special issues to the Mint's business.

In the 40 years since Decimalisation there have been changes to the obverse portrait of Her Majesty The Queen with the exception of the Silver Maundy coins which retain the Mary Gillick design. The new effigy for the introduction of the decimal series was by Arnold Machin, followed then by Raphael Maklouf, and the current portrait is by Ian Rank - Broadley.

Previous editions of the catalogue listed coins according to the portrait rather than by denomination. After discussion with dealers and contributors, it has been decided that a radical change should be made so that users of the catalogue can see all issues of a particular denomination in sequence, starting with the lowest value and progressing to the highest. This will help collectors of, for example, £1, £2 and crown size coins. Catalogue numbers have been retained from the previous edition.

BRONZE

Obverse portrait by Arnold Machin

     4239   4240

4239 Half new penny. ℞. The Royal Crown and the inscription '1/2 NEW PENNY'
   (Reverse design: Christopher Ironside)

1971 .... £0.50	1975 .... £0.50	1979 .... £0.50
— Proof *FDC** £1	— Proof *FDC** £1	— Proof *FDC** £1
1972 Proof *FDC** £2	1976 .... £0.50	1980 .... £0.50
1973 .... £0.50	— Proof *FDC** £1	— Proof *FDC** £1
— Proof *FDC** £1	1977 .... £0.50	1981 .... £0.50
1974 .... £0.50	— Proof *FDC** £1	— Proof *FDC** £1
— Proof *FDC** £1	1978 .... £0.50	
	— Proof *FDC** £1	

4240 Half penny. 'New' omitted. As illustration

1982 .... £0.50	1983 .... £0.50	1984* £2
— Proof *FDC** £1	— Proof *FDC** £1	— Proof *FDC** £2

Obverse portrait by Arnold Machin

    4237   4238   4381

4237 One new penny. ℞. A portcullis with chains royally crossed, being the badge of Henry
   VII and his successors, and the inscription 'NEW PENNY' above and the figure '1' below.
   (Design: Christopher Ironside)

1971 .... £0.50	1975 .... £0.50	1979 .... £0.50
— Proof *FDC** £1	— Proof *FDC** £1	— Proof *FDC** £1
1972 Proof *FDC** £2	1976 .... £0.50	1980 .... £0.50
1973 .... £0.50	— Proof *FDC** £1	— Proof *FDC** £1
— Proof *FDC** ... £1	1977 .... £0.50	1981 .... £0.50
1974 .... £0.50	— Proof *FDC** £1	— Proof *FDC** £1
— Proof *FDC** £1	1978 .... £0.50	
	— Proof *FDC** £1	

4238 One penny. 'New' omitted, As illustration

1982 .... £0.50	1983 .... £0.50	1984 .... £1
— Proof *FDC** £1	— *FDC** £1	— Proof *FDC** £1

Obverse portrait by Raphael Maklouf

4381 One penny. ℞. Crowned portcullis with chains

1985 .... £0.50	1988 .... £0.50	1991 .... £0.50
— Proof *FDC** £1	— Proof *FDC** £1	— Proof *FDC** £1
1986 .... £0.50	1989 .... £0.50	1992 .... £0.50
— Proof *FDC** £1	— Proof *FDC** £1	— Proof *FDC** £1
1987	1990	
— Proof *FDC** £1	— Proof *FDC** £1	

* Coins marked thus were originally issued in Royal Mint sets.

COPPER PLATED STEEL

4391 **One penny** R. Crowned portcullis with chains

1992 .... £0.50	1995 .... £0.50	1997 .... £0.50
1993 .... £0.50	— Proof *FDC** £1	— Proof *FDC** £1
— Proof *FDC** £1	1996 .... £0.50	
1994 .... £0.50	— Proof *FDC** £1	
— Proof *FDC** £1	— Proof in silver *FDC** £15	

Obverse portrait by Ian Rank-Broadley

4710

4710 **One penny.** R. Crowned portcullis with chains. (Illus. as 4381)

1998 .... £1	2004 .... £1
— Proof *FDC* £3	— Proof *FDC** £3
1999 .... £1	2005 .... £1
— Proof *FDC* £3	— Proof *FDC** £3
2000 .... £1	2006 .... £1
— Proof *FDC* £3	— Proof *FDC** £3
— Proof in silver FDC (see PSS08) *	£8 ... — Proof in silver *FDC* (see PSS22)*
£8	
2001 .... £1	2007 .... £1
— Proof *FDC* £3	— Proof *FDC* £3
2002 .... £1	2008 .... £1
— Proof *FDC* £3	— Proof *FDC* £3
— Proof in gold *FDC* (see PGJS1)*£200	— Proof in silver *FDC* (see PSS27)* .. £8
2003 .... £1	— Proof in gold *FDC* (see PGEBCS)*....
£275	£275
— Proof *FDC* £3	— Proof in platinum *FDC*
	(see PPEBCS)* £350

4711

4711 **One penny.** R. A section of Our Royal Arms showing elements of the first and third quartering accompanied by the words 'ONE PENNY'(Reverse design: Matthew Dent)

2008 ....£3
— Proof *FDC* (in 2008 set, see PS96)* £3
— Proof in silver *FDC* (in 2008 set, see PSS28)* £8
— Proof piedfort in silver *FDC* (in 2008 set, see PSS29)* £15
— Proof in gold *FDC* (in 2008 set, see PGRSAS)* £275
— Proof in platinum *FDC* (in 2008 set, see PPRSAS)*...£350

* Coins marked thus were originally issued in Royal Mint sets.

2009
— Proof *FDC* (in 2009 set, see PS97)*
— BU in silver £15
— Proof in silver *FDC* (in 2009 set, see PSS 37)* £15
2010
— Proof *FDC* (in 2010 set, see PS101)* £3
— BU in silver £15
— Proof in silver *FDC* (in 2010 set, Edition: 3,500, see PSS41)* £15
2011 ....£3
— Proof *FDC* (in 2011 set, see PS104) * £3
— BU in silver..£15
— Proof in silver *FDC* (in 2011 set, Edition: 2,500, see PSS44) *............£15
2012 ....£3
— Proof *FDC* (in 2012 set, see PS107) * £3
— BU in silver...£23
— Proof in silver *FDC* (Edition: 995, see PSS47)* £30
— Proof in silver with selected gold plating *FDC* (Edition: 2,012, see PSS48) *......£30
— Proof in gold *FDC* (Edition: 150 see PGDJS)*...................................£275

BRONZE

Obverse portrait by Arnold Machin

4235	4236

4235 Two new pence. R. The badge of the Prince of Wales, being three ostrich feathers enfiling a coronet of cross pattee and fleur de lys, with the motto 'ICH DIEN', and the inscription '2 NEW PENCE' (Reverse design: Christopher Ironside)

1971 .... £0.50	1976 ....£0.50	1979..........................£0.50
— Proof *FDC*...... £1	— Proof *FDC* £1	— Proof *FDC*..........£1
1972 Proof *FDC*...... £2	1977 ....£0.50	1980..........................£0.50
1973 Proof *FDC*...... £2	— Proof *FDC* £1	— Proof *FDC*..........£1
1974 Proof *FDC*...... £2	1978 ....£0.50	1981..........................£0.50
1975.................... £0.50	— Proof *FDC* £1	— Proof *FDC*..........£1
— Proof *FDC*....... £1		

4236 Two pence. 'New' omitted. As illustration

| 1982*........................ £1 | 1983* ....£1 | 1984*..........................£1 |
| — Proof *FDC*....... £2 | — Proof *FDC* ....£2 | — Proof *FDC*..........£2 |

4236A — Error reverse. The word 'new' was dropped from the reverse of the currency issues in 1982 but a number of 2 pence coins were struck in 1983 with the incorrect reverse die, similar to coins listed as 4235. Reports suggest that the error coins, or 'Mules' were contained in some sets packed by the Royal Mint for Martini issued in 1983 ....£750

* Coins marked thus were originally issued in Royal Mint sets.

Obverse portrait by Raphael Maklouf

4376

4376   Two pence. R. Prince of Wales feathers

1985 .... £0.50	1988 .... £0.50	1991 .... £0.50
— Proof *FDC** £1	— Proof *FDC** £1	— Proof *FDC** £1
1986 .... £0.50	1989 .... £0.50	1992 .... £0.50
— Proof *FDC** £1	— Proof *FDC** £1	— Proof *FDC** £1
1987 .... £0.50	1990 .... £0.50	
— Proof *FDC** £1	— Proof *FDC** £1	

COPPER PLATED STEEL

4386   Two pence R. Plumes

1992 .... £1	1995 .... £1	1997 .... £0.50
1993 .... £1	— Proof *FDC** £1	— Proof *FDC** £1
— Proof *FDC** £1	1996 .... £1	
1994 .... £1	— Proof *FDC** £1	
— Proof *FDC** £1	— Proof in silver *FDC** £15	

Obverse portrait by Ian Rank-Broadley

4700

4700   Two pence. R. Prince of Wales feathers.
1998 .... £0.50

* *Coins marked thus were originally issued in Royal Mint sets.*

COPPER PLATED STEEL

4690 Two pence. R. Prince of Wales feathers.

1998	£1	2004	£1
— Proof *FDC**	£3	— Proof *FDC**	£3
1999	£1	2005	£1
— Proof *FDC**	£3	— Proof *FDC**	£3
2000	£1	2006	£1
— Proof *FDC**	£3	— Proof *FDC**	£3
— Proof in silver FDC (see PSS08)*	£8	— Proof in silver *FDC* (see PSS22)*	£8
2001	£1	2007	£1
— Proof *FDC**	£3	— Proof *FDC**	£3
2002	£1	2008	£1
— Proof *FDC**	£3	— Proof *FDC**	£3
— Proof in gold *FDC* (see PGJS1)*	£400	— Proof in silver *FDC* (see PSS27)*	£10
2003		— Proof in gold *FDC* (see PGEBCS)*	£550
— Proof *FDC**	£3	— Proof in platinum *FDC* (see PPEBCS)*	£700

4691

4691 Two pence. R. A section of Our Royal Arms showing elements of the second quartering accompanied by the words 'TWO PENCE'(Reverse design: Matthew Dent)

2008	£3
— Proof *FDC* (in 2008 set, see PS96)*	£3
— Proof in silver *FDC* (in 2008 set, see PSS28)*	£10
— Proof piedfort in silver *FDC* (in 2008 set, see PSS29)*	£20
— Proof in gold *FDC* (in 2008 set, see PGRSAS)*	£550
— Proof in platinum *FDC* (in 2008 set, see PPRSAS)*	£700
2009	£3
— Proof *FDC* (in 2009 set, see PS97)*	£3
— Proof in silver *FDC* (in 2009 set, see PSS 37)*	£10
2010	£3
— Proof *FDC* (in 2010 set, see PS101)*	£3
— Proof in silver *FDC* (in 2010 set, Edition: 3,500 see PSS41)*	£10
2011	£3
— Proof *FDC* (in 2011 set, see PS104) *	£3
— Proof in silver *FDC* (in 2011 set, Edition: 2,500, see PSS44) *	£15
2012	£3
— Proof *FDC* (in 2012 set, see PS107) *	£3
— Proof in silver *FDC* (Edition: 995, see PSS47)*	£30
— Proof in silver with selected gold plating *FDC* (Edition: 2,012, see PSS48) *	£30
— Proof in gold *FDC* (Edition: 150 see PGDJS)*	£550

* Coins marked thus were originally issued in Royal Mint sets.

CUPRO-NICKEL

Obverse portrait by Arnold Machin

4233   4234

4233 Five new pence. ℞. A thistle royally crowned, being the badge of Scotland, and the inscription '5 NEW PENCE' (Reverse design: Christopher Ironside)

1968 .... £0.50	1974 Proof *FDC** £4	1979 ....£0.50
1969 .... £0.50	1975 ....£0.50	— Proof *FDC** £2
1970 .... £0.50	— Proof *FDC** £2	1980 ....£0.50
1971 .... £0.50	1976 Proof *FDC** £4	— Proof *FDC** £2
— Proof *FDC** £2	1977 .... £0.50	1981 Proof *FDC** £4
1972 Proof *FDC** £4	— Proof *FDC** £2	
1973 Proof *FDC** £4	1978 .... £0.50	
	— Proof *FDC** £2	

4234 Five pence. 'New' omitted. As illustration

1982* £2	1983* £2	1984* £2
— Proof *FDC** £4	— Proof *FDC** £4	— Proof *FDC** £4

Obverse portrait by Raphael Maklouf

4371   4372

4371 Five pence. ℞. Crowned thistle

1985* £2	1988 ....£1	1990* £2
— Proof *FDC** £4	— Proof *FDC** £2	— Proof *FDC** £2
1986* £2	1989 ....£1	— Proof in silver *FDC** £12
— Proof *FDC** £4	— Proof *FDC** £2	
1987 .... £1		
— Proof *FDC** £2		

4372 Five pence. ℞. Crowned thistle: reduced diameter of 18mm

1990 ....£1	1992 ....£1	— Proof *FDC** £2
— Proof *FDC** £2	— Proof *FDC** £2	1996 ....£1
— Proof in silver *FDC** £10	1993* £2	— Proof *FDC** £2
— Proof piedfort in silver	— Proof *FDC** £4	— Proof in silver *FDC** £15
FDC (Issued:20,000)£20	1994 ....£1	1997 ....£1
1991 ....£1	— Proof *FDC** £2	— Proof *FDC** £2
— Proof *FDC** £2	1995 ....£1	

Obverse portrait by Ian Rank-Broadley

4670

4670 Five pence. R. Crowned thistle

1998.................................£1	2004 ....£1
— Proof *FDC* *...........................£3	— Proof *FDC** £3
1999 ....£1	2005 ....£1
— Proof *FDC* ¹ £3	— Proof *FDC*ered* £3
2000...................................£1	2006 ....£1
— Proof *FDC* *...........................£3	— Proof *FDC** £3
— Proof in silver FDC (see PSS08)*£12	— Proof in silver *FDC* (see PSS22)* £12
2001...................................£1	2007 ....£1
— Proof *FDC* *...........................£3	— Proof *FDC** £3
2002...................................£1	2008 ....£1
— Proof *FDC* *...........................£3	— Proof *FDC* * £3
— Proof in gold *FDC* (see PGJS1) £275	— Proof in silver *FDC* (see PSS27)* £12
2003...................................£1	— Proof in gold *FDC* (see PGEBCS)* £275
— Proof *FDC* *...........................£3	— Proof in platinum *FDC*
	(see PPEBCS)* £400

4671

4671 Five pence. R. A section of Our Royal Arms showing elements of all four quarterings accompanied by the words 'FIVE PENCE'(Reverse design: Matthew Dent)

2008..£3
— Proof *FDC* (in 2008 set, see PS96)*...£3
— Proof in silver *FDC* (in 2008 set, see PSS28)*...£12
— Proof piedfort in silver *FDC* (in 2008 set, see PSS29)* £25
— Proof in gold *FDC* (in 2008 set, see PGRSAS)* £275
— Proof in platinum *FDC* (in 2008 set, see PPRSAS)*...£400
2009...£1
— Proof *FDC* (in 2009 set, see PS97)*...£3
— Proof in silver *FDC* (in 2009 set, see PSS 37 ....£12
2010...£1
— Proof *FDC* (in 2010 set, see PS101)*...£3
— Proof in silver *FDC* (in 2010 set, Edition: 3,500 see PSS41)* £12
2011 ....£3
— Proof *FDC* (in 2011 set, see PS104) * £3
— Proof in silver *FDC* (in 2011 set, Edition: 2,500, see PSS44) * £12
2012 ....£3
— Proof *FDC* (in 2012 set, see PS107) * £3
— Proof in silver *FDC* (Edition: 995, see PSS47) *...£30
— Proof in silver with selected gold plating *FDC* (Edition: 2,012, see PSS48) *......£30
— Proof in gold *FDC* (Edition: 150 see PGDJS)* £275

* Coins marked thus were originally issued in Royal Mint sets.

Obverse portrait by Arnold Machin

4231   4232

4231 Ten new pence. R. Lion passant guardant being royally crowned, being part of the crest of England, and the inscription 'Ten New Pence' (Reverse design: Christopher Ironside)

1968 .... £0.50	1974 .... £0.50	1978 Proof FDC* £4
1969 .... £0.50	— Proof FDC* £3	1979 .... £0.50
1970 .... £0.50	1975 .... £0.50	— Proof FDC £3
1971 .... £0.50	— Proof FDC* £3	1980 .... £1
— Proof FDC* £3	1976 .... £0.50	— Proof FDC* £3
1972 Proof FDC* £4	— Proof FDC* £3	1981 .... £1
1973 .... 0.40	1977 .... 0.50	— Proof FDC* £3
— Proof FDC* £3	— Proof FDC* £3	

4232 Ten pence. 'New' omitted. As illustration

1982* £3	1983* £3	1984* £3
— Proof FDC* £4	— Proof FDC* £4	— Proof FDC* £4

Obverse portrait by Raphael Maklouf

4366

4366 Ten pence. R. Lion passant guardant

1985* £3	1988* £3	1991* £4
— Proof FDC * £4	— Proof FDC* £4	— Proof FDC* £4
1986* £3	1989* £4	1992* £3
— Proof FDC* £4	— Proof FDC* £4	— Proof FDC* £4
1987* £3	1990* £4	— Proof in silver FDC* £14
— Proof FDC* £4	— Proof FDC* £4	

* Coins marked thus were originally issued in Royal Mint sets.

4367   4650

4367 Ten pence R Lion passant guardant: reduced diameter of 24.5mm

1992	£1	1995	£1
— Proof *FDC**	£3	— Proof *FDC**	£3
— Proof in silver *FDC** £10		1996	£1
— Proof piedfort in silver *FDC** (Issued: 14,167)	£30	— Proof *FDC**	£3
1993*	£3	— Proof in silver *FDC**	£15
— Proof *FDC**	£4	1997	£1
1994*	£3	— Proof *FDC**	£3
— Proof *FDC**	£4		

Obverse portrait by Ian Rank-Broadley

4650 Ten pence. R. Lion passant guardant. (Illus. as 4232)

1998*	£3	2004	£1
— Proof *FDC**	£4	— Proof *FDC**	£3
1999*	£3	2005	£1
— Proof *FDC**	£4	— Proof *FDC**	£3
2000	£1	2006	£1
— Proof *FDC**	£3	— Proof *FDC**	£3
— Proof in silver FDC (see PSS08)*	£15	— Proof in silver *FDC* (see PSS22)*	£15
2001	£1	2007	£1
— Proof *FDC**	£3	— Proof *FDC*	£3
2002	£1	2008	£1
— Proof *FDC**	£3	— Proof *FDC**	£3
— Proof in gold *FDC* (see PGJS1)*	£500	— Proof in silver *FDC* (see PSS27)*	£15
2003	£1	— Proof in gold *FDC* (see PGEBCS)*	£500
— Proof *FDC**	£3	— Proof in platinum *FDC* (see PPEBCS)*	£800

4651

4651 Ten pence. R. A section of Our Royal Arms showing elements of the first quartering accompanied by the words 'TEN PENCE'(Reverse design: Matthew Dent)

2008	£3
— Proof *FDC* (in 2008 set, see PS96)*	£6
— Proof in silver *FDC* (in 2008 set, see PSS28)*	£15
— Proof piedfort in silver *FDC* (in 2008 set, see PSS29)*	£25
— Proof in gold *FDC* (in 2008 set, see PGRSAS)*	£500
— Proof in platinum *FDC* (in 2008 set, see PPRSAS)*	£800

2009...£3
— Proof *FDC* (in 2009 set, see PS97)*..£6
— Proof in silver *FDC* (in 2009 set, see PSS 37)*...£15
2010...£3
— Proof *FDC* (in 2010 set, see PS101)*..£6
— Proof in silver *FDC* (in 2010 set, Edition: 3,500 see PSS 41)*..............................£15
2011...£3
— Proof *FDC* (in 2011 set, see PS104) *..£3
— Proof in silver *FDC* (in 2011 set, Edition: 2,500, see PSS44) *.............................£15
2012...£3
— Proof *FDC* (in 2012 set, see PS107)*..£3
— Proof in silver *FDC* (Edition: 995, see PSS47)*..£30
— Proof in silver with selected gold plating *FDC* (Edition: 2,012, see PSS48)*.......£30
— Proof in gold *FDC* (Edition: 150 see PGDJS)*...£550

Obverse portrait by Arnold Machin

4230

4230 Twenty pence. R. The Royal Badge of the Rose of England represented as a double rose
barbed and seeded, slipped and leaved and ensigned by a Royal Crown and the date of the
year with the inscription 'TWENTY PENCE' and the figure '20' superimposed on the stem
of the rose.(Reverse design: William Gardner)
1982...£0.50
— Proof *FDC**...£3
— Proof piedfort in silver *FDC* (Issued: 10,000) £30
1983...£0.50
1984...£0.50
— Proof *FDC**...£3

Obverse portrait by Raphael Maklouf

4361

4361 Twenty pence. R. Crowned double rose

1985 ....£1	1990 ....£1	1995..............................£1
— Proof *FDC** £3	— Proof *FDC** £3	— Proof *FDC**...........£3
1986*.........................£3	1991 ....£1	1996..............................£1
— Proof *FDC** £4	— Proof *FDC** £3	— Proof *FDC**...........£3
1987..........................£1	1992...........................£1	1997..............................£1
— Proof *FDC** £3	— Proof *FDC** £3	— Proof in silver *FDC** £18
1988..........................£1	1993 ....£1	— Proof *FDC**...........£3
— Proof *FDC** £3	— Proof *FDC** £3	
1989..........................£1	1994 ....£1	
— Proof *FDC** £3	— Proof *FDC** £3	

* Coins marked thus were originally issued in Royal Mint sets.

Obverse portrait by Ian Rank-Broadley

4630   4631

4630 Twenty pence. ℞. Crowned double rose.

1998..£1		2004 ....£1
— Proof *FDC** £3		— Proof *FDC** £3
1999..£1		2005 ....£1
— Proof *FDC** £3		— Proof *FDC** £3
2000...£1		2006 ....£1
— Proof *FDC** £3		— Proof *FDC** £3
— Proof in silver *FDC* (see PSS08) *£20		— Proof in silver *FDC* (see PSS22)* £20
2001...£1		2007 ....£1
— Proof *FDC** £3		— Proof *FDC** £3
2002...£1		2008 ....£1
— Proof *FDC** £3		— Proof *FDC** £3
— Proof in gold *FDC* (see PGJS1)*£450		— Proof in silver *FDC* (see PSS27)*..........£20
2003...£1		— Proof in gold *FDC* (see PGEBCS)* £450
— Proof *FDC** £3		— Proof in platinum *FDC*
		(see PPEBCS)* £700

4631 Twenty pence. ℞. A section of Our Royal Arms showing elements of the second and forth quartering accompanied by the words 'TWENTY PENCE'(Reverse design: Matthew Dent)

2008...£3
— Proof *FDC* (in 2008 set, see PS96)* £3
— Proof in silver *FDC* (in 2008 set, see PSS28)* £20
— Proof piedfort in silver *FDC* (in 2008 set, see PSS29)* £40
— Proof in gold *FDC* (in 2008 set, see PGRSAS)* £450
— Proof in platinum *FDC* (in 2008 set, see PPRSAS)*...............................£700
2009...£3
— Proof *FDC* (in 2009 set, see PS97)* £6
— Proof in silver *FDC* (in 2009 set, see PSS 37)* £20
2010...£3
— Proof *FDC* (in 2010 set, see PS101)* £6
— Proof in silver *FDC* (in 2010 set, Edition: 3,500 see PSS 41)* £20
2011...£3
— Proof *FDC* (in 2011 set, see PS104) * £3
— Proof in silver *FDC* (in 2011 set, Edition: 2,500, see PSS44) * £15
2012...£3
— Proof *FDC* (in 2012 set, see PS107)* £3
— Proof in silver *FDC* (Edition: 995, see PSS47)*.....................................£30
— Proof in silver with selected gold plating *FDC* (Edition: 2,012, see PSS48)*.......£30
— Proof in gold *FDC* (Edition: 150 see PGDJS)* £450

4631A — Error obverse – known as a Mule. The new reverse design by Matthew Dent does not include the year date and this should have appeared on the obverse. A number of coins were struck using the undated obverse die that had previously been used with the dated reverse of the crowned double rose. (See Illus. 4630) £100

* Coins marked thus were originally issued in Royal Mint sets.

Obverse portrait by Arnold Machin

4223

4223 **Fifty new pence** (seven-sided). R. A figure of Britannia seated beside a lion, with a shield resting against her right side, holding a trident in her right hand and an olive branch in her left hand; and the inscription '50 NEW PENCE'. (Reverse design: Christopher Ironside)

1969 .... £3	1976 .... £2	1979 .... £2
1970 .... £4	— Proof *FDC** £3	— Proof *FDC** £3
1971 Proof *FDC** £5	1977 .... £2	1980 .... £2
1972 Proof *FDC** £5	— Proof *FDC** £3	— Proof *FDC** £3
1974 Proof *FDC** £5	1978 .... £2	1981 .... £2
1975 Proof *FDC** £5	— Proof *FDC** £3	— Proof *FDC** £3

4224   4225

4224 Accession to European Economic Community. R. The inscription 'FIFTY PENCE' and the date of the year, surrounded by nine hands, symbolizing the nine members of the community, clasping one another in a mutual gesture of trust, assistance and friendship. (Reverse design: David Wynne)

1973 .... £3
— Proof *FDC* ** £6

4224A — Design as 4224 above, but struck in very small numbers in silver on thicker blank. Sometimes referred to as a piedfort but not twice the weight of the regular cupro-nickel currency issue. The pieces were presented to EEC Finance Ministers and possibly senior officials on the occasion of the United Kingdom joining the European Economic Community £2500

4225 **Fifty pence.** 'New' omitted. As illustration

1982 .... £3	1983 .... £2	1984* £3
— Proof *FDC** £3	— Proof *FDC** £3	— Proof *FDC** £3

* *Coins marked thus were originally issued in Royal Mint sets*
** *Issued as an individual proof coin and in the year set*

Obverse portrait by Raphael Maklouf

4351

4351   Fifty pence. R. Britannia

1985.............................£3	1990*................................£4	1996*...............................£3
— Proof *FDC*.........£3	— Proof *FDC*............£5	— Proof *FDC*............£4
1986*................................£3	1991*....................................£4	— Proof in silver *FDC* £20
— Proof *FDC*.........£3	— Proof *FDC*.............£5	1997...............................£2
1987*............................£3	1992*...............................£4	— Proof *FDC*............£4
— Proof *FDC*............£3	— Proof *FDC*...................£5	— Proof in silver *FDC*£20
1988*............................£3	1993*................................£4	
— Proof *FDC*.........£4	— Proof *FDC*.............£4	
1989*............................£4	1995*................................£3	
— Proof *FDC*.........£3	— Proof *FDC*.............£4	

4352

4352 Fifty pence Presidency of the Council of European Community Ministers and completion
of the Single Market. R A representation of a table on which are placed twelve stars, linked
by a network of lines to each other and also to twelve chairs, around the table, on one of
which appear the letters 'UK', and with the dates '1992' and '1993' above and the value
'50 PENCE' below. (Reverse design: Mary Milner Dickens)

1992-1993 ....£12
— Proof *FDC*...£12
— Proof in silver *FDC** (Issued: 26,890 .... £28
— Proof piedfort in silver *FDC* (Issued: 10,993) £60
— Proof in gold *FDC* (Issued: 1,864)...£1000

* Coins marked thus were originally issued in Royal Mint sets

4353

4353 Fifty pence 50th Anniversary of the Normandy Landings on D-Day. R: A design representing the Allied invasion force of the D-Day landings heading for Normandy and filling the sea and sky, Together with the value '50 PENCE' (Reverse design: John Mills)

1994 ....£3
—   Specimen in presentation folder...£5
—   Proof *FDC** £5
—   Proof in silver *FDC* (Issued: 40,000)..£35
—   Proof piedfort in silver *FDC* (Issued: 10,000) £60
—   Proof in gold *FDC* (Issued: 1,877)...£1000

4354 Fifty pence R. Britannia: reduced diameter of 27.3mm

1997 ....£2
—   Proof *FDC** £4
—   Proof in silver *FDC* (Issued: 1,632)..£25
—   Proof piedfort in silver *FDC* (Issued: 7,192) £40

Obverse portrait by Ian Rank-Broadley

4610

4610 Fifty pence. R. Britannia. (Illus. as 4351)

1998 .... £3		2006 ....£3	
— Proof *FDC** £3		— Proof *FDC** £3	
1999 .... £3		— Proof in silver *FDC* (see PSS22)* £25	
— Proof *FDC** £3		2007 ....£3	
2000 .... £3		— Proof *FDC** £3	
— Proof *FDC** £3		2008 ....£3	
— Proof in silver *FDC* (see PSS08)*£25		— Proof *FDC** £3	
2001 .... £3		— Proof in silver *FDC* (see PSS27)* £30	
— Proof *FDC** £3		— Proof in gold *FDC* (see PGEBCS)* £600	
2002 .... £3		— Proof in platinum *FDC* (see PPEBCS)* £800	
— Proof *FDC** £3		2009	
— Proof in gold *FDC* (see PGJS1)* £450		— Proof *FDC* (in 2009 set, see PS100)* £15	
2003 ....£3		— Proof in silver *FDC* (in 2009 set,	
— Proof *FDC** £3		see PSS40)*.......................£30	
2004 ....£3		— Proof in gold *FDC* (in 2009 set,	
— Proof *FDC**	£3	see PG50PCS)* £600	
2005	£3	— Proof piedfort in gold *FDC*	
— Proof *FDC**	£3	(see PG50PPCS)* £1500	

4611   4612   4613

4611 Fifty pence. R. Celebratory pattern of twelve stars reflecting the European flag with the dates 1973 and 1998 commemorating the 25th Anniversary of the United Kingdom's membership of the European Union and Presidency of the Council of Ministers. (Reverse design: John Mills)

1998 ....£2
— Proof *FDC** £5
— Proof in silver *FDC* (Issued: 8,859) £30
— Proof piedfort in silver *FDC* (Issued: 8,440) £60
— Proof in gold *FDC* (Issued: 1,177)...£600
2009
— Proof *FDC* (in 2009 set, see PS100)* £15
— Proof in silver *FDC* (in 2009 set, see PSS40)* £30
— Proof in gold *FDC* (in 2009 set, see PG50PCS)* £600
— Proof piedfort in gold *FDC* (see PG50PPCS) * £1500

4612 Fifty pence. R. A pair of hands set against a pattern of radiating lines with the words 'FIFTIETH ANNIVERSARY' and the value '50 PENCE' accompanied by the initials 'NHS' which appear five times on the outer border. (Reverse design: David Cornell)

1998 ....£2
— Specimen in presentation folder £3
— Proof in silver *FDC* (Issued: 9,032) £30
— Proof piedfort in silver *FDC* (Issued: 5,117) £60
— Proof in gold *FDC* (Issued: 651)...£600
2009
— Proof *FDC* (in 2009 set, see PS100)* £15
— Proof in silver *FDC* (in 2009 set, see PSS40)* £30
— Proof in gold *FDC* (in 2009 set, see PG50PCS)* £600
— Proof piedfort in gold *FDC* (see PG50PPCS) * £1500

4613 Fifty pence. Library commemorative. R. The turning pages of a book above the dates '1850 – 2000'and the value '50 PENCE', all above a classical library building on which the words 'PUBLIC LIBRARY' and, within the pediment , representations of compact discs. (Reverse design: Mary Milner Dickens)

2000 ....£2
— Specimen in presentation folder £5
— Proof *FDC** £5
— Proof in silver *FDC* (Issued: 7,634)...£28
— Proof piedfort in silver *FDC* (Issued: 5,721) £60
— Proof in gold *FDC* (Issued: 710)...£600
2009
— Proof *FDC* (in 2009 set, see PS100)* £15
— Proof in silver *FDC* (in 2009 set, see PSS40)* £30
— Proof in gold *FDC* (in 2009 set, scc PG50PCS)* £600
— Proof piedfort in gold *FDC* (see PG50PPCS) * £1500

* Coins marked thus were originally issued in Royal Mint sets.

4614 4615 4616

4614 Fifty pence. Anniversary of the Suffragette Movement commemorative. R. The figure of a suffragette chained to railings and holding a banner on which appear the letters 'WSPU', to the right a ballot paper marked with a cross and the words 'GIVE WOMEN THE VOTE', to the left the value '50 PENCE' and below and to the far right the dates '1903' and '2003'. (Reverse design: Mary Milner Dickens)

2003...£2
— Specimen in presentation folder (Issued: 9,582)...£5
— Proof *FDC* (in 2003 set, see PS78)*...£5
— Proof in silver *FDC* (Issued: 6,267) £28
— Proof piedfort in silver *FDC* (Issued 6,795) £60
— Proof in gold *FDC* (Issued: 942)..£600
2009
— Proof *FDC* (in 2009 set, see PS100)*...£15
— Proof in silver *FDC* (in 2009 set, see PSS40)*..£30
— Proof in gold *FDC* (in 2009 set, see PG50PCS)*...£600
— Proof piedfort in gold *FDC* (see PG50PPCS) *...£1500

4615 Fifty pence. 50th anniversary of the first sub four-minute mile. R. The legs of a running athlete with a stylised stopwatch in the background and, below, the value '50 PENCE'. (Reverse design: James Butler)

2004...£2
— Specimen in presentation folder (Issued: 10,371)...£5
— Proof *FDC* (in 2004 set, see PS81)*...£5
— Proof in silver *FDC* (Issued: 4,924)..£28
— Proof piedfort in silver *FDC* (Issued: 4,054) £60
— Proof in gold *FDC* (Issued: 644)..£600
2009
— Proof *FDC* (in 2009 set, see PS100)*...£15
— Proof in silver *FDC* (in 2009 set, seePSS40)*..£30
— Proof in gold *FDC* (in 2009 set, see PG50PCS)*...£600
— Proof piedfort in gold *FDC* (see PG50PPCS)*... £1500

4616 Fifty pence. 250th anniversary of the publication of Samuel Johnson's Dictionary of the English Language. R. Entries from Samuel Johnson's Dictionary of the English Language for the words 'FIFTY' and 'PENCE', with the figure '50' above, and the inscription 'JOHNSON'S DICTIONARY 1755' below. (Reverse design: Tom Phillips)

2005...£2
— Proof *FDC* (in 2005 set, see PS84)*...£5
— Proof in silver *FDC* (Issued: 4,029)..£28
— Proof piedfort in silver *FDC* (Issued: 3,808) £60
— Proof in gold *FDC* (Issued: 584)..£600
2009
— Proof *FDC* (in 2009 set, see PS100)*...£15
— Proof in silver *FDC* (in 2009 set, see PSS40)*..£30
— Proof in gold *FDC* (in 2009 set, see PG50PCS)*...£600
— Proof piedfort in gold *FDC* (see PG50PPCS)*...£1500

* Coins marked thus were originally issued in Royal Mint sets.

4617   4618   4619

4617 Fifty pence. 150th anniversary of the institution of the Victoria Cross. R. A depiction of the
obverse and reverse of a Victoria Cross with the date '29. JAN 1856' in the centre of the
reverse of the Cross, the letters 'VC' to the right and the value 'FIFTY PENCE'. (Reverse
design: Claire Aldridge)

2006..£2
— Specimen in presentation folder with 4618..£7
— Proof *FDC* (in 2006 set, see PS87)*...£5
— Proof in silver *FDC* (Edition: 7,500) £30
— Proof piedfort in silver *FDC* (see PSS27)..£60
— Proof in gold *FDC* (Edition: 1,000) £600
2009
— Proof *FDC* (in 2009 set, see PS100)*...£15
— Proof in silver *FDC* (in 2009 set, see PSS40)*...£30
— Proof in gold *FDC* (in 2009 set, see PG50PCS)*...£600
— Proof piedfort in gold *FDC* (see PG50PPCS)*...£1500

4618 Fifty pence. 150th anniversary of the institution of the Victoria Cross. R. A Depiction of
a soldier carrying a wounded comrade with an outline of the Victoria Cross surrounded
by a sunburst effect in the background and the value 'FIFTY PENCE'. (Reverse design:
Clive Duncan)

2006..£2
— Specimen in presentation folder with 4617..£7
— Proof *FDC* (in 2006 set, see PS87)*...£5
— Proof in silver *FDC* (Edition: 7,500) £30
— Proof piedfort in silver *FDC* (see PSS27)..£60
— Proof in gold *FDC* (Edition: 1,000) £600
2009
— Proof *FDC* (in 2009 set, see PS100)*...£15
— Proof in silver *FDC* (in 2009 set, see PSS40)*...£30
— Proof in gold *FDC* (in 2009 set, see PG50PCS)*...£600
— Proof piedfort in gold *FDC* (see PG50PPCS)*...£1500

4619 Fifty pence. Centenary of the Founding of the Scouting Movement. R. A Fleur-de-lis
superimposed over a globe and surrounded by the inscription 'BE PREPARED', and the
dates '1907' and '2007' and the denomination 'FIFTY PENCE' (Reverse design:
Kerry Jones)

2007..£2
— Specimen in presentation folder...£7
— Proof *FDC** (in 2007 set, see PS90) £5
— Proof in silver *FDC* (Issued: 10,895) £30
— Proof piedfort in silver *FDC** (Issued; 1,555) £60
— Proof in gold *FDC* (Issued: 1,250) £600
2009
— Proof *FDC* (in 2009 set, see PS100)*...£15
— Proof in silver *FDC* (in 2009 set, see PSS40)*...£30
— Proof in gold *FDC* (in 2009 set, see PG50PCS)*...£600
— Proof piedfort in gold *FDC* (see PG50PPCS)*...£1500

* *Coins marked thus were originally issued in Royal Mint sets.*

4620   4621

4620 Fifty pence. R. A section of Our Royal Arms showing elements of the third and fourth quarterings accompanied by the words 'FIFTY PENCE' (Reverse design: Matthew Dent)

2008 ....£3
— Proof *FDC* (in 2008 set, see PS96)* £5
— Proof in silver *FDC* (in 2008 set, see PSS28)* £30
— Proof piedfort in silver *FDC* (in 2008 set, see PSS29)* £60
— Proof in gold *FDC* (in 2008 set, see PGRSAS)* £600
— Proof in platinum *FDC* (in 2008 set, see PPRSAS)* £800
2009 ....£3
— Proof *FDC* (in 2009 set, see PS97)* £5
— Proof in silver *FDC* (in 2009 set, see PSS37)* £30
— Proof in gold *FDC* (in 2009 set, see PG50PCS)* £600
— Proof piedfort in gold *FDC* (see PG50PPCS)* £1500
2010 ....£3
— Proof *FDC* (in 2010 set, see PS101)* £5
— Proof in silver *FDC* (in 2010 set, Edition: 3,500, see PSS41)* £30
2011 ....£3
— Proof *FDC* (in 2010 set, see PS104)* £3
— Proof in silver *FDC* (in 2011 set, Edition: 2,500, see PSS44) * £15
2012 ....£3
— Proof *FDC* (in 2012 set, see PS107)* £3
— Proof in silver *FDC* (Edition: 995, see PSS47)* £30
— Proof in silver with selected gold plating *FDC* (Edition: 2,012, see PSS48) £30
— Proof in gold *FDC* (Edition: 150 see PGDJS)* £600

4621 Fifty pence 250th Anniversary of the foundation of the Royal Botanical Gardens, Kew. R. A design showing the pagoda, a building associated with the Royal Botanical Gardens at Kew, encircled by a vine and accompanied by the dates '1759' and '2009', with the word 'KEW' at the base of the pagoda.(Reverse design: Christopher Le Brun)

2009 ....£3
— Specimen in presentation pack (Edition: 50,000) £7
— Proof *FDC* (in 2009 set, see PS97)* £7
— Proof in silver *FDC* (Edition: 20,000 including coins in sets) £30
— Proof piedfort in silver *FDC* (Edition: 3,500 including coins in sets) £55
— Proof in gold *FDC* (Edition: 1,000 including coins in sets) £600
— Proof piedfort in gold *FDC* (see PG50PPCS)* £1500

4622 Fifty new pence R. Britannia (See 4223).
— Proof *FDC* (in 2009 set, see PS100)* £15
— Proof in silver *FDC* (in 2009 set, see PSS40)* £30
— Proof in gold *FDC* (in 2009 set, see PG50PCS)* £600
— Proof piedfort in gold *FDC* (in 2009 set, see PG50PPCS)* £1500

* Coins marked thus were originally issued in Royal Mint sets.

4623 Fifty new pence Accession to European Economic Community R. Clasped hands.
(See 4224)

— Proof *FDC* (in 2009 set, see PS100)* £15
— Proof in silver *FDC* (in 2009 set, see PSS40)* £30
— Proof in gold *FDC* (in 2009 set, see PG50PCS)* £600
— Proof piedfort in gold *FDC* (in 2009 set, see PG50PPCS)* £1500

4624 Fifty pence R. Presidency of the Council of European Community Ministers and
completion of the Single Market. R. Conference table top and twelve stars. (See 4352)

— Proof *FDC* (in 2009 set, see PS100)* £15
— Proof in silver *FDC* (in 2009 set, see PSS40)* £30
— Proof in gold *FDC* (in 2009 set, see PG50PCS)* £600
— Proof piedfort in gold *FDC* (in 2009 set, see PG50PPCS)* £1500

4625 Fifty pence 50th Anniversary of the Normandy Landings on D-Day. R. Allied Invasion
Force (See 4353)

— Proof *FDC* (in 2009 set, see PS100)* £15
— Proof in silver *FDC* (in 2009 set, see PSS40)* £30
— Proof in gold *FDC* (in 2009 set, see PG50PCS)* £600
— Proof piedfort in gold *FDC* (in 2009 set, see PG50PPCS)* £1500

4626   4627

4626 Fifty pence. 100th Anniversary of Girl Guides. R. A design which depicts a repeating
pattern of the current identity of Girl Guiding, UK, accompanied by the inscription
'CELEBRATING ONE HUNDRED YEARS OF GIRLGUIDING UK' and the
denomination 'FIFTY PENCE' (Reverse design: Jonathan Evans and Donna Hainan)
2010 ....£1

— Specimen on presentation card (Edition: 75,000) £5
— Specimen in presentation folder (Edition: 50,000) £7
— Proof *FDC* (in 2010 set, see PS101)* £7
— Proof in silver *FDC* (Edition: 20,000 including coins in sets) £30
— Proof piedfort in silver *FDC* (Edition: 5,000 including coins in sets) £55
— Proof in gold *FDC* (Edition: 1,000) £650

4627 Fifty pence. Fifth Anniversary of the World Wildlife Fund. R. A design which features 50
different icons symbolising projects and programmes that the World   Wildlife Fund has
supported over the course of the last 50 years, with the Panda logo of the organisation in
the centre and the date '2011' below. (Reverse design: Matthew Dent)
2011 ....£1

— Specimen in presentation folder £7
— Proof *FDC* (in 2011 set, see PS104)...£7
— Proof in silver *FDC* (Edition: 40,000 including coins in sets) £42
— Proof piedfort in silver *FDC* (Edition: 3,500 including coins in set) £73
— Proof in gold *FDC* (Edition: 1,500)...£900

* Coins marked thus were originally issued in Royal Mint sets.

NICKEL-BRASS

Obverse portrait by Arnold Machin

4221   4222

4221 One pound R. The Ensigns Armorial of Our United Kingdom of Great Britain and
Northern Ireland with the value 'ONE POUND' below and the edge inscription
'DECUS ET TUTAMEN' (Reverse design: Eric Sewell)

1983 ....£5
— Specimen in presentation folder (Issued: 484,900) £5
— Proof *FDC* (in 1983 set, seePS33)* £5
— Proof in silver *FDC* (Issued: 50,000) £35
— Proof piedfort in silver *FDC* (Issued: 10,000) £125

4222 One pound (Scottish design). R. A thistle eradicated enfiling a representation of Our
Royal Diadem with the value 'ONE POUND' below and the edge inscription 'NEMO
ME IMPUNE LACESSIT' (Reverse design: Leslie Durbin)

1984 ....£5
— Specimen in presentation folder (Issued: 27,960) £5
— Proof *FDC* (in 1984 set, see PS34)* £5
— Proof in silver *FDC* (Issued: 44,855) £30
— Proof piedfort in silver *FDC* (Issued: 15,000) £60

Obverse portrait by Raphael Maklouf

4331   4332   4333

4331 One pound (Welsh design). R. A leek eradicated enfiling a representation of Our Royal
Diadem with the value 'ONE POUND' below and the edge inscription 'PLEIDIOL
WYF I'M GWLAD". (Reverse design: Leslie Durbin)

1985 ....£4
— Specimen in presentation folder (Issued: 24,850) £4
— Proof *FDC* (in 1985 set, see PS35)* £5
— Proof in silver *FDC* (Issued: 50,000) £30
— Proof piedfort in silver *FDC* (Issued: 15,000) £60
1990 ....£5
— Proof *FDC* (in 1990 set, see PS45)* £6
— Proof in silver *FDC* (Issued: 23,277) £28

* *Coins marked thus were originally issued in Royal Mint sets.*

4332   One pound (Northern Irish design). R. A flax plant eradicated enfiling a representation
of Our Royal Diadem with value 'ONE POUND' below and **the** Edge inscription
'DECUS ET TUTAMEN'. (Reverse design: Leslie Durbin)
1986 ....£5
— Specimen in presentation folder (Issued: 19,908) £5
— Proof *FDC* (in 1986 set, see PS37)* £4
— Proof in silver *FDC* (Issued: 37, 958) £30
— Proof piedfort in silver *FDC* (Issued: 15,000) £60
1991 ....£5
— Proof *FDC* (in 1991 set, see PS47)* £6
— Proof in silver *FDC* (Issued: 22,922) £28

4333   One pound (English design). R. An oak tree enfiling a representation of Our Royal
Diadem **w**ith the value 'ONE POUND' below and the edge inscription 'DECUS ET
TUTAMEN'. (Reverse design: Leslie Durbin)
1987 ....£4
— Specimen in presentation folder (Issued: 72,607) £4
— Proof *FDC* (in 1987 set, see PS39)* £6
— Proof in silver *FDC* (Issued: 50,000) £30
— Proof piedfort in silver *FDC* (Issued: 15,000) £60
1992 ....£5
— Proof *FDC* (in 1992 set, see PS49)* £6
— Proof in silver *FDC* (Issued: 13,065) £30

4334   One pound (Royal Shield). R. A Shield of Our Royal Arms ensigned by a representation
of Our Royal Crown with the value 'ONE POUND' below and the Edge inscription
'DECUS ET TUTAMEN'. (Reverse design: Derek Gorringe)
1988 ....£5
— Specimen in presentation folder (Issued: 29,550) £6
— Proof *FDC* (in 1988 set, see PS41)* £6
— Proof in silver *FDC* (Issued: 50,000) £35
— Proof piedfort in silver *FDC* (Issued: 10,000) £60

4335   One pound (Scottish design). Edge 'NEMO ME IMPUNE LACESSIT' (Illus. as 4222)
1989 ....£5
— Proof *FDC* (in 1989 set, see PS43)* £6
— Proof in silver *FDC* (Issued: 22,275) £30
— Proof piedfort in silver *FDC* (Issued: 10,000) £60

4336   One pound (Royal Arms design). Edge 'DECUS ET TUTAMEN' (Illus. as 4221)
1993 ....£5
— Proof *FDC* (in 1993 set, see PS51)* £6
— Proof in silver *FDC* (Issued: 16,526) £30
— Proof piedfort in silver *FDC* (Issued: 12,500) £60

4337   One pound (Scottish design). R: A Lion rampant within a double tressure flory counter-
flory, being that quartering of Our Royal Arms known heraldically as Scotland with
the value 'ONE POUND' below and the edge inscription 'NEMO ME IMPUNE
LACESSIT'. (Reverse design: Norman Sillman)
1994 ....£4
— Specimen in presentation folder £5
— Proof *FDC* (in 1994 set, see PS53)* £6
— Proof in silver *FDC* (Issued: 25,000) £30
— Proof piedfort in silver *FDC* (Issued: 11,722) £60

* Coins marked thus were originally issued in Royal Mint sets.

4338 One pound (Welsh design). R. A dragon passant, being Our badge for Wales with the value 'ONE POUND' below and the edge inscription 'PLEIDIOL WYF I'M GWLAD'. (Reverse design: Norman Sillman)

1995 ....£4
— Specimen in presentation folder, English version £5
— Specimen in presentation folder, Welsh version £10
— Proof *FDC* (in 1995 set, see PS55)* £5
— Proof in silver *FDC* (Issued: 27,445) £30
— Proof piedfort in silver *FDC* (Issued: 8,458) £70

4339 One pound (Northern Irish design). R. A Celtic cross charged at the centre with an Annulet therein a Pimpernel flower and overall an ancient Torque, symbolizing that part of Our Kingdom known as Northern Ireland with the value 'ONE POUND' below and the edge inscription 'DECUS ET TUTAMEN'. (Reverse design: Norman Sillman)

1996 ....£4
— Specimen in presentation folder £6
— Proof *FDC* (in 1996 set, see PS57)* £6
— Proof in silver *FDC* (Issued: 25,000) £30
— Proof piedfort in silver *FDC* (Issued: 10,000 ....£60

4340

4340 One pound (English design) R. Three lions passant guardant, being that quartering of Our Royal Arms known heraldically as *England*, with the value 'ONE POUND' below and the edge inscription 'DECUS ET TUTAMEN.(Reverse design: Norman Sillman)

1997 ....£4
— Specimen in presentation folder (Issued 56,996) £5
— Proof *FDC* (in 1997 set, see PS59)* £5
— Proof in silver *FDC* (Issued: 20,137) £30
— Proof piedfort in silver *FDC* (Issued: 10,000) £60

Obverse portrait by Ian Rank-Broadley

4590

4590 One pound (Royal Arms design). Edge: 'DECUS ET TUTAMEN' (rev. as 4221)

1998 ....£5
— Proof *FDC* (in 1998 set, see PS61)* £6
— Proof in silver *FDC* (Issued: 13,863) £30
— Proof piedfort in silver *FDC* (Issued: 7,894) £60

2003 ....£3
— Specimen in presentation folder (Issued: 23,760) £5
— Proof *FDC* (in 2003 set, see PS78)* £6
— Proof in silver *FDC* (Issued: 15,830) £30
— Proof piedfort in silver *FDC* (Issued: 9,871) £60
2008
— Specimen in presentation folder (Issued: 18,336) £7
— Proof *FDC* (in 2008 set, see PS93)* £6
— Proof in silver *FDC* (Issued: 8,441) £30
— Proof in gold *FDC* (Issued: 674) £750
— Proof in platinum *FDC* (in 2008 set, see PPEBCS)* £1000
4590A 2008
— Proof in silver with selected gold plating on reverse *FDC* (in 2008 set,
see PSS30)* £40
4591   One pound. (Scottish lion design). Edge: 'NEMO ME IMPUNE LACESSIT' (rev as 4337)
1999 ....£3
— Specimen in presentation folder £5
— Proof *FDC* (in 1999 set, see PS63)* £6
— Proof in silver *FDC* (Issued: 16,328) £30
— Proof piedfort in silver *FDC* (Issued: 9,975 .... £60
2008
— Proof in gold *FDC* (in 2008 set, see PG1PCS)* £750
4591A 1999
— Proof in silver *FDC,* with reverse frosting, (Issued: 1,994)* £50
4591B 2008
— Proof in silver with selected gold plating on reverse *FDC* (in 2008 set, see PSS30)* £40
4592   One pound. (Welsh design). Edge: 'PLEIDIOL WYF I'M GWLAD' (rev. as 4338)
2000 ....£3
— Proof *FDC* (in 2000 set, see PS65)* £6
— Proof in silver *FDC* (Issued: 15,913) £30
— Proof piedfort in silver *FDC* (Issued: 9,994) £60
2008
— Proof in gold *FDC* (in 2008 set, see PG1PCS)* £750
4592A 2000
— Proof in silver *FDC*, with reverse frosting, (Issued: 1,994)* £50
4592B 2008
— Proof in silver with selected gold plating on reverse *FDC* (in 2008 set,
see PSS30)* £40

* Coins marked thus were originally issued in Royal Mint sets.
4593   One pound. (Northern Irish design). Edge: 'DECUS ET TUTAMEN' (rev. as 4339)
2001 ....£3
— Proof *FDC* (in 2001 set, see PS68)* £6
— Proof in silver *FDC* (Issued: 11,697) £30
— Proof piedfort in silver *FDC* (Issued: 8,464) £60
2008
— Proof in gold *FDC* (in 2008 set, see PG1PCS)* £750
4593A 2001
— Proof in silver *FDC*, with reverse frosting, (Issued: 1,540)* £60
4593B 2008
— Proof in silver with selected gold plating on reverse *FDC* (in 2008 set, see PSS30)* £40

* Coins marked thus were originally issued in Royal Mint sets.

4594 One pound. (English design) Edge: 'DECUS ET TUTAMEN' (rev. as 4340)

2002 ....£3

— Proof *FDC* (in 2002 set, see PS72)* £6

— Proof in silver *FDC* (Issued: 17,693) £30

— Proof piedfort in silver *FDC* (Issued: 6,599) £60

— Proof in gold *FDC* (in 2002 set, see PGJS1)* £750

2008

— Proof in gold *FDC* (in 2008 set, see PG1PCS)* £750

4594A2002

— Proof in silver *FDC*, with reverse frosting, (Issued: 1,540)* £60

4594B2008

— Proof in silver with selected gold plating on reverse *FDC* (in 2008 set,
see PSS30)* £40

4595   4595B

4595 One pound. Scotland R. A representation of the Forth Railway Bridge with a border of
railway tracks and beneath, the value 'ONE POUND' and an incuse decorative feature
on the edge symbolising bridges and pathways. (Reverse design: Edwina Ellis)

2004 ....£3

— Specimen in presentation folder (Issued: 24,014) £5

— Proof *FDC* (in 2004 set, see PS81)* £6

— Proof in silver *FDC* (Issued: 11,470) £30

— Proof piedfort in silver *FDC* (Issued: 7,013) £60

— Proof in gold *FDC* (Issued: 2,618)..£750

2008

— Proof in gold *FDC* (in 2008 set, see PG1PCS)* £750

4595A One pound pattern. Scotland. R. Forth Railway Bridge but dated 2003 with plain edge
and hallmark, reading "PATTERN" instead of "ONE POUND"

— Proof in silver *FDC** £25

— Proof in gold *FDC** £700

4595B One pound pattern. Scotland. R. Unicorn with the word "Pattern" below with plain
edge and hallmark and dated 2004. (Reverse design: Timothy Noad)

— Proof in silver *FDC** £25

— Proof in gold *FDC** £700

4595C..2008

— Proof in silver as 4595 with selected gold plating on reverse *FDC* (in 2008 set, see
PSS30)* £40

* Coins marked thus were originally issued in Royal Mint sets.

| 4596 | 4596B | 4597 | 4597B |

4596 One pound. Wales. ℞. A representation of the Menai Straits Bridge with a border of railings and stanchions, the value 'ONE POUND' and an incuse decorative feature on the edge symbolising bridges and pathways. (Reverse design: Edwina Ellis)

2005 ....£3
— Specimen in presentation folder (Issued: 24,802) £6
— Proof *FDC* (in 2005 set, see PS84)* £6
— Proof in silver *FDC* (Issued: 8,371) £35
— Proof piedfort in silver *FDC* (Issued: 6,007) £60
— Proof in gold *FDC* (Issued: 1,195) £750
2008
— Proof in gold *FDC* (in 2008 set, see PG1PCS)* £750

4596A One pound pattern. Wales. ℞. Menai Straits Bridge but dated 2003 with plain edge and hallmark
— Proof in silver *FDC* (in 2003 set, see PPS1)* £25
— Proof in gold *FDC* (in 2003 set, see PPS2)* £700

4596B One pound pattern. Wales. ℞ Dragon and the word "Pattern" below with plain edge and hallmark and dated 2004. (Reverse design: Timothy Noad)
— Proof in silver *FDC* (in 2004 set, see PPS3)* £25
— Proof in gold *FDC* (in 2004 set, see PPS4)* £700

4596C 2008
— Proof in silver as 4596 with selected gold plating on reverse *FDC* (in 2008 set, see PSS30)* £40

4597 One pound. Northern Ireland. ℞. A representation of the Egyptian Arch Railway Bridge in County Down with a border of railway station canopy dags, the value 'ONE POUND' and an incuse decorative feature on the edge symbolising bridges and pathways. (Reverse design: Edwina Ellis)

2006 ....£4
— Specimen in presentation folder £6
— Proof *FDC* (in 2006 set, see PS87)* £8
— Proof in silver *FDC* (Edition: 20,000) £30
— Proof piedfort in silver *FDC* (Edition: 7,500) £60
— Proof in gold *FDC* (Edition: 1,500) £750
2008
— Proof in gold *FDC* (in 2008 set, see PG1PCS)* £750

4597A One pound pattern. Northern Ireland. ℞. MacNeill's Egyptian Arch Railway Bridge but dated 2003 with plain edge and hallmark
— Proof in silver *FDC* (in 2003 set, see PPS1)* £25
— Proof in gold *FDC* (in 2003 set, see PPS2)* £700

4597B One pound pattern. Northern Ireland. ℞ Stag and the word 'Pattern' below with plain edge and hallmark and dated 2004. (Reverse design: Timothy Noad)
— Proof in silver *FDC* (in 2004 set, see PPS3)* £25
— Proof in gold *FDC* (in 2004 set, see PPS4)* £700

4597C 2008
— Proof in silver as 4597 with selected gold plating on reverse *FDC* (in 2008 set, see PSS30)* £40

* Coins marked thus were originally issued in Royal Mint sets.

4598 4598A 4598B

4598 One pound. England. R. A representation of the Gateshead Millennium Bridge with a border of struts, the value 'ONE POUND' and an incuse decorative feature on the edge symbolising bridges and pathways. (Reverse design: Edwina Ellis)

2007...£4
— Specimen in presentation folder..£7
— Proof *FDC** (in 2007 set, see PS90) £8
— Proof in silver *FDC* (Issued: 10,110) £30
— Proof piedfort in silver *FDC* (Issued: 5,739) £60
— Proof in gold *FDC* (Issued: 1,112) £750

2008
— Proof in gold *FDC* (in 2008 set, see PG1PCS)* £750

4598A One pound pattern. England. R. Millennium Bridge but dated 2003 with plain edge and hallmark
— Proof in silver *FDC* (in 2003 set, see PSS1)* £25
— Proof in gold *FDC* (in 2003 set, see PPS2)* £700

4598B One pound pattern. England. R. Lion with the word 'Pattern' below with plain edge and hallmark and dated 2004. (Reverse design: Timothy Noad)
— Proof in silver *FDC* (in 2004 set, see PPS3)* £25
— Proof in gold *FDC* (in 2004 set, see PPS4)* £700

4598C 2008
— Proof in silver as 4598 with selected gold plating on reverse *FDC* (in 2008 set, see PSS30)* £40

4599 One pound. (Scottish design). Edge 'NEMO ME IMPUNE LACESSIT' (rev. as 4222)
2008
— Proof in gold *FDC* (in 2008 set, see PG1PCS)* £750

4599A 2008
— Proof in silver with selected gold plating on reverse *FDC* (in 2008 set, see PSS30)* £40

4600 One pound. (Welsh design). Edge 'PLEIDOL WYF I'M GWLAD' (rev. see 4331)
2008
— Proof in gold *FDC* (in 2008 set, see PG1PCS)* £750

4600A 2008
— Proof in silver with selected gold plating on reverse *FDC* (in 2008 set, see PSS30)* £40

4601 One pound. (Northern Irish design). Edge 'DECUS ET TUTAMEN' (rev. see 4332)
2008
— Proof in gold *FDC* (in 2008 set, see PG1PCS)* £750

4601A 2008
— Proof in silver with selected gold plating on reverse *FDC* (in 2008 set, see PSS30)* £40

4602 One pound. (English design). Edge 'DECUS ET TUTAMEN' (rev. see 4333)
2008
— Proof in gold *FDC* (in 2008 set, see PG1PCS)* £750

4602A 2008
— Proof in silver with selected gold plating on reverse *FDC* (in 2008 set, see PSS30)* £40

* *Coins marked thus were originally issued in Royal Mint sets.*

4604   4605

4604 One pound. R. A shield of Our Royal Arms with the words 'ONE' to the left and
'POUND' to the right and the edge inscription 'DECUS ET TUTAMEN' (Reverse
design: Matthew Dent)

2008 ....£3
— Proof *FDC* (in 2008 set, see PS96)* £5
— Proof in silver *FDC* (Issued: 5,000) £30
— Proof piedfort in silver *FDC* (Edition: 8,000) £50
— Proof in gold *FDC* (Issued: 860)* £750
— Proof in platinum *FDC* (in 2008 set, see PPRSAS)* £1000
2009 ....£3
— Specimen in presentation folder (Edition: 15,000) £7
— Proof *FDC* (in 2009 set, see PS97)* £5
— BU in silver (Edition: 50,000)...£30
— Proof in silver *FDC* (Edition: 20,000 including coins in sets)..........................£35
— Proof in gold *FDC* (Edition: 1,000) £750
2010 ....£3
— Proof *FDC* (in 2010 set, see PS101)* £5
— BU in silver (Edition: 50,000)...£30
— Proof in silver *FDC* (Edition: 20,000 including coins in sets)..........................£35
2011 ....£3
— Proof *FDC* (in 2011 set, see PS104) * £5
— BU in silver...£30
— Proof in silver *FDC* (in 2011 set, Edition: 2,500, see PSS44) *.........................£35
2012 ....£3
— Proof *FDC* (in 2012 set, see PS107)* £3
— BU in silver £25
— Proof in silver with selected gold plating *FDC* (Edition: 2,012, see PSS48) £40
— Proof in gold *FDC* (Edition: 150 see PGDJS)* £750

4605 – One pound. London. R. A design which depicts the official badges of the capital
cities of the United Kingdom, with the badge of London being the principal focus,
accompanied by the name 'LONDON' and the denomination 'ONE POUND' with the
edge inscription 'DOMINE DIRIGE NOS'. (Reverse design: Stuart Devlin)

2010 ....£3
— Specimen on presentation card (Edition: 25,000) £5
— Specimen in presentation folder with 4606 (Edition: 10,000) £13
— Proof *FDC* (in 2010 set, see PS101)* £5
— Proof in silver *FDC* (Edition: 20,000 including coins in sets)..........................£35
— Proof piedfort in silver *FDC* (Edition: 5,000 including coins in sets) £55
— Proof in gold *FDC* (Edition: 2,500) £750

* Coins marked thus were originally issued in Royal Mint sets.

4606

4606 – One pound. Belfast. R. A design which depicts the official badges of the capital cities of the United Kingdom, with the badge of Belfast being the principal focus, accompanied by the name 'BELFAST' and the denomination 'ONE POUND' with the edge inscription 'PRO TANTO QUID RETRIBUAMUS' (Reverse design: Stuart Devlin)

2010 ....£3
— Specimen on presentation card (Edition: 25,000) £5
— Specimen in presentation folder with **4605** (Edition: 10,000) £13
— Proof *FDC* (in 2010 set, see PS101)* £5
— Proof in silver *FDC* (Edition: 20,000 including coins in sets).............................£35
— Proof piedfort in silver *FDC* (Edition: 5,000 including coins in sets) £55
— Proof in gold *FDC* (Edition: 2,500) £750

4607   4608

4607 One pound. Edinburgh. R. A design which depicts the official badges of the capital cities of the United Kingdom, with the badge of Edinburgh being the principal focus, accompanied by the name 'EDINBURGH' and the denomination 'ONE POUND' with the edge inscription 'NISI DOMINUS'. (Reverse design: Stuart Devlin)

2011 ....£3
— Specimen in presentation folder with **4608** (Edition: 10,000) £14
— Proof *FDC* (in 2011 set, see PS104)* £8
— Proof in silver *FDC* (Edition: 20,000 including coins in sets) £45
— Proof piedfort in silver *FDC* (Edition: 5,000 including coins in sets) £78
— Proof in gold *FDC* (Edition: 2,500)...£1200

4608 One pound. Cardiff. R. A design which depicts the official badges of the capital cities of the United Kingdom, with the badge of Cardiff being the principal focus, accompanied by the name 'CARDIFF' and the denomination 'ONE POUND' with the edge inscription 'Y DDRAIG GOCH DDYRY CYCHWYN ' (Reverse design: Stuart Devlin)

2011 ....£3
— Specimen in presentation folder with **4607** (Edition: 10,000)...............................£14
— Proof *FDC* (in 2011 set, see PS104) * £8
— Proof in silver *FDC* (Edition: 20,000 including coins in sets) £45
— Proof piedfort in silver *FDC* (Edition: 5,000 including coins in sets) £78
— Proof in gold *FDC* (Edition: 2,500)...£1200

* Coins marked thus were originally issued in Royal Mint sets.

NICKEL-BRASS

Obverse portrait by Raphael Maklouf

4311

4311 **Two pounds.** R. St. Andrew's cross with a crown of laurel leaves and surmounted by a thistle of Scotland with date '1986' above. Edge 'XIII COMMONWEALTH GAMES SCOTLAND' (Reverse design: Norman Sillman)

1986 ....£5
— Specimen in presentation folder £8
— Proof *FDC** £10
— 500 silver (Issued: 58,881) £18
— Proof in silver *FDC* (Issued: 59,779) £35
— Proof in gold *FDC* (Issued: 3,277)..£650

4312   4313

4312 **Two pounds** 300th Anniversary of Bill of Rights. R Cypher of W&M (King William and Queen Mary) interlaced surmounting a horizontal Parliamentary mace and a representation of the Royal Crown above and the dates '1689'and '1989' below, all within the inscription 'TERCENTENARY OF THE BILL OF RIGHTS'. (Reverse design: John Lobban)

1989 ....£5
— Specimen in presentation folder £8
— Proof *FDC* (in 1989 set, see PS43)* £10
— Proof in silver *FDC* (Issued: 25,000) £35
— Proof piedfort in silver *FDC* (in 1989 set, seePSS01)* £60

4313 **Two pounds** 300th Anniversary of Claim of Right (Scotland). R. As 4312, but with Crown of Scotland and the inscription 'TERCENTENARY OF THE CLAIM OF RIGHT'. (Reverse design: John Lobban)

1989 ....£15
— Specimen in presentation folder £20
— Proof *FDC* (in 1989 set, see PS43)* £15
— Proof in silver *FDC* (Issued: 24,852) £35
— Proof piedfort in silver *FDC* (in 1989 set, seePSS01)* £60

* Coins marked thus were originally issued in Royal Mint sets.

| 4314 | 4315 | 4316 |

4314 Two pounds 300th Anniversary of the Bank of England. R: Bank's original Corporate Seal, with Crown & Cyphers of William III & Mary II and the dates '1694' and '1994'. Edge 'SIC VOS NON VOBIS'on the silver and base metal versions. (Reverse design: Leslie Durbin)

1994 ....£5
— Specimen in presentation folder £8
— Proof *FDC* (in 1994 set, see PS53)* £10
— Proof in silver *FDC* (Issued: 27, 957) £35
— Proof piedfort in silver *FDC* (Issued: 9,569) £60
— Proof in gold *FDC* (Issued: 1,000)..£700

4314A— Gold Error – known as a Mule coin. £2500
The obverse of the 1994 Bank of England issue should have included the denomination 'TWO POUNDS' as this was not included in the design of the commemorative reverse. An unknown number of coins were struck and issued in gold using the die that was reserved for the Double Sovereign or Two Pound coins in the sovereign series. The Royal Mint wrote to its retail customers inviting them to return the error coin for replacement with the correct design. No details are known as to how many were returned, nor how many exist in the market. The incorrect obverse can be seen at **4251** below in the section listing Gold Sovereigns; the correct obverse is at **4311** above.

4315 Two pounds 50th Anniversary of the End of World War II. R: A stylised representation of a dove as the symbol of Peace. Edge '1945 IN PEACE GOODWILL 1995'. (Reverse design: John Mills)

1995 ....£5
— Specimen in presentation folder £8
— Proof *FDC* (in 1995 set, see PS55)* £10
— Proof in silver *FDC* (Issued: 35,751) £35
— Proof piedfort in silver *FDC* (Edition: 10,000)...£60
— Proof in gold *FDC* (Issued: 2,500)..£650

4316 Two pounds 50th Anniversary of the Establishment of the United Nations. R: 50th Anniversary symbol and a fanning pattern of flags with the inscription 'NATIONS UNITED FOR PEACE' above and the dates '1945-1995'below. (Reverse design: Michael Rizzello)

1995 ....£5
— Specimen in presentation folder £7
— Specimen in card (issued as part of multi country United Nations Collection)..........£7
— Proof in silver *FDC* (Edition: 175,000) £35
— Proof piedfort in silver *FDC* (Edition: 10,000)..£60
— Proof in gold *FDC* (Edition: 17,500) £650

* Coins marked thus were originally issued in Royal Mint sets.

4317

4317 Two pounds European Football Championships. R: A stylised representation of a football
with the date '1996' centrally placed and surrounded by sixteen small rings. Edge:
'TENTH EUROPEAN CHAMPIONSHIP'. (Reverse design: John Mills)
1996...£6
— Specimen in presentation folder..£8
— Proof *FDC* (in 1996 set, see PS57)* £10
— Proof in silver *FDC* (Issued: 25,163)...£35
— Proof piedfort in silver *FDC* (Issued: 7,634) £60
— Proof in gold *FDC* (Issued: 2,098)..£650

4317A Incorrect blank. When struck the coins have a dished appearance on both the obverse
and reverse but several pieces in gold have been reported where the surface of the coins
is flat. Enquiries at the Mint are continuing with a view to understanding how this could
have occurred..£1500

Bimetallic issues

4318

4318 Two pounds Bimetallic currency issue. R. Four concentric circles representing the Iron
Age, 18th Century industrial development, silicon chip, and Internet. Edge: 'STANDING
ON THE SHOULDERS OF GIANTS'. (Reverse design: Bruce Rushin)
1997...£5
— Specimen in presentation folder..£8
— Proof *FDC* (in 1997 set, see PS59)* £10
— Proof in silver FDC (Issued: 29,910) £32
— Proof piedfort in silver *FDC* (Issued: 10,000) £60
— Proof in gold *FDC* (Issued: 2,482)..£650

* Coins marked thus were originally issued in Royal Mint sets.

Obverse portrait by Ian Rank-Broadley

4570

4570 Two pounds. Bimetallic currency issue. R. Four concentric circles, representing the Iron Age, 18th Century industrial development, silicon chip and Internet. Edge: 'STANDING ON THE SHOULDERS OF GIANTS'. (Rev. as 4318)

1998	£5
— Proof *FDC* (in 1998 set, see PS61)*	£10
— Proof in silver *FDC* (Issued: 19,978)	£32
— Proof piedfort in silver *FDC* (Issued: 7,646)	£60
1999	£4
2000	£4
— Proof *FDC* (in 2000 set, see PS65)*	£10
— Proof in silver *FDC* (in 2000 set, see PSS10)*	£35
2001	£4
— Proof *FDC* (see PS68)*	£10
2002	£4
— Proof *FDC* (in 2002 set, see PS72)*	£10
— Proof in gold *FDC* (in 2002 set, see PGJS1)*	£650
2003	£4
— Proof *FDC* (see PS78)*	£10
2004	£4
— Proof *FDC* (in 2004 set, see PS81)*	£10
2005	£4
— Proof *FDC* (see PS84)*	£10
2006	£4
— Proof *FDC* (in 2006 set, see PS87)*	£10
— Proof in silver *FDC* (in 2006 set, see PSS22)*	£35
2007	£4
2008	£4
— Proof *FDC* (in 2008 set, see PS93) *	£10
2009	£4
— Proof *FDC* (in 2009 set, see PS97)	£10
— Proof in silver *FDC* (in 2009 set, see PSS37)*	£35
2010	£4
— Proof *FDC* (in 2010 set, see PS101) *	£10
— Proof in silver *FDC* (in 2010 set, see PSS41)*	£35
2011	£4
— Proof *FDC* (in 2010 set, see PS104) *	£10
— Proof in silver *FDC* (in 2010 set, see PSS44)*	£35
2012	£4
— Proof *FDC* (in 2012 set, see PS107)*	£3
— Proof in silver *FDC* (Edition: 2,012, see PSS47)*	£30
— Proof in gold *FDC* (Edition: 150 see PGDJS)*	£1000

* Coins marked thus were originally issued in Royal Mint sets.

4571A   4572

4571 Two pounds. Rugby World Cup. R. In the centre a rugby ball and goal posts surrounded
by a stylised stadium with the denomination 'TWO POUNDS' and the date '1999'. Edge:
'RUGBY WORLD CUP 1999'. (Reverse design: Ron Dutton)

1999 ....£5
—   Specimen in presentation folder £8
—   Proof *FDC* (in 1999 set, see PS63)* £10
—   Proof in silver *FDC* (Issued: 9,665) £40
—   Proof in gold *FDC* (Issued: 311) £700

4571A— Proof piedfort in silver with coloured hologram on reverse *FDC* (Issued: 10,000) ..£150

4572 Two pounds. Marconi commemorative. R. Decorative radio waves emanating from a spark
of electricity linking the zeros of the date to represent the generation of the signal that crossed
the Atlantic with the date '2001' and the denomination 'TWO POUNDS'. Edge: 'WIRELESS
BRIDGES THE ATLANTIC MARCONI 1901'. (Reverse design: Robert Evans)

2001 ....£5
—   Specimen in presentation folder £7
—   Proof *FDC* (in 2001 set, see PS68)* £10
—   Proof in silver *FDC* (Issued: 11,488) £35
—   Proof piedfort in silver *FDC* (Issued: 6,759) £60
—   Proof in gold *FDC* (Issued: 1,658) £650

4572A— Proof in silver *FDC*, with reverse frosting. (Issued: 4,803 in a 2-coin set with a
Canadian $5 Marconi silver proof) £60

* Coins marked thus were originally issued in Royal Mint sets.

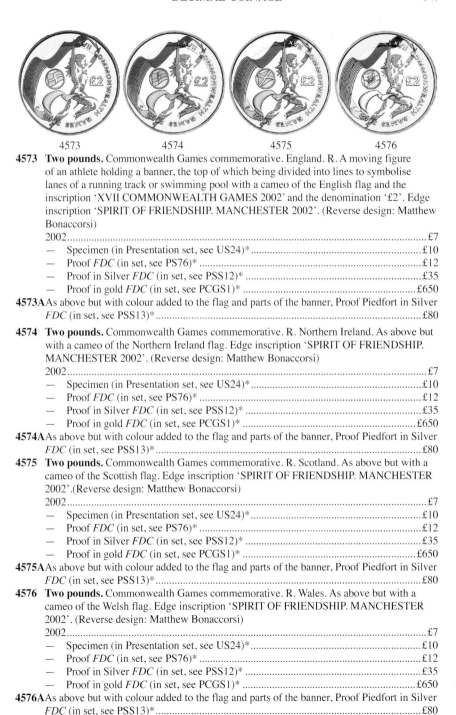

4573   4574   4575   4576

4573 **Two pounds.** Commonwealth Games commemorative. England. R. A moving figure of an athlete holding a banner, the top of which being divided into lines to symbolise lanes of a running track or swimming pool with a cameo of the English flag and the inscription 'XVII COMMONWEALTH GAMES 2002' and the denomination '£2'. Edge inscription 'SPIRIT OF FRIENDSHIP. MANCHESTER 2002'. (Reverse design: Matthew Bonaccorsi)

2002 ....£7
— Specimen (in Presentation set, see US24)* £10
— Proof *FDC* (in set, see PS76)* £12
— Proof in Silver *FDC* (in set, see PSS12)* £35
— Proof in gold *FDC* (in set, see PCGS1)* £650

4573A As above but with colour added to the flag and parts of the banner, Proof Piedfort in Silver *FDC* (in set, see PSS13)* £80

4574 **Two pounds.** Commonwealth Games commemorative. R. Northern Ireland. As above but with a cameo of the Northern Ireland flag. Edge inscription 'SPIRIT OF FRIENDSHIP. MANCHESTER 2002'. (Reverse design: Matthew Bonaccorsi)

2002 ....£7
— Specimen (in Presentation set, see US24)* £10
— Proof *FDC* (in set, see PS76)* £12
— Proof in Silver *FDC* (in set, see PSS12)* £35
— Proof in gold *FDC* (in set, see PCGS1)* £650

4574A As above but with colour added to the flag and parts of the banner, Proof Piedfort in Silver *FDC* (in set, see PSS13)* £80

4575 **Two pounds.** Commonwealth Games commemorative. R. Scotland. As above but with a cameo of the Scottish flag. Edge inscription 'SPIRIT OF FRIENDSHIP. MANCHESTER 2002'.(Reverse design: Matthew Bonaccorsi)

2002 ....£7
— Specimen (in Presentation set, see US24)* £10
— Proof *FDC* (in set, see PS76)* £12
— Proof in Silver *FDC* (in set, see PSS12)* £35
— Proof in gold *FDC* (in set, see PCGS1)* £650

4575A As above but with colour added to the flag and parts of the banner, Proof Piedfort in Silver *FDC* (in set, see PSS13)* £80

4576 **Two pounds.** Commonwealth Games commemorative. R. Wales. As above but with a cameo of the Welsh flag. Edge inscription 'SPIRIT OF FRIENDSHIP. MANCHESTER 2002'. (Reverse design: Matthew Bonaccorsi)

2002 ....£7
— Specimen (in Presentation set, see US24)* £10
— Proof *FDC* (in set, see PS76)* £12
— Proof in Silver *FDC* (in set, see PSS12)* £35
— Proof in gold *FDC* (in set, see PCGS1)* £650

4576A As above but with colour added to the flag and parts of the banner, Proof Piedfort in Silver *FDC* (in set, see PSS13)* £80

* Coins marked thus were originally issued in Royal Mint sets.

                4577   4578   4579

4577 Two pounds. Discovery of the structure of DNA. England. R. In the centre the spiralling
double helix structure of DNA with the inscription 'DNA DOUBLE HELIX' and the
dates '1953' and '2003' separated by the denomination 'TWO POUNDS' Edge:
'DEOXYRIBONUCLEIC ACID'. (Reverse design: John Mills)

2003 .... £5
— Specimen in presentation folder (Issued: 41,568) £10
— Proof *FDC* (in set, see PS78)* £10
— Proof in Silver *FDC* (Issued: 11,204) £35
— Proof piedfort in silver *FDC* (Issued: 8,728) £60
— Proof in gold *FDC* (Issued: 1,500) £650

4578 Two pounds. R.In the centre a depiction of Trevithick's Locomotive Penydarren and
the denomination 'TWO POUNDS' surrounded by a cog representing the Industrial
Revolution and the inscription 'R.TREVITHICK 1804 INVENTION INDUSTRY
PROGRESS 2004' Patterned Edge. (Reverse design: Robert Lowe)

2004 .... £5
— Specimen in presentation folder (Issued: 56,871) £10
— Brilliant uncirculated in silver (Issued: 1,923) £25
— Proof *FDC* (in 2004 set, see PS81)* £10
— Proof in Silver *FDC* (Issued: 10,233) £35
— Proof piedfort in silver *FDC* (Issued: 5,303) .... £ 65
— Proof in gold *FDC* (1,500) £650

4579 Two pounds. 400th Anniversary of the Gunpowder Plot. R. An arrangement of crosiers,
maces and swords, surrounded by stars, with the dates '1605' and '2005' above, and the
denomination 'TWO POUNDS' below, and the edge inscription REMEMBER
REMEMBER THE FIFTH OF NOVEMBER'. Reverse design: Peter Forster)

2005 .... £5
— Specimen in presentation folder (Issued: 12,044) £7
— Proof *FDC* (in 2005 set, see PS84)* £10
— Proof in Silver *FDC* (Issued: 4,394) £40
— Proof piedfort in silver *FDC* (Issued: 4,585) £65
— Proof in gold *FDC* (Issued: 914) £650

* Coins marked thus were originally issued in Royal Mint sets.

4580   4581   4582

4580 **Two pounds.** 60th Anniversary of the end of World War II. R. In the centre a depiction of the front of St.Paul's Cathedral in full floodlights with the denomination 'TWO POUNDS' and the dates '1945 - 2005' with the edge inscription 'IN VICTORY MAGNANIMITY IN PEACE GOODWILL'. (Reverse design: Robert Elderton)

2005 ....£5
— Specimen in presentation folder with medal (Issued: 53,686) £10
— Proof in Silver *FDC* (Issued: 21,734) £35
— Proof piedfort in silver *FDC* (Issued: 4,798) £65
— Proof in gold *FDC* (Issued: 1,578 single coins and 1,346 in sets) £650

4581 **Two pounds.** 200th Anniversary of the birth of Isambard Brunel. R. In the centre a portrait of the engineer with segments of a wheel and bridge in the background surrounded by links of a heavy chain and the date '2006' and the denomination 'TWO POUNDS', with the edge inscription '1806 - 1859 ISAMBARD KINGDOM BRUNEL ENGINEER'. (Reverse design: Rod Kelly)

2006 ....£5
— Specimen in presentation folder (with **4582**) £10
— Proof *FDC* (in 2006 set, see PS87)* £10
— Proof in silver *FDC* (Edition: 20,000) £35
— Proof piedfort in silver *FDC* (see PSS25)* £65
— Proof in gold *FDC* (1,500) £650

4582 **Two pounds.** 200th Anniversary of the birth of Isambard Brunel. R. In the centre a section of the roof of Paddington Station with 'BRUNEL' below and the date '2006' and the denomination 'TWO POUNDS', with the edge inscription 'SO MANY IRONS IN THE FIRE'. (Reverse design: Robert Evans)

2006 ....£4
— Specimen in presentation folder (with **4581**) £10
— Proof *FDC* (in 2006 set, see PS87)* £10
— Proof in silver *FDC* (Edition: 20,000) £35
— Proof piedfort in silver *FDC* (see PSS25)* £65
— Proof in gold *FDC* (1,500) £650

* Coins marked thus were originally issued in Royal Mint sets.

      4583   4584   4585

4583 **Two pounds.** Tercentenary of the Act of Union between England and Scotland. R. A
design dividing the coin into four quarters, with a rose and a thistle occupying two of the
quarters, and a portcullis in each of the other two quarters. The whole is overlaid with a
linking jigsaw motif and surrounded by the dates '1707' and '2007' and the denomination
'TWO POUNDS', with an edge inscription 'UNITED INTO ONE KINGDOM' (Reverse
design : Yvonne Holton)

2007...£5
— Specimen in presentation folder..£8
— Proof *FDC* (in 2007 set, see PS90)* £10
— Proof in Silver *FDC* (Issued: 8,310) £35
— Proof piedfort in silver *FDC* (Issued: 4,000) £60
— Proof in gold *FDC* (Issued: 750)..£850

4583A – Error edge. The obverse and reverse designs of the Act of Union silver proof
combined with the edge inscription of the Abolition of Slave Trade issue (4584 below).
The edge inscription is impressed on the blanks prior to the striking of the obverse and
reverse designs and whilst one example has been reported, and confirmed as genuine by
the Royal Mint, it seems possible that a small batch may have been produced and other
pieces have yet to be detected. £1000

4584 **Two pounds.** Bicentenary of the Abolition of the Slave Trade in the British Empire. R.
The date '1807' with the '0' depicted as a broken chain link , surrounded by the inscription
'AN ACT FOR THE ABOLITION OF THE SLAVE TRADE', and the date '2007', with
an edge inscription 'AM I NOT A MAN, AND A BROTHER' (Reverse design : David
Gentleman)

2007...£5
— Specimen in presentation folder with..£8
— Proof *FDC* (in 2007 set, see PS90)* £10
— Proof in Silver *FDC* (Issued: 7,095) £35
— Proof piedfort in silver *FDC* (Issued: 3,990)* £60
— Proof in gold *FDC* (Issued: 1,000)..£700

4585 **Two pounds.** 250th Anniversary of the birth of Robert Burns. R. A design featuring a
quote from the song *Auld Lang Syne* 'WE'LL TAK A CUP A' KINDNESS YET, FOR
AULD LANG SYNE ', the calligraphy of which is based on the handwriting of Robert
Burns with the inscription '1759 ROBERT BURNS 1796' and the denomination 'TWO
POUNDS' with the edge inscription 'SHOULD AULD ACQUAINTANCE BE FORGOT'
(Reverse design: Royal Mint Engraving Team)

2009...£5
— Specimen in celebration card £6
— Specimen in presentation folder (Edition: 50,000) £8
— Proof *FDC* (in 2009 set, see PS97)* £10
— Proof in Silver *FDC* (Edition: 20,000 including coins in sets)..............................£35
— Proof piedfort in silver *FDC* (Edition: 3,500 including coins in sets)....................£60
— Proof in gold *FDC* (Edition: 1,000) £700

* Coins marked thus were originally issued in Royal Mint sets.

4586 4587

4586 Two pounds. 200th Anniversary of the birth of Charles Darwin. ℞ A design showing a portrait of Charles Darwin facing an ape surrounded by the inscription '1809 DARWIN 2009' and the denomination 'TWO POUNDS' and the edge inscription 'ON THE ORIGIN OF SPECIES 1859' (Reverse design: Suzie Zamit)

2009..£5
— Specimen in presentation folder (Edition: 25,000) £8
— Proof *FDC* (in 2009 set, see PS97)* £10
— Proof in Silver *FDC* (Edition: 20,000 including coins in sets)................................£35
— Proof piedfort in silver *FDC* (Edition: 3,500 including coins in sets).....................£60
— Proof in gold *FDC* (Edition: 1,000) £700

4587 Two pounds. The Centenary of the death of Florence Nightingale and the One hundred and fiftieth Anniversary of the publication of *NOTES ON NURSING*. ℞. A design depicting the pulse of a patient being taken, surrounded by the inscription 'FLORENCE NIGHTINGALE – 1910' and the denomination 'TWO POUNDS'. The design being set against a background texture of lines symbolising rays of light from a lamp with the edge inscription '150 YEARS OF NURSING' on the precious metal versions. (Reverse design: Gordon Summers)

2010..£3
— Specimen on presentation card £5
— Specimen in presentation folder (Edition: 25,000) £8
— Proof *FDC* (in 2010 set, see PS101)* £10
— Proof in silver *FDC* (Edition: 20,000 including coins in sets)................................£35
— Proof piedfort in silver *FDC* (Edition: 5,000 including coins in sets).....................£60
— Proof in gold *FDC* (Edition: 1,000) £700

4588

4588 Two pounds. 500th Anniversary of the launch of the Mary Rose. R. A depiction of the ship based on a contemporary painting, surrounded by a cartouche bearing the inscription 'THE MARY ROSE' above, the denomination 'TWO POUNDS' below, and a rose to the left and right. The lettering on the reverse is rendered in the Lombardic style employed on the coins of Henry VII, and with the edge inscription 'YOUR NOBLEST SHIPPE 1511' (Reverse design: John Bergdahl)

2011..£3
— Specimen in presentation folder (Edition: 20,000)...£8
— Proof *FDC* (in 2011 set, see PS104)* £10
— Proof in silver *FDC* (Edition: 20,000 including coins in sets) £50
— Proof piedfort in silver *FDC* (Edition: 4,000 including coins in sets)........................£88
— Proof in gold *FDC* (Edition: 1,511) £1000

* *Coins marked thus were originally issued in Royal Mint sets.*

4589

4589 Two pounds. The 400th Anniversary of the King James Bible. R. A design focusing
on the opening verse of St John's Gospel, 'IN THE BEGINNING WAS THE WORD',
showing the verse as printing blocks on the left and the printed page on the right, with
the inscription' KING JAMES BIBLE' above and the dates '1611-2011'below with the
edge inscription 'THE AUTHORISED VERSION'. (Reverse design: Paul Stafford and
Benjamin Wright)

2011 ....£3
—   Specimen in presentation folder (Edition: 20,000)..£8
—   Proof *FDC* (in 2011 set, see PS104)* £10
—   Proof in silver *FDC* (Edition: 20,000 including coins in sets) £50
—   Proof piedfort in silver *FDC* (Edition: 3,500 including coins in sets).........................£88
—   Proof in gold *FDC* (Edition: 1,000)...£1000

4590

4590 Two pounds. The 200th Anniversary of the birth of Charles Dickens. R. A silhouette
profile of the writer through the titles of his works, greater prominence being given to
those that are more well known, with the inscription 'CHARLES DICKENS 1870' to the
left with the edge inscription 'SOMETHING WILL TURN UP' (Reverse design:)

2012 ....£3
—   Specimen in presentation folder (Edition: 20,000) £8
—   Proof *FDC* (in 2012 set, see PS107)* £10
—   Proof in silver *FDC* (Edition: 8,000 including coins in sets) £50
—   Proof piedfort in silver *FDC* (Edition: 2,000)...£88
—   Proof in gold *FDC* (Edition: 1,000) £1000

For further £2 commemorative issues, see Olympic and Paralympic coins on pages 608-609.

CUPRO-NICKEL

Note for Collectors

The collecting of crown size coins is one of the most popular pursuits among new and established coin collectors. Before decimalisation in 1971, crowns had a nominal denomination of five shillings and this was then changed to twenty five pence in 1972 when the Silver Wedding commemorative was issued. Over time with increasing metal, manufacturing and distribution costs, the production of coins with such a low face value was not economic and the decision was taken to change to a higher value that would last for many years. The first of the five pound crowns was issued in 1990 to mark the ninetieth birthday of The Queen Mother. It seems sensible to group all of the crown size coins together and therefore the earlier twenty five pence issues are not listed between the twenty pence and fifty pence denominations but appear below.

Obverse portrait by Arnold Machin

4226

4226 Twenty-five pence. (Crown) Silver Wedding Commemorative R. The initials E P on a background of foliage, figure of Eros above the Royal Crown with the inscription 'ELIZABETH AND PHILIP' above and the dates '20 NOVEMBER 1947 – 1972' below.(Reverse design: Arnold Machin)

1972...£2
— Proof *FDC* (in 1972 Set, See PS22)*..£6
— Silver proof *FDC* (Issued: 100,000) £45

* Coins marked thus were originally issued in Royal Mint sets.

4227

4227 Twenty-five pence. (Crown) Silver Jubilee Commemorative R. The Ampulla and Anointing Spoon encircled by a floral border and above a Royal Crown. (Obverse and reverse design: Arnold Machin)

1977...£2
—   Specimen in presentation folder...£2
—   Proof *FDC* (in 1977 Set, See PS27)* £5
—   Silver proof *FDC* (Issued: 377,000) £40

4228   4229

4228 Twenty-Five pence. (Crown) Queen Mother 80th Birthday Commemorative R. In the centre a portrait of The Queen Mother surrounded by bows and lions with the inscription 'QUEEN ELIZABETH THE QUEEN MOTHER 4 AUGUST 1980' (Reverse design: Richard Guyatt)

1980...£3
—   Specimen in presentation folder...£5
—   Silver proof *FDC* (Issued: 83,672) £45

4229 Twenty-five pence. (Crown)Royal Wedding Commemorative R.Portrait of the Prince of Wales and Lady Diana Spencer with the inscription 'HRH THE PRINCE OF WALES AND LADY DIANA SPENCER 1981' (Reverse design: Philip Nathan)

1981...£3
—   Specimen in presentation folder...£5
—   Silver proof *FDC* (Issued: 218,142) £45

* Coins marked thus were originally issued in Royal Mint sets.

Obverse portrait by Raphael Maklouf

4301

4301 Five pounds (crown). Queen Mother's 90th birthday commemorative. R. A Cypher in the letter E in duplicate above a Royal Crown flanked by a rose and a thistle all within the inscription 'QUEEN ELIZABETH THE QUEEN MOTHER' and the dates '1900 – 1990' (Reverse design: Leslie Durbin)

1990..£10

— Specimen in presentation folder (Issued: 45,250)..£12

— Proof in silver *FDC* (Issued: 56,102)...£45

— Proof in gold *FDC* (Issued: 2,500)...£1600

4302

4302 Five pounds (crown). 40th Anniversary of the Coronation. ℞. St Edward's Crown
encircled by forty trumpets all within the inscription 'FAITH AND TRUTH I WILL BEAR
UNTO YOU' and the dates '1953 – 1993'(Reverse design: Robert Elderton)
1993...£7
   —   Specimen in presentation folder...£9
   —   Proof *FDC* (in 1993 set, see PS51)* £12
   —   Proof in silver *FDC* (Issued: 58,877)...£45
   —   Proof in gold *FDC* (Issued: 2,500)...£1600

4303

4303 Five pounds (crown). 70th Birthday of Queen Elizabeth II. ℞. A representation of
Windsor Castle with five flag poles, two holding forked pennants with anniversary dates
'1926' and '1996', the other flags are Royal Arms, the Union flag and Our Personal flag.
Edge inscription: 'VIVAT REGINA ELIZABETHA'. (Reverse design: Avril Vaughan)
1996..£10
   —   Specimen in presentation folder (issued: 73,311) £12
   —   Proof *FDC* (in 1996 set, See PS57)* £12
   —   Proof in silver *FDC* (Issued: 39,336)...£50
   —   Proof in gold *FDC* (Issued: 2,127)...£1600

* Coins marked thus were originally issued in Royal Mint sets.

4304

4304 Five pounds (crown). Golden Wedding of Queen Elizabeth II and Prince Philip. Conjoint portraits of The Queen and Prince Philip. R. A pair of shields, chevronwise, on the left, OurRoyal Arms, on the right, the shield of Prince Philip, above a Royal Crown separating the dates '1947' and '1997' with the date '20 NOVEMBER', below an anchor cabled with the denomination 'FIVE POUNDS'. (Obverse design: Philip Nathan, reverse design: Leslie Durbin)

1997..£7
— Specimen in presentation folder...£10
— Proof *FDC* (in 1997 set, See PS59)* £15
— Proof in silver *FDC* (Issued: 33,689)...£50
— Proof in gold *FDC* (Issued: 2,574)..£1600

Obverse portrait by Ian Rank-Broadley

4550

4550 Five pounds (crown). Prince Charles' 50th Birthday. R. A portrait of Prince Charles and in the background words relating to the work of The Prince's Trust. A circumscription of 'FIFIETH BIRTHDAY OF HRH PRINCE OF WALES' and below 'FIVE POUNDS' flanked by the anniversary dates '1948' and '1998'. (Reverse design: Michael Noakes / Robert Elderton)

1998..£7
— Specimen in presentation folder...£10
— Proof *FDC* (in 1998 set, see PS 61)* £15
— Proof in silver *FDC* (Issued: 13,379)..£60
— Proof in gold *FDC* (Issued: 773)..£1600

* Coins marked thus were originally issued in Royal Mint sets.

4551

4551 **Five pounds** (crown). Diana, Princess of Wales Memorial. ℞. A portrait of Diana, Princess of Wales with the dates '1961' and '1997', and the circumscription 'IN MEMORY OF DIANA, PRINCESS OF WALES' with the value 'FIVE POUNDS' (Reverse design: David Cornell)

1999 ....£7
— Specimen in presentation folder..£12
— Proof *FDC* (in 1999 set, see PS63)* £15
— Proof in silver *FDC* (Issued: 49,545)...£50
— Proof in gold *FDC* (Issued: 7,500)..£1600

4552　　　　　　　　　　4552A

4552 **Five pounds** (crown). Millennium commemorative. ℞. A representation of the dial of a clock with hands set at 12 o'clock with a map of the British Isles and the dates '1999' and '2000' and the words 'ANNO DOMINI' and the value 'FIVE POUNDS'. Edge: 'WHAT'S PAST IS PROLOGUE' in serif or sans serif font. (Reverse design: Jeffrey Matthews)

1999 ....£7
— Specimen in presentation folder..£10
— Proof in silver *FDC* (Issued: 49,057)...£50
— Proof in gold *FDC* (Issued: 2,500)..£1600

2000
— Specimen in presentation folder..£20
— Proof *FDC* (in 2000 set, see PS65)* £15
— Proof in gold *FDC* (Issued: 1,487)..£1600

4552A 2000
— Specimen in presentation folder with Dome mint mark £20
(See illustration above - the mintmark is located within the shaded area at 3 o'clock).

4552B 2000
— Proof in silver *FDC* (Issued: 14,255)...£60
(The reverse design is the same as the 1999 issue but with the British Isles highlighted with 22 carat gold)

* *Coins marked thus were originally issued in Royal Mint sets.*

4553   4554

4553 Five pounds (crown). Queen Mother commemorative. ℞. A portrait of the Queen Mother flanked by groups of people with the circumscription 'QUEEN ELIZABETH THE QUEEN MOTHER' the anniversary dates '1900' and '2000' below, and the denomination 'FIVE POUNDS'. Below the portrait a representation of her signature. (Reverse design: Ian Rank-Broadley)

2000 ....£7
— Specimen in presentation folder £10
— Proof in silver *FDC* (Issued: 31,316) £50
— Proof piedfort in silver *FDC* (Issued: 14,850) £80
— Proof in gold *FDC* (Issued: 3,000) £1600

4554 Five pounds (crown) Victorian anniversary. ℞. A classic portrait of the young Queen Victoria based on the Penny Black postage stamp with a V representing Victoria, and taking the form of railway lines and in the background the iron framework of the Crystal Palace, and the denomination '5 POUNDS' and the dates '1901' and '2001'. (Reverse design: Mary Milner-Dickens)

2001 ....£7
— Specimen in presentation folder £10
— Proof *FDC* (in 2001 set, see PS68)* £15
— Proof in silver *FDC* (Issued: 19,216) £55
— Proof in gold *FDC* (Issued: 2,098) £1600

4554A— Proof in silver *FDC* with 'reverse frosting' giving matt appearance (Issued:596) (Crown issued with sovereigns of 1901 and 2001)* £200

4554B— Proof in gold *FDC* with 'reverse frosting' giving matt appearance.(Issued:733) (Crown issued with four different type sovereigns of Queen Victoria, - Young Head with shield, and Young Head with St.George reverse, Jubilee Head and Old Head.)* £1700

* Coins marked thus were originally issued in Royal Mint sets.

4555

4555 **Five pounds.** (crown) Golden Jubilee commemorative 2002. O. New portrait of The
Queen with the denomination 'FIVE POUNDS'. ℞. Equestrian portrait of The Queen with
the inscription 'ELIZABETH II DEI GRA REGINA FID DEF' around the circumference
and 'AMOR POPULI PRAESIDIUM REG' within, and the date '2002' below separated
by the central element of the Royal Arms. (Obverse and reverse designs:
Ian Rank-Broadley)

2002..£7
— Specimen in presentation folder...£10
— Proof *FDC* (in 2002 set, see PS 72)* £15
— Proof in silver *FDC* (Issued: 54,012) £55
— Proof in gold *FDC* (Issued: 3,500)...£1600

4556

4556 **Five pounds,** (crown) Queen Mother Memorial 2002. ℞. Three quarter portrait of the
Queen Mother within a wreath with the inscription 'QUEEN ELIZABETH THE QUEEN
MOTHER' and the dates '1900' and '2002', with an edge inscription 'STRENGTH,
DIGNITY AND LAUGHTER'. (Reverse design: Avril Vaughan)

2002..£8
— Specimen in presentation folder...£15
— Proof in silver *FDC* (Issued: 16,117) £55
— Proof in gold *FDC* (Issued: 2,086)...£1600

* Coins marked thus were originally issued in Royal Mint sets.

4557

4557 Five pounds. (crown) Coronation commemorative 2003. O. Profile portrait of The Queen in linear form facing right with the inscription 'ELIZABETH II DEI GRATIA REGINA F D'. R. In the centre the inscription 'GOD SAVE THE QUEEN' surrounded by the inscription 'CORONATION JUBILEE' the denomination 'FIVE POUNDS' and the date '2003'. (Obverse and reverse designs: Tom Phillips)

2003 ....£8
— Specimen in presentation folder (Issued: 100,481) £10
— Proof *FDC* (in 2003 set, see PS 78)* £15
— Proof in silver *FDC* (Issued: 28,758) £55
— Proof in gold *FDC* (Issued: 1,896) £1600

4558

4558 Five pounds. (crown) Centenary of Entente Cordiale 2004. R. In the centre the head and shoulders of Britannia and her French counterpart Marianne with the inscription 'ENTENTE CORDIALE' separated by the dates '1904' and '2004'. Obv. as 4556. (Reverse design: David Gentleman)

2004 ....£8
— Specimen in presentation folder (Issued: 16,507) £20
— Proof *FDC* with reverse frosting (Issued: 6,065) £20
— Proof in silver *FDC* (Issued: 11,295) £60
— Proof Piedfort in silver *FDC* (Issued: 2,500) £150
— Proof in gold *FDC* (Issued: 926) £1600
— Proof Piedfort in platinum *FDC* (Issued: 501) £4500

* Coins marked thus were originally issued in Royal Mint sets.

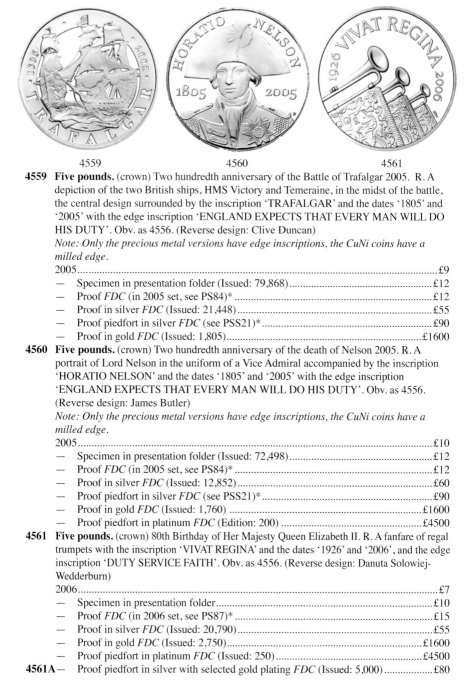

4559   4560   4561

4559 **Five pounds.** (crown) Two hundredth anniversary of the Battle of Trafalgar 2005. ℞. A depiction of the two British ships, HMS Victory and Temeraine, in the midst of the battle, the central design surrounded by the inscription 'TRAFALGAR' and the dates '1805' and '2005' with the edge inscription 'ENGLAND EXPECTS THAT EVERY MAN WILL DO HIS DUTY'. Obv. as 4556. (Reverse design: Clive Duncan)

Note: Only the precious metal versions have edge inscriptions, the CuNi coins have a milled edge.

2005...£9
— Specimen in presentation folder (Issued: 79,868)...£12
— Proof *FDC* (in 2005 set, see PS84)* £12
— Proof in silver *FDC* (Issued: 21,448)..£55
— Proof piedfort in silver *FDC* (see PSS21)* £90
— Proof in gold *FDC* (Issued: 1,805)...£1600

4560 **Five pounds.** (crown) Two hundredth anniversary of the death of Nelson 2005. ℞. A portrait of Lord Nelson in the uniform of a Vice Admiral accompanied by the inscription 'HORATIO NELSON' and the dates '1805' and '2005' with the edge inscription 'ENGLAND EXPECTS THAT EVERY MAN WILL DO HIS DUTY'. Obv. as 4556. (Reverse design: James Butler)

Note: Only the precious metal versions have edge inscriptions, the CuNi coins have a milled edge.

2005...£10
— Specimen in presentation folder (Issued: 72,498)...£12
— Proof *FDC* (in 2005 set, see PS84)* £12
— Proof in silver *FDC* (Issued: 12,852)..£60
— Proof piedfort in silver *FDC* (see PSS21)* £90
— Proof in gold *FDC* (Issued: 1,760) £1600
— Proof piedfort in platinum *FDC* (Edition: 200) £4500

4561 **Five pounds.** (crown) 80th Birthday of Her Majesty Queen Elizabeth II. ℞. A fanfare of regal trumpets with the inscription 'VIVAT REGINA' and the dates '1926' and '2006', and the edge inscription 'DUTY SERVICE FAITH'. Obv. as 4556. (Reverse design: Danuta Solowiej-Wedderburn)

2006..£7
— Specimen in presentation folder...£10
— Proof *FDC* (in 2006 set, see PS87)* £15
— Proof in silver *FDC* (Issued: 20,790)..£55
— Proof in gold *FDC* (Issued: 2,750)...£1600
— Proof piedfort in platinum *FDC* (Issued: 250)...£4500

4561A— Proof piedfort in silver with selected gold plating *FDC* (Issued: 5,000) £80

* Coins marked thus were originally issued in Royal Mint sets.

4562

4562 Five pounds. (crown) Diamond Wedding Anniversary of Her Majesty Queen Elizabeth II and The Duke of Edinburgh. O. Conjoint portrait of The Queen and Prince Philip. R. The Rose window of Westminster Abbey with the inscription 'TVEATVR VNITA DEVS', the dates '1947' and '2007', the denomination 'FIVE POUNDS', and the edge inscription 'MY STRENGTH AND STAY' (Obverse design: Ian Rank-Broadley, reverse design: Emma Noble) 2007..£7
— Specimen in presentation folder..£10
— Proof *FDC* (in 2007 set, see PS90)*...£15
— Proof in silver *FDC* (Issued: 15,186)...£55
— Proof piedfort in silver *FDC* (Issued: 2,000) £80
— Proof in gold *FDC* (Issued: 2,380)...£1600
— Proof piedfort in platinum *FDC* (Issued: 250)..£4500

4563   4564

4563 Five pounds. (crown) 450th Anniversary of the Accession of Queen Elizabeth I. R A portrait of Queen Elizabeth I surrounded by four Tudor roses placed at the centre points of connecting arches, with two side panels containing details taken from carvings made by Robert Dudley, Earlof Leicester, found at the Tower of London, the design being encircled by the inscription 'ELIZABETH REGINA' with the dates 'MDLVIII' and 'MMVIII' with the edge inscription 'I HAVE REIGNED WITH YOUR LOVES' on the precious metal versions. Obv. as 4556. (Reverse design: Rod Kelly). 2008...£7
— Specimen in presentation folder (Issued: 26,700)...£10
— Proof *FDC* (in 2008 set, see PS93)*..£15
— Proof in silver *FDC* (Issued: 10,398)..£60
— Proof piedfort in silver *FDC* (Edition: 5,000)..£90
— Proof in gold *FDC* (Issued: 1,500)..£1600
— Proof piedfort in platinum *FDC* (Issued: 150)...£4500

* Coins marked thus were originally issued in Royal Mint sets.

4564 **Five pounds.** (crown) Prince of Wales 60th Birthday. R. A profile portrait of His Royal Highness The Prince of Wales with the inscription 'THE PRINCE OF WALES' above and '1948 ICH DIEN 2008' below with the edge inscription 'SIXTIETH BIRTHDAY' on the precious metal versions. Obv. as 4556. (Reverse design : Ian Rank-Broadley)

2008 .... £7
— Specimen in presentation folder (Issued: 54,746) £10
— Proof *FDC* (in 2008 set, see PS93)* £15
— Proof in silver *FDC* (Issued: 7,446) £60
— Proof piedfort in silver *FDC* (Edition: 5,000) £90
— Proof in gold *FDC* (Issued: 867) £1600
— Proof in platinum *FDC* (Issued: 54) £4500

4565   4566

4565 **Five pounds.** (crown) 500th Anniversary of the accession of Henry VIII. R. A design inspired By a Holbein painting of King Henry VIII, set within a tressure and surrounded by the inscription 'THE ACCESSION OF HENRY VIII 1509' and the denomination 'FIVE POUNDS', with the edge inscription 'ROSA SINE SPINA' on the precious metal versions. Obv. as 4551. (Reverse design: John Bergdahl)

2009 .... £7
— Specimen in presentation folder (Edition: 100,000) £10
— Proof *FDC* (in 2009 set, see PS97)* £15
— Proof in silver *FDC* (Edition: 20,000 including coins in sets) £60
— Proof piedfort in silver *FDC* (Edition: 4,009 including coins in sets) £90
— Proof in gold *FDC* (Edition: 1,509) £1600
— Proof piedfort in platinum *FDC* (Edition: 100) £4500

4566 **Five pounds. (crown)** Commemorating the three hundred-and fiftieth anniversary of the restoration of the Monarchy. R. A design featuring a crown, a spray of oak leaves, interlinked 'C's, the date '1660', the inscription 'RESTORATION OF THE MONARCHY' and the denomination 'FIVE POUNDS' with the edge inscription 'A QUIET AND PEACEFUL POSSESSION' on the precious metal versions. Obv. as 4551. (Reverse design: David Cornell)

2010 .... £7
— Specimen on presentation card (Edition: 150,000) £8
— Specimen in presentation folder (Edition: 50,000) £10
— Proof *FDC* (in 2010 set, see PS101)* £15
— Proof in silver *FDC* (Edition: 20,000 including coins in sets £50
— Proof piedfort in silver *FDC* (Edition: 5,000 including coins in sets) £90
— Proof in gold *FDC* (Edition: 1,200) £1600
— Proof piedfort in platinum *FDC* (Edition: 100) £4500

---

* Coins marked thus were originally issued in Royal Mint sets.

4567

4567 Five pounds. (crown) Royal Wedding Commemorative. R.A design featuring facing
portraits of His Royal Highness Prince William and Miss Catherine Middleton with the
inscription 'WILLIAM AND CATHERINE' above and the date '29 APRIL 2011 below.
(Reverse design: Mark Richards)
2010

— Specimen in presentation folder (Edition: 250,000) £18
— Proof in silver *FDC* (Edition: 50,000) £75
— Proof in silver with gold plating *FDC* (Edition: 3,000) £90
— Proof piedfort in silver *FDC* (Edition: 3,000) £120
— Proof in gold *FDC* (Edition: 3,000) £1550
— Proof piedfort in platinum *FDC* (Edition: 200) £5600

4568

4568 Five pounds. (crown) 90th Birthday of Prince Philip. R. A profile portrait of His Royal
Highness The Duke of Edinburgh with the inscription 'PRINCE PHILIP 90TH BIRTHDAY '
and the denomination 'FIVE POUNDS' and the date '2011' (Reverse design: Mark Richards)
2011

— Specimen in presentation folder (Edition: 50,000)..£10
— Proof *FDC* (in 2011 set, see PS104)*..£15
— Proof in silver *FDC* (Edition: 20,000 including coins in sets) £83
— Proof piedfort in silver *FDC* (Edition: 4,000 including coins in sets) £145
— Proof in gold *FDC* (Edition: 1,200) £2400
— Proof piedfort in platinum *FDC* (Edition: 90)..£6350

* Coins marked thus were originally issued in Royal Mint sets.
For further £5 commemorative issues, see Olympic and Paralympic coins on pages 610-619.

4569

4569 Five pounds (crown). Diamond Jubilee commemorative 2012. O. For the obverse
impression, Our Effigy, inspired by the sculpture mounted in the entrance to the
Supreme Court building on Parliament Square, with the inscription 'ELIZABETH. II.
D. G. REG. F. D. FIVE POUNDS', and for the reverse an adaptation of Our Effigy first
used on United Kingdom coins from 1953, with an olive branch and ribbon below, the
date '2012' to the left and the inscription 'DIRIGE DEVS GRESSVS MEOS' to the
right. With the edge inscription 'A VOW MADE GOOD' on the precious metal coins.
(Obverse and reverse designs: Ian Rank-Broadley)
2012
  — Specimen in presentation folder £13
  — Proof *FDC* (in 2012 set, see PS107)* £10
  — Proof in silver *FDC* (Edition: 75,000 including coins in sets) £83
  — Proof in silver with gold plating *FDC* (Edition: 12,500) £100
  — Proof piedfort in silver *FDC* (Edition: 3,250) £145
  — Proof in gold *FDC* (Edition: 3,850) £2,400
  — Proof piedfort in platinum *FDC* (Edition: 250)... £6,400

4600

4600 Ten pounds (five ounce). Diamond Jubilee commemorative 2012. O. For the obverse
impression, Our Effigy, inspired by the sculpture mounted in the entrance to the Supreme
Court building on Parliament Square, with the inscription 'ELIZABETH. II. D. G. REG. F.
D. TEN POUNDS', and for the reverse an enthroned representation of Ourself surrounded
by the inscription 'DILECTA REGNO MCMLII – MMXII' (Obverse and reverse design:
Ian Rank-Broadley)
2012
  — Proof in silver *FDC* (Edition: 1,952) £450
  — Proof in gold *FDC* (Edition: 250) £9,500
  Illustration shown at reduced size – actual coin diameter 65 mm.

* *Coins marked thus were originally issued in Royal Mint sets.*

4610

4610 Five hundred pounds (one kilo). Diamond Jubilee commemorative 2012. O. For the obverse impression, Our Effigy, inspired by the sculpture mounted in the entrance to the Supreme Court building on Parliament Square, with the inscription 'ELIZABETH. II. D. G. REG. F. D. 500 POUNDS', and for the reverse a full achievement of the Royal Arms based on those mounted on the front gates of Buckingham Palace with the date '2012' below. (Obverse and reverse design: Ian Rank-Broadley)
2012
— Proof in silver *FDC* (Edition: 1,250) £2,600
Illustration shown at reduced size – actual coin diameter 100 mm.

4620

4620 One thousand pounds (one kilo). Diamond Jubilee commemorative 2012. O. For the obverse impression, Our Effigy, inspired by the sculpture mounted in the entrance to the Supreme Court building on Parliament Square, with the inscription 'ELIZABETH. II. D. G. REG. F. D. 1000 POUNDS', and for the reverse a full achievement of the Royal Arms based on those mounted on the front gates of Buckingham Palace with the date '2012' below. (Reverse design:
2012
— Proof in gold *FDC* (Edition: 60) £60,000

* Coins marked thus were originally issued in Royal Mint sets.

GOLD SOVEREIGN ISSUES

Obverse portrait by Ian Rank-Broadley

4445

4445 Quarter sovereign. R. The image of St George armed, sitting on horseback, attacking the
dragon with a sword, and a broken spear upon the ground, and the date of the year. (Reverse
design: Benedetto Pistrucci)

2009 Bullion type (Edition: 50,000) £110
—   Proof *FDC* (Edition: 25,000 including coins in sets) £130
2010 Bullion type (Edition: 250,000) £110
—   Proof *FDC* (Edition: 25,000 including coins in sets) £130
2011 Bullion type (Edition: 50,000) £110
—   Proof *FDC* (Edition: 15,000 including coins in sets) £130

4446

4446 Quarter sovereign. R. The image of St George on horseback, attacking the dragon with a
lance, with date of the year to the left. (Reverse design: Paul Day)

2012 Bullion type (Edition: 250,000) £99
—   Proof *FDC* (Edition: 10,744 including coins in sets)...£130

Obverse portrait by Arnold Machin

4205

4205 Half-sovereign. R. The image of St George armed, sitting on horseback, attacking the
dragon with a sword, and a broken spear upon the ground, and the date of the year.
(Reverse design: Benedetto Pistrucci)

1980 Proof *FDC* (Issued: 76.700) . £200   1983 Proof *FDC* (Issued: 19,710)** £200
1982 Unc .... £150   1984 Proof *FDC* (Issued: 12,410) £200
—   Proof *FDC* (Issued: 19,090).. £200

* Coins marked thus were originally issued in Royal Mint sets.

Obverse portrait by Raphael Maklouf

4276

4276 Half-sovereign. R. St. George (as 4205)

1985 Proof *FDC* (Issued: 9,951)... £225	1992 Proof *FDC* (Issued: 3,783) £250
1986 Proof *FDC* (Issued: 4,575)... £225	1993 Proof *FDC* (Issued: 2,910) £250
1987 Proof *FDC* (Issued: 8,187)... £225	1994 Proof *FDC* (Issued: 5,000) £225
1988 Proof *FDC* (Issued: 7,074)... £225	1995 Proof *FDC* (Issued: 4,900) £225
1990 Proof *FDC* (Issued: 4,231)... £250	1996 Proof *FDC* (Issued: 5,730) £225
1991 Proof *FDC* (Issued: 3,588)... £250	1997 Proof *FDC* (Issued: 7,500) £225

4277

4277 Half-sovereign 500th Anniversary of Sovereign. For the obverse impression a representation Of Ourself as at Our Coronation, seated in King Edward's Chair and having received the Sceptre with the Cross and the Rod with the Dove, all within the circumscription 'ELIZABETH. II.DEI.GRA.REG.FID.DEF' and for the reverse a Shield of Our Royal Arms ensigned by an open Royal Crown, the whole superimposed upon a double Rose, and with the circumscription 'ANNIVERSARY OF THE GOLD SOVEREIGN 1489-1989' (Designs: Bernald Sindall)

1989 Proof *FDC* (Issued: 8,888)...£450

Obverse portrait by Ian Rank-Broadley

4440	4441	4442	4443

4440 Half sovereign. R. St.George

1998 Proof *FDC* (Issued: 6,147)... £225	2004 Bullion type (Issued: 34,924) £165
1999 Proof *FDC* (Issued: 7,500)... £225	— Proof *FDC* (Issued: 4,446) £225
2000 Bullion type (Issued: 146,822). £165	2006 Bullion type £165
— Proof *FDC* (Issued: 7,458).... £225	— Proof *FDC* (Issued: 4,173) £225
2001 Bullion type (Issued: 94,763) .£165	2007 Bullion type (Edition: 75,000)........£165
— Proof *FDC* (Issued: 4,596).... £225	— Proof *FDC* (Issued: 2,442) £225
2003 Bullion type (Issued: 47,818)£165	2008 Bullion type (Edition: 75,000)........£165
— Proof *FDC* (Issued: 4,868).... £225	— Proof *FDC* (Issued: 2,465) £225

* Coins marked thus were originally issued in Royal Mint sets.
** Numbers include coins sold in sets

4441 Half sovereign R. The Shield of Arms of Our United Kingdom of Great Britain and Northern Ireland within an open wreath of laurel and ensigned by Our Royal Crown and beneath the date of the year. (Reverse design: Timothy Noad)

2002 Bullion type (Issued: 61,347) £180
— Proof *FDC* (Issued: 10,000) £300

4442 Half sovereign. R. A depiction of St George, carrying a shield and a sword, slaying the dragon, with the date '2005' beneath the wing of the dragon.(Reverse design: Timothy Noad)

2005 Bullion type (Issued: 30,299) £180
— Proof *FDC* (Issued: 5,011) £300

4443 Half sovereign. R. St George. Based on the original design of 1893 with reduced ground below design and larger exergue with no BP initials

2009 Bullion type (Edition: 50,000) £165
— Proof *FDC* (Edition: 6,000 including coins in sets) £225
2010 Bullion type (Edition: 250,000) £165
— Proof *FDC* (Edition: 7,000 including coins in sets) £225
2011 Bullion type (Edition: 50,000) £160
— Proof *FDC* (Edition: 7,500 including coins in sets) £250

4444

4444 Half sovereign. R. The image of St George on horseback, attacking the dragon with a lance, with date of the year to the left. (Reverse design: Paul Day)

2012 Bullion type (Edition: 250,000) £195
— Proof *FDC* (Edition: 4,894 including coins in sets) £250

Obverse portrait by Arnold Machin

4204

4204 Sovereign. R. The image of St George armed, sitting on horseback, attacking the dragon with a sword, and a broken spear upon the ground, and the date of the year.(Reverse design: Benedetto Pistrucci)

1974 Unc £325	1981 Unc...£325
1976 Unc £325	— Proof *FDC* (Issued: 32,960) £350
1976 VIP Proof *FDC*......*Extremely rare*	1982 Unc...£325
1978 Unc £325	— Proof *FDC* (Issued: 20,000) £350
1979 Unc £325	1983 Proof *FDC* (Issued: 21,250)** £350
— Proof *FDC* (Issued: 50,000) £350	1984 Proof *FDC* (Issued: 12,880) £350
1980 Unc £325	
— Proof *FDC* (Issued: 81,200) £350	

* Coins marked thus were originally issued in Royal Mint sets.

Obverse portrait by Raphael Maklouf

4271 4272

4271 Sovereign. ℞. St. George (as 4204)

1985 Proof *FDC* (Issued: 11,393) . £375	1992 Proof *FDC* (Issued: 4,772) £450
1986 Proof *FDC* (Issued: 5,079)... £375	1993 Proof *FDC* (Issued: 4,349) £500
1987 Proof *FDC* (Issued: 9,979)... £375	1994 Proof *FDC* (Issued: 4,998) £450
1988 Proof *FDC* (Issued: 7,670)... £375	1995 Proof *FDC* (Issued: 7,500) £400
1990 Proof *FDC* (Issued: 4,767)... £450	1996 Proof *FDC* (Issued: 7,500) £400
1991 Proof *FDC* (Issued: 4,713)... £450	1997 Proof *FDC* (Issued: 7,500) £400

4272 Sovereign. 500th Anniversary of Sovereign. For the obverse impression a representation Of Ourself as at Our Coronation, seated in King Edward's Chair and having received the Sceptre with the Cross and the Rod with the Dove, all within the circumscription 'ELIZABETH.II.DEI.GRA.REG.FID.DEF' and for the reverse a Shield of Our Royal Arms ensigned by an open Royal Crown, the whole superimposed upon a double Rose, and with the circumscription 'ANNIVERSARY OF THE GOLD SOVEREIGN 1489-1989' (Designs: Bernald Sindall)

1989 Proof *FDC* (Issued: 10,535) £1200

Obverse portrait by Ian Rank-Broadley

4430

4430 Sovereign. ℞. St.George

1998 Proof *FDC* (Issued: 10,000). £400	2004 Bullion type (Issued: 30,688) £325
1999 Proof *FDC* (Issued: 10,000). £450	— Proof *FDC* (Issued: 10,175) £400
2000 Bullion type (Issued: 129,069) .£325	2006 Bullion type £325
— Proof *FDC* (Issued: 9,909).... £400	— Proof *FDC* (Issued: 9,195) £400
2001 Bullion type (Issued: 49,462)£325	2007 Bullion type (Edition: 75,000)........£325
— Proof *FDC* (Issued: 8,915).... £400	— Proof *FDC* (Issued: 8,199) £400
2003 Bullion type (Issued: 43,230)£325	2008 Bullion type (Edition: 75,000)........£325
— Proof *FDC* (Issued: 12,433)..£400	— Proof *FDC* (Edition: 12,500)...........£400

* *Coins marked thus were originally issued in Royal Mint sets.*
Where numbers of coins issued or the Edition limit is quoted, these refer to individual coins. Additional coins were included in sets which are listed in the appropriate section.

4431   4433   4434

4431 Sovereign R. The Shield of Arms of Our United Kingdom of Great Britain and Northern Ireland within an open wreath of laurel and ensigned by Our Royal Crown and beneath the date of the year. (Reverse design: Timothy Noad)

2002 Bullion type (Issued: 75,264) £400
—   Proof *FDC* (Issued: 12,500) £500

4432 Sovereign R. A depiction of St George, carrying a shield and a sword, slaying the dragon, with the date '2005' beneath the wing of the dragon.(Reverse design: Timothy Noad)

2005 Bullion type (Issued: 45,542) £400
—   Proof *FDC* (Issued: 12,500) £500

4433 Sovereign. R. St George. Based on the original design of 1820 with the plumed helmet without its streamer.

2009 Bullion type (Edition: 75,000)...£325
—   Proof *FDC* (Edition: 16,000 including coins in sets) £400
2010 Bullion type (Edition: 250,000)...£325
—   Proof *FDC* (Edition: 16,000 including coins in sets) £400
2011 Bullion type (Edition: 250,000) £325
—   Proof *FDC* (Edition: 15,000 including coins in sets) £450

4434 Sovereign. R. The image of St George on horseback, attacking the dragon with a lance, with date of the year to the left. (Reverse design: Paul Day)

2012 Bullion type (Edition: 250,000)...£380
—   Proof *FDC* (Edition: 8,144 including coins in sets) £495

* *Coins marked thus were originally issued in Royal Mint sets.*

Obverse portrait by Arnold Machin

4203

4203 **Two pounds** R. The image of St George armed, sitting on horseback, attacking the dragon with a sword, and a broken spear upon the ground, and the date of the year.(Reverse design: Benedetto Pistrucci)

1980 Proof *FDC* (see PGS01)* ....£650   1983 Proof *FDC* (Issued: 12,500) ** £650
1982 Proof *FDC* (see PGS03)* £650

Obverse portrait by Raphael Maklouf

4261

4261 **Two pounds.** R. St. George (as 4203)

1985 Proof *FDC* (see PGS06)* ....£650   1991 Proof *FDC* (Issued: 620) £650
1987 Proof *FDC* (Issued: 1,801) ....£650   1992 Proof *FDC* (Issued: 476) £650
1988 Proof *FDC* (Issued: 1,551) ....£650   1993 Proof *FDC* (Issued: 414) £650
1990 Proof *FDC* (Issued: 716) ....£650   1996 Proof *FDC* (see PGS24)* £650

4262

4262 **Two pounds** 500th Anniversary of Sovereign. For the obverse impression a representation Of Ourself as at Our Coronation, seated in King Edward's Chair and having received the Sceptre with the Cross and the Rod with the Dove, all within the circumscription 'ELIZABETH. II.DEI.GRA.REG.FID.DEF' and for the reverse a Shield of Our Royal Arms ensigned by an open Royal Crown, the whole superimposed upon a double Rose, and with the circumscription 'ANNIVERSARY OF THE GOLD SOVEREIGN 1489-1989' (Designs: Bernald Sindall)

1989 Proof *FDC* (Issued: 2,000) £900

* *Coins marked thus were originally issued in Royal Mint sets.*

Obverse portrait by Ian Rank-Broadley

4420

4420 Two pounds. R. St. George

1998 Proof *FDC* (see PGS28)* ....£600　　2000 Proof *FDC* (see PGS32)* £600
2003 Proof *FDC* (see PGS38)* ....£600　　2006 Proof *FDC* (see PGS44)* £600
2007 Proof *FDC* (see PGS46)* ....£600　　2008 Proof *FDC* (see PGS49)* £600

4421　　　　　　　　4422　　　　　　　　4423

4421 Two pounds. R. The Shield of Arms of Our United Kingdom of Great Britain and
Northern Ireland within an open wreath of laurel and ensigned by Our Royal Crown and
beneath the date of the year. (Reverse design: Timothy Noad)
2002 Proof *FDC* (see PGS36)* £750

4422 Two pounds. R. A depiction of St George, carrying a shield and a sword, slaying the
dragon, with the date '2005' beneath the wing of the dragon.(Reverse design: Timothy
Noad)
2005 Proof *FDC* (see PGS42)* £750

4423 Two pounds. R. St George. Based on the original design of 1820 with greater detail on
the dragon.
2009 Proof *FDC* (see PGS52)* £600
2010 Proof *FDC* (Edition: 2,750 in sets)*...£600
2011 Proof *FDC* (Edition: 2,950 in sets)*...£900

4424

4424 Two pounds. R. The image of St George on horseback, attacking the dragon with a
lance, with date of the year to the left. (Reverse design: Paul Day)
2012 BU (Edition: 60 in three coin set, see PGS6)* £1400
—　Proof *FDC* (Edition: 1,944 including coins in sets)*

* Coins marked thus were originally issued in Royal Mint sets.

Obverse portrait by Arnold Machin

4201

4201 Five pounds. R. The image of St George armed, sitting on horseback, attacking the dragon with a sword, and a broken spear upon the ground, and the date of the year.(Reverse design: Benedetto Pistrucci)

1980 Proof *FDC* (see PGS01)*... £1550	1982 Proof *FDC* (see PGS03)* £1550
1981 Proof *FDC* (Issued: 5,400) ** £1550	1984 Proof *FDC* (Issued: 905) £1550

4202 As 4201 but, 'U' in a circle to left of date
1984 (Issued: 15,104) *Unc* £1550

Obverse portrait by Raphael Maklouf

4251 4253

4251 Five pounds. R. St. George (as 4201)

1985 Proof *FDC* (see PGS06)*... £1550	1990 Proof *FDC* (see PGS12)* £1550
1991 Proof *FDC* (see PGS14)*... £1550	1992 Proof *FDC* (see PGS16)* £1550
1993 Proof *FDC* (see PGS18)*... £1550	1994 Proof *FDC* (see PGS20)* £1550
1995 Proof *FDC* (see PGS22)*... £1550	1996 Proof *FDC* (see PGS24)* £1550
1997 Proof *FDC* (see PGS26)*.. £1550	

4252 Five pounds R. St George, 'U' in a circle to left of date.

1985 (Issued: 13,626)..................£1550	1993 (Issued: 906) £1550
1986 (Issued: 7,723).....................£1550	1994 (Issued: 1,000) £1550
1990 (Issued: 1,226)....................£1550	1995 (Issued: 1,000) £1550
1991 (Issued: 976)........................£1550	1996 (Issued: 901) £1550
1992 (Issued: 797)........................£1550	1997 (Issued: 802) £1550

4253 Five pounds Uncouped portrait of Queen Elizabeth II. As illustration. R. St. George, 'U' in a circle to left of date.

1987 (Issued: 5,694)....................£1550	1988 (Issued: 3,315) £1550

4254

4254 Five pounds 500th Anniversary of Sovereign. For the obverse impression a representation
Of Ourself as at Our Coronation, seated in King Edward's Chair and having received
the Sceptre with the Cross and the Rod with the Dove, all within the circumscription
'ELIZABETH.II.DEI.GRA.REG.FID.DEF' and for the reverse a Shield of Our Royal
Arms ensigned by an open Royal Crown, the whole superimposed upon a double Rose,
and with the circumscription 'ANNIVERSARY OF THE GOLD SOVEREIGN 1489-
1989' (Designs: Bernald Sindall)

1989 (Issued: 2,937)...£1650
—   Proof *FDC* (see PGS10)*...£2000

Obverse portrait by Ian Rank-Broadley

4400

4400 Five pounds. R. St.George

1998 Proof *FDC* (see PGS28)*... £1550	2004 Unc (Issued: 1,000)........................£1550
1999 Proof *FDC* (see PGS30)*... £1550	— Proof *FDC* (see PGS40)* £1550
2000 Bullion type........................ £1550	2006 Unc (Issued: 731)...........................£1550
— Proof *FDC* (see PGS32)*.... £1550	— Proof *FDC* (see PGS44)* £1550
2001 Proof *FDC* (see PGS34)*... £1550	2007 Unc (Issued: 768)...........................£1550
2003 Unc (Issued: 812) £1550	— Proof *FDC* (see PGS46)* £1550
— Proof *FDC* (see PGS38)*.... £1550	2008 Unc (Issued: 750)...........................£1550
	— Proof *FDC* (see PGS49)* £1550

* Coins marked thus were originally issued in Royal Mint sets.

4401 4402 4403

4401 Five pounds. R. The Shield of Arms of Our United Kingdom of Great Britain and Northern Ireland within an open wreath of laurel and ensigned by Our Royal Crown and beneath the date of the year. (Reverse design: Timothy Noad)

2002 Unc (Issued: 1,370) £1650

— Proof *FDC* (see PGS36)* £1800

4402 Five pounds. R. A depiction of St George, carrying a shield and a sword, slaying the dragon, with the date '2005' beneath the wing of the dragon.(Reverse design: Timothy Noad)

2005 Unc (Issued: 936) £1650

— Proof *FDC* (see PGS42)* £1800

4403 Five pounds. R. St George. Based on the original pattern piece of 1820 with the designer's name, 'PISTRUCCI', shown in full in the exergue, and with a broader rim.

2009 BU (Edition: 1,000)...............£1550 — Proof *FDC* (see PGS52)*...............£1550

2010 BU (Edition: 1,000)...............£1550 — Proof *FDC* (Edition: 2,000 in sets)* £1550

2011 BU (Edition: 1,000)...............£2100 — Proof *FDC* (Edition: 2,000 in sets)* £2100

4404

4404 Five pounds. R. The image of St George on horseback, attacking the dragon with a lance, with date of the year to the left. (Reverse design: Paul Day)

2012 BU (Edition: 1,250)...£2400

— Proof *FDC* (Edition: 999 coins in sets)*

4410 Five pounds. R. St. George, 'U' in a circle to left of date

1998 (Issued: 825) ....£1550 2000 (Issued: 994) £1550

1999 (Issued: 970) ....£1550 2001 (Issued: 1,000) £1550

* Coins marked thus were originally issued in Royal Mint sets.

BRITANNIA COIN ISSUES

In 1987 the Mint decided to enter the market for bullion coins and launched a series of four gold coins with weights that corresponded to those already issued by a number of gold producing countries such as Canada, South Africa and China. The plan was to sell bullion quality coins in quantity to trade customers and investors at modest premiums over the ruling gold market price, and also to sell proof versions in limited editions to collectors.

Due to market reaction, particularly from the Far East, silver rather than copper was alloyed with the gold in 1990 in an effort to increase demand but in the absence of sales figures, it appears that the major interest is now to be found among collectors of the proof collector versions.

To mark the 10th anniversary of the first design, silver coins struck in Britannia silver (0.958) were introduced in the same four weights. Again the main interest seems to have been among collectors of the proof versions although the one ounce silver bullion coin of £2 face value has proved popular as silver prices have risen.

There are some attractive and different interpretations of Britannia with the gold and silver issues sharing the same designs as they are changed. The range of designs thus far are shown below, and the complete sets are listed in the appropriate sections towards the end of the catalogue.

BRITANNIA SILVER

Obverse portrait by Raphael Maklouf

4300C

4300C Britannia. Twenty pence. (1/10 oz of fine silver) 10th Anniversary of Britannia issue R. The figure of Britannia standing in a chariot drawn along the seashore by two horses, with the word 'BRITANNIA', the inscription. '1/10 OUNCE FINE SILVER' and the date of the year. (Reverse design: Philip Nathan).
  1997 Proof *FDC* (Issued: 8,686, plus coins issued in sets, see PSB01) £20

Obverse portrait by Ian Rank-Broadley

4530   4531

4530 Britannia. Twenty pence. (1/10 oz of fine silver) R. The figure of Britannia standing upon a rock in the sea, her right hand grasping a trident and her left hand resting on a shield and holding an olive branch, with the word 'BRITANNIA', the date of the year, and the inscription '1/10 OUNCE FINE SILVER'. (Reverse design: Philip Nathan). (See 4500)
  1998 — Proof *FDC* (Issued: 2,724, plus coins issued in sets, see PSB02) £20
  2006 BU version £15
  2012 — Proof *FDC* (Edition: 2,600 in sets see PBS14)*

4531 Britannia. Twenty pence. (1/10 oz of fine silver) R. The figure of Britannia, as guardian, with a shield in her left hand and a trident in her right hand, accompanied by a lion and, against the background of a wave motif, the words '1/10 OUNCE FINE SILVER' to the left and 'BRITANNIA' and the date of the year to the right. (Reverse design: Philip Nathan).
  2001 — Proof *FDC* (Issued: 826, plus coins issued in sets, see PSB03) £20

* *Coins marked thus were originally issued in Royal Mint sets.*

4532 4534 4536

4532 Britannia. Twenty pence. (1/10 oz fine silver) ℞. Helmeted head of Britannia with, to the left, the word 'BRITANNIA' and, to the right, the inscription '1/10 OUNCE FINE SILVER' and the date of the year, the whole being overlaid with a wave pattern. (Reverse design: Philip Nathan)
2003 — Proof *FDC* (Issued: 1,179, plus coins issued in sets, see PBS04) £20

4533 Britannia. Twenty pence. (Previously listed as 4515) (1/10 oz of fine silver) ℞. Seated figure of Britannia facing to the left holding a trident with a shield at her side, with the word 'BRITANNIA', the inscription '1/10 OUNCE FINE SILVER' and the date of the year. (Reverse design: Philip Nathan)
2005 — Proof *FDC** (Issued: 913, plus coins issued in sets, see PBS06) £20

4534 Britannia. Twenty pence. (1/10 oz of fine silver) ℞. Seated figure of Britannia facing right holding a trident in her right hand and a sprig of olive in the left hand with a lion at her feet with the inscription '1/10 OUNCE FINE SILVER' and the word 'BRITANNIA' and the date of the year (Reverse design: Christopher Le Brun)
2007 — Proof *FDC* (Issued: 901, plus coins issued in sets, see PBS08) £20

4535 Britannia. Twenty pence. (1/10 oz of fine silver) ℞. A Standing figure of Britannia holding a trident with a shield at her side, the folds of her dress transforming into a wave, with the word 'BRITANNIA' and the date of the year and the inscription '1/10 OUNCE FINE SILVER' (Reverse design: John Bergdahl). (See 4506)
2008 — Proof *FDC* (Edition: 2,500, plus coins issued in sets, see PBS1010).................£20

4536 Britannia. Twenty pence. (1/10 oz fine silver) ℞. Standing figure of Britannia in horse drawn chariot. (See 4501)
2009 — Proof *FDC* (Edition; 3,500 including coins in sets)...£25

4537

4537 Britannia. Twenty pence. (1/10 oz fine silver) ℞. A design depicting a profile bust of Britannia wearing a helmet, accompanied by the name 'BRITANNIA', the inscription '1/10 OUNCE FINE SILVER' and the date '2010'. (Reverse design: Suzie Zamit)
2010 Proof *FDC* (Edition: 8,000 including coins in sets)...£25

4538 Britannia. Twenty pence. (1/10 oz fine silver) ℞. A design depicting a seated figure of Britannia set against a background of a rippling Union Flag accompanied by the words '1/10 OUNCE FINE SILVER BRITANNIA' and the date '2011'. (Reverse design: David Mach)
2011 Proof *FDC* (Edition: 6,000 including coins in sets)

* *Coins marked thus were originally issued in Royal Mint sets.*

Obverse portrait by Raphael Maklouf

4300B

4300B **Britannia. Fifty pence.** (1/4 oz of fine silver) 10th Anniversary of Britannia issue R. The figure of Britannia standing in a chariot drawn along the seashore by two horses, with the word 'BRITANNIA', the inscription. '1/4 OUNCE FINE SILVER' and the date of the year. (Reverse design: Philip Nathan).
1997 Proof *FDC* (in 1997 sets, see PSB01)* £30

Obverse portrait by Ian Rank-Broadley

4520   4521   4522   4524

4520 **Britannia. Fifty pence.** (1/4 oz of fine silver) R. The figure of Britannia standing upon a rock in the sea, her right hand grasping a trident and her left hand resting on a shield and holding an olive branch, the word 'BRITANNIA', the date of the year, and the inscription '1/4 OUNCE FINE SILVER'. (Reverse design: Philip Nathan). (See 4500)
1998 — Proof *FDC* (in 1998 set, see PSB02)* £25
2012 — Proof *FDC* (Edition: 2,600 in sets see PBS14)*

4521 **Britannia. Fifty pence.** (1/4 oz of fine silver) R. The figure of Britannia, as guardian, with a shield in her left hand and a trident in her right hand, accompanied by a lion and, against the background of a wave motif, the words '(1/4 OUNCE FINE SILVER' to the left and 'BRITANNIA' and the date of the year to the right. . (Reverse design: Philip Nathan).
2001 — Proof *FDC* (in 2001 set, see PSB03)* £25

4522 **Britannia. Fifty pence.** (1/4 oz fine silver) R. Helmeted head of Britannia with, to the left, the word 'BRITANNIA' and, to the right, the inscription '1/4 OUNCE FINE SILVER' and the date of the year, the whole being overlaid with a wave pattern. (Reverse design: Philip Nathan)
2003 — Proof *FDC** £25

4523 **Britannia. Fifty pence.** (Previously listed as 4514) (1/4 oz of fine silver) R. Seated figure of Britannia facing to the left holding a trident with a shield at her side, with the word 'BRITANNIA', the inscription '1/4 OUNCE FINE SILVER' and the date of the year. (Reverse design: Philip Nathan). (See 4504)
2005 — Proof *FDC** £25

4524 **Britannia. Fifty pence.** (1/4 oz of fine silver) R. Seated figure of Britannia facing right holding a trident in her right hand and a sprig of olive in the left hand with a lion at her feet with the inscription '1/4 OUNCE FINE SILVER' and the word 'BRITANNIA' and the date of the year (See 4505) (Reverse design: Christopher Le Brun)
2007 — Proof *FDC** £25

* Coins marked thus were originally issued in Royal Mint sets.

4525   4527

4525 Britannia. Fifty pence. (1/4 oz of fine silver) ℞. A Standing figure of Britannia holding a
trident with a shield at her side, the folds of her dress transforming into a wave, with the word
'BRITANNIA' and the date of the year and the inscription '1/4 OUNCE FINE SILVER'
(Reverse design: John Bergdahl)
2008 — Proof *FDC**..£25

4526 Britannia. Fifty pence. (1/4 oz fine silver) ℞. Standing figure of Britannia in horse drawn
chariot. (see 4300B above)
2009 — Proof *FDC**..£30

4527 Britannia. Fifty pence. (1/4 oz fine silver) ℞. A design depicting a profile bust of Britannia
wearing a helmet, accompanied by the name 'BRITANNIA', the inscription '1/4 OUNCE
FINE SILVER' and the date '2010'. (Reverse design: Suzie Zamit)
2010 Proof *FDC* *..£30

4528 Britannia. Fifty pence. (1/4 oz fine silver) ℞. A design depicting a seated figure of Britannia
set against a background of a rippling Union Flag accompanied by the words '1/4 OUNCE
FINE SILVER BRITANNIA' and the date '2011'. (Reverse design: David Mach)
2011 Proof *FDC* (Edition: 5,000 including coins in sets)..£30

Obverse portrait by Raphael Maklouf

4300A

4300A Britannia. One pound. (1/2 oz of fine silver) 10th Anniversary of Britannia issue. ℞. The
figure of Britannia standing in a chariot drawn along the seashore by two horses, with the
word 'BRITANNIA', the inscription. '1/2 OUNCE FINE SILVER' and the date of the year.
(Reverse design: Philip Nathan).
1997 Proof *FDC**..£40

* *Coins marked thus were originally issued in Royal Mint sets.*

Obverse portrait by Ian Rank-Broadley

4510

4510 Britannia. One pound. (1/2 oz of fine silver) R. The figure of Britannia standing upon a
rock in the sea, her right hand grasping a trident and her left hand resting on a shield and
holding an olive branch, with the word 'BRITANNIA', the date of the year, and the
inscription '1/2 OUNCE FINE SILVER' (Reverse design: Philip Nathan).
1998 — Proof *FDC** £40
2012 — Proof *FDC* (Edition: 4,620 in sets see PBS14 and PBS15)*
4510A 2007 Proof with satin finish on reverse (see 2007 set, PBS09) * £40

4511   4512

4511 Britannia. One pound. (1/2oz of fine silver) R The figure of Britannia, as guardian, with a
shield in her left hand and a trident in her right hand, accompanied by a lion and, against the
background of a wave motif, the words '1/2 OUNCE FINE SILVER' to the left and
'BRITANNIA' and the date of the year to the right. (Reverse design: Philip Nathan).
2001 — Proof *FDC** £40
2012 — Proof *FDC* (Edition: 2,012 in sets see PBS15)*
4511A 2007 Proof with satin finish on reverse (see 2007 set, PBS09) * £40
4512 Britannia. One pound. (1/2 oz fine silver) R. Helmeted head of Britannia with, to the
left, the word 'BRITANNIA' and, to the right, the inscription '1/2 OUNCE FINE
SILVER' and the date of the year, the whole being overlaid with a wave pattern. (Reverse
design: Philip Nathan)
2003 — Proof *FDC** £40
2012 — Proof *FDC* (Edition: 2,012 in sets see PBS15)*
4512A2007 Proof with satin finish on reverse (see 2007 set, PBS09) * £40
4513 Britannia. One pound. (1/2 oz of fine silver) R. Seated figure of Britannia facing to the
left holding a trident with a shield at her side, with the word 'BRITANNIA', the inscription
'1/2 OUNCE FINE SILVER' and the date of the year. (Reverse design: Philip Nathan).
(See 4504)
2005 — Proof *FDC** £40
2012 — Proof *FDC* (Edition: 2,012 in sets see PBS15)*
4513A 2007 Proof with satin finish on reverse (see 2007 set, PBS09) * £40

* Coins marked thus were originally issued in Royal Mint sets.

4514 4516 4517

4514 Britannia. One pound. (1/2 oz of fine silver) R̶. Seated figure of Britannia facing right
holding a trident in her right hand and a sprig of olive in the left hand with a lion at her feet
with the inscription '1/2 OUNCE FINE SILVER' and the word 'BRITANNIA' and the date
of the year. (Reverse design: Christopher Le Brun)
2007 Proof *FDC* * £40
2012 — Proof *FDC* (Edition: 2,012 in sets see PBS15)*

4514A 2007 Proof with satin finish on reverse (see 2007 set, PBS09) * £40

4515 Britannia. One pound. (1/2 oz of fine silver) R̶. Standing figure of Britannia in horse
drawn chariot. (See 4300A)
2007 Proof with satin finish on reverse (see 2007 set, PBS09) * £40

4516 Britannia. One pound. (1/2 oz of fine silver) R̶. A Standing figure of Britannia holding
a trident with a shield at her side, the folds of her dress transforming into a wave, with
the word 'BRITANNIA' and the date of the year and the inscription '1/2 OUNCE FINE
SILVER' (Reverse design: John Bergdahl)
2008 Proof *FDC* * £40
2012 — Proof *FDC* (Edition: 2,012 in sets see PBS15)*

4517 Britannia. One pound. (1/2 oz fine silver) R̶. Standing figure of Britannia in horse drawn
chariot. (Reverse design: Philip Nathan) (See 4300A above)
2009 — Proof *FDC* * £40
2012 — Proof *FDC* (Edition: 2,012 in sets see PBS15)*

4518 4519

4518 Britannia. One pound. (1/2 oz fine silver) R̶. A design depicting a profile bust of
Britannia wearing a helmet, accompanied by the name 'BRITANNIA', the inscription '1/2
OUNCE FINE SILVER' and the date '2010'. (Reverse design: Suzie Zamit)
2010 Proof *FDC* * £40
2012 — Proof *FDC* (Edition: 2,012 in sets see PBS15)*

4519 Britannia. One pound. (1/2 oz fine silver) R̶. A design depicting a seated figure of Britannia
set against a background of a rippling Union Flag accompanied by the words '1/2 OUNCE
FINE SILVER BRITANNIA' and the date '2011'. (Reverse design: David Mach)
2011 Proof *FDC* (Edition: 5,000 including coins in sets) £40
2012 — Proof *FDC* (Edition: 2,012 in sets see PBS15)*

* Coins marked thus were originally issued in Royal Mint sets.

Obverse portrait by Raphael Maklouf

4300

4300 Britannia. Two pounds. (1 oz fine silver) 10th Anniversary of Britannia issue R. The
figure of Britannia standing in a chariot drawn along the seashore by two horses, with the
word 'BRITANNIA', the inscription. 'ONE OUNCE FINE SILVER' and the date of the
year. (Reverse design: Philip Nathan)
1997 Proof *FDC* (Issued: 4,173) £120

Obverse portrait by Ian Rank-Broadley

4500

4500 Britannia. Two pounds. (1 oz of fine silver) R. The figure of Britannia standing upon a
rock in the sea, her right hand grasping a trident and her left hand resting on a shield and
holding an olive branch, with the word 'BRITANNIA', the date of the year, and the
inscription' ONE OUNCE FINE SILVER'. (Reverse design: Philip Nathan)

1998 (Issued: 88,909) £40	2006 (Edition 100,000) £40
— Proof *FDC* (Issued: 2,168) £80	— Proof *FDC* (Issued: 2,529) £65
2000 (Issued: 81,301) £40	2012 (Edition 100,000) £58
2002 (Issued: 36,543) £40	— Proof *FDC* (Edition 5,550 including coins
2004 (Edition: 100,000) £40	in sets) £93
— Proof *FDC* (Issued: 2,174) £65	

4500A Britannia. Two pounds. (1 oz of fine silver) R. Standing figure of Britannia
2006 - Proof *FDC** with selected gold plating of obverse and reverse (See PBS07).......£70

* Coins marked thus were originally issued in Royal Mint sets.

4501 4502

4501 Britannia. Two pounds. (1oz fine silver) ℞. Standing figure of Britannia in horse drawn chariot.(Reverse design: Philip Nathan)

1999 (Issued: 69,394)..£40

2009 (Issued: 100,000)...£40

— Proof *FDC* (Edition: 12,000 including coins in sets)..£65

4501ABritannia. Two pounds. (1 oz of fine silver) ℞. Standing figure of Britannia in horse drawn chariot

2006 — Proof *FDC** with selected gold plating of obverse and reverse (See PBS07)....£70

4502 Britannia. Two pounds. (1 oz of fine silver) ℞. The figure of Britannia, as guardian, with a shield in her left hand and a trident in her right hand, accompanied by a lion and, against the background of a wave motif, the words 'ONE OUNCE FINE SILVER' to the left and 'BRITANNIA' and the date of the year to the right. (Reverse design: Philip Nathan)

2001 (Issued: 44,816)...£40

— Proof *FDC* (Issued: 3,047) £60

4502ABritannia. Two pounds. (1 oz of fine silver) ℞. Helmeted figure of Britannia holding a trident and a shield with a lion in the background

2006 — Proof *FDC** with selected gold plating of obverse and reverse (See PBS07)....£70

4503 4504

4503 Britannia. Two pounds. (1oz fine silver) ℞. Helmeted head of Britannia with, to the left, the word 'BRITANNIA' and, to the right, the inscription 'ONE OUNCE FINE SILVER' and the date of the year, ... the whole being overlaid with a wave pattern. (Reverse design: Philip Nathan)

2003 (Issued: 73,271)..£40

— Proof *FDC* (Issued: 2,016)...£65

* Coins marked thus were originally issued in Royal Mint sets.

4503A Britannia. Two pounds. (1oz fine silver) R. Helmeted figure of Britannia with stylised waves
2006 — Proof *FDC** with selected gold plating of obverse and reverse (See PBS07)....£70

4504 Britannia. Two pounds. (1 oz of fine silver) R. Seated figure of Britannia facing to the
left holding a trident with a shield at her side, with the word 'BRITANNIA', the inscription
'ONE OUNCE FINE SILVER' and the date of the year. (Reverse design: Philip Nathan)
2005 (Edition: 100,000) £40
— Proof *FDC* (Issued: 1,539)..£65

4504A Britannia. Two pounds. (1 oz of fine silver) R. Seated figure of Britannia facing left
2006 — Proof *FDC** with selected gold plating of obverse and reverse (See PBS07)....£70

4505   4506

4505 Britannia. Two pounds. (1 oz of fine silver) R. Seated figure of Britannia facing right
holding a trident in her right hand and a sprig of olive in the left hand with a lion at her feet
with the inscription 'ONE OUNCE FINE SILVER' and the word 'BRITANNIA' and the
date of the year (See 4505) (Reverse design: Christopher Le Brun)
2007 (Edition: 100,000) £40
— Proof *FDC* (Issued: 5,157 ....£65

4506 Britannia. Two pounds. (1 oz of fine silver) R. A Standing figure of Britannia holding a
trident with a shield at her side, the folds of her dress transforming into a wave, with the word
'BRITANNIA' and the date of the year and the inscription 'ONE OUNCE FINE SILVER'
(Reverse design: John Bergdahl)
2008 (Edition: 100,000) £40
— Proof *FDC* (Edition: 2,500) £65

4507   4508

4507 Britannia. Two pounds. (1 oz fine silver) R. A design depicting a profile bust of
Britannia wearing a helmet, accompanied by the name 'BRITANNIA', the inscription
'ONE OUNCE FINE SILVER' and the date '2010'. (Reverse design: Suzie Zamit)
2010 (Edition: 100,000) £40
— Proof *FDC* (Edition: 8,000 including coins in sets)................................£65

* Coins marked thus were originally issued in Royal Mint sets.

4508 Britannia. Two pounds. (1 oz fine silver) R. A design depicting a seated figure of Britannia set against a background of a rippling Union Flag accompanied by the words 'ONE OUNCE FINE SILVER BRITANNIA' and the date '2011'. (Reverse design: David Mach)
2011 (Edition: 500,000) ....£58   Proof *FDC* (Edition: 10,000)......................£90

BRITANNIA GOLD
Obverse portrait by Raphael Maklouf

4296

4296 Britannia. Ten pounds. (1/10oz of fine gold alloyed with copper). R. The figure of Britannia standing upon a rock in the sea, her right hand grasping a trident and her left hand resting on a shield and holding an olive branch, with the inscription '1/10 OUNCE FINE GOLD BRITANNIA' and the year of the date. (Reverse design: Philip Nathan)

1987..£130	1989 ....£130
— Proof *FDC* (Issued: 3,500).... £150	— Proof *FDC* (Issued: 1,609) £150
1988..£130	
— Proof *FDC* (Issued: 2,694).... £150	

4297 Britannia. Ten pounds. (1/10oz of fine gold alloyed with silver). R. Britannia standing.

1990..£130	1994 ....£130
— Proof *FDC* (Issued: 1,571).... £150	— Proof *FDC* (Issued: 994) £150
1991..£130	1995 ....£130
— Proof *FDC* (Issued: 954).......£150	— Proof *FDC* (Issued: 1,500) £150
1992..£130	1996 ....£130
— Proof *FDC* (Issued: 1,000)....£150	— Proof *FDC* (Issued: 2,379) £150
1993..£130	
— Proof *FDC* (Issued: 997).......£150	

4298

4298 Britannia. Ten pounds. (1/10 oz fine gold, alloyed with silver) 10th Anniversary of Britannia issue. R. The figure of Britannia standing in a chariot drawn along the seashore by two horses, with the word 'BRITANNIA', .the inscription '1/10 OUNCE FINE GOLD' and the date of the year. (Reverse design: Philip Nathan)
1997 Proof *FDC* (Issued: 1,821) £180

NB. The spot price of gold at the time of going to press was £1092 per oz.

Obverse portrait by Ian Rank-Broadley

4480   4481   4482   4483

4480 **Britannia. Ten pounds.** (1/10 oz fine gold alloyed with silver) R. The figure of Britannia standing upon a rock in the sea, Her right hand grasping a trident and her left hand resting on a shield and holding an olive branch, with the word 'BRITANNIA', the date of the year, and the inscription '1/10 OUNCE FINE GOLD'. (Reverse design: Philip Nathan)

1998 Proof *FDC* (Issued: 392)......£150	2002 Proof *FDC* (Issued: 1,500) £150
1999...£130	2004 Proof *FDC* (Issued: 929) £1500
1999 Proof *FDC* (Issued: 1,058)...£150	2006 Proof *FDC* (issued: 700).................£150
2000...£130	2012 ....£150
2000 Proof *FDC* (Issued: 659)......£150	2012 Proof *FDC* (Edition: 2,500)............£225
2002...£130	

4481 **Britannia. Ten pounds.** (1/10 oz fine gold alloyed with silver) R. The figure of Britannia, as guardian, with a shield in her left hand and a trident in her right hand, accompanied by a lion and, against the background of a wave motif, and the words '1/10 OUNCE FINE GOLD' to the left and 'BRITANNIA' and the date of the year to the right. (Reverse design: Philip Nathan)

    2001...£130   2001 Proof *FDC* (Issued: 1,557) £150

4482 **Britannia. Ten pounds.** (1/10 oz fine gold alloyed with silver) R. . Helmeted head of Britannia with, to the left, the word 'BRITANNIA' and, to the right, the inscription '1/10 OUNCE FINE GOLD' and the date of the year, the whole being overlaid with a wave pattern. (Reverse design: Philip Nathan)

    2003...£130   2003 Proof *FDC* (Issued: 1,382) £150

4483 **Britannia. Ten pounds.** (1/10 oz fine gold alloyed with silver) R. Seated figure of Britannia facing to the left holding a trident with a shield at her side, with the word 'BRITANNIA', the inscription '1/10 OUNCE FINE GOLD' and the date of the year. (Reverse design: Philip Nathan)

    2005 Proof *FDC* (issued: 1,225) £150

4484   4485   4486   4487

4484 **Britannia. Ten pounds.** (1/10 oz fine gold alloyed with silver) R. Seated figure of Britannia facing right holding a trident in her right hand and a sprig of olive in the left hand with a lion at her feet with the inscription '1/10 OUNCE FINE GOLD' and the word 'BRITANNIA' and the date of the year. (Reverse design: Christopher Le Brun)

    2007...£130   2007 Proof *FDC* (Issued: 893) £150

4484A(1/10 oz platinum)

    2007 Proof *FDC* (Issued: 691)..£225

* Coins marked thus were originally issued in Royal Mint sets.

NB. The spot price of gold at the time of going to press was £1092 per oz.

4485 Britannia. Ten pounds. (1/10 oz fine gold alloyed with silver) R. A Standing figure of
Britannia holding a trident with a shield at her side, the folds of her dress transforming
into a wave, with the word 'BRITANNIA' and the date of the year and the inscription '1/10
OUNCE FINE GOLD' (Reverse design: John Bergdahl)
2008 Proof *FDC* (Issued: 748 plus coins issued in sets, see PBS30) £150
4485A(1/10 oz platinum)
2008 Proof *FDC* (Issued: 268 plus coins issued in sets, see PPBCS2) £225
4486 Britannia. Ten pounds. (1/10 oz fine gold alloyed with silver) R. Standing figure of
Britannia in horse drawn chariot.
2009...£130   2009 Proof *FDC* (Edition: 750)...............£160
4487 Britannia. Ten pounds. (1/10 oz fine gold alloyed with silver) R. A design depicting a
profile bust of Britannia wearing a helmet, accompanied by the name 'BRITANNIA', the
inscription '1/10 OUNCE FINE GOLD' and the date '2010'. (Reverse design: Suzie Zamit)
2010 Proof *FDC* (Edition: 3,000 including coins in sets)..£160
4488 Britannia. Ten pounds. (1/10 oz fine gold alloyed with silver) R. A design depicting a
seated figure of Britannia set against a background of a rippling Union Flag accompanied by
the words '1/10 OUNCE FINE GOLD BRITANNIA, and the date '2011'. (Reverse design:
David Mach)
2011 Proof *FDC (*Edition: 8,000 including coins in sets) £225

Obverse portrait by Raphael Maklouf

4291

4291 Britannia. Twenty five pounds. (1/4oz of fine gold alloyed with copper). R. The figure
of Britannia standing upon a rock in the sea, her right hand grasping a trident and her left
hand resting on a shield and holding an olive branch, with the inscription '1/4 OUNCE
FINE GOLD BRITANNIA' and the year of the date. (Reverse design: Philip Nathan)

1987.. £325	1989 ....£325	
— Proof *FDC* (Issued: 3,500).... £350	— Proof *FDC* (see PBS05)* £350	
1988.. £325		
— Proof *FDC* (see PBS03)* £350		

4292 Britannia. Twenty five pounds. (1/4oz of fine gold alloyed with silver). R. Britannia standing.

1990.. £325	1994 ....£325
— Proof *FDC* (see PBS07)* £350	— Proof *FDC* (see PBS11)*................£350
1991.. £325	1995 ....£325
— Proof *FDC* (see PBS08)* £350	— Proof *FDC* (see PBS12)* £350
1992.. £325	1996 ....£325
— Proof *FDC* (see PBS09)* £350	— Proof *FDC* (see PBS13.................. £350
1993.. £325	
— Proof *FDC* (see PBS10)* £350	

* Coins marked thus were originally issued in Royal Mint sets.
NB. The spot price of gold at the time of going to press was £1092 per oz.

4293

4293 **Britannia. Twenty five pounds.** (1/4 oz fine gold, alloyed with silver) 10th Anniversary of Britannia issue. R. The figure of Britannia standing in a chariot drawn along the seashore by two horses, with the word 'BRITANNIA', ..the inscription. '1/4 OUNCE FINE GOLD' and the date of the year. (Reverse design: Philip Nathan)
1997 Proof *FDC* (Issued: 923) £350

Obverse portrait by Ian Rank-Broadley

4470   4471   4472

4470 **Britannia. Twenty five pounds**. (1/4 oz fine gold alloyed with silver) R. The figure of Britannia standing upon a rock in the sea, her right hand grasping a trident and her left hand resting on a shield and holding an olive branch, with the word 'BRITANNIA', the date of the year, and the inscription' 1/4 OUNCE FINE GOLD'. (Reverse design: Philip Nathan)

1998 Proof *FDC* (Issued: 560) £350	2002 Proof *FDC* (Issued: 750) £350
1999..£325	2004 Proof *FDC* (Issued: 750) £350
1999 Proof *FDC* (Issued: 1,000) ... £350	2006 Proof *FDC* (Edition: 1,000)............£350
2000..£325	2012 Proof *FDC* (Edition: 1,750) £500
2000 Proof *FDC* (Issued: 500) £350	

4471 **Britannia. Twenty five pounds.** (1/4 oz fine gold alloyed with silver) R. The figure of Britannia, as guardian, with a shield in her left hand and a trident in her right hand, accompanied by a lion and, against the background of a wave motif, the words '1/4 OUNCE FINE GOLD' to the left and 'BRITANNIA' and the date of the year to the right. (Reverse design: Philip Nathan)

2001 ....£325	2006 Proof *FDC* (see PBS28)* £350
2001 Proof *FDC* (Issued: 500) £350	

4472 **Britannia. Twenty five pounds.** (1/4 oz fine gold alloyed with silver) R. Helmeted head of Britannia with, to the left, the word 'BRITANNIA' and, to the right, the inscription '1/4 OUNCE FINE GOLD' and the date of the year, the whole being overlaid with a wave pattern. (Reverse design: Philip Nathan)

2003 Proof *FDC* (Issued: 609) £325	2006 Proof *FDC* (see PBS28)* £350

* Coins marked thus were originally issued in Royal Mint sets.
NB. The spot price of gold at the time of going to press was £1092 per oz.

4475   4476

4473 Britannia. Twenty five pounds. (1/4 oz fine gold alloyed with silver) R. Seated figure of
Britannia facing to the left holding a trident with a shield at her side, with the word
'BRITANNIA', the inscription '1/4 OUNCE FINE GOLD' and the date of the year.
(Reverse design: Philip Nathan)
2005 Proof *FDC* (Issued: 750)...... £325   2006 Proof *FDC* (seePBS28)* £350

4474 Britannia. Twenty five pounds. (1/4 oz fine gold alloyed with silver) R. Standing figure
of Britannia in horse drawn chariot. (See 4293)
2006 Proof *FDC* (see PBS28)* ..... £325   2009 Proof *FDC* (Edition: 1,000) £350

4475 Britannia. Twenty five pounds. (Previously listed as 4474) (1/4 oz fine gold alloyed
with silver) R. Seated figure of Britannia facing right holding a trident in her right
hand and a sprig of olive in the left hand with a lion at her feet with the inscription '1/4
OUNCE FINE GOLD' and the word 'BRITANNIA' and the date of the year. (Reverse
design: Christopher Le Brun)
2007.. £325   2007 Proof *FDC* (Issued: 1,000) £350

4475A(1/4 oz platinum)
2007 Proof *FDC* (Issued: 210)... £450

4476 Britannia. Twenty five pounds. (1/4 oz fine gold alloyed with silver) R. A Standing figure
of Britannia holding a trident with a shield at her side, the folds of her dress transforming
into a wave, with the word 'BRITANNIA' and the date of the year and the inscription '1/4
OUNCE FINE GOLD' (Reverse design: John Bergdahl)
2008 Proof *FDC* (Edition: 1,000) £350

4476A(1/4 oz platinum)
2008 Proof *FDC* (Edition: 500) £450

4477 Britannia. Twenty five pounds. (1/4 oz fine gold alloyed with silver) R. A design depicting
a profile bust of Britannia wearing a helmet, accompanied by the name 'BRITANNIA', the
inscription '1/4 OUNCE FINE GOLD' and the date '2010'. (Reverse design: Suzie Zamit)
2010 Proof *FDC* (Edition: 3,000 including coins in sets).. £350

4477

4478 Britannia. Twenty Five pounds. (1/4 oz fine gold alloyed with silver) R. A design
depicting a seated figure of Britannia set against a background of a rippling Union Flag
accompanied by the words ' 1/4 OUNCE FINE GOLD BRITANNIA, and the date '2011'.
(Reverse design: David Mach)
2011 Proof *FDC* (Edition: 7,000 including coins in sets).. £500

* Coins marked thus were originally issued in Royal Mint sets.
NB. The spot price of gold at the time of going to press was £1092 per oz.

Obverse portrait by Raphael Maklouf

4286

4286 Britannia. Fifty pounds. (1/2oz of fine gold alloyed with copper). R. The figure of
Britannia standing upon a rock in the sea, her right hand grasping a trident and her left
hand resting on a shield and holding an olive branch, with the inscription '1/2 OUNCE
FINE GOLD BRITANNIA' and the year of the date. (Reverse design: Philip Nathan)

1987.. £650   1989 ....£650
— Proof *FDC* (Issued: 2,486).... £700   — Proof *FDC* (see PBS05)* £700
1988.. £650
— Proof *FDC* (see PBS03)* £700

4288

4287 Britannia. Fifty pounds. (1/2oz of fine gold, alloyed with Silver). R. Britannia standing.

1990.. £650   1994 ....£650
— Proof *FDC* (see PBS07)* ...... £700   — Proof *FDC* (see PBS11)* £700
1991.. £650   1995 ....£650
— Proof *FDC* (see PBS08)* ...... £700   — Proof *FDC* (see PBS12)* £700
1992.. £650   1996 ....£650
— Proof *FDC* (see PBS09)* ...... £700   — Proof *FDC* (see PBS13)* £700
1993.. £650
— Proof *FDC* (see PBS10)* £700

4288 Britannia. Fifty pounds. (1/2 oz fine gold, alloyed with silver) 10th Anniversary of
Britannia issue. R.The figure of Britannia standing in a chariot drawn along the seashore
by two horses, with the word 'BRITANNIA', the inscription. '1/2 FINE GOLD' and the
date of the year.(Reverse design: Philip Nathan)

1997 Proof *FDC* (see PBS14)* £700

* Coins marked thus were originally issued in Royal Mint sets.
NB. The spot price of gold at the time of going to press was £1092 per oz.

Obverse portrait by Ian Rank-Broadley

4460   4461

4460 **Britannia. Fifty pounds.** (1/2 oz fine gold alloyed with silver). R. The figure of Britannia standing upon a rock in the sea, her right hand grasping a trident and her left hand resting on a shield and holding an olive branch, with the word 'BRITANNIA', the date of the year, and the inscription' 1/2 OUNCE FINE GOLD'. (Reverse design: Philip Nathan)

1998 Proof *FDC* (see PBS15)* £700	2002 Proof *FDC* (see PBS19)* £700
1999... £650	2004 Proof *FDC* (see PBS23)* £700
1999 Proof *FDC* (see PBS16)* £700	2006 Proof *FDC* (see PBS27)* £700
2000... £650	2012 Proof *FDC* (Edition: 1,000)............ £700
— Proof *FDC* (see PBS17)* £700	

4461 **Britannia. Fifty pounds.** (1/2 oz fine gold alloyed with silver). R. The figure of Britannia, as guardian, with a shield in her left hand and a trident in her right hand, accompanied by a lion and, against the background of a wave motif, the words '1/2 OUNCE FINE GOLD' to the left and 'BRITANNIA' and the date of the year to the right. (Reverse design: Philip Nathan)

2001... £650   2001 Proof *FDC* (see PBS18)* £700

4462 **Britannia. Fifty pounds.** (1/2 oz fine gold alloyed with silver) R. Helmeted head of Britannia with, to the left, the word 'BRITANNIA' and, to the right, the inscription '1/2 OUNCE FINE GOLD' and the date of the year, the whole being overlaid with a wave pattern. (Reverse design: Philip Nathan)

2003... £650   2003 Proof *FDC* (see PBS20)* £700

4463   4464

4463 **Britannia. Fifty pounds.** (1/2 oz fine gold alloyed with silver) R. Seated figure of Britannia facing to the left holding a trident with a shield at her side, with the word 'BRITANNIA', the inscription '1/2 OUNCE FINE GOLD' and the date of the year. (Reverse design: Philip Nathan)

2005 Proof *FDC* * £700

4464 **Britannia. Fifty pounds.** (1/2 oz fine gold alloyed with silver) R. Seated figure of Britannia facing right holding a trident in her right hand and a sprig of olive in the left hand with a lion at her feet with the inscription '1/2 OUNCE FINE GOLD' and the word 'BRITANNIA' and the date of the year (See 4505) (Reverse design: Christopher Le Brun)

2007... £650   2007 Proof *FDC* (see PBS29)* £700

4464A (½ oz platinum)

2007 Proof *FDC* * (see 2007 set, PPBCS1)..£800

* *Coins marked thus were originally issued in Royal Mint sets.*

NB. The spot price of gold at the time of going to press was £1092 per oz.

4465   4466   4467

4465 Britannia. Fifty pounds. (1/2 oz fine gold alloyed with silver) R. A Standing figure of
Britannia holding a trident with a shield at her side, the folds of her dress transforming
into a wave, with the word 'BRITANNIA' and the date of the year and the inscription ' 1/2
OUNCE FINE GOLD' (Reverse design: John Bergdahl)
2008 Proof *FDC* * £700

4465A (1/2 oz platinum)
2008 Proof *FDC* (see PPBCS2)* £800

4466 Britannia. Fifty pounds. (1/2oz fine gold alloyed with silver) R.Standing figure of
Britannia in horse drawn chariot.(see 4288 above)
2009... £650   2009 Proof *FDC* (see PBS31)* £700

4467 Britannia. Fifty pounds. (1/2 oz fine gold alloyed with silver) R. A design depicting a
profile bust of Britannia wearing a helmet, accompanied by the name 'BRITANNIA', the
inscription '1/2 OUNCE FINE GOLD' and the date '2010' (Reverse design: Suzie Zamit)
2010 Proof *FDC* (Edition: 1,750 in sets)* £700

4468 Britannia. Fifty pounds. (1/2 oz fine gold alloyed with silver) R. A design depicting a
seated figure of Britannia set against a background of a rippling Union Flag accompanied
by the words ' 1/2 OUNCE FINE GOLD BRITANNIA, and the date '2011'. (Reverse
design: David Mach)
2011 Proof *FDC* (Edition: 2,000 including coins in sets)*...£700

Obverse portrait by Raphael Maklouf

4281

4281 Britannia. One hundred pounds. (1oz of fine gold alloyed with copper) R. The figure
of Britannia standing upon a rock in the sea, her right hand grasping a trident and her left
hand resting on a shield and holding an olive branch, with the inscription ...'ONE OUNCE
FINE GOLD BRITANNIA' and the year of the date. (Reverse design: Philip Nathan)
1987.. £1300   1989 ....£1300
  —   Proof *FDC* (Issued: 2,485).. £1350   —   Proof *FDC* (Issued: 338) £1350
1988.. £1300
  —   Proof *FDC* (Issued: 626)..... £1350

* *Coins marked thus were originally issued in Royal Mint sets.*
NB. The spot price of gold at the time of going to press was £1092 per oz.

4282 **Britannia. One hundred pounds.** (1oz of fine gold alloyed with silver) R. Britannia standing.

1990 .... £1300	1994 .... £1300
— Proof *FDC* (Issued: 262)** . £1350	— Proof *FDC* (see PBS11)* £1350
1991 .... £1300	1995 .... £1300
— Proof *FDC* (Issued: 143)** . £1350	— Proof *FDC* (see PBS12)* £1350
1992 .... £1300	1996 .... £1300
— Proof *FDC* (see PBS09)* £1350	— Proof *FDC* (see PBS13)* £1350
1993 .... £1300	
— Proof *FDC* (see PBS10)* £1350	

4283

4283 **Britannia. One Hundred pounds.** (1 oz of fine gold, alloyed with silver) 10th
Anniversary of Britannia issue. R. The figure of Britannia standing in a chariot drawn
along the seashore by two horses, with the word 'BRITANNIA', the inscription. 'ONE
OUNCE FINE GOLD' and the date of the year. (Reverse design: Philip Nathan)

1997 .... £1400   1997 Proof *FDC* (Issued: 164) £1600

Obverse portrait by Ian Rank-Broadley

4450   4451

4450 **Britannia. One Hundred pounds.** (1oz fine gold alloyed with silver) R. The figure of
Britannia standing upon a rock in the sea, her right hand grasping a trident and her left hand
resting on a shield and holding an olive branch, with the word 'BRITANNIA', the date of the
year, and the inscription' ONE OUNCE FINE GOLD'. (Reverse design: Philip Nathan)

1998 Proof *FDC* (see PBS15)* ... £1350	2004 .... £1300
1999 .... £1300	2004 Proof *FDC* (see PBS23)* £1350
1999 Proof *FDC* (see PBS16)* ... £1350	2006 Proof *FDC* (see PBS27)* £1350
2000 .... £1300	2012 .... £1300
2000 Proof *FDC* (see PBS17)* ... £1350	2012 Proof *FDC* (see PBS36) £1500
2002 Proof *FDC* (see PBS19)* ... £1350	

* Coins marked thus were originally issued in Royal Mint sets.
** Where numbers of coins are quoted, these refer to individual coins. Additional coins were
included in sets which are listed in the appropriate section.
NB. The spot price of gold at the time of going to press was £1092 per oz.

4451 Britannia. One Hundred pounds. (1oz fine gold alloyed with silver) R. The figure
of Britannia, as guardian, with a shield in her left hand and a trident in her right hand,
accompanied by a lion and, against the background of a wave motif, the words 'ONE
OUNCE FINE GOLD' to the left and 'BRITANNIA' and the date of the year to the right.
(Reverse design: Philip Nathan)
2001 .... £1300   2001 Proof *FDC* (see PBS18)* £1350

4452   4453

4452 Britannia. One Hundred pounds. (1oz fine gold alloyed with silver) R. Helmeted head
of Britannia with, to the left, the word 'BRITANNIA' and, to the right, the inscription
'ONE OUNCE FINE GOLD' and the date of the year, the whole being overlaid with a
wave pattern. (Reverse design: Philip Nathan)
2003 .... £1300   2003 Proof *FDC* (see PBS20)* £1350

4453 Britannia. One Hundred pounds. (1oz fine gold alloyed with silver) R. Seated figure
of Britannia facing to the left holding a trident with a shield at her side, with the word
'BRITANNIA', the inscription 'ONE OUNCE FINE GOLD' and the date of the year.
(Reverse design: Philip Nathan)
2005 Proof *FDC* (see PBS25)* £1350

4454   4455

4454 Britannia. One Hundred pounds. (1 oz fine gold alloyed with silver) R. Seated figure
of Britannia facing right holding a trident in her right hand and a sprig of olive in the left
hand with a lion at her feet with the inscription 'ONE OUNCE FINE GOLD' and the word
'BRITANNIA' and the date of the year (See 4505) (Reverse design: Christopher Le Brun)
2007 .... £1300   2007 Proof *FDC* (see PBS29)* £1350

4454A(1 oz platinum)
2007 Proof *FDC* (see 2007 set, PPBCS1)* £1500

4455 Britannia. One Hundred pounds. (1oz fine gold alloyed with silver) R. A Standing figure
of Britannia holding a trident with a shield at her side, the folds of her dress transforming
into a wave, with the word 'BRITANNIA', and the date of the year, and the inscription
'ONE OUNCE FINE GOLD' (Reverse design: John Bergdahl)
2008 .... £1300   2008 Proof *FDC* (see PBS30)* £1350

* Coins marked thus were originally issued in Royal Mint sets.
NB. The spot price of gold at the time of going to press was £1092 per oz.

4455A (1 oz platinum)
　　2008 Proof *FDC*　(see 2008 set, PPBCS2)* £1500
4456　Britannia. One Hundred pounds. (1oz fine gold alloyed with silver) R. Standing figure
　　of Britannia in horse drawn chariot.
　　2009 ....£1300　　　2009 Proof *FDC* (see PBS31)* £1350

　　　　4456　　　　　　　　　　　4457　　　　　　　　　　　4458

4457　Britannia. One Hundred pounds. (1oz fine gold alloyed with silver) R. A design
　　depicting **a** profile bust of Britannia wearing a helmet, accompanied by the name
　　'BRITANNIA', the inscription 'ONE OUNCE FINE GOLD' and the date '2010'.
　　(Reverse design: Suzie Zamit)
　　2010 ....£1300　　　2010 Proof *FDC* (Edition: 1,250 in sets)*£1350
4458　Britannia. One Hundred pounds. (1 oz fine gold alloyed with silver) R. A design
　　depicting a seated figure of Britannia set against a background of a rippling Union Flag
　　accompanied by the words 'ONE OUNCE FINE GOLD BRITANNIA, and the date
　　'2011'. (Reverse design: David Mach)
　　2011 Proof *FDC* (Edition: 3,000 including coins in sets) * £1500

* Coins marked thus were originally issued in Royal Mint sets.
NB. The spot price of gold at the time of going to press was £1092 per oz.

The Royal Mint plan to issue a considerable number of coins to mark the London 2012 Olympic and Paralympic Games. It has been decided that it will be easier for collectors if these coins are grouped together rather than be included with other coins of the same denomination. As a consequence the £2 coins issued in 2008 (previously listed as 4585 and 4586) have been renumbered and are now part of the Olympic group.

LONDON 2012 OLYMPIC AND PARALYMPIC GAMES

As part of their Programme of Olympic commemorative issues the Royal Mint has struck and released into circulation a series of 29 different 50 pence coins and details are given below. In addition to the circulating coins there is a series of numbered coin packs each containing the cupro-nickel versions of the coins but of higher quality. There are also sterling silver brilliant uncirculating examples.

The artist for each coin in the series has received a gold version of their design and a further example has been placed in the Mint museum. No value is shown at the present time.

4960   4961

4960 Fifty pence. To commemorate the London 2012 Olympic and Paralympic Games. R. A design which depicts an athlete clearing a high jump bar, with the London 2012 logo above and the denomination '50 pence' below. (Reverse design: Florence Jackson)
2009
  —   Specimen in presentation folder (Edition: 100,000) £3
  —   Gold FDC – presented to the artist
2011 ....£1
  —   Specimen in card (3/29) £3
  —   Specimen in presentation folder signed by Daley Thompson (Edition: 500) £50
  —   Specimen in presentation folder signed by Dame Kelly Holmes (Edition: 500) £50
  —   Specimen in presentation folder signed by Lord Sebastian Coe (Edition: 500) £50
  —   Silver BU (Edition: 30,000) £35
4961 Fifty pence. To commemorate the London 2012 Olympic and Paralympic Games. R. A design which depicts a cyclist in a velodrome, with the London Olympic logo above and the denomination '50 PENCE' below. (Reverse design: Theo Crutchley- Mack)
2010
  —   Gold *FDC* – presented to the artist
2011 ....£1
Specimen in card (9/29) £3
  —   Silver BU (Edition: 30,000)..£35

4962   4963

4962 Fifty pence. To commemorate the London 2012 Olympic and Paralympic Games. R. A design which depicts a swimmer submerged in water, with the London Olympic logo above and the denomination '50 PENCE' below. (Reverse design: Jonathan Olliffe)

2011... £1   Specimen in card (1/29)...............................£3

— Silver BU (Edition: 30,000)..... £35   — Gold *FDC* – presented to the artist

4963 Fifty pence. To commemorate the London 2012 Olympic and Paralympic Games. R. A design which depicts a bow being drawn, with the London Olympic logo above and the denomination '50 PENCE' below. (Reverse design: Piotr Powaga)

2011... £1   Specimen in card (2/29)...............................£3

— Silver BU (Edition: 30,000)..... £35   — Gold *FDC* – presented to the artist

4964   4965

4964 Fifty pence. To commemorate the London 2012 Olympic and Paralympic Games. R. A design which depicts a shuttlecock and a diagram of badminton actions, with the London Olympic logo above and the denomination '50 PENCE' below. (Reverse design: Emma Kelly)

2011... £1   Specimen in card (4/29)...............................£3

— Silver BU (Edition: 30,000)..... £35   — Gold *FDC* – presented to the artist

4965 Fifty pence. To commemorate the London 2012 Olympic and Paralympic Games. R. A design which depicts basketball players against a textured background of a large basketball, with the London Olympic logo above and the denomination '50 PENCE' below. (Reverse design: Sarah Payne)

2011... £1   Specimen in card (5/29)...............................£3

— Silver BU (Edition: 30,000)..... £35   — Gold *FDC* – presented to the artist

4966   4967

4966 Fifty pence. To commemorate the London 2012 Olympic and Paralympic Games. ℞. A design
which depicts a boccia player in a wheelchair throwing a ball, with the London Olympic logo
above and the denomination "50 PENCE" below. (Reverse design: Justin Chung)
2011 .... £1   Specimen in card (6/29) £3
—   Silver BU (Edition: 30,000) ..... £35   —   Gold *FDC* – presented to the artist

4967 Fifty pence. To commemorate the London 2012 Olympic and Paralympic Games. ℞. A design
which depicts a pair of boxing gloves against the background of a boxing ring, with the London
Olympic logo above and the denomination "50 PENCE" below. (Reverse design: Shane Abery)
2011 .... £1   Specimen in card (7/29) £3
—   Silver BU (Edition: 30,000) ..... £35   —   Gold *FDC* – presented to the artist

4968   4969

4968 Fifty pence. To commemorate the London 2012 Olympic and Paralympic Games. ℞. A
design which depicts a figure in a canoe on a slalom course, with the London Olympic logo
above and the denomination "50 PENCE" below. (Reverse design: Timothy Lees)
2011 .... £1   Specimen in card (8/29) £3
—   Silver BU (Edition: 30,000) ..... £35   —   Gold *FDC* – presented to the artist

4969 Fifty pence. To commemorate the London 2012 Olympic and Paralympic Games. ℞. A
design which depicts a horse and rider jumping over a fence, with the London Olympic logo
above and the denomination "50 PENCE" below. (Reverse design: Thomas Babbage)
2011 .... £1   Specimen in card (10/29) £3
—   Silver BU (Edition: 30,000) ..... £35   —   Gold *FDC* – presented to the artist

4970   4971

4970 Fifty pence. To commemorate the London 2012 Olympic and Paralympic Games. R. A design which depicts two figures fencing, with the London Olympic logo above and the denomination "50 PENCE" below. (Reverse design: Ruth Summerfield)

2011 .... £1   Specimen in card (11/29) £3
—   Silver BU (Edition: 30,000) ..... £35   —   Gold *FDC* – presented to the artist

4971 Fifty pence. To commemorate the London 2012 Olympic and Paralympic Games. R. A diagrammatic explanation of the offside rule in football, with the London Olympic logo above and the denomination "50 PENCE" below. (Reverse design: Neil Wolfson)

2011 .... £1   Specimen in card (12/29) £3
—   Silver BU (Edition: 30,000) ..... £35   —   Gold *FDC* – presented to the artist

4972   4973

4972 Fifty pence. To commemorate the London 2012 Olympic and Paralympic Games. R. A design which depicts a goalball player throwing a ball, with the London Olympic logo above and the denomination "50 PENCE" below. (Reverse design: Jonathan Wren)

2011 .... £1   Specimen in card (13/29) £3
—   Silver BU (Edition: 30,000) ..... £35   —   Gold *FDC* – presented to the artist

4973 Fifty pence. To commemorate the London 2012 Olympic and Paralympic Games. R. A design which depicts a gymnast with a ribbon, with the London Olympic logo above and the denomination "50 PENCE" below. (Reverse design: Jonathan Olliffe)

2011 .... £1   Specimen in card (14/29) £3
—   Silver BU (Edition: 30,000) ..... £35   —   Gold *FDC* – presented to the artist

4974   4975

4974 Fifty pence. To commemorate the London 2012 Olympic and Paralympic Games. ℞. A design which depicts a handball player throwing a ball against a background of a handball court, with the London Olympic logo above and the denomination '50 PENCE' below. (Reverse design: Natasha Ratcliffe)

2011 ....£1	Specimen in card (15/29)...............................£3	
— Silver BU (Edition: 30,000).....£35	— Gold *FDC* – presented to the artist	

4975 Fifty pence. To commemorate the London 2012 Olympic and Paralympic Games. ℞. A design which depicts two hockey players challenging for the ball, with the London Olympic logo above and the denomination "50 PENCE" below. (Reverse design: Robert Evans)

2011 ....£1	Specimen in card (16/29)...............................£3	
— Silver BU (Edition: 30,000).....£35	— Gold *FDC* – presented to the artist	

4976   4977

4976 Fifty pence. To commemorave the London 2012 Olympic and Paralympic Games. ℞. A depiction of a judo throw, with the London Olympic logo above and the denomination '50 PENCE' below. (Reverse design: David Cornell)

2011 ....£1	Specimen in card (17/29)...............................£3	
— Silver BU (Edition: 30,000).....£35	— Gold *FDC* – presented to the artist	

4977 Fifty pence. To commemorate the London 2012 Olympic and Paralympic Games. ℞. A montage of the five sports which form the modern pentathlon, with the London Olympic logo above and the denomination '50 PENCE' below. (Reverse design: Daniel Brittain)

2011 ....£1	Specimen in card (18/29)...............................£3	
— Silver BU (Edition: 30,000).....£35	— Gold *FDC* – presented to the artist	

4978   4979

4978 Fifty pence. To commemorate the London 2012 Olympic and Paralympic Games. R. A design which depicts a rowing boat accompanied by a number of words associated with the Olympic movement, with the London Olympic logo above and the denomination '50 PENCE' below. (Reverse design: David Podmore)

2011 ....£1
— Specimen in card (19/29) £3
— Specimen in presentation folder signed by Sir Steve Redgrave (Edition: 500).............£50
— Silver BU (Edition: 30,000) £35

4979 Fifty pence. To commemorate the London 2012 Olympic and Paralympic Games. R. A design which depicts three sailing boats accompanied by a map of the coast of Weymouth, with the London Olympic logo above and the denomination '50 PENCE' below. (Reverse design: Bruce Rushin)

2011 ....£1   Specimen in card (20/29) £3
— Silver BU (Edition: 30,000).....£35   — Gold *FDC* – presented to the artist

4980   4981

4980 Fifty pence. To commemorate the London 2012 Olympic and Paralympic Games. R. A design which depicts a figure shooting, with the London Olympic logo above and the denomination '50 PENCE' below. (Reverse design: Pravin Dewdhory)

2011 ....£1   Specimen in card (21/29) £3
— Silver BU (Edition: 30,000).....£35   — Gold *FDC* – presented to the artist

4981 Fifty pence. To commemorate the London 2012 Olympic and Paralympic Games. R. A design which depicts two table tennis bats against the background of a table and net, with the London Olympic logo above and the denomination "50 PENCE" below. (Reverse design: Alan Linsdell)

2011 ....£1   Specimen in card (22/29) £3
— Silver BU (Edition: 30,000).....£35   — Gold *FDC* – presented to the artist

4982   4983

4982 Fifty pence. To commemorate the London 2012 Olympic and Paralympic Games. ℞. A design which depicts two athletes engaged in Taekwondo, with the London Olympic logo above and the denomination "50 PENCE" below. (Reverse design: David Gibbons)
2011 .... £1   Specimen in card (23/29) £3
  —   Silver BU (Edition: 30,000) ..... £35   —   Gold *FDC* – presented to the artist

4983 Fifty pence. To commemorate the London 2012 Olympic and Paralympic Games. ℞. A design which depicts a tennis net and tennis ball, with the London Olympic logo above and the denomination "50 PENCE" below. (Reverse design: Tracy Baines)
2011 .... £1   Specimen in card (24/29) £3
  —   Silver BU (Edition: 30,000) ..... £35   —   Gold *FDC* – presented to the artist

4984   4985

4984 Fifty pence. To commemorate the London 2012 Olympic and Paralympic Games. ℞. A montage of the three sports which form the triathlon, with the London Olympic logo above and the denomination "50 PENCE" below. (Reverse design: Sarah Harvey)
2011 .... £1   Specimen in card (25/29) £3
  —   Silver BU (Edition: 30,000) ..... £35   —   Gold *FDC* – presented to the artist

4985 Fifty pence. To commemorate the London 2012 Olympic and Paralympic Games. ℞. A design which depicts three figures playing beach volleyball, with the London Olympic logo above and the denomination "50 PENCE" below. (Reverse design: Daniela Boothman)
2011 .... £1   Specimen in card (26/29) £3
  —   Silver BU (Edition: 30,000) ..... £35   —   Gold *FDC* – presented to the artist

4986 4987

4986 Fifty pence. To commemorate the London 2012 Olympic and Paralympic Games. R. A design which depicts the outline of a weightlifter starting a lift, with the London Olympic logo above and the denomination "50 PENCE" below. (Reverse design: Rob Shakespeare)

2011 ....£1   Specimen in card (27/29) £3
— Silver BU (Edition: 30,000)...£35   — Gold *FDC* – presented to the artist

4987 Fifty pence. To commemorate the London 2012 Olympic and Paralympic Games. R. A design which depicts a wheelchair rugby player in action, with the London Olympic logo above and the denomination "50 PENCE" below. (Reverse design: Natasha Ratcliffe)

2011 ....£1   Specimen in card (28/29) £3
— Silver BU (Edition: 30,000)...£35   — Gold *FDC* – presented to the artist

4988

4988 Fifty pence. To commemorate the London 2012 Olympic and Paralympic Games. R. A design which depicts two figures wrestling in a stadium, with the London Olympic logo above and the denomination "50 PENCE" below. (Reverse design: Roderick Enriquez)

2011 ....£1   Specimen in card (29/29) £3
— Silver BU (Edition: 30,000)...£35   — Gold *FDC* – presented to the artist

4951

4951 Two pounds. (Previously listed as 4585) Centenary of the Olympic Games of 1908 held
  in London. ℞. A running track on which is superimposed the date '1908' accompanied
  by the denomination 'TWO POUNDS' and the date '2008', the whole design being
  encircled by the inscription 'LONDON OLYMPIC CENTENARY' with the edge
  inscription 'THE 4ᵀᴴ OLYMPIAD LONDON' (Reverse design: Thomas T Docherty)
  2008 .... £5
  —   Specimen in presentation folder (Issued: 29,594) £10
  —   Proof *FDC* (in 2008 set, see PS93)* £15
  —   Proof in Silver *FDC* (Issued: 8,023) £35
  —   Proof piedfort in silver *FDC* (Edition: 5,000)..£55
  —   Proof in gold *FDC* (Issued: 1,908 including coins in sets) £700

4952

4952 Two pounds. (Previously listed as 4586) London Olympic Handover Ceremony. ℞.
The Olympic flag being passed from one hand to another, encircled by the inscription
'BEIJING 2008 LONDON 2012' and with the London 2012 logo below with the edge
inscription 'I CALL UPON THE YOUTH OF THE WORLD' (Reverse design: Royal
Mint Engraving Team)

2008 ....£5
— Specimen in presentation folder (Edition: 250,000) £10
— Proof in Silver *FDC* (Issued: 30,000) £38
— Proof piedfort in silver *FDC* (Issued: 3,000) £60
— Proof in gold *FDC* (Edition: 3,250 including coins in sets)...............................£700

4953

4953 Two pounds. London to Rio Olympic Handover coin. ℞. A design which depicts a
baton being passed from one hand to another, accompanied by the conjoined Union
and Brazilian Flags. The reverse design is set against the background of a running track
motif, with the London 2012 logo above and the surrounding inscription 'LONDON
2012 RIO 2016'. With the edge inscription 'I CALL UPON THE YOUTH OF THE
WORLD'. (Reverse design: Jonathan Olliffe)

2012
— Specimen in presentation card..£10
— Proof in silver *FDC* (Edition: 12,000) £60
— Proof piedfort in silver *FDC* (Edition: 2,000)...£105
— Proof in gold *FDC* (Edition: 1,200) £1,195

4920

4920 Five pounds. (crown) UK countdown to 2012 Olympic Games. R. In the centre a
depiction of two swimmers as faceted figures accompanied by the number '3' with
a section of a clock face to the right and the London 2012 logo to the left printed in
coloured ink on the precious metal versions and surrounded by a plan view of the main
Olympic Stadium incorporating the date '2009' with the words 'COUNTDOWN' above
and the inscription 'XXX OLYMPIAD' below. (Reverse design: Claire Aldridge) (Obv.
as 4556)

2009 (Edition: 500,000) £8
—   Specimen in presentation folder (Edition: 500,000) £10
—   Proof in silver *FDC* (Issued: 30,000) £95
—   Proof piedfort in silver *FDC* (Issued: 6,000) £175
—   Proof in gold *FDC* (Edition: 4,000) £2000

4921

4921 Five pounds. (crown) UK countdown to 2012 Olympic Games. R. In the centre a
depiction of two runners as faceted figures accompanied by the number '2' with a section
of a clock face to the right and the London 2012 logo to the left printed in coloured
ink on the precious meta versions and surrounded by a plan view of the main Olympic
Stadium incorporating the date '2010' with the words 'COUNTDOWN' above and the
inscription 'XXX OLYMPIAD' below.(Reverse design: Claire Aldridge) (Obv. as 4556)

2010
—   Specimen in presentation card   (Edition: 250,000) £8
—   Specimen in presentation folder (Edition: 250,000) £10
—   Proof in silver *FDC* (Edition: 30,000) £80
—   Proof piedfort in silver *FDC* (Edition: 4,000) £200
—   Proof in gold *FDC* (Edition: 3,000) £2000

4922

4922 Five pounds. (crown) UK countdown to 2012 Olympic Games. R. In the centre a depiction of a cyclist as a faceted figure, accompanied by the number '1' with a section of a clock face to the right, below and to the left, and the London 2012 logo to the right printed in coloured ink on the precious metal versions and surrounded by a plan view of the main Olympic Stadium incorporating the date '2011' with the words 'COUNTDOWN' above and the inscription 'XXX OLYMPIAD' below. (Reverse design: Claire Aldridge)

2011
— Specimen in presentation card (Edition: 250,000) £8
— Specimen in presentation folder (Edition: 250,000)..£10
— Proof in silver *FDC* (Edition: 30,000) £100
— Proof piedfort in silver *FDC* (Edition: 4,000) £175
— Proof in gold *FDC* (Edition: 3,000)..£2880

4923

4923 Five pounds. (crown) UK countdown to 2012 Olympic Games. R. A depiction of three athletes as faceted figures standing on a victory podium, with a section of a clock-face to the right, to the left and above, and the London 2012 logo to the right. The reverse design is surrounded by a plan view of the main Olympic Stadium, incorporating the date '2012' at the top, and the word 'COUNTDOWN' above and the inscription 'XXX OLYMPIAD' below. (Reverse design: Claire Aldridge)

2012
— Specimen in presentation card (Edition: 250,000) £8
— Specimen in presentation folder (Edition: 250,000) £13
— Proof in silver *FDC* (Edition: 30,000) £100
— Proof piedfort in silver *FDC* (Edition: 4,000)..£175
— Proof in gold *FDC* (Edition: 3,000) £2,880

4924

4924 Five pounds. (crown) The London 2012 Olympic Games. R. An image of the skyline of some of the most well-known landmarks and buildings in London reflected in the River Thames, with the inscription 'LONDON 2012' above. Surrounding the skyline image is a selection of sports from the London 2012 Games with the London 2012 logo at the top. (Reverse design: Saiman Miah)

2012

— Specimen in presentation folder £15
— Proof in silver *FDC* (Edition: 100,000) £100
— Proof in silver with gold plating *FDC* (Edition: 12,500) £125
— Proof piedfort in silver *FDC* (Edition: 7,000) £175
— Proof in gold *FDC* (Edition: 5,000) £2880

4925

4925 Five pounds. (crown) The London 2012 Paralympic Games. R. A design showing segments of a target, a spoked wheel, a stopwatch and the clock face of the Palace of Westminster. The inscription 'LONDON 2012' appears on the target and the London 2012 Paralympic logo appears on the stopwatch. On the gold and silver coins the London Paralympic logo will be printed in coloured ink , while on the cupro-nickel coin the logo will be struck into the surface. (Reverse design: Pippa Anderson)

2012

— Specimen in presentation folder (Edition: 250,000) £15
— Proof in silver *FDC* (Edition: 10,000) £100
— Proof in silver with gold plating *FDC* (Edition: 3,000) £125
— Proof piedfort in silver *FDC* (Edition: 2,012) £175
— Proof in gold *FDC* (Edition: 2,012) £2880

4930

4930 Five pounds. (crown) The Mind of Britain. R. A depiction of the clock-face of the Palace of Westminster accompanied by the London 2012 logo, printed in coloured ink and a quotation From Walter Bagehot, 'NATIONS TOUCH AT THEIR SUMMITS'. (Reverse design: Shane Greeves and the Royal Mint Engraving Department)
2009
— Proof *FDC* (Edition: 100,000)£20 — Proof silver *FDC* (Edition: 95,000) £100

4931

4931 Five pounds. (crown). The Mind of Britain. R. A depiction of Stonehenge accompanied by the London 2012 logo, printed in coloured ink on the silver version and a quotation from William Blake 'GREAT THINGS ARE DONE WHEN MEN AND MOUNTAINS MEET' (Reverse design: Shane Greeves and the Royal Mint Engraving Department)
2009
— Proof silver *FDC* (Edition: 95,000) £100

4932   4933

4932 **Five pounds.** (crown). The Mind of Britain. R. A depiction of the Angel of the North accompanied   by the London 2012 logo printed in coloured ink on the silver version and a quotation from William Shakespeare 'I HAVE TOUCHED THE HIGHEST POINT OF MY GREATNESS' (Reverse design: Shane Greeves and the Royal Mint Engraving Department) 2009
— Proof silver *FDC* (Edition: 95,000) £100

4933 **Five pounds.** (crown). The Mind of Britain. R. A depiction of the Flying Scotsman accompanied   by the London 2012 logo printed in coloured ink on the silver version and a quotation from William Shakespeare 'TRUE HOPE IS SWIFT' (Reverse design: Shane Greeves and the Royal Mint Engraving Department) 2009
— Proof silver *FDC* (Edition: 95,000) £100

4934

4934 **Five pounds.** (crown). The Mind of Britain. R. A depiction of Eduardo Paolozzi's sculpture of Isaac Newton North accompanied by the London 2012 logo printed in coloured ink on the silver version and a quotation from William Shakespeare 'MAKE NOT YOUR THOUGHTS YOUR PRISONS' (Reverse design: Shane Greeves and the Royal Mint Engraving Department) 2009
— Proof silver *FDC* (Edition: 95,000) £100

4935

4935 **Five pounds.** (crown). The Mind of Britain. R. A depiction of the Globe Theatre accompanied by the London 2012 logo printed in coloured ink on the silver version and a quotation from William Shakespeare 'WE ARE SUCH STUFF AS DREAMS ARE MADE ON' (Reverse design: Shane Greeves and the Royal Mint Engraving Department) 2009

— Proof silver *FDC* (Edition: 95,000) £100

4936   4937

4936 **Five pounds.** (crown). The Body of Britain. R. A depiction of Rhossili Bay accompanied by the London 2012 logo printed in coloured ink, and a quotation from William Blake 'TO SEE A WORLD IN A GRAIN OF SAND' (Reverse design: Shane Greeves and the Royal Mint Engraving Department) 2010

— Proof silver *FDC* (Edition: 95,000) £100

4937 **Five pounds.** (crown). The Body of Britain R. A depiction of Giant's Causeway accompanied by the London 2012 logo printed in coloured ink, and a quotation from Alice Oswald 'WHEN THE STONE BEGAN TO DREAM' (Reverse design: Shane Greeves and the Royal Mint Engraving Department) 2010

— Proof silver *FDC* (Edition: 95,000) £100

4938   4939

4938 Five pounds. (crown). The Body of Britain R. A depiction of the River Thames accompanied
by the London 2012 logo printed in coloured ink, and a quotation from Percy Bysshe Shelley,
'TAMELESS, AND SWIFT AND PROUD' (Reverse design: Shane Greeves and the Royal
Mint Engraving Department)
2010
—   Proof silver *FDC* (Edition: 95,000)..£100

4939 Five pounds. (crown). The Body of Britain. R. A depiction of a barn owl accompanied by
the London 2012 logo printed in coloured ink, and a quotation from Samuel Johnson 'THE
NATURAL FLIGHTS OF THE HUMAN MIND' (Reverse design: Shane Greeves and the
Royal Mint Engraving Department)
2010
—   Proof silver *FDC* (Edition: 95,000)..£100

4940   4941

4940 Five pounds. (crown). The Body of Britain. R. A depiction of oak leaves and an acorn
accompanied by the London 2012 logo printed in coloured ink, and a quotation from Alfred,
Lord Tennyson, 'TO STRIVE, TO SEEK......AND NOT TO YIELD' (Reverse design: Shane
Greeves and the Royal Mint Engraving Department)
2010
—   Proof silver *FDC* (Edition: 95,000)..£100

4941 Five pounds. (crown). The Body of Britain. R. A depiction of a weather-vane accompanied by
the London 2012 logo printed in coloured ink, and a quotation from Charlotte Bronte, NEVER
MAY A CLOUD COME O'ER THE SUNSHINE OF YOUR MIND' (Reverse design:
Shane Greeves and the Royal Mint Engraving Department)
2010
—   Proof silver *FDC* (Edition: 95,000)..£100

4942 4943

4942 Five pounds. (crown). The Spirit of Britain. R. A depiction of the intertwined national emblems of England, Scotland, Wales and Northern Ireland accompanied by the London 2012 logo, printed in coloured ink, and a quotation from John Lennon, 'AND THE WORLD WILL BE ONE' (Reverse design: Shane Greeves and the Royal Mint Engraving Department) 2010

— Proof silver *FDC* (Edition: 95,000)..£100

4943 Five pounds. (crown).The Spirit of Britain. R. A depiction of the White Rabbit from Lewis Carroll's *Alice in Wonderland* accompanied by the London 2012 logo, printed in coloured ink, and a quotation from T S Eliot, 'ALL TOUCHED BY A COMMON GENIUS' (Reverse design: Shane Greeves and the Royal Mint Engraving Department) 2010

— Proof silver *FDC* (Edition: 95,000)..£100

4944 4945

4944 Five pounds. (crown).The Spirit of Britain. R. A view down the Mall of cheering crowds accompanied by the London 2012 logo, printed in coloured ink, and a quotation from Alfred, Lord Tennyson, 'KIND HEARTS ARE MORE THAN CORONETS' (Reverse design: Shane Greeves and the Royal Mint Engraving Department) 2010

— Proof *FDC* (Edition; 100,000)...£20

— Proof silver *FDC* (Edition: 95,000)..£100

4945 Five pounds. (crown).The Spirit of Britain. R. A DEPICTION OF THE STATUE OF Winston Churchill in Parliament Square accompanied by the London 2012 logo, printed in coloured ink, and a quotation from Anita Roddick, 'BE DARING, BE FIRST, BE DIFFERENT, BE JUST' (Reverse design: Shane Greeves and the Royal Mint Engraving Department) 2010

— Proof *FDC* (Edition; 100,000)...£20

— Proof silver *FDC* (Edition: 95,000)..£100

4946

4946 Five pounds. (crown).The Spirit of Britain. R An arrangement of musical instruments based on a well known sculpture accompanied by the London 2012 logo, printed in coloured ink, and a quotation from John Lennon and Paul McCartney, 'ALL YOU NEED IS LOVE'. (Reverse design: Shane Greeves and the Royal Mint Engraving Department) 2010

— Proof silver *FDC* (Edition: 95,000) £100

4947

4947 Five pounds. (crown).The Spirit of Britain. R. An image of the nineteenth-century anti-slavery campaigner Equiano accompanied by the London 2012 logo, printed in coloured ink, and a quotation from William Shakespeare, 'TO THINE OWN SELF BE TRUE'. (Reverse design: Shane Greeves and the Royal Mint Engraving Department) 2010

— Proof silver *FDC* (Edition: 95,000) £100

4950

4950 Ten pounds. (Five ounce). R. A design of the winged horse Pegasus rearing on its hind
legs surrounded by the inscription 'LONDON OLYMPIC GAMES', and the London 2012
logo and the date '2012'.(Reverse design: Christopher Le Brun)
2012
— Proof in 0.999 fine silver *FDC* (Edition: 7,500) £525
— Proof in 0.999 fine gold *FDC* (Edition: 500) £11,500
Illustration shown at reduced size – actual coin diameter 65 mm.

4905

4905 Twenty five pounds. Faster. R. An image of Diana accompanied by a depiction of the
sport of cycling, specifically pursuit racing ,with Olympic Rings above, the name 'DIANA'
to the left, the Latin word for faster 'CITIUS', to the right, and the inscription 'LONDON
2012' below. (Reverse design: John Bergdahl)
2010
— Proof in gold *FDC* (Edition: 20,000) £600

4906

4906 Twenty five pounds. Faster. R. An image of Mercury accompanied by a depiction of
the sport of running, with Olympic Rings above, the name 'MERCURY' to the left, the
Latin word for faster 'CITIUS', to the right, and the inscription 'LONDON 2012' below.
(Reverse design: John Bergdahl)
2010
— Proof in gold *FDC* (Edition: 20,000) £600

4907

4907 Twenty five pounds. Higher. ℞. An image of Apollo accompanied by a depiction of the
sport of rhythmic gymnastics, with Olympic Rings above, the name 'APOLLO' to the
left, the Latin word for higher 'ALTIUS', to the right, and the inscription 'LONDON
2012' below. (Reverse design: John Bergdahl)
2011
— Proof in gold *FDC* (Edition: 20,000 including coins in sets) £600

4908   4909   4910

4908 Twenty five pounds. Higher. ℞. An image of Juno accompanied by a depiction of the
sport of pole vaulting, with Olympic Rings above, the name 'JUNO' to the left, the Latin
word for higher 'ALTIUS', to the right, and the inscription 'LONDON 2012' below.
(Reverse design: John Bergdahl)
2011
— Proof in gold *FDC* (Edition: 20,000 including coins in sets) £600

4909 Twenty five pounds. Stronger. ℞. An image of Vulcan accompanied by a depiction of
the sport of hammer throwing, with the Olympic Rings above, the name 'VULCAN'
to the left, and the Latin word for stronger 'FORTIUS', to the right, and the inscription
'LONDON 2012' below. (Reverse design: John Bergdahl)
2012
— Proof in gold *FDC* (Edition: 20,000 including coins in sets) £600

4910 Twenty five pounds. Stronger. ℞. An image of Minerva accompanied by a depiction
Of the sport of javelin throwing, with the Olympic Rings above, the name 'MINERVA'
to the left , the Latin word for stronger, 'FORTIUS', to the right, and the inscription
'LONDON 2012@ below. (Reverse design: John Bergdahl)
2012
— Proof in gold *FDC* (Edition: 20,000 including coins in sets) £600

4915

4915 One hundred pounds. Faster. R. An image of Neptune, accompanied by a depiction of the sport of sailing, with the Olympic Rings above, the name 'NEPTUNE' to the left, the Latin word for faster 'CITIUS' to the right, and the inscription 'LONDON 2012' below. (Reverse design: John Bergdahl)
2010
— Proof in gold *FDC* (Edition: 7,500) £2300

4916

4916 One hundred pounds. Higher. R. An image of Jupiter, accompanied by a depiction of the sport of diving, with the Olympic Rings above, the name 'JUPITER' to the left, the Latin word for higher 'ALTIUS' to the right, and the inscription 'LONDON 2012' below. (Reverse design: John Bergdahl)
2011
— Proof in gold *FDC** £2300

4917

4917 One hundred pounds. Stronger. R. An image of Mars accompanied by a depiction of the sport of boxing, with the Olympic Rings above, the name 'MARS' to the left, the Latin word for stronger, 'FORTIUS', to the right, and the inscription 'LONDON 2012' below. (Reverse design: John Bergdahl)
2012
— Proof in gold *FDC* (Edition: 7,500 including coins in sets) £2300

4920

4920 Five hundred pounds. (One kilo). R. A design consisting of celebratory pennants and the
inscription 'XXX OLYMPIAD' surrounded by the epigram 'UNITE OUR DREAMS TO
MAKE THE WORLD A TEAM OF TEAMS' (Reverse design: Tom Phillips)
2012
—   Proof in silver (Edition: 2,012) £3000
Illustration shown at reduced size – actual coin diameter 100 mm

4921

4921 One thousand pounds. (One kilo). R. . A design depicting individual pieces of sporting
equipment encircled by a laurel of victory. (Reverse design: Sir Anthony Caro)
2012
—   Proof in gold (Edition: 60) £100,000
Illustration shown at reduced size – actual coin diameter 100 mm

The practice of issuing annual sets of coins was started by the Royal Mint in 1970 when a set of the £SD coins was issued as a souvenir prior to Decimalisation. There are now regular issues of brilliant uncirculated coin sets as well as proofs in base metal, and issues in gold and silver. In order to simplify the numbering system, and to allow for the continuation of the various issues in the future, the Prefix letters have been changed. The base metal proof sets will continue the series of numbers from the 1970 set, PS20. Other sets, such as those of uncirculated coins, silver and gold now have their numbering series commencing with number 01 in each case.

In addition to the annual sets of uncirculated and proofs coins sold by the Royal Mint to collectors and dealers, the Mint has produced specially packaged sets and single coins for companies. No details are made available of these issues and therefore no attempt has been made to include them in the listings below. The Mint also sells 'Christening' and 'Wedding' sets in distinctive packaging but the numbers circulating in the market are relatively modest and of limited appeal after the year of issue.

The Mint has recently offered sets of coins to collectors that consist of coins obtained from the market e.g. silver proofs, crowns and gold sovereigns showing different portraits. Although these are available in limited numbers from the Mint, it has been decided not to list them in the section devoted to sets.

Following the comprehensive review of the layout, it has been decided to move the folder containing the two 50 pence coins of 1992 to the list below of uncirculated coins. This was formerly included as 4352A, and is now US13 with all subsequent numbers adjusted by one.

Uncirculated Sets

			£
US01–**1982**	Uncirculated (specimen) set in Royal Mint folder, 50p to ½p, new reverse type, including 20 pence (Issued: 205,000)	(7)	9
US02–**1983**	'U.K.' £1 (4221) to ½p (Issued: 637,100)	(8)	15
US03–**1984**	'Scottish' £1 (4222) to ½p (Issued: 158,820)	(8)	15
US04–**1985**	'Welsh' £1 (4331) to 1p, new portrait of The Queen (Issued: 102,015)	(7)	15
US05–**1986**	'Commonwealth Games' £2 (4311) plus 'Northern Irish' £1 (4332) to 1p, (Issued: 167,224)	(8)	18
US06–**1987**	'English' £1 (4333) to 1p, (Issued: 172,425)	(7)	15
US07–**1988**	'Arms' £1 (4334) to 1p, (Issued: 134,067)	(7)	15
US08–**1989**	'Scottish' £1 (4335) to 1p, (Issued: 77,569)	(7)	20
US09–**1989**	'Bill of Rights' and 'Claim of Right' £2s (4312 and 4313) in Royal Mint folder (Issued: not known)	(2)	25
US10–**1990**	'Welsh' £1 (4331) to 1p plus new smaller 5p, (Issued: 102,606)	(8)	20
US11–**1991**	'Northern Irish' £1 (4332) to 1p, (Issued: 74,975)	(7)	20
US12–**1992**	'English' £1 (4333), 'European Community' 50p (4352) and 'Britannia' 50p, 20p to 1p plus new smaller 10p (Issued: 78,421)	(9)	25
US13-**1992**	'European Community' 50p (4352) and 'Britannia' 50p (4351) in presentation folder previously listed as 4352A	(2)	20
US14–**1993**	'UK' £1 (4336), 'European Community' 50p (4352) to 1p ((Issued: 56,945)	(8)	25
US15–**1994**	'Bank of England' £2 (4314), 'Scottish' £1 (4337) and 'D-Day' 50p (4353) to 1p, (Issued: 177,971)	(8)	15
US16–**1995**	'Peace' £2 (4315) and 'Welsh' £1 (4338) to 1p (Issued: 105, 647)	(8)	15
US17–**1996**	'Football' £2 (4317) and 'Northern Irish' £1 (4339) to 1p (Issued: 86,501)	(8)	15
US18–**1997**	'Bimetallic' £2 (4318), 'English' £1 (4340) to 1p plus new smaller 50p (Issued: 109,557)	(9)	15
US19–**1998**	'Bimetallic' £2 (4570), 'UK' £1 (4590) and 'EU' 50 pence (4611) to1 pence (Issued: 96,192)	(9)	25
US20–**1998**	'EU' and 'Britannia' 50 pence (4611 and 4610) in Royal Mint folder.	(2)	6
US21–**1999**	'Bimetallic' 'Rugby' £2 (4571), 'Scottish' £1 (4591) to 1p (Issued: 136,696)	(8)	18
US22–**2000**	'Bimetallic' £2 (4570), 'Welsh' £1 (4592) to 1p plus 'Library' 50 pence (4613) (Issued: 117,750)	(9)	18
US23–**2001**	'Bimetallic' £2 (4570), 'Bimetallic' 'Marconi' £2 (4572), 'Irish' £1 (4594) to 1p (Issued: 57,741)	(9)	18

£

US46–**2011**	'Bimetallic' £2 (4570), 'Royal Shield' £1 (4604), 50 pence to 1 pence (4620, 4631, 4651, 4671, 4691 4711)	(8)	21
US47–**2011**	'Edinburgh' £1 (4607) and 'Cardiff' £1 (4608) (Edition: 10,000)	(2)	14
US48–**2012**	Diamond Jubilee £5, struck in c/n (4569), 'Bimetallic' 'Charles Dickens' £2 (4590), 'Bimetallic' £2 (4570) 'Royal Shield' £1(4604), 50 pence to 1 pence (4620, 4631, 4651, 4671, 4691 and 4711	(10)	39
US 49–**2012**	'Bimetallic' £2 (4570) 'Royal Shield' £1(4604), 50 pence to 1 pence (4620, 4631, 4651, 4671, 4691 and 4711	(8)	21

Proof Sets

PS21–**1971**	Decimal coinage set, 50 new pence 'Britannia' to $^1/_2$ new pence, in sealed plastic case with card wrapper (Issued: 350,000)	(6)	18
PS22–**1972**	Proof 'Silver Wedding' Crown struck in c/n (4226) plus 50p to ½p (Issued: 150,000)	(7)	20
PS23–**1973**	'EEC' 50p (4224) plus 10p to ½p, (Issued: 100,000)	(6)	15
PS24–**1974**	'Britannia' 50p to ½p, as 1971 (Issued: 100,000)	(6)	15
PS25–**1975**	'Britannia'50p to ½p (as 1974), (Issued: 100,000)	(6)	12
PS26–**1976**	'Britannia' 50p to ½p, as 1975, (Issued: 100,000)	(6)	12
PS27–**1977**	Proof 'Silver Jubilee' Crown struck in c/n (4227) plus 50p to ½p, (Issued: 193,000)	(7)	12
PS28–**1978**	'Britannia' 50p to ½p, as 1976, (Issued: 86,100	(6)	12
PS29–**1979**	'Britannia' 50p to ½p, as 1978, (Issued: 81,000)	(6)	12
PS30–**1980**	'Britannia' 50p to ½p, as 1979, (Issued: 143,000)	(6)	15
PS31–**1981**	'Britannia' 50p to ½p, as 1980, (Issued: 100,300)	(6)	15
PS32–**1982**	'Britannia' 50p to ½p including 20 pence (Issued: 106,800)	(7)	15
PS33–**1983**	'U.K.' £1 (4221) to ½p in new packaging (Issued: 107,800)	(8)	20
PS34–**1984**	'Scottish' £1 (4222) to ½p, (Issued: 106,520)	(8)	20
PS35–**1985**	'Welsh' £1 (4331) to 1p, (Issued: 102,015)	(7)	20
PS36–**1985**	As last but packed in deluxe red leather case (Included above)	(7)	20
PS37–**1986**	'Commonwealth Games' £2 (4311) plus 'Northern Irish' £1 (4332) to 1p, (Issued: 104,597)	(8)	20
PS38–**1986**	As last but packed in deluxe red leather case (Included above)	(8)	23
PS39–**1987**	'English' £1 (4333) to 1p, (Issued: 88,659)	(7)	20
PS40–**1987**	As last but packed in deluxe leather case (Included above)	(7)	23
PS41–**1988**	'Arms' £1 (4334) to 1p, (Issued: 79,314)	(7)	25
PS42–**1988**	As last but packed in deluxe leather case (Included above)	(7)	29
PS43–**1989**	'Bill of Rights' and 'Claim of Right' £2s (4312 and 4313), 'Scottish' £1 (4335) to 1p, (Issued: 85,704)	(9)	30
PS44–**1989**	As last but packed in red leather case, (Included above)	(9)	35
PS45–**1990**	'Welsh' £1 (4331) to 1p plus new smaller 5p, (Issued: 79,052)	(8)	27
PS46–**1990**	As last but packed in red leather case (Included above)	(8)	32
PS47–**1991**	'Northern Irish' £1 (4332) to 1p, (Issued: 55,144)	(7)	27
PS48–**1991**	As last but packed in red leather case (Included above)	(7)	33
PS49–**1992**	'English' £1 (4333), 'European community' 50p (4352) and 'Britannia' 50p, 20p to 1p plus new smaller 10p, (Issued: 44,337)	(9)	28
PS50–**1992**	As last but packed in red leather case (Issued: 17,989)	(9)	33
PS51–**1993**	Proof 'Coronation Anniversary' £5 struck in c/n (4302), 'U.K.' £1 (4336), 50p to 1p, (Issued: 43,509)	(8)	30
PS52–**1993**	As last but packed in red leather case (Issued: 22,571)	(8)	35
PS53–**1994**	'Bank' £2 (4314), 'Scottish' £1 (4337), 'D-Day' 50p (4353) to 1p, (Issued: 44,643)	(8)	30
PS54–**1994**	As last but packed in red leather case (Issued: 22,078)	(8)	35
PS55–**1995**	'Peace' £2 (4315), 'Welsh' £1 (4338) to 1p, (Issued: 42,842)	(8)	32
PS56–**1995**	As last but packed in red leather case (Issued: 17,797)	(8)	35

£

PS57–**1996**	Proof '70th Birthday' £5 struck in c/n (4303), 'Football' £2 (4317), 'Northern Irish' £1 (4339) to 1p, (Issued: 46,295)	(9)	32
PS58–**1996**	As last but packed in red leather case (Issued: 21,286)	(9)	37
PS59–**1997**	Proof 'Golden Wedding' £5 struck in c/n (4304), 'Bimetallic' £2 (4318), 'English' £1 (4340) to 1p plus new smaller 50p (Issued: 48,761)	(10)	33
PS60–**1997**	As last but packed in red leather case (Issued: 31,987)	(10)	40
PS61–**1998**	Proof 'Prince of Wales 50th Birthday'£5 struck in c/n (4550), 'Bimetallic' £2 (4570), 'UK'. £1 (4590), 'EU' 50 pence (4611) to 1p. (Issued: 36,907)	(10)	33
PS62–**1998**	As last, but packed in red leather case. (Issued: 26,763)	(10)	40
PS63–**1999**	Proof 'Diana, Princess of Wales' £5 struck in c/n (4551), 'Bimetallic' 'Rugby' £2 (4571), 'Scottish' £1 (4591) to 1p. (Issued: 40,317)	(9)	34
PS64–**1999**	As last, but packed in red leather case. (Issued: 39,827)	(9)	40
PS65–**2000**	Proof 'Millennium' £5 struck in c/n (4552), 'Bimetallic' £2 (4570), 'Welsh' £1 (4592), 'Library' 50 pence (4613) and 'Britannia' 50 pence (4610) to 1p.Standard Set, (Issued: 41,379)	(10)	30
PS66–**2000**	As last, but Deluxe set (Issued: 21,573 above)	(10)	30
PS67–**2000**	As last, but Executive set (Issued: 9,517)	(10)	60
PS68–**2001**	Proof 'Victoria' £5 struck in c/n (4554), 'Bimetallic' £2 (4570), 'Bimetallic' 'Marconi' £2 (4572), 'Irish' £1 (4593) to 1p. Standard Set. (Issued: 28,244).	(10)	34
PS69–**2001**	As last, but Gift Set (Issued: 1,351)	(10)	30
PS70–**2001**	As last, but packed in red leather case (Issued: 16,022)	(10)	48
PS71–**2001**	As last, but Executive Set (Issued: 3,755)	(10)	60
PS72–**2002**	Proof 'Golden Jubilee' £5 struck in c/n (4555), 'Bimetallic' £2 (4570), 'English' £1 (4594) to 1p. Standard set. (Issued: 30,884)	(9)	32
PS73–**2002**	As last, but Gift Set (Issued: 1,544)	(9)	30
PS74–**2002**	As last, but packed in red leather case (Issued: 23,342)	(9)	46
PS75–**2002**	As last, but Executive Set (Issued: 5,000)	(9)	70
PS76–**2002**	'Bimetallic' 'Commonwealth Games'£2 (4573, 4574, 4575 and 4576) (Issued: 3,358)	(4)	36
PS77–**2002**	As last, but Display Set (Issued: 673)	(4)	33
PS78–**2003**	Proof 'Coronation'£5 struck in c/n (4557), 'Bimetallic' 'DNA' £2 (4577), 'Bimetallic' £2 (4570), 'UK' £1 (4590), 'Suffragette' 50 pence (4614) and 'Britannia' 50 pence (4610) to 1p. Standard set. (Issued: 23,650)	(11)	34
PS79–**2003**	As last, but packed in red leather case (Issued: 14,863)	(11)	47
PS80–**2003**	As last, but Executive Set (Issued: 5,000)	(11)	70
PS81–**2004**	'Bimetallic' 'Penydarren engine' £2 (4578), 'Bimetallic' £2 (4570), 'Forth Rail Bridge' £1 (4595), 'Sub four-minute mile' 50 pence (4615) and 'Britannia' 50 pence (4610) to 1p. Standard set. (Issued: 17,951)	(10)	35
PS82–**2004**	As last, but packed in red leather case (Issued: 12,968)	(10)	45
PS83–**2004**	As last, but Executive Set (Issued: 4,101)	(10)	65
PS84–**2005**	Proof 'Trafalgar'£5 struck in c/n (4559), Proof 'Nelson'£5 struck in c/n (4560) 'Bimetallic' 'Gunpowder Plot' £2 (4579), 'Bimetallic' £2 (4570), 'Menai Straits Bridge' £1 (4596), 'Samuel Johnson's Dictionary' 50 pence (4616) and 'Britannia' 50 pence (4610) to 1p. (Issued: 21,374)	(12)	40
PS85–**2005**	As last, but packed in red leather case (Issued: 14,899)	(12)	50
PS86–**2005**	As last, but Executive Set (Issued: 4,290)	(12)	75
PS87–**2006**	Proof '80th Birthday'£5 struck in c/n (4561), 'Bimetallic' 'Isambard Brunel' £2 (4581), 'Bimetallic' 'Paddington Station' £2 (4582), 'Bimetallic' £2 (4570), 'MacNeill's Egyptian Arch' £1 (4597), 'Victoria Cross' 50 pence (4617), 'Wounded soldier' 50 pence (4618) and 'Britannia' 50 pence (4610) to 1p (Issued: 17,689)	(13)	42
PS88 –**2006**	As last, but packed in red leather case (Issued: 15,000)	(13)	50
PS89 –**2006**	As last, but Executive Set (Issued: 5,000)	(13)	78

£

PS90 –**2007**	Proof 'Diamond Wedding'£5 struck in c/n (4562), 'Bimetallic' 'Act of Union' £2 (4583), 'Bimetallic' 'Abolition of Slave Trade' £2 (4584), 'Gateshead Millennium Bridge' £1 (4598), 'Scouting Movement' 50 pence (4619), and 'Britannia' 50p (4610) to 1p (Issued: 18,215)	(12)	40
PS91 –**2007**	As last, but packed in red leather case (Issued: 15,000)	(12)	50
PS92 –**2007**	As last, but Executive Set (Issued: 5,000)	(12)	78
PS93 –**2008**	Proof 'Prince Charles 60th Birthday' £5 struck in c/n (4564), Proof 'Elizabeth I Anniversary' struck in c/n (4563), 'Bimetallic' 'London Olympics Centenary' £2 (4951), 'Bimetallic' £2 (4570) 'UK' £1 (4590), and 'Britannia' 50p (4610) to 1p (Issued: 17,719)	(11)	40
PS94 – **2008**	As last, but packed in black leather case (Issued: 13,614)	(11)	50
PS95 – **2008**	As last, but Executive Set (Issued: 5,000)	(11)	80
PS96 – **2008**	'The Royal Shield of Arms', 'Royal Shield' £1 (4604) to 1p (4611, 4631, 4651, 4671, 4691, 4711) (Issued: 20,000)	(7)	45
PS97 – **2009**	Proof 'Henry VIII' £5 struck in c/n (4565), 'Bimetallic' 'Charles Darwin' £2 (4586), 'Bimetallic' 'Robert Burns' £2 (4585) 'Bimetallic' £2 (4570), 'Royal Shield' £1 (4604), 'Kew Gardens' 50 pence (4621) 50 pence (4620), 20 pence (4631), 10 pence (4651), 5 pence (4671), 2 pence (4691) and 1 pence (4711) (Edition: 20,000)	(12)	40
PS98 – **2009**	As last, but packed in black leather case (Edition: 15,000)	(12)	50
PS99 – **2009**	As last, but Executive Set (Edition: 5,000)	(12)	80
PS100–**2009**	Set of sixteen 50 pence reverse designs marking the 40th Anniversary of the introduction of the 50 pence denomination (4610- 4625) (Edition: 5,000)	(16)	195
PS101–**2010**	Proof 'Restoration of the Monarchy' £5 struck in c/n (4566), 'Bimetallic' 'Florence Nightingale' £2 (4587), 'Bimetallic' £2 (4570), 'London' £1 (4605), 'Belfast' £1 (4606), Royal Shield £1 (4604), 'Girl Guiding' 50 pence (4626), and 50 pence to 1 pence (4620, 4631, 4651, 4671, 4691and 4711) (Edition: 20,000)	(13)	40
PS102–**2010**	As last, but packed in black leather case (Edition: 15,000)	(13)	50
PS103–**2010**	As last, but Executive Set (Edition: 5,000)	(13)	80
PS104–**2011**	Proof 'Prince Philip 90th Birthday' £5 struck in c/n (4568),'Bimetallic' 'Mary Rose' £2 (4588), 'Bimetallic' King James Bible'£2 (4589), 'Bimetallic' £2 (4570) 'Edinburgh' £1 (4607), 'Cardiff' £1 (4608), 'Royal Shield '£1(4604), 50 pence, 'WWF' (4627), 50 pence to 1 pence (4620, 4631, 4651, 4671, 4691, and 4711) (Edition: 20,000)	14)	45
PS105–**2011**	As last, but packed in black leather case (Edition: 15,000)	(14)	52
PS106–**2011**	As last, but Executive Set (Edition: 5,000)	(14)	82
PS107–**2012**	Diamond Jubilee £5, struck in c/n (4569), 'Bimetallic' 'Charles Dickens' £2 (4590), 'Bimetallic' £2 (4570) 'Royal Shield '£1(4604), 50 pence to 1 pence (4620, 4631, 4651, 4671, 4691 and 4711) (Edition: 30,000)	(10)	55
PS108–**2012**	Premium Proof set, Proof Diamond Jubilee £5, struck in c/n (4569), 'Bimetallic' 'Charles Dickens' £2 (4590), 'Bimetallic' £2 (4570) 'Royal Shield '£1(4604), 50 pence to 1 pence (4620, 4631, 4651, 4671, 4691, 4711) and Mint medal (Edition:.3,500)	(10)	99

Silver Maundy Sets

4211   Maundy Set (4p, 3p, 2p and 1p). Uniform dates. Types as 4131

	FDC £		FDC £
1971 *Tewkesbury Abbey*	225	1992 *Chester Cathedral*	200
1972 *York Minster*	200	1993 *Wells Cathedral*	200
1973 *Westminster Abbey*	200	1994 *Truro Cathedral*	200
1974 *Salisbury Cathedral*	200	1995 *Coventry Cathedral*	200
1975 *Peterborough Cathedral*	200	1996 *Norwich Cathedral*	200
1976 *Hereford Cathedral*	200	1997 *Bradford Cathedral*	200
1977 *Westminster Abbey*	200	1998 *Portsmouth Cathedral*	200
1978 *Carlisle Cathedral*	200	1999 *Bristol Cathedral*	200
1979 *Winchester Cathedral*	200	2000 *Lincoln Cathedral*	200
1980 *Worcester Cathedral*	200	2001 *Westminster Abbey*	225
1981 *Westminster Abbey*	225	2002 *Canterbury Cathedral*	200
1982 *St. Davidís Cathedral*	200	2002 *Proof in gold from set *(see PCGS1)*	1750
1983 *Exeter Cathedral*	200	2003 *Gloucester Cathedral*	200
1984 *Southwell Minster*	200	2004 *Liverpool Cathedral*	200
1985 *Ripon Cathedral*	200	2005 *Wakefield Cathedral*	200
1986 *Chichester Cathedral*	200	2006 *Guildford Cathedral*	200
1987 *Ely Cathedral*	200	2007 *Manchester Cathedral*	200
1988 *Lichfield Cathedral*	200	2008 *Armagh Cathedral*	350
1989 *Birmingham Cathedral*	200	2009 *St. Edmundsbury Cathedral*	350
1990 *Newcastle Cathedral*	200	2010 *Derby Cathedral*	400
1991 *Westminster Abbey*	225	2011 *Westminster Abbey*	500

4212   — fourpence, 1971-2010 .... *from* 50
4213   — threepence, 1971-2010 .... *from* 50
4214   — twopence, 1971-2010 .... *from* 50
4215   — penny, 1971-2010 .... *from* 75
The place of distribution is shown after each date.

Silver Sets

			£
PSS01–**1989**	'Bill of Rights' and 'Claim of Right' £2s (4312 and 4313), Silver piedfort proofs (Issued: 10,000)	(2)	85
PSS02–**1989**	As last but Silver proofs (Not known)	(2)	65
PSS03–**1990**	2 x 5p Silver proofs (4371 and 4372), (Issued: 35,000)	(2)	30
PSS04–**1992**	2 x 10p Silver proofs (4366 and 4367), (Not known)…	(2)	34
PSS05–**1996**	25th Anniversary of Decimal Currency (4339, 4351, 4361, 4367, 4372, 4386, 4391) in Silver proof (Edition: 15,000)	(7)	125
PSS06–**1997**	2 x 50p silver proofs (4351 and 4354) (Issued: 10,304)	(2)	45
PSS07–**1998**	'EU' and 'NHS' Silver proofs (4611 and 4612)	(2)	60
PSS08–**2000**	'Millennium' £5, 'Bimetallic' £2, 'Welsh' £1, 50p to 1p, and Maundy coins, 4p-1p, in silver proof (4552, 4570, 4592, 4610, 4630, 4650, 4670, 4212-4215) (Issued: 13,180)	(13)	275
PSS09–**2002**	'Commonwealth Games' 'Bimetallic' £2 (4573, 4574, 4575 and 4576) in silver (Issued: 2,553)	(4)	140
PSS10–**2002**	As above with the addition of colour and piedfort in silver. (4573A, 4574A, 4575A and 4576A) (Issued: 3,497)	(4)	240
PSS11–**MD**	'Golden Jubilee' £5 (4555) and 'Coronation' £5 (4557) silver proofs	(2)	110
PSS12–**2003**	'Coronation' £5 (4557), 'Britannia' £2 (4503), 'Bimetallic' 'DNA' £2 (4577), 'UK' £1 (4590) and 'Suffragette' 50 pence (4614) silver proofs (Edition:)	(5)	165
PSS13–**2004**	'Entente Cordiale' £5 (4558), 'Britannia' £2 (4500), 'Bimetallic' 'Penydarren engine' £2 (4578) 'Forth Rail Bridge' £1 (4595) and 'Sub four-minute mile' 50 pence (4615) silver proofs (Edition:)	(5)	165
PSS14–**2004**	'Bimetallic' 'Penydarren engine' £2 (4578), 'Forth Rail Bridge' £1 (4595), 'Sub four-minute mile' 50 pence (4615) Silver piedfort proofs	(3)	145

£

PSS15–**2005**	'Bimetallic' 'Gunpowder Plot' £2 (4579), Bimetallic' 'World War II' £2 (4580), 'Menai Straits Bridge' £1 (4596), 'Samuel Johnson's Dictionary' 50 pence Silver piedfort proofs.....................	(4)	190
PSS16–**2005**	'Trafalgar' £5 (4559) and 'Nelson' £5 (4560) silver piedfort proofs, (Issued: 2,818)................	(2)	175
PSS17–**2006**	'H M The Queen's 80th Birthday' £5, 'Bimetallic' £2, 'Northern Ireland' £1, 50p to 1p,(4561, 4570, 4597, 4610, 4630, 4650, 4670, and Maundy Coins, 4p – 1p, in silver proof, (4212 – 4215) (Edition: 8,000)	(13)	275
PSS18–**2006**	'Bimetallic' 'Isambard Brunel' £2 (4581) and 'Bimetallic' 'Paddington Station' £2 (4582) silver proofs (Edition: taken from individual coin limits)	(2)	70
PSS19–**2006**	As last but silver piedforts (Edition: 5,000)	(2)	130
PSS20–**2006**	'Victoria Cross' 50 pence (4617) and 'Wounded soldier' 50 pence (4618) silver proofs (Edition: taken from individual coin limits)................	(2)	65
PSS21–**2006**	As last but silver piedforts (Edition: 5,000)	(2)	115
PSS22–**2006**	'80th Birthday' £5 (4561), 'Bimetallic' 'Isambard Brunel' £2 (4581) and 'Bimetallic' 'Paddington Station' £2 (4582), 'MacNeill's Egyptian Arch' £1 (4597), 'Victoria Cross' 50 pence (4617), 'Wounded soldier' 50 pence (4618) silver piedforts (Edition: taken from individual coin limits)..................	(6)	325
PSS23–**2007**	'Diamond Wedding' £5, Britannia £2, 'Bimetallic' 'Act of Union' £2, 'Bimetallic' 'Abolition of Slavery' £2, 'Millennium Bridge' £1 and 'Scout Movement'50p in silver proof (4562, 4505, 4583, 4584, 4598 and 4619) (Edition: taken from individual coin limits)	(6)	200
PSS24–**2007**	'Diamond Wedding' £5, 'Bimetallic' 'Act of Union'£2, 'Bimetallic' 'Abolition of Slavery' £2, 'Millennium Bridge' £1 and 'Scout Movement'50p in silver piedfort (4562, 4583, 4584, 4598 and 4619) (Edition: taken from individual coin limits	(5)	250
PSS25–**MD**	Set of four £1 coins 'Forth Rail Bridge' (4595), 'Menai Straits Bridge' (4596) 'MacNiell's Egyptian Arch' (4597) and 'Gateshead Millennium Bridge' (4598) in silver proof (Edition: taken from individual coin limits)	(4)	115
PSS26–**MD**	As above but in silver piedfort (Edition: 1,400 taken from individual coin limits)...……………………………………………………………	(4)	200
PSS27–**2008**	'Emblems of Britain', 'UK' £1 (4590), 'Britannia' 50 pence (4610), 20 pence to 1p silver proofs (Issued: 8,168)...........	(7)	150
PSS28–**2008**	'The Royal Shield of Arms', 'Royal Shield' £1 (4604) to 1p (4611, 4631, 4651, 4671, 4691, 4711) silver proof (Issued: 10,000)	(7)	160
PSS29–**2008**	As above but silver piedforts (Issued: 3,000)................	(7)	295
PSS30–**2008**	Set of 14 different £1 with selected gold plating to the reverse designs (4590 to 4603) (Edition: 15,000 collections)................	(14)	395
PSS31–**2008**	Set of 3 £1 Regional designs for Scotland with selected gold plating to the reverse designs (4591B, 4595C and 4599A) (Edition: 750, taken from above)	(3)	95
PSS32–**2008**	Set of 3 £1 Regional designs for Wales with selected gold plating to the reverse designs (4592B, 4596C and 4600A) (Edition: 750, taken from above)...........	(3)	95
PSS33–**2008**	Set of 3 £1 Regional designs for Northern Ireland with selected gold plating to the reverse designs (4593B, 4597C and 4601A) (Edition: 750, taken from above)	(3)	95
PSS34–**2008**	Set of 3 £1 Regional designs for England with selected gold plating to the reverse designs (4594B, 4598C and 4602A) (Edition: 750, taken from above)	(3)	95
PSS35–**2008**	'Prince Charles 60th Birthday' £5 (4563), 'Elizabeth I Anniversary' £5 (4564), Britannia £2 (4506), 'London Olympic Centenary' £2 (4951) and 'UK' £1 (4590) silver proofs (Edition: 5,000)................	(5)	180
PSS36–**2008**	'Prince Charles 60th Birthday' £5 (4563), 'Elizabeth I Anniversary' £5 (4564), 'London Olympic Centenary' £2 (4951) and 'Royal Shield' £1 (4604) silver piedforts (Edition: 3,000)	(4)	250

£

PSS37–**2009** 'Henry VIII" £5 (4565), 'Bimetallic' 'Charles Darwin' £2 (4586), Bimetallic 'Robert Burns' £2 (4585) 'Bimetallic'£2 (4570), 'Royal Shield' £1 (4604), 'Kew Gardens' 50 pence (4621), 50 pence (4620), 20 pence (4631), 10 pence (4651), 5 pence (4671), 2 pence (4691) and 1 pence (4711) silver proofs (Edition: 7,500 .... (12) 270

PSS38–**2009** 'Henry VIII' £5 (4565), Britannia £2 (4501), 'Charles Darwin' £2 (4586), 'Robert Burns' £2 (4585), 'Royal Shield' £1 (4604) and 50 pence 'Kew Gardens' (4621) silver proofs (Edition; 1,500).. (6) 200

PSS39–**2009** 'Henry VIII' £5 (4565), 'Charles Darwin' £2 (4586), 'Robert Burns' £2 (4585) and 50 pence 'Kew Gardens' (4621) silver piedforts (Edition: 2,500)........... (4) 255

PSS40–**2009** Set of sixteen 50 pence reverse designs marking 40th Anniversary of the introduction of the 50 pence denomination (4610- 4625) silver proofs (Edition: 2,500) .... (16) 425

PSS41–**2010** 'Restoration of the Monarchy' £5 (4566), 'Bimetallic 'Florence Nightingale' £2 (4587), 'Bimetallic'£2 (4570), 'London' £1 (4605), 'Belfast' £1 (4606), Royal Shield £1 (4604), 'Girl Guiding' 50 pence (4626), and 50 pence to 1p (4620, 4631, 4651, 4671, 4691and 4711) silver proofs (Edition: 3,500) .... (13) 300

PSS42–**2010** 'Restoration of the Monarchy' £5 (4566), 'Bimetallic 'Florence Nightingale' £2 (4587), 'London' £1 (4605), 'Belfast' £1 (4606), and 'Girl Guiding' 50 pence (4626) silver proofs (Edition: 2,500) .... (5) 180

PSS43–**2010** 'Restoration of the Monarchy'£5 (4566), 'Bimetallic 'Florence Nightingale' £2 (4587), 'London' £1 (4605), 'Belfast' £1 (4606), and 'Girl Guiding' 50 pence (4626) silver piedforts (Edition: 2,500) .... (5) 300

PSS44-**2011** Proof 'Prince Philip 90th Birthday' £5 (4568),'Bimetallic' 'Mary Rose' £2 (4588), 'Bimetallic' King James Bible'£2 (4589),'Bimetallic' £2 (4570) 'Edinburgh' £1 (4607), 'Cardiff' £1 (4608), 'Royal Shield '£1(4604), 50 pence,' WWF' (4627), 50 pence to 1 pence (4620, 4631, 4651, 4671, 4691 and 4711) silver proofs (Edition: 2,500) .... (14) 450

PSS45-**2011** Proof 'Prince Philip 90th Birthday' £5 (4568),'Bimetallic' 'Mary Rose' £2 (4588), 'Bimetallic' King James Bible'£2 (4590), 'Edinburgh' £1 (4607), 'Cardiff' £1 (4608), 50 pence,' WWF' (4627), silver proofs (Edition: 1,500) .... (6) 285

PSS46-**2011** Proof 'Prince Philip 90th Birthday' £5 (4568),'Bimetallic' 'Mary Rose' £2 (4589), 'Bimetallic' King James Bible'£2 (4589), 'Edinburgh' £1 (4607), 'Cardiff' £1 (4608), 'WWF' (4627), silver piedforts (Edition: 2,000) .... (6) 455

PSS47–**2012** Proof Diamond Jubilee £5, (4569), 50 pence to 1 pence (4620, 4631, 4651, 4671, 4691 and 4711) silver proofs, (Edition: 995) .... (7) 395

PSS48–**2012** Proof Diamond Jubilee £5, (4569), 'Bimetallic' 'Charles Dickens' £2 (4590), 'Bimetallic' £2 (4570) 'Royal Shield '£1(4604), 50 pence to 1 pence (4620, 4631, 4651, 4671, 4691 and 4711) silver proofs, the £2s to 1 pence with selected gold plating (Edition: 2,012) .... (10) 490

PSS49–**MD** Proof Silver Wedding Crown, 25pence, Golden Wedding Crown, £5 and Diamond Wedding Crown, £5 (4226, 4304 and 4562) silver proofs (Edition: 250 taken from the original sales and obtained from the secondary market). (3) 150

Britannia Silver Proof Sets

PBS01–**1997** £2 – 20 pence (4300, 4300A, 4300B, 4300C) (Issued: 11,832) .... (4) 175

PBS02–**1998** £2 – 20 pence (4500, 4510, 4520, 4530) (Issued: 3,044) .... (4) 160

PBS03–**2001** £2 – 20 pence (4502, 4511, 4521, 4531) (Issued: 4,596) .... (4) 150

PBS04–**2003** £2 – 20 pence (4503, 4512, 4522, 4532) (Issued: 3,669) .... (4) 150

PBS05–**MD** Britannia set of four different £2 designs, 1999- 2003 (4500, 4501,4502, 4503) (Edition: 5,000) .... (4) 160

£

PBS06–**2005**	Britannia proofs, £2 – 20 pence (4504, 4513, 4523, 4533) (Issued: 2,360).....	(4)	150
PBS07–**2006**	Britannia set of five different £2 designs with selected gold Plating of obverse and reverse (4500A, 4501A, 4502A, 4503A, 4504A) (Issued: 3,000).............	(5)	350
PBS08–**2007**	Britannia proofs, £2 - 20 pence, (4505, 4514, 4524, 4534) (Issued: 2,500).....	(4)	150
PBS09–**2007**	Britannia set of six different proof £1 designs with satin finish on reverse (4510A, 4511A, 4512A, 4513A, 4514A, 4515) (Issued: 2,000)......................	(6)	225
PBS10–**2008**	Britannia proofs, £2 – 20p (4506, 4516, 4525, 4535) (Issued: 2,500).............	(4)	150
PBS11–**2009**	Britannia proofs, £2 – 20p (4501, 4517, 4526, 4536) (Issued: 2,500).............	(4)	150
PBS12–**2010**	Britannia proofs, £2 – 20p (4502, 4518, 4527, 4537) (Edition: 3,500)...........	(4)	150
PBS13–**2011**	Britannia proofs, £2 – 20p (4508, 4519, 4528, 45387) (Edition: 3,500).......	(4)	195
PBS14–**2012**	Britannia proofs, £2 – 20p, (As PB02) (Edition: 2,600)...............................	(4)	195
PBS15–**2012**	Britannia £1 proofs, set of nine different reverse designs (4510 to 4514, and 4516 to 4519) (Edition: 1,612 sets)	(9)	00

Gold Sovereign Proof Sets

Many of the coins that appear in the Gold proof sets were also offered for sale as individual coins in presentation cases with appropriate certificates. There are collectors of particular denominations such as £2 pieces, sovereigns and half sovereigns who request coins as issued i.e. in their cases with certificates rather than buying coins taken from sets. As a consequence, many of these individual coins command a premium over those that might have come from cased sets. As a result the prices for sets are often less than the sum of the individual coins.

PGS01–**1980**	Gold £5 to half-sovereign (4201, 4203-4205) (Issued: 10,000)......................	(4)	2600
PGS02–**1981**	U.K. Proof coin Commemorative collection. (Consists of £5, sovereign, 'Royal Wedding' Crown (4229) in silver, plus base metal proofs 50p to ½p), (Not known)	(9)	1850
PGS03–**1982**	Gold £5 to half-sovereign (as 1980 issue) (Issued: 2,500).............................	(4)	2600
PGS04–**1983**	Gold £2, sovereign and half-sovereign, (4203 – 4205) (Not known)	(3)	1100
PGS05–**1984**	Gold £5, sovereign and half-sovereign, (4201, 4204 and 4205) (Issued: 7,095)	(3)	2000
PGS06–**1985**	Gold £5 to half-sovereign (4251, 4261, 4271, 4276) (Issued: 5,849)	(4)	2600
PGS07–**1986**	Gold Commonwealth games £2, sovereign and half-sovereign (4311, 4271 and 4276) (Issued: 12,500)..	(3)	1100
PGS08–**1987**	Gold £2, sovereign and half-sovereign (4261, 4271 and 4276) (Issued: 12,500)	(3)	1100
PGS09–**1988**	Gold £2 to half-sovereign, (as 1987 issue) (Issued: 11,192)...........................	(3)	1100
PGS10–**1989**	Sovereign Anniversary Gold £5 to half-sovereign (4254, 4263, 4272, 4277), (Issued: 5,000)	(4)	4000
PGS11–**1989**	Gold £2 to half-sovereign (4263, 4272 and 4277) (Issued: 7,936)	(3)	2250
PGS12–**1990**	Gold £5 to half-sovereign (as 1985 issue), (Issued: 1,721)............................	(4)	2600
PGS13–**1990**	Gold £2 to half-sovereign (as 1988 issue), (Issued: 1,937)............................	(3)	1200
PGS14–**1991**	Gold £5 to half-sovereign (as 1985 issue) (Issued: 1,336).............................	(4)	2600
PGS15–**1991**	Gold £2 to half-sovereign (as 1987 issue (Issued: 1,152).............................	(3)	1200
PGS16–**1992**	Gold £5 to half-sovereign (as 1985 issue) (Issued: 1,165).............................	(4)	2600
PGS17–**1992**	Gold £2 to half-sovereign (as 1987 issue) (Issued: 967)................................	(3)	1200
PGS18–**1993**	Gold £5 to half-sovereign with silver Pistrucci medal in case (Issued: 1,078)	(5)	2700
PGS19–**1993**	Gold £2 to half-sovereign (as 1985 issue) (Issued: 663)................................	(3)	1250
PGS20–**1994**	Gold £5, £2, sovereign and half-sovereign (4251, 4314, 4271 and 4276) (Issued: 918)	(4)	2650
PGS21–**1994**	Gold £2, sovereign and half-sovereign (4314, 4271 and 4276) (Issued: 1,249)	(3)	1150
PGS22–**1995**	Gold £5,£2,sovereign and half-sovereign (4251,4315,4271and 4276) (Issued: 718)...	(4)	2600
PGS23–**1995**	Gold £2, sovereign and half-sovereign (4315, 4271 and 4276) (Issued: 1,112)	(3)	1200

£

PGS24–**1996**   Gold £5 to half-sovereign (as 1985 issue) (Issued: 742)................................... (4) 2600
PGS25–**1996**   Gold £2 to half-sovereign (as 1987 issue) (Issued: 868)................................ (3) 1200
PGS26–**1997**   Gold £5,£2,sovereign and half-sovereign (4251,4318,4271 and 4276)
                 (Issued: 860) .... (4) 2600
PGS27–**1997**   Gold £2 to half-sovereign (4318, 4271 and 4276) (Issued: 817) .... (3) 1200
PGS28–**1998**   Gold £5 to half sovereign (4400, 4420, 4430, 4440) (Issued: 789) .... (4) 2600
PGS29–**1998**   Gold £2 to half sovereign (4420, 4430, 4440) (Issued: 560) .... (3) 1200
PGS30–**1999**   Gold £5, £2, sovereign and half sovereign (4400, 4571, 4430 and 4440)
                 (Issued: 991) .... (4) 2600
PGS31–**1999**   Gold £2, sovereign and half sovereign (4571, 4430 and 4440) (Issued: 912) . (3) 1200
PGS32–**2000**   Gold £5 to half-sovereign (as 1998 issue) (Issued: 1,000)............................. (4) 2600
PGS33–**2000**   Gold £2 to half-sovereign (as 1998 issue) (Issued: 1,250)............................. (3) 1100
PGS34–**2001**   Gold £5,£2,sovereign and half sovereign (4400, 4572, 4430 and 4440)
                 (Issued: 1,000) .... (4) 2600
PGS35–**2001**   Gold £2 , sovereign and half sovereign (4572,4430 and 4440)(Issued: 891) .. (3) 1000
PGS36–**2002**   Gold £5 to half sovereign (4401, 4421, 4431, 4441) (Issued: 3,000) .... (4) 3250
PGS37–**2002**   Gold £2 to half sovereign (4421, 4431, 4441) (Issued: 3,947) .... (3) 1400
PGS38–**2003**   Gold £5 to half sovereign (as 1998 issue) (Issued: 2,050) .... (4) 2600
PGS39–**2003**   Gold £2, sovereign and half sovereign (4577, 4430 and 4440) (Issued: 1,737) (3) 1100
PGS40–**2004**   Gold £5 to half sovereign (as 1998 issue) (Issued: 1,749) .... (4) 2600
PGS41–**2004**   Gold £2, sovereign and half sovereign (4578, 4430 and 4440) (Issued: 761) . (3) 1100
PGS42–**2005**   Gold £5 to half sovereign (4402, 4422, 4432, 4442 (Issued: 2,161)............... (4) 3250
PGS43–**2005**   Gold £2 to half sovereign (4422, 4432, 4442) (Issued: 797) .... (3) 1400
PGS44–**2006**   Gold £5 to half sovereign (as 1998 issue) (Issued: 1,750) .... (4) 2600
PGS45–**2006**   Gold £2 to half sovereign (as 1998 issue) (Issued: 540) .... (3) 1100
PGS46–**2007**   Gold £5 to half sovereign (as 1998 issue) (Issued: 1,750) .... (4) 2600
PGS47–**2007**   Gold £2 to half sovereign (as 1998 issue) (Issued: 651) .... (3) 1100
PGS48–**2007**   Gold sovereign and half sovereign (4430 and 4440) (Issued: 818) .... (2)   600
PGS49–**2008**   Gold £5 to half sovereign (as 1998 issue) (Issued: 1,750) .... (4) 2600
PGS50–**2008**   Gold £2 to half sovereign (as 1998 issue) (Issued: 583) .... (3) 1100
PGS51–**2008**   Gold sovereign and half sovereign (as 2007 issue) (Issued: 804, in
                 addition to individual coin issues)... (2)   600
PGS52–**2009**   Gold £5, £2, sovereign, half sovereign, and quarter sovereign (4403, 4423,
                 4433, 4443, and 4445) (Issued: 1,750)... (5) 3000
PGS53–**2009**   Gold £2, sovereign and half sovereign (4423, 4433 and 4445) (Edition: 750) (3) 1200
PGS54–**2009**   Gold sovereign and half sovereign (4433 and 4443) (Edition: 1,000)............ (2)   600
PGS55–**2010**   Gold £5 to quarter sovereign (as 2009 issue) (Edition: 1,750) ..………....... ..(5) 3000
PGS56–**2010**   Gold £2 to half sovereign (as 2009 issue) (Edition: 750)…………..……. ….(3) 1200
PGS57–**2010**   Gold sovereign, half sovereign and quarter sovereign (4433, 4443 and 4445)
                 (Edition: 1,500) .... (3)   725
PGS58–**2011**   Gold £5 to quarter sovereign (as 2010 issue) (Edition: 1,500) .... (5) 4000
PGS59–**2011**   Gold £2 to quarter sovereign (4423, 4433, 4443 and 4445) (Edition: 200)..... (4) 2000
PGS60–**2011**   (Previously listed as PGS59) Gold £2 to half sovereign (as 2010 issue)
                 (Edition: 750) .... (3) 1650
PGS61–**2011**   (Previously listed as PGS60) Gold sovereign, half sovereign and quarter
                 sovereign (4433, 4443 and 4445) (Edition: 1,000) .... (3)   825
PGS62–**2012**   Gold £5, £2, sovereign, half sovereign and quarter sovereign (4404, 4424,
                 4434, 4444 and 4446) (Edition: 999) .... (5) 4000
PGS63–**2012**   Gold £2 to quarter sovereign (4424, 4434, 4444 and 4446) (Edition: 159)..... (4) 2000
PGS64–**2012**   Gold £2 to half sovereign (4424, 4434 and 4444) (Edition: 750) .... (3) 1650
PGS65–**2012**   Gold sovereign, half sovereign and quarter sovereign (4433, 4443 and 4445)
                 (Edition: 700) .... (3)   825
PGS66–**2012**   BU Gold £2 to half sovereign (4424, 4434 and 4444) (Edition: 60)............... (3) 2000

£

Britannia Gold Proof Sets

PBS01–**1987**	Britannia Proofs £100, £50, £25, £10 (4281, 4286, 4291, and 4296), alloyed with copper (Issued: 10,000)	(4) 2400
PBS02–**1987**	Britannia Proofs £25, £10 (4291 and 4296) (Issued: 11,100)	(2) 450
PBS03–**1988**	Britannia Proofs £100–£10 (as 1987 issue) (Issued: 3,505)...........................	(4) 2400
PBS04–**1988**	Britannia Proofs £25, £10 (as 1987 issue) (Issued: 894)................................	(2) 450
PBS05–**1989**	Britannia Proofs £100–£10 (as 1987) (Issued: 2,268)....................................	(4) 2400
PBS06–**1989**	Britannia Proofs £25, £10 (as 1987 issue) (Issued: 451)................................	(2) 450
PBS07–**1990**	Britannia Proofs, £100–£10, gold with the addition of silver alloy (4282, 4287, 4292, 4297) (Issued: 527)..	(4) 2400
PBS08–**1991**	Britannia Proofs, as PBS07 (Issued: 509)	(4) 2400
PBS09–**1992**	Britannia Proofs, as PBS07 (Issued: 500)	(4) 2400
PBS10–**1993**	Britannia Proofs, as PBS07 (Issued: 462)	(4) 2400
PBS11–**1994**	Britannia Proofs, as PBS07 ((Issued: 435)	(4) 2400
PBS12–**1995**	Britannia Proofs, as PBS07 (Issued: 500)	(4) 2400
PBS13–**1996**	Britannia Proofs, as PBS07 (Issued: 483)	(4) 2400
PBS14–**1997**	Britannia proofs £100, £50, £25, £10 (4283, 4288, 4293, 4298) (Issued: 892)	(4) 2600
PBS15–**1998**	Britannia proofs £100, £50, £25, £10 (4450, 4460, 4470, 4480) (Issued: 750)	(4) 2400
PBS16–**1999**	Britannia Proofs, as PBS15 (Issued: 740)	(4) 2400
PBS17–**2000**	Britannia Proofs, as PBS15 (Issued: 750)	(4) 2400
PBS18–**2001**	Britannia Proofs £100, £50, £25, £10 (4451, 4461, 4471, 4481) (Issued: 1,000)	(4) 2400
PBS19–**2002**	Britannia Proofs, as PBS15 (Issued: 945)	(4) 2400
PBS20–**2003**	Britannia Proofs £100, £50, £25, £10 (4452, 4462, 4472, 4482) (Issued: 1,250)	(4) 2400
PBS21–**2003**	Britannia Proofs £50, £25, £10 (4462, 4472, 4482) (Issued: 825)	(3) 1050
PBS22–**MD**	Britannia **BU** £100 set of four different designs, 1987, 1997, 2001, 2003 (4281, 4283, 4451, 4452) (Edition: 2,500)	(4) 5200
PBS23–**2004**	Britannia Proofs, as PBS15 (Issued: 973)	(4) 2400
PBS24–**2004**	Britannia Proofs, £50, £25, £10 (4460, 4470, 4480) (Issued: 223)	(3) 1100
PBS25–**2005**	Britannia Proofs, £100, £50, £25, £10 (4453, 4463, 4473, 4483) (Issued: 1,439)	(4) 2400
PBS26–**2005**	Britannia Proofs, £50, £25, £10 (4463, 4473, 4483) (Issued: 417)	(3) 1100
PBS27–**2006**	Britannia Proofs, as PBS15 (Issued: 1,163)	(4) 2400
PBS28–**2006**	Britannia set of five different proof £25 designs (4470, 4471, 4472, 4473, 4474) (Edition: 250)	(5) 1700
PBS29–**2007**	(Previously listed as **PBS28**) Britannia Proofs, £100, £50, £25, £10 (4454, 4464, 4475, 4484) (Issued: 1,250)...	(4) 2400
PBS30–**2008**	Britannia Proofs, £100, £50, £25, £10 (4455, 4465, 4476, 4485) (Issued: 1,250)	(4) 2400
PBS31–**2009**	Britannia Proofs, £100, £50, £25, £10 (4456, 4466, 4474, 4486) (Edition: 1,250)	(4) 2400
PBS32–**2010**	Britannia Proofs, £100, £50, £25, £10 (4457, 4467, 4477, 4487) (Edition: 1,250)	(4) 2400
PBS33–**2010**	Britannia Proofs, £50, £25, £10 (4467, 4475, 4487) (Edition: 500).….............	(3) 1200
PBS34–**2011**	Britannia Proofs, £100, £50, £25, £10 (4458, 4468, 4478, 4488) (Edition: 1,000)	(4) 3600
PBS35–**2011**	Britannia Proofs, £50, £25, £10 (4468, 4478, 4488) (Edition: 250)	(3) 1900
PBS36–**2012**	Britannia Proofs, as PBS15 (Edition: 550)...	(4) 3600
PBS37–**2012**	Britannia Proofs, £50, £25 and £10 (4460, 4470 and 4480) (Edition: 100).....	(3) 1900
PBS38–**MD**	Britannia Proof set of 1987 (£100 to £10, struck in copper alloyed gold, see PBS01), and set of 2012 (£100 to £10, struck in silver alloyed gold, see PBS36) (Edition: 15, sets of 1987 from the secondary market).......................	(8) 6,600

Gold Coin Proof Sets

PCGS1–**2002**	Commonwealth Games 'Bimetallic' £2 (4573, 4574, 4575 and 4576) in gold (Issued: 315)	(4)	2600
PGJS1–**2002**	'Golden Jubilee' £5, 'Bimetallic' £2, 'English' £1, 50p to 1p and Maundy coins, 4p-1p, in gold proof (4555, 4570, 4594, 4610, 4630, 4650, 4670, 4212-4215) (Issued: 2,002)	(13)	6500
PGBNS–**2006**	'Bimetallic' 'Isambard Brunel' £2 (4581) and 'Bimetallic' 'Paddington Station' £2 (4582) gold proofs (Edition: taken from individual coin limits)	(2)	1300
PGVCS–**2006**	'Victoria Cross' 50 pence (4617), 'Wounded Colleague' 50 pence (4618) gold proof (Edition: taken from individual coin limits)	(2)	1200
PGBS1–**MD**	Set of four £1 coins 'Forth Rail Bridge' (4595), 'Menai Straits Bridge' (4596) 'MacNiell's Egyptian Arch' (4597) and 'Gateshead Millennium Bridge' (4598) in gold proof (Edition: 300 sets taken from individual coin limits)	(4)	3000
PGEBCS–**2008**	'Emblems of Britain', 'UK' £1 (4590), 'Britannia' 50 pence (4610), 20 pence to 1p gold proofs (Issued: 708)	(7)	3200
PGRSAS–**2008**	'The Royal Shield of Arms', 'Royal Shield' £1 (4604) to 1p gold proof (4611, 4631, 4651, 4671, 4691, and 4711) (Issued: 886)	(7)	3200
PG1PCS–**2008**	Set of 14 different £1 reverse designs (4590 to 4603) (Issued: 150)	(14)	10500
PG50PCS–**2009**	Set of sixteen 50 pence reverse designs marking 40th Anniversary of the introduction of the 50 pence denomination (4610- 4625) gold proofs (Edition: 125)	(16)	9600
PG50PPCS–**2009**	Set of sixteen 50 pence reverse designs marking 40th Anniversary of the introduction of the 50 pence denomination (4610- 4625) gold proof piedfort (Edition: 40)	(16)	25000
PGDJS–**2012**	Diamond Jubilee £5, (4569), 'Bimetallic' 'Charles Dickens' £2 (4590), 'Bimetallic' £2 (4570) 'Royal Shield '£1(4604), 50 pence to 1 pence (4620, 4631, 4651, 4671, 4691 and 4711) gold proofs (Edition: 150)	(10)	8500
PGCS–**2012**	Diamond Jubilee £5, (4569) and Golden Jubilee £5, (4555) (Edition: 60)	(2)	4000
PGCS2–**2012**	Diamond Jubilee £5, (4569) and £2 (Sovereign design, 4424) set of two (Edition : 60, taken from individual coins limits)	(2)	3200
PGCS3–**MD**	Set of six £2 with Sporting connections, Commonwealth Games 1986 (4311), European Football Championship 1996 (4317) and Commonwealth Games 2002 (4573 to 4576), coins obtained from the secondary market (Edition: 50)	(6)	4000

Platinum Coin Proof sets

PPBCS1–**2007**	Britannia Proofs £100, £50, £25, £10 (4454A, 4464A, 4474A and 4484A) (Issued: 250)	(4)	3500
PPBCS2–**2008**	Britannia Proofs £100, £50, £25, £10 (4455A, 4465, 4476A, and 4485A) (Edition: 250)	(4)	3500
PPEBCS–**2008**	'Emblems of Britain', 'UK' £1 (4590), 'Britannia' 50 pence (4610) and 20 pence to 1p (Issued: 250)	(7)	4500
PPRSAS–**2008**	'The Royal Shield of Arms', 'Royal Shield' £1 (4604) to 1p (4611, 4631, 4651, 4671, 4691, 4711) (Issued: 184)	(7)	4500

Pattern Proof sets

PPS1–**2003**	Silver proof set of £1 designs with plain edge and hallmark (4595A, 4596A, 4597A, 4598A) (Edition: 7,500)	(4)	75
PPS2–**2003**	Gold proof set of £1 designs with plain edge and hallmark (4595A, 4596A, 4597A, 4598A) (Edition: 3,000)	(4)	2850

£

| PPS3–**2004** | Silver proof set of £1 designs with plain edge and hallmark (4595B, 4596B, 4597B, 4598B) (Edition: 5,000) .... | (4) | 75 |
| PPS4–**2004** | Gold proof set of £1 designs with plain edge and hallmark (4595B, 4596B, 4597B, 4598B) (Edition: 2,250 .... | (4) | 2850 |

LONDON 2012 OLYMPIC AND PARALYMPIC GAMES

OCNS1–**MD**	Set of 29 50 pence coins in individual card packs (4960 to 4988)	(29)	90
OCNS2	Gold Medal Winners set of 50 pence Cuni and £5 Olympic 2012 £5, (Athletics, 4960, Boxing, 4967, Canoeing, 4968, Cycling, 4961, Equestrian, 4969, Rowing, 4978, Sailing, 4979, Shooting, 4980, Taekwondo, 4982, Tennis, 4983, Triathlon, 4984 and £5, 4924) (Edition: 2,012)	(12)	45
OCNS3	Five pounds.(crowns). Set of the four Countdown issues and the Official Olympic and Paralympic £5 cuni coins. (4920 to 4925). (Edition: 2,012)	(6)	70
OCNS4	Five pounds. (crowns). Set of four Countdown issues (4920 – 4923)	(4)	45

Silver coin sets.

OSS1–**2009**.	The Mind of Britain. Set of six £5 silver proofs (4930, 4931, 4932, 4933, 4934 and 4935) (Edition: each coin 95,000)	(6)	300
OSS2–**2010**	The Body of Britain. Set of six £5 silver proofs (4936, 4937, 4938, 4939, 4940 and 4941) (Edition: each coin 95,000)	(6)	300
OSS3–**2010**	The Spirit of Britain. Set of six £5 silver proofs (4942, 4943, 4944, 4945, 4946 and 4947) (Edition: each coin 95,000)	(6)	300
OSS4–**MD**	Great British Icons. Set of 6 £5 silver proofs (4930,4931,4938,4944,4945, 4946)........ (Edition: 10,000 taken from individual coin limits of 95,000)		550
OSS5–**MD**	The Mind, Body and Spirit of Britain. Set of 18 £5 silver proofs (4930 to 4947)...		1650
OSS6–**2011**	Set of 29 50 pence silver brilliant uncirculated coins (4960 to 4988		900
OSS7–**2011**	Gold Medal Winners set of 50 pence silver brilliant uncirculated coins and £5 Olympic 2012 silver proof, (Athletics, 4960, Boxing, 4967, Canoeing, 4968, Cycling, 4961, Equestrian, 4969, Rowing, 4978, Sailing, 4979, Shooting, 4980, Taekwondo, 4982, Tennis, 4983, Triathlon, 4984 and £5, 4924), (Edition: 999 but coins taken from individual issue limits)	(12)	550
OSS8–**2011**	Accuracy. Set of six 50 pence silver brilliant uncirculated coins depicting various sports (Badminton, 4964, Basketball, 4965, Fencing, 4970, Football, 4971, Hockey, 4975, and Tennis, 4983) (Edition: 2,012 but taken from individual issue limits)...	(6)	280
OSS9–**2011**	Agility. Set of six 50 pence silver brilliant uncirculated coins depicting various sports (Boxing, 4967, Equestrian, 4969, Gymnastics, 4973, Judo, 4976, Sailing, 4979, and Taekwondo, 4982) (Edition: 2,012 but taken from individual issue limits)...	(6)	280
OSS10–**2011**	Speed. Set of six 50 pence silver brilliant uncirculated coins depicting various sports (Athletics, 4960, Aquatics, 4962, Canoeing, 4968, Cycling, 4961, Rowing, 4978, Triathlon, 4984) (Edition: 2,012 but taken from individual issue limits)...	(6)	280
OSS11–**MD**	Five pounds.(crowns). Set of the four Countdown issues and the Official Olympic and Paralympic £5 proof silver coins. (4920 to 4925). (Edition: 800 taken from individual issue limits)....................................	(6)	500

£

Gold coin sets.

OGS1–**2008**   (**Previously listed as PG2PCS**). 'Bimetallic' 'Centenary of Olympic Games of
1908' £2 (4585) and 'Bimetallic' 'United Kingdom Olympic Handover
Ceremony' £2 (4951) gold proofs (Edition: 250) ....   (2) 1000

OGS2–**2010**   'Faster' 2-coin proof set, two £25, (4905 and 4906) (Edition: taken from
individual coin Limits) ....   (2) 1200

OGS3–**2010**   'Faster' 3-coin proof set, £100, and two £25, (4915, 4905 and
4906) (Edition: 4,000) ....   (3) 3500

OGS4–**2011**   'Higher' 2-coin proof set, two £25, (4907 and 4908) (Edition: taken from
individual coin limits)..   (2) 1200

OGS5–**2011**   'Higher' 3-coin proof set, £100, and two £25, (4916, 4907 and
4908) (Edition: 4,000) ....   (3) 3500

OGS6–**2012**   'Stronger' 2-coin proof set, two £25, (4909 and 4910) (Edition: taken from
individual coin limits) ....   (2) 1200

OGS7–**2012**   'Stronger' 3-coin proof set, £100, and two £25, (4917, 4909 and 4910)
(Edition: 4,000) ....   (3) 3500

OGS8–**MD**   'Faster', 'Higher' and 'Stronger' set of three £100 (4915 – 4917) and six
£25 (4905 – 4910) (Edition: 1,000 taken from individual coin limits)........   .(9)10500

OGS9–**MD**   'Countdown to London' set of four £5 gold proof coins (4920 – 4923)......   (4)11500

OGS10–**2012**   Set of £5 proof London Olympic Games and Paralympic Games (4924
and 4925) (Edition: taken from individual coin limits) ....   (2) 5500

A SELECT NUMISMATIC BIBLIOGRAPHY

Listed below is a selection of general books on British numismatics and other works that the specialist collector will need to consult.

General Books:

BROOKE, G. C. *English Coins*. 3rd ed., 1966.

CHALLIS, C. E. (ed.) *A New History of the Royal Mint*. 1992

GRUEBER, H. A. *Handbook of the Coins of Great Britain and Ireland*. Revised 1970

KENYON, R. Ll. *Gold Coins of England*. 1884

NORTH, J. J. *English Hammered Coinage*, Vol. I, c. 650-1272. 1994; Vol. II, 1272-1662. 1991

STEWARTBY, Lord. *English Coins 1180-1551*. 2009

SUTHERLAND, C. H. V. *English Coinage, 600-1900*. 1972

Specialist Works:

ABRAMSON, T. Sceattas, *An Illustrated Guide*. 2006

ALLEN, D. *The Origins of Coinage in Britain: A Reappraisal*. Reprint 1978

ALLEN, D. F. *The Coins of the Coritani*. (SCBI no. 3) 1963

ALLEN, D. F. *English Coins in the British Museum: The Cross-and-Crosslets ('Tealby') type of Henry II*. 1951

ALLEN, M. *The Durham Mint*. 2003

ARCHIBALD, M. M. and BLUNT, C. E. *British Museum. Anglo-Saxon Coins. Athelstan to the reform of Edgar*. 924-c.973. 1986

ASKEW, G. *The Coinage of Roman Britain*. (1951) Reprinted 1980.

BESLY, E. M. *Coins and Medals of the English Civil War*. 1990

BLACKBURN, M. A. S. *Anglo-Saxon Monetary History*. 1986

— — *Viking Coinage and Currency in the British Isles*. 2011

BLUNT, C. E. and WHITTON, C. A. *The Coinages of Edward IV and of Henry VI (Restored)*.

BLUNT, C. E., STEWART, B.H.I.H. and LYON, C.S.S. *Coinage in Tenth-Century England. From Edward the Elder to Edgar's Reform*. 1989

BOON, G. C. *Coins of the Anarchy. 1135-54*. 1988

BRAND, J. D. *The English Coinage 1180-1247: Money, Mints and Exchanges* 1994

BROOKE, G. C. *English Coins in the British Museum: The Norman Kings*. 1916

BROWN, I. D., COMBER, C. H. & WILKINSON, W. *The Hammered Silver coins produced at the Tower Mint during the reign of Elizabeth I*. 2006

BROWN, I. D. and DOLLEY, M. *Bibliography of Coin Hoards of Great Britain and Ireland 1500-1967*. 1971

BUCK, I. *Medieval English Groats*. 2000

CARSON, R. A. G. *Mints, Dies and Currency. Essays in Memory of Albert Baldwin*. 1971

CHICK, D. *The Coinage of Offa and his Contemporaries*. 2010

DAVIES, P. J. *British Silver Coins Since 1816 with Engravers' Patterns and Proofs and Unofficial Pieces*. 1982

DE JERSEY, P. *Coinage in Iron Age Armorica*. 1994

DOLLEY, R. H. M. (ed.). *Anglo-Saxon Coins; studies presented to Sir Frank Stenton*. 1964

EAGLEN, R. J. *The Abbey and Mint of Bury St. Edmunds to 1279.* 2006

EVERSON, T. *The Galata Guide to The Farthing Tokens of James I & Charles I.* 2007

FREEMAN, M. J. *The Bronze Coinage of Great Britain.* 2006

GRIERSON, P. and BLACKBURN, M. A. S. *Medieval European Coinage, vol. 1, The Early Middle Ages.* 1986

HOBBS, R. *British Iron Age Coins in the British Museum.* 1996

KEARY, C. and GREUBER, H. *English Coins in the British Museum: Anglo-Saxon Series.* 1887, reprinted, 1970, 2 volumes.

LAKER, A. J. *The portrait Groats of Henry VIII.* 1978

LAWRENCE, L. A. *The Coinage of Edward III from 1351.*

LINECAR, H. W. A. *The Crown Pieces of Great Britain and the British Commonwealth.* 1962

— — *English Proof and Pattern Crown-Size Pieces.* 1968

MACK, R. P. *The R. P. Mack Collection, Ancient British, Anglo-Saxon and Norman Coins.* (SCBI no. 20) 1973

MANVILLE, H. E. *Encyclopedia of British Numismatics. Numismatic Guide to British and Irish Periodicals 1731-1991.* 1993

MANVILLE, H. E. and ROBERTSON, T. J. *An Annotated Bibliography of British Numismatic Auction Catalogues from 1710 to the Present.* 1986

MARSH, M. A. *The Gold Half Sovereign.* 2nd Edition, revised 2004

MARSH, M. A. *The Gold Sovereign.* 2nd Edition 1999

MASS, J. P. *The J. P. Mass collection of English Short Cross Coins 1180-1247. (SCBI 56).* 2001

NAISMITH, R. *The Coinage of Southern England, 796-c.865.* 2011

NORTH, J. J. *Edwardian English Silver Coins 1279-1351. (SCBI 39)* 1989

NORTH, J. J. and PRESTON-MORLEY, P. J. *The John G. Brooker Collection: Coins of Charles I. (SCBI 33)* 1984

PECK, C. W. *English Copper, Tin and Bronze Coins in the British Museum, 1558-1958.* 1970

RAYNER, P.A. *The English Silver Coinage from 1649.* 5th ed. 1992

REECE, R. *Coinage in Roman Britain,* 1987

ROBINSON, Dr. B. *The Royal Maundy.* 1992

RUDD, C. *Ancient British Coins (ABC).* 2009

RUDING, REV. R. *Annals of the Coinage of Great Britain.* 3rd Edition 1840

SEAR, D. R. *Roman Coins and their Values.* 4th Edition (1999) Reprinted 2000

SILLS, J. *Gaulish and Early British Gold Coinage.* 2003

THOMPSON, J. D. A. *Inventory of British Coin Hoards, A.D. 600-1500.* 1956

VAN ARSDELL, R. *Celtic Coinage of Britain.* 1989

VAN ARSDELL, R. D. *The Coinage of the Dobunni.* 1994

WHITTON, C. A. *The Heavy Coinage of Henry VI.*

WILSON, A. and RASMUSSEN, M. *English Patten, Trial and Proof Coin in Gold, 1547-1968.* 2000

WITHERS, P. & B. R. *The Galata Guide to the Pennies of Edward I and II and the Coins of the mint of Berwick-upon-Tweed.* 2006

WOODHEAD, P. *English Gold Coins 1257-1603. The Herbert Schneider Collection, vol. 1 (SCBI 47)* 1996

— — *English Gold Coins 1603-20th Century. The Herbert Schneider Collection, vol. 2 (SCBI 57)* 2002

WREN, C. R. *The Short-cross coinage 1180-1247. Henry II to Henry III. An illustrated Guide to Identification.* 1992
— — *The Voided Long-Cross Coinage 1247-1279. Henry III and Edward I.* 1993
— — *The English Long-Cross Pennies 1279-1489. Edward I-Henry VII.* 1995

For further references to British hammered coinage see *Sylloge of Coins of the British Isles*, a serial publication now comprising 62 volumes cataloguing collections in private hands and institutions. For a full list of the volumes published to date in this series, please contact Spink at the address below.

Other authoritative papers are published in the *Numismatic Chronicle, British Numismatic Journal and Spink's Numismatic Circular.* A complete book list is available from Spink & Son Ltd., 69 Southampton Row, Bloomsbury, London WC1B 4ET. Tel: 020 7563 4046 Fax: 020 7563 4068. Email: Books@spink.com

Further information regarding membership of the British Numismatic Society can be found at www.britnumsoc.org

www.timelineauctions.com

MIDLAND COIN FAIR	
National Motorcycle Museum Coventry Road, Bickenhill Solihull, West Midlands, B92 0EJ, UK	
13 January 2013	10 am – 3.30 pm
10 February 2013	10 am – 3.30 pm
10 March 2013	10 am – 3.30 pm
14 April 2013	10 am – 3.30 pm
12 May 2013	10 am – 3.30 pm
9 June 2013	10 am – 3.30 pm
14 July 2013	10 am – 3.30 pm
11 August 2013	10 am – 3.30 pm
8 September 2013	10 am – 3.30 pm
13 October 2013	10 am – 3.30 pm
10 November 2013	10 am – 3.30 pm
8 December 2013	10 am – 3.30 pm

Northern Fairs Attendance Calendar

HARROGATE COIN FAIR	
Old Swan Hotel, Swan Road Harrogate HG1 2SR, UK	
22 March 2013	11 am – 6 pm
23 March 2013	10 am – 2 pm

COIN & STAMP FAIR	
The Grandstand, York Racecourse York, YO23 1EX, UK	
18 January 2013	11 am – 6 pm
19 January 2013	10 am – 4 pm
19 July 2013	11 am – 6 pm
20 July 2013	10 am – 4 pm

TimeLine Auctions are pleased to announce that we have a comprehensive calendar of coin fairs scheduled for 2013. Either ourselves or our representative, will be on hand at the following fairs to accept entries, answer queries and give valuations. Viewings of lots in upcoming auctions will be possible, by request.

Please note that all dates may be subject to change.

LATIN OR FOREIGN LEGENDS ON ENGLISH COINS

A DOMINO FACTUM EST ISTUD ET EST MIRABILE IN OCULIS NOSTRIS. (This is the Lord's doing and it is marvellous in our eyes: *Psalm 118.23.*) First used on 'fine' sovereign of Mary.

AMOR POPULI PRAESIDIUM REGIS. (The love of the people is the King's protection.) Reverse legend on angels of Charles I.

ANNO REGNI PRIMO, etc. (In the first year of the reign, etc.) Used around the edge of many of the larger milled denominations.

CHRISTO AUSPICE REGNO. (I reign under the auspice of Christ.) Used extensively in the reign of Charles I.

CIVIUM INDUSTRIA FLORET CIVITAS. (By the industry of its people the State flourishes.) On the 1951 Festival Crown of George VI.

CULTORES SUI DEUS PROTEGIT. (God protects His worshippers.) On gold double crowns and crowns of Charles I.

DECUS ET TUTAMEN. (An ornament and a safeguard: Virgil, *Aenid*, v.262.) This inscription on the edge of all early large milled silver was suggested by Evelyn, he having seen it on the vignette in Cardinal Richelieu's Greek Testament, and of course refers to the device as a means to prevent clipping. This legend also appears on the edge of U.K. and Northern Ireland one pound coins.

DIEU ET MON DROIT. (God and my right.) On halfcrowns of George IV and later monarchs

DIRIGE DEUS GRESSUS MEOS. (May God direct my steps: *Psalm 118.133.*) On the 'Una' Five pounds of Queen Victoria.

DOMINE NE IN FURORE TUO ARGUAS ME. (O Lord, rebuke me not in Thine anger: *Psalm 6, 1.).* First used on the half-florin of Edward III and then on all half-nobles.

DomiNus Deus Omnipotens REX. (Lord God, Almighty King.) Viking coins.

DUM SPIRO SPERO. (Whilst I live, I hope.) On the coins struck at Pontefract Castle during the Civil War after Charles I had been imprisoned.

EXALTABITUR IN GLORIA. (He shall be exalted in glory: *Psalm 111.9.*) On all quarter-nobles.

EXURGAT DEUS ET DISSIPENTUR INIMICI EIUS. (Let God arise and let His enemies be scattered: *Psalm* 68, 1.) On the Scottish ducat and early English coins of James I (VI) and was chosen by the King himself. Also on Charles I, civil war, and Declaration coins,

FACIAM EOS IN GENTEM UNAM. (I will make them one nation: *Ezekiel, 37, 22.)* On unites and laurels of James I.

FLORENT CONCORDIA REGNA. (Through concord kingdoms flourish.) On gold unite of Charles I and broad of Charles II.

HANC DEUS DEDIT. (God has given this, i.e. the crown .) On siege-pieces of Pontefract struck in the name of Charles II.

HAS NISI PERITURUS MIHI ADIMAT NEMO. (Let no one remove these [letters] from me under penalty of death.) On the edge of crowns and half-crowns of Cromwell.

HENRICUS ROSAS REGNA JACOBUS. (Henry united the roses, James the kingdoms.) On English and Scottish gold coins of James I (VI).

HONI SOIT QUI MAL Y PENSE. (Evil to him who evil thinks.) The Motto of the Order of the Garter, first used on the Hereford (?) halfcrowns of Charles I. It also occurs on the Garter Star in the centre of the reverse of the silver coins of Charles II, but being so small it is usually illegible; it is more prominent on the coinage of George III.

ICH DIEN. (I serve.) Aberystwyth Furnace 2d, and Decimal 2p. The motto of The Prince of Wales.

INIMICOS EJUS INDUAM CONFUSIONE. (As for his enemies I shall clothe them with shame: *Psalm* 132, 18.) On shillings of Edward VI struck at Durham House, Strand.

JESUS AUTEM TRANSIENS PER MEDIUM ILLORUM IBAT. (But Jesus, passing through the midst of them, went His way: *Luke iv. 30.*) The usual reverse legend on English nobles, ryals and hammered sovereigns before James I; also on the very rare Scottish noble of David II of Scotland and the unique Anglo-Gallic noble of Edward the Black Prince.

JUSTITIA THRONUM FIRMAT. (Justice strengthens the throne.) On Charles I half-groats and pennies and Scottish twenty-penny pieces.

LUCERNA PEDIBUS MEIS VERBUM EST. (Thy word is a lamp unto my feet: *Psalm 119, 105.*) Obverse legend on a rare half-sovereign of Edward VI struck at Durham House, Strand.

MIRABILIA FECIT. (He made marvellously: *Psalm 97.1.*) On the Viking coins of (?) York.

NEMO ME IMPUNE LACESSIT. (No-one provokes me with impunity.) On the 1984 Scottish one pound. Motto of The Order of the Thistle.

NUMMORUM FAMULUS. (The servant of the coinage.) The legend on the edge of the English tin coinage at the end of the seventeenth century.

O CRUX AVE SPES UNICA. (Hail! O Cross, our only hope.) On the reverse of all half-angels.

PAX MISSA PER ORBEM. (Peace sent throughout the world.) The reverse legend of a pattern farthing of Anne.

PAX QUÆRITUR BELLO. (Peace is sought by war.) The reverse legend of the Cromwell broad.

PER CRUCEM TUAM SALVA NOS CHRISTE REDEMPTOR. (By Thy cross, save us, O Christ, our Redeemer.) The normal reverse of English angels.

PLEIDIOL WYF I'M GWLAD. (True am I to my country.) Used on the 1985 Welsh one pound. Taken from the Welsh National Anthem.

POST MORTEM PATRIS PRO FILIO. (After the death of the father for the son.) On siege-pieces struck at Pontefract in 1648 (old style) after the execution of Charles I.

POSUI DEUM ADJUTOREM MEUM. (I have made God my Helper: *comp. Psalm* 54, 4.) Used on many English and Irish silver coins from Edward III until 1603. Altered to POSUIMUS and NOSTRUM on the coins of Philip and Mary.

PROTECTOR LITERIS LITERÆ NUMMIS CORONA ET SALUS. (A protection to the letters [on the face of the coin], the letters [on the edge] are a garland and a safeguard to the coinage.) On the edge of the rare fifty-shilling piece of Cromwell.

QUÆ DEUS CONJUNXIT NEMO SEPARET. (What God hath joined together let no man put asunder: *Matthew 19, 6.*) On the larger silver English and Scottish coins of James I after he succeeded to the English throne.

REDDE CUIQUE QUOD SUUM EST. (Render to each that which is his own.) On a Henry VIII type groat of Edward VI struck by Sir Martin Bowes at Durham House, Strand.

RELIGIO PROTESTANTIVM LEGES ANGLIÆ LIBERTAS PARLIAMENTI. (The religion of the Protestants, the laws of England, the liberty of the Parliament.) This is known as the 'Declaration' and refers to Charles I's declaration to the Privy Council at Wellington, 19 September, 1642; it is found on many of his coins struck at the provincial mints during the Civil War. Usually abbreviated to REL:PROT:LEG: ANG:LIB:PAR:

ROSA SINE SPINA. (A rose without a thorn.) Found on some gold and small coins of Henry VIII and later reigns.

RUTILANS ROSA SINE SPINA. (A dazzling rose without a thorn.) As last but on small gold only.

SCUTUM FIDEI PROTEGET EUM or EAM. (The shield of faith shall protect him, or her.) On much of the gold of Edward VI and Elizabeth.

SIC VOS NON VOBIS (Thus we labour but not for ourselves). 1994 £2 Bank of England.

TALI DICATA SIGNO MENS FLUCTUARI NEQUIT. (Consecrated by such a sign the mind cannot waver: from a hymn by Prudentius written in the fourth century, entitled 'Hymnus ante Somnum'.) Only on the gold 'George noble' of Henry VIII.

TIMOR DOMINI FONS VITÆ. (The fear of the Lord is a fountain of life: *Proverbs, 14, 27.*) On many shillings of Edward VI.

TVAETVR VNITA DEVS. (May God guard these united, i.e. kingdoms.) On many English Scottish and Irish coins of James I.

VERITAS TEMPORIS FILIA. (Truth, the daughter of Time.) On English and Irish coins of Mary Tudor.

Some Royal Titles:

REX ANGL*orum*—King of the English.

REX SAXONIORVM OCCIDENTALIVM —King of the West Saxons.

DEI GRA*tia* REX *ANGL*iae ET FRANC*iae DomiNus HYBerniae ET AQVITaniae*—By the Grace of God, King of England and France, Lord of Ireland and Aquitaine.

D*ei GRAtia Magnae Britanniae, FRanciae ET Hiberniae REX Fidei Defensor BRunsviciensis ET Luneburgen-sis Dux, Sacri Romani Imperii Archi-THesaurarius ET ELector*=By the Grace of God, King of Great Britain, France and Ireland, Defender of the Faith, Duke of Brunswick and Luneburg, High Treasurer and Elector of the Holy Roman Empire.

BRITANNIARUM REX —King of the Britains (i.e. Britain and British territories overseas).

BRITT:OMN:REX:FID:DEF:IND:IMP: —King of all the Britains, Defender of the Faith, Emperor of India.

VIVAT REGINA ELIZABETHA — Long live Queen Elizabeth. On the 1996 £5 Queen's 70th birthday £5 crown.

APPENDIX III

NUMISMATIC CLUBS AND SOCIETIES

Coin News, The Searcher and *Treasure Hunting*, are the major monthly magazines covering numismatics. Spink's *Numismatic Circular* is long established, its first issue appeared in December 1892, and is now published 6 times a year. Many local clubs and societies are affiliated to the British Association of Numismatic Societies, (B.A.N.S) which holds an annual Congress. Details of your nearest numismatic club can be obtained from the Hon. Secretary, Phyllis Stoddart, British Association of Numismatic Societies, c/o Dept. of Numismatics, Manchester Museum, Oxford Road, Manchester M13 9PL email: phyllis.stoddart@manchester.ac.uk.

The two principal learned societies are the Royal Numismatic Society, c/o Department of Coins and Medals, the British Museum, Great Russell Street, Bloomsbury, London WC1B 3DG, and the British Numismatic Society, c/o The Secretary, Peter Preston-Morley, c/o Dix, Noonan, Webb, 16 Bolton Street, London, W1J 8BQ, email: ppm@dnw.co.uk. Both these societies publish an annual journal.

MINTMARKS AND OTHER SYMBOLS ON ENGLISH COINS

A Mintmark (*mm.*), is a term borrowed from Roman and Greek numismatics where it showed the place of mintage; it was generally used on English coins to show where the legend began (a religious age preferred a cross for the purpose). Later, this mark, since the dating of coins was not usual, had a periodic significance, changing from time to time. Hence it was of a secret or 'privy' nature; other privy marks on a coin might be the code-mark of a particular workshop or workman. Thus a privy mark (including the *mintmark.*) might show when a coin was made, or who made it. In the use of precious metals this knowledge was necessary to guard against fraud and counterfeiting.

Mintmarks are sometimes termed 'initial marks' as they are normally placed at the commencement of the inscription. Some of the symbols chosen were personal badges of the ruling monarch, such as the rose and sun of York, or the boar's head of Richard III, the dragon of Henry Tudor or the thistle of James I; others are heraldic symbols or may allude to the mint master responsible for the coinage, e.g. the *mm.* bow used on the Durham House coins struck under John Bowes and the WS mark of William Sharrington of Bristol.

A table of mintmarks is given on the next page. Where mintmarks appear in the catalogue they are sometimes referred to only by the reference number, in order to save space, i.e. *mm. 28* (=mintmark Sun), *mm.28/74 (=mm.* Sun on obverse, *mm.* Coronet on reverse), *mm. 28/- (=mm.* Sun on obverse only).

+44 [0]1708 222 824
enquiries@timelineauctions.com

THE LONDON COIN FAIR	
Holiday Inn, Coram St. Bloomsbury London, WC1, UK	
2 February 2013	9.30 am – 5 pm
1 June 2013	9.30 am – 5 pm
7 September 2013	9.30 am – 5 pm
2 November 2013	9.30 am – 5 pm
BLOOMSBURY COIN FAIR	
The Bloomsbury Hotel 16-22 Great Russell Street London, WC1 3NN, UK	
5 January 2013	9.30 am – 1 pm
2 March 2013	9.30 am – 1 pm
6 April 2013	9.30 am – 1 pm
COINEX 2013	
The Ballroom, Millennium Hotel, London Mayfair Grosvenor Square, London W1K 2HP, UK	
27 September 2013	11 am – 5.30 pm
28 September 2013	10 am – 5 pm

London Fairs Attendance Calendar

TimeLine Auctions are pleased to announce that we have a comprehensive calendar of coin fairs scheduled for 2013. Either ourselves or our representative, will be on hand at the following fairs to accept entries, answer queries and give valuations. Viewings of lots in upcoming auctions will be possible, by request.

Please note that all dates may be subject to change.

MINTMARKS AND OTHER SYMBOLS

1 Edward III, Cross 1 (Class B+C).
2 Edward III, broken Cross 1 (Class D).
3 Edward III, Cross 2 (Class E)
4 Edward III, Cross 3 (Class G)
5 Cross Potent (Edw. III Treaty)
6 Cross Pattée (Edw. III Post Treaty Rich. III).
7 (a) Plain of Greek Cross. (b) Cross Moline.
8 Cross Patonce.
9 Cross Fleuree.
10 Cross Calvary (Cross on steps).
11 Long Cross Fitchée.
12 Short Cross Fitchée.
13 Restoration Cross (Hen. VI).
14 Latin Cross.
15 Voided Cross (Henry VI).
16 Saltire Cross.
17 Cross and 4 pellets.
18 Pierced Cross.
19 Pierced Cross & pellet.
20 Pierced Cross & central pellet.
21 Cross Crosslet.
22 Curved Star (rayant).
23 Star.
24 Spur Rowel.
25 Mullet.
26 Pierced Mullet.
27 Eglantine.
28 Sun (Edw. IV).
29 Mullet (Henry V).
30 Pansy.
31 Heraldic Cinquefoil (Edw. IV).
32 Heraldic Cinquefoil (James I).
33 Rose (Edw. IV).
34 Rosette (Edw. IV).
35 Rose (Chas. I).
36 Catherine Wheel.
37 Cross in circle.
38 Halved Sun (6 rays) & Rose.
39 Halved Sun (4 rays) & Rose.
40 Lis-upon-Half-Rose.
41 Lis-upon-Sun & Rose.
42 Lis-Rose dimidiated.
43 Lis-issuant-from-Rose.
44 Trefoil.

45 Slipped Trefoil, James I (1).
46 Slipped Trefoil, James I (2).
47 Quatrefoil.
48 Saltire.
49 Pinecone.
50 Leaf (-mascle, Hen. VI).
51 Leaf (-trefoil, Hen. VI).
52 Arrow.
53 Pheon.
54 A.
55 Annulet.
56 Annulet-with-pellet.
57 Anchor.
58 Anchor & B.
59 Flower & B.
60 Bell.
61 Book.
62 Boar's Head (early Richard III).
63 Boar's Head (later Richard III).
64 Boar's Head, Charles I.
65 Acorn   (a) Hen. VIII
                  (b) Elizabeth.
66 Bow.
67 Br. (Bristol, Chas. I).
68 Cardinal's Hat.
69 Castle (Henry VIII).
70 Castle with H.
71 Castle (Chas. I).
72 Crescent   (a) Henry VIII
                  (b) Elizabeth.
73 Pomegranate. (Mary; Henry VIII's is broader).
74 Coronet.
75 Crown.
76 Crozier   (a) Edw. III
                  (b) Hen. VIII.
77 Ermine.
78 Escallop (Hen. VII).
79 Escallop (James I).
80 Eye (in legend Edw. IV).
81 Eye (Parliament).
82 Radiate Eye (Hen. VII).
83 Gerb.
84 Grapes.
85 Greyhound's Head.
86 Hand.
87 Harp.
88 Heart.
89 Helmet.
90 Key.
91 Leopard's Head.

91A Crowned Leopard's Head with collar (Edw. VI).
92 Lion.
93 Lion rampant.
94 Martlet.
95 Mascle.
96 Negro's Head.
97 Ostrich's Head.
98 P in brackets.
99 Pall.
100 Pear.
101 Plume.
102 Plume. Aberystwyth and Bristol.
103 Plume. Oxford.
104 Plume. Shrewsbury.
105 Lis.
106 Lis.
107 Portcullis.
108 Portcullis, Crowned.
109 Sceptre.
110 Sunburst.
111 Swan.
112 R in brackets.
113 Sword.
114 T (Henry VIII).
115 TC monogram.
116 WS monogram.
117 y or Y.
118 Dragon (Henry VII).
119 (a) Triangle
       (b) Triangle in Circle.
120 Sun (Parliament).
121 Uncertain mark.
122 Grapple.
123 Tun.
124 Woolpack.
125 Thistle.
126 Figure 6 (Edw. VI).
127 Floriated cross.
128 Lozenge.
129 Billet.
130 Plume. Bridgnorth or late declaration
131 Two lions.
132 Clasped book.
133 Cross pommée.
134 Bugle.
135 Crowned T (Tournai, Hen VIII)
136 An incurved pierced cross

The reign listed after a mintmark indicates that from which the drawing is taken. A similar mm. may have been used in another reign and will be found in the chronological list at the beginning of each reign.

1	2	3	4	5	6	7a	7b	8	9
10	11	12	13	14	15	16	17	18	19
20	21	22	23	24	25	26	27	28	29
30	31	32	33	34	35	36	37	38	39
40	41	42	43	44	45	46	47	48	49
50	51	52	53	54	55	56	57	58	59
60	61	62	63	64	65a	65b	66	67	68
69	70	71	72a	72b	73	74	75	76	77
78	79	80	81	82	83	84	85	86	87
88	89	90a	90b	90c	91	92	93	94	95
96	97	98	99	100	101	102	103	104	105
106	107	108	109	110	111	112	113	114	115
116	117a	117b	118	119a	119b	120	121	122	123
124	125	126	127	128	129	130	131	132	133
134	135	136							

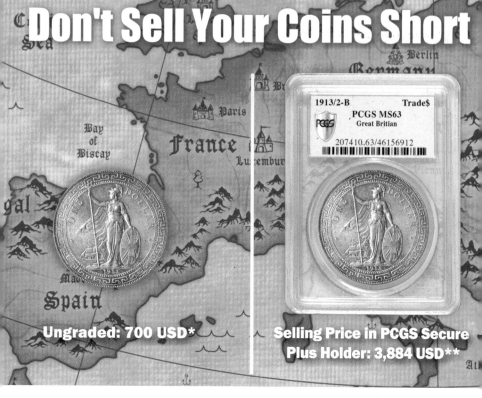